ESSAYS ON
THE PHILOSOPHY
OF SOCRATES

ESSAYS ON
THE PHILOSOPHY
OF SOCRATES

EDITED BY

Hugh H. Benson

New York   Oxford
OXFORD UNIVERSITY PRESS
1992

Oxford University Press

Oxford   New York   Toronto
Delhi   Bombay   Calcutta   Madras   Karachi
Kuala Lumpur   Singapore   Hong Kong   Tokyo
Nairobi   Dar es Salaam   Cape Town
Melbourne   Auckland

and associated companies in
Berlin   Ibadan

Library of Congress cataloging-in-Publication Data
Essays on the philosophy of Socrates / edited by Hugh H. Benson.
p.   cm.
Includes bibliographical references and index.
ISBN 0-19-506756-8
ISBN 0-19-506757-6 (pbk.)
1. Socrates.   2. Philosophy, Ancient.
I. Benson, Hugh H., 1956–   .
B317.E88   1992
183'.2—dc20   91–10002   CIP

2 4 6 8 9 7 5 3

Printed in the United States of America
on acid-free paper

To Mom and Dad

Preface

The study of Socratic philosophy has blossomed since the publication in 1971 of Gregory Vlastos' *The Philosophy of Socrates: A Collection of Critical Essays*. A number of important books have appeared. To name a few, there is Terence Irwin's *Plato's Moral Theory*, Gerasimos Santas' *Socrates*, Richard Kraut's *Socrates and the State*, Thomas Brickhouse and Nicholas Smith's *Socrates on Trial*, and Vlastos' own *Socrates, Ironist and Moral Philosopher* (in press at the time of this writing). These books have spawned, and been spawned by, a vast body of literature in journals. Nevertheless, to date there has been no attempt to make any of this exhaustive research more readily accessible. In this volume I attempt to do just that. Restricting myself to the two decades since the publication of Vlastos' collection, I have attempted to gather together essays of the highest quality, representing the range and diversity of this vast literature. In the pages which follow, the reader will find both essays devoted to a single Platonic dialogue as well as those devoted to a number of dialogues, essays concerned with the Socratic method, Socratic epistemology, and Socratic ethics, plus historical and philosophical essays. I only wish there was room to include more.

In the interest of making this diverse research as accessible as possible to the nonscholar, I have transliterated all of the Greek (accents have been omitted), appended to each essay a short list of suggested further readings, and provided a brief summary of the arguments of each of the essays in my general introduction. Finally, for the scholar I have included an extensive bibliography of Socratic research covering the last two decades as well as an index locorum.

I owe a debt of gratitude to a number of people who in various ways have provided much needed assistance. I am grateful to Gregory Vlastos and Geoffrey Sayre-McCord for encouraging me to take on this project; to Nicholas Smith, Mark McPherran, Gregory Vlastos, and two anonymous reviewers for their suggestions concerning which essays to include; to Cynthia Read for her patience and encouragement during the preparation of this volume; and to the Department of Philosophy at the University of Oklahoma—in particular to Neera Badhwar and Monte Cook for reading drafts of the introduction, to Catherine Blaha for her flawless and timely clerical assistance and Mark Hulbert for the preparation of the index locorum. I am especially grateful to Roslyn Weiss, who always seemed willing to drop everything to offer encouragement, suggestions, and criticism. All remaining mistakes and instances of poor judgment are, of course, my own. Finally, I would like to thank Ann and Thomas Benson for their patience and love.

Norman, Okla.   H.B.
March 1991

Acknowledgments

"The Formal Charges Against Socrates," by Thomas C. Brickhouse and Nicholas D. Smith originally appeared in *Journal of the History of Philosophy* 23 (1985), 457–81. Reprinted by permission of *Journal of the History of Philosophy*.

"Did Plato Write Socratic Dialogues?" by Charles H. Kahn originally appeared in *Classical Quarterly* 31 (1981), 305–20. Reprinted by permission of *Classical Quarterly*.

"Socratic Midwifery, Platonic Inspiration" by Myles F. Burnyeat originally appeared in *Bulletin of the Institute of Classical Studies* 24 (1977), 7–16. Reprinted by permission of the author and *Bulletin of the Institute of Classical Studies*.

"Socratic Irony" by Gregory Vlastos originally appeared in *Classical Quarterly* 37 (1987), 79–96. Reprinted by permission of *Classical Quarterly*.

"Plato's Early Theory of Knowledge" by Paul Woodruff originally appeared in *Epistemology*, ed. S. Everson (Cambridge, Eng. 1990), 60–84. Copyright 1990 Cambridge University Press. Reprinted with the permission of Cambridge University Press.

"Does Socrates Commit the Socratic Fallacy?" by John Beversluis originally appeared in *American Philosophical Quarterly* 24 (1987), 211–23. Reprinted by permission of the *American Philosophical Quarterly*.

"Misunderstanding the 'What-is-F-ness?' Question" by Hugh H. Benson originally appeared in *Archiv für Geschichte der Philosophie* 72 (1990), 125–42. Reprinted by permission of the *Archiv für Geschichte der Philosophie*.

"Elenchus and Mathematics: A Turning-Point in Plato's Philosophical Development" by Gregory Vlastos originally appeared in *American Journal of Philology* 109 (1988), 362–96. Reprinted by permission of *American Journal of Philology*.

"The Unity of Virtue" by Terry Penner is reprinted from *Philosophical Review* 82 (1973), 35–68, by permission of the publisher and the author.

"Socrates' Use of the Techne-Analogy" by David L. Roochnik originally appeared in *Journal of the History of Philosophy* 24 (1986), 295–310. Reprinted by permission of *Journal of the History of Philosophy*.

"Socrates the Epicurean" by Terence H. Irwin originally appeared in *Illinois Classical Studies* 11 (1986), 85–112. Copyright 1986, The Board of Trustees, University of Illinois. Reprinted by permission of the author and *Illinois Classical Studies*.

"Socratic Piety in the *Euthyphro*" by Mark L. McPherran originally appeared in *Journal of the History of Philosophy* 23 (1985), 283–309. Reprinted by permission of *Journal of the History of Philosophy*.

"Ho Agathos as *Ho Dunatos* in the *Hippias Minor"* by Roslyn Weiss originally appeared in *Classical Quarterly* 31 (1981), 287–304. Reprinted by permission of *Classical Quarterly*.

"Socrates on Desire for the Good and the Involuntariness of Wrongdoing: *Gorgias* 466a–468e" by Kevin McTighe originally appeared in *Phronesis* 29 (1984), 193–236. Reprinted by permission of *Phronesis*.

"Meno's Paradox and Socrates as a Teacher" by Alexander Nehamas originally appeared in *Oxford Studies in Ancient Philosophy* 3 (1985), 1–30. Reprinted by permission of the author.

Contents

read this

Abbreviations

Aelian
Var. Hist.   *Varia Historia*

Albinus
Epit.   *Epitome*

Antipater (Antip.)

Apuleius
De Plat.   *De dogmate Platonis*

Aristophanes (Arist.)

Aristotle (A.)
EE   *Eudemian Ethics*
EN   *Nicomachean Ethics*
Met.   *Metaphysics*
MM   *Magna Moralia*
Phys.   *Physics*
Po. An.   *Posterior Analytics*
Pol.   *Politics*
Rhet.   *Rhetoric*
Soph. El.   *De Sophisticis Elenchis*
Top.   *Topics*

Augustine
Civ. Dei   *De Civitate Dei*
Conf.   *Confessions*

Cicero
Acad.   *Academica*
de Fin.   *De Finibus*
de Rep.   *De Republica*
N.D.   *De Natura Deorum*
Parad.   *Paradoxa Stoicorum*
Tusc. Disp.   *Tusculanae Disputationes*
                                (Tusculan Dispositions)

Democritus (Democ.)

Diogenes Laertius (D.L.)

Epictetus
Disc.   *Discourses*

Herodotus (Hdt.)

Hippocrates
On Anc. Med.   *On Ancient Medicine*

Hippolytus
Ref.   *Refutation of all Heresies*

Isocrates
In Callim.   *In Callimachus*

Libanius
Apol.   *Apology*

Marcus Aurelius
Medit.   *Meditations*

Olympiodorus
in Plat. Alc.   *in Platonis Alcibiadem Commentarii*
in Plat. Gorg.   *in Platonis Gorgiam Commentaria*
in Plat. Phaed.   *in Platonis Phaedonem Commentaria*

Plato (Pl.)
Alc. I   *Alcibiades I*
Alc. II   *Alcibiades II*
Apol.   *Apology*
Ax.   *Axiochus*
Charm.   *Charmides*
Cr.   *Crito*
Crat.   *Cratylus*
Def.   *Definitions*
Ep.   *Epistles*
Eu.   *Euthyphro*
Eud.   *Euthydemus*
Gorg.   *Gorgias*
H.Ma.   *Hippias Major*
H.Mi.   *Hippias Minor*
I.   *Ion*
La.   *Laches*
Lg.   *Laws*
Ly.   *Lysis*
M.   *Meno*
Phdo.   *Phaedo*
Phdr.   *Phaedrus*
Phil.   *Philebus*

Plato (Pl.) (*continued*)

Pltc.	*Politicus*
Prot.	*Protagoras*
Rep.	*Republic*
Soph.	*Sophist*
Sym.	*Symposium*
Tht.	*Theaetetus*
Tim.	*Timaeus*

Plutarch (Plut.)

Plat. Quaest.	*Quaestiones Platonicae*

Proclus

in Plat. Alc. I	*in Platonis Alcibiadem I*

Quintillian

Inst. Or.	*Institutio Oratoria*

Sextus

Hypotyp.	*Purroneioi Hupotuposeis* (*Outlines of Pyrrhonism*)
Adv. Math.	*Adversus Mathematicos* (*Against the Prefessors*)

Thucydides (Th.)

Xenophon

Apol.	*Apology*
Hell.	*Hellenica*
Mem.	*Memorabilia*
Symp.	*Symposium*

ESSAYS ON
THE PHILOSOPHY
OF SOCRATES

1

Editor's Introduction

The Socrates discussed in this book, like the Socrates of Gregory Vlastos' earlier collection of essays on the philosophy of Socrates, is the Socrates of Plato's early dialogues.[1] This is the Socrates who engages individuals from a variety of backgrounds and occupations in discussions of such questions as: "What is the nature of courage (or temperance, or rhetoric)?" "Is virtue teachable?" "Is the one who commits evil intentionally or unintentionally the good man?" He is also the Socrates who is accused and found guilty of impiety and yet refuses to escape from jail and save his life because to do so would be unjust. He espouses such nontraditional—in some cases even paradoxical—theses as: "No one ever does wrong willingly," "it is wrong to harm one's enemies," and "knowledge is virtue" and yet disavows his own wisdom. Finally, he is the Socrates with whom many teachers of philosophy introduce the subject to their students. As Paul Woodruff has put it, "He is our model of a philosopher."[2] It is this Socrates whose philosophy will be examined in the following pages. But how many aspects of Socrates are there, and which one, if any, is the historical Socrates? This question is commonly referred to as the "Socratic problem."

Let me introduce this volume by briefly sketching what seems the most plausible and generally accepted solution to this problem. I believe this is a problem that must be faced, if only to put it aside, by anyone approaching the philosophy of the Platonic Socrates for the first time. Those who want to pursue this most vexing of problems further are encouraged to consult the list of suggested readings at the end of this introduction.

We have essentially four sources for the historical Socrates: Aristophanes, a fifth-century comic poet and social critic; Xenophon, a military general and probably only a casual acquaintance of Socrates; Plato, a philosopher of the highest rank and an intimate companion of Socrates; and Aristotle, another philosopher of the highest rank and a pupil of Plato. From these sources three Socrateses have emerged: (1) the Aristophanic Socrates, a sophistic natural philosopher who was willing to teach anyone who would pay how to make the weaker argument appear the stronger and who denied the existence of the gods of common opinion; (2) the Xenophontean Socrates, an unexciting didactician, who was quick to give advice concerning the most common matters and who was a paragon of common morality and religious practice; and (3) the Platonic Socrates, a nondogmatic, perhaps even skeptical, moral philosopher, who examined and exposed others' pretenses to wisdom, denied that he taught anything, and espoused the nontraditional theses mentioned earlier that "no one ever does wrong willingly," "it is wrong to harm one's enemies," and "knowledge is virtue."[3] Presently, many scholars would agree that the Platonic Socrates is the most historically accurate.[4] The reasons for this preference are diverse and complex, but in very general terms they come down to the following.

The Aristophanic Socrates is, after all, a character in a comedic play. As a result, although we should expect sufficient historical accuracy to make the character identifiable, we should also expect exaggeration and distortion. In fact, the Aristophanic Socrates appears to be an amalgam of stereotypical characteristics of fifth-century natural philosophers and fifth-century sophists. As such he serves as the butt of Aristophanes' general attack on fifth-century intellectualism.[5] The Xenophontean Socrates, on the other hand, is too good to be true. In attempting to defend Socrates against his accusers, Xenophon paints a picture of a person so commonsensically virtuous and religious that it is difficult to imagine why such a person would have been brought to trial in the first place. As Gerasimos Santas succinctly puts it, "Xenophon really makes it impossible for us to see why the Athenians were upset or why Plato was inspired."[6] Only the Platonic Socrates is sufficiently profound and complex that one can imagine why the same character who was convicted and sentenced to death for "rejecting the gods of the state," "introducing strange deities," and "corrupting the youth," could have also inspired such diverse characters as Critias, an oligarchic tyrant, Alcibiades, an aristocratic demagogue, Chaerephon, a harmless democrat, and of course Xenophon and Plato themselves. None of this, of course, is to suggest that Aristophanes and Xenophon are of no value in discovering the historical Socrates. When their Socrateses accord with Plato's, we can be all the more confident that we have found the historical Socrates, coming as he does from such diverse sources. But when their pictures of Socrates do not accord with Plato's, it appears to be Plato's Socrates with whom we must side.[7]

Once the Socratic problem has been decided in favor of Plato, we are faced with yet another problem. As is becoming generally recognized, there appears to be more than one Socrates in the dialogues of Plato. In his masterful essay "Socrates," Gregory Vlastos claims to discover in the Platonic dialogues two very different philosophers that go by the name of Socrates. The one is "a moral philosopher, pure and simple."[8] He has no interest in mathematics, metaphysics, epistemology, or ontology. He professes no moral knowledge, practices a populistic philosophy, and becomes identified with a method of question and answer known as the *elenchos*. The other is a first-rate mathematician, metaphysician, epistemologist, and ontologist, as well as a moral philosopher. This Socrates is confident of the philosopher's capacity to gain moral knowledge, practices an elitist philosophy, and "scuttles" the *elenchos* in favor of a new method, the method of hypothesis. Although some Socratic scholars disagree with Vlastos' descriptions of the two philosophers, few would nowadays dispute Vlastos' central claim that there is more than one Socrates in the Platonic dialogues. But then which of the Platonic philosophers is the historical Socrates? The attempt to solve this "second Socratic problem" depends in part on the order of composition of the Platonic dialogues, another diverse and complex issue but one that has also achieved some measure of agreement.

It is generally believed that the dialogues can be roughly divided into the following three periods:

EARLY	MIDDLE	LATE
Apology	*Cratylus*	*Critias*
Charmides	*Phaedo*	*Laws*
Crito	*Phaedrus*	*Parmenides*
Euthydemus	*Republic*	*Philebus*
Euthyphro	*Symposium*	*Politicus*
Gorgias		*Sophist*
Hippias Major		*Theaetetus*
Hippias Minor		*Timaeus*[9]
Ion		
Laches		
Lysis		
Menexenus		
Meno		
Protagoras[10]		

Admittedly, opinion is sharply divided concerning the order of composition within these periods. (I have simply listed them in alphabetical order.) In the case of the early period, Gregory Vlastos, for example, argues that the *Gorgias* is the last of the completely "Socratic" dialogues. It is followed only by the *Lysis, Hippias Major, Euthydemus,* and *Meno,* all of which are transitional in character: the *elenchos* has been abandoned and Socrates the mathematician is gradually emerging.[11] Charles Kahn, however, argues that the *Gorgias* precedes all of the following "pre-middle" or "Socratic" dialogues: *Laches, Charmides, Lysis, Euthyphro, Protagoras, Euthydemus,* and *Meno.*[12] While, as Kahn points out, Vlastos' chronology appears to be the prevailing one (even if the philosophical implications he draws from it are not), the issue remains hotly disputed. Still, the *Meno* does appear to be generally recognized to be the latest of this early period and as such to be a transitional dialogue: the Socrates of the early period remains, but the Socrates of the *Republic* and *Phaedo* is beginning to emerge.[13] More important, there appears to be general agreement that there is a single Socrates to be found somewhere within this early period and that this Socrates is the historical one.[14]

Once again the reasons for this agreement are diverse and complex, but they can be condensed as follows. If the historical Socrates is to be found anywhere in the Platonic dialogues it presumably will be in Plato's early work when the influence of his mentor remains strong. As Plato begins to philosophically mature, we should expect him to gradually move away from the views of Socrates to his own original positions. Furthermore, this view of Plato's philosophical development is reinforced in two ways. First, the one dialogue that is most likely to be historically accurate is the *Apology*. If this dialogue is to serve its purpose as a defense of Socrates it must at least purport to be reasonably historically accurate.[15] But it is the Socrates of the early dialogues that comes closest to Socrates' description of himself in the *Apology*. This is the Socrates who, whenever he meets someone who professes to care for wisdom, truth, or the perfection of his soul, questions, examines, and tests him. And if he discovers, as he always does, that despite his professions the individual does not really care for these things, this is the Socrates who reproves him and exhorts him to care for the most important things.[16]

Second, when Aristotle distinguishes between the philosophical views of Socrates and Plato, the distinction reflects the difference between the philosophy of the earlier and later periods.[17] It is the Socrates of the early dialogues who occupies himself with ethics and definitions, who correctly does not make universals exist apart, and who disavows knowledge.[18]

Thus, the dialogues of this early period are the focus of the essays that follow.[19] Of course, passages from the later period may occasionally be included, but only if they support theses independently testified to in the early dialogues themselves. Thus, the Socrates of this volume is indeed the Socrates of Plato's early dialogues. He is the Socrates of, for example, the *Apology, Crito, Laches, Gorgias, Protagoras,* perhaps of the *Euthydemus, Lysis,* and *Hippias Major,* and of parts of the *Meno.* He is also the Socrates who was an intimate of Alcibiades, who fought in the retreat of the Athenians from Delium, and who was put to death by Athens in 399 B.C. for "rejecting the gods of the state," "introducing strange deities," and "corrupting the youth."

The selection of the essays included in this volume has been guided by a number of considerations. First, all have been published after the appearance of Gregory Vlastos' *The Philosophy of Socrates: A Collection of Critical Essays.* The two decades following its publication has seen a virtual explosion of research in the philosophy of Socrates.[20] Second, I have attempted to represent the diversity of this research. The reader will find essays on a group of dialogues and on a single dialogue, essays devoted to Socratic method and to Socratic ethics, historical essays and philosophical essays.[21] Finally, and most important, I have sought to include essays of only the highest quality. Many of those selected have already enjoyed a well-deserved influence on subsequent research. Unfortunately, many essays of comparable quality and influence have unavoidably been left out. It is in this respect that I have most of all felt the exasperation of an editor. The problem has not been one of finding enough excellent essays to include but of finding too many. I hope only that the essays I have selected will prompt the reader to explore the depths of this extraordinary research.

Let me conclude this introduction with an explanation of the arrangement of the essays in this volume and a brief summary of their contents. The first essay is fairly historical. Thomas Brickhouse and Nicholas Smith discuss the formal charges leveled against Socrates by his three accusers, Meletus, Anytus, and Lycon. As I have noted earlier, Socrates is formally charged with "rejecting the gods of the state," "introducing strange deities," and "corrupting the youth." Brickhouse and Smith argue against a tradition according to which neither Socrates nor his accusers take these formal charges seriously, so that Socrates' refutation of these charges in Plato's *Apology* is not serious either. Brickhouse and Smith argue, on the contrary, that there are good reasons to think that the three accusers take very seriously the formal charges leveled at Socrates, and that not only is Socrates' defense of these charges a serious attempt to demonstrate their incoherence but that it very nearly convinces the jury.

We turn next to the Socratic dialogues, properly so called, and begin with a general discussion concerning how they should be read: Charles Kahn's penetrating critique of what he calls the "historicist" assumption. According to Kahn, the historicist assumption is the assumption that Plato began his philosophical writing career by attempting to produce "historically faithful portrayals [of Socrates], which gradually changed into something else," namely original philosophical exposition. Kahn argues against the prevailing ordering of the early dialogues and claims that his "pre-middle" or "Socratic'' dialogues (subgroup a: *Laches, Charmides, Lysis, Euthyphro,* and subgroup b: *Protagoras, Euthydemus,* and *Meno*) should be read ''proleptically.'' They should be read, that is, not as looking backward toward Socrates, as the historicist would have it, but as looking forward toward middle Platonism. This essay is the first of a series of essays in which Kahn defends his original and distinctive proleptic interpretation of the early dialogues.[22]

The next nine essays are concerned with two topics that have received considerable attention in the secondary literature of the last two decades: Socratic method and Socratic moral theory. In the case of Socratic method, we begin with two familiar images associated with that method: Socrates, the midwife, and Socrates, the ironist. Myles Burnyeat argues that the midwife image is not an image used of himself by the historical Socrates, but rather is a Platonic invention. Plato introduces this image in a later dialogue, the *Theaetetus,* to serve two functions. First, it brings us ''back to Socrates''— to the philosopher of the early dialogues who knows nothing, who has no metaphysical (perhaps even theoretical) commitments, and whose mission is simply to help others become aware of their epistemological limits. Second, it introduces to the old Socratic method of question and answer known as the *elenchos* the aspect of discovering what one really believes, and thereby engenders a more productive role for the method.

Gregory Vlastos argues that the image of Socrates the ironist plays a fundamental role in the meaning of the Greek word *eironeia.* According to Vlastos, *eironeia* originally meant intentional deceit, but its later more traditional sense is that of irony— that is, meaning to express one thing but uttering its contrary. Socratic *eironeia,* Vlastos points out, involves no intention to deceive; rather, its two classic examples, Socrates' disavowal of knowledge and Socrates' disavowal of teaching, are cases of ''complex'' irony. A complex irony is one in which ''what is said both is and isn't what is meant.'' In disavowing knowledge, Socrates means what he says in the sense in which knowledge means certainty, but he does not mean what he says in the sense in which knowledge means justified true belief. In disavowing teaching, Socrates means what he says in the sense in which teaching means the transfer of knowledge from the teacher to the pupil, but he does not mean what he says in the sense in which teaching means encouraging the pupil to discover truths independently.

Paul Woodruff continues the discussion concerning Socrates' disavowal of knowledge. Woodruff's discussion arises within the context of a formidable problem in Socratic scholarship: How are we to understand Socrates' disavowal of knowledge, in light of his frequent knowledge claims?[23] Woodruff contends that Plato ''has shown Socrates making a distinction in use between two conceptions of knowledge with different epistemic standards:'' (p. 88) expert and non-expert knowledge.[24] Expert knowledge, according to Woodruff, is teachable, specialized, complete (i.e., it covers the entire range of its specific subject), adequate (i.e., it must aim at the good), and definitional (i.e., it entails the ability to say without contradiction what the specific subject's good is). It is this sort of knowledge that Socrates disavows. It is also this knowledge that Socrates discovers others lack. Non-expert knowledge, on the other hand, is ''common knowledge,'' ''the common property of ordinary people.'' It is neither teachable, specialized, complete, adequate, nor definitional. It is what we all ''really'' believe. This is the kind of knowledge that Socrates avows and that his *elenchos* can uncover.

Next, John Beversluis attacks a long-standing tradition in Socratic scholarship according to which Socrates commits what Peter Geach has called the Socratic Fallacy.[25] The Socratic Fallacy, as Beversluis examines it, consists in assuming that if a person fails to know the definition of F-ness, then he or she cannot know anything about it, neither that something is an example of F-ness nor that F-ness has some property or other (the priority of definition principle).[26] For example, if Socrates fails to know what holiness is, then he can know neither that prosecuting Euthyphro's father is holy nor that holiness is teachable. One result of this assumption is that it would appear to be impossible to search for definitions of F-ness by appealing to examples of things that are F (Geach's [B] and Beversluis' [B*]). If the definition of F-ness is unknown, then what things are examples of F-ness will be unknown as well. Beversluis' challenge to this tradition consists of two parts. First, he argues that the early dialogues not only fail to provide evidence for Socrates' commitment to the priority of definition principle, but they testify against such a commitment. According to Beversluis, Socrates' use of the *elenchos* is incompatible with this principle, for the *elenchos* depends upon knowledge of examples and properties in order to achieve knowledge of the definition. Second, he argues against two popular attempts to defend Socrates against the charge of fallacy on the assumption that he is committed to the priority of definition principle, what Beversluis calls the Correct Use Theory[27] and the True Belief Theory.[28]

In the next essay, I examine the question the priority-of-definition principle encourages, Socrates' "What is F-ness?" question. There is a traditional view according to which Socrates' interlocutors frequently misunderstand his "What is F-ness?" question by providing concrete particular instances of F-ness as their initial answers, when what Socrates' question calls for is a universal. Alexander Nehamas has recently challenged this tradition.[29] He argues that the initial answers of Socrates' interlocutors are not concrete particular instances of the relevant F-ness, but universals, albeit not sufficiently broad universals to count as the correct answer to the question. After briefly reviewing and endorsing Nehamas' argument, I point to a problem that his argument raises. In the case of four answers (Euthyphro's and Laches' first and Meno's first and third) and no others, Socrates responds that the interlocutors have misunderstood his question. According to Socrates, these four answers are not merely incorrect answers, they are incorrect sorts of answers. This suggests that Socrates takes these four answers to be in some way formally incorrect, not merely materially incorrect. But how, I ask, is this distinction between formal and material correctness to be made once we accept Nehamas' claim that these four answers are indeed universals, just not sufficiently broad universals to correctly answer the "What is F-ness?" question? By drawing on some contemporary work on the logic of questions, I argue that these four answers remain formally incorrect because they violate a completeness requirement. That is, these four answers have the form "x is one of the universals that are F-ness" when Socrates' question calls for an answer of the form "x is the one and only universal that is F-ness." Understanding the Socratic question in this way highlights one of its most controversial presuppositions. According to Socrates, there is one and only one universal that is F-ness.

From the Socratic question we turn to a direct discussion of the Socratic *elenchos,* Socrates' philosophical method of question and answer. In the next essay, Gregory Vlastos traces the development of Plato's philosophical method from the early Socratic dialogues, through the transitional dialogues (the *Euthydemus, Lysis,* and *Hippias Major*), to the *Meno.* According to Vlastos, the *elenchos* as practiced by Socrates in the early dialogues (Vlastos' "elenctic dialogues") is "peirastic" in form: "A thesis is refuted when, and only when, its negation is derived 'from the answerer's own beliefs'" (p. 139). (In an earlier essay Vlastos coined the phrase "the say what you believe rule.")[30] Focusing on this feature, Vlastos uncovers the following four characteristics of the *elenchos:* (1) it is adversative; (2) it must "worm" the truth out the interlocutor; (3) it presupposes that the interlocutors always carry with them the truth, at least implicitly; and finally (4) as a truth-seeking device it fails to yield certainty. Vlastos argues that this method is abandoned in the transitional dialogues and explains this abandonment by discovering evidence for Plato's newfound interest in higher mathematics. With mathematics Plato has found an alternative to the messy *elenchos*. He has found a method, the method of hypothesis, which holds the promise of reaching certainty. In the *Meno* this change becomes explicit.

From Socratic method we turn to Socratic moral theory. Terry Penner's classic essay challenges yet another tradition in Socratic scholarship, that concerning the Socratic doctrine of the unity of virtues. According to the view that Penner challenges, Socrates' view that the virtues are unified is simply the view that a person is brave just in case he is pious, and pious just in case temperate, and temperate just in case just, and just just in case wise. No one who has one of the virtues fails to have any of the others. Penner argues that the unity-of-virtues doctrine is stronger than mere equivalence. It is to be understood as an identity. The virtue terms "bravery," "piety," "temperance," "justice," and "wisdom" refer to the motivating forces or states of the soul that are responsible for the individual's being brave, pious, temperate, just, and wise, and according to the unity-of-virtues doctrine, as Penner understands it, these five terms all refer to the same motivating force or state of the soul. Penner argues for his interpretation of the unity-of-virtues doctrine by defending both its philosophical respectability (section II) and its textual superiority (sections III and IV).

Next we turn to an essay that challenges probably the most influential book in Socratic philosophy in the last two decades, Terence Irwin's *Plato's Moral Theory*. David Roochnik challenges Irwin's interpretation of Socrates' use of the *techne* analogy. (*Techne* is frequently translated "craft," and is so translated by Irwin; Roochnik disputes the accuracy of this translation.) The analogy, which likens moral knowledge to *techne,* is interpreted by Irwin as likening moral knowledge to specifically craft (i.e., productive) knowledge. If Irwin is correct, then Socrates' adoption of the *techne* analogy would strongly suggest his subscription to an instrumental moral theory according to which virtue is desirable for its production of some end other than itself. Roochnik objects to this interpretation on two grounds. First, he argues that Socrates does not always use *techne* to refer to craft knowledge, but uses it in a broader, more flexible sense. Hence, even if moral knowledge is a *techne,* it need not be productive, and so virtue need not be desirable for some end other than itself. Second, he argues more generally that Irwin's view of the function of the *techne* analogy goes beyond what is actually warranted by the passages upon which it is based. According to Roochnik, the *techne* analogy functions dialectically and is used not to make a theoretical claim about moral knowledge, but rather either to refute or to exhort individual interlocutors within particular exchanges. (This second objection, which Roochnik takes to be characteristic of two schools of Socratic/Platonic interpretation, is taken up in greater detail in the exchange between Roochnik and Irwin in Charles Griswold's interesting collection, *Platonic Writings, Platonic Readings.*)[31]

In the next essay Terence Irwin continues the work of his *Plato's Moral Theory* and argues that Socrates is committed to what he calls an adaptive account of happiness. According to Irwin, Socrates accepts the thesis that virtue is sufficient for happiness (Irwin's "sufficiency thesis"). This thesis, Irwin points out, is difficult to square with two formal criteria for happiness that are plausibly Socratic: (1) happiness is complete (i.e., it achieves all that we want); and (2) happiness is self-sufficient (i.e., it lacks nothing that we need to achieve all that we desire). It would seem that, given such criteria, virtue could not be sufficient for happiness since various goods other than virtue (Irwin's "external goods") would be necessary (e.g., wealth in order to purchase what we want, fair weather on the seas in order to reach our destination, and good health in order to pursue our various projects). Irwin attempts to resolve this tension by arguing that Socrates is committed to an adaptive account of happiness according to which we adapt our desires to what is feasible under the circumstances. The wise (i.e., virtuous) person on this account will recognize that he is better off with desires that are possible to satisfy. So, if the external conditions change making some of his or her desires unsatisfiable or unfeasible, he or she will simply give them up. "By adapting his desires to suit the external conditions, he will secure his happiness whatever the conditions may be." (p. 206). Hence, virtue (i.e., wisdom) is indeed sufficient for happiness.

The final four essays in this volume are concerned with individual dialogues. First Mark McPherran argues for an interpretation of Socrates' view of piety (*hosiotes* or *eusebeia*) in the *Euthyphro* that lies somewhere between what he calls constructivist interpretations and anticonstructivist interpretations. According to the constructivists, beneath surface refutations of the various definitions of piety the careful reader can discover a definition of piety that Socrates accepts in the *Euthyphro*. According to the anticonstructivists, no such definition is to be found. McPherran argues that the constructivists are correct to the extent that the careful reader can discover that Socrates accepts Euthyphro's claim that "Piety is that part of justice which is service . . . of men to the gods, assisting the gods in their work . . . , a work which produces some good result" (p. 223). The anticonstructivists, however, are correct as well in that Socrates does not accept Euthyphro's claim as a definition. Socrates does not accept it as a definition because he does not think that it is complete. It fails to specify the chief work that the pious assist the gods in doing. In fact, according to McPherran, it is necessarily incomplete because it is beyond human cognitive abilities to know what this chief work is. Indeed, on McPherran's view, a major thrust of the *Euthyphro* is to undercut the confident belief of humans that they know what piety is and what acts are pious.

Next we turn to the *Hippias Minor*. Roslyn Weiss defends this dialogue's logical and ethical respectability. First, she contends that Socrates validly argues at 363a1–369b7 that the one skilled at speaking falsehoods (the *pseudes,* whom Hippias identifies with the *polutropos,* the wily one) is no worse than, indeed no different from, the one skilled at speaking truths (the *alethes*). Second, she contends that Socrates validly argues at 373c7–376c6 that the one who does unjust things intentionally is better than the one who does them unintentionally and that he who does unjust things intentionally is the *agathos,* the good man. Finally, Weiss argues that neither of these conclusions is immoral. The first is not immoral because it "is not the paradoxical and scandalous view that the man who typically lies is the same as the man who typically tells the truth . . . , but rather the reasonable view that since the man who is able to lie in a given art or science . . . is the same as the man who is able to speak truthfully in the same art or science . . . , neither, with respect to his ability alone, is better or worse than the other'' (p. 248). The second is not immoral because it does not claim that intentional unjust acts are better than unintentional ones, but rather only that the agent that intentionally acts unjustly is better (i.e., more skilled) than the agent who unintentionally acts unjustly. Nor in claiming that the *agathos* is the one who does unjust things intentionally need Socrates be claiming that the man we normally call good is the one who does unjust things intentionally. For in the context of this argument the *agathos* is the one skilled in justice, not the just person. The question remains, however, why Socrates would devote considerable effort to deriving a paradoxical-sounding and seemingly immoral conclusion concerning a nonstandard *agathos*.

Once again we turn to an essay that challenges a tradition in Socratic scholarship. Kevin McTighe disputes the widely held view that Socrates supports the distinction he himself draws at *Gorgias* 466a–468e between ''doing what one desires'' and ''doing what seems good to one'' (McTighe's DG). According to McTighe, this distinction has been taken to be Socratic for primarily two reasons: (1) Socrates is viewed as intending to put forward a sound argument at *Gorgias* 466a–468e against Polus' view that tyrants and orators are powerful, an argument in which this distinction figures essentially; and (2) the Socratic Paradox that no one is voluntarily unjust depends essentially upon this distinction. McTighe argues, however, that Socrates rejects the view that ''doing what one desires'' is distinct from ''doing what seems good to one'' and that rather than intending to offer a sound argument against Polus at *Gorgias* 466a–468e, Socrates quite intentionally offers a fallacious, ad hominem argument for the purpose of eliminating Polus' conceit. Furthermore, McTighe argues that the Socratic Paradox is not the view that no one desires to act unjustly, a view that, as it is typically understood, does essentially rely upon the distinction between ''doing what one desires'' and ''doing what seems good to one.'' Rather, says McTighe, the Socratic Paradox is the view that no one who acts unjustly is blameworthy, for unjust action is necessarily a result of a certain sort of ignorance. The Socratic Paradox so understood, McTighe points out, does not depend upon the distinction between ''doing what one desires'' and ''doing what seems good to one.''

In the last essay we turn to the *Meno,* a dialogue that is generally recognized to be transitional between the early Socratic dialogues and the middle Platonic dialogues. In this dialogue a new Platonic philosophy begins to emerge. In his essay Alexander Nehamas examines three central features of this dialogue: (1) Meno's paradox that learning is impossible; (2) Socrates as a teacher of *arete* (variously translated as ''virtue'' or ''excellence''); and (3) the theory of recollection. According to Nehamas, Meno has good reasons to raise his paradox at *Meno* 80d, especially in light of Socrates' avowed ignorance of the nature of *arete.* For while Socrates' avowed ignorance is what makes him safe to approach when one is ignorant of the nature of *arete,* it is also what gives rise to the question at the bottom of Meno's paradox: ''How do two people who are ignorant of the answer to a given question discover that answer and how do they realize that they have discovered it?'' (p. 306). This problem is particularly pressing for Plato who comes to regard Socrates, despite Socrates' protestations, as perhaps the best teacher of *arete* to be found. Nehamas then goes on to provide an account of the theory of recollection that purports to solve this ethical and pragmatic problem as well as Plato's own more theoretical problems involving the nature of understanding. Nehamas' essay, like the dialogue with which it is concerned, provides a nice transition from the philosophy of Socrates to the philosophy of Plato, Socrates' most famous pupil.

NOTES

1. G. Vlastos (ed.), *The Philosophy of Socrates* (Garden City, N.Y., 1971). In many ways I intend this collection of essays to be a companion to, not a replacement for, Vlastos' earlier collection.
2. P. Woodruff, "Expert Knowledge in the *Apology* and *Laches:* What a General Needs to Know," *Proceedings of the Boston Area Colloquium in Ancient Philosophy* 3 (1987), 81.
3. Most scholars have found that the Aristotelian Socrates agrees with the Platonic Socrates in all essentials, at least the Socrates of Plato's early dialogues. See G. Vlastos, "The Paradox of Socrates," in G. Vlastos (ed.) *The Philosophy of Socrates,* 1, n. 1.
4. At least this is the common assumption of all of the authors represented in this volume who have anything to say concerning this issue.
5. See, e.g., T. C. Brickhouse and N. D. Smith, *Socrates on Trial* (Princeton, N.J., 1989), 69.
6. G. Santas, *Socrates: Philosophy in Plato's Early Dialogues* (London and Boston, 1979), 5.
7. For defenders of the Aristophanic Socrates, see, e.g., M. Nussbaum, "Aristophanes and Socrates on Learning Practical Wisdom," *Yale Classical Studies* 26 (1980), 43–97, and L. Edmunds "Aristophanes' Socrates," *Proceedings of the Boston Area Colloquium in Ancient Philosophy* 1 (1985), 209–30. For defenders of the Xenophontean Socrates, see, e.g., D. Morrison, "On Professor Vlastos' Xenophon," *Ancient Philosophy* 7 (1987), 9–22.
8. G. Vlastos, "Socrates," *Proceedings of the British Academy* 74 (1988), 91.
9. I here reflect the traditional placement of the *Timaeus.* For the debate concerning its date of composition, see G. E. L. Owen, "The Place of the *Timaeus* in Plato's Dialogues," *Classical Quarterly* (1953), 79–95, and H. F. Cherniss, "The Relation of the *Timaeus* to Plato's Later Dialogues," *American Journal of Philology* (1957), 225–66, both of which are usefully reprinted in R. E. Allen (ed.), *Studies in Plato's Metaphysics* (London, 1965), 313–38 and 339–78.
10. I have not listed the following works whose Platonic authorship has been doubted: *Alcibiades* I, *Alcibiades* II, *Definitions, Epinomis, Epistles* I–XII, *Hipparchus, Kleitophon, Minos, Rivales,* and *Theages.* Their authenticity or spuriousness is of no consequence to the arguments of the essays that follow. Of those I have listed, only the *Hippias Major* has been doubted by one or more of the authors of this collection. See C. Kahn, "The Beautiful and the Genuine: A Discussion of Paul Woodruff, *Plato, Hippias Major," Oxford Studies in Ancient Philosophy* 3 (1985), 261–87.
11. See G. Vlastos, "Elenchus and Mathematics: A Turning Point in Plato's Philosophical Development," reprinted in this collection.
12. See C. Kahn, "On the Relative Date of the *Gorgias* and the *Protagoras," Oxford Studies in Ancient Philosophy* 6 (1988), 69–102.
13. The theory of recollection, the method of hypothesis, and the doctrine that true belief is sufficient for virtuous action, all of which are found in the *Meno,* are views characteristic of the middle dialogues.
14. This does not mean that most scholars believe that the early dialogues fail to represent Platonic views. Many, if not most scholars, would accept Vlastos' "grand methodological hypothesis" that "Plato puts into the persona of Socrates only what at the time he himself considers true." (See p. 155, n. 39.) On this view, in the early dialogues Plato is at once exposing his own philosophical views, as well as what he understands to be the philosophical views of his teacher, Socrates.
15. See G. Vlastos, "The Paradox of Socrates," 3–4; see also Brickhouse and Smith, *Socrates on Trial,* 2–10.
16. *Apol.* 29d–30b.
17. See, for example, T. Irwin, *Plato's Moral Theory* (Oxford, 1977), 291 n. 33, and Vlastos, "Socrates," 102–7.

18. A., *Met.* 1078b and *Soph. El.* 183b.
19. The only exception is the first book of the *Republic*. It is usually included as a "Socratic" dialogue whether or not one thinks that it was originally written as an independent dialogue (perhaps entitled the *Thrasymachus*) and only later used to introduce Plato's magnum opus.
20. Gregory Vlastos' responsibility for this explosion should not be underestimated. In addition to the collection of essays, he has contributed substantial and significant work of his own (see the bibliography at the end of this volume). Furthermore, he has encouraged the work of others. Three of the contributors to this volume were his students at Princeton, while five others were participants in his seminars on the philosophy of Socrates given under the auspices of the National Endowment for the Humanities.
21. It has, of course, been impossible to cover every aspect of recent research in the philosophy of Socrates. Some readers, for example, will miss discussions of Socratic views concerning democracy or obedience to the law.
22. See the bibliography at the end of this volume.
23. A similar problem that Woodruff does not address concerns how we are to understand these Socratic disavowals in light of the Socratic doctrine that knowledge is necessary for virtue and Socrates' expressed confidence in his own virtue. See, for example, T. C. Brickhouse and N. D. Smith, "What Makes Socrates a Good Man," *Journal of the History of Philosophy* 28 (1990), 169–79.
24. The previous discussion by Vlastos suggests a distinction between certain knowledge and justified true belief (what Vlastos calls "elenctic knowledge"), the former of which Socrates disavows, the latter of which he avows.
25. P. T. Geach, "Plato's *Euthyphro*," *Monist* 50 (1966), 369–82.
26. The priority of definition principle as I have formulated it is the conjunction of Beversluis' (A1) and (A2). Geach's (A) is equivalent (A1) and so is an immediate consequence of the priority of definition principle. Geach's (B) is also a consequence of the priority of definition principle as Geach himself points out (371).
27. See R. M. Hare, *Plato* (Oxford, 1924).
28. See, especially, Irwin, *Plato's Moral Theory*.
29. A. Nehamas, "Confusing Universals and Particulars in Plato's Early Dialogues," *Review of Metaphysics* 29 (1975), 287–306.
30. See G. Vlastos, "The Socratic Elenchus," *Oxford Studies in Ancient Philosophy* 1 (1985), 27–58. This is a classic essay and has led to a number of essays devoted to the study of the Socratic *elenchos*. It should be read by everyone even remotely interested in Socratic philosophy. Unfortunately, it could not be reprinted here.
31. See the suggestions for further reading at the end of Roochnik's essay.

FURTHER READING

Guthrie, W. K. C. 1971. "Problems and Sources." *Socrates,* 5–57. Cambridge, Eng.

Lacey, A. R. 1971. "Our Knowledge of Socrates." In *The Philosophy of Socrates,* ed. Gregory Vlastos, 22–49. Garden City, N.Y.

Nussbaum, M. 1980. "Aristophanes and Socrates on Learning Practical Wisdom." *Yale Classical Studies* 26:43–97.

Ross, W. D. 1933. "The Problem of Socrates." *Proceedings of the Classical Association* 7–24.

Vlastos, G. 1988. "Socrates." *Proceedings of the British Academy* 74:87–109.

Vogel, C. J. de. 1955. "The Present State of the Socrates Problem." *Phronesis* 1:26–35.

2

The Formal Charges
Against Socrates

THOMAS C. BRICKHOUSE AND NICHOLAS D. SMITH

At 19A of Plato's *Apology*, Socrates begins his defense against what he calls the "first" accusers, whose slanders he sees as posing an even greater threat to him than those of the newer accusers, Meletus, Anytus, and Lycon. Because these older accusations are the most dangerous, he undertakes first to defend himself against them. But from 24B to 28A Socrates elects to address the charges of the "new" accusers by an interrogation of one of them, Meletus, the official[1] author of the indictment against him. This interrogation has been the source of a good deal of puzzlement to scholars, for during the interrogation Meletus seems to many readers to be ill prepared to defend his own charges coherently. To some, this is a decisive sign that the entire interlude is largely, if not wholly, invented by Plato to discredit Socrates' prosecutors as inept and unprincipled.[2] Other readers see the interrogation as showing that neither Socrates nor even Meletus takes the formal charges as the real motive for the prosecution. To Meletus and his collaborators, the formal charges, we are told, are a legal pretext for other complaints that could not themselves legally be prosecuted, but could nonetheless comprise such a bias against Socrates as to ensure his conviction on the charges they could bring. And on this view, the legal fiction involved was so evident that Socrates would not honor the formal charges with a serious refutation. Instead, he undertook in his interrogation of their nominal author merely to demonstrate to the jury that his prosecutors had shown a careless unconcern for morality and the law by employing such patently senseless and unsupportable charges against him.[3]

In this essay we wish to challenge such established interpretations by showing that both Socrates and his prosecutors may sensibly be taken as having viewed the formal charges as reflecting important issues to be decided by the court, even if (as we are wholly disinclined to doubt) other concerns also influenced the prosecution and outcome of the case.[4] In Part 1 we review the meaning of the specific charges themselves. In Part 2 we argue that the three prosecutors can reasonably be assumed to have intended the official indictment to be taken as specifying serious crimes actually committed by Socrates. In Part 3 we argue that Socrates' principles require that he do everything (within the bounds of those principles) to prove that the formal charges are false. In Part 4 we show that the arguments Socrates develops during his interrogation of Meletus are designed not merely, as other commentators have claimed, to confuse Meletus, and thus discredit him before the jury, but rather to refute the legal charges themselves by showing that they are based upon incoherent and thus indefensible prejudices. Finally, in Part 5 we consider Socrates' response to the jury's vote to convict him and argue that it can only be understood if he himself believes that he has actually refuted the formal accusations during the interrogation. We also show that his belief in the success of the interrogation in proving his innocence of the formal accusations is shared by many, perhaps even a majority of the jury.

1. THE FORMAL CHARGES AGAINST SOCRATES

At 24C, Socrates recalls the formal charges against him as follows: "Socrates is unjust both because he corrupts youth and because he does not recognize the gods the state recognizes, but rather other new divinities" (24C). According to Diogenes Laertius, the precise wording of the indictment (reported by Favorinus to be preserved in the Metroon—the temple of Cybele, where the Athenians kept their state archives) was as follows: "This indictment and affidavit is sworn by Meletus, the son of Meletus of Pitthos, against Socrates, the son of Sophroniscus of Alopece: Socrates is guilty of refusing to recognize the gods the state recognizes, and of introducing other new divinities. He is also guilty of corrupting the youth. The penalty demanded is death"[5] (2.40). Diogenes' report is supported by the fact that Xenophon offers the same version with only one word changed.[6]

Despite the differences in wording in the three accounts, the nature of the charges is the same in each. There are thus three distinct charges:[7]

1. Socrates does not recognize the gods the state recognizes.
2. Socrates introduces new divinities.
3. Socrates corrupts the youth.

Let us consider these in order.

1.1 *Hous men he Polis Nomizei Theous Ou Nomizon* *(The Gods the State Recognizes [Socrates] Does Not Recognize)*

Noting the connection between *nomizein* (to recognize) and *nomos* (custom, common practice), John Burnet, A. E. Taylor, and Reginald Allen[8] argue that this charge must be construed as saying that Socrates did not conform in religious practice to the religion sanctioned by the law of Athens, not that Socrates was some form of atheist. The arguments for this view have been effectively refuted, in our opinion, by R. Hackforth, W. K. C. Guthrie, James Beckman, and especially J. Tate,[9] and so we need not repeat their refutations at length. Rather a few simple observations will suffice here.

First, the distinction Burnet et al. attempt to secure between *ou nomizein theous* (not to recognize the gods) and *ou nomizein einai theous* (literally, not to recognize the gods to be),[10] only the latter of which would imply atheism on their view, is neglected by the very people to whom it would mean the most: Socrates himself, who uses the two expressions interchangeably in his interrogation of Meletus on this point (at 26B–28A; cf. also 29A), and Meletus, whose *"parapan* (completely) *ou nomizeis theous"* without the allegedly necessary *einai* (to be) at 26C nonetheless leaves his meaning clear. His charge is not that Socrates completely neglects proper religious practice; it is that Socrates is a complete atheist.

Secondly, and despite Burnet's explicit claim to the contrary,[11] that Xenophon also understood the charges against Socrates to involve atheism is clear from his rendering of the issue at *Memorabilia* 1.1.2–5.[12] Burnet's point that Xenophon so carefully stresses Socrates' orthopraxy in his *Apology* is quite correct, but irrelevant; after all, such activities would naturally be taken as good behavioral evidence that Socrates was no atheist. Nor is the emphasis in Greek law on proper practice evidence that orthodox belief was not a major concern; the two are inextricably tied together. The argument in pseudo-Lysias, "Against Andocides" (32) is illuminating on this point: people will become more atheistic if the law allows its citizens to ignore or violate established practices.

Finally, there is the matter of the psephism of Diopeithes under which Anaxagoras was allegedly tried, the relevance of which Burnet greatly overestimates. Even if we uncritically accept the existence of the psephism, as Burnet does, the fact that it would have been nullified by the general Amnesty under the archonship of Eucleides provides no reason to suppose that a charge of atheism could no longer be legally valid.[13] Socrates was not charged with violating the psephism of Diopeithes, but of violating the law against impiety.[14] Since this law was vague,[15] its extension would almost certainly be determined in each instance ad hoc, first and provisionally at the *anakrisis* before the trial[16] by the King-archon, and then decisively by the jury at the trial. Greek religious sentiments would be remarkable indeed if they saw atheism as not impious of itself, so long as proper rituals were performed (in utter hypocrisy, *ex hypothesi*) by the atheist. The very existence of the psephism of Diopeithes, and in any case the action against Anaxagoras, whether or not it was done under the psephism, would by themselves provide sufficient evidence against the claim that intellectual orthodoxy was of no particular concern to the Athenians, for the psephism explicitly concerned ideology and the case against Anaxagoras was based upon his teachings and not upon any specific violation of ritual. Nor would the annulment of the psephism (as one of all prior *psephismata*—it was hardly singled out for invalidation) by the Amnesty provide any evidence that its effects could not be obtained by subsumption under a constitutional law, in this case, the one proscribing impiety. This, on our view, is precisely what happened in Socrates' case and explains why he does not undertake to dispute the legality of the charges against him,[17] despite Meletus' interpretation of them at 26C and despite Socrates' willingness to challenge the Athenians' conceptions of the laws when he thinks those conceptions incorrect, even when doing so involves great risk to himself (cf. 32B).[18]

1.2 Hetera de Kaina Daimonia, Eisegoumenos
(Introducing New Divinities)

In order to introduce new divinities, one need not give up the traditional ones; and giving up the traditional gods does not necessitate replacing them with new divinities. So the two explicitly religious charges against Socrates are independent of one another, and thus each must be given independent support and interpretation.

The first thing to notice about this second charge is that it does not say that Socrates introduces new *theoi* (gods); it makes instead the less specific accusation that he introduces new *daimonia* (divinities).[19] But he leaves the second charge vague: is it that Socrates introduces new gods, or is it that he introduces new divinities of other sorts, or is it perhaps that he introduces some of each?

Equally important to this charge is the sense of illegitimacy inherent in the *daimonia* so described. The *daimonia* Socrates introduces cannot be real divinities that the Athenian simply had not heard of before, for then Socrates' introducing them would be a boon to the city. For the charge to make any sense as a charge of impiety, the sense of it has to be that Socrates introduces as divinities new entities that are not really divinities at all. Hence, even if Socrates called these new divinities *theoi,* they would not merit that label from Meletus; the only *real* gods, on Meletus' view, are the gods identified in the first part of the indictment, the gods the state recognizes. It is not necessarily to be assumed, moreover, that Socrates introduces them with a sincere (but mistaken) belief in their divinity,[20] though this is hardly ruled out. But what sorts of new *daimonia* is Socrates being charged with introducing?

At 31C–D in Plato's *Apology,* Socrates reminds the jury about the "something divine and spiritual"[21] that he has had since his childhood, and that warns him away from doing what he should not do. Both Plato and Xenophon explicitly tie the second charge to this *daimonion,*[22] to which Socrates refers frequently in various places in the accounts of both men.[23] Given that our two principal sources for information about Socrates interpret the charge in this way, and are contradicted in this by no other ancient sources, we see no reason to doubt them.

However, as a number of scholars have noted,[24] the charge of "introducing new divinities" almost certainly reflects a strategic decision on the part of the prosecution, for it accords very well with the portrayal of Socrates in Aristophanes' *Clouds,* and in general the "first" accusers' slander that Socrates is a nature philosopher. Such men, the jury might be convinced, replace the old gods with new sorts of (often explicitly called "divine")[25] powers. This is no doubt why the second charge is in the plural, so as to be purposefully vague. Socrates' *daimonion* can be cited directly in court; the other "new divinities" need not ever be cited by the prosecution directly, for given the work against Socrates already done by the "first" accusers, insinuation is all that is needed to remind the jury of them. In this, however, his prosecutors gravely underrated Socrates, for as we shall argue, seeking to preserve these insinuations leads them into inconsistency.

1.3 *Adikei de kai Tous Neous Diaphtheiron*
(*[Socrates] Is Also Unjust by Corrupting the Youth*)

Youth may be corrupted in any of a great number of ways, but it is worth considering precisely how Socrates is supposed to be construed as corrupting them. And though both Plato and Xenophon may plausibly be supposed, we believe, to wish to absolve Socrates of this charge no matter how it is construed, at 26B of Plato's *Apology* we find Socrates requesting clarification of this very point from Meletus: "In what way is it that you say I corrupt the youth, Meletus? Or is it clear, according to the indictment you wrote, that it is by teaching them not to recognize the gods the state recognizes, but rather other new divinities. Is this not what you say, that by teaching I corrupt them?" (26B2–6) To this, Meletus unhesitatingly replies, "That is exactly what I say" (26B7). Thus, the third charge of the indictment, as Meletus himself interprets it, is intrinsically related to the first two parts, at least in Plato's account (the sense of which is repeated at *Euthyphro* 3B).

It might be thought that the connection Meletus makes between this part of the indictment and the part explicitly concerning religious matters is a tactical mistake; after all, it might be easier to obtain a conviction if any evidence of corruption will count as relevant. But the purpose of the *anakrisis* or preliminary hearing was to decide whether the evidence warranted a trial and, if it did, to delimit the issues to be decided by the court.[26] It is extremely unlikely that the King-archon would have forwarded only the vague accusation that Socrates corrupted the youth unless Meletus specified in the indictment the actual manner in which Socrates has actually caused the harm. In addition, there is no record of any law proscribing corruption of the youth.[27] Yet, as we have already noted,[28] one of the conditions of the Amnesty required that a defendant be charged with violating some particular, written statute. In order, therefore, to bring the charge of corruption within the jurisdiction of the court, Meletus may have been obliged during the *anakrisis* to link formally the two parts of the indictment by charging that Socrates corrupted the youth by teaching them his own impious beliefs.

There is no reason to suppose, however, that corrupting youth could not in a general way be subsumed under the law proscribing impiety, especially given the powerful religious sanction for showing proper respect to one's parents and elders. If Socrates could be shown to encourage children, as the character of that name plainly does in Aristophanes' *Clouds,* to turn against their parents with scorn and disobedience (especially, again, on religious issues), he might well be viewed as guilty of impiety.[29] And in any case, regardless of its legal status, Socrates' nasty reputation in Athens was most assuredly on the minds of both accusers and jurors. Once again, the "first" accusers have a great deal to say about such things, and Socrates' two initial responses to this charge in the *Apology* (about which we will say more in section 4 of this essay) interpret its scope more broadly than Meletus applies it. And that such broader concerns are serious issues, even if they lacked legal status, is supported by all of the ancient sources. Aeschines flatly states that Socrates was put to death for being the teacher of Critias.[30] The pamphlet of Polycrates, though not dependable as a representation of anything actually said at Socrates' trial, relied heavily upon Socrates' alleged connections with Alcibiades and Critias as their teacher,[31] and this allegation may at least be supposed to reflect a real source of hostility toward Socrates. And though Burnet is certainly right in saying that these charges could not be official after the Amnesty,[32] they were taken seriously enough for Xenophon to refute them explicitly in his lengthy rebuttal of "the accuser" (no doubt Polycrates) in his *Memorabilia.*[33] Isocrates also defends Socrates against Polycrates' charge that he was the teacher of Alcibiades.[34] So whether or not Socrates' accusers wished, by innuendo or otherwise, to make more of the charge that he corrupted the youth than Meletus did explicitly, it is certain that there was a good deal more to it in the air at the trial.

2. THE PROSECUTION'S COMMITMENT TO THE CHARGES

It is not hard to see how Burnet and the others who share his interpretation of the indictment came to the conclusion that the formal charges against Socrates were not intended to be taken literally, and accordingly that Socrates in Plato's *Apology* does not take them seriously. After all, we have not the slightest evidence that Socrates failed to observe the established Athenian religious rituals, yet the Socrates of Plato's *Apology* makes no effort to document this fact (unlike the one of Xenophon's *Apology*—cf. esp. 11). But their conclusion is not necessarily avoided by removing, as we have done, the evidence Burnet et al. would cite for it, for other evidence might yet be found to show that neither the charges nor Socrates' specific reaction to them were seriously at issue.

Does Meletus intend the charges to be taken literally? One reason to suppose that he does can (curiously) be derived from the view tentatively offered by Burnet, and repeated with confidence by Hackforth and others,[35] that the Meletus who indicted Socrates was the same as the man who prosecuted Andocides in the same year. But if we also suppose that this Meletus' speech against Andocides is preserved even in the version attributed to Lysias, we have some grounds to think that Socrates' accuser was a bona fide religious fanatic, unlikely to employ religion casually as a mere pretext for more serious concerns. As Burnet points out, moreover, the Meletus who prosecuted Andocides was one of the men sent by the Thirty to arrest Leon,[36] a gross injustice in which Socrates himself would take no part (32D). Now Burnet may be right in arguing that Plato's Socrates would not stoop to the *ad hominem* appeal of reminding the jury of Meletus' past misdeeds,[37] but that the same lofty restraint would have silenced Xenophon as well, who recalls the incident at *Memorabilia* 4.4.3, seems implausible.[38] It is also hard to imagine that the Meletus who had been involved in such a notorious scandal could reasonably have been described as an ''unknown,'' as he is in Plato's *Euthyphro* (2B). Nor for that matter could the prosecutor of Andocides be so described, assuming that the trial of Andocides preceded that of Socrates.[39] Finally, whatever the order of the two trials, they could not have been so far apart as to render it likely that the prosecutor of Andocides would so near in time join forces with Anytus, whom Andocides calls on his behalf (cf. 1.150). The best, indeed the only, evidence that can be claimed in support of the identity of the two prosecutors, is that they bear the same name (Burnet claims it is an unusual one, but himself cites too many instances of it to be convincing)[40] and prosecute a charge of *asebeia* against two very different men, in two very different cases. And though we might well imagine that Andocides' accuser would have much against Socrates, the evidence, in our opinion, weighs against his being the man Socrates interrogates in the *Apology*. If we are wrong about this, however, there is good reason to suppose that Socrates' prosecutor is a sufficiently narrow dogmatist to intend the charges he brings very seriously.

Whatever one believes about this issue, however, it remains true that Meletus, Anytus, and Lycon managed not only to persuade a King-archon to forward the case to trial before 500 or 501 paid jurors—an expensive and politically risky decision to make on a private prejudice—but also to persuade 280 of the Athenians on the jury to convict Socrates and sentence him to death. Of course, all of these people (including his fellow prosecutors) may have ignored the interpretation of these charges offered by Meletus at 26C, or for that matter all of the formal charges, but such flagrant and widespread disregard for the letter of the law, however compatible with Plato's and Xenophon's unfriendly assessment of the honor of their fellow citizens, needs some imagination to endorse without at least some uneasiness. More important, Socrates himself seems to think that the jury is predisposed to find him guilty, because the ''first'' accusers have insinuated that he is a sophist and a nature philosopher. It is worth noting that if these ''first'' accusations are believed, the formal charges against Socrates would appear at least superficially to be quite appropriate in the eyes of a contemporary Athenian. That sophists corrupt young people by teaching them disregard for their elders and the laws is exactly the point of Aristophanes' *Clouds,* the one instance of a "first" accusation Socrates explicitly cites. That sophists and nature philosophers convince the young that the gods are dubious inventions of old-fashioned fogeys is also explicitly a part of that comedy. Moreover, the religious skepticism of such intellectuals is both notorious and well documented. Since the essence of the "first" accusations is the charge that Socrates is in some way or other a dangerous innovator against established religious beliefs and a corrupter of youth—that is, the sense of these charges is the same as that of those lodged by the "new" accusers—these "new" accusers have every reason to believe that their accusations will be seen as important and serious ones. And since so many jurors may be supposed to be convinced by the prejudices thus aroused by Socrates' "first" accusers, there is at least equal reason to suppose that such blind prejudices (no doubt among others) may also have infected his "new" accusers. Hence, there is at least this much reason to allow that the "new" accusers may have believed their own accusations to be true.

But the purpose of these remarks is not to endorse what would plainly be the unwarranted view that the motives of Socrates' prosecutors were all the same, or to suggest that they would all have endorsed the formal charges with equal vigor. In fact, it remains impossible to determine the degree to which any of them privately believed in the accuracy of their accusations. Their choice of accusations may have been wholly insincere and tactical. Socrates himself suggests that the three have somewhat different motives for making their accusations (23E–24A), and we see no reason to doubt at least the effect of his suggestion. There is, of course, at least some reason to suppose that the main instigator of the charges was not their nominal author, Meletus, but rather Anytus,[41] a man of great political influence at the time,[42] and according to Plato, a man with a mindless and fanatical hatred of the sophists.[43] Such hatred could easily enough apply itself to Socrates, especially given the long-standing slanders of the "first" accusers, or for that matter could ensue upon a conversation of just the sort Plato portrays in the *Meno* from 90A–95A. But our argument is only that the prosecutors had good reason to select the charges they did, for they had excellent reason to suppose that such charges would be taken seriously by the jurors they had to convince. The degree to which the private motives of the prosecutors are expressed in the formal charges, however, is both impossible to determine and irrelevant. At least this much can be said, however: we have good reason to suppose that the prosecutors, the King-archon, and the jury took the formal charges seriously as issues to be argued before the court, whatever other reasons each may have had for acting as they did.

3. SOCRATES' RESPONSE TO THE CHARGES

Despite the differences between scholars' opinions about the specific meaning of the charges, there is virtual unanimity to be found in their assessments of Socrates' interrogation of Meletus: Socrates, they say, makes no attempt to refute the specific charges, but rather demonstrates his own dialectical ability to "entrap"[44] Meletus into confusion and contradiction.

The initial appeal of the established interpretation is evident enough. For one thing, the discrediting of Meletus seems to be all that Socrates intends to achieve through the interrogation: before he begins his questioning, he tells the jury only that he will show that Meletus is"joking by lightly involving men in a law suit" (24C); he does not explicitly say that he will actually refute the charges. Moreover, the interrogation itself is unmistakably similar to the *elenctic* refutations Socrates has always employed with such devastating efficiency against others who claim to know what they do not. Such a process is, after all, an essential part of his mission in Athens. And if the *elenchus* is taken to demonstrate only a contradiction in his opponent's assertions, and not the truth or falsity of individual propositions,[45] it is difficult to see how the interrogation could possibly result in a proof of Socrates' innocence of the formal charges.[46] Finally, as we have said, Socrates' association with the notorious Critias and Alcibiades is affirmed by many ancient sources as being the motive for bringing Socrates to trial, and it is not at all unlikely that his prosecutors would seek to arouse the same bias in the jury. But the Amnesty prohibits Socrates' "new" accusers from addressing such issues directly.[47] It would not be surprising then, were Socrates preemptively to dismiss the formal charges as a purely superficial legal maneuver by showing that even their author has given them only little thought. The irony of Meletus' position would therefore be evident to all. The charges he actually prosecutes are ones for which he cares little;[48] and the charges he considers to be serious are ones he cannot prosecute.

But despite its initial plausibility, the established interpretation is not unproblematical. Socrates begins his speech by telling the jury that he is hopeful that his defense will succeed (19A). Nevertheless, he is keenly aware that acquittal is possible only if he can remove the long-standing prejudice against him that has been engendered by the "first" accusations. And the same reasoning as we applied previously to the prosecutors and jurors also applies to Socrates' own response to each set of accusers. Insofar as there is good reason to suppose that the prosecutors, accusers, and jury would take the charges seriously, there is equal reason for Socrates to recognize that fact. And even if he believes, as he says he does, that the "first" accusers are the more dangerous, since (as we have shown) the charges of each set of accusers are in essence the same, Socrates cannot sensibly take those of one set seriously and reject the others as patently absurd. If one set is serious, both are; if one is beneath serious regard, both are. Of course, Socrates may take the "first" accusers more seriously as adversaries, despite the fact that they charge him with the same crimes as do the "new" accusers, and this seems to be the sense of what he says in assessing the relative dangers of each. He says that he fears the "first" more than the "new" accusers because the former have been at it for such a long time, insinuating their biases in Socrates' jurors from childhood (18B, C); they are many (18C); the case they have made has gone without rebuttal by a defense (presumably until now) (18C); they are for the most part anonymous, except for the comedy writers (18C–D); and, most important, they cannot be cross-examined (*elegxai*—18D).

But Meletus can be cross-examined, unlike the "first" accusers. In the cross-examination he accordingly undertakes, shall Socrates neglect his thereby improved opportunity to demonstrate his innocence, in favor of a flashy demonstration of his ability to "entrap" Meletus with verbal tricks, a strategy certain only to confirm in his jurors' minds the connection made by his most dangerous enemies (18B) with the slick dialectical skills of the sophists? Such behavior would not only be imprudent in the extreme, it would constitute an unnecessary incitement to the jury to follow prejudice instead of law, and thus to come to a verdict that was both inappropriate and immoral. It would make little sense, then, were Socrates to dismiss the formal accusations and to use his opportunity to question Meletus only to make an ironical or rhetorical point, having already expressed his recognition of the danger posed to him by the formal accusations and his desire for his defense to be successful. Yet such verbal trickery is precisely what the established view portrays Socrates as employing in his interrogation of Meletus.

Although Socrates' initial remarks suggests that he will defend himself against both sets of accusations, his principles do not allow him to defend himself in any way whatever, no matter how great the danger each presents. Unlike both the older and the newer accusers, who have engaged in slanders and deceptions, he must tell only the truth (18A, 20D, 22B, 28A, 31E, 32A, 33C). No doubt his concern to tell the truth derives at least in part from the requirement for his mission that he encourage all men to pursue virtue through philosophical examination. Therefore, he would convict himself of impiety for having disobeyed the command of the god were he not to use the occasion of the trial to attempt once again to convince his fellow Athenians, especially those jurors who confuse philosophy with sophistry, that he has done no wrong in pursuing his mission.

Now Socrates' principles do not allow him to say whatever happens to be true in order to promote a just decision. He cannot, for instance, attempt to arouse the compassion of the jury even if what he says is true and would have the effect of preventing the jury from condemning an innocent man (cf. 34B–C). In telling the truth he must enable the jury to perform its assigned legal function. Thus, at the close of his speech rather than issuing a final emotional plea for acquittal, as was the usual practice of defendants, Socrates chooses instead to lecture the jurors once again about his and their respective duties. A speaker, he says, ought to "inform and persuade" (35C2) and "the juror does not take his place in court to grant favors," but "to judge these matters" (C2–3). And in order to leave no doubt about the domain of the specific judgment the jury is to make, he reminds them that the oath they have taken obliges them "to judge with respect to the laws" (C5).[49] Socrates is thus committed to promoting the jury's performance of its proper legal function by telling the truth relevant to the question of his guilt or innocence of the charges. Given his conception of these restraints, therefore, he must attempt to "inform and persuade them" that he has not violated the laws.

Now the law the jury is sworn to consider in this case is the statute proscribing impiety. In order, then, to clarify the issues for consideration by the jury, Meletus has been required to state in the indictment the specific ways in which he is accusing Socrates of impiety.[50] And it is clear that, in Socrates' view, neither he nor the jury may carelessly disregard the formal accusations, given the importance he places on the jury's duty "to judge with respect to the laws" and hence to judge with respect to the truth about the way in which those laws apply in this case. On the contrary, if justice is to be done, Socrates must do everything in his power in the short time allotted to him to convince the jury that Meletus' accusations are false. Were he, then, to have simply ignored these formal accusations in favor of an attempt only to discredit Meletus in the eyes of the jurors, as the established interpretation claims, he would be guilty of engaging in a diversion of the sort he is committed to avoiding, and thus in effect of misleading the jury about the very thing he so adamantly insists they must decide: whether or not he has violated the laws of Athens.[51]

Of course, it might be argued that exposing Meletus' thoughtlessness and confusion goes a long way towards discrediting his accusation, and so the established view of the interrogation need not be seen as requiring Socrates to abandon his own defense. But though we do not deny that the discrediting of Meletus would contribute to Socrates' defense at lease in some sense, we believe that doing so cannot of itself be a goal for Socrates. For one thing, the fact that Socrates is able to confuse Meletus in court is entirely consistent with his charges' being true, and thus with Socrates' having violated the law in the relevant ways. So long as Socrates' interrogation of Meletus involves no actual argument against the truth of the charges, therefore, it is no more than an *ad hominem* diversion from the issue before the court. The issue, after all, is not whether Meletus can survive a clever cross-examination without becoming flustered and foolish-looking; the issue is whether or not his charges are true. If Socrates can show that Meletus is a stupid, impulsive man, that would most assuredly assist Socrates in securing acquittal. But it would do so irrelevantly, for it would have this consequence whether or not Meletus' charges were in fact true. In other words, such an *ad hominem* display would encourage the correct verdict for the wrong reasons, for it would function only by the creation of a bias against Meletus himself, and not by securing a judgment against the truth of the charges. Hence, even though the established view need not convict Socrates of abandoning his defense, it does convict him of failing to adhere to the principles he repeats throughout his speech. If Socrates seeks to demonstrate an incoherency or confusion in this part of the speech, therefore, that incoherency or confusion cannot merely be one he induces ad hoc in Meletus himself. Rather, it must have its source in the actual charges to be considered by the jury.

4. SOCRATES' INTERROGATION OF MELETUS

As we said in part 1 of this essay, before he calls Meletus forward to be questioned, Socrates recalls the indictment in such a way as to reverse the order of the charges from the way they appear in both Diogenes Laertius' and Xenophon's accounts. Hence, when he takes the charges up in order, Socrates considers the corruption charge first.

Surprisingly, Socrates' two initial arguments regarding the corruption charge treat the phrase "corrupts the youth" as if its meaning were unproblematical. The first argument (24C9–25C4) is formulated on the basis of Meletus' agreement with the proposition that "all Athenians make the youth excellent and Socrates alone corrupts them." Socrates immediately points out that such a claim violates the rules suggested by analogous cases, since it is plain in the case of horses and all other animals that only the one person with the appropriate knowledge, namely the trainer, actually improves the animals under his care, whereas all other men injure them (25A13–B6). Moreover, if Meletus' assertion were true, it is unlikely that the youth have been harmed at all, since it is unlikely that one man could succeed in corrupting them when everyone else is acting to make them better off (25B7–C1).

It is not uncommon for defenders of the established interpretation to suggest that this argument is in some way unfair to Meletus.[52] But Socrates in no way forces Meletus to assert that he alone corrupts the young, and in any case, the view that the great majority of Athenian citizens are good men who work to improve those around them was widely held.[53] And far from being disingenuous, Socrates' use of the analogy between the improvement of animals and the improvement of persons is a familiar one in the works of Plato and Xenophon,[54] as is the point he seeks to make with it here, namely, that the majority of his fellow citizens are thoroughly incapable of improving anyone.[55] Finally, although this argument does not show that Socrates is innocent of the accusation, it does succeed in showing that he is at worst no more culpable than most other men, since the analogy indicates that they too injure the young because they lack the knowledge of how to improve them. Thus, if the jury is to convict Socrates on this ground, they must convict virtually all of Athens as well.

The second argument (25C5–26A7), like the first, develops a familiar Socratic doctrine. Meletus agrees that bad men do something evil to those who are with them (25C7–8), and that no one wishes to be harmed rather than benefited (25D1–2). When Meletus subsequently claims that Socrates has corrupted the youth voluntarily, Socrates is quick to point out that this is completely unbelievable given his former admissions (25E4–6), for no one would voluntarily make those around him worse, for from bad people one can only expect to receive harm and evil. Thus, either he has not corrupted the youth at all, or if he has, he has done so involuntarily. Either way, Meletus' accusation is a sham, since the law has no interest in prosecuting the innocent or those who act involuntarily (26A1–7).

The obvious ease with which Socrates derives this conclusion might well have the effect of making Meletus look foolish in the eyes of the jury. But even if some of the jurors take this argument to be no more than a bit of sophistical trickery, it does not follow that Socrates is dissembling or insincere in what he asserts in it. In fact, since the argument is a version of one we see elsewhere in Plato's Socratic writings,[56] there is every reason to take it here as being presented with the utmost seriousness, despite what the jurors, or for that matter we, might think of it. And although this argument, like the first, does not show that he has not actually corrupted the youth, it does show something of considerable importance regarding the accusation: corrupting his youthful followers is something Socrates would never willingly do.

Socrates says that he is convinced that he has never corrupted anyone. And because he must provide the jury with the full truth about his mission, he does not want them to think that his philosophical pursuits have ever harmed anyone, even unintentionally. In order, then, to show that the corruption accusation is actually false, Socrates asks Meletus about the manner in which he allegedly corrupts the youth, and as we said in Part 1, Meletus replies in such a way as to make clear that he predicates the corruption charge upon the religious charges (26B). On Meletus's own interpretation of the charges, therefore, Socrates can prove the corruption charge false by showing that the religious charges are false.[57]

In turning to these parts of the indictment, Socrates' first move is to have Meletus clarify the phrase, "does not recognize the gods the state recognizes." In doing so, Socrates might be supposed only to be baiting a rhetorical trap. But we must not forget that in the Athenian legal system, individuals charged and prosecuted other individuals; Athens had no legal equivalent of our district attorney, who is duly authorized by the state to prosecute charges in the state's name. Hence the prosecutors' interpretation of the charges is *the only* interpretation that is legally at issue before the court, and on this point Meletus must be supposed to speak officially for his fellow prosecutors no less than himself. It could not be that each of the three prosecutors had a different but equally official interpretation of the charges, each of which had to be disproved by Socrates in order for him to defend himself successfully. Of course, other interpretations of the charges might be open to the jurors *psychologically* speaking, and to the extent that

Socrates can anticipate this, it would be prudent for him to defend himself in such a way as to cover these as well. But it is not sensible, and certainly not legally necessary, for Socrates to have to anticipate and defend himself against any possible interpretation of the charges.

Under the circumstances, moreover, Socrates might well be puzzled by the locution "the gods the state recognizes"; neither Athenian law nor custom prescribed the recognition of a clearly specified set of deities, even if, as we argued in Part 1, atheism was impermissible. But, of course, atheism was just what Meletus was charging Socrates with, and thus to make sure that both he and the jury understand the charge, Socrates asks Meletus: "Do you say that I teach that I recognize some gods to be, and therefore I myself recognize gods to be, and that I am not a complete atheist nor unjust in that way, but that these gods are not the ones the state recognizes, but different ones? Is this what you accuse me for, that I recognize the different ones? Or do you say that I do not myself recognize any gods at all, and that I teach this to others?" (26C1–6)

Meletus' unequivocal answer is that Socrates does not recognize any gods at all (26C7). Now the established view of this is that Meletus has been "entrapped" into answering as he does. But the first thing we should notice about the way this argument proceeds is that Socrates has hardly tricked Meletus into his answer. Instead, Socrates plainly lays out all of the options Meletus might take, clearly offering as one of them that Socrates is not a complete atheist, but only a theistic innovator. Meletus' answer, then, is in no way forced; rather, it seems to be freely and eagerly contributed.

Of course, Meletus' answer does in fact allow Socrates subsequently to derive a contradiction in the charges so conceived, and thus it might be thought that Meletus has made an unbelievable blunder that he would eagerly wish to retract if given the slightest opportunity; surely a more careful and evasive answer could be given. But as we argued in Part 2, there is every reason to suppose that Meletus and his collaborators actually believed they could convince the jury that Socrates was an atheist. Many Athenians would have thought this about any number of the sophists and nature philosophers, and insofar as they were inclined to see no important distinction between those fellows and Socrates, a charge of complete atheism would come naturally to mind. Playing upon such a presumption would not be tactically unreasonable either, even if the prosecutors themselves did not believe it. Given the long-standing suspicion that Socrates is one of these "atheistic" nature philosophers, a prejudice upon which the prosecution has relied so heavily in daring to bring Socrates to trial in the first place, Meletus and the others would lose a major advantage if they were to attempt to revise that prejudice. One could hardly expect the jury to abandon what they had supposed all along and suddenly believe that the danger Socrates posed to society was actually quite unlike that supposed to be posed by the stereotypical sophist or nature philosopher, namely, complete irreligion. Had Meletus attempted to select Socrates' other option, therefore, he would be committed to showing Socrates in a very new light, in which the old prejudices must be abandoned, for now it would turn out that Socrates was in fact religious in some recognizable sense, even though his religious beliefs were not the customary ones. Of course, it is still possible that Meletus would be able to convince the jurors that Socrates was guilty of impiety even on these grounds, but now he would have to do so without the aid of the "first accusers." Understandably, Meletus seeks to avoid incurring such a loss by maintaining the stereotypical portrayal of Socrates as an atheist.

But once it is clear that the charge of "not recognizing the gods the state recognizes" is really an accusation of atheism, Socrates can point out its implausibility. For one thing, even if this conception of the accusation were true, the youth of Athens would hardly have needed to come to Socrates to learn such a doctrine, since the books of Anaxagoras, which are filled with the very sorts of views Meletus has in mind, are so easily accessible (26D–E). But Socrates also advances an additional argument that, he says, will show that the indictment is "insolent, unrestrained, and rashly conceived" (26E). The first point is that anyone who believes in (again, *nomizei*—recognizes) "*daimonia pragmata*" (divine matters) of whatever sort must also believe in the existence of *daimones* in the same way, for example, that anyone who believes in matters pertaining to horses must believe in the existence of horses (27B3–C10). The second point is that recognition of the existence of *daimones* requires recognition of the existence of gods (*theoi*), since *daimones* are themselves either gods or the children of gods. The two points taken together form the premises of a hypothetical syllogism, the conclusion of which is that anyone who recognizes any sort of divinities must also believe in gods. Since the additional premise, that Socrates recognizes some divinities, is provided by the indictment itself, the senselessness of Meletus' charge is apparent: on the one hand, Meletus accuses Socrates of not believing in any gods; but the last part of the indictment can be true only if Socrates does believe in gods.

Some have found treachery in one of the vital premises of this argument, arguing that it is unthinkable that Socrates could really believe in *daimones* as they are conceived in the argument.[58] But though we do know that Socrates was critical of some aspects of the religious orthodoxy of his day,[59] in not one of the ancient sources do we find any reason to suppose that Socrates did not hold orthodox beliefs as regards the nature of *daimones*. And even if he did not, his argument is not thereby reduced to an *ad hominem*, as the established view would hold,[60] for it still shows that the indictment, as Meletus himself would interpret it, cannot be maintained sensibly. In other words, it is not that Meletus has been confused into admitting what he did not really mean. Rather, in relying on the prejudicial stereotypes against Socrates, Meletus has trapped himself in incoherency: atheistic sophists and nature philosophers do not believe in new divinities; they do not believe in divinities at all.

Could Meletus not have avoided such an embarrassing conclusion? Let us reconsider his options. As we have said, he could have selected the alternative Socrates offered him by saying that Socrates does recognize some gods, just not the gods of the state. But again, that would actually support Socrates' defense against the "first accusers," for now Socrates could say, "you see, even Meletus and his supporters do not believe I am really like the character of my name in the *Clouds;* even Meletus and his supporters realize that I am no Anaxagoras." If Socrates is right about the relative dangers posed by the two sets of accusers, then it would be a great advantage to his defense to be able to call his current accusers as witnesses, as it were, against the more dangerous "first accusers." Meletus could have selected Socrates' other proffered interpretation of the charges, then, only by undermining the very thing most dangerous to Socrates: the well-established prejudice that he is an atheistic nature philosopher like Anaxagoras.

What if Meletus denies the connection between *daimones* and *theoi?* If anything, this would be an even worse strategy, for now he would have to deny one of the standard religious beliefs of his day, an odd position for the prosecutor of an impiety charge to have to endorse in open court. But could Meletus not simply deny that Socrates would make any such connection? No, for not only could Meletus not provide evidence for such a claim, but any such denial would appear implausible to the average Athenian; such distinctions were simply not made. We know of not one case of someone who held sincere beliefs in *daimones* but denied the existence of any gods. Finally, Meletus could also not deny that Socrates' belief in *daimones* was sincere. After all, Socrates' belief in his "divine sign" was apparently well known,[61] and provided Meletus one natural ground for the second charge. Any attempt to say that Socrates did not really believe in the existence of his "divine sign" would be instantly rejected by anyone with sense on the jury.

But now it might appear that Socrates' arguments are so easily won that Meletus and his fellow accusers could not have failed to see them coming when they undertook to write the charges. Certainly Meletus shows great reluctance to answer Socrates' questions in the courtroom, but this might only represent uneasiness about being interrogated by one so renowned for dialectical wizardry. It is more likely that Meletus and the other accusers were blinded by the same prejudices upon which they relied, as Socrates says, in bringing the case before the court, prejudices deriving from the "first accusers" (19A–B). Prejudice, as we know, does not work according to rational processes; where prejudice is at work incompatible things may be endorsed in ways that are unthinkable to those viewing the issue rationally. The prejudiced man says of his enemy both that he is dull-witted and that he is treacherously clever; both that he is worthless and weak and that he is a dangerous threat. One worries that one's enemy may woo one's friends into his alliance, all the while saying (what one does not believe about one's friends) that only fools and evildoers would ever consider befriending such a man. If Meletus et al. are guilty of prejudice, then, to that extent their critical faculties as regards Socrates' real character and beliefs were at their worst, and the charges they sought to bring may well have reflected that fact.

Nor can it be that the King-archon would of necessity prevent incoherent charges from being brought to trial. If Socrates' reputation was as bad as we might suppose, there is no reason to suppose that the King-archon would not be infected with the same prejudice. We may even suppose that the prosecutors charged Socrates when they did (and not earlier or later) because they felt confident that the current King-archon, an elected official, would forward their charges without resistance or interference of any kind. Anytus, after all, was a man with many powerful connections in Athens at the time.

And if this is the case, it would not even matter if one or more of the prosecutors recognized that Socrates could not both be a complete atheist and hold a sincere belief in his *daimonion,* for example. That prosecutor or those prosecutors might still be willing to go to court with flawed charges on the tactical assumption that the prejudice such charges would further inflame or arouse would weigh more heavily than any incoherence Socrates *might* (and it turns out does) expose in them. Whatever the prosecutors believed, their tactics worked; for the jury, despite Socrates' refutation of Meletus' charges, convicts Socrates anyway.

5. THE JURY'S VERDICT

But Plato tells us that the margin by which Socrates is convicted is remarkably narrow.[62] Socrates takes the closeness of the vote to be compelling evidence that he has thoroughly refuted Meletus' formal accusation (36A) and he attributes his conviction to the fact that

Anytus and Lycon also spoke against him (36A–B) and to his own refusal to be in any way obsequious to the jury (38D–39A). Indeed, he says that he would actually have succeeded in overcoming even these difficulties had he only been given more time to speak (37A–B). He makes it clear, however, that had he been given more time, he would have continued to present precisely the same kind of defense. It is decidedly implausible, then, that Socrates would have set aside nearly one-fifth of the time allotted for his defense to interrogate Meletus had he only sought, as the orthodox interpretation maintains, merely to reveal Meletus' incompetence *ad hominem,* especially when he can make Meletus' foolishness abundantly clear to all by showing that the charges rely on prejudices that are incoherent and thus indefensible.[63]

But one last worry must be addressed. It might be argued that the reason for conviction was at least in part that Socrates' interrogation of Meletus had the effect of leaving intact in the jurors' minds the one interpretation of the charges that does render them consistent not only with one another, but also with Socrates' sincere belief in his *daimonion:* Socrates does not recognize the gods of the state, but introduces new divinities in which he sincerely believes, but that are nonetheless false and offensive to orthodox religion. Socrates plainly does not ever explicitly refute any such interpretation of the charges; for example, not once in the *Apology* does he ever directly assert his belief in the gods of the state under that description. Moreover, though his claim to have a personal divine guide may well have troubled many jurors, he never tries to defend its compatibility with conventional religious belief.[64] Taking these two facts together with Socrates' suggestion at *Euthyphro* 6A that the motive for his prosecution is his skepticism concerning many of the generally accepted myths and characterizations of the gods, we might even suppose that he could not defend himself convincingly before the jury against this interpretation of the charges.

A number of considerations count against this supposition, however, though we do not believe that any decisive resolution of this issue is possible. For one thing, we must recall that the interpretation of the charges in question is not the one in fact before the court, and hence Socrates is under no legal obligation to "inform and persuade" (35C2) the court about this issue. And if we take seriously Socrates' remarks about the influence of the "first accusers," since this interpretation of the charges diverges so far from their slanders, in which Meletus follows suit, it may be for all practical purposes moot. Socrates does not consider it, on this line of reasoning, since no one else in the courtroom is likely to be concerned by it either. Moreover, what Socrates says in the *Euthyphro* is for at least a few reasons not strong evidence for the view at issue. For one thing, Socrates in the *Euthyphro* has not yet been through the *anakrisis,* and so does not yet know what the specific interpretation of the charges to be argued before the court is going to be. His speculation about the motive and meaning of the charges at 6A, therefore, is not an informed one, and turns out, as what actually happens in the *Apology* would appear to show, to be incorrect. Again, since Meletus in fact put another interpretation on the charges, we have no reason to suppose that the issues Socrates raises in the *Euthyphro* were ever considered (at least explicitly) by anyone at the actual trial. Secondly, what Socrates there says may have caused his prosecutors to take action against him does not in any way entail that he disbelieves in the gods of the state. Rather, all he says is that he finds it difficult to believe the stories about them that would seem to degrade and diminish them. Finally, it is not at all clear to us at least that this kind of doubt would qualify as criminally impious even to the most orthodox Athenians. After all, though it is clear that the fanatical Euthyphro does believe all of the stories Socrates doubts, the former shows no pious outrage at Socrates' confession of skepticism, and we must suppose that what would qualify as acceptably orthodox allowed some degree of latitude, at least.

It cannot, of course, be doubted that Socrates does not undertake to address the one coherent and factually arguable conception of the charges that could have been, though it was not in fact, offered. But, for the reasons outlined, we find the evidence favoring the claim that his silence on this point weighed against him at the trial to be insufficient and thus believe that any conclusions on this issue can be at best only prohibitively speculative.

6. SUMMARY AND CONCLUSION

The arguments of this paper should not be taken as saying that the interrogation provides Socrates' only, or even the principal part of his defense, for that is far from true. As Socrates himself says, the "first" accusations have always been the most dangerous, and whatever the jury may think of it, it is plain that Socrates believes that his philosophical activity in Athens is an expression of the highest sort of piety, as an "assistance" (23B), "obedience" (29D), and "service" (30A) to the god. Our view is only that his interrogation of Meletus is not merely a defensive diversion from Socrates' refutation of the charges against him, but rather contributes substantive grounds to those capable of perceiving them for believing him innocent.

We have argued that the charges against Socrates are intended to be taken seriously, and that Socrates' interrogation of Meletus addresses the formal charges directly in an attempt to convince the jury that these charges have no merit. Such an approach, we believe, is required by the principles Socrates refers to in his speech. But these principles also require that he make clear Meletus' ignorance and lack of concern for matters of the greatest importance. It is testimony to Socrates' consummate philosophical skill that he accomplishes both goals with such precision and economy of argument, for by questioning Meletus directly he demonstrates that not even his most fanatical enemy can coherently believe that he is guilty of charges in the indictment.

NOTES

We are indebted to Gregory Vlastos, Charles M. Reed, Jean Roberts, Mark McPherran, David M. Halperin, Walter Englert and the editorial staff of *Journal of the History of Philosophy* for their helpful suggestions and criticisms of various earlier drafts of this paper, and to the National Endowment for the Humanities for helping to fund our research on this topic. All errors, however, are ours alone.

1. Meletus is at least nominally the principal prosecutor of the case, but this of course does not rule out his acting on someone else's behalf. Many believe that Anytus was the real force behind the prosecution (about which, see note 41).
2. The clearest statement of this position can be found in the treatment of this issue by Reginald Hackforth in *The Composition of Plato's Apology* (Cambridge, Eng., 1933), 104–10. An absurd extreme of this view is argued by Thomas G. West, *Plato's Apology of Socrates* (Ithaca and London, 1979), 134–50, who dismisses Socrates' arguments in this section as

"among the most ridiculous used by him anywhere in Plato" and sees this as proof that the entire interrogation is Plato's attempt at comedy writing (135). Though we do not take the arguments of this paper as providing evidence for or against the view that Plato's Socrates is an accurate representation of the actual man himself, we do oppose the view that Plato's account in this case must be seen as providing Socrates no serious and substantive defense, for such is precisely what we propose can be found, even if the defense in question is only one of Plato's invention.

One reason for wondering whether this part of Plato's account is his own invention, however, we will not take seriously. Someone might wonder whether the incident could take place at all. But even Hackforth (109–10) recognizes that Athenian law allowed Socrates to interrogate Meletus, and notes that such an interrogation (though different in substance) also occurs at Xen. *Apol.* 19–21. For more on the legal permissibility of such an interrogation, see John Burnet, *Plato's Euthyphro, Apology of Socrates, and Crito* (London, 1924), note on 24C9 (106).

3. Clear examples of this view can be found in Burnet, 100–101, and note on 24C9 (106–7) and also, *Greek Philosophy* (Melbourne, London, and Toronto, 1968), 146–47; A. E. Taylor, *Plato: The Man and His Work* (London, 1977), 162–63; A. E. Taylor, *Socrates* (New York, 1933), 100; James Beckman, *The Religious Dimension of Socrates' Thought* (Waterloo, 1979), 60–63; Roman Guardini, *The Death of Socrates*, tr. B. Wrighton (New York, 1948), 43; E. H. Blakeney, *The Apology of Socrates* (London, 1929), 118.

4. For an extensive list of such possible motives, see Coleman Phillipson *The Trial of Socrates* (London, 1928), 157–67, 200–212. See also, K. J. Dover, "Freedom of the Intellectual in Greek Society," *Talanta* 7 (1975): 24–54, esp. 51–54. We agree that such motives may have encouraged Socrates' accusers to make their charges, but we disagree with the inference often made from this view that the formal charges were not themselves seriously at issue before the court. (For someone who questions the extent of political motive, see Hackforth, 71–79.)

5. Tr. after R. D. Hicks.

6. Xenophon's version has *eispheron* instead of *eisegoumenos*, which does not change the sense of the indictment (*Mem.* 1.1.1).

7. Some commentators refer to only two accusations, the corruption charge and the impiety charge, and thus take "not recognizing the gods the state recognizes, and introducing other new divinities" to be one accusation. As will be made clear in our argument to follow, Socrates and Meletus in Plato's *Apology* understand the explicitly religious part of the indictment as making two distinct charges.

8. Burnet (1924) notes on *Eu.* 3B3 (15), and *Apol.* 18C3 and 24C1 (78, 104–5); A. E. Taylor (1933), 98; R. E. Allen, *Plato's "Euthyphro" and the Earlier Theory of Forms* (London, 1970), 62.

9. Hackforth, 58–70; W. K. C. Guthrie, *A History of Greek Philosophy* (Cambridge, 1969), 3:237, n. 2; J. Beckman, 55–56; J. Tate, "Greek for Atheism," *Classical Review* 50 (1936): 3–5, and "More Greek for Atheism," *Classical Review* 51 (1937): 3–6.

10. For example, see Burnet (1924), note on *Apol.* 26C2, 111.

11. Burnet (1924), note on *Apol.* 24C1, 104.

12. See esp. *"ouk einai theous"* at *Mem.* 1.1.5.

13. The Amnesty created during the archonship of Eucleides called for the complete revision and codification of the laws of Athens. It further required that all prosecutions be for alleged violations of the newly codified laws and that there could be no prosecutions for alleged violations of *psephismata*, or edicts passed by the Assembly, one of which may have been the psephism of Diopeithes. For more on the Amnesty, see Burnet (1924), 100–101; A. W. R. Harrison, *The Law of Athens* (Oxford, 1971), 1:47–48.

Recently, however, Dover has questioned the existence of the disputed psephism (39–41), and of the action against Anaxagoras (27–32). But whether or not there ever was such a psephism, even Dover admits that "we do not have to suppose that the legislation of 403 (the Amnesty) redefined piety in such a way as explicitly to include types of behaviour proscribed by Diopeithes; to be the victim of a *graphe* at Athens it was not necessary to have committed an act which was forbidden by the law in so many words" (41). In any case, we do not believe that sufficient sense can be made of what Socrates says at *Apol.* 26D (about which Dover is surprisingly silent) unless there had been an action against Anaxagoras, or at the very least, unless such an action were conceivable, on the very sorts of grounds specified in the disputed psephism. Hence, though Dover is right when he points out that the evidence for these incidents is inconclusive, we remain convinced that there is some justification of our view to be found in the stories about the prosecution of Anaxagoras, whether or not there really was such a prosecution, and whether or not it was performed under the psephism of Diopeithes. Again, our point is only that there is no reason to suppose that the charge of impiety, on the grounds of atheism, would be viewed by the Athenians as either illegal or even perverse.

14. This is made obvious by the fact that Socrates is being tried in the Heliastic court, the principal court in Athens. (See also *Eu.* 12E.)
15. See Douglas M. MacDowell, *The Law in Classical Athens* (Ithaca, 1978), 199–200.
16. On the importance of the *anakrisis* in clarifying the issues to be set forth in the indictment, see MacDowell, 240–42.
17. Plato could quite naturally have reminded us of such an illegality in any number of dialogues, and the same goes for Xenophon, yet there is complete silence among the ancients on this issue.
18. See also *Gorg.* 474A. For other ancient references to the Arginusae affair, see Xen. *Mem.* 1.1.18, 4.4.2, *Hell.* 1.7.12–15; *Axiochus* 368; D. L. 2.24.
19. At *Eu.* 3B2, however, Socrates says that Meletus is charging him with making new gods (*"Phesi gar me poieten einai theon, kai hos kainous poiounta theous, tous d' archaious ou nominzonta, egrapsato touton auton heneka, hos phesin"*). This discrepancy, we believe, is sufficiently accounted for by our following analysis of the specific charge, by the fact that Socrates at *Eu.* 3B2 is not reporting the actual words of the charge, but is rather speaking loosely, and by the fact that Euthyphro, immediately after Socrates' remark, unhesitatingly infers that the "new gods" are no other than Socrates' private *daimonion* (about which, more below).
20. As Gregory Vlastos has pointed out to us, this would fit nicely with the picture of Socrates Aristophanes offers in the *Clouds,* for there Socrates says that "the gods have no currency here" (247) and flatly denies the existence of Zeus (366); instead, he calls the Clouds "our divinities" (*tais hemeteraisi daimosi*—252). This would also explain the otherwise peculiar qualifications in pseudo-Lysias' speech, "Against Andocides" 51: "the gods in whom we believe and whom we worship and to whom we sacrifice in purity and pray . . ."; that is, the *real* gods, not just anything that might be called by that name.
21. *"Theion ti kai daimonion";* on the vagueness of Socrates' terminology, see Burnet (1924) note on *Eu.* 3B5, 16–17.
22. Plato, *Apol.* 31D, *Eu.* 3B5–7; Xen., *Apol.* 12. Burnet (1924) doubts this connection (see his notes on *Eu.* 3B5 [15–17], *Apol.* 24C1 [105], 31C7 and D1 [127–28]).
23. Plato, *Apol.* 31D, 40C, 41D; *Eu.* 3D; *Eud.* 272E; *Rep.* 496C; *Phdr.* 242B; and the spurious *Theages* 128D–131A; Xen. *Mem.* 1.1.2–4, 4.8.1; *Apol.* 4–5, 8, 12–13; *Sym.* 8.5.
24. For examples, see Burnet (1924) note on *Eu.* 3B2 (14); Beckman, 57; Taylor (1933), 101–2.
25. For one of many examples of this, see the references to Anaximenes in Hippolytus, *Ref.* 1.7.1; Aetius 1.7.13; Cicero *N.D.* 1.10.26; Augustinus *Civ. Dei.* 8.2. See also Aristotle's more general remark at *Phys.* 3.203b7ff.
26. See note 16.
27. See Burnet (1924) note on 24B9, 103–4, and our next paragraph, however.
28. See note 13.

29. This is also the interpretation of this charge Meletus offers during Socrates' cross-examination of him in Xen. *Apol.* 20. W. A. Heidel takes Plato's *Euthyphro* as providing a defense against this more general conception of the charge, in "the emphatic utterance Socrates gives to his surprise at Euthyphro's conduct toward his father. Socrates was often charged with inciting sons to disrespect and even violence to their parents. What more effective means of meeting this calumny than this could be devised by his friend?" ("On Plato's *Euthyphro*," *Transactions and Proceedings of the American Philological Society* 31 [1900]: 166). Heidel's view is perhaps somewhat supported by the fact that Diogenes Laertius claims that Euthyphro abandoned his suit against his father as a result of his conversation with Socrates (2.29).

Yet another sense of this charge might be derived from *Crito* 53C, where Socrates seems to assume that inducing disrespect for the laws in the youth would count as corrupting them, and that if Socrates were to be guilty of this he would thereby prove that the verdict of his trial had been the right one. (We owe this point to Gregory Vlastos.)

30. Aischines, 1.173.
31. For a reconstruction and discussion of this, see Anton-Hermann Chroust, *Socrates, Man and Myth* (Notre Dame, 1957), 69–100.
32. Burnet (1924), 101; see also Hackforth, 72.
33. Xen. *Mem.* 1.2.9–61. See also Libanius, *Apol.*, esp. 135, 136, 148.
34. Isoc. *Busiris* 5. Despite this evidence, Hackforth doubts that the connections to Critias and Alcibiades had as much effect on the prosecutors as the ancient authors proposed (71–79).
35. Burnet (1924) notes on *Eu.* 2B9, 9–11, and *Apol.* 32D6, 137; Taylor (1933), 95; Hackforth, 78; Beckman, 60. This identification is denied by Eduard Zeller in *Socrates and the Socratic Schools*, tr. O. J. Reichel (London, 1877), 193–94, n. 6; A. N. W. Saunders in *Greek Political Oratory* (Bungay, Suffolk, 1970), 65 n. 5; W. D. Ross in the *Oxford Classical Dictionary*, 2d ed. (Oxford, 1970), 667. *q.v.* Meletus, and Kahrstedt in *R. E.* 15.1, cols. 503–4, *q.v.* Meletus. For more on Meletus, see F. Stoessl in supplemental volume 12 of the *R. E.*, col. 852–54, *q.v.* Meletus.
36. Andocides, *On the Mysteries*, 94.
37. Burnet (1924) note on *Apol.* 32D6, 137.
38. In fact, such a connection is made by none of the ancient sources (see, e.g., Diogenes Laertius' silence at 2.24).
39. See the relative dates given by Saunders, 270–71.
40. Burnet (1924) note on *Eu.* 2B9, 9–11. Guthrie flatly claims that "the name is not common" (381, n. 2). Saunders, on the contrary, says "There were several persons called Meletus" (65 n. 5). On this issue, Saunders seems to us to be right. See also D. M. MacDowell, *Andocides on the Mysteries* (Oxford, 1962), 208ff.
41. This view is lent some support by Diogenes Laertius' endorsement of it at 2.38, and by Plato's first reference to his accusers in the *Apology* (18D3) as *tous amphi Anuton* (see also 29C1, 30B8, 31A5). Many commentators endorse this view of the matter without hesitation; for examples, see Guthrie, who calls Meletus "a puppet whose strings were pulled by the powerful Anytus" (381); Blakeney, who calls Meletus "one of the creatures of Anytus" (22); and Burnet, who says that Anytus "stooped to make use of the fanaticism of Meletus" (101). This account of the matter is not, however, universally accepted; see Hackforth (77–78), for example. The outcome of this particular debate would not affect the position we seek to establish in this essay, however.
42. See Plato's description of him at *Meno* 90A–B. For other ancient references to Anytus, see Zeller, 194 n. 1; P. J. Rhodes, *A Commentary on the Aristotelian Athenaion Politeia* (Oxford, 1981), 343–44, 431–33; J. K. Davies, *Athenian Propertied Families, 600–300 B.C.* (Oxford, 1971), 40–41; and *R. E.* vol. 1.2, col. 2656, *q.v.* Anytus.
43. See *M.* 91C, 92A.
44. It is interesting to see how often this word or one of its derivatives is used in describing the

interrogation. See, for examples, Burnet (1924) notes on 24C9 (107), 26A4 (110) and 26D4 (112); Taylor (1933), 100; Hackforth (104); Beckman (61).

45. For the view that the *elenchus* demonstrates only the inconsistency of a set of propositions, see, for examples, Gregory Vlastos, *Protagoras* (Indianapolis and New York, 1956), xxvi–xxxi (Vlastos has subsequently abandoned the view he argues here, however); Richard Robinson, *Plato's Earlier Dialectic* (New York and London, 1980), 17–18. Recently, however, T. H. Irwin in *Plato's Moral Theory* (Oxford, 1977), chapter 3, argues that individual propositions may be established. Though the general arguments for each position cannot be considered here, it will be plain from our interpretation of this instance of a Socratic argument that we believe it intended to provide a positive proof of Socrates' innocence. Hence, at least for this case, we are committed to something like Irwin's view.

46. It might be thought that by reducing Meletus to a state of *aporia* Socrates would have proved his innocence, since the prosecution would not have carried its burden of proof. But Athenian law recognizes no such burden and it is unlikely that an Athenian jury would acquit a defendant simply on the grounds that the prosecutor had failed to provide a strong case against him, especially (as in this instance) if the jury felt it had independent grounds for finding the defendant guilty of the prosecutor's charges.

47. See n. 13. It is worth noting that Anytus was very active in the passage of the Amnesty (see Isoc. *In Callim.* 23), and hence would be unlikely to want to violate it in fact or in spirit.

48. It is likely that Socrates is punning on Meletus' name throughout the interrogation. "Meletus" is a cognate of *melein* ("to care for" or "to be an object of care"), yet Socrates shows how little Meletus cares about a series of vital issues.

49. According to Demosthenes (24.149–51) the exact wording of the juror's oath is as follows: "I will judge according to the laws and decrees of Athens, and matters about which there are no laws I will judge by the justest opinion." We cannot, of course, be certain that precisely the same oath was administered to jurors in 399. However, Socrates' references to the oath suggest that they are very similar. For more on the oath taken by jurors, see MacDowell (1978), 43–44.

50. At the *anakrisis* before the trial; see note 16.

51. In addition to the above reasons, Socrates' rhetoric suggests that he intends his interrogation of Meletus to be seen as a defense against the formal charges. The expression Socrates uses to complete his interrogation of Meletus (*hikana kai tauta*—28A3–4) is a standard sign employed by forensic orators to mark the completion of a refutation. A like and equally standard forensic marking expression (*hikane apologia*) is used at 24B4 to mark the end of his defense against the older accusers. (On the use of these expressions in forensic rhetoric, see Burnet [1924], note on 28A4, 117).

52. See, for examples, Burnet (1924) note on 26D4 (112); Taylor (1977), 164; West, 137, 144.

53. See, for example, Plato, *Prot.* 323A–328D, where Protagoras endorses the view that every citizen is capable of improving the youth by teaching them what virtue is. Of course, he also believes that some sophists provide better training, and he the best of all. The former view, but most strenuously not the latter, is averred by Anytus in the *Meno* (92E).

54. Plato, *Eu.* 13B–C; *Rep.* 342C; Xen. *Mem.* 4.1.3–4.

55. Plato, *Cr.* 47A–48A.

56. Related arguments are to be found at *M.* (77B–78A), and *Prot.* (351B–358D). See also Arist., *EN* 1145b23–28 and Xen., *Mem.* 3.9.4–5.

57. Strictly, to show that the corruption charge is false Socrates must show that it is false that he teaches the young not to recognize the gods the state recognizes *and* that this is the *only* way in which he corrupts the youth according to the indictment. It is clear from what follows, however, that both Meletus and Socrates are assuming the proper conjunction.

58. Guardini, for example, proclaims that "it is hardly to be assumed that Socrates believed

seriously in 'illegitimate children of the gods, either by the nymphs or by other mothers'" (43).

59. See, e.g., *Eu.* 6A.

60. See, e.g., Guardini, 43.

61. Socrates tells the jury that they have heard him talk about his *daimonion* "at many times in many places" (31C–D). See also *Eu.* 3B.

62. See *Apol.* 36E. Of the 501 jurors, 221 apparently voted for acquittal. Thus, had only thirty additional jurors voted for Socrates, he would have won the case.

63. On the supposition that Plato's account of the trial is essentially accurate, the closeness of the jury's vote would itself give some evidence that Socrates' interrogation of Meletus was taken seriously by them. If we assume that the widespread pre-trial hostility to Socrates was real, and that the "first" accusations were the cause of it, then the jury's acceptance or rejection of his defense against these accusations will have the greatest effect on the outcome of the trial. But the center of his defense against these accusations is the oracle story, and in both Plato's and Xenophon's account this part of Socrates' speech particularly outraged the jurors (Plato, *Apol.* 21A; Xen., *Apol.* 14). Hence, whatever (however incomplete) success in his defense speech may be implied by the closeness of the vote to convict Socrates would not likely have derived from his defense against the "first" accusers. We might thus suppose the interrogation of Meletus to have been one of the most persuasive parts of the speech.

64. Xenophon argues that Socrates' belief is no novelty in *Mem.* 1.1.3–4. But the very fact that Xenophon feels he must undertake this defense in the first place leaves one with the sense that there might have been something in Socrates' belief that troubled the jury after all. It is also true that when Euthyphro is told that Socrates is being charged with impiety, he immediately supposes that the charge is based on Socrates' belief in the *daimonion* (see *Eu.* 3B). Euthyphro's readiness to make such an inference indicates that Socrates' belief was potentially troublesome to those of traditional convictions. Nonetheless, it remains true that Socrates himself sees nothing wrongful or impious in his belief in his *daimonion* and gives no indication that he perceived it as being a significant concern to the jury.

FURTHER READING

Allen, R. E. 1980. *Socrates and Legal Obligation.* Minneapolis, Minn.

Brickhouse, T. C., and Smith, N. D., 1989. "Socrates' Defense, Part II (24b3–30c1)." *Socrates on Trial,* 109–53. Princeton, N.J.

Kraut, R. 1984. *Socrates and the State.* Princeton, N.J.

Reeve, C. D. C. 1990. "The Defense Against Meletus." *Socrates in the "Apology,"* 74–107. Indianapolis, Ind.

3

Did Plato Write
Socratic Dialogues?

CHARLES H. KAHN

My title is deliberately provocative, since I want to challenge both the chronology and the philosophical interpretation generally accepted for the dialogues called Socratic. I am not primarily interested in questions of chronology, or even in Plato's intellectual "development." But the chronological issues are clear-cut, and it will be convenient to deal with them first. My aim in doing so will be to get at more interesting questions concerning philosophical content and literary design.

Interpreters should perhaps think more often about such questions as: why did Plato write dialogues after all? Why does a little dialogue like the *Laches* have such a stellar cast, with so many major figures from Athenian history? Why does Plato re-create the schoolboy atmosphere of the *Charmides* and *Lysis?* Why does he compose such a large and vivid fencing-match between Socrates and the long-dead Protagoras, in a conversation supposed to have taken place before Plato himself was born? The view I wish to challenge tends to assume that Plato's motivation in such dialogues was primarily historical: to preserve and defend the memory of Socrates by representing him as faithfully as possible. From this is would seem to follow that the philosophic content of these dialogues must be Socrates' own philosophy, which Plato has piously preserved somewhat in the way that Arrian has preserved the teachings of Epictetus. The counterpart assumption tends to be that when Plato ceases to write as an historian he writes like any other philosopher: using Socrates as a mouthpiece to express whatever philosophical doctrines Plato himself holds at the time of writing.

Although there must be some truth in both assumptions—for Plato surely does attempt to give a lifelike portrait of Socrates, and he also sometimes puts in Socrates' mouth views which must be Plato's—yet neither assumption takes seriously into account the fact that the dialogues are works of dramatic art, and in most cases of dramatic fiction. As works of art they produce an effect of literary "distancing" between author and audience which prevents us, even in works as late as the *Parmenides* and *Theaetetus*, from simply reading off the author's thoughts in any straightforward way from what is said by some character in the dialogues. The Socrates of the dialogues is an ambiguous figure, at once Plato's historical master and his literary puppet. A parallel ambiguity attaches to the portraits of Protagoras, Alcibiades, and most characters in these works.

The dialogue itself is a unique art form: a piece of rigorous philosophical discussion wrapped in a dramatic, personal setting and projected into the historical past. We have only to compare it with Cicero's elegant but pallid imitations to see what a rich and vibrant artistic structure the Platonic dialogue has. To such artful cunning on the part of the writer there should correspond a degree of hermeneutical subtlety on the part of the reader. But let us begin with chronology.

The standard view, admirably presented by Professor Guthrie in the fourth volume of his *History*, is that Plato's earliest writings form a "Socratic" group, in which he "is imaginatively recalling, in form and substance, the conversations of his master without as yet adding to them any distinctive doctrines of his own" (p. 67). For Guthrie this group includes *Apology, Crito, Euthyphro, Laches, Lysis, Charmides, Hippias Major, Hippias Minor,* and *Ion.* At the end of this group comes the *Protagoras,* which "takes the argument further than the others," but contains nothing specifically Platonic (p. 214). The *Gorgias* on the other hand is clearly later, more Platonic: "Socrates the ignorant questioner has turned into a man of positive and strongly expressed convictions," and we have "the first of the great eschatological myths" (p. 284). Then comes the *Euthydemus,* and the *Meno* which introduces Pythagorean themes such as reincarnation and mathematics.[1] Writing independently at about the same time, Terence Irwin bases his account of Plato's moral theory upon what is essentially the same chronology, which he regards as "fairly widely accepted": first a Socratic period, then the *Protagoras,* interpreted as "Plato's first systematic defence of Socratic ethics," followed by the *Gorgias,* which represents a new departure but still works with "the inadequate resources of the Socratic theory."[2] Only in the *Meno* does Plato begin to develop a theory of his own, with the doctrine of recollection and the distinction between knowledge and true belief.

As far as the *Meno* is concerned, I think the prevailing view is correct that sees this work as a curtain-raiser for the middle dialogues—and by middle dialogues here I mean *Symposium, Phaedo, Cratylus, Republic,* and *Phaedrus:* the dialogues in which we find the classical theory of Forms. Hence I shall not question the standard ordering of the dialogues from the *Meno* on. But I hasten to point out that the entire construction of a chronology prior to the *Meno* rests on sand. Stylometry can tell us that all these dialogues belong to the same "early" group, but it cannot tell us in what order they were written.[3] And if stylometry is quite useless here, external evidence is extremely meagre. Of course the death of Socrates in 399 is a *terminus post quem* for *Apology,* and *Crito,* and presumably for all the rest. Otherwise the only significant datum, in my opinion, is the statement of the *Seventh Epistle* that Plato was about forty years old when he gave up hope of a political career in Athens and set off for Italy and Sicily.[4] I think Dodds and others are correct to see the impact of this momentous decision in the passionate conflict between political and philosophical careers in the *Gorgias.*[5] If this is right, we can date the *Gorgias* around 390–386; and the *Menexenus,* which reflects a similar emotional involvement in Athenian imperial politics, dates itself in (or immediately after) 386. But aside from these clues for *Gorgias* and *Menexenus,* and some hints for dating the *Ion* in the 390s, we have no external evidence worth mentioning for the date of any dialogue earlier than *Meno* and *Symposium.*[6] There are some grounds for putting both *Meno* and *Symposium* in the general neighbourhood of 380, which gives us a plausible *terminus ante quem* for the entire early group.[7] Hence we have thirteen dialogues to locate in some twenty years (399–380), where the only fixed points are the

Gorgias (390–386, with some probability) and the *Menexenus* (386 or 385, with near certainty).

So I propose to begin by sweeping away the historical mirage of an "early Socratic" period, and clearing the ground for a new construction. This means redating the four dialogues of "definition" (using this term loosely, to include the *Lysis*), and the *Protagoras* which is their sequel, after the *Gorgias* rather than before. I shall offer positive reasons for this move in due course. But for the moment I insist on a *negative* reason: in order to break the spell of habit and tradition, the sheer inertial weight of so many books in which this order is taken for granted. I submit that the dating of these dialogues in the 390s, in the years immediately after Socrates' death, rests upon *no evidence whatsoever,* but only on two unsupported assumptions: (*a*) that Plato began by faithfully recalling the conversations of his master, and (*b*) that this is what we find in the *Laches, Charmides, Lysis,* and *Euthyphro.* I hope to *show* that the second assumption is false. But I want to cast doubt on the first as well.

This first assumption defines an "early" group where Plato reproduces Socratic conversations "without as yet adding to them any distinctive doctrines of his own" (to quote Guthrie again, who is following Field and many others). I submit that such a group must either be an empty set or contain at most one member. I shall not dispute the status of the *Apology,* which is after all not a dialogue and may have preceded the creation of the dialogue form. The very partial account of Socrates' philosophical activity and beliefs could well be historically accurate, even if the *Apology* itself is clearly a work of Platonic art. But as soon as we come to the *Crito* (which has some claim to be the earliest *dialogue*), the situation is quite different. Here we have the text of what purports to be a private conversation at which Plato cannot have been present, and which he is therefore free to invent. Now it would be strange if he had used this freedom to misrepresent Socrates' basic position of respect for law, or his loyalty to moral principles that have withstood the test of rational criticism. But the Socratic conclusion not to escape from prison is argued here on the basis of a highly original theory of tacit contract or consent which we have no reason to ascribe to the historical Socrates.[8] The situation is similar in the *Ion,* where the view of poetry as *enthousiasmos* may be genuinely Socratic, but where it is supported by an elaborate theory of poetry as magnetism which is much more likely to be Plato's own invention. Thus in such brief and early ventures as the *Crito* and the *Ion,* Plato is not only a creative artist but a creative philosopher as well.

The *Ion* is one of the very few dialogues which we have some external evidence for dating in the 390s.[9] Next to it I would put the *Hippias Minor,* which recalls the *Ion* in its brevity, its formal simplicity, and its abundant use of Homeric material. Both works illustrate the Socratic "mission" of exposing pretenders to wisdom; and both seek to characterize the kind of knowledge that qualifies as *technē.* I suggest that these are the *only* two dialogues, with *Apology* and *Crito,* to be dated before the *Gorgias,* in the first ten years after Socrates' death. (I ignore the *Hippias Major,* since I am not convinced that it was written by Plato at all.)[10] The *Gorgias* itself is un-Socratic in many respects, and not least in its focus upon a choice between two careers, politics or philosophy, a choice which Plato obviously made with some reluctance, but which Socrates never had to face.

On the hypothetical chronology which I propose, then, before the turning-point of the *Gorgias* Plato is only an occasional author of dialogues, all of them very short; he is practising his art on the small jar—as other followers of Socrates may have done at this time, in the 390s. Plato's attention is focused elsewhere, on the political arena; but Socrates and the life of philosophy remain very much on his mind. Then comes the explosion of the *Gorgias,* followed after his return from Sicily by its "tail-piece," the *Menexenus.*[11] (The *Menexenus* will seem less strange if Plato had written very few dialogues at the time.) It is only after he has broken with Athenian political life and settled down to the full-time practice of philosophy that Plato becomes a systematic writer. It is only then, after Socrates has been dead for a dozen years, that the typical "Socratic" dialogue takes shape, as a regularly unsuccessful search for definition. Plato now begins to experiment with new literary forms: the *Laches* is the first dialogue to be introduced by a dramatic episode with several speakers; the *Charmides* and the *Lysis* are the first to use the form of a reported conversation to sketch a vivid *mise en scène.* Plato is here working out the formal techniques he will use to more powerful effect in the *Protagoras, Symposium,* and *Phaedo.* After the sporadic composition of the *Ion, Hippias Minor,* and *Menexenus,* the dialogues now seem to be planned in coherent groups, and were probably written in quick succession. This would explain why we have (on my view) only five or six dialogues in the first dozen years after Socrates' death, but seven or more in the half-dozen years after Plato's return from Sicily, followed immediately by the middle dialogues in the 370s.

The chronological order I propose is indicated on the following chart.

I   Early or "pre-systematic" dialogues
    Apology (after 399)
    Crito
    Ion
    Hippias Minor
    Gorgias (390–386)
    Menexenus (386–385)
II   Pre-middle or "Socratic"
  A   *Laches*
    Charmides
    Lysis
    Euthyphro
  B   *Protagoras*
    Euthydemus
    Meno
III   Middle dialogues (the doctrine of Forms)
    Symposium (after 385, before 378)
    Phaedo
    Cratylus
    Republic
    Phaedrus
IV   Post-middle
    Parmenides
    Theaetetus (shortly after 369)
    Second Sicilian voyage, 367–365

It would be foolish to insist upon absolute dates, but on my hypothesis the seven dialogues in group II (*Laches, Charmides, Lysis, Euthyphro, Protagoras, Euthydemus,*

Meno) must all have been written c. 386–380, if Dover is correct in dating the *Symposium* before 378. I do not see anything implausible here: it would be quite arbitrary to suppose that the composition of dialogues must be evenly spaced over the 390s and 380s. And looking back, from the date of the *Theaetetus,* it seems clear that the middle dialogues must have been largely composed in the 370s.[12]

So much for chronology. My heresy consists in removing the *Protagoras* and the four dialogues of definition (*Laches, Charmides, Lysis, Euthyphro*) from their usual place before the *Gorgias,* in the 390s, and relocating them after the *Gorgias,* in the middle and late 380s. Now, what is the significance of such a redating? From the point of view of Plato's "development," it means that these five works—which in some sense form a unit—belong much closer in time to the middle dialogues, and hence to the doctrine of Forms, than is usually supposed. More important, however, than any guesswork about Plato's biography is the question how we are to understand the dialogues. And in this perspective the point of my non-standard chronology is to suggest that we read these five works *proleptically,* looking forward rather than backward for their meaning: reading them not to find out what Socrates said so long ago but to see how Plato will pursue his paths of inquiry from one dialogue to the next, and ultimately on to the doctrines of the middle dialogues. If I am right, the interpreters who regard these dialogues as essentially Socratic *in content* have been taken in by a kind of optical illusion, the measure of Plato's success in re-creating the atmosphere of the fifth century and making Socrates so lifelike.[13] Instead, I suggest we read them as the work of a philosopher in his forties, who is organizing his own school in the Academy, and is writing to prepare the minds of his audience—both inside and outside the school—for the reception of his mature philosophy.

My chronological and biographical hypothesis can be regarded simply as a likely story—and I submit that it is, historically speaking, much more likely than the usual view of Plato as memorialist of Socrates' thought. The real choice, however, is not between two historical claims but between two frameworks, two sets of hermeneutical assumptions, two different ways of reading the dialogues. I doubt that there is enough properly historical evidence to decide the chronological issue either way; and in any case chronology limits, but does not determine, the choice of an interpretive scheme. Thus one might accept my chronology and refuse to read the dialogues proleptically; or one might stick to the standard arrangement but doubt the faithfully "Socratic" character of our five dialogues (group IIA plus the *Protagoras*). The choice of a hermeneutical assumption can be justified only by its fruits: its success in making possible a more adequate interpretation of the texts. Thus Irwin's reconstruction of Socratic moral theory on the basis of the orthodox chronology can be regarded as evidence in favour of the standard view: anyone who finds Irwin's interpretation of the *Protagoras* and *Gorgias* persuasive has to that extent a reason to maintain the standard view and the standard chronology. (Again, the converse does not hold: you might reject Irwin's interpretation but stick to his chronology and to the general "Socratic" framework.) I cannot deal with Irwin's important book here except to point out where our positions become incompatible: if I am right about the chronology, Irwin must be wrong, at least on the *Gorgias,* since his interpretation requires the *Gorgias* to be later than the *Protagoras* and the four dialogues of definition. More fundamentally, our assumptions conflict in that he sees the shorter dialogues before the *Protagoras* as statements of a single, static theory; whereas I insist upon the movement forward from one work to another, in the gradual exploration of problems whose solution will only come with the doctrine of Forms and with the moral psychology and theory of education of the *Republic*. In effect, I deny the existence of a distinct Socratic moral theory in the dialogues.[14]

I have applied my principles of interpretation elsewhere to the doctrine of the unity of the virtues, and have attempted to show that an adequate explication of this thesis in the *Protagoras* requires the theory of philosophic eros and philosophic virtue which Plato will provide in the *Symposium, Phaedo,* and *Republic*.[15] I want here to offer a general defence of this proleptic approach to the dialogues in my group II by tracing a number of major themes that emerge in this group but are wholly absent from or at best marginal in, the dialogues of group I, which includes the *Gorgias*. Many of these thematic interconnections have been noted before and some of them have contributed to the notion of the Socratic dialogues as a unified group. (Cf. Guthrie iv, pp. 68f.) What has not generally been noticed is (1) the systematic and progressive nature of these interconnections, and (2) the fact that they tie my group II closely to the middle dialogues, but *not* to group I. In terms of continuity of theme and conceptual elaboration, the Socratic dialogues and the *Protagoras* have more in common with the *Phaedo* and *Republic* than with the *Gorgias*.[16] The prominence of one or more of themes I have selected serves as my primary criterion for assigning a work to group II rather than to group I. These themes are the philosophic topics Plato chose to explore in the dialogues composed to prepare the readers' minds for the statement of his mature philosophy, while at the same time developing the dialogue into a rich and flexible art form, capable of re-creating a simulacrum of the Socratic world within which Plato's own theories would be expounded and discussed. Thus the thesis I am defending is not about the unity of Plato's thought but about the unity of his literary project in a dozen dialogues from the *Laches* to the *Republic*. The *Gorgias*, like the *Apology* and *Crito*, falls outside this project; the second half of the *Phaedrus* points beyond it to something new.

The six themes to be surveyed are: (1) the theory of definition, (2) the theory of the definiendum, (3) the theory of virtue, its unity and its teachability, (4) the theory of friendship, (5) the concept of dialectic, and (6) the method of hypothesis.

1. The theory of definition is first elaborated by Socrates' practice in the *Laches*, where he neatly illustrates the criterion of coextensivity (namely, that the definiens must be true of the definiendum and of nothing else) by first rejecting a definition of courage that is too narrow, standing firm in battle, and then one that is too broad, psychic endurance or perseverance (*karteria*). The *Laches* goes on to consider two definitions that might pass muster: wise endurance, and the knowledge of what is and is not to be feared. But the positive development of these ideas comes later, in the *Protagoras* and the *Republic*. Our next lesson in the methodology of definition is provided by the *Euthyphro*, which spends little time on the criterion of coextensivity (6D); that criterion is quickly satisfied by Euthyphro's definition of piety as what is pleasing to the gods. (On my view of how Plato writes dialogues, the speed with which Euthyphro catches on to coextensivity should be seen less as a sign of his intelligence than as a reflection of the fact that the reader is supposed to be acquainted with the *Laches*.) On the basis of Euthyphro's theology, however, his definition will generate a contradiction, since the gods may disagree: an explicit assumption of unanimity is required to make the definition coherent (*Hupothemenos* 9D 8). The definition now applies exclusively to pious action; it specifies what we may call a *proprium* of piety, a condition both necessary and sufficient. But this definition cannot show *why* an action is pious; hence it is rejected as

giving not the essence (*ousia*) of piety but only a derivative property (*pathos*) (11A–B). The *Euthyphro* thus insists that a definition must be explanatory as well as coherent and coextensive. The same dialogue introduces the first careful notice of extensional relations between genus and species (identified here as "whole" and "part"), and sketches an example of definition *per genus et differentiam* (12C–F).

In the *Laches* and *Euthyphro* the theory of definition is practiced rather than discussed. The *Meno* takes up the topic in an explicit way, offering a variety of sample definitions to illustrate the requirement of unity in the definiens (72Aff.), insisting that a definition must be non-circular and make use of terms that are already familiar (75E–76A; cf. 79D). The extensional relations between genus and species, mentioned in the *Euthyphro*, are here more fully discussed (73E 1ff., 74D, 79 A 3, D6–7). I take it that the sequence *Laches–Euthyphro–Meno* is the only natural order for reading these three dialogues on the topic of definition; and this is confirmed by the development of the next theme.

2. The theory of the definiendum. The *Laches* tells us that a proper answer to the question "what is courage?" must specify some item which is "the same in all these cases" of conduct recognized as courageous (191 E 10 *ti on en pasi toutois tauton estin;* cf. 192 B 6–7), something of such a nature (*pephukos*) as to be present in them all or apply "throughout" (*dia pantōn,* 192 C1). This is probably the first clear statement we have of the notion of a *universal* (anticipating *Meno* 74A9, 77A6, etc.). In the *Laches* this common item is presented as some kind of "power" or capacity (*dunamis* 192B6). The *Euthyphro* speaks more neutrally of a "form," "structure," or "type" of thing (*idea* at 5D, *eidos* in 6D), but that dialogue goes on to elaborate this notion of a universal property. In addition to the positive form it recognizes a negative opposite: besides the pious, "which is the same with itself in every action," we have the impious, which is likewise "similar to itself and possessed of one single form (*idea*) in regard to its impiety" (5D). The characterization in terms of opposites (*enantia*) connects the new notion with an older, Presocratic conception of causal principles. But its originality is defined by its contrast with a multitude of particulars: "the many pious things" (*ta polla hosia*) are to be distinguished from "that very form (*eidos*) itself by which all pious things are pious" (6D10–11). And this form is described as a model (*paradeigma*) to which we might refer (*apoblepein*) in deciding whether any given action is properly said to be pious (6E). This role of the definiendum as a standard or criterion for predication, and as that *by which* or *in virtue of which* things are as they are, answers to the requirement on the definiens that it must be explanatory if it is to specify the *ousia* or *"what-it-is"* of a thing (11A). If the definition of F tells us what-it-is for anything to be F, it will give us a standard for deciding disputed instances of F.

These passages of the *Euthyphro* obviously have certain features in common with the terminology used to describe the Forms in the *Phaedo* and the *Republic*. But the distinctive metaphysics and epistemology of the middle dialogues is entirely lacking: there is no trace here of Eleatic oppositions between Being and Becoming, the Intelligible and the Sensible—what Aristotle called the "separation" of the Forms. So we can imagine that the *Euthyphro* represents an earlier, less "Platonic" notion of paradigmatic essences.[17] Or we can prudently leave open the question of Plato's metaphysical convictions at the time of writing.[18] What is clear in either case is that the reader is presented with a new way of envisaging the object of definition—in terms of *eidos, idea, ousia, paradeigma,* "that in virtue of which things are F"—and that this way will be exploited later by Plato in the formulation of his most characteristic doctrine.

The *Meno* makes use of the same terminology as the *Euthyphro* (*ousia* at 72B1, *eidos* at 72C7) with slight variations of phrasing; the definiendum is "one thing true of many" (*hen kata pantōn* at 73D1), or "the same for all cases" (*to epi pasin toutois tauton* 75A4–5). Plato seems deliberately to leave open the question of questions concerning universals: whether the form which all these instances "have" is something *present* in them (as several formulations suggest) or something *distinct* (as might be implied by the notion of *paradeigma* in the *Euthyphro*). The *Meno* seems slightly more non-committal on this point, since the term *paradeigma* does not recur (but cf. *apoblepein* at *M*.72C8). I think it would be unwise to look for a difference of doctrine between these two dialogues as far as the definiendum is concerned: Plato is simply unwilling to clarify here the ontological status of these "forms" or "essences." The unveiling of his ontology is reserved for a separate occasion, in a dialogue specially designed for this purpose, where the priestess Diotima will reveal the Form of Beauty in a marvellous vision to climax an initiation into the mysteries of love (*Sym.* 210–11).

On my view the *Protagoras* comes between the *Euthyphro* and the *Meno*.[19] Here we find no search for definitions and hence no terminology for definiendum: Plato does not pursue the same theme in every dialogue. Nevertheless, the *Protagoras* makes use of the terminology of *dunamis* and *ousia* in a way exactly parallel to the *Laches* and the *Euthyphro* (*Prot.* 330A4, 6, B1; 349B4, 5, C5). In the *Gorgias,* by contrast, where both terms occur, neither one is used in the semi-technical sense connected with questions of definition and conceptual unity.[20] It is a striking fact that the *Gorgias* shows no interest in the theory, methodology and terminology of definition which we have just illustrated from *Laches–Euthyphro–Meno,* and all the more striking because in that dialogue Socrates does *practise* definition, in the lengthy exchange by which he obliges Gorgias to make more and more precise an initially vague characterization of rhetoric (449D–454B). I take it that such procedures were genuinely Socratic, and that to this extent Aristotle is justified in crediting the historical Socrates with the practice of definition. But when Aristotle refers at *Met. M.* 4, 1078b 18 to general definitions of the moral virtues, he probably has in mind *Laches, Euthyphro,* and *Meno,* which is something else again. In the *Gorgias* there is no clear focus on universal concepts, no formal concern either with definiens or definiendum. The question about rhetoric is presented in an informal, pre-technical way, introduced by an exchange between Socrates and Chaerephon to indicate just what kind of question is going to be asked (447C 9ff.). There is no trace here of the logical sophistication we find in the *Laches* or the *Euthyphro.* I do not see how anyone who reflects upon the lack of theoretical interest in the procedure of definition in the *Gorgias* can believe that it belongs to the series of dialogues that leads from the *Laches* to the *Meno* and the *Phaedo.*[21]

3. The theory of virtue: (*a*) its parts and its unity, and (*b*) its teachability. If we know anything at all about the historical Socrates, we know he was passionately devoted to the pursuit of *aretē* or moral excellence, and that his practice of philosophy was a kind of exhortation to virtue. In the *Gorgias* Socrates appears as the embodiment of this pursuit, and his concern for moral education is presented as the only true exercise of the political art. (And in this respect, in the concern for politics as moral education, Plato remained a faithful Socratic all his life.) The *Gorgias* also contains an argument for the unity of the virtues, maintaining that the temperate man must be just, pious, brave, and perfectly good (507 A–C). What the *Gorgias* shows no trace of, and what is characteristic of the

Laches, Protagoras, and *Meno,* is (i) a systematic discussion of the "parts" of virtue and how they are related to the whole, and (ii) an explicit raising of the question whether virtue can be taught. The *Gorgias* insists upon the importance of moral education; it expresses some doubt whether the sophists succeed in teaching virtue (519c–520e) and implies that Socrates might do better (517b, 521d). But it does not discuss in detail the problems of teaching and learning any more than it attempts to analyse the virtues. Now it is precisely this question of *paideuein anthrōpous,* how to train men in excellence and make their souls as good as possible, which is systematically raised in the *Laches,* where it leads to the request for a definition (185b–190e2). This is the central issue not only in the *Protagoras* and *Meno,* but also in the *Euthydemus* and the *Republic;* it is an important underlying theme in the *Lysis, Charmides,* and *Symposium.* The doctrine of Forms itself is introduced in the *Symposium* as the final stage of erotic pedagogy; in the *Republic* this doctrine defines the goal of the entire training programme for the guardians. From the *Laches* to the *Republic,* the theory of virtue and how it is to be produced is *the* unifying theme that ties all the dialogues together. (The *Cratylus* is probably the only dialogue from this period in which the topic of moral education is not an essential component.) For understanding the continuity in Plato's treatment of these themes, the division between Socratic and middle dialogues may be more of a hindrance than a help.

The *Laches* is the first dialogue to confront both the question of teachability for virtue and the question of its parts or species. Issues to be discussed at length in the *Protagoras* and *Meno* are here raised in a preliminary way, with some of the problems left implicit in the situation: why do men eminent in *aretē* not succeed in training eminent sons? Is such excellence teachable? If so, who are the teachers? If not, how can it be a *technē,* or form of knowledge? The specific goal of defining courage, in order to know how it may be acquired, is not formulated until half-way through this brief dialogue. The length and weight of the dramatic introduction, the extraordinary prestige of the interlocutors (Nicias and Laches) or of their fathers (Aristides and Thucydides son of Melesias), underline the importance of the topic to be discussed, and suggest that we have here an introduction not to the *Laches* alone but to the whole series of dialogues on virtue and education. A similar motivation is suggested by the choice of interlocutors in the *Charmides,* which is probably the second dialogue in this group. The later career of Critias and Charmides, ringleader and member of the notorious Thirty, casts a grim shadow over the discussion of "temperance." We have here a conversation on virtue with the conspicuously bad, to match the conversation with the eminent examples of *aretē* in the *Laches,* thus suggesting in a vivid way the range of possibilities for the young men whose moral future is still open. And the cast of these two dialogues, from Aristides the Just to Critias, spans not only the moral spectrum but also the whole history of Athens in the fifth century. The dramatic framework here restates implicitly the claim that was explicit in the *Gorgias:* that a study of *aretē* is the key to understanding what happens in history.

After the *Laches* and *Euthyphro* have shown, in different ways, that any definition of the virtues in isolation is bound to fail, the *Protagoras* addresses itself to their connections and alleged unity, while the *Meno* goes on to seek a general definition of virtue (and notes, retrospectively, the error of earlier attempts to define the parts separately, 79c8). Taking up the question of teachability where the *Protagoras* had left it, the *Meno* first proposes a positive answer on the basis of an assumption (suggested in *Laches* and *Charmides* and argued for in the *Protagoras*) that virtue is a kind of knowledge. But Socrates is still baffled by the question of teachability, and hence he goes on to offer an alternative account of virtue based upon right opinion. The *Meno* points beyond itself in many ways, and not only in the doctrine of Recollection and the myth of rebirth. The account of virtue based upon right opinion, which is suggested at the end of the *Meno,* is in fact not provided until *Republic* 4.

It will be obvious that this concern with wisdom, excellence, and the possibility of education fits smoothly enough into the biographical framework of a philosopher recently returned from Sicily and busy with the educational scheme of the Academy. I suggest that the seven dialogues in my group II, from *Laches* to *Meno* and *Euthydemus,* be regarded less as a defence for Socrates than as an advertisement for the Academy. They represent both a protreptic to philosophic work and an object for philosophic study. Their ideal reader, capable of following up the hints and movement of thought from one dialogue to the next, would be a pupil or associate of Plato in the Academy.

4. The *Lysis* is the only "Socratic" dialogue devoted not to the definition of virtue but to the theory of friendship (*philia*). To show that this puzzling dialogue is to be interpreted as a preparation for the *Symposium* and the theory of philosophic *eros* in the middle dialogues would require more discussion than is appropriate here.[22] I will refer only to the one point where the dialogue seems most palpably proleptic. I doubt that any good sense can be made of "the primary *philon,* for the sake of which all other things are dear" (219D), without looking ahead to the Form of Beauty in the *Symposium* and the Form of the Good in the *Republic,* "which every soul pursues, and for the sake of which it does whatever it does" (*Rep.* 6, 505D11). The characteristic language of *Symposium* and *Republic* is foreshadowed both in the reference to other dear things as "images" (*eidōla*) of the primary object of affection, and also in the phrases *ekeino ho estin prōton philon . . . ekeino to prōton, ho hōs alēthōs esti philon* (219C8–D5). This is a cunning anticipation of the technical terminology for the doctrine of Forms, not used again until *Symposium* 211C (cf. *eidōla* at 212A4), and then generalized at *Phaedo* 75A: "all the things on which we set the seal of *to auto ho esti*"[23] (cf. 92D9: *hē ousia echousa tēn epōnumian tēn tou ho estin*). If we deny any forward reference and insist on limiting our framework of interpretation to the confines of the *Lysis,* these formulae must be hopelessly enigmatic. I think they were meant to be recognized by the original readers as puzzles and hints of things to come.

That Plato was capable of planting such deliberate anticipations, in a context where they could at first be regarded only as cryptic or unintelligible, seems certain from the parallel case concerning dialectic.

5. In the *Meno* dialectic is defined as a friendly mode of discussion, to be contrasted with the disputatious practice of eristic, since in dialectic "one not only gives true answers but answers by means of things [i.e., terms and premises] which the interlocutor would agree that he knows" (75D). This is only a slight variant on the pre-technical use of *dialegesthai* in the *Gorgias* (448D10, 449B4) for a methodical discussion by questions and short answers, in contrast to oratory (*rhētorikē*) or the making of long speeches. No doubt this was a genuine conversational practice of the historical Socrates: but it was not superficially different from the procedures of some whom we (following Plato) would call Sophists.[24]

It is this superficial resemblance which underlies and justifies such a strange dialogue as the *Euthydemus,* where the Sophists' art is called *dialegesthai* (295E2) and hinges on the demand that Socrates give short and unconditional answers to their questions (295A4,

10, B6–10, 297B8, D3, 8). This is precisely the eristic perversion which Plato has in view when he defines dialectic in the *Meno* (75D). The extent to which the *Euthydemus* is dominated by a caricature of dialectic makes it all the more remarkable that, in an earlier context, dialecticians (*hoi dialektikoi*) have been introduced as practitioners of a master art, to whom mathematicians hand over the truths (*ta onta*) which they have discovered but do not know how to use: the dialectician stands to the mathematician as the statesman or king stands to the general (290C–D; 291C). When this doctrine is ascribed to the boy Clinias, Crito expresses disbelief; Socrates is not sure from whom he has heard it, except that it was *not* from the eristic brothers, Euthydemus and Dionysidorus: perhaps it was spoken by some superior power or divinity present? (290E–291A). The passage is thus frankly labelled a mystery, and it is hard to see how this mystery could be unravelled by anyone who had not read the account of dialectic in *Republic* 6 and 7, or heard Plato give some comparable explanation.

To this deliberate teaser there is a parallel in the *Cratylus,* where a partially similar account of dialectic is introduced by a summary of our passage from the *Euthydemus,* including the same illustration: the cithara-player as judge of the lyre-maker's art.[25] The *Cratylus* defines the dialectician as one who knows how to ask and answer questions, along the lines of *Gorgias* and *Meno;* but here his art is said to stand as judge over the work of the name-giver or lawmaker, since the dialectician is the user of the product—namely, words—of which the *nomothetēs* is the manufacturer (390C–D). Since the correct assignment of names is said to require insight into the form (*eidos*) and essence (*ousia*) of the thing named, this passage in the *Cratylus* connects the new and loftier conception of dialectic with the doctrine of Forms (390E; cf. 386E, 389B–390A, etc.). To this extent it is less mysterious, and may serve as partial exegesis of the reference to dialectic in the *Euthydemus.* But the *Cratylus* does *not* explain why the dialectician is set up as an authority over mathematics. For an explanation of this point, and for a full understanding of both passages, there is really no substitute for the central books of the *Republic.*

Some scholars may be tempted on other grounds to date the *Cratylus* later than the *Republic.* I think this would be a mistake; the close parallel to the *Euthydemus* on dialectic tends to confirm the standard dating of the *Cratylus* as roughly contemporary with *Symposium* and *Phaedo.* But even if we leave the *Cratylus* out of account, we have two clear examples of deliberately proleptic writing in the pre-middle dialogues: the anticipation of the Form of Beauty or Form of Good in the *Lysis* and the anticipation of the theory of dialectic as meta-mathematics in the *Euthydemus.*

6. I want to conclude by mentioning another thematic development that culminates in the dialectic of *Republic* 6–7, namely, the method of hypothesis. This method is first sketched in the *Meno* and applied to the question whether virtue can be taught, which question can be answered in the affirmative if we accept the assumption (*hupothesis*) that virtue is knowledge (86E–87C). We then go on to justify this assumption on the basis of a further premiss (*hupothesis*) that virtue is something good (87D2–3; cf. *hupotithesthai* for the parallel assumption concerning temperance in the *Charmides,* 160D1–2, referring back to 159C1). If this double use of *hupothesis* seems confusing,[26] the confusion can be dispelled by looking ahead to the fuller statement of dialectical method in the *Phaedo,* where the notion of a second hypothesis is introduced systematically, in the account of how one justifies a particular premiss by positing another hypothesis, "the one that seems best among those higher up, until you reach something adequate" (101D4–E1).

This upward path is more fully spelled out in the discussion of dialectic at the end of *Republic* 6, where the place of *hikanon* is taken by "the unconditional" or non-hypothetical first principle (*to anupotheton, ti*), which in this context can only be the Form of the Good.[27] The *Meno*, *Phaedo*, and *Republic* do not provide a static theory of hypothesis that could just as well be presented in a handbook or a Discourse on Method. But they do present progressively more complete pictures of a single, flexible view, and the *Phaedo* can help us understand the *Meno* in much the same way as the doctrine of *Republic* 6 helps us understand the talk about "higher hypotheses" in the *Phaedo*. What I want to suggest now is that just as the *Laches* and *Euthyphro* practise the art of definition without pronouncing the word "definition," so the final argument of the *Protagoras* practises the method of hypothesis without employing the term *hupothesis* in this connection.

I cannot here argue for the view that the identification of pleasure with the good in the *Protagoras* should be regarded as a convenient dialectical hypothesis, proposed because the many (and even the sophists) can be brought to accept it, and because on the basis of this assumption Socrates can then produce a plausible derivation of his paradoxical conclusion, that virtue is knowledge. That view has been defended by others.[28] I have three points to add. (1) Since the *Gorgias* had already made Plato's position on hedonism quite clear, no informed reader of the *Protagoras* would have been in any doubt as to the hypothetical nature of the argument. (2) The argument is an exercise in the method described in the *Meno*, in that (*a*) a conclusion (in this case, that virtue is knowledge) is reached *ex hupotheseōs*, on the basis of premiss, and (*b*) that the premiss is itself not established[29] but can be accepted by the interlocutors, in the way characteristic of dialectic according to *Meno* 75D. (Note that the conclusion in the *Protagoras* becomes the *hupothesis* in the *Meno*.) (3) But this premiss is itself subject to criticism or defence on the basis of some "higher" *hupothesis*, and ultimately on the basis of something still more adequate and non-hypothetical. The hedonistic premiss is explicitly rejected in the *Phaedo* (68D–69B) on the strength of a higher notion of philosophical wisdom tied to the doctrine of Forms; and this notion of wisdom and virtue is in turn derived from the unconditional *archē tou pantos*, the Form of the Good, in *Republic* 6. Thus the method of hypothesis, proceeding by an upward path, leads us from the hedonism of the *Protagoras* to the philosophic *eros* of the *Phaedo* and finally to the ultimate Good of the *Republic*. This progression is exactly parallel to the step-by-step clarification of the doctrine of the unity of the virtues, which the *Protagoras* defends by the dialectical *hupothesis* in question, but which cannot be understood without the *Symposium*, the *Phaedo*, and the *Republic*. Just as the *Phaedo* picks up the *Meno* on the topic of Recollection, so it corrects the assumption of the *Protagoras* and replaces it by something more adequate. The conception of philosophic virtue resting on the erotic passion for the Forms permits us to "rise above" the *hupothesis* of hedonism and to defend the same true conclusion from premises much closer to the truth, as Plato saw it.

In closing, let me make clear that in attacking the notion of Socratic dialogues I do not mean to attack the portrait of Socrates which Plato has given us. Where this portrait is unfaithful, we are in no position to correct it. As far as we are concerned, the Socrates of the dialogues *is* the historical Socrates. He is certainly the only one who counts for the history of philosophy.

Hence I regard as authentically Socratic the conception of philosophy as psychic therapy or "tendence for one's soul," regularly exercised in *elenchos* or cross-examination, and supported by a central core of paradoxes: no one does wrong voluntarily, it is better to suffer than to do wrong, virtue is knowledge, and no evil can happen to a good man. For without these paradoxes and this conception of philosophy, we would not be able to recognize Socrates at all. But it does not follow that any arguments used to support these paradoxes in the dialogues, or any further consequences as to the nature of virtue and wisdom, can be attributed to Socrates himself. On these matters it is better to admit our ignorance. Hence, although I do not doubt the historicity of the figure of Socrates as presented in the dialogues, I do indeed doubt the historicity of the dialogues themselves as reports of philosophical conversations in the fifth century.[30] The dialogues belong to Plato and to the fourth century. So do the doctrines and arguments contained in them. Even where the inspiration of Socrates is clear, the dialogues are all Platonic.

NOTES

This is a revised text of the paper read to the Cambridge Philological Society on 1 November 1979. It has since been presented to several different audiences, including the Société Française de Philosophie in Paris, February 1980. I am indebted to a number of friends, colleagues and auditors for helpful criticism, and in particular to Julia Annas, Pierre Aubenque, Jonathan Barnes, and Anthony Long.

1. *A History of Greek Philosophy*, IV (Cambridge, Eng., 1975), p. 236. Guthrie hesitates about the relative date of *Meno* and *Gorgias*, and discusses *Meno* first; but he recognizes that most scholars place it after the *Gorgias*.
2. T. Irwin, *Plato's Moral Theory: the Early and Middle Dialogues* (Oxford, 1977), pp. 2, 102, 131. For his chronology see pp. 291–3, n. 33. The area of agreement diminishes, however, if we look beyond recent British and American scholarship. Consider, for example, the five lists cited by Ross in *Plato's Theory of Ideas* (Oxford, 1951, p. 2): almost the only relevant point on which they all agree is in placing the *Gorgias* after the *Protagoras*. Even on this point the "consensus" was challenged by A. E. Taylor (*Plato: The Man and His Work* (New York, 1956), pp. 20, 235), Grube (*Plato's Thought* (Indianapolis, 1980), p. xii), and Ernst Kapp, who (writing after 1942, published only in 1968) regarded *Apology, Crito, Gorgias* as the three earliest dialogues and the only ones to be "attributed with practical certainty to the period between 399 and 389" ("The Theory of Ideas in Plato's Earlier Dialogues," in *Ausgewählte Schriften* (Berlin, 1968), p. 80). In his recent *Studies in the Styles of Plato* (Acta Philosophica Fennica xx, 1967), H. Thesleff partially follows R. Böhme (*Von Sokrates zu Ideenlehre* (Bernae, 1959)) in placing the *Gorgias* earlier than the *Protagoras* (p. 21 with n. 1).
   More recently still, J. Kube, on the basis of a careful study of Plato's theory of *technē*, has proposed an order which largely anticipates the chronology suggested here: his arrangement of the first five dialogues is exactly the same as mine (*Apology, Crito, Ion, Hippias Minor, Gorgias*), and the four dialogues of definition also follow in my proposed order (*Laches, Charmides, Lysis, Euthyphro*). Only in regard to the three major "pre-middle" dialogues (*Protagoras, Meno, Euthydemus*) do we diverge, since Kube inserts these among the four dialogues of definition. See *Technē und Aretē* (Berlin, 1969), pp. 122ff., with table of contents, p. x. Kube does not claim chronological accuracy for his arrangement, but he does suggest (p. 121) that it should correspond roughly to the chronological sequence.
3. Lutoslawski thought otherwise, but he was mistaken, as Ritter pointed out. See C. Ritter, *Platon* 1 (Munich, 1910–1923), pp. 246, 261. For Ritter's unsuccessful later attempt to

subdivide the group on stylometric grounds see E. R. Dodds, *Plato's Gorgias* (Oxford, 1959), p. 19, nn. 1 and 2.

I am indebted to a recent letter from Dr. Leonard Brandwood, confirming "that stylometry has so far been unsuccessful in indicating any chronological order *within* this [early] group beyond the probability that certain works, e.g. *Phaedo, Symposium, Cratylus,* are at or near the end of it." See his Ph.D. thesis, "The Dating of Plato's Works by the Stylistic Method—a Historical and Critical Survey," University of London (1958).

4. I have no doubt of the authenticity of the *Seventh Letter* (which may or may not entail that of the *Eighth,* but surely none of the rest: see Thesleff (op. cit. in n. 2) p. 16. n. 1). If, on the other hand, one shares the scepticism of Edelstein and others, we are left with no information on Plato's early career and hence no basis for dating the *Gorgias* beyond the thematic and emotional links to the *Menexenus,* whose date is secure. These links point, however, to roughly the same date as the evidence from the *Seventh Letter,* i.e. the early 380s.

5. For the connection between the *Seventh Epistle* and the *Gorgias,* See Kapp, "Theory of Ideas," pp 98ff., as well as Dodds, *Gorgias,* pp. 25–31, and Guthrie, *History* iv, p. 284.

6. For example, the first chapter of Isocrates' *Helen* mentions with contempt a doctrine of the unity of the virtues in knowledge, which it is natural to read as a reference to Plato's *Protagoras* (and perhaps to the *Meno* as well, though this is much less certain). Unfortunately the date of the *Helen* is unknown; recent scholars place it anywhere from 390 to 380. Since no one doubts that the *Protagoras* was written before 380 (and probably the *Meno* as well), this bit of external evidence is of no real use to us. It has been argued that the apparent reference to Isocrates at *Euthydemus* 304D, 305Bff. must be later than the *Panegyricus* of 380 BC, which would be more surprising (but not impossible, in my view): see G. Matthieu in *Mélanges Glotz* II, pp. 558–60. But there is too much guesswork involved for this kind of (possible) cross-reference to count as historical evidence.

7. The mention of Ismenias of Thebes at *Meno* 90A could reflect any date after 395; but Ismenias' career came to a dramatic end in 382, and it may be that event which recalled his name to Plato's attention (cf. Guthrie iv, p. 236, n. 4). This is only guesswork, of course; but the later date fits well with Dover's carefully argued case for dating the *Symposium* after 385 and before 378 (*Phronesis* 10 [1965], 1–20).

8. No reason, that is, beyond the mere fact that Plato puts it in his mouth. As a principle of historical interpretation, this leads straight to the Taylor–Burnet view of Socrates as author of the theory of Forms (not to mention the fact that a similar principle would saddle Socrates with all the foolish things that Xenophon makes him say). Of course there is a special attraction to the principle in this case: why should Plato wish to mislead us concerning Socrates' motives for such a momentous decision? But we must distinguish between (*a*) Socrates' moral stance, and (*b*) the theories and arguments by which it is defended. I suggest that Plato had every reason to represent the former as faithfully as he could, but that with regard to the latter he felt free (or even obliged) to provide the strongest arguments available. Hence in the *Phaedo* Socrates' attitude in the face of death will be grounded in the theory of Forms. In the *Crito* and the *Gorgias* we have the same tendency at work; only the theory is less elaborate.

9. See H. Flashar, *Der Dialog Ion as Zeugnis Platonischer Philosophie* (Berlin, 1958), pp. 96–100. Note that the "dramatic date" of the dialogue would be 394–393 BC (or soon thereafter), to judge by contemporary allusions, e.g. to Athenian rule over Ephesus. (So Flashar, and similarly Méridier in the Budé Plato, vol. v. 1, p. 24.) In fact such allusions can only count as evidence for the date of composition: since Socrates was not available in 394–393, the dialogue has no dramatic date! And of course the same is true for the *Menexenus,* where Socrates alludes to the King's Peace of 386. The *Gorgias* is also notoriously indeterminate with regard to a dramatic date. (See Dodds, *Gorgias,* p. 17.) Plato is not yet consciously recreating the quasi-historical background characteristic of the *Protagoras* and the *Symposium,* where it makes sense to speak of anachronisms. I suggest that the careful invocation of a

particular time and place in the *Laches, Charmides, Lysis,* and *Euthyphro* should be recognized as an artistic innovation, like the use of the reported form. The earlier use of a specific setting in the *Crito* is quite different, since that is not a free invention on Plato's part, given the topic of the dialogue.

10. My doubts on the *Hippias Major* are essentially the same as those expressed by Thesleff, p. 13, n. 4. For the early date of *Ion* and *Hippias Minor,* see Thesleff's view, p. 19, and Méridier (Budé, Plato v. 1, pp. 27f.), who cites Wilamowitz and others.

11. See Dodds, *Gorgias,* p. 24; Guthrie iv, p. 213.

12. For dating *Phaedo, Republic,* etc. in the 370s, cf. Dodds, *Gorgias,* p. 25; Kapp, "Theory of Ideas," pp. 90f.

13. The first to be taken in was apparently Aristotle, whose account of Socrates' position on definition, *epagōgē, akrasia,* and the like seems largely based upon a reading of the Platonic dialogues as historical documents. In this sense, the conception of Socratic dialogues which I am attacking can be traced directly back to Aristotle (as Pierre Aubenque has reminded me). In effect Aristotle gives Socrates credit for everything in the dialogues before the doctrine of Forms and the theory of Recollection. When he arrived in Athens thirty-three years after Socrates' death, the memory even of those who had known the man personally would inevitably be coloured by the brilliant literary portrayal that had been presented in the meantime. Of course, there would still be informants enough to remind Aristotle that the theory of Forms was an innovation, and he could see for himself that it was not there in the more typically "Socratic" dialogues.

Aristotle had no real taste or talent for the history of philosophy, and I see no reason to take his account of Socrates and Plato at face value. (What sensitive reader of the *Cratylus* can believe that the namesake of that dialogue was a teacher from whom Plato believed he had learned something of great importance?) Aristotle systematically neglects the crucial role played by Parmenidean ontology in the formation of Plato's theory, and emphasizes instead a debt to the Pythagoreans which must have been fashionable to proclaim at the time (see W. Jaeger, *Aristotle,* tr. R. Robinson, p. 97), but whose historical reality is extremely doubtful. There is generally a kernel of historical truth in Aristotle's statements about his predecessors, but in order to extract that kernel we must first be able to interpret their doctrine on independent grounds. He is certainly not a model to follow on how to read a Platonic dialogue!

For the documentation and discussion see Th. Deman, *Le Témoignage d' Aristote sur Socrate* (Paris, 1942), and W. D. Ross, *Aristotle's Metaphysics* I, xxxiv ff.

14. I do not deny a recognizably Socratic normative ethics (above all in the *Apology* and *Crito*), with some more general claims (no one does wrong willingly, the unity of virtue in knowledge). But how far and in what directions Socrates himself developed these claims *theoretically* is anyone's guess. What I deny is that Plato's theoretical developments (in *Gorgias, Charmides, Protagoras,* etc.) should be regarded primarily as attempts to reproduce Socrates' own thought.

15. "Plato on the Unity of the Virtues," in *Facets of Plato's Philosophy,* ed. W. H. Werkmeister (*Phronesis* suppl. vol. II, 1976, 21–39).

16. Of course the *Gorgias* and the *Republic* have one major theme in common (the theory of justice and the defence of morality), but the latter is in no sense a *sequel* to the former: Plato begins over again from scratch, with the attack by Thrasymachus (reformulated by Glaucon and Adeimantus) as a replacement for Polus and Callicles.

I cannot deal here with all the arguments brought forward to show that the *Gorgias* must be later than the *Protagoras* (e.g. Dodds, *Gorgias,* pp. 21f. with reference there to Rudberg's article in *Symbolae Osloensis* 30 [1953]). To answer only two points: (1) the arguments which claim that the depiction of Socrates in *Protagoras* is more lifelike ("with no wart or wrinkle smoothed out of the portrait," in Vlastos' memorable phrase) and more aporetic, whereas in the *Gorgias* he is more idealized and more dogmatic, all rely for their chronological inference on the assumption that Plato began by an historically faithful portrayal, which gradually changed into something else. But this is precisely the historicist assumption I wish to challenge. Furthermore, even the pursuit of historical verisimilitude seems to be a secondary development, part of the literary project that begins *after* the *Gorgias*. (See n. 9 on the notion of a dramatic date.) (2) It is true that the contrast between *pistis* and *mathēsis* (or *epistēmē*) at *Gorg.* 454c–455A partially anticipates the distinction between true opinion (*doxa*) and knowledge which is first drawn at *M.* 97Bff., but here again there is no thematic or conceptual continuity. On the one hand, *pistis* in the *Gorgias* belongs to the language of rhetoric: it is the subjective state of "persuasion," whatever the audience is convinced of, with no intrinsic connection with the truth; since the audience is gullible, *pistis* is more likely than not to be false. The term plays no part in the positive account of knowledge in the *Gorgias*, which is built on the contrast between *technē* and *empeiria* (463Bff., 465A, 501A). The standard Platonic distinction, on the other hand, opposes knowledge to *true* opinion, where the latter characterizes not the ignorant mob but the statesman (*M.* 98cff.) and even the philosopher (*Sym.* 202A with 203D–204B), or is an essential point of contrast for the cognition of Forms (*Rep.* 477Bff. *Timaeus* 51D–E). Nothing connects the discussion of *pistis* in the *Gorgias* with the theory of *doxa* in the *Meno*, in the way that the latter is directly continued by the treatment of *doxa* in the *Symposium* and later works.

17. So R. E. Allen, *Plato's "Euthyphro" and the Earlier Theory of Forms* (New York, 1970), and "Plato's Earlier Theory of Forms," in G. Vlastos, ed., *The Philosophy of Socrates* (Garden City, N.Y., 1971).

18. I think myself that Plato will have had the metaphysics of the *Symposium-Phaedo* in mind when he wrote the *Euthyphro*. There is nothing in the text to show that it *must* be so: but the Parmenidean vein is opened by the characterization of the "forms" in terms of self-identity, self-similarity, and contrariety (compare *Euthyphro* 5D 1–3 with Parmenides frr. 8, 29 and 55–9). In the case of *Lysis* and *Euthydemus*, there are more unmistakable signs of things to come, as we shall see. And in the *Meno* it seems to me certain that Plato has in mind eternal and intelligible Forms as objects previously cognized by the disembodied soul and recollected here, since (*a*) the immortal soul requires an eternal object, and (*b*) unless prenatal cognition was different *in kind* from ordinary learning it could not help to solve the paradox of inquiry. But Plato does not tell us this in the *Meno*: he is still not ready to reveal his mysteries, though he has begun the initiation by invoking the authority of learned priests and priestesses (*M.* 81A10). And the proleptic reading of the *Meno* is confirmed by Plato's explicit backward reference on the topic of recollection at *Phdo.* 73A–B.

19. Or perhaps one should say at roughly the same time as the *Euthyphro*. Both dialogues presuppose the *Laches*, and both are presupposed by the *Meno*. But the priority of *Euthyphro* to *Protagoras* is suggested by two considerations (other than the sheer scale of the latter): (i) *Euthyphro*, like *Laches* and *Charmides*, prepares for the thesis of unity without mentioning this thesis (cf. 12D, the designation of piety as a "part" of justice): and (ii) the semi-technical use of *ousia* is motivated by the *hoti pot' estin* question at *Eu.* 11A7 but simply taken for granted at *Prot.* 349B4.

20. At *Gorg.* 509E 1, 510A4, *dunamis* is used as an equivalent for *technē*, as at *H. Mi.* 375D–376A. At *Gorg.* 472B6 and 486c1 *ousia* means "property," in the former instance with a play (pace Dodds) on the sense of "truth" or "reality," but no reference to "essence" or "entity" as at *Prot.* 349B4, *Charm.* 168D2.

One might find the more technical usage of *dunamis* prefigured at *Gorg.* 447c2 (*tis hē dunamis tēs technēs tou andros*, in connection with the *ti esti* question): but the same phrase is used by Gorgias in a colloquial sense ("the power of rhetoric") at 455D7 (cf. 456A5, A8, c6, etc). Of course the *Gorgias* does draw a distinction between *poia tis* and *tis* (at 448E6: cf. 462c10–D1) which provides the basis for the *pathos-ousia* opposition in the *Euthyphro*. But the terminological precision of the latter reflects a theoretical interest which is lacking in the *Gorgias*.

21. The absence of theoretical concern with definition in the *Gorgias* may also be contrasted with the *Charmides*. Although the latter does not focus our attention on formal conditions for correct definition, it clearly describes *sōphrosunē* as a psychic *dunamis* at 160D6ff. (without using the term) and discusses the conditions of competence that should permit the interlocutor to discover a definition (158E7–159A10), elaborating the point made at *Laches* 190c4–6. Both *dunamis* and *ousia* are used in their semi-technical sense at *Charm.* 168B3–5, D1–2, E5; cf. 169A3.

22. Compare Friedländer, *Plato,* tr. Meyerhoff, II. pp. 102–4.

23. So Burnet. Better read (with Gallop) *touto to ho esti.*

24. See parallels in Dodds' note on *Gorg.* 449c2. For confirmation of Socratic practice, cf. Xenophon, *Mem.* 4. 6. 13–15.

25. *Crat.* 390B5–10, echoing *Eud.* 289B10–c4; note the mention of Euthydemus at *Crat.* 386D.

26. So R. Robinson in the first edition of *Plato's Early Dialectic* (Oxford, 1953, p. 121), corrected in the second edition, pp. 117f.

27. Robinson (*Plato's Early Dialectic,* 2nd ed. pp. 137f.) denies any connection between *hikanon ti* in the *Phaedo* and *to anupotheton* in *Republic* 6, but he reads *hikanon ti* as if it were equivalent *hikanēn tina* (sc. *hupothesin*), which it is not.

28. See, e.g. A. E. Taylor, *Socrates,* p. 144n., *Plato: the Man and His Work,* pp. 258–61; G. M. A. Grube, *Plato's Thought,* p. 61; and the detailed exegesis by J. P. Sullivan in *Phronesis* 6 (1961), 10ff. For recent interpretations which ascribe the hedonism to Socrates (or to Plato) see Irwin, *Plato's Moral Theory,* ch. IV, and C. C. W. Taylor, *Plato's Protagoras* (1976), pp. 208–10 (with bibliography). Other views in N. Gulley, *The Philosophy of Socrates* (1968), pp. 111–18; G. Vlastos, "Socrates on Acrasia," *Phoenix* 23 (1969), 75f.

29. It is true that the many are first described as unready to accept the hedonist view (351c3), just as Protagoras himself is unwilling to do so (351c7ff.). Discussion and clarification is required to get him to assent to it first in the name of the many (354c–E), and then in agreement with the others (358B2–3). So the procedure is not exactly that of the *Meno* (as Geoffrey Lloyd reminds me), where the argument from the *hupothesis* is given first (87B–c), and the *hupothesis* itself defended afterwards (87c11ff.). (Note that the *Meno* ends by regarding its own *hupothesis* as at least doubtful, since virtue may rest on true belief as well as on knowledge: the *hupothesis* remains a problematic assumption.) But the function of *hupothesis* is essentially the same in *Meno* and in our argument from *Protagoras:* a useful preliminary (*proürgou, M.* 87A2) permitting one to solve a problem that cannot be attacked directly.

30. Thus I very much doubt the historicity of the *Symposium* as an account of Agathon's party, but I do not doubt that Socrates sometimes stood still in the street or in the snow at Potidea, and that Alcibiades was passionately attached to him in the way his speech indicates. The historicity of the meeting with Protagoras in the house of Callias (before Plato's birth . . .) is at least doubtful. The encounter with Parmenides and Zeno is almost certainly pure fiction.

For those who feel that Plato's artistic simulacra must have some prima facie claim to historical accuracy, I refer to Christopher Gill, "The Death of Socrates," *Classical Quarterly* n.s. 23 (1973), 25–8.

FURTHER READING

Griswold, C. L., Jr. 1988. "Unifying Plato." *Journal of Philosophy* 85:550–51.

Kahn, C. H. 1986. "Plato's Methodology in the *Laches.*" *Revue Internationale de Philosophie* 40:7–21.

———. 1988. "On the Relative Date of the *Gorgias* and the *Protagoras.*" *Oxford Studies in Ancient Philosophy* 6:69–102.

———. 1988. "Plato's *Charmides* and the Proleptic Reading of Socratic Dialogues." *Journal of Philosophy* 85:541–49.

McPherran, M. L. 1990. "Comments on Charles Kahn, 'The Relative Date of the *Gorgias* and the *Protagoras.*'" *Oxford Studies in Ancient Philosophy* 8:211–36.

Vlastos, G. 1988. "Socrates." *Proceedings of the British Academy* 74:87–109.

4

Socratic Midwifery, Platonic Inspiration

MYLES F. BURNYEAT

There are certain famous passages in literature which are so well known that, paradoxically, they become extremely difficult to read. The words are so familiar, their appeal so direct and powerful, that the reader, drawn in, does not ask the questions which would lead to a critical and explicit awareness of what is actually in the text. One such passage, I believe, is the fine and deservedly famous section of Plato's *Theaetetus* (148e–151d) where Socrates compares himself to a midwife and his method of dialectical questioning to the midwife's art of delivery.

It is a passage often referred to in accounts of Socrates but seldom examined in detail. The scholarly literature shows little recognition of the interesting and sometimes remarkable things that are stated or implied, commented upon or not commented upon, in this and in certain related texts, such as the equally famous speech of Diotima in the *Symposium*. Consider, for example (to make our start at a reasonably mundane level), the question whether the midwife comparison is to be attributed to the historical Socrates. Not a few scholars have accepted, with more or less confidence, that it is;[1] there are many more who, while they have not formally expressed a view on the historical point, must acknowledge in themselves the accuracy of Richard Robinson's observation that the image of Socrates as a midwife of ideas "has so gripped our minds that we usually think of it as a feature of all the Socratic literature and of the real Socrates."[2] This is high testimony to the power of the image. For the fact is, Plato makes it abundantly clear that the comparison is *not*, in any sense, to be attributed to the historical Socrates.

The conversation is so contrived that Theaetetus distinguishes, item by item, those elements of the comparison which are familiar to him because they are common gossip about Socrates and those which are not. He has heard what sort of questions Socrates is accustomed to ask (148e); that Socrates is the son of a midwife with the astonishingly appropriate name Phainarete, "she who brings virtue to light" (149a);[3] that he has an extraordinary way of reducing people to perplexity (149ab). Further he knows that the art of midwifery is reserved for women who are past the age for having children themselves (149bc). He has not, however, heard that Socrates is following his mother's art of midwifery when he asks his questions and induces perplexity. He has not heard this for the good reason that Socrates has not let it be known and would not like Theaetetus to make a public accusation of it either (149a). Nor did he know that midwives pride themselves on being the best matchmakers—again for the good reason that they are reluctant to practise this skill for fear they will be accused of pandering (149d–150a). Such concern to tell us exactly which details of the comparison a young man could be expected to know already can have no other motive than to sift fact from imagination, putting Socratic midwifery firmly in the realm of the imaginary.

It must, then, be the power of the image, its striking one as so absolutely the "right" representation of what Socrates does, that blinds people to Plato's explicit sign-posting and convinces them that this was how Socrates himself viewed his role as educator of the young.[4] The image has indeed great power—one may surmise that it touches certain chords in the reader's own psyche—but the question we have to ask is why, given that the midwife figure is not historical, Plato should have chosen to develop it for this particular dialogue. We shall find that the answer lies, first, in some pointed contrasts with the treatment of related themes in other dialogues (notably the *Meno* and *Symposium*), and second, in the design of the *Theaetetus* itself: the midwifery passage prepares us for a highly important feature of Part I of the dialogue, the like of which is not to be met with in Plato's work elsewhere.

The necessary background to the picture of Socrates as midwife, without which the whole elaborate fancy would lose its sense, is, of course, the metaphor of the mind giving birth to ideas it has conceived. The compelling naturalness of this image is a matter of common experience and needs no argument. But it can be taken more or less seriously. At a superficial level it is a metaphor like any other, based on a sense of resemblance between physical and mental creativity. The resemblance seems so fitting, however, so familiar even, as to invite the thought that the metaphor corresponds, in some deeper sense, to psychological reality. The response it evokes is more like recognition than ordinary appreciation, a recognition of an aspect of one's own experience which may not be fully acknowledged. It is not only that we do often represent the originating of thoughts in terms of parturition, but that a significant emotional charge attaches to the idea that the mind is no less capable of conception and birth than the body of a woman. To take the metaphor seriously is to recognize it as embodying an important part of the meaning that the creative process can have for someone. In Plato's case, that his seriousness was of this order is something to be felt rather than proved, but felt it can be in the sustained use he makes of the imagery both here and in the *Symposium,* where the idea of mental pregnancy and birth is central to Diotima's discourse on love; but the development it receives is interestingly different from, even antithetical to, the *Theaetetus.*

Diotima's thesis is that "all men are pregnant both in body and in soul, and when they come of age our nature desires to give birth; it cannot give birth in anything ugly, only in what is beautiful" (206c), and this desire to give birth in what is beautiful is love (206e).[5] Notice the strange reversal: the pregnancy is the cause, not the consequence, of love; and the birth is love's expressive manifestation. Although Diotima speaks of "our nature," it is a male pregnancy she is describing, and the birth is the lover engendering offspring, at the physical level in bodily union with a woman, at the spiritual level in artistic and intellectual creation of every kind but most especially in passionate communion with a beautiful boy, who inspires his lover to deliver himself of discourses on virtue and other educative topics (208e–209e, 210aff.). In short, at either level pregnancy precedes intercourse, because birth and intercourse are imaginatively equated. So striking a reversal could only be contrived in a realm of imagination and metaphor, but for that reason it may reveal something about Plato's mind. To this we shall return.

Meanwhile, it is to be remarked that in the *Symposium* the great lover in the spiritual sense is Socrates himself, as we learn from Alcibiades' speech in his praise. It is Socrates whose talk with the young is rich with images of virtue (222a) and productive of improving effects (216b–217a), he therefore who is most fruitfully pregnant, while it is not Socrates but Beauty, present in the boy, who has the midwife's office of relieving travail (206d). In keeping with this, the *Symposium* envisages none but worthy children of the mind, namely, wisdom and the other virtues (209a, 212a), embodied in (and promoted by) a lover's improving discourses (209bc), advances in practical or theoretical knowledge (209a with 197ab, 210d), or the protreptic force of poetry and laws (209a, de).

What a change to move to the *Theaetetus* and find Socrates barren, like other midwives (150cd).[6] The youth has the pregnancy (how he got to be pregnant is left as mysterious as in the *Symposium*); Socrates merely helps to bring forth his conception. Correspondingly, not all a young mind's offspring are worthy to be reared. Socrates' most important task, and one that has no analogue in ordinary midwifery, is that of testing whether the thought-product he has delivered is genuine and true or a false counterfeit, a "wind-egg" with no life in it (150ac, 151cd, 151e, 157d, 160e–161a, 210b).

There can be no doubt which of the two representations of Socrates is more appropriate to the Socratic method as that is practised in the *Theaetetus,* especially its first part. (That it is primarily Part I of the dialogue which the midwifery section introduces is clear from this, that reminders of the comparison between the Socratic method and the midwife's art recur at intervals throughout Part I [151e, 157cd, 160e–161b, 161e, 184b] but not again until the brief concluding remarks which bring the dialogue to a close [210bd]. The discussion in Parts II and III makes no pretence to exemplify Socrates' art of midwifery; the definition in Part III is not even, strictly speaking, Theaetetus' own conception but a view which suddenly comes to mind as one that he heard someone else put forward [201c].) The *Symposium* presents a middle period Socrates, argumentative still but with positive doctrine of his own or learned from Diotima. The *Theaetetus* starts by introducing Socrates as a lover of young Athenians, in contrast to Theodorus who would not like to be thought susceptible to beauty (143de; cp. 146a, 185e, 210d), but on its own this is no more than a trait from the early dialogues brought in to help with the scene-setting (cf. e.g. *Charm.* 154bff., *Ly.* 223b, *Prot.* 309a, *Gorg.* 481d, *M.* 76b; cp. *Sym.* 216d), after which it virtually drops out of view. The midwife figure signals a return to the aporeutic style of those early dialogues and to the Socratic method which is the substance of that style.[7]

So much is clear. Less obvious, perhaps, is the survival into the *Theaetetus* of a devalued version of the *Symposium*'s sexualized view of teaching—devalued in that it has become separated from the metaphor of mental conception and birth and is now associated with sophistic education in pointed *contrast* to Socrates' own approach. The first hint of this development comes in the argument with which Socrates overrules Theaetetus' surprise at the inclusion of matchmaking among the skills of the ordinary midwife. Taking a thoroughly agricultural view of marriage, Socrates maintains that knowledge of cultivating and harvesting is inseparable from, belongs to the same field of competence as, knowledge of what seeds to plant in what ground; hence the midwife, who is the harvester of human crop, is the best person to tell which man should sow his seed in which woman in order to produce the best children (149de). Pure invention, as we have already seen, but why? Simply to provide Socrates with an analogue for one of his own practices. It being part of a midwife's job to discern who is pregnant and who is not (149c), when he thinks that a young man who has come to him has no need of his assistance because he is not pregnant and has no conception for him to deliver, he kindly arranges to "marry him off" to Prodicus or some other suitable teacher, so that the youth can receive the marvellous benefits of his instruction (151b; cp. *La.* 200d). The ironical implication, which Socrates refrains from spelling out, is not kindly: an empty mind which has no conceptions of its own (cf. 148e) is fitted only to be sown with another's seed. As for Prodicus, a "marriage" arranged with him would be a "good match" both in the conventional sense, since Prodicus stood high in popular esteem,[8] and also, one suspects, because the ideas he implanted in the young man's empty mind would be correspondingly empty and anodyne.[9]

Here, then, are two contrasting notions of education. The sophist treats his pupil as an empty receptacle to be filled from the outside with the teacher's ideas. Socrates respects the pupil's own creativity, holding that, with the right kind of assistance, the young man will produce ideas from his own mind and will be enabled to work out for himself whether they are true or false. Like childbirth, the process can be painful, for it hurts to be made to formulate one's own ideas and, having done so, to find out for oneself what they are worth (151a, c); many turn on Socrates in angry resentment at seeing some nonsense they have produced exposed by him (151a, cd). But the other side of the coin is the progress that can be made this way, progress measured not only by the valuable truths found within oneself and brought to birth (150de),[10] but also by the accompanying growth in self-knowledge, the awareness of what one knows and does not know (210bc). Self-knowledge is the benefit peculiarly associated with the Socratic method, and Theaetetus is already dimly aware that he is in travail with a conception of what knowledge is (151b with 148e). Orthodox teaching, even when it is a reputable man like Theodorus (cf. 143de) rather than Prodicus giving the instruction, does not have the same effect, save *per accidens,* because the thoughts imparted to the pupil are not his to begin with and do not have their roots in his experience and attachments.

This contrast, between putting ideas into the pupil's mind and drawing them out from within, is not new in Plato. It is the key contrast in the *Meno's* exposition of the theory that learning is recollection (cf. 81e–82a, 82b, e, 84cd, 85bd). Many have assumed, accordingly, that the midwife figure is a continuation or reworking of that theory, or at least that it casts middle period shadows on the argument ahead by alluding, right at the outset of the inquiry, to the theory of recollection and the philosophical doctrines associated with it.[11] Surprising as that would be in a dialogue which shows every sign that Plato intends to make a fresh start on fundamental questions in epistemology, it can be seen to be incorrect from a careful reckoning of differences.

The *Meno's* theory that learning is the recollecting of knowledge possessed by the soul before birth stands or falls by the contention that *any* soul, throughout its embodied life, has true opinions within it which can be elicited by the right kind of questioning; hence the test case in which Socrates' questions lead an uneducated slave to the solution of a mathematical problem (82aff.). The *Theaetetus* makes no such general claim, since,

since, as we have seen, not all souls conceive, and even those that do are not necessarily pregnant at all times (cf. 210bc). The *Meno* appears to hold, further, that all knowledge is to be gained by recollection, from within (81cd, 85ce). There are interpretative problems about how this is to be taken, but, once again, the *Theaetetus* is more modest: it is not said or implied that all truths, or all knowable truths, are to be got from within, only that many important ones are delivered by Socrates' skill (150d), and nothing at all is indicated as to how these might become *knowledge*. That would prejudge the discussion to come, while any hint that Socratic midwifery could encompass all (knowable) truths would be inconsistent with one of the more positive of later results, that perception, the use of the senses, is necessary for knowledge of various empirical matters (185e, 201b) and in some cases even for mistaken judgements about them (193a–194b). Thirdly, the theory of recollection was introduced in the *Meno* (80dff.) to meet a puzzle about seeking to know what one does not know (how is this possible unless one knows what one is looking for, in which case how can inquiry be needed?): now the same problem, or a closely related puzzle about knowing and not knowing the same thing, is very much alive in Part II of the *Theaetetus* (188aff.); yet not only is no connection drawn with Socratic midwifery but Plato at once discounts as beside the point any solution which appeals, as the *Meno* does, to intermediate internal states like learning and forgetting (188a). Add, finally, that the *Theaetetus* has nothing to say in these contexts about the soul existing independently of the body and it is clear that the bolder claims which accompanied the inner/outer contrast in the *Meno* are withdrawn in the later work.[12]

The fact is, the doctrine of recollection served at least two purposes for Plato. It offered the beginnings of a general theory of knowledge which would tie in logically with other central doctrines of his middle period philosophy such as the independence and immortality of the soul and the theory of Forms (cf. *Phdo.* 76d–77a). At the same time, in the *Meno* at least, it was, more specifically, a theory of the Socratic method, designed to explain how the dialectical process of eliciting an interlocutor's beliefs and testing them for consistency need not be wholly negative and destructive; if the discussion is pursued with sincerity and determination, Socratic inquiry can lead to knowledge. Now our *Theaetetus* passage confines itself to aspects of the Socratic method and, as we have seen, its claims are carefully limited. So far from the midwife figure drawing into the dialogue ideas pertaining to Plato's middle period theory of knowledge, this is put into abeyance and a fresh start prepared by the return to the style and method of the early dialogues. Even on the method itself the *Theaetetus* is cautious: unlike the theory of recollection, the metaphor of conception and birth offers no assurance that the answer sought is already within us waiting to be found. Theaetetus' answers to the question "What is knowledge?" all fail, and the dialogue is content to leave him empty and conscious of his own ignorance. He will be the better for this, intellectually and morally, but Socrates holds out no definite prospect that he will become pregnant again, still less that he will ever really know what knowledge is (210bc).[13] The only assurance the *Theaetetus* has to give is on the value of the self-knowledge to which Socratic inquiry leads.

So far, what is distinctive about the midwife figure, when the *Theaetetus* is compared with the *Meno* and *Symposium,* is its restraint. The passage presents a method of education which is at the same time a method of doing philosophy, and does so in a way that avoids, and seems designed to avoid, metaphysical commitments. It goes over some of the same ground as the theory of recollection in the *Meno,* emphasizing again the contrast between putting ideas into a pupil's mind and drawing them out from within, but the positive doctrine that Plato had once built on this contrast is conspicuously left out. And Socrates himself, instead of being a mouthpiece for Platonic views, is restored to something like his original role as the man who knows nothing on his own account but has a mission to help others by his questioning. All this can be understood as a move "back to Socrates" for the purpose of a dialogue which is critical in intent and deliberately restrained in its positive commitments.

Yet things are not quite the same as they were in the early, Socratic dialogues. The characteristically Socratic procedure of subjecting the interlocutor's ideas to critical scrutiny is now preceded by the process of bringing his conception to birth, and the description and dramatic display of this process is where the midwife figure exhibits its major innovations. It is not simply that the conception may prove to be genuine and true (that possibility was not ruled out in the early period),[14] nor that if the conception is false, it is well to see it for the nonsense it is and be rid of it. These are but the end-results of a process which begins with Socrates awakening or allaying perplexity, and perplexity, (*aporia*) is the sign of a conception struggling to be born (148e, 151ab). Where earlier dialogues had valued perplexity merely as a necessary step towards disencumbering someone of the conceit of knowledge (*I. 532bc, 533cd, H. Mi.* 369ac, *Eu.* 11bc, *La.* 194ac, 200e–201a, *Charm.* 169c, *Ly.* 213cd, *Prot.* 348c, and esp. *M.* 72a, 80ad, 84ad), the *Theaetetus* treats it as a productive state, the first stirring of creative thought.

With this difference goes another. Socrates' earlier interlocutors, once they have grasped what is asked of them, are prompt enough to produce a definition,[15] after which Socrates proceeds immediately to testing and refutation. Theaetetus, however, begins in doubt and perplexity about answering the question "What is knowledge?" (148be), and has to be encouraged to formulate a reply (151d), which he manages to do only with hesitation and expressions of uncertainty:

> Well, then, *it seems to me* that one who knows something perceives what he knows, and knowledge, *at least as it looks at the moment,* is simply perception. (151e)

Socrates responds, quite in his old manner, by announcing his intention that the two of them should now set about testing whether the definition is genuine or a wind-egg. But then he checks himself[16] with the remark that Theaetetus has come out with the same view of knowledge as was held by Protagoras (151e)—and there begins the long process of drawing out the epistemological implications of the thesis that knowledge is perception. In the event, Theaetetus' child is not fully born, ready for testing, until 160e. This extended elaboration of a thesis—a tour de force without parallel in any other dialogue—is what the midwife figure is evidently meant to prepare us for.

It is not my concern here to study how, and with what justification, Socrates involves the thesis that knowledge is perception ever more deeply in the doctrines of Protagoras and Heraclitus. As he does so, however, he has occasion to induce more perplexity in Theaetetus (cf. e.g. 155cd, 158ab), and to alleviate it by taking the argument further. At one point (157c), when he has rounded off a particularly extravagant-seeming set of Heraclitean thoughts and asks how Theaetetus likes the taste of them, the young man is reduced to the puzzled admission that he does not know whether he should accept them as his own, still less can he tell whether Socrates actually believes the ideas he has been expounding or is just putting him to the test. To which Socrates replies, in a significant statement:

> You are forgetting, my friend, that I neither know nor claim as my own anything of the sort. None of them are my offspring. It is you I am delivering, and that is why I chant incantations and offer you tastes from each of the wise, until I bring your opinion into the light of the world—when it has been brought forth, then will be the time to examine whether it is a wind-egg or quick with life. Until then, take heart and persevere with your answers, telling me bravely, whatever I ask about, exactly what appears to you. (157cd).

The reference is to the incantations and medicines which a midwife uses to bring on and alleviate the pains of labour (cf. 149cd). The equivalent in Socrates' art of spiritual midwifery is his arousing and allaying the pains of perplexity (151ab),[17] thereby stimulating the further creative thought needed to bring to birth the opinion Theaetetus has conceived. That is to say, the entire process of elaborating Theaetetus' definition of knowledge with the aid of medicinal tastings from Protagoras and Heraclitus is represented as one of discovering what Theaetetus' own opinion really is. This is clearly of great importance for understanding the logic of Socrates' treatment of the definition, but it is important also for the present discussion of the more psychological aspects of his procedure.

What Theaetetus has to discover is not, presumably, the right words to express his opinion—he managed that when he gave his definition—but whether he really does believe them. In philosophy at least, to know what one's opinion is, it is not enough to have formulated a proposition in words; one must have thought through its implications in a systematic way, confronting it with other relevant beliefs and considering whether these require it to be withdrawn or revised. This is, of course, exactly what happens in a discussion conducted by the Socratic method,[18] but, more than that, it offers a purchase for the somewhat elusive notion that the real reward of Socratic inquiry is a certain kind of self-knowledge.

This idea is most explicit at the end of the dialogue when the midwife image recurs and Socrates talks about the benefits of not thinking one knows what one does not know (210bc). The recommendation to become aware of the limits of one's knowledge, which will in turn limit the tendency to be over-bearing to others and promote temperance (*sophrosune*—210c2–3), is the Socratic version of the traditional Apolline precept "Know thyself" (cf. esp. *Charm.* 164dff., but also *Apol.* 21b–23b, *Tim.* 72a, *Soph.* 230be, *Phil.* 48cff.). But whereas the inscription at Delphi was not a call to self-exploration but a god's reminder that man is limited and should think mortal thoughts, Socrates engaged his fellow men in the task of finding out for themselves what they knew and what they did not. And to discover the limits of one's knowledge in this sense it is necessary first to find out what one really believes. The opinion will need to be tested, but to have formulated it and thought through its implications and connections with other beliefs is already a step towards self-knowledge.

A further aspect of self-knowledge is deployed in the description Socrates gives (150e–151a) of what happens to certain of his pupils who will not acknowledge the debt they owe to his obstetric skills. It is entirely in the spirit of the traditional Greek notion of self-knowledge to expect them to recognize the part played in the birth of their ideas by Socrates and his divine patron.[19] But unlike Theaetetus, who in the dialogue is well aware of the extent to which Socrates' assistance has contributed to his fecundity (210b), these youths take all the credit for themselves. The outcome of this sorry failure of self-knowledge is, first, that they leave Socrates prematurely, on their own initiative or under the influence of others, and second, that their further conceptions miscarry on account of the bad company they fall into and the ones Socrates delivered for them are lost by bad nurture, since they value false counterfeits more than the truth.[20] (How can they value the ideas they owe to Socrates' midwifery if they do not want to admit that they needed his assistance? It is psychologically right that they would prefer to neglect and destroy them.) Only when their ignorance eventually becomes obvious to themselves as well as to others do they plead with Socrates to take them back, and if his "divine sign" does not say "No" to his resuming the association, as sometimes happens, then they make progress again. In other words, Socratic education can only be successful with someone like Theaetetus who is aware of, and can accept, his need for it; that much self-knowledge is an indispensable motivating condition, for always the greatest obstacle to intellectual and moral progress with Socrates is people's unwillingness to confront their own ignorance.

Self-knowledge, then, is not only the goal of Socratic education. It is also, right from the beginning, a vital force in the process itself, which involves and is sustained by the pupil's growing awareness of his own cognitive resources, their strengths and their limitations. That being so, it is all the more surprising (to return to the meaning of creativity) that no question is raised as to the origin of conceptions. Socrates gives no sign of interest in the matter and he seems not to expect the pupil to think about it either. Why should the recommendation to self-knowledge stop short at this critical point?

The inquiry is addressed, of course, to Plato. The metaphor of mental conception and birth is his and he is responsible for the use made of it in the passage under discussion: his too is the emotional seriousness which the writing conveys. Why, then, is it that some conceive and others do not? Where do the conceptions come from? Even within the realm of metaphor the imagery invites these questions, but Plato forestalls the obvious answer, in the *Symposium* by placing the intercourse after the pregnancy, in the *Theaetetus* by setting up a contrast between the pupil conceiving for himself and impregnation by a teacher.

Some readers may think it inappropriate to press such a point. But it does seem significant that Plato should return time and again to sexual imagery for mental creativity without ever raising the question whether a conception does not need to be brought about by a metaphorical intercourse within the mind. The *Symposium* and *Theaetetus* are not the only dialogues in which this occurs. In the *Phaedrus,* where morally improving discourses are represented as a man's true sons, they are simply found within him, carrying a seed that will generate similar offspring in other souls (278ab; cf. 276b–277a). The *Republic* comes closer to what we are seeking when it describes an intercourse with the Forms which begets understanding and truth (490b; cf. the degenerate version at 496a, a marriage of unworthy persons with philosophy which begets sophistries), but the Forms are impersonal entities outside the mind. Perhaps the most revealing evidence comes from Plato's theorizing about creative inspiration in such dialogues as the *Ion* and the *Phaedrus.*

Here he is very much alive to the part played by unconscious forces (as we would put it) but nearly always opposes this to the work of reason. Either ideas come in an uncontrolled eruption of inspired material, as in the case of the poet or seer, who is possessed, temporarily loses his reason and knows not what he says, or they are the product of reason (*I.* 533e ff., *Phdr.* 244a–245a; cf. *Apol.* 22bc. *M.* 99cd, also *Tim.* 71e–72b). The rigid "either-or" character of this approach is obvious. For the most part Plato is unable, or unwilling, to envisage the possibility of a marriage of interaction between the two modes of mental functioning within a single mind. Yet if anything is clear in this area, it is that some such interaction of intuitive inspiration and controlled thinking is a vital element in any kind of creative process. And in one quite exceptional passage, as highly wrought and inspired as any Plato ever wrote, he broke through to a realization of this fundamental point. I refer to the account of philosophic madness in the *Phaedrus* myth (cf. 249bff.), which essays to describe an interaction of reason and inspiration as intimate as could be wished.[21] This is indeed exceptional, an exception so impressive as to confirm that our questions were on the mark. What Plato would never countenance, however, is that a very natural way to represent the creative interaction, especially if one is going on to use the metaphor of conception and birth, is the sexual imagery of a marriage or intercourse between masculine and feminine aspects of the self.[22]

We thus confront a "blind-spot" in Plato. Ultimately, no doubt, it stems from a failure of self-knowledge in the area of his own creativity, but at this distance in time and with only his writings to go on, there is little hope of uncovering the cause. One may conjecture a connection with his need to resist allowing physical expression to the strong homosexual feelings which were so clearly part of his make-up.[23] Many readers have felt that a certain tendency to self-laceration over his own artistic creativity shows through in the *Republic* when Plato banishes poetry from his ideal commonwealth (cf. *Rep.* 607b–608b); and there is the story that he burned his own poems after listening to Socrates (D. L.iii 5, Aelian, *Var. Hist.* ii 30). But one may prefer to say simply that here and there in the dialogues, not least in the midwifery passage we have been discussing, we catch a glimpse into a dark corner of Plato's personality.

NOTES

This paper was prepared during the leisure generously provided by a Radcliffe Fellowship. I am grateful to the Radcliffe Trust for the tenure of the Fellowship and to University College London for allowing me to take it up. The paper itself benefited from comments by James Dybikowski, Malcolm Schofield, Richard Sorabji and Bernard Williams.

1. Thus e.g. A. E. Taylor, *Varia Socratica* (Oxford 1911), 148ff.; John Burnet, "The Socratic Doctrine of the Soul," *Proc. Brit. Acad.* 7 (1916): cited from his *Essays and Addresses* (London 1929), 161; Francis Macdonald Cornford, *Plato's Theory of Knowledge* (London 1935), 28; W. K. C. Guthrie, *A History of Greek Philosophy* iii (Cambridge 1969), 397 n. 1, 444; also Jean Humbert, *Socrate et les petits Socratiques* (Paris 1967), 90–3.

2. Richard Robinson, "Forms and Error in Plato's *Theaetetus*," *Philosophical Review* 59 (1950), 4; compare A. R. Lacey, "Our Knowledge of Socrates," in Gregory Vlastos, ed., *The Philosophy of Socrates* (New York 1971), 42: "The comparison . . . is so apt for what seems to emerge as our general picture of Socrates that one feels tempted to say that if Plato had not written it we would have had to invent it." Robinson himself, in *Plato's Earlier Dialectic,* 2d ed., (Oxford 1953), 83–4, strongly dissents from the view he describes; like Heinrich Maier, *Sokrates: sein Werk und seine geschichtliche Stellung* (Tübingen 1913), 359–60, he thinks the midwife figure is a purely Platonic invention.

3. As remarked by Guthrie, 378 n. 1, this combination of biographical details takes some believing but appears to be true. "Phainarete" was in use as a name and (if it is independent evidence) is again given as the name of Socrates' mother at *Alc. I* 131e.

4. It is true that the authors cited in note 1 (Humbert excepted) find outside support for their view in a phrase that occurs in Aristophanes' *Clouds* 137, where one of Socrates' students

complains that a sudden noise at the door has caused the miscarriage of a newly discovered idea (*phrontid' exēmblōkas exēurēmenēn*): supposedly, this is a fifth-century allusion to Socrates' use of the midwife figure, confirming its historicity. But, as a recent editor of the play observes (K. J. Dover, *Aristophanes Clouds* [Oxford 1968], xlii–xliii), if the midwife figure was so important and well known that the single word *exēmblōkas* would suffice for a humorous allusion (*exambloun* is used at *Tht.* 150e but Aristophanes ends his phrase with *exēurēmenēn* rather than a term appropriate to conception and the following lines produce no supporting terminological anticipations of the Platonic Socrates), it is surprising that there should be no trace of it in Plato's representations of Socrates before a late dialogue like the *Theaetetus*. Given that verbs such as *tiktein* and *gennān* were freely used to speak of giving birth to something in metaphorical senses, it is simpler to explain the joke of an intellectual miscarriage as a humorous twist on talk of giving birth to an idea (metaphors of mental birth and productivity are found, admittedly not earlier than the *Clouds,* in Cratinus, *Pytine* frag. 199 Kock, Arist. *Frogs,* 96, 1059; cf. Xen. *Cyr.* 5.4.35, where a soul is pregnant with a thought).

Guthrie, 444 finds additional support in Xenophon's portrait of Socrates as a pander (*Sym.* 3.10, 4.56–60; cf. also 8.5 and 42). But (a) Socrates' pandering turns out to mean that he makes people attractive and agreeable to others—a far cry from intellectual midwifery; Xenophon goes on (61–4) to describe something akin to the academic matchmaking of *Tht.* 151b, but the activity is ascribed to Antisthenes rather than Socrates and its purpose is quite different from that which guides Socrates in the *Theaetetus*. And (b) the pandering which Socrates practises in Xenophon's *Symposium* is in the *Memorabilia* (2.6.36–9) an art he learned from Pericles' mistress Aspasia; now there was a dialogue *Aspasia* written by the Socratic philosopher Aeschines of Sphettus in which Socrates presented Aspasia as his instructress in much the same kind of educative pandering as Xenophon describes (which would, of course, be entirely appropriate to the figure of a great courtesan), and there is reason to believe that Xenophon's Socratic pandering is simply his development of this Aeschinean theme, with borrowings from Plato's *Symposium* and even from the *Theaetetus* itself: cf. Barbara Ehlers, *Eine vorplatonische Deutung des sokratischen Eros: der Dialog Aspasia des Sokratiker Aischines* (Munich 1966), 63ff. These are not the materials to make history with. Neither Aristophanes nor Xenophon offer anything that could reasonably be thought to outweigh Plato's own dramatic indications that the midwife figure is not historical.

5. The vocabulary allows no backing away from the implications of the metaphor, for although in its literal sense *tiktein* (to beget or give birth to) is commonly used of the father no less than the mother (cf. LSJ s.v.), *kuein* (to have conceived, be pregnant) is not. What is withdrawn is the initial suggestion that all men are pregnant in soul as well as body (cf. 209a). Nevertheless, the idea of paternal pregnancy arouses resistance in some readers, e.g. Diskin Clay, "Platonic Studies and the Study of Plato," *Arion* 2.1 (1975), 174–5, arguing against Gregory Vlastos, *Platonic Studies* (Princeton 1973), 21 with n. 59; according to Clay, the meaning of *kuein* here is simply human fecundity or ripeness (similarly Léon Robin, *La théorie platonicienne de l'amour* (Paris 1933), 16–17). Clay refers for support to the midwifery passage of the *Theaetetus*. But clearly, to deny that *kuein* in the *Theaetetus* means to be pregnant is to refuse to accept that the metaphor of midwifery is the metaphor it is; the same holds, *mutatis mutandis,* for Diotima's imagery in the *Symposium*.

6. Unlike Artemis, the virgin goddess of childbirth, the ordinary midwife has not always been barren—being human, she needs first-hand experience of childbirth if she is to help others (149bc). Some have inferred, therefore, that Socrates too had once been fruitful; thus the anonymous Academic commentator on the dialogue whose work has been preserved on papyrus from the second century A.D. (H. Diels and W. Schubart edd., *Anonymer Kommentar zu Platos Theaetet* [Berlin 1905], 54, 2–13; Herman Schmidt, "Exegetischer Commentar zu Platos Theatet" (*Jahrbücher für klassische Philologie,* 12. Suppl. Bd,

Leipzig 1881), 96; A. E. Taylor, *Plato—The Man and His Work* (London 1926), 324 n. 2. A better view is that of Lewis Campbell, *The Theaetetus of Plato*, 2d ed., (Oxford 1883), 28: "This point is dropped in the comparison: unless Plato means to hint that the art of Socrates was superhuman." For Socrates says quite clearly that he has never given birth (150cd). By the same token, the anonymous commentator 57, 15–42 and others are wrong to treat the *Symposium* and *Theaetetus* together as constituting a coherent complex of ideas: Taylor, *Varia Socratica*, 149–51; Burnet, 161; and Guthrie, 397 n. 1, 444; also R. G. Bury, *The Symposium of Plato*, 2d ed., (Cambridge 1932), 110; Robin, 174–5.

7. On the Socratic method in the *Theaetetus* I may refer to my paper "Examples in Epistemology: Socrates, Theaetetus and G. E. Moore," *Philosophy* 52 (1977) 381–98.

8. Cf. Dover, lv: "Prodicus was the most distinguished and respected intellectual of the day, and achieved in his lifetime . . . something like the 'proverbial' status of Thales"—this on the evidence of comedy and other sources, though missing the irony in the present passage.

9. Prodicus is the sophist whom Plato names most often in passing references but discusses least. Nowhere are his views accorded serious treatment. His trite and unoriginal moral fable on the choice of Heracles is briefly mentioned (*Sym.* 177b; cf. *Prot.* 340d), but it was Xenophon who thought its content worth preserving (*Mem.* 2.1.21ff.). His speciality, the drawing of excessively neat distinctions between closely related words (on display at *Prot.* 337ac), is referred to in the dialogues with dismissive irony and seldom found relevant to any matter of real philosophical substance (*Charm.* 163bd; *Prot.* 358ab, de; *Eud.* 277e–278a with 278b; *M.* 75e; *La.* 197bd is hardly more favourable, *Prot.* 340aff. is parody, and at *Crat.* 384bc Socrates relates how Prodicus' one-drachma show-lecture did not entice him to enroll for the fifty-drachma session it was designed to advertise). Opinions have differed on what is to be made of Socrates describing himself as Prodicus' pupil (*Prot.* 341a, *M.* 96d; for discussion, with further references, cf. R. S. Bluck, *Plato's Meno* [Cambridge 1961], 400–1; Guthrie, 222–3, 275–6), but both passages are highly ironical and it is irony without a trace of respect. There is no respect, either, in the portrait of Prodicus in the opening scene of the *Protagoras* (315c–316a), where the sophist keeps himself wrapped up in bed in a disused storeroom, as if unable to compete with his rivals discoursing outside, and the booming of his bass voice in the small space makes his words too indistinct for Socrates to catch any sense from them (!). This is cruel, but in our dialogue too Plato regards it as a mark of a mean and captious mind to insist on linguistic exactitude unless some serious purpose requires it (164cd, 165a, 166c, 168bc, and esp. 184c; cf. *Pltc.* 261e). A couple of further references to Prodicus' ideas merely reinforce the impression of mediocrity (*Eud.* 305c, *Phdr.* 267b); Plato says nothing of Prodicus' views on the origins of religion, which sound more interesting but are not easy to reconstruct from the confusion of later doxographical material (cf. Guthrie, 238ff.). On the whole, it is hard not to concur with Plato's implied judgement of the man.

10. 150d7–8 speaks only of "many fine things" brought to birth, but it is not in the spirit of the passage for Socrates to describe in such terms ideas which are false (cf. 151d), and their truth is in fact certified at 150e7.

11. Plutarch, *Plat. Quaest.* 1000de (cp. Olympiodorus, *in Plat. Phaed.* 159, 1–3 Norvin); the anonymous commentator 47, 31ff., 55, 26ff.; Proclus in *Plat. Alc. I* 28, 16–29, 3 Creuzer; David Peipers, *Untersuchungen über das System Platos, Erster Theil; Die Erkenntnistheorie Platos, mit besonderer Rücksicht auf den Theätet* (Leipzig 1874), 232 ff.; Schmidt, 99; Cornford, 27–8; Léon Robin, *Platon* (Paris 1935), 72; Norman Gulley, "Plato's Theory of Recollection," *CQ* n.s. 4 (1954) 200 n. 1.

12. Others who agree that the midwife figure does not allude to recollection use the argument that conceptions in the *Theaetetus* may be false, which recollections cannot be, at least so far as concerns the theory of recollection in the *Phaedo* (72e ff.) and *Phaedrus* (249b ff.) where what is recollected is (knowledge of) Forms (Robinson, "Forms and Error in Plato's *Theaetetus*," 4, R. Hackforth, "Notes on Plato's *Theaetetus*," *Mnemosyne* series 4, 10 (1957), 128–9,

John McDowell, *Plato: Theaetetus* (Oxford 1973), 116–7). This is true, but I do not emphasize the point because in the *Meno* the term "recollection" covers the whole dialectical process leading up to successful recollection of a correct answer, in which process the eliciting and testing of false opinions has an essential part to play (cf. *M*. 82e, 84a).

13. Contrary to the opinion of Proclus, *in Plat. Alc. I* 28, 4–8, that after cleansing Theaetetus of false opinions Socrates lets him go as now being capable of discovering the truth by himself.

14. Robinson, *Plato's Earlier Dialectic,* 83–4, describes the midwife figure as a subterfuge to allow the mature Plato to present in a constructive light the essentially destructive Socratic method of dialectical refutation; cf. the similar view taken by Gilbert Ryle, *Plato's Progress* (Cambridge 1966), 120–1. But for all his irony Socrates always did hope to find truth by his examination of other people's minds (*Apol.* 21bff., *Crito* 46b, *H. Mi. 369ce, 372c, Eu.* 11de, *Gorg.* 453ab, 486eff.); and when he found nothing but false pretensions to wisdom and knowledge he hoped, by exposing this, to enlist his interlocutor in a common search for truth and virtue (*Apol.* 29dff., *Charm.* 165b, 176ad, *Prot.* 348cd, 361cd, *M*. 80d). The most that can be said on this score is that he goes beyond the early dialogues in declaring positively that he has brought many fine conceptions to birth (150d).

15. Charmides hestitates to say what *sophrosune* (temperance, modesty) is, but that is because he is supposed to have the virtue himself and fears it will look immodest if he describes the qualities involved (*Charm.* 159ab).

16. That is the force of *mentoi* at 151e 8, which must be adversative; it is not here the affirmative "Well now" and the like favoured by most translators and by J. D. Denniston, *The Greek Particles,* 2d ed., (Oxford 1954), 400. Otherwise the dramatic structure falls apart, since, as we are about to see, the testing is in fact postponed until 160e.

17. The comparison of Socrates' dialectical questioning to incantations composed for psychiatric effect was a theme of the *Charmides* (156dff., 175e, 176b; cp. *M*. 80a).

18. See my paper cited in n. 7.

19. Socrates' special patron is usually Apollo (*Apol.* 23bc, *Phdo.* 85b). Accordingly, Gottfried Stallbaum, *Platonis Theaetetus (Platonis omnia opera* VIII.I, Gotha and Erfurt 1839), 69 and Campbell, 31-2 suppose that the reference of the masculine *ho theos* in 150cd is to Apollo. On the other hand, a midwife's allegiance is to Apollo's elder sister Artemis, and at 210c Socrates and his mother are said to have their art of midwifery "from God" (*ek theou*), as if there was but one deity for the two of them to serve. *Ho theos* in Greek can refer to a goddess (cf. Hdt. i.31.3, 105.4, ii 133.2, vi 82.1–2), but it would probably be better to say that the divinity in charge of midwifery is thought of in a fairly indeterminate, generic way and assumes masculine guise when the art is practiced by a man on men.

20. One such man is mentioned by name: Aristeides, son of Lysimachus (151a). Aristeides is one of the two youths whose education is discussed in the *Laches,* where Lysimachus and Melesias are pathetically anxious that their sons should make more of a name for themselves than they have managed to do (179cd). It emerges that the youths have already encountered Socrates and have come away full of praise for him (180d–181a), and the dialogue ends with some prospect that he will continue to take an interest in the question of their education; but it is implied that he will recommend a teacher rather than take charge of them himself (cf. 200d–201c). At all events, so far as we know Aristeides' career when he grew up was as undistinguished as his father's. Plato's reason for mentioning him in the *Theaetetus* is probably just to remind us of the *Laches* and of a young man whose dealings with Socrates led to nothing. (The pseudo-Platonic *Theages* 130ae fills out his story in some detail, but since the author gives an entirely different explanation for his departure from Socrates, namely, military service, the account can safely be set aside as a later invention.)

21. The importance of the passage is remarked by Vlastos, 27 n. 80.

22. For a wise and jargon-free exploration of this difficult topic see Marion Milner, *On Not Being Able to Paint,* 2d ed. (London 1957).

23. Clay, 124, denies it can be known that Plato was homosexual. Certainly, the fact cannot be documented in a manner likely to satisfy a determined sceptic: who would expect it to be? It is no more, but also no less, than a conclusion to which most readers of Plato are irresistibly drawn. More important, it is a conclusion which, once accepted, must be central to any attempt at a sympathetic understanding of Plato's recurring preoccupation with the mysterious links, which at some level we all feel, between creativity and sexuality. This is amply clear from the very paper that Clay is criticizing: Gregory Vlastos' brave and magnificent essay "The Individual as an Object of Love in Plato" (in *Platonic Studies,* cited n. 5).

FURTHER READING

Burnyeat, M. F. 1977. "Examples in Epistemology: Socrates, Theaetetus, and G. E. Moore." *Philosophy* 52:381–98.
Robinson, R. 1953. *Plato's Earlier Dialectic,* 2d ed., esp. 7–60. Oxford.
Tarrant, H. 1988. "Midwifery and the Clouds." *Classical Quarterly* 38:116–22.
Tomin, J. 1987. "Socratic Midwifery." *Classical Quarterly* 37:97–102.
Vlastos, G. 1983. "The Socratic Elenchus." *Oxford Studies in Ancient Philosophy* 1:27–58.
———. "Afterthoughts." *Oxford Studies in Ancient Philosophy* 1:71–74.

5

Socratic Irony

GREGORY VLASTOS

"Irony," says Quintilian, is that figure of speech or trope "in which something contrary to what is said is to be understood" (*contrarium ei quod dicitur intelligendum est*).[1] His formula has stood the test of time. It passes intact into Dr. Johnson's dictionary ("mode of speech in which the meaning is contrary to the words" [1755]). It survives virtually intact in ours:

> Irony is the use of words to express something other than, and especially the opposite of, [their] literal meaning. (Webster's)

Here is an example, as simple and banal as I can make it: a British visitor, landing in Los Angeles in the middle of a downpour, is heard to remark: "What fine weather you are having here." The weather is foul, he calls it "fine," and has no trouble making himself understood to mean the contrary of what he says.

Why should we want to put such twists on words, making them mean something so different from their "literal"—that is, their established, commonly understood—sense that it could even be its opposite? What purpose could this serve? For one thing, humour. For another, mockery. Or, perhaps, both at once, as when Mae West explains why she is declining President Gerald Ford's invitation to a state dinner at the White House: "It's an awful long way to go for just one meal." The joke is *on* someone, a put-down made socially acceptable by being wreathed in a cerebral smile.

A third possible use of irony has been so little noticed[2] that there is no name for it. Let me identify it by ostension. Paul, normally a good student, is not doing well today. He stumbles through a tutorial, exasperating his tutor, who finally lets fly with, "Paul, you are positively brilliant today." Paul feels he is being consigned to the outer darkness. But what for? What has he done that is so bad? Has he been rambling and disorganized, loose and sloppy in his diction, ungrammatical, unsyntactical, ill-prepared, uninformed, confused, inconsistent, incoherent? For which sub-class of these failings is he being faulted? He hasn't been told. He has been handed a riddle and left to solve it for himself. Though certainly not universal, this form of irony is not as rare as one might think. Only from its most artless forms, as in my first example, is it entirely absent. There is a touch of it in the second. Mae West puts us off teasingly from her reasons for turning down that gilt-edged invitation. She is implying: "If you are not an utter fool you'll know this isn't my real reason. Try guessing what that might be."

When irony riddles it risks being misunderstood. At the extreme the hearer might even miss the irony altogether. If Paul had been fatuously vain, sadly deficient in self-criticism, he could have seized on that remark to preen himself on the thought that he must have said *something* brilliant after all. If so, we would want to say that the deception occurred contrary to the speaker's intent. For if the tutor had meant to speak ironically he could not have meant to deceive. Those two intentions are at odds; insofar as the first is realized the second cannot be. That in fact there was no intention to deceive should be obvious in all three of my examples. And that this is not a contingent feature of these cases can be seen by referring back to the definition at the start. Just from that we can deduce that if the visitor had wanted to deceive someone—say, his wife back in London—that the weather just then was fine in L.A., he could not have done it by saying to her *ironically* over the phone, "the weather is fine over here." For to say this ironically is to say it intending that by "fine" she should understand the contrary; if she did, she would not be deceived: the weather in L.A. *was* the contrary of "fine" just then.

This is so basic that a further example may not be amiss. A crook comes by a ring whose stone he knows to be fake, and he goes around saying to people he is trying to dupe, "Can I interest you in a diamond ring?" To call this "irony" would be to show one is all at sea about the meaning of the word. Our definition tells us why: to serve his fraud the literal sense of "diamond" has to be the one he intends to convey. To see him using the word ironically we would have to conjure up circumstances in which he would have no such intention—say, telling his ten-year-old daughter with a tell-tale glint in his eye, "Luv, can I interest you in a diamond ring?" Now suppose he had said this to her without that signal. Might we still call it "irony?" We might, provided we were convinced he was not trying to fool her: she is ten, not five, old enough to know that if that trinket were a diamond ring it would be worth thousands and her father would not let it out of his sight. If we thought this is what he was about—testing her intelligence and good sense—we could still count it irony: a pure specimen of the riddling variety. It would not be disqualified as such if the little girl were to fail the test, for the remark had not been made with the intention to deceive. Similarly, the tutor might have said, "brilliant" well aware there was a chance Paul might miss the irony and mistake censure for praise—knowing this, and for good reasons of his own willing to take that chance.

Once this has sunk in we are in for a surprise when we go back to classical Greece and discover that the intention to deceive, so alien to our word for irony, is normal in its Greek ancestor *eirōneia, eirōn, eirōneuomai*.[3] The difference is conspicuous in its first three uses in the surviving corpus of the Attic texts—all three of them in Aristophanes. In *Wasps* 173, *hōs eirōnikōs* refers to Philocleon's lying to get his donkey out of the family compound to make a dicast out of him. In *Birds* 1210, it is applied to Iris for lying her way into the city of the birds. In *Clouds* 415, *eirōn* sandwiched in between two words for "slippery," *masthlēs, gloios*, figures "in a catalogue of abusive terms against a man who is a tricky opponent in a lawsuit" (K. Dover, ad loc.).[4] We meet more of the same in the fourth-century usage. Demosthenes (I *Phil.* 7) uses it of citizens who prevaricate to evade irksome civic duty. Plato uses it in the *Laws* (901e) when prescribing penalties for heretics: the hypocritical ones he calls *to eirōnikon eidos* of the class; for them he legislates death or worse; those equally wrong-headed but honestly outspoken are let off with confinement and admonition. In the *Sophist,* pronouncing Socrates' dialectic a superior form of *sophistikē* (*hē genei gennaia sophistikē*, 231b), Plato contrasts it with the run-of-the-mill *sophistikē* practised by ordinary sophists: these are the people he puts into the *eirōnikon eidos* of the art; not Socrates, but his arch-rivals, whom Plato thinks imposters, are the ones he calls *eirōnes* (268a–b).

How entrenched in disingenuousness is the most ordinary use of *eirōn* at this time we can see from the picture of the *eirōn* in Aristotle and Theophrastus. Strikingly different though the *eirōn* is in each—odious in Theophrastus, aimiable in Aristotle[5]—in one respect he is the same in both: he wilfully prevaricates in what he says about himself. Aristotle takes a lenient view of such dissembling in the case of Socrates. Casting him as an *eirōn*, Aristotle contrasts him with his opposite, the braggart *alazōn*, and finds him incomparably more attractive, because the qualities he disclaims are the prestigious ones and his reason for disclaiming them—"to avoid pompousness"—is commendable (*EN*, 1127b23–6), though still, it should be noted, not admirable in Aristotle's view. When he expresses admiration for Socrates' personal character he shifts to an entirely different trait; it is for indifference to the contingencies of fate (*apatheia*), not at all for *eirōneia*, that he calls Socrates *megalopsuchos* (*Po. An.* 98a16–24; cf D.L. 6.2). In Theophrastus the *eirōn* is flayed mercilessly,[6] portrayed as systematically deceitful,[7] venomously double-faced,[8] adept at self-serving camouflage.

This too is how Thrasymachus views Socrates in that famous passage in the *Republic* (337a) in which he refers to Socrates' "customary" *eirōneia*:

> **T1** "Heracles!" he said. "This is Socrates' habitual shamming (*eirōneia*). I had predicted to these people that you would refuse to answer and would sham (*eirōneusoio*) and would do anything but answer if the question were put to you."

Thrasymachus is charging that Socrates lies in saying he has no answer of his own to the question he is putting to others: he most certainly does. Thrasymachus is protesting, but pretends he hasn't to keep it under wraps so he can have a field-day pouncing on ours and tearing it to shreds while his is shielded from attack. So there is no excuse for rendering *eirōneia* here by "irony" (Bloom, Grube, Shorey):[9] if that translation were correct, lying would be a standard form of irony.[10]

From the behaviour of *eirōneia* and *eirōneuein* in all of the foregoing Attic texts from Aristophanes to Theophrastus one could easily jump to a wrong conclusion: *because* they are so commonly used to denote sly, intentionally deceptive speech or conduct throughout this period, *must* they be always so used of Socrates by Plato? This is what many noted Hellenists have assumed: Burnet,[11] Wilamowitz,[12] Guthrie[13] among them. Let me point out how unsafe is this kind of inference. From the fact that a word is used in a given sense in a multitude of cases it does not follow that it cannot be used in a sharply different sense in others. Such statistical inferences are always risky. This one is certainly wrong. Consider the following:

> **T2** *Gorg.* **489d5–e4:** [a]Socrates: "Since by 'better' you don't mean 'stronger,' tell me again from the beginning what you mean. And teach me more gently, admirable man, so that I won't run away from your school." Callicles: "You are mocking me (*eirōneuēi.*" [b] Socrates: "No, by Zethus, whom you used earlier to do a lot of mocking against me (*polla eirōneuou pros me*)."

In part (a) Callicles is protesting Socrates' casting himself as a pupil of his—a transparent irony, since Callicles no doubt feels that, on the contrary, it is Socrates who has been playing the school-master right along. In (b) Socrates is retorting that Callicles had used the figure of Zethus to mock him earlier on, associating him with the latter's brother, the pathetic Amphion, who "despite a noble nature, puts on the semblance of a silly juvenile'' (485e7–486a1). In both cases mockery is being protested without the slightest imputation of intentional deceit. In neither case is there any question of shamming, slyness or evasiveness—no more so than if they had resorted to crude abuse, like calling each other ''pig'' or ''jack-ass.''[14]

No less instructive for my purpose is the following from the *Rhetorica ad Alexandrum* (a late fourth-century treatise of uncertain authorship):[15]

T3 *Eirōneia* is [a] saying something while pretending (*prospoioumenon*) not to say it or [b] calling things by contrary names (21).

At [a] we get nothing new: *eirōneuein* is one of the many tricks of the trade this handbook offers the rhetorician.[16] Not so at [b], as becomes even clearer in his example:

T4 Evidently, those good people (*houtoi men hoi chrēstoi*) have done much evil to the allies, while we, the bad ones (*hēmeis d' hoi phauloi*) have caused them many benefits (loc. cit.).

The way *chrēstoi* is used here reminds us of the line Aristophanes gives Strepsiades in the opening monologue of the *Clouds: ''ho chrēstos houtosi neanias,''* the old man says of his good-for-nothing son.[17] This is irony of the purest water: mockery without the slightest insinuation of deceit.

Can we make sense of this state of affairs: in a mass of Attic texts (eight of those to which I have referred; I could have added many more of the same ilk) we find *eirōneia* implying wilful misrepresentation; yet in the ninth we see it standing for mockery entirely devoid of any such connotation and so too again in part [b] of the tenth, where a rhetorician who is thoroughly at home in fourth-century Attic usage gives a definition of *eirōneia* which anticipates Quintilian so perfectly that the two definitions are precisely equivalent: each is a description of the same speech-act, viewed from the speaker's point of view in T3[b], from the hearer's in Quintilian. Is this linguistic phenomenon understandable? Yes, perfectly so, if we remind ourselves of the parallel behaviour of our own word ''pretending.'' To say that a malingerer is ''pretending'' to be sick and that a con man is ''pretending'' to have high connections is to say that these people are deceivers: ''to allege falsely'' is the basic use of ''to pretend.'' Even so, there are contexts where ''to pretend'' by-passes false allegation because it by-passes falsehood, as when we say that the children are ''pretending'' that their coloured chips are money (''pretend-money'' they call them) or that their dolls are sick or die or go to school. In just the same way we could say that the crook in my example is ''pretending'' that the stone on the trinket he offers his daughter is a diamond, which is as far as anything could be from his ''pretending'' it is a diamond when putting it up to the people he is trying to hook. That the latter should be the most common and, in point of logic, the primary use of ''pretending'' does nothing to block a secondary use of the word, tangential to the first—a subsidiary use of ''pretending'' which is altogether innocent of intentional deceit, predicated on that ''willing suspension of disbelief'' by which we enter the world of imaginative fiction in art or play. This is the sense of ''pretending'' we could invoke to elucidate ironical diction, as in Mae West's remark: we could say she is ''pretending'' that the length of the journey is her reason for declining, which would be patently absurd if ''pretending'' were being used in its primary sense; there is no false allegation because there is no allegation: she is pulling our leg.

This, I suggest, gives a good explanation of the fact that though *eirōn, eirōneuein, eirōneia* are commonly used to imply wilfull disingenuousness, even so, *pace* Wilamowitz, Burnet, Guthrie,[18] Dover,[19] they are suseptible of an alternative use which is completely free of such evocation. What happened, I suggest, is this. When *eirōneia* gained currency in Attic speech (by the last third of the fifth century at the latest), its semantic field was as wide as is that of "pretending" in present day English, and *eirōn, eirōneuein, eirōneia* had strongly unfavourable connotations—were used as terms of denigration or abuse—because the first of those two uses predominated heavily over the second: to be called an *eirōn* would be uncomplimentary at best, insulting at the worst. But turn the pages of history some three hundred years—go from Greece in the fourth century B.C. to Rome in the first, and you will find a change that would be startling if long familiarity had not inured us to it. The word has now lost its disagreeable overtones. When Cicero, who loves to make transliterated Greek enrich his mother tongue, produces in this fashion the new Latin word, *ironia*, the import has an altogether different tone. Laundered and deodorized, it now betokens the height of urbanity, elegance, and good taste:

> **T5 Cicero,** *de Oratore* **2.67 (269–70):** Urbana etiam dissimulatio est, cum alia dicuntur ac sentias . . . Socratem opinor in hac *ironia* dissimulantiaque longe lepore et humanitate omnibus praestitisse. Genus est perelegans et cum gravitate salsum.[20]

And when Quintilian, two generations later, consolidating Cicero's use of the term, encapsulates its meaning in the definition cited earlier, we are no longer in any doubt that *ironia* has shed completely its disreputable past, has already become in their prose[21] what it will come to be in the languages and sensibility of modern Europe: speech used to express something contrary to what is said—the perfect medium for mockery innocent of deceit. Subsidiary in the use of the parent word in classical Greece, this now becomes the standard use. *Eirōneia* has metastasized into irony.

Exactly what made this happen we cannot say: we lack the massive linguistic data we would need to track the upward mobility of the word. What, I submit, we can say is *who* made it happen: Socrates. Not that he ever made a frontal assault upon the word. There is no reason to believe he ever did. In none of our sources does he ever make *eirōneia* the *F* in a "What is *F*?" question or bring it by some other means under his elenctic hammer. He changes the word not by theorizing about it but by creating something new for it to mean: a new form of life realized in himself which was the very incarnation of *eirōneia* in that second of its contemporary uses, as innocent of intentional deceit as is a child's feigning that the play chips are money, as free of shamming as are honest games, though, unlike games, serious in its mockery (*cum gravitate salsum*), dead earnest in its playfulness (*severe ludens*), a previously unknown, unimagined type of personality, so arresting to his contemporaries and so memorable forever after that the time would come, centuries after his death, when educated people would hardly be able to think of *ironia* without its bringing Socrates to mind. And as this happened the meaning of the word altered. The image of Socrates as the paradeigmatic *eirōn* effected a change in the previous connotation of the word.[22] Through the eventual influence of the after-image of its Socratic incarnation, the use which had been marginal in the classical period became its central, its normal and normative, use: *eirōneia* became *ironia*.

I have made a very large claim. What is there in our sources to show that Socrates was really the arch-ironist Cicero and Quintilian thought him?

Nothing in Aristophanes. The anti-hero of the *Clouds* is many things to many men, but an ironist to none: too solemn by half as natural philosopher, sage or hierophant, too knavish[23] as a preceptor of the young. Nor is he represented as an ironist in the sideswipe at him in the *Frogs* (1491–9).[24] We turn to Xenophon. At first it looks as though here too we shall get nothing better. Through most of the *Memorabilia* this tirelessly didactic, monotonously earnest, Socrates appears to have no more jesting, mocking or riddling in his soul than does the atheistic natural philosopher and "high-priest of subtlest poppycock"[25] in the Aristophanic caricature. But once in a while we get a flash of something different,[26] and then, in chapter 11 of Book III, we get a big break. Here Socrates turns skittish and goes to pay a visit to the beautiful Theodote.[27] He offers her suggestions on how she might enlarge her clientele and she invites him to become her partner in the pursuit of *philoi*. He demurs, pleading much public business (*dēmosia*), and adding:

> **T6 Xenophon,** *Mem.* **3.11.16:** I have my own girlfriends (*philai*) who won't leave me day or night, learning from me filtres and enchantments.

Since she is meant to see, and does see, that these "girlfriends" are philosophers, depressingly male and middle-aged, there is no question of her being misled into thinking that her visitor has a stable of pretty women to whom he teaches love-potions. So here at last we do get something Cicero and Quintilian would recognize as *ironia*, though hardly a gem of the genre: its humour is too arch and strained.

After the visit to Theodote, Socrates in the *Memorabilia* resumes his platitudinously wholesome moralizing. But he snaps out of it for good in Xenophon's *Symposium*.[28] There we see what he might have been in the *Memorabilia* if the severely apologetic aims of that work had not darkened the hues of its Socratic portrait into shades of gray. The convivial *mise-en-scène* of the *Symposium* prompts Xenophon to paint bright, even garish, colours into the picture. Asked what is that art of his in which he takes great pride he says it is the art of the procurer (*mastropos,* 4.56). Challenged to a beauty contest with the handsome Critoboulus (5.1ff.), he pleads the superior beauty of his own ugliest features—his snub nose, his oversized flaring nostrils—on the ground that useful is beautiful (5.6). Here we see a new form of irony, unprecedented in Greek literature to my knowledge, which is peculiarly Socratic. For want of a better name, I shall call it "complex irony" to contrast it with the simple ironies I have been dealing with in this essay heretofore. In "simple" irony what is said is simply not what is meant. In "complex" irony what is said both is and isn't what is meant. Thus when Socrates says he is a "procurer" he does not, and yet does, mean what he says. He obviously does not in the common, vulgar, sense of the word. But nonetheless he does in another sense which he gives the word ad hoc, making "procurer" mean simply someone "who makes the procured attractive to those whose company he is to keep" (4.57). Xenophon's Socrates can claim he does exactly that. Again, when he says that his flat, pushed-in, nose and his oversized flaring nostrils are beautiful, he does not, and yet does, mean what he says. In the ordinary sense of that word he would be the first to deny they are. But if by "beautiful" he were allowed to mean "well made or constituted for their required function" (5.4), then he would have us know that his particular sort of eyes and nose are superlatively beautiful: his eyes, unlike the deep-set ones of fashion-models, can see sidewise, not merely straight ahead; his nose is a more efficient vent than that of the currently admired profile. (5.5–6).

Undoubtedly then there is an authentic streak of irony in Xenophon's depiction of

Socrates. But for the purpose of assuring us that it was really Socrates who played the critical role in the mutation of *eirōneia* into irony, what Xenophon tells us about Socrates would still be defective in two ways.

In the first place, the ironies Xenophon puts into the portrait have little doctrinal significance. They contribute nothing vital to the delineation of Socrates' philosophy, because Xenophon systematically ignores those very features of it which can only be understood as complex ironies of the sort he illustrates in making his hero say he is a procurer and has a charming nose. I mean, of course, the two great philosophical paradoxes of Socrates' disavowal of knowledge and of teaching. Each of these is intelligible only as a complex irony. When he professes to have no knowledge he both does and does not mean what he says. In one sense of "knowledge," the traditional one, in which it implies certainty, Socrates means just what he says: he wants it to be understood that in the moral domain there is not a single proposition he claims to know with certainty. But in another sense of "knowledge," where the word refers to justified true belief, justified through the peculiarly Socratic method of elenctic argument, there are many propositions he does claim to know. So too, I would argue, Socrates' parallel disavowal of teaching should be understood as a complex irony. In the conventional sense, where to "teach" is simply to transfer knowledge from the teacher's to the learner's mind, Socrates means what he says: that sort of "teaching" he does not want to do and cannot do. But in the sense which *he* would give to "teaching"—engaging would-be learners in elenctic argument to make them aware of their own ignorance and give them opportunity to discover for themselves the truth the teacher had held back—in that sense of "teaching" Socrates would want to say he is a teacher, the best of teachers in his time, the only true teacher.

In the second place, the words *eirōn, eirōneia, eirōneuomai* are never applied to Socrates by Xenophon himself or by anyone else in his account of Socrates. If we had only his picture of Socrates we would have no reason to think that Socrates' contemporaries had thought of *eirōneia* as a distinctively Socratic trait. That noun and its cognate verb, so conspicuous in the attack on Socrates by Thrasymachus in T1, are omitted when an identical reproach is ventilated by Hippias in the *Memorabilia*. This is how the complaint is now made to read:

> **T7 Xenophon, *Mem.* 4.4.9:** You are content to make a laughing-stock of others, questioning and refuting them, while you yourself will not submit to questioning or state your own opinion about anything.

The reference to Socrates' "habitual *eirōneia*" with which Thrasymachus' attack begins T1, and the verb *eirōneusoio* that follows, have dropped out.

Fortunately, we have Plato's Socratic dialogues. Here what Xenophon has denied us is supplied in such abundance that to go through all of it would be work for a whole book. Forced to be harshly selective, I shall concentrate on one piece of it—the half dozen pages or so that make up the speech of Alcibiades in the *Symposium*. Despite the provenance of this composition from a dialogue of Plato's middle period, its Socrates is unmistakably the philosopher of the earlier ones: he voices that total disavowal of knowledge (T15) which separates the Socrates who speaks for Socrates from the *Apology* through the first part of the *Meno* from Plato's proxy in what follows. The reported dialogue with Diotima put into the mouth of Socrates in the *Symposium* is as strong an affirmation of Plato's *un*-Socratic doctrine, the theory of transcendent Forms, as is anything he ever wrote. But Alcibiades has not heard that discourse. He joins the banquet after Socrates has finished. In that last speech of the *Symposium* Plato brings back to life the earlier *un*-Platonic Socrates as surely as he does also in Book I of the *Republic*. He ushers us into the *Republic* through a Socratic portico and escorts us out of the *Symposium* through a Socratic back-porch.

The key sentence in Alcibiades' speech is

> **T8 *Sym*. 216e4–5:** *eirōneuomenos de kai paizōn panta ton bion pros tous anthrōpous diatelei.*

How shall we read the first word? When Quintilian (*Inst. Or.* 9.2.46) remarks that *ironia* may characterize not just a text or a speech but "an entire life" (*vita universa*), Socrates is his only example. So we know how *he* would read *eirōneuomenos* in this text. But time and again it is read differently by scholars. Guthrie[29] takes it to refer to "the way in which Socrates deceives everyone as to his real character." Dover,[30] assimilating it to T1, denying that the word means "irony" here, takes it to refer to Socrates' pretended ignorance. Suzy Groden translates, "He *pretends* [my emphasis] to be ignorant and spends his whole life putting people on," and W. Hamilton, "He spends his whole life *pretending* [my emphasis] and playing with people." If we follow Quintilian, we shall understand Alcibiades to be saying that Socrates is a life-long ironist. If we follow Guthrie & Co. we shall understand him to be saying that Socrates is a life-long deceiver. Since, as I explained, the latter was the most common of the current uses of the word, the presumption should indeed be that these scholars are right. So if one believes that, on the contrary, Quintilian's reading is the right one, one must assume the burden of proof. I gladly assume it.

But I must start with another sentence in Alcibiades' speech which is almost as important for my thesis, for here again the critical word is applied not to what Socrates says on this or that occasion but to his usual, characteristic, way of speaking:

> **T9 *Sym*. 218d6–7:** *kai houtos akousas, mala eirōnikōs kai sphodra heautou te kai eiōthotōs elexen.*

Here Groden translates, "He answered in that extremely *ironical* [my emphasis] way he always uses, very characteristic of him," and Hamilton, "He had a thoroughly characteristic reply in his usual *ironical* [my emphasis] style." Thus of their own accord both of them now give me all I want. Do they realize what they are doing? Do they see that they are welshing on their previous translation of *eirōneuomenos* in T8? I don't know and don't need to know. It suffices that here Plato's text gives them no other choice.

Let us recall the context. T9 comes at the climax of the *pièce de résistance* of Alcibiades' speech: his narration of an episode from his distant youth, when he was still in his "bloom"—that final stage in a boy's transition to manhood, which in that culture marked the peak of his physical attractiveness to males older than himself. The story begins as follows:

> **T10 *Sym*. 217a:** Believing that he was seriously smitten by my bloom, I thought it a windfall, a wonderful piece of luck, since by allowing him my favours I would be able to hear from him all he knew.

The project of swapping sex for moral wisdom may seem incredible today. It would not have seemed so *in the least* to someone in Alcibiades'circumstances at the time. Let me enumerate them:

1. As we know from Pausanias' speech in the *Symposium,* this is the norm (*nomos*)[31] in the higher form of pederastic love: the boys gives "favours," the man gives intellectual and moral improvement (218d6–219a).

2. Alcibiades already had (and knew he had: 217a5–6) that asset to which he was to owe throughout his life so much of his unprincipled success: stunning beauty and grace.[32]

3. We know from other Platonic dialogues (*Prot.* 309a; *Gorg.* 481d; *Charm.* 155c–e; *M.* 76c1–2) and from Xenophon too (*Sym.* 8.2) that Socrates has a high susceptibility to male beauty to which a sexy teenager could hardly have failed to resonate.

4. Socrates does not answer questions, does not expound his "wisdom." Pieces of it spill out in elenctic arguments, leaving the interlocutor wondering how much more is being held back.

5. We know that the speaker is a highly acratic personality. He starts his whole speech with a confession:

> **T11** *Sym.* **216b3–5:** I know that I cannot contradict him and I should do as he bids, but when I am away from him I am defeated by the adulation of the crowd.

There is no reason to think he had been different as a teenager.

Put these five things together and it should not seem strange if a boy who longs to become *kalos kagathos* should get it into his head that the key to what he wanted was hidden away in that vast undisclosed store of the wisdom of Socrates who might be induced to slip him the key were he to offer as a *quid pro quo* something as irresistibly attractive to all the men of his acquaintance as was his own superlative "bloom." He pursues the project methodically, going through all the ploys in the current repertoire of homosexual seduction. But nothing works. Socrates remains friendly and distant. When Alcibiades waits to hear the sweet nothings of love all he gets is elenctic argument— more of the same old thing. Finally he sets Socrates up and blurts out his proposition. T9 introduces the response he gets:

> **T12** *Sym.* **218d6–219a1:** He heard me out and then *mala eirōnikōs,* in his most characteristic, habitual manner [T9 above], he said "Dear Alcibiades, it looks as though you are not stupid (*phaulos*), if what you say about me is true and there really is in me some power which could make you a better man: you must be seeing something inconceivably beautiful in me, enormously superior to your good looks. If that is what you see and you want to exchange beauty for beauty, you mean to take a huge advantage of me: you are trying to get true beauty in exchange for seeming beauty—"gold for brass" (*Iliad* 6.236)."

Here, I submit, it is incontestably clear that "ironically" *has* to be the sense of *eirōnikōs,* for the context gives absolutely no foothold to the notion of pretence or deceit. Socrates is turning down flat the proposed exchange, saying it is a swindle. He starts off with a simple irony, saying to Alcibiades, "you are not stupid," when he clearly means: you *are* stupid, very stupid: what could be more stupid than to think I would fall for a barter of gold for brass? When such a thing happens in those verses of the *Iliad* he echoes here— Glaucus exchanging his golden armour for one of brass—the poet explains that "Zeus had taken away his wits" [6.234]. Socrates is saying to Alcibiades: I would have to be out of my head to buy your proposal; what a fool you must be, a complete ass, to think you could pull it off.

He winds up with a "complex"[33] irony:

> **T13** *Sym.* **219a1–4:** But look more closely, blessed boy, lest you have missed that I am nothing. The mind's vision becomes acute only when the eyesight has passed its peak, and you are still far from that.

Alcibiades is told that the "gold" he has been looking for—the sort of wisdom that could be handed over in a swap—isn't there after all. That sort of wisdom Socrates does not have, though he does have another sort, which Alcibiades could have for free if he would seek it for himself, looking to Socrates not as a guru but as a partner in the search. To find deception anywhere in this speech we would have to plant it there ourselves: there is not a shadow of the will to mislead in what Socrates has said to Alcibiades *mala eirōnikōs*.

Does that settle the sense of *eirōneuomenos* at T8? No, but it does create a powerful presumption that there too the sense is the same. It would be most unlikely that *eirōnikōs* would be used as we have now seen it used in T9 if just two Stephanus pages earlier *eirōneuomenos panta ton bion . . . diatelei* had carried the thought that Socrates went through life "deceiv[ing] everyone as to his real character."[34] So let us look as closely into the context there—the paragraphs in Alcibiades' speech which precede immediately the seduction story. They are pursuing the famous simile with which the whole speech had begun:

> **T14** *Sym.* **215a7–b3:** I assert that he is very like those Sileni that sit in the workshops of the statuaries . . . who, when opened into two, turn out to have images of gods inside.

This is the piture of a man who lives behind a screen—a mysterious, enigmatic figure, a man nobody knows: "You should know that none of you know him" (216c–d), says Alcibiades to Socrates' friends. To say this is not at all to imply that Socrates has been deceiving them: to be reserved and to be deceitful are not the same thing. All we can get from the simile is concealment, not deceit. Even so, we have to ask if Alcibiades does not insinuate deceit in his own explication of the simile:

> **T15** *Sym.* **216d2–5:** You see that [a] Socrates is erotically attracted to beautiful youths, always hanging around them, smitten by them; and again [b] that he knows nothing and is ignorant of everything. Isn't this like Silenus? Enormously so.

The allusion to Socrates' eroticism in part [a] of this text is amply corroborated elsewhere in Plato and in Xenophon as well.[35] But here, after putting Socrates' bloom-chasing into the centre of the picture, Alcibiades seems to take it all back:

> **T16** *Sym.* **216d7–e1:** You should know he does not care at all if someone is beautiful: you wouldn't believe how he scorns that sort of thing.

He says the same thing again no less than four times at the climax of the attempted seduction:

> **T17** *Sym.* **219c3–5:** He was so superior, so scornful and derisive of my bloom, so insulting of it.

So on one hand we are told that Socrates is "smitten" by the male beauty, on the other, that he is utterly scornful of it. Isn't this what Guthrie might have cited as good reason for reading deceit into *eirōneuomenos* at T8? If Socrates is so contemptuous of such beauty, how could his pursuit of it be anything but a sham?

This is a highly pertinent question. I must meet it head on. To do so I must say something about Socratic *erōs*, distinguishing it from Platonic *erōs*, with which it is so often conflated—most recently in Dover's *Greek Homosexuality* (1978) and again in volume two of Foucault's *Histoire de la Sexualité* (1984). There are four differences:

1. In Platonic *erōs* what is loved in a beautiful boy is the transcendent form of Beauty whose image he is. Socrates' ontology has no transcendent forms. So what he loves in a beautiful body is a beautiful boy, and that is all.

2. In Platonic *erōs* passionate body-contact is normal: the lovers in the *Phaedrus* touch, kiss, "lie down together," and "sleep together" (255e).[36] In the Socratic counterpart erotic intimacy is limited to mind and eye contact.[37]

3. While both Plato and Socrates interdict terminal gratification, they do so for different reasons. In Plato's case these are ultimately metaphysical, for he regards the soul's conjunction with the body as a doom calling for a life-long discipline whose aim is to detach soul from body, so far as possible, in the present life and liberate the soul from the wheel of reincarnation after death: sexual bliss defeats this endeavour, nails the soul to the body, distorts its sense of reality (*Phdo.* 83d). This doctrine is utterly foreign to Socrates. In none of our sources does Socrates object to orgasmic pleasure as such—only to that form of it which is pursued in pederastic coupling,[38] and there only for moral, not metaphysical, reasons: because he thinks it bad for the boy,[39] viewing it as a form of predation in which a younger male is exploited ("devoured"[40]) by his lover, used for the latter's one-sided gratification.[41]

4. Platonic *erōs* generates an emotion which has torrential force, matching that imputed by the poets to all forms of sexual passion: pederastic, lesbian, or heterosexual. Like the poets, Plato calls *erōs* "madness" and so describes it:

> **T18** *Phdr.* **251d–252b:** . . . and so between joy and anguish [the lover] is distraught at being in such a strange condition; perplexed and frenzied, with madness upon him, can neither sleep by night nor sit still by day. . . . Mother, brother, friends, he forgets them all, not caring if his property is being ruined by neglect; those rules and graces in which he previously took pride he now scorns, welcoming a slave's estate, sleeping anywhere at all, if only it can be as close as possible to his darling.

For such amiable insanity Socratic *erōs* has no place. It is even-keeled, light-hearted, jocular, cheerfully and obstinately sane.[42] Not that Socrates is sexually anorexic (I stressed the contrary a moment ago) or that he anticipates the Cynic and Christian determination to expunge the joy of sex from the economy of happiness. The sliver of it he allows himself he pursues openly, without the least embarrassment, and in any case without fear that it could get out of control, for in the dynamics of his psyche it is held in the field of force of an incomparably mightier drive: when Alcibiades comes to speak of the glimpse he once got of the "images of gods" concealed by the satyr's bestial exterior, his language becomes ecstatic. It dissolves in a shimmer of glittering, evocative adjectives:

T19 *Sym.* **216e–217a:** I saw them once and they seemed so divine, golden, altogether beautiful, wonderful.

What is this dazzling, enchanting thing Socrates keeps hidden inside his own soul? His *sōphrosunē,* says Alcibiades:

T20 *Sym.* **216d7–8:** But, oh my fellow-drinkers, how full of *sōphrosunē* [he would be seen to be] inside, if he were opened up.

But it could hardly be only that, since that is in the public view. What no one but Socrates himself can see is, I suggest, the happiness he finds in that *sōphrosunē,* which is so much more alluring than anything he could hope to get from physical beauty or from any other mundane good—health, wealth, honour, life itself—that he can enjoy each of these for what each is worth, flavouring in each its own sweet little quota of contentment or delight—that, and no more, thumbing his nose at it (''scorning'' it) when it promises more. A maxipassion keeps all the minipassions effortlessly under control. It has been recently said,[43] following Foucault, that ''sex is a hard knot of anxiety'' in all Western discourse about love. If that is true, then Socrates is an exception. From what we learn about Socratic *erōs* from Plato, in it there is no *inquiétude* at all.[44]

Once we take this into account it becomes arbitrary to read deceit or pretence into Socrates' dalliance with youthful ''bloom.'' We can understand Socratic *erōs* as a ''complex'' irony[45] of the same sort as the other irony Alcibiades allows him in part (b) of T15—that of ''knowing nothing and being ignorant of everything.'' Just as when maintaining ''he knows nothing'' Socrates both does and does not mean what he says, so too when he says he is erotically attracted to beautiful young men, he both does and does not mean what he says. In the currently understood sense of pederastic love Socrates does not ''love'' Alcibiades or any of those other youths he pursues.[46] But in the other sense which *erān* has in the doctrine and practice of Socratic *erōs,* he does love them: their physical beauty gives special relish to his affectionate encounters with their mind. So there is no pretence and no deceit in his saying to others that he is Alcibiades' lover (*Gorg.* 481d) or saying the same thing, as he no doubt did, to Alcibiades himself.

''But surely,'' it will be said, ''to court those giddy young things, whose head is swimming with the compliments being paid to them by swarms of powerful Athenians, will deceive them. So isn't Socrates guilty of intentional deceit after all?'' How it was in other cases we do not know. But in the case of Alcibiades we do have the data for a confident reply. Yes, Alcibides was deceived, for otherwise he would not have hatched that crazy scheme of bartering bloom for wisdom and would not have stuck to it for who knows how long, while Socrates kept refusing to take the bait. Deceived he was, but by whom? Not by Socrates, but by himself. He believed what he did because he wanted to believe it. We might have guessed as much; but we don't need to guess. Just from his own story we can tell this is what happened. At T12 Socrates is saying ''No'' to the offer, doing so as emphatically as would a Zen Roshi responding to a foolish question by bringing down his staff full strength on the questioner's head. Alcibiades could not but see that Socrates is saying ''No.'' And still he refuses to believe it. He jumps into Socrates' bed as though he had been told ''Yes'' or, at least, ''Maybe.'' And if this is what happened then, there is no reason to believe that Socrates had ever said or done anything intended to deceive Alcibiades into thinking that skin-love was what he wanted from the youth.

But I may be asked: "Even so, can we not gather from the account that long before that night Socrates was aware of what was going on in the boy's head, and yet was willing to let his young friend wallow in self-deceit without taking any decisive action to dispel it?" To this we surely have to answer: Yes. Over and over again before that night Socrates would have had ample opportunity to explain that Alcibiades was making a fool of himself, duped by his own wishful thinking. Yet Socrates said nothing. Day after day Socrates watched and kept still. Why so? The only reasonable answer is that he wanted Alcibiades to find out the truth for himself by himself. The irony in his love for Alcibiades, riddling from the start, persisted until the boy found the answer the hard way, in a long night of anguished humiliation, naked next to Socrates, and Socrates a block of ice.

This essay has been an investigation of the meaning of two words, "irony" and *eirōneia*, a good part of it devoted to the meaning of just two tokens of the latter occurring in Alcibiades' speech: *eirōneuomenos* at T8, *eirōnikōs* at T9. It does, however, have wider implications. A word about these by way of conclusion.

A question always hanging over our head as we work in Plato's Socratic dialogues is whether or not their protagonist allows himself deceit as a debating tactic. Some of Socrates' most devoted students have taken it for granted that he does. For Kierkegaard Socrates is the anti-sophist who by sophistry tricks sophists into truth.[47] For Paul Friedländer, whose three-volume work on Plato is as learned a work of scholarship as any produced in his time, Socrates is "the living witness to the fact that he who knows the truth can deceive better than he who does not, and that he who deceives voluntarily is better than he who deceives involuntarily" (*Plato* 2, Eng. tr. [1964], p. 145). This point of view has been widely influential. One sees it at the centre of Michael O'Brien's brilliant book, *The Socratic Paradoxes*[48] and at the edges of much distinguished work on Plato.[49] The obvious objection is in what Plato makes Socrates say:

> **T21 *Gorg*. 458a1–b1:** As for me, I would be pleased to cross-question you, provided you are the same sort of man as I. Of what sort is that? One of those who would be pleased to refute another if *he* says something untrue, but more pleased to be refuted than to refute—as much more as being rid of the greatest evil is better than ridding another of it; for I do not believe that anything could be as evil for a man as to harbour false beliefs about the things we are now discussing.

These words are familiar to those scholars. We ask them if they doubt their sincerity and they assure us they do not. Well then, if Socrates would rather lose than win the argument when the truth is on the other side, what could he stand to gain by deceit: how could he hope to advance his search for truth by slipping in a false premise or a sophistical inference? But this argument, which ought to be conclusive, falls flat on scholars who tell us that just making it we are revealing we have been reading Plato's text with a tin ear for irony. It should be obvious, they say, that what would be out of the question in the usual mode of philosophical discourse may be normal in the ironical one: that Socrates should outsophist the sophists is no paradox if the sophistries with which he plies them are ironical.

In this essay I have tried to nail down the mistake in the conception of irony which underlies this point of view. For this purpose I have gone back to the primary, down-to-earth, meaning of the living word which "irony" has been in all the languages of the Western world, beginning with Cicero's Latin. In this primary use from which all philosophically invented ones are derived (including the one Kierkegaard fished out of Hegel: "infinite absolute negativity"),[50] what irony means is simply expressing what we mean by saying something contrary to it. This is something we do all the time—even children do it—and if we choose to do it we forfeit in that very choice the option of speaking deceitfully. To think otherwise is to mistake *ironia* for *eirōneia* thereby reversing the process by which the former evolved out of the latter, denying Socrates one of his chief titles to fame: his contribution to the sensibility of Western Europe, no less memorable an achievement than is his contribution to our moral philosophy.

But in the course of this inquiry I stumbled upon something I had not reckoned on at the start: that in the persona of Socrates depicted by Plato there is something which helps explain what Kierkegaard's genius and Friedländer's learning have read into Socrates. In that small segment of the evidence I have scrutinized one can see how Socrates could have deceived without intending to deceive. If you are young Alcibiades courted by Socrates your are left to your own devices to decide what to make of his riddling ironies. If you go wrong and he sees you have gone wrong, he may not lift a finger to dispel your error, far less the obligation to knock it out of your head. If this were happening over trivia no great harm would be done. But what if it concerned the most important matters—whether or not he loves you? He says he does in that riddling way of his which leaves you free to take it one way though you are meant to take it in another, and when he sees you have gone wrong he lets it go. What would you say? Not, surely, that he does not care that you should know the truth, but that he cares more for something else: that if you are to come to it at all, it must be by yourself for yourself.

The concept of moral autonomy never surfaces in Plato's Socratic dialogues—which does not keep it from being the deepest thing in their Socrates, the strongest of his moral concerns. What he is building on is the fact that in almost everything we say we put a burden of interpretation on the hearer. When we speak a sentence we do not add a gloss on how it should be read. We could not thus relieve the hearer of that burden, for that would be an endless business: each gloss would raise the same problem and there would have to be gloss upon gloss *ad infinitum*. Socratic irony is not unique in acknowledging the burden of freedom which is inherent in all significant communication. It is unique in playing that game for bigger stakes than anyone ever has in the philosophy of the West. Socrates doesn't say that the knowledge by which he and we must live is utterly different from what anyone has ever understood or even imagined moral knowledge could be. He just says he has no knowledge, though without it he is damned, and lets us puzzle out for ourselves what that could mean.[51]

ADDITIONAL NOTE

Erōs Kalos: *Its Hazards for the Boy*

Third parties close to him who are concerned for his own good—parents and friends within his peer group—think he would be well out of such affairs:

> Fathers put tutors in charge of the boy and won't let him talk with lovers: the tutors are ordered to forbid it. And friends of his own age reproach him (*oneidizōsin:* cf. *oneidos, Phdr.* 231e3–4) if they see him going in for anything of this sort, and their reproaching isn't vetoed by their elders—they don't say the blame is undeserved. (*Sym.* 183c5–d2)

If formerly, bad-mouthed by his friends, who had been saying that dallying with a lover is a disgrace (*aischron*), he had repelled the lover. (*Phdr.* 255a4–6)

However glamorized in the fashionable *nomos,* the boy's role remains *risqué*: he is placed in an ambiguous and vulnerable position. Still in mid-teens, emotionally immature, his character barely formed, without seasoned judgement of men and the world, suddenly, if he happens to be *kalos,* he finds himself in possession of an asset in short supply and high demand,[52] for access to which an older man will grovel[53] at his feet, prepared to offer great prizes in return for "favours." Would he not be under the strongest of temptations to barter his new-found treasure in ways which would corrupt him?

Suppose he does form an honorable liaison within which his lover gets all he wants. Will the boy escape the stigma which in Greek opinion taints the sexual pathic?[54] So Dover thinks because, he holds (*GH*, pp.103 and passim), within the *nomos* orgasmic contact remains solely intercrural. Deeply conscious of my debt to him for what little understanding I have of this difficult matter, I remain strongly sceptical of this particular thesis of his. The vase paintings supply his evidential ground for it. But can we exclude the possibility that prevailing conventions screened out the depiction of what was in fact the normal mode of gratification? That this is no idle conjecture we know from the literary evidence. As Dover recognizes,[55] his thesis gets no support from this quarter:

In Greek comedy [anal copulation] is assumed (save in *Birds* 706)[56] to be the only mode of [homosexual consummation]; and when Hellenistic poetry makes a sufficiently unambiguous reference to what actually happens on the bodily plane, we encounter only anal, never intercrural copulation. (*GH* 99)

But even if the thesis were to be accepted *in toto,* it would still not obliterate the shadow on the boy's good name. If submitting to anal copulation carries a stigma, the boy would always be under suspicion of it. Who is to know what goes on between him and his lover in the privacy of their *amours?*

NOTES

Originally read in Cambridge, this essay was also presented at Cornell (as a Townsend Lecture), at Columbia (as a Trilling Seminar) and at Brown (as a Robinson Memorial Lecture). It has benefited from critical comments received at each of these occasions, most particularly from those of Professors Ahl at Cornell and Charles Kahn who was a fellow-symposiast at the Trilling Seminar, from a reply by Don Addams, a graduate student in my Cornell seminar, and from corrections received subsequently from Sir Kenneth Dover who did me the kindness of reading the essay in typescript at my request. I am most grateful for this help.

1. *Institutio Oratorica* 9.22.44. Much the same definition at 6.2.15 and 8.6.54.
2. The samples in D.C. Muecke, *The Compass of Irony* (London, 1969), pp. 15–19, several of them perfect gems, include no pure specimen of this variety. Neither in this nor in that other excellent book, *The Rhetoric of Irony,* by Wayne C. Booth (Chicago, 1974) is this dimension of irony noticed, far less explored.
3. On *eirōn* as *Schimpfwort* in its common use in the classical period see the groundbreaking paper of O. Ribbeck, 'Uber den Begriff des *Eiron,* " Rhein. Mus. 31 (1876), 381ff. [hereafter "Ribbeck"]: it has not been superseded by later studies which I shall not undertake to review in the present essay.

4. In his invaluable edition of the *Clouds* (Oxford, 1968).
5. In his reference to Socrates in the *EN, EE,* and *MM,* but perhaps not in the *Rhet.,* where *eirōneia* is reckoned a "disdainful" trait (*kataphronētikon,* 1179b31–2).
6. "Such men are more to be avoided than adders" (I, *sub fin.*).
7. "He pretends (*prospoeistha*) not to have heard what he heard, not to have seen what he saw, to have no recollection of the thing to which he agreed" (I.5).
8. "He will praise to their faces those he attacks behind their backs" (I.2). I find it astonishing that Friedländer (*Plato,* I [English tr., New York, 1938], p. 138) should remark that Theophrastus ("the moral botonist") portrays, but "does not evaluate," irony: could there be a more emphatic devaluation than the remarks quoted in this and the two preceding notes? By leaving Socrates out of it, Theophrastus feels free to vent on the *eirōn* the scorn he well deserves in the common view.
9. Bloom and Grube take this to be the sense of both *eirōneia* and *eirōneusoio.* Shorey too takes "irony" to be the sense of *eirōneia* (referring to *Sym.* 216e: to be discussed); but he shifts to "dissemble" for the latter, offering no explanation for the shift. I suspect he is confused about the meaning of the English word "irony," taking *it* to mean "dissembling." (Translations and commentaries to which I refer by name of author only [can be found in the bibliography at the end of this volume].
10. For correct translation consult Cornford ("shamming ignorance"), Robin ("feinte ignorance"). That "shamming," "feigning" *is* the sense should be completely clear from the context.
11. Burnet *ad* Plato, *Apol.* 38a1: "The words *eirōn, eirōneia, eirōneuomai* (in Plato) are only used of Socrates by his opponents, and have always an unfavorable meaning." He is not overlooking *eirōneuomenōi* at *Apol.* 38a1 (taking it, quite rightly, to mean "regarding this pretence as a sly evasion"; the same sense in R.E. Allen's translation, "I am being sly and dishonest"). But he is ignoring (or misunderstanding?) both of the notable uses of the word in Alcibiades' speech in the *Symposium* (to be discussed).
12. *Platon* (3rd ed., 1948), p. 451 n. 1: "Wo [die Ironie] dem Sokrates beigelegt wird [im Platon] geschieht es immer als Vorwurf, auch von Alkibiades, *Sym.* 216e." Neither he nor Burnet (preceding note) takes any notice of Ribbeck's discussion of *Rep.* 337a, which captures exactly the sense of *eiōthuia eirōneia* here.
13. "In Plato it retains its bad sense, in the mouth either of a bitter opponent like Thrasymachus or of one pretending to be angry at the way in which Socrates deceives everyone as to his real character (Alcibiades at *Sym.* 216e, 218d)," *History of Greek Philosophy* (Cambridge, 1969) [hereafter *"HGPh"*] III, p. 446. He is taking no notice of *Gorg.* 489d–e (to be discussed directly in the text) and assumes that in *Rep.* 337a above *eiōthuia eirōneia* has the same sense as does *eirōnikōs . . . eiōthotōs* in *Sym.* 218d and *mala eirōnikōs* in *Sym.* 218d6.
14. My translation follows Croiset-Bodin. Woodhead's "you are ironical" is acceptable in [a] where the mockery *is* ironical: it takes the form of saying something contrary to what the speaker believes to be true, but not at [b], where this is not the case. Irwin's "sly" will not do: there is nothing particularly "cunning, wily or hypocritical" (*O.E.D.* for "sly") in the tone or content. We must also reject Ribbeck's understanding of the sense at [a]: inexplicably, he reads "chicaniren" into *eirōneuēi* at [a]. But there is nothing wrong with his gloss on *eirōneuou* at [b] ("Art der Verhöhnung durch nicht aufrichtig gemeinten, unwahres Lob"), rightly connecting the use of *eirōneuein* here with Pollux 2.78, *kai ton eirōna enioi muktēra kalousi,* and the sillographer Timon's reference to Socrates (fr. 25d, *ap.* D.L. 2.19), *muktēr rhētoromuktos hupattikos eirōneutēs.* Ribbeck remarks *a propos* of [b]: "so muss der gangbar Begriff des *eirōneuesthai* ein weiterer gewesen sein, als man gewöhnlich annimmt" (loc. cit.) He should have specified more definitely this "wider" use. That it is to express mockery pure and simple without any insinuation of deceit Ribbeck does not seem to have grasped clearly, else why "chicaniren" as the sense at [a]?

15. Long attributed to Aristotle (included in the Berlin edition of Aristotle's works), this treatise then came to be ascribed to Anaximenes of Lampsacus, a contemporary of Theophrastus (see the introduction to the treatise by H. Rackham in his translation of it in the Loeb Classical Library: *Aristotle, Problems* II and *Rhetorica ad Alexandrum* [London, 1937], pp. 258ff.). The ascription is far from certain, but its date cannot be much later. Its linguistic and political ambience is that of fourth-century Athens, echoing Isocrates' *Techne Rhetorike.* Eight fragments of the treatise turn up in a papyrus dated by its editors in the first half of the third century (Grenfell & Hunt, *Hibeh Papyri,* Pt. 1, No. 26, pp. 114ff.).

16. E.M. Cope (in his *Introduction to Aristotle's Rhetoric* [London, 1867], pp. 401ff.) describes the form of persuasion recommended by the treatise as "a system of tricks, shifts and evasions, showing an utter indifference to right and wrong, truth and falsehood."

17. Should the reader be reminded that the occurrence of ironical speech-acts is independent of the availability of a desciption of them as such in the speaker's language? The use of irony, as distinct from reflection upon it, is no doubt as old as the hills. We can imagine a caveman offering a tough piece of steak to his mate with the remark, "Try this tender morsel."

18. For Burnet, Wilamowitz, Guthrie see, respectively, nn. 11, 12, 13.

19. Cf. his gloss on *Sym.* 216e4: *eirōneia* (unlike "irony") is "mock-modesty," "pretended ignorance"; in *Rep.* 337a Thrasymachus speaks (in no friendly tone) of "Socrates' accustomed *eirōneia.*" He is assuming that *eirōneia* is used in the same sense in both passages.

20. If we translate *dissimulatio* here by "dissembling" (as we may, with good warrant from the dictionaries), we should bear in mind that *deceitful* concealment, normally conveyed by the English word, is completely absent from the figue of speech Cicero has in view. Deceitful speech would not be what he calls "*urbane* dissimulation . . . where the whole tenor of your speech shows that you are gravely jesting (*severe ludens*) in speaking differently from what you think" (loc. cit.).

21. Though not perhaps in that of their Greek contemporaries, as Professor Fred Ahl pointed out to me when I presented this essay at Cornell. How soon the change came to be shared by the Greek rhetoricians, whose diction was likely to be governed more strictly by classical models, is a topic calling for special research which falls outside the scope of the present study.

22. A change so drastic as to eclipse the original meaning of the word from Cicero's and Quintilian's view. The occultation seems total: from what the say about *ironia* we would never guess that in texts they knew well its Greek original had been a *Schimpfwort.* The authority of the Socratic paradigm becomes so definitive for Cicero that he is content to understand by the word simply "that *ironia* . . . found in Socrates, which he deploys in the dialogues of Plato, Xenophon and Aeschines" (*Brutus* 292). And when Quintilian remarks that "*ironia* may characterize a man's whole life" he refers (only) to Socrates (*Inst. Or.* 9.2.46).

23. Though he does not himself inculcate crooked argument, he panders to the demand for it. He keeps both the *dikaios* and the *adikos logos* on the premises and the client has his choice.

24. The portrait is not appreciably different: outside the Thinkery (else the question of an ordinary Athenian picking a seat next to him [*Sōkratei parakathēmenon,* 1491–2] would not arise), no longer a sinister figure, Socrates is still a quibbler whose hair-splitting solemnities (*epi semnoisi logoisi/kai skariphēsmoisi lērōn,* 1496–7) engulf his interlocutors in tasteless triviality. No hint of irony in this pretentious idler's chatter.

25. *Leptotatōn lērōn hiereu,* 359, in Arrowsmith's amusingly inventive translation.

26. Kierkegaard (*The Concept of Irony* [Eng. tr. 1965: to be cited hereafter only by the author's name], pp. 58–9 and 64) notes flashes of irony in the dialogue with Charicles (1.2.36) and Hippias (4.4.6).

27. Here Kierkegaard's taste, usually faultless, deserts him. He finds the episode "disgusting" (pp. 61–2).

28. For shrewd appreciation of irony in this work see the comments on the goings-on at the

drinking party in W.E. Higgins, *Xenophon the Athenian* (Albany, N.Y., 1977), pp. 15–20. Full discussion of the same material also in Emma Edelstein, *Xenophonitisches und Platonisches Bild des Sokrates* (Berlin, 1935), pp. 11–12, though curiously enough she does not percieve it as irony.

29. *HGPh* 3, p. 446.
30. See n. 19.
31. *Sym.* 182a–e, 183c, 184a-b, on which see K. J. Dover, "Eros and Nomos," *BICS* II (1964), 31–42, and *Greek Homosexuality* [hereafter *"GH"*] (London, 1978), "Pursuit and Flight," pp. 81–91.
32. Cf. W. Ferguson in the *Cambridge Ancient History,* 5 (1935), p. 263: "Arrestingly handsome, he received from men in Athens the recognition and privileges ordinarily given in other societies to extraordinary beauty in women; and his insolence he draped in such charm of manner that when he showed respect for neither gods nor man, age nor authority, guardian nor wife, the outrageousness of the act was often forgotten and only the air of the actor remembered."
33. Cf. p. 71.
34. So Guthrie: n. 29.
35. References in Dover, *GH,* pp. 154–5.
36. This physical intimacy, so explicit in the text of the *Phaedrus,* is seldom noticed in accounts of Platonic *erōs*. It is ignored in comment on the passage where we would most expect it: Wilamowitz (n. 12), pp. 368–9; Guthrie, *HGPh* IV pp. 404–6. Earlier translations blunt the force of Plato's words: in Jowett *sunkatakeisthai* becomes "embrace," *en tēi sunkoimēsei,* "when they meet together."
37. In Xenophon, Socrates' fear of physical contact with an attractive youth is obsessive (to kiss a pretty face is "to become forthwith a slave instead of a free man," *Mem.* 1.3.11; a momentary contact of his nude shoulder with that of the beautiful Critoboulos affects Socrates like "the bite of a wild beast," his shoulder stings for days, *Sym.* 4.27–8). There is nothing so extreme in the Platonic portrait; Socrates there shows no terror of skin-contact with a beautiful body (wrestling in the nude with Alcibiades happens "often" on the latter's initiative [*Sym.* 217c] and makes no dent in Socrates' resistence to the youth's advances); but neither is there anything in Plato to suggest that Socrates would ever encourage physical endearments from any of the youths he "loves."
38. Cf. Xen. *Mem.* 2.6.22: Socrates counsels "those who delight in the sexual charms of boys in bloom" (*tois tōn hōraiōn aphrodisiois hēdomenoi*) to resist the attraction "in order to cause no distress to those who should be spared it (*hōste mē lupein hous mē prosēkei*)."
39. See "Additional Note" at the end of this essay.
40. *Charmides* 155d–e: "And I thought how well Cydias understood the ways of *erōs;* giving advice to someone about a beautiful boy, he warned: Don't bring the fawn too close to the lion that would devour his flesh." *Phdr.* 241d1: "As wolves are fond of lambs, so lovers love a boy."
41. Xen. *Sym.* 8.19: the man "reserves the pleasure for himself, the most shameful things for the boy." Ibid. 21 (translation, in part, after E. C. Marchant): "the boy does not share, like a woman, the delight of sex with the man, but looks on, sober, at another in love's intoxication."
42. It is so pictured in both Plato's and Xenophon's Socratic dialogues. Nor does the reference to Socrates' *erōs* for Alcibiades in the eponymous dialogue by Aeschines Socraticus (fr. II, Dittmar) tell a materially different story. Though there is a suggestion here of greater intensity in Socrates' sentiment for the youth than there is in Alcibiades' narrative in Plato, neither is there any call for blowing it up into "fine frenzy" as in A. E. Taylor's fanciful interpretation of the fragment (*Philosophical Studies* [London, 1934], 15). His reading of part *c* of the fragment has lost track of what was said just before in parts *a* and *b*. If so read, it will be seen

that Taylor misunderstands the point of comparison with the bacchantes in part *c*. It is not said there that Socrates is like them in being made *entheos* by his love for the youth, but that just as they achieve wonderful results (''draw milk and honey from wells where others cannot even draw water'') by divine possession (hence not through art or science), so too Socrates hopes to achieve the improvement of Alcibiades (a wonderful result) not through art or science (whose possession he disclaims by suggestion at *a* and by explicit denial at *c*) but by love (*dia to erān*).

43. Michael Ignatieff, in his review of M. Foucault, *Histoire de la Sexualité* (vols. 2 and 3) in the *Times Literary Supplement,* 28 Sept. 1984, p. 1071.

44. This fundamental feature of Socratic *erōs* has been missed in all accounts of it known to me, from Kierkegaard, whose romantic fancy reads ''passionate turmoil'' into it (88), to Foucault, whose highly discerning discussion of ''le véritable amour'' in Plato reveals its residual blind-spot in the hyphenated expression, ''l'Erotique socratico-platonicenne'' (op. cit. vol. 2, p. 225) by which he refers to it.

45. Cf. p. 71.

46. Admitting the allegation that he has been ''chasing'' Alcibiades' bloom (standard metaphor for pederastic courting), Socrates proceeds to smother it in irony (*Prot.* 309a1–d2).

47. ''Socrates tricks Protagoras out of every concrete virtue; by reducing each virtue to unity, he completely dissolves it; while the sophistry lies in the power through which he is able to accomplish this. Hence we have at once an irony borne by a sophistic dialectic and a sophistic dialectic reposing in irony.'' (96).

48. Whose contribution to our understanding of Socrates is sidetracked because the author, misapplying the use of irony in the Socratic dialogues, is prepared to jettison some of Socrates' most fundamental doctrines. Thus, if *kalos* at *Prot.* 352d4 means the contrary of what it says, the whole Socratic doctrine of the impossibility of *acrasia* goes down the drain; to cite its Aristotelian attestation would be useless: it would be met by the retort that he too missed the irony.

49. Most recently in Charles Kahn, ''Drama and Dialectic in Plato's *Gorgias,*'' *Oxford Studies In Ancient Philosophy,* 1 (1983), 75ff. He speaks of ''the trickery'' by which Socrates rebuts Polus (*Gorg.* 474dff.). I would not accept his description of my analysis of the argument (*AJP* 88 [1967], 454ff.) as ''Socrates tricks Polus'' (90); I argued *against* the suggestion that Socrates' argument is intentionally fallacious.

50. 276 and passim. His treatment of Socratic irony is hopelessly perplexed by this dazzling mystification. It seduces him into finding in the Platonic texts he purports to be glossing the vagaries of a romantic novella: ''the disguise and mysteriousness which it [irony] entails, . . . the infinite sympathy it assumes, the elusive and ineffable moment of understanding immediately displaced by the anxiety of misunderstanding'' etc. (p. 85).

51. My guess at the riddle is stated and argued for in ''Socrates' Disavowal of Knowledge'' (*Philosophical Quarterly* 35 [1985], 1ff.).

52. The demographic facts should not be overlooked: bloomers are to potential bloom chasers as are the *kaloi* within a five-year age-group to most of the adult males. Of the scarcity of the *kaloi* within their own age-group we get some sense in the opening scene of the *Charmides:* droves of youngsters in the palaestra and one *kalos,* all eyes on him, ''gazing on him as if a statue'' (154c).

53. ''Praying, entreating, supplicating, vowing upon oath, sleeping at the door, willingly enduring slavery worse than any slave's'' (*Sym.* 183a4–7).

54. Dover, *GH,* pp. 103–4: ''By assimilating himself to a woman in the sexual act the submissive male rejects his role as a male citizen'' and chooses ''to be the victim of what would be, if the victim were unwilling, hubris.''

55. He is misrepresented in Martha Nussbaum's account of his view (*The Fragility of Goodness,* Cambridge, 1986, p. 188): ''But two things [the boy] will not allow, in the works of art *and*

the literary testimonies [my emphasis] that have come down to us: he will not allow any opening of his body to be penetrated'' etc.

56. I would not concede that this verse of Aristophanes is an exception. There is no textual evidence for the supposition (*GH,* p. 98) that the word used here, *diamērizein,* was ''almost certainly'' the original term for intercrural copulation or that it ever meant anything but genital intercourse with females or anal with males, as it uncontroversially does in Zeno Stoicus (H. von Arnim, *SVF* 250 and 251, *ap.* Sextus Empiricus, *Hypotyp.* 3.245, *Adv. Math.* 11.190). Its three earliest literary occurrences are in the *Birds.* In 1024 it refers unambiguously to vaginal copulation, as Dover recognizes. I submit that it must refer likewise to the usual type of intercourse in the other two occurrences as well: Euelpides, declaring, *diamērizoim' an autēn hēdeōs* (699), could hardly be lusting after *ersatz* gratification. And if it were agreed that the word is used to signify phallic penetration in 699 and then again in 1024, as it is by Zeno in the Stoic fragments cited previously, we would have no good reason for supposing that in 706 Aristophanes has shifted to a different sense which is never unambiguously attested in a single surviving Greek text and is not required by its immediate context: no reason is discernible in the text why the birds' vaunted power to fulfil men's longings should accord to their favourites something less than the usual thing.

FURTHER READING

Austin, S. 1987. ''The Paradox of Socratic Ignorance (How to Know That You Don't Know).'' *Philosophical Topics* 15:23–34.

Brickhouse, T. C. and N. D. Smith. 1984. ''Irony, Arrogance, and Sincerity in Plato's Apology.'' In *New Essays on Socrates,* ed. E. Kelly, 29–46. Lanham, MD.

Vlastos, G. 1985. ''Socrates' Disavowal of Knowledge.'' *Philosophical Quarterly* 35:1–31.

6

Plato's Early Theory
of Knowledge

PAUL WOODRUFF

In Plato's early dialogues, Socrates states or assumes a number of views about knowledge.[1] Although he never examines these views critically or develops them into a theory, they can be interpreted as mutually consistent, and as such constitute what I shall loosely call Plato's early theory of knowledge. This is mainly a theory of expert knowledge, and concerns what sort of thing an expert ought to know. The theory says little about what it is for an expert or anyone else to know what she knows, and for this reason is not very like epistemology as we know it, despite a number of misleading appearances. There is nothing here about the grounds of knowledge or the justification of belief, and Plato's early theory of knowledge stands outside the sort of sceptical debate that stimulates epistemology. Anyone who brings standard epistemological questions to a reading of early Plato is bound to misunderstand him. That would be too bad, for what he offers is attractive in many ways. It is the least academic of philosophical theories, for by itself it carries no reference to earlier philosophers. The basic distinction that it makes is familiar and practical—between the knowledge anyone can have, and the knowledge for which we must depend on specialised experts. Still, the theory is heavy with the seeds of later epistemology, and deserves to be examined in any history of the subject.

I shall follow the usual convention of assuming that Plato's early theory is the theory, that he represents Socrates as holding. For convenience of reference, I shall use "Socrates" to refer to the fictional character in Plato's early dialogues. By "early" I mean the family of dialogues, largely aporetic, that cluster around themes of the *Apology*, and do not explicitly advance theories of epistemology or metaphysics: *Euthyphro, Charmides, Laches, Lysis, Hippias Major, Hippias Minor, Euthydemus, Protagoras, Gorgias,* and *Ion.* Later dialogues that apparently reflect on the approach of the early dialogues may be admitted as evidence, but only with caution: *Theaetetus* 148e ff., *Sophist* 230c, and possibly *Phaedo* 100b ff. Elsewhere Plato develops theories to mitigate the paradoxes of the early dialogues. In the *Meno* he does this through his model of learning by recollection and his distinction of knowledge from true belief. Though the *Meno* theories do not belong to early Plato, they were adduced to explain certain difficulties in early Plato; and for that reason I shall cover the *Meno* briefly in an appendix.

I

Plato and the Sceptical Debate

Which came first, the sceptic or the epistemologist? The answer is, "Neither: Plato came first." Epistemology asks what knowledge is and how it can be acquired. Scepticism, aiming to detach the epistemologist from his enterprise, raises hard questions as to whether knowledge, as the epistemologist defines it, can be acquired at all. Early Plato does something quite different from either of these, though it smacks of both.

Much of modern epistemology has tried to answer scepticism, and this tempts us to think of epistemology as second in the order of thought and of history—as the sort of theory given by dogmatic philosophers in answer to what sceptics have already said. But classical scepticism cannot come first in any order of things. Unwilling to take a position on anything, true scepticism has nothing to say except in response to a philosopher who already has views about knowledge. In fact, scepticism did not properly emerge until after Aristotle, by which time it could develop against a rich background of dogmatic epistemology. After a form of scepticism made its professional début in the Academy, philosophers on both sides expanded the debate in mutual responses that grew in sophistication. But if this story is correct, how could Plato be a major part of it? If epistemology and scepticism can flourish only in the sort of dialogue that began long after Plato's death, what could Plato say about either one?

Of course the matter is not so simple. Elements of proto-scepticism occur in the remains of Xenophanes, Parmenides, Democritus and some of the sophists, but Plato did not reply to them in any of his earlier works. On the contrary, Plato's earlier works themselves seem to carry out a proto-sceptical programme: they include a series of fictions that show Socrates refuting men who directly or indirectly lay strong claims to knowledge. Socrates gives no general reasons for disputing human claims to knowledge, however, and so his programme is not in itself sceptical. Nor is his procedure strictly sceptical, for Socrates must introduce criteria of knowledge that are his own.

In short, Plato took no part in any of the historical dialogues that pitted scepticism against epistemology; instead, he wrote dialogues, a whole series of them, that set Socrates in unequal combat against naive dogmatists—unequal because in this discussion Socrates supplies *both* the dogmatic theory *and* the negative arguments, while his partner grows tongue-tied. Even the negative arguments are not sceptical on familiar modern or even ancient models.

When Socrates disclaims knowledge or undermines the claim of another, he does not do so by attacking the truth, the certainty, or even the source of the particular item of knowledge that is in question. Instead, he challenges the reliability of the person who claims knowledge, by asking him for a definition that would hold for all circumstances. The point is not to ascertain whether he is right in this case, but to see whether his claim could hold for every case. This is close to the sceptical issue, but deceptively so.

The Sceptical Academy of Arcesilaus and Carneades used Socrates as an icon; but so far as we know they showed no interest in the sort of argument Socrates actually used in the early dialogues. Surprisingly, it is the later sceptics of the Pyrrhonist revival who use arguments reminiscent of Plato, and who return to the issue of reliability as it arises in later Plato, in the context of the reliability of the senses.[2]

Socrates' Disavowal of Knowledge

Socrates' disavowal of knowledge has been a commonplace in the history of philosophy since Aristotle (*de Sophisticis Elenchis* 183b6–8), and indeed was the one point on which the Academic Arcesilaus declined to follow Socrates (Cicero, *Academica* I.45): a sceptic would hold back from disavowing knowledge because of the same attitude that balks at avowing it. The very formulation of the disavowal seems a paradox: "I know of myself that I am wise in neither much nor little" (21b4–5); "I know of myself that I am expert in hardly anything" (22d1).[3] Without wisdom, how does Socrates know that he is not wise?

Disavowals of knowledge occur in a number of contexts. Besides *Apology* 21b2–5 and 22d1, we have *Apology* 21d2–6, where Socrates comments on his examination of the claim of a politician to knowledge: "Perhaps I am wiser than this man. For it turns out that neither of us knows anything fine or good, but he thinks he knows something when he doesn't, while I, on the grounds that I do not know, do not think that I do." General disavowals of knowledge are implied in the *Gorgias* at 506a3–5 ("I do not say what I say as one who knows") and 509a4–6 ("the same saying always applies to me: I do not know that these things are so"). The disavowal of the *Meno* ("I do not know anything about virtue"—71b3) could be taken as an ironical attempt to draw on Socrates' partner; but the similar disavowals at *Euthyphro* 16d and *Hippias Major* 304b cannot be dismissed so easily, as these come after the discussions have reached their impasse.

On the other hand, Socrates does say that he *knows* of his ignorance at *Apology* 21b4 and 22d1 (cf. *Phaedrus* 235c7). At 37b7–8 he speaks of alternative penalties that he "knows well" to be evil, and at *Gorgias* 486e5–6 he says, "I know well that if you [Callicles] agree with me on what my soul believes, then these opinions are true." Of Socrates' knowledge claims the most significant is at *Apology* 29b6–9, for it invokes knowledge of the sort of moral subject that Socrates takes up in his elenchus of others: "to do injustice, that is, to disobey my superior, god or man, this I *know* to be evil and base" (cf. *Crito* 51b). Had anyone else based a decision on this principle, we would expect Socrates to have asked how he knew this: "Come, tell me, what is the evil and base?"

The basic problem has been brought into focus by Gregory Vlastos in a masterful article: though Socrates is sincere in disavowing knowledge, he says or implies that he knows a good many things.[4]

The difficulty shows up in several ways. Socrates applies outrageously difficult epistemic criteria in some areas, but in others he uses the word "knowledge" as in ordinary language. He sets out to purge other people of their dogmatic conceits of knowledge, yet he does so by demonstrating their ignorance on the basis of a thesis he holds dogmatically about knowledge—that one who knows knows definitions. Again, in view of his success in proving the ignorance of anyone he meets, it would seem foolish for anyone to aspire to knowledge; yet Socrates at least aspires to virtue, and this, in his analysis, is knowledge.

Readers of Plato have not agreed on a solution. Perhaps, when Socrates says that he does not know, he means to deceive his hearers.[5] Perhaps, when Socrates says that he does know, he means merely that he has true belief.[6] More likely, Socrates means most of what he says on this score, but means the verb "to know" differently on different occasions.

We need a distinction between the sort of knowledge Socrates claims, and the sort he disavows. Nothing like this is explicit in Plato. We shall have to supply a distinction that Socrates recognises merely in use. Some have attempted to solve the difficulty by distinguishing among the subjects of knowledge: there is a kind of thing Socrates knows, and a kind of thing he does not. For example, he might consistently and unambiguously say (1) that he *does* know the moral character of specific actions but (2) that he *does not* know basic theses about virtue and related terms.[7] But this line will not work. Nothing can disguise the fact that Socrates does not apply the same stringent standards for knowledge in all cases; and different standards mean different working conceptions. When Euthyphro says he knows it is pious to prosecute the guilty, Socrates thinks this confidence should be backed up by a definition of piety (4e–5d); but Socrates does not consider such a test for certain assertions he makes with equal certainty—for example, that he knows it is wrong to disobey the gods, though he emphasises his confidence in this claim by contrasting it with his uncertain beliefs about life after death (*Apology* 29b). In each case what is said to be known is the same kind of thing exactly—a moral judgement about a certain sort of action—and the two believers show equal confidence. Even if different kinds of things were presumed known in the two cases, the fact would remain that Socrates applies different epistemic standards in them, and thereby uses different working conceptions of knowledge. Either Plato (1) has failed to represent him consistently, or (2) has succeeded in representing him as an inconsistent thinker, or (3) has shown Socrates making a distinction in use between two conceptions of knowledge with different epistemic standards. This last is the most likely hypothesis if the texts will accommodate an adequate account of the distinction.

What we need, then, is a distinction between two kinds of knowledge. Vlastos has argued that Socrates makes a dual use of the various words for "know" and "knowledge": what he disavows is knowledge in a strong technical sense, certain knowledge ("knowledge$_C$"), while what he claims is knowledge in a weak sense ("knowledge$_E$"). Knowledge$_E$ is knowledge that is justifiable by the elenchus, that is, by Socrates' method of cross-examination. But some have complained that Socrates, who sought always for unity of definition, would not want to multiply senses of "know," and therefore would not respond to the failure of elenchus to achieve knowledge$_C$ by falling back on a second conception of knowledge. This complaint is right as far as it goes, but it does not answer Vlastos' point, which was that elenchus is totally inappropriate for knowledge$_C$. If knowledge$_C$ had been Socrates' goal, he would have been mad to propose the elenchus as a route to it.[8]

Vlastos' distinction between knowledge$_C$ and knowledge$_E$ is promising, but raises several difficulties. To do its job, the distinction should at least assign all of the moral knowledge Socrates claims or assumes to knowledge$_E$. But not all of such knowledge claims could be based on the elenchus. When Socrates claims certainty, as he does by implication at *Apology* 29b, he cannot mean to appeal merely to the elenchus, since that, as Vlastos concedes, leaves a "security gap."

Moreover, premises of the elenchus (for example that courage is fine—*Laches* 192c) must be known when this is demonstrative, but these could not be justified without circularity by the elenchus that uses them. In fact, it is odd to think of the elenchus as *justifying* a knowledge claim at all; at most it *fails to disconfirm*. But to call the latter an *epistemic justification* is misleading. If elenchus were enough for knowledge, then justification, as it is usually understood, is not required. Better to say, on this view, that knowledge is *examined* true belief.

In any case, degree of certainty does not appear to be the important difference between the knowledge Socrates claims and the knowledge he denies. The difference is that the knowledge he denies is supposed to be backed up by an ability to give a certain sort of account, a Socratic definition. But what does that have to do with certainty? You can be quite certain in the ordinary way of any number of things, without being able to give a Socratic definition; again, you can give any number of Socratic definitions, and still be subject to doubt. If Socrates wants extraordinary philosophical certainty, he would be wrong to pursue it through definitions, which do nothing by themselves to banish doubt. Charity demands that we attribute to Socrates a better reason for asking after definitions.

Expert and Non-expert Knowledge

Let us begin with two loosely defined categories which we can fill out from the texts. What Socrates disavows is a certain sort of *expert knowledge,*[9] while the sort of knowledge Socrates claims, or allows for others, need not meet expert standards; indeed, Socrates claims knowledge in non-expert contexts as if it need not meet any standards at all (as at *Apology* 29b). Socrates' conception of expert knowledge is based on, but broader than, the view his contemporaries held. Expert knowledge is mainly the specialised knowledge of professionals, but it extends to a less specialised sort of knowledge that Socrates thinks should meet similar standards.

The *Apology* makes it plain that expert knowledge is what Socrates means to disavow. Our initial paradox was that Socrates said he knew that he lacked wisdom and knowledge (21b, 22d). The words for what Socrates says he lacks (*sophia* and *epistēmē*) can be used interchangeably with *technē,* his word for professional knowledge. In the immediate context of 22d, expertise is plainly what Socrates has in mind; and his procedure for testing the oracle by questioning well-known experts suggests that he has the same idea at 21b. It is professional knowledge, expertise, that he knows he lacks, and that he looks for elsewhere, asking, in effect: if there is no subject in which I can claim expertise, what did the oracle mean by saying no one was wiser? The people he questions turn out either not to be experts at all, or to suppose mistakenly that they are experts on a grand scale, a mistake serious enough to eclipse their small expertise.

Because Socrates employs two conceptions of knowledge, we shall have to reconstruct two types of epistemology: (1) the theory of *expert knowledge* Socrates tacitly uses in discrediting people's claims to expertise; (2) the theory of *non-expert knowledge* we must supply to make sense of the knowledge that Socrates himself confidently displays, and which he sometimes recognises in others. Under each heading, we will need to make further distinctions. Expert knowledge will include quite ordinary skills; and non-expert knowledge will include the quite extraordinary human knowledge that Socrates connects with virtue—an understanding of one's own epistemic limitations. It will also be the foundation for Socrates' practice of questioning people and exhorting them to virtue.[10]

I must emphasise before going on that these are technical terms; they do not have their ordinary English meanings, and the meanings they have here are special to the early dialogues. Expert knowledge is the sort of knowledge that a specialised professional ought to have, such that we would be right to trust him or her to make decisions on our behalf. Doctors, generals, sea-pilots and teachers should have expert knowledge. Non-expert knowledge is the sort of knowledge you can have without being an expert. Socrates uses his concept of expert knowledge often in his contests with alleged experts, so that we can confidently sketch a detailed account of a Socratic view on this matter. But the concept of non-expert knowledge is obscure. We know that he uses such a concept, since he says he knows certain things, without implying that he is an expert; but because he does not depend on the concept in argument, we have little basis for assigning him a definite view about it.

Still, it helps to see that the two concepts of knowledge play different roles in Socratic argument. Expert knowledge is something for which there are criteria that an expert must satisfy. Socrates uses arguments—a form of elenchus—that test people's claims to expert knowledge against these criteria. Non-expert knowledge is never at issue in the same way; the elenchus uses it, reveals it, and may in some manner support it. But we must see at the outset that ordinary knowledge does not need the kind of support that is required for expertise.

The concept of expert knowledge is based on criteria that experts must satisfy; but there are no criteria for being a non-expert. This way of making the distinction is not arbitrary. It makes sense to ask the credentials of a presumed expert, but it would be absurd in other cases. An expert has specialised knowledge; she makes decisions on our behalf. Before we trust her to do this we naturally want to know if she is qualified. Hence the need for criteria in this area. Before you trust your life to a doctor—before you accept her as an expert in medicine—it is reasonable to ask where she studied and how many patients she has cured or killed. But if someone tells you he knows what time of day it is, you do not ask to see his diploma (though you may want to know who made his watch).

Socrates never investigates a claim to non-expert knowledge; for him it is never an issue whether a person knows in the ordinary way the things that he believes.[11] Indeed, this has led to confusion among Plato's modern readers, who have been unsure whether Plato in a given context had in mind *knowledge* or *true belief* for assertions he saw no reason to test. (On the distinction, see pp. 103–4.)

Evidence for Early Platonic Epistemology

Most of Plato's speakers show that they have views about knowledge which they do not state, though none of them directly presents an epistemological theory. These views show themselves in two ways. On the positive side, each time a character says that he knows something, or even acts as though he did, we can ask what sort of view he would have to take about knowledge in order to defend his claim. On the negative side, whenever Socrates disclaims knowledge on his own account, or fails to find grounds for another man's claim to knowledge, then we can ask by what criteria of knowledge the characters are supposed to fall short of their ambitions.

We must be cautious about our results. The dialogues, after all, are works of fiction about a Socrates who assumes different tones with different antagonists, and who may sometimes, but not always, be Plato's spokesman, but who does not always speak even for himself.

Socrates does not have the same attitude towards every theoretical view he uses in the elenchus. Of these, some appear to be his own views, and others are the expressed views of his partners in debate, while still others are supplied by Socrates dialectically as being necessary to support the expressed views of his partners. Socrates' theory of expert knowledge is certainly not the expressed view of any of his interlocutors; none of them proposes it, and scarcely any shows that he understands it. Moreover, Socrates does not adjust his view of expert knowledge to meet the need of each argument; his view is much the same, no matter whose case it is used against. Nevertheless, we would be naive to conclude that this simply is Socrates' analysis of what it is to be an expert. He uses it dialectically, especially when he applies it to moral expertise.[12] It is safer to say Socrates supplies this view of expert knowledge as necessary in his view to support the claims made by his partners.

II

Expert Knowledge

To be an expert is to be someone on whom others may reasonably rely in difficult, perilous, or highly technical matters. Plato indicates expert knowledge by *technē* and its cognates, and in many contexts also by *sophia* and *epistēmē*.

Socrates has a way of knowing whether or not one is an expert. In the *Apology* he says that he knows he is not an expert (22d1), and that he has demonstrated that poets are not experts (22c9). Socrates' test for expertise is evidently cross-examination, what modern scholars have called the elenchus. Poets and politicians (*Meno* 99d), orators and rhapsodes (*Gorgias* 462b ff. and *Ion,* passim), even a pair of experienced generals (*Laches*), all fail this examination in one way or another; and Socrates' confident disavowal of expert knowledge must rest on the same foundation. Socrates must think he has failed his own test, for he refers poignantly to his self-criticism at the end of the *Hippias Major* (304de; cf. 286cd with 298b11). A natural reading of *Apology* 38a takes it to imply the value of self-criticism, and this practice is shown indirectly in a number of early dialogues that test Socratic views after disposing of his first partner's amateur efforts. For example, in the *Hippias Major* Socrates takes both roles for the greater part of the debate, putting forward definitions with one hand while rejecting them with the other. In the *Laches* he finds his own teaching presented by Nicias, and proves that it does not represent expert knowledge. These passages are controversial, but their combined weight supports attributing a practice of self-criticism to Socrates.

The standards Socrates uses explicitly or implicitly to test for expertise give us a basis for constructing an early Platonic theory of expert knowledge. But a curious double standard runs through the early dialogues, making for a complex theory. There is the ordinary expertise of cobblers and shipwrights, which Socrates uses as a model, and the extraordinary expertise Socrates looks for in a teacher of virtue, a politician, or a poet. In the *Apology* he finds no expertise at all in politicians (21c8) and poets (22bc), but allows a sort of expertise to handcraftsmen: they "know many fine things" (22d2) and each practises his *technē* to good effect (22d6), though this results in a false conceit of *sophia* that obscures the *sophia* they actually have.

Socrates does not say what he is doing, but he appears to be using *technē* in two ways when he applies higher standards to poets and politicians than to men who work with their hands. The crafts to which Socrates readily grants expert status are humble; I shall call them *subordinate technai,* and suppose that Socrates is content to speak with the vulgar in these cases. Socrates applies his own strict theory of *Technē* to other cases, however, to professions that claim higher status. A *Technē* in strict Socratic usage would be adequate, and would not need the guidance of a superior body of knowledge (*Republic* 1.342ab). Subordinate *technai* and *Technē* are the two categories of expert knowledge which I shall consider here.[13]

The Subordinate Technai

Though he normally reserves the word *technē* for the highest sort of expertise, Socrates needs to appeal to ordinary examples of *technai* to build his arguments. Generally, he allows the term for vulgar lines of work that are in no danger of being ennobled by it, as in the *Apology;* and he withholds the term from poets, politicians, and the like, who would have considerable authority even without expert status. That is, he allows the term for crafts that are plainly subordinate, and withholds it from those that might masquerade as a Ruling *Technē.*

Socrates is clear that there is a class of *technai* that ought to be subordinate to a ruling *Technē.* Subordinate *technai* are ones you can master without knowing exactly when it is good to apply them, or how their products are best used. A sensible sea-pilot holds his knowledge cheap, because although it tells him how to save lives at sea, it does not tell him which lives it is good to save (*Gorgias* 511c–513c). A sensible general turns his captured city over to statesmen, because he recognises that he does not know how to use what he knew how to capture (*Euthydemus* 290d; cf. 291c). The Ruling *Technē* turns out to be elusive (291b–292e), but this does not vitiate his earlier point that the subordinate *technai* are defective without it.

Standards for Subordinate Technai

Not surprisingly, the standards for *technai* at this level are as ordinary and as familiar as the doctor's diploma on the examining room wall; you can establish expert status by pointing to your education or your success; and, to be an expert, you must possess a body of knowledge that is teachable, deals with a specialised subject, and covers it completely. Fine as it may be, such a *technē* is specialised and so cannot be adequate in itself; that is why it deserves to be a subordinate *technē.*

Sufficient Conditions

(*a*) *Education.* Apparently it suffices for an expert to show that he has had good teachers (*Laches* 185b, *Euthyphro* 16a1, *Meno* 90b, *Gorgias* 514a–c). The condition is not necessary (*Laches* 185e7); you might establish expertise by pointing to your pupils as well.

(*b*) *Success.* If all else fails, you might still establish expertise by pointing to a body of work well done (*Laches* 185e9ff.).

Necessary Conditions

(*c*) *Teachability.* If you are an expert, you can pass your expertise on to others; if you cannot, your success must be due to some other cause. But, presumably, the only way to prove that you can teach is to do it (*Protagoras* 319eff.: cf. 348eff., *Meno* 99b).

This is a corollary of the common Greek view that any *technē* is teachable. But Socrates may have held an unconventional view of what it is to teach, and this is part of the difference between Socrates and Protagoras in the dialogue *Protagoras*. Protagoras holds the conventional view that training people in non-intellectual ways is still teaching them; while Socrates evidently does not.[14]

Intuitively this condition is sound: expert knowledge must be teachable. Nevertheless, the principle becomes awkward on a narrow view of what it is to teach. For this reason, Socrates will introduce a model of non-teachable knowledge in the *Meno*.

(*d*) *Specialisation*. If you are an expert, you are a specialist with a well-defined subject or ability. This is the condition that poets, orators, and rhapsodes most signally fail, since they speak equally well on anything and to any effect. Such is the argument of the *Ion* (especially 541e) and the *Gorgias* (447c, 448e, 450b, 455b, 456a). *Republic* I treats justice as a *technē* when it asks after its specific function—in what sphere it yields benefits to friends (332c ff.).

This too is a corollary of a commonplace about *technē*: that a *technē* involves specialisation. That is why Plato represents gentlemen of leisure as having no interest in acquiring *technai*, and contrasts education (*paideia*) with technical training (*Protagoras* 312b). Protagoras holds a similar view (317c); and though he treats political virtue on the analogy with *technē* (because it is teachable) he stresses this difference: political virtue is not the province of specialists but of all normal civilised humans (322d, 327d).

This requirement is even more awkward than that of teachability. If *technai* are specialised, then each one has its specific goal, the good of its object, which it pursues to the exclusion of all others: doctoring cures patients, but money-making collects the bills (*Republic* 341d ff., 342c; cf. 346e, 347a). This leads to paradox if each *technē* operates without fault, as Socrates recognises at *Charmides* 174b ff. (cf. *Republic* I 342b3–5). To operate faultlessly, a *technē* would need to know what really promotes the advantage of its object. It would have to ask, for example, whether a mutilated patient is really better off alive or dead; but that would be beyond the scope of specialised doctoring. Socrates recognises that for this reason you will not be able to acquire rhetoric as a *technē* unless you also acquire, as a *technē*, the ability to avoid committing injustice (*Gorgias* 510a; cf. 509e). It follows that no ordinary specialised *technē* is adequate in itself, and that all such *technai* must be subordinate as rhetoric is subordinate: you could not be *technikos* in rhetoric without being *technikos* in justice. But this undermines the principle of specialisation.

Again, within the confines of a given *technē* there is no way of marking off good uses of the relevant skill from bad ones (*Hippas Minor* 367e, 375bc, and passim). If *technai* (or *epistēmai*, treated as *technai*) are specialised, then no *technē* can judge either its own work or the work of another, as Socrates infers at *Charmides* 165e–166a: cf. 171c, 172d. The principle will make it impossible to find in this category a *technē* that judges other *technai*. The same principle, which confines each *technē* to its specific subject-matter, will not allow one *technē* to be subordinate to another, and so undermines the concept with which we began. A *technē* of life-saving saves lives, but does not know whether it is good to do so; but an equally specialised Ruling *Technē*, if it knew this, would be interfering in a subject it is supposed to know nothing about—life-saving.

These paradoxes about subordinate *technai* are symptoms of deep confusions in the ordinary conception of *technē*; to Socrates they probably indicate that subordinate *technai* are not *technai* in the true sense. In his strict theory, the vulgar idea that there are *multiple* specialised *technai* must wither away. The only way Plato could save the notion of a *technē* that is adequate in itself, without violating the principle of specialisation, would be to suppose that there is but one true *Technē*. The principle of specialisation is not dispensable; Socrates' larger project depends upon it—the guarding of Athens against deception by the opinions of experts off their own ground (*Apology* 22e). If you are an expert on poetry, as Ion would be if he were expert on anything, then I would be a fool to rely on you for moral knowledge; if you are an expert on grammar, I should not be a slave to your view of international politics. The price of preserving the principle of specialisation is high, but it is worth paying.

(*e*) *Completeness*. A *technē* is complete in that it covers the entire range of its specific subject. Socrates' theory of *technai* rides on an implicit theory about the integrity of each body of knowledge. Just how this theory works in general is never clear, though the specific examples are intuitively satisfactory. The assumption of the integrity of each body of knowledge shows up in the *Laches* at a crucial point, where it will not allow Nicias and Socrates to claim that knowing future goods and knowing all goods are different things (198d1–199a8). The principle is used as a test for *technē* most notably in the *Ion*, where Ion claims to be an expert in Homer only, and not in poetry as a whole. There Socrates concludes that Ion's ability to talk about Homer is not due to expertise; if it were, Ion could talk equally well of other poets (532c). To claim expertise is to claim knowledge of a body of material.

The Adequacy of Technē

Technai on the strict theory must satisfy all the conditions for the subordinate *technai* plus the necessary condition that it should be adequate in itself. The defect of the subordinate *technai* is that they were too specialised to know how to put their skills to good use, and so would have to be subordinate to a *technē* that did specialise in the relevant good. But any true *technē*, it now appears, must aim at the good, and must therefore know what this is. In some cases Socrates expects the expert to give a Socratic definition in order to demonstrate his ability to say precisely what good it is that he brings about (at *Laches* 190b, but not at *Gorgias* 449dff., *Protagoras* 318aff.).

Technē aims at the good as an end, and is consciously part of a teleological ordering. This principle, which no doubt came to Aristotle from Plato (*Nicomachean Ethics* I.1), puts Plato's epistemology firmly in the service of his values; a value-free *technē* would not be worthy of the name.

Of course, the principle is not true of the *subordinate technai*, from which most of his examples are drawn; nor is it true of *technē* as it is usually understood. Hence at *Protagoras* 356d, where Socrates is using *technē* as he supposes Protagoras would use it, he does not subordinate the measuring *technē* to independent knowledge of the good. Where Socrates does mention the principle, it often leads to paradox (*Charmides* 174bff., *Republic* I.342b, *Gorgias* 510a), and this may be a further reason for Plato's not giving it full play until he is ready to give the vulgar examples subordinate status in the *Gorgias*.

Texts implying that *Technē* aims at the good occur before the *Gorgias*, however. Some of these concern the corollary that an expert knows what are the goals of his profession, not merely the means of achieving those goals. At *Laches* 185cd Socrates makes a related point for medicine of the eyes: the expert takes thought not about the medicine but about the eye; he is an expert in the care of eyes. At *Euthyphro* 14e, on similar grounds, Socrates claims it is not *technikos* to give the gods what they do not need. An expert in piety, on this view, would know what the gods need, but this would require him to know also what is good for them. In the *Gorgias* the principle becomes explicit (502d–504a: cf. 506de, 464c; cf. 501b, 500a). It is clearest at 521d, where Socrates claims alone to practise true political *Technē,* because he alone aims not at pleasure but at what is best. It is an implicit consequence of this principle that the same basic knowledge is essential to every *Technē*—knowledge of the good. If this is so, then either the principle of specialisation must be scrapped, or, as I have suggested, any adequate *Technē* in the final analysis will turn out to be essentially the same as expert knowledge of the good.

This is the feature of *Technē* that will be carried most significantly into Plato's middle epistemology (e.g., *Republic* vi.508e).

Definition

If you are an expert, and know the relevant good, then you should be able to say what it is without contradicting yourself—to give a Socratic sort of definition of the good that you produce. This is the rule that will disqualify the most confident self-styled experts. Since this rule guides the disqualifying elenchus of the early dialogues, we must suppose (though we cannot prove) that this is the rule Socrates used in refuting the experts mentioned in the *Apology,* and this the principle that left him in the condition he describes there—"not expert with their expertise, or wrongheaded with their mistakes" (22e), but recognising that he is truly worthless so far as expertise goes (23b).

The requirement is explicit at *Gorgias* 465a (cf. 500b–501a): If you are an expert, you are able to give a certain sort of *logos* or account. What sort of account Socrates has in mind emerges at *Laches* 190aff., and generally in the practice of the elenchus: you must be able to give a Socratic definition of whatever it is that your *technē* produces. Socratic definition tells the *ousia* or essence of something like courage, and in doing so explains why anything that partakes of that essence will in fact be courageous; furthermore, any adequate definition of a virtue like courage will explain why the thing that is courage is good and noble in every instance. For our purposes, this is the most important feature of Socratic definition. An expert doctor must know that what he imparts to you under the name "health" is in fact always healthy and good; similarly, an expert moral teacher must know that what he imparts to you under the name "courage" is always brave and noble. There is no point in paying a teacher to train you in a quality that is good only in certain circumstances. A quality that looks brave only in conventional hoplite battle is not true courage, for it would fail you in the cavalry or whenever lateral or retrograde troop movements are required (*Laches* 190eff.). To be an expert is to know that what you produce has the qualities you say it has *in virtue of its essential nature,* and so will continue to have those qualities so long as it survives, whatever the circumstances.

This is the point that marks the difference between Socrates and the epistemologist. A modern epistemologist, in the spirit of Descartes, would ask whether Euthyphro can entertain doubt as to whether it is pious to prosecute his father, and would proceed to look for an unshakeable foundation for this view. But that is not Socrates' question. He asks whether Euthyphro's expertise is so exact that he does not fear lest prosecuting his father turn out to be impious (4e). "Exact," and not "certain," is the correct word for the knowledge Socrates wants: exact knowledge is evidently *unqualified* knowledge. The danger, as we learn from 8ab, is not that Euthyphro's original judgement would turn out to be incorrect, but that, if correct, it would turn out to be compatible with an opposed judgement. This would happen if his action were pious to one god and impious to another; and then his answer would be true only under a qualification. Euthyphro might fend off even that consequence, and issue a judgement that all the gods would approve; but even then he would still not be an expert, unless his account of piety stated the essence of piety (11ab). Only in that case would there be, not just the fact that the gods agreed, but a guarantee that what Euthyphro called piety would be piety, and never impiety, in any circumstance.

This requirement, which goes beyond anything an epistemologist would require for certainty, is appropriate for expertise. Euthyphro is being tested for knowledge on which others may rely, and this must therefore be not merely true, and not merely certain, but transferable without loss to any number of situations. Socrates is looking for a teacher whose expertise would support the defence of Socrates, whose circumstances are gravely different from Euthyphro's. To look for such an expert in Euthyphro is a joke, of course; but it is not a joke to insist that such an expert should know the essential nature of his subject—what it is in all circumstances.

Here is the main bridge from early Plato's theory of *Technē* to later Plato's theory of Forms: if you have a *Technē,* you know the essential nature of your product; essential natures will turn out in the middle dialogues to be Forms, entities so special that you must be oriented in a special direction in order to know them.

Expert Knowledge and the Sceptic

A classical sceptic has no theory about knowledge; he borrows his enemy's theory and uses it against him. In effect, he helps the dogmatist see that he does not satisfy his own epistemological standards. An argument that does this is rhetorical and not demonstrative; its aim is not truth but an attitude of detachment from the truth, and its method commits the sceptic to no views whatever.

Socrates cannot play the sceptic's role. The dogmatic characters he confronts have nothing like a theory of knowledge. Socrates supplies the necessary theory, brings them to agree to it, and then shows on that basis that they are not experts.[15] His use of this theory bars us from claiming a consistently sceptical attitude for Socrates.

But Socrates is not on the other side either, for his theory has little to do with the central issues of epistemology. It is a theory about what it is to be an expert, not a theory about what it is to know. The theory assumes that we understand what is meant by "know," and insists that an expert must know a certain kind of thing: if you are an expert you will know the essential nature of your product. Socrates also makes the obvious assumptions that you should be able to say what you know without contradicting yourself. But he gives nothing approaching a definition of knowledge, or a sufficient condition, or even an account of how knowledge is to be acquired.

Infallibility

Two kinds of infallibility must be distinguished: the infallibility of what is known, and the infallibility of the expert who knows it. An infallible expert is one who cannot fail to know; an infallible truth is one that cannot fail to be true in any circumstance. Socrates shows no interest in the infallibility of experts, but enormous interest in the infallibility of what is to be known. Socrates tests would-be experts not to see if they can make mistakes, but to see if there is a circumstance in which what they claim to know fails to be true. When Socrates claims to know that it is wrong to disobey one's superior, he does not mean to arrogate to himself the infallibility of a god; what makes this a matter of knowledge is that, if true, it cannot fail to be true for gods or men, above, below, or on the earth, while no claim about Hades can have this feature (*Apology* 29b: cf. *Crito* 51b).

Later Plato will distinguish knowledge from other cognitive attitudes as being (1) *infallible* (*Republic* 447e; cf. *Theaetetus* 152c5 and 166d), and (2) *resistant to persuasion* (*Timaeus* 51e). These may be characterisations Socrates has in mind for the knowledge he disavows.[16] For (1), infallibility, the *Republic* and the early dialogues agree that knowledge knows only the sort of thing that stays true no matter what. A fallible belief could be true or false depending on the circumstances (compare *Hippias Major* 289c5 and *Euthyphro* 8ab with *Republic* 479aff.). The danger is that your view may be true for the cases you have in mind but for no other cases: Euthyphro could be right about prosecuting his father, and be quite certain that he is right, and still fail condition (1) if doing that sort of thing is not always pious.

As for (2), resistance to persuasion, the early dialogues give the only helpful examples: people who are easily persuaded to drop their views cannot have known those views; while Socrates cites his success at resisting persuasion as evidence that his views were right (*Gorgias* 509a). The example makes it clear that he has in mind the resistance of the belief, not the believer: clinging stubbornly to your views is a bad sign. The beliefs that satisfy condition (2) are the ones that you are left with after a lifetime of the sort of strenuous discussion that threatens to refute your most cherished ideas.

Notice that you can satisfy either condition without being an expert. Socrates' knowledge that it is bad to disobey one's superior is infallible in Plato's sense (*Apology* 29b); but this cannot be expert knowledge. Again, Socrates more than anyone satisfies condition (2): after a lifetime of self-scrutiny, and of submission to the scrutiny of others, he could still say, "It is always the same story with me; I don't know how these things are . . ."(*Gorgias* 509a). This is borne out by the *Crito,* where he is shown at the end of his life still open, for a while, to persuasion. There he does not claim the status of the expert he mentioned at 47d, whose judgement would simply carry the day; instead, he asks Crito to try to speak against him (48e1). If, in the end, he is beyond listening to counter-arguments, it is not because he is certain, but because the guiding beliefs of his whole long life are singing to him so loudly at this point that he can listen to nothing else (54d).

Notice also that neither of these conditions is necessary for *certainty*. Certainty, in epistemological discussions, is immunity from doubt and a shield against scepticism. You can satisfy condition (1), in that your attitude is towards an unchanging object, and still be uncertain that you have it right. Again, as we have seen, Socrates could resist persuasion in the elenchus for a lifetime, satisfying condition (2), and still not be certain. But satisfying these conditions makes you *reliable* nonetheless.

Reliability and certainty serve different sorts of interests. Descartes seeks to know in a manner that will satisfy himself as being certain; he himself recognises that the immediate result of his meditation is of no interest to anyone but himself. But Socrates seeks an expert on whom others should rely. Reliability has nothing to do with certainty—with your ability to answer an internal sceptic; but it has everything to do with your knowing something that will be as useful for others as it is for you. I may know how to be truly brave in trench warfare, but that would not qualify me to train soldiers who might fight anywhere. I may know enough to build a particular house, and may even be able to defend my beliefs about my nails and my beams to the fiercest sceptic; but unless I know principles that would apply to any structure in any circumstance I am not fit to give general advice.

III

Non-expert Knowledge

In practice, Socrates allows that one can know many things without being an expert. I shall discuss these under one heading, although no general concept of this sort is treated in the early dialogues. There will be much less to say than there was on expert knowledge. We have no practical interest in testing other people for non-expert knowledge, and neither did Socrates.

There are five overlapping categories of non-expert knowledge to which Socrates is committed, either for himself or for others:

a. *Cases Socrates explicitly distinguishes from expert knowledge.* This category includes whatever Socrates says he knows, when he claims knowledge in a context governed by his disavowal of knowledge (especially *Apology* 21b4–5).

b. *Things Socrates says he knows.* These include (i) the knowledge that he, Socrates, is not an expert (*Apology* 21b2–5, 22d1), (ii) the moral truth that it is bad to disobey one's superior (*Apology* 29b6–7), (iii) certain methodological principles (*Gorgias* 485e5–6). (Some of Socrates' moral and methodological views belong also in category d, as presuppositions of elenchus.)

c. *Things Socrates says other people know.* These fall into two groups, expert and non-expert: (i) ascriptions of expert knowledge to ordinary experts (e.g. *Apology* 22d, *Crito* 47aff.), (ii) claims as to what other people know (non-expertly). Most of this relates to the paradox that vice is ignorance (*Protagoras* 357d7–e1, *Republic* 1.351a5–6 with 350c10–11, *Gorgias* 512b1–2).

Curiously, the things Socrates says other people know are often views which he holds, but which the others do not consciously share. He must think that the elenchus finds this knowledge in them, when it brings forward surprising consequences of beliefs that they do hold consciously.

d. *Presuppositions of the elenchus, where this is demonstrative.* Socrates uses the elenchus at times to demonstrate certain conclusions. Where this is so, he must think that he knows that his methodological principles and premises are correct. These comprise (i) his theory of expert knowledge (which he uses to demonstrate that others are not experts), (ii) certain views about the subjects under discussion (most prominently Socrates' view that each virtue is good and noble, as at *Laches* 192c and *Charmides* 159c1), and (iii) certain examples and counter-examples, which Socrates treats as known (e.g. *Laches* 191c, the courage of the Spartans at the battle of Plataia).

e. *Results of the elenchus, where this is demonstrative.* These fall into two groups: (i) negative results, when Socrates concludes that none of a series of answers indicates expert knowledge. Socrates treats these conclusions as established in their contexts, and in the *Apology* refers to his negative results as demonstrated (e.g. 22b7), (ii) positive results, which are explicitly claimed only in the *Gorgias* (479e8, 508e6–509a5).

Pragmatic Differences Between Expert and Non-expert Knowledge

Imagine a sceptic challenging Socrates to explain why he tests claims to expert, but not to non-expert, knowledge. What could Socrates say in reply? An expert is a well-qualified specialist on whom others may safely rely. Socrates can say that it is reasonable for us non-specialists to ask a presumed expert to prove his credentials before we give him our trust. In such a case we need to choose whom to believe, and it makes sense to seek grounds for reasonable choices because there plainly are grounds in ordinary cases: a true expert can point to his accomplishments, or to his pupils, or at least to an established teacher. On the other hand, since we are not invited to trust non-experts, we do not have the same reason to test their credentials; we would be foolish to ask them to have expert credentials anyway. Socrates' reply would be that he is right to treat the two cases differently because the cases are different: experts have credentials and non-experts do not. Moreover, practically, we need to ask experts for credentials, but not non-experts.

Though this may explain why Socrates treats the two cases differently, it would not answer a sceptical challenge: no sceptic would agree that the differences between experts and non-experts are relevant to his question: the credentials that mark experts do not establish knowledge; even the Pyrrhonists followed the dictates of *technai*. Again, although there is no practical need to test non-experts, the sceptical challenge remains: does the non-expert know what he thinks he knows?

Common Knowledge

Suppose a sceptic asks Socrates to explain why he may say that he knows certain things when even the best-trained people he questions cannot meet his standards for expert knowledge. If they fail, and if Socrates is no better, on what grounds can he claim to know? Socrates can answer that, unlike the presumed experts, he does not arrogate to himself a special position; he claims no more for himself than he does for everyone else. His knowledge is the common property of ordinary people; anyone knows enough to join in the elenchus. Though it makes sense to ask an expert to establish his credentials, it is absurd to ask an ordinary person to prove that he has ordinary accomplishments.

But this common-knowledge defence is particularly vulnerable to sceptical objections. A sceptic could turn against Socrates an argument like the one Socrates will use against Protagoras in the *Theaetetus:* ordinary people do not always agree with each other, and they especially disagree with the sort of thing Socrates often says he knows to be the case. But then if Socrates' views are knowledge, the opposed views of the "ordinary people" are not.

But Socrates would not concede the point that disagreement occurs. In the last analysis, he would say, no one disagrees with him on the matters he thinks he knows. The elenchus derives what people *really* believe from what they initially say they believe, and this method, Socrates believes, resolves apparent disagreement at a deep level.[17] So the sceptical argument from disagreement would fail to get a grip on Socrates, as long as he denied that disagreement occurred. Still the sceptic would be unsatisfied: how does Socrates know which way the deep-level agreement will fall? How can he be sure that he will not find himself agreeing that his opponents are in the right? And even if the right sort of agreement were secured, on what grounds could that be called knowledge?

Knowledge and the Elenchus

Socrates has a method, the elenchus, to which he sometimes appeals for proof of his beliefs. Could the elenchus be the ground for Socrates' knowledge? Socrates says that some of what he believes was proved in the elenchus (*Gorgias* 479e, 509a). Vlastos infers that Socrates held all his human knowledge to be elenctically justifiable.

What this means is not clear; "justifiable" cannot carry its usual sense in epistemology, as Vlastos makes plain. The justification is not epistemic, since it warrants no claims to knowledge. Socrates appeals to these elenctic arguments not as a reason for claiming that his beliefs have the status of knowledge, but simply as a reason for believing them.

Elenctic justification would not explain Socrates' fierce confidence in some of his views (*Apology* 29b, e.g.). That confidence must have another source. Also, the weak role that elenchus could play in justifying belief does not fit the enormous place that the method has in Socrates' life. Weak or strong, justification holds little charm for Socrates. His cherished elenchus must have other purposes.

Among other things, elenchus guards against the error of taking someone else as an authority on a matter in which no one is more expert than another. On moral questions, it appears, members of Socrates' audience are all in the same boat. The pretensions of the poets and politicians, the rhapsodes and the sophists—none of them bears Socratic examination. The elenchus leaves its audience near dangerous moral shoals, without a specialist to guide them to shore. Every search for an expert leads to an impasse, leaving the ordinary person to fall back on his own resources.

But the elenchus finds that these resources are not so meagre as they had perhaps seemed. The same argument that unmasked the pretenders disclosed an impressive consensus on its moral premises. We have seen that elenchus discovers beliefs the believer never knew he had, and evidently does the same for knowledge (see n. 17). Socrates holds that, in the last analysis, you believe the consequences of whatever views you are left with after the elenchus has done its work. The elenchus thus exposes what you believe in the last analysis, and simply treats this sort of belief, without apology, as non-expert knowledge. The early elenchus is a direct ancestor to the method Socrates will introduce in the *Meno* for recovering knowledge from oblivion. Discovery, not justification, is the positive legacy of the elenchus. In Plato's early theory, special pretensions are to be challenged, but ordinary knowledge is to be found.

APPENDIX

The Transitional Theory of Knowledge in the Meno

The *Meno* shows Socrates sketching out views of knowledge that go beyond anything presupposed in Plato's earlier works.[18] New in the *Meno* are the theory that what we call learning is really recollection, and a distinction between knowledge and true belief. A consequence of these developments is that the *technē*-model for knowledge is abandoned, for here Socrates considers a sort of knowledge that is always present in the knower, and so never taught.

The first stage of the dialogue follows a familiar pattern. Socrates demonstrates that Meno, for all his studies with Gorgias, cannot adequately say what virtue is, and the discussion ends in a stalemate. Meno is stymied and Socrates is no better off: he disclaims knowledge of virtue (80d1:cf. 71b3). The discussion does not end here, however, for Socrates offers to continue the enquiry, and Meno counters with a methodological question (80d5–8), the same question, in fact, that has perplexed our study of the earlier dialogues: how, in view of Socrates' disclaimer of knowledge, can he proceed in his enquiry? Now, for the first time, Socrates considers questions as to how knowledge is to be acquired.

The Eristic Paradox

After disclaiming knowledge of virtue, Socrates proposes to enquire, along with Meno, what virtue is. Now Meno worries how enquiry can proceed without knowledge: "In what way will you seek to know something that you do not know at all? What sort of thing, among those things you do not know, will you propose to seek? Or if you really find it, how will you know that this is the thing you did not know before?" (80d). Socrates thinks Meno has in mind the eristic paradox: "that it is not possible for a human being to seek to know either what he knows or what he does not know; for he would not seek what he knows—for he knows it already, and has no need to seek it—nor would he seek what he does not know—for he does not know what he will seek" (80e).

Recollection

Socrates answers by proposing that what we call learning is actually the recollection of lessons learned before birth (81de). He plainly thinks this solves the paradox (81d5: cf. 86bc), though he does not say how he thinks it does so. Evidently he supposes that when he seeks to know what virtue is, he is seeking something that falls neither into the class of the simply known nor into the class of the simply unknown, but into a third class, that of lessons once learned but now forgotten. Apparently, memory can guide a search for items in this third class. The theory of recollection reappears at *Phaedo* 72e ff. and

Phaedrus 249c, in connection with metaphysical and psychological ideas of Plato's middle period; but it is never more than a sketch of a theory.

Socrates' attitude towards the theory in the *Meno* is puzzling. On the one hand, he says that he believes it to be true (81e1); on the other, he declines to affirm the theory with any strength (86b7). The most he will fight for is his view that we are better off not submitting to the eristic paradox (86c: cf.81de). His attitude towards the theory of recollection illustrates a general view on which much of the argument of the *Meno* depends: Socrates evidently holds that we have beliefs on which we may rely for the guidance of our enquiries, but which cannot be securely affirmed (cf. 85c6–7).

This must fill out his unstated solution to the eristic paradox. The paradox (like Meno's worry) presupposed that any enquiry must be guided by knowledge of what the enquiry is about; but Socrates implicitly denies this. Enquiry, he must think, can be guided by beliefs that are not yet known to be true.[19]

It is a consequence of the theory of recollection that what we call learning does not come by teaching; on this point Socrates is emphatic (82a1, 82e4, 84d1). Instead of teaching Meno that his theory is true, he illustrates the theory through an exercise with a slave boy, and presumably leaves it to Meno to recollect what truth there is in the theory. Instead of teaching the slave boy, Socrates questions him, and so brings the boy to learn a truth of geometry. Socrates points out that all of the boy's answers expressed beliefs that were his own (85bc). Socrates then infers first that those beliefs were always in the boy, and then that they were not implanted by teaching.

I will not stay here to evaluate this chain of inferences. The outline of Socrates' theory is clear enough. It entails (a) that a person may have true beliefs of which he is not aware (85c9: cf. the passages cited in n. 17), and (b) that, after becoming aware of such beliefs and being questioned about them, a person may come to know in the full sense the subject of those beliefs (85d1). From this follows the important but unstated conclusion that one may learn and know things that one was never taught.

Readers may think that Socrates has indeed taught the slave boy, and done it so well that he never had to ask the boy to accept a belief that the boy had not already reached by himself. But this would be to miss the point that this theory in the *Meno* marks Socrates' abandonment of the *technē* model for knowledge. For on that model, a person can learn and know only what he has been taught. Socrates may have been one kind of teacher to the slave boy, but he was not the kind of teacher who passes a *technē* by precept and example to a pupil. The concept of knowledge that Socrates treats in the *Meno* is something new: its standards are as high as the standards for a *technē* in the earlier dialogues; but it is not a *technē,* and it is not teachable as a *technē* is teachable.

In the *Protagoras* Socrates argued that virtue is not teachable by any method he accepts as teaching (319bff.), and the same point is made later here (*Meno* 94e2, 96c10). But in the theory of recollection, the *Meno* has implicitly developed a concept of knowledge such that virtue could be knowledge and still not teachable. This new concept has developed out of Socrates' earlier theory of unteachable non-expert knowledge. It is a break from his theory of teachable expert knowledge.

To be sure, the *Meno* is not consistent on this point. The thesis that there can be knowledge without teaching, virtually explicit in 85c, is resisted in the balance of the dialogue. Socrates infers that what is not teachable is not knowledge (99ab) on the basis of a hypothesis repeated at 87c and 89d. These passages represent the pre-*Meno* theory of knowledge as *technē*. Why Socrates retreats to his earlier view after 86c is a serious puzzle about the construction of the *Meno*. We shall encounter a parallel difficulty about true belief.

True and Right Belief

The distinction between knowledge and true belief in the *Meno* is emphatic at 85c7; Socrates distinguishes with equal force between knowledge and right belief (*orthē doxa*) at 98b, where Socrates says that he knows this distinction if he knows anything. But Socrates does not clearly specify the standards for knowledge as opposed to true belief, nor does he say clearly how far true belief is reliable without knowledge.

The following considerations bear on *criteria* for knowledge as opposed to true or right belief:

1. *Origins*. The *Meno* is not consistent as to whether true belief and knowledge have different origins. In the recollection-passage, true belief is considered on a par with knowledge: it is present from birth and brought to light through questioning (85c). But in the last part of the dialogue, right belief is said to be acquired (98d); it is differentiated from knowledge as something not acquired by teaching (99bc); and it is therefore equivalent to a sort of inspiration, given to individuals by the gods (99cd: cf. *Ion* 533dff., *Apology* 22c). Again, as for the teachability of knowledge, the recollection-passage takes Socrates beyond the theory of the earlier dialogues, while the later passages do not. True belief and right belief may represent two different theories awkwardly married in the *Meno* at 97e–98a.

2. *Definition*. It is necessary to know what virtue is in order to know whether it can be taught (71a, 86d), though enquiry on this topic can proceed by hypothesis (86e).

3. *Refutability*. True beliefs are said to become knowledge when they have been awakened by questioning (86a7) or tethered by an explanatory account (98a3), but these metaphors are not clearly explained. A likely hypothesis is that a tethered belief is one that cannot be refuted. Socrates likens beliefs to the wandering statues of Daedalus (97de, 98a1); he had used a similar image at *Euthyphro* 11cd, where a wandering belief is evidently one that can be refuted. We may infer that knowledge, unlike true belief, cannot be refuted.

4. *Reliability*. Insofar as it is right or true, Socrates insists that a right or true belief is no less useful than knowledge (97c, 98c; but see *Republic* VI.506c7). This does not entail that true belief is reliable; indeed, Socrates implies that it is not (98a1). The tone of the last pages of the *Meno* is ironical and derogatory of inspired true belief, which, as in the *Ion,* has little in common with knowledge. In the recollection passage, on the other hand, true belief plays an entirely positive role in the recovery of knowledge.

NOTES

1. This essay owes much to G. Vlastos, "Socrates' Disavowal of Knowledge," *Philosophical Quarterly* (1985), 1–31, and to his generous correspondence with me on the subject. The views presented here are my own, however.

2. P. Woodruff, "The Skeptical Side of Plato's Method," *Revue internationale de philosophie* (1986), 22–37.

3. For the translation of *sunoida*, see *Phaedrus* 235c7 ("knowing my own ignorance"), which shows that *sunoida* is at least as strongly epistemic as *oida* ("I know"). There, Socrates uses *ennenoēka* and *eu oida* in the same context and to the same effect as *sunoida*. Some translators have wrongly chosen a weaker translation for 21b4: e.g. Tredennick: "I am only too conscious."

4. Vlastos, "Socrates' Disavowal of Knowledge."

5. The interpretation of the disavowal as an act of deception (first bruited by Thrasymachus— *Republic* I 337a) has been represented in recent years by N. Gulley, *The Philosophy of Socrates* (1968), 69, and roundly refuted by Vlastos, "Socrates' Disavowal of Knowledge," 3–5, followed on this point by J. H. Lesher, "Socrates' Disavowal of Knowledge," *Journal of the History of Philosophy* (1987), 275–88.

   On the crucial distinctions between deception, simple irony and complex irony, see G. Vlastos, "Socratic Irony," reprinted in this volume: "In 'simple' irony what is said is simply not what is meant. In 'complex' irony what is said both is and isn't what is meant" (p. 71).

6. So T. H. Irwin, *Plato's Moral Theory* (1977), 39–40, on which see Vlastos' persuasive reply in, "Socrates' Disavowal of Knowledge," 5–11.

7. Lesher, "Socrates' Disavowal of Knowledge," esp. p. 282.

8. Vlastos, "Socrates' Disavowal of Knowledge"; the objection is stated by Lesher, "Socrates' Disavowal of Knowledge," 277–8.

9. By "expert knowledge" I mean what Socrates most often refers to by *technē*. On the use of this word in Plato, see D. L. Roochnik, "Socrates' Use of the Techne-Analogy," reprinted in this volume. Interest in *technē* in moral and political contexts grew out of the increasing complexity of public affairs in Athens in the later fifth century. On this theme see W. R. Connor, *The New Politicians of Fifth-Century Athens* (1971), 125 and 126, n. 68.

10. Socrates calls this practice a *political technē*, without meaning to claim for it any special epistemic status: at *Gorgias* 521d he claims to practise the true political *technē*, on the grounds that his sights are set not on what is most pleasant but on what is best (cf. *Apology* 30a, 36de). This is not expert knowledge, because it does not satisfy the conditions of teachability and specialisation, and so the knowledge on which it is based must be non-expert. But Socrates' *practice* of the elenchus remains a *technē* in this special Socratic sense.

11. A possible exception is *Charmides* 166c7–d4; but that must refer to Socrates' concern not to mistake his ordinary views for *expert* knowledge, if definitions are required only to support a claim to expert knowledge.

12. See Roochnik, "Socrates' Use of the Techne-Analogy," p. 193.

13. There is a tradition that divides *technē* also into productive and theoretical *technai*, a division that cuts across the one I make here between subordinate *technai* and an adequate *Technē*. See Roochnik, "Socrates' Use of the Techne-Analogy," p. 186.

14. The difference shows up in the contrast between Socrates' argument that virtue is not taught (319aff.) and Protagoras' reply that it is taught, like language, by all to all (327eff.). It is obvious again in the discussion of courage at 351aff., where Protagorean teaching includes the nurture (*eutrophia*) of the soul, and Socrates takes the narrower view that teaching is imparting a *technē*, and leads to professional confidence.

15. For a detailed discussion of such an elenchus, and an argument that it is indeed intended as demonstrative, see P. Woodruff, "Expert Knowledge in the *Apology* and *Laches:* What a General Needs to Know," *Proceedings of the Boston Area Colloquium in Ancient Philosophy* (1987), 79–115.

16. Vlastos, "Socrates' Disavowal of Knowledge," 18.

17. As at *Gorgias* 471d, 473a, 475e, and 482b. The same principle underlies the ascriptions of knowledge to other people, category c(ii) above. Cf. *Symposium* 202c and Socrates' general

practice of imputing to historical figures the views he thinks they ought to have held (e.g. *Theaetetus* 152d, which gives Protagoras a view he would have held if, like Socrates, he thought that no consistent relativist could continue to use the verb "to be").

18. The interpretation of these matters is controversial. For a fine recent study, see A. Nehamas, "Meno's Paradox and Socrates as a Teacher," reprinted in this volume.

19. True beliefs are awakened in the course of enquiry only one step ahead of knowledge. It is therefore hard to see how *these* beliefs could guide the first stage of the enquiry (Nehamas "Meno's Paradox and Socrates as a Teacher," p. 310). But even the negative elenchus is, as we have seen, guided by Socratic beliefs about the criteria of knowledge. So the early stage of the enquiry must be guided either unconsciously by beliefs not yet awakened or (more likely) consciously by beliefs awakened in the course of a different enquiry.

FURTHER READING

Kraut, R. 1984. "Definition, Knowledge, and Teaching." *Socrates and the State*, 245–309. Princeton, N.J.

Lesher, J. 1987. "Socrates' Disavowal of Knowledge." *Journal of the History of Philosophy* 25:275–88.

Vlastos, G. 1985. "Socrates' Disavowal of Knowledge." *Philosophical Quarterly* 35:1–31.

Woodruff, P. 1986. "The Skeptical Side of Plato's Method." *Revue Internationale de Philosophie* 40:22–37.

———. 1987. "Expert Knowledge in the *Apology* and *Laches:* What a General Needs to Know." *Proceedings of the Boston Area Colloquium in Ancient Philosophy* 3:79–115.

7

Does Socrates Commit
the Socratic Fallacy?

JOHN BEVERSLUIS

Ever since P. T. Geach's famous assault[1] on a "style of mistaken thinking" underlying Socrates' What-is-*F?* question the specter of the Socratic Fallacy has haunted the literature. Unlike many less searching allegations, the charge of a specifically "Socratic" fallacy cuts deep and calls for radical reappraisal. It bespeaks not simply error but monumental error—a mistake in principle which fatally undercuts Socrates' whole theoretical enterprise and is "quite likely to be morally harmful"[2] as well.

How is it that the man who claimed never intentionally to have wronged anyone should have come under such severe censure? What, exactly, is the Socratic Fallacy?

According to Geach, it consists in making two assumptions:

    (A) [I]f you know that you are correctly predicating a given term "T" you must "know what it is to be a T," in the sense of being able to give a general criterion for a thing's being T,

and

    (B) [I]t is no use to try and arrive at the meaning of "T" by giving examples of things that are T.[3]

That Socrates makes both assumptions Geach has no doubt. I will argue that he makes neither and hence does not commit the Socratic Fallacy.[4]

I. THE CHARGE AND ITS HISTORY

The charge is based on a cluster of misconceptions about the methodology which Socrates tacitly employs in the early dialogues. First, it presupposes a mistaken *philosophical* interpretation, not an uncontroversial textual exegesis, of the epistemic relation between definitional knowledge of *F* and extensional knowledge of things that are *F*. Geach thinks that, for Socrates, the former is epistemically prior to, and a necessary condition for, the latter. Second, in imputing to Socrates a "contemptuous attitude toward the particular case,"[5] it misconstrues the epistemic status and elenctic role of the numerous examples he employs. Third, it misunderstands the peculiarly Socratic conception of knowledge (not to be confounded with the Platonic) and how it differs from true belief.

Geach is not the first to have ascribed (A) to Socrates.[6] So had many prominent commentators of the 50s and early 60s[7] who, on this point, were themselves following well-trodden logical and epistemological trails already blazed by some of the most respected names in early twentieth century Platonic scholarship.[8] What distinguishes Geach from his like-minded predecessors is that he not only ascribes (A) to Socrates but proceeds to advance the polemical thesis that, in holding it, he commits a fallacy of grievous proportions. Whether he is right about this is a much-debated and still-unresolved question.[9] In any event, since my contention that Socrates does not hold (A) goes far beyond a mere disagreement with Geach and challenges a long-standing interpretive tradition, I will not only deny the charge of the fallacy but also argue that the methodology at work in the early dialogues requires that we reject the entire traditional interpretation on which it is based.

So as to bring under (A)'s rubric the kindred views of many commentators, past and present, who concur with Robinson about the impression "vaguely given" by the early dialogues that no truth whatever about *F* can be known without a definition of *F*, I will embellish Geach's original formulation by distinguishing two forms that it may take:

(A1) If you do not know the definition of *F*, you cannot know that anything is an *F*,

and

(A2) If you do not know the definition of *F*, you cannot know anything about *F* (e.g. that *F*, say Justice, is *Y*, say beneficial).

I will also reformulate (B). Since the futility to which Geach refers in claiming that, for Socrates, it is "no use" searching for definitions by means of examples is not the futility of excessive difficulty but of sheer impossibility, I will hereafter render (B) as:

(B*) It is impossible to search for a definition of *F* by means of examples of things that are *F*.

I will begin by re-examining the Socratic theory of Definition and the doctrine of epistemic priority which, according to a great cloud of exegetical witnesses, lies at its very heart.

II. THE TEXTS

Geach's charge is based on a single passage from the *Euthyphro*. Although he claims that the early dialogues are the *"locus classicus"* of the Socratic Fallacy and that the same "fallacious" reasoning is "paralleled" in "many other" places, he does not document these somewhat sweeping generalizations with further textual support. We are left, then, with *Eu.* 6D9–E6 where Socrates, in quest of what Holiness (*to hosion*) is, says:

> [T]ell me what is the essential form (*auto to eidos*) of holiness which makes all holy actions holy . . . so that, with my eye on it, and using it as a standard (*paradeigma*), I can say that any action done by you or anyone else is holy if it resembles this ideal, or, if it does not, can deny that it is holy.

Geach thinks that here we catch Socrates in the very act of committing the Socratic Fallacy, that is, of affirming (A1). Hence since neither he nor Euthyphro knows the definition of Holiness, they cannot know that any action is holy. Geach then formulates this thesis in full generality: since throughout the early dialogues Socrates and his interlocutors *never* arrive at definitions of Courage, Temperance, Justice, and so on, it follows that they cannot know that any action is courageous, temperate, just, etc. Universal eidetic ignorance entails a correspondingly universal lack of extensional knowledge of which actions any moral term is correctly predicable. Add to this already disquieting situation the further methodological stricture that, given (B*), they cannot even minimally extricate themselves from their predicament by pondering examples, and the result is a hopeless epistemic impasse.

These "Socratic" theses strike Geach as scandalous. But does Socrates hold them?

First, (B*). If Socrates really thinks that it is impossible to search for a definition of F by means of examples of things that are F, he is guilty of repeated self-contradiction;[10] for that is exactly what he urges his interlocutors to do in every early dialogue in which the What-is-F? question is raised.[11] The dialogues of search abound with passages in which he not only unproblematically accepts examples of the virtue under discussion from interlocutors who manifestly lack a definition of it but heartily endorses examples as the primary data from which the definition is to be extracted.

Asked what Courage is, Laches responds with an example: the courageous man "remains at his post and fights against the enemy." (*La.* 190E5–6) Now if Socrates holds (B*), he should immediately rebuke Laches for appealing to an example of a courageous action with no definition of Courage. But he does not. He ignores Laches' apparent transgression of (B*), *accepts* his example, and then flagrantly violates (B*) himself by producing additional examples: courage amid perils at sea, in disease, poverty, pain (*La.* 191D1–E2). Thereupon he exhorts Laches to attend to this inventory of particular cases and search for the common character which is the same in each. That he is not merely describing general action-types but identifying particular action-tokens, that is, predicating "F" of specific actions and persons without a definition of F, is clear from his reference to the courage of the Scythian cavalry and from his concluding summation, "Now all these are courageous" (*Oukoun andreioi men pantes houtoi eisin, La.* 191E4). Similarly, at *Charm.* 159C3–160B5 Socrates easily disposes of Charmides' definition of Temperance as Quietness by producing examples of temperate actions which do not require quietness but quickness and agility, and then urges him to resume his search for a definition by investigating a wider range of cases. Euthyphro, too, is directed to "the numerous actions that are holy" (*tōn pollōn hosiōn*) and asked to state the *idea* "by which" they are holy (*Eu.* 6D9–E1). Far from eschewing examples until he has discovered the definition of the relevant moral or evaluational term, Socrates habitually operates on the opposite methodological principle that it is by means of a scrutiny of examples that the definition is to be achieved. For only by examining diverse instantiations of F can the inquirer be in a position to discern the *eidos* which is "the same in all cases," "includes all the various uses of the term," and constitutes "the universal nature that pervades them all" (*La.* 191E10–192B4). How could it be otherwise? If it is the F-ness common to things that are F that he wishes to discover, how could he systematically disallow a scrutiny of the very Fs *to which* it is common? What sense could anyone make of a request for that which all Fs have in common which included as one of its procedural stipulations that, in complying with it, one must not take into account any Fs?[12]

Not only does Socrates fail to rebuke his interlocutors for unlawful trafficking in examples as they search for definitions, he makes copious use of examples himself in refuting the definitions they proffer. Refutation by counterexample, typically a single counterexample, is one of his most characteristic elenctic strategies. Since in any adequate Socratic definition the members of the classes denoted by the *definiens* and the *definiendum* must be coextensive, counterexamples can be employed in a variety of ways. At *La.* 191D1–E2 Socrates rejects a definition by producing examples of the *definiendum* which are not covered by the *definiens:* there are cases of Courage other than remaining at one's post: at *La.* 191E1–3 by citing an example which is covered by the *definiens* but is clearly not a case of the *definiendum:* if Courage is wise endurance, then whoever endures in spending money wisely is courageous: at *Charm.* 159C3–160B5 by uncovering cases of the *definiendum* which have the opposite property of that expressed by the *definiens:* some temperate actions require not quietness but quickness; and at *Rep.* 331C5–9 by demonstrating that the *definiens* entails a moral judgment that is patently false: in response to Cephalus' definition of Justice as rendering to everyone his due, Socrates produces the celebrated counterexample of returning weapons to their mad, though rightful, owner—an action which must be pronounced just if the definition is to stand.

If Socrates holds (B*), how are these passages to be understood? How in *Rep.* I can Socrates' maneuver count as a refutation of Cephalus' definition if his philosophical methodology categorically prohibits him from employing the very counterexamples by which the refutation is accomplished? All these passages bear witness to the fact that Socrates does not hold (B*). He not only encourages his interlocutors to search for definitions by means of examples, he also proceeds in a manner which implies that any adequate definition must be compatible with those examples. Deny this compatibility requirement and Socrates' elenctic use of examples and counterexamples loses not only all cogency but all intelligibility. Socrates, then, has no *general* methodological objection to employing examples.

To say this is not to deny that there is a sense in which Socrates does invariably reject examples. But he does so only in one exceptional and methodologically isolated context, namely, whenever his interlocutor offers an example *as an answer* to the What-is-*F*? question. This move he never tolerates. Yet even as he rejects the example as an answer to his question, he is usually perfectly willing to accept it *as an example*.[13] Hence whatever "contemptuous" attitude Socrates may harbor toward the particular case, it is not a contempt *überhaupt* but rather a context-dependent and context-provoked protest against confusing definition with enumeration of instances—a protest which would be wholly superfluous if he really holds that without a definition it is impossible to enumerate instances. Why forbid the doing of what cannot be done? Hence those (perhaps too familiar) passages in which Socrates does reject examples as answers to the What-is-*F*? question entitle us to infer neither that the elenctic method makes no use of examples nor that he prohibits his interlocutors from searching for definitions by means of them. Once his interlocutor has assimilated the distinction between definition and enumeration of instances, Socrates is only too happy to work with examples. In fact, the elenchus could not get along without them.

I turn next to (A1). Since Geach rests his entire case on *Eu.* 6D9–E6, that passage warrants close scrutiny. Does Socrates here assert that knowing the definition of Holiness is a necessary condition for knowing that any action is holy? He does not. He does, however, make two other assertions: first, that knowing the definition of Holiness would be a sufficient condition for knowing what actions are holy; second, that such definitional knowledge alone can provide him with the "standard" he needs in the situation at hand. Clearly, then, he thinks that knowing the definition of Holiness is a necessary condition for doing *something*. But what? The answer is provided by the perplexity which precipitated the whole discussion: Socrates needs to know the definition of Holiness in order to adjudicate the controversial and borderline case of Euthyphro's pending suit against his father, i.e. in order to know whether Euthyphro's action is holy. That it is the extraordinary circumstances surrounding the Euthyphro case, rather than some general epistemic inability, which prompts the need for a "standard" is evident from the overall context of the dialogue as well as from the further textual consideration that of all the early, elenctic dialogues it is in the *Euthyphro* alone that this appeal to the eidetic standard as a necessary condition for advancing a knowledge-claim about a particular case occurs.[14] Little wonder, then, that Geach cites only this passage in support of ascribing (A1) to Socrates. His claim that its "fallacious" content is "paralleled" in "many other" places is not only undocumented but undocumentable.

My contention that, for Socrates, definitional knowledge of *F* is not a necessary condition for knowing that anything is an *F* should not be confused with a very different claim recently put forth by Santas:

> Socrates does not say or imply that without having a definition of holiness it would be impossible for him to say, in the sense of forming a judgment or belief, that a given action is holy. He says only that by using such a definition he would be able to tell whether a given action is holy. In short, the use of such a definition would be sufficient for determining whether a given action is of the defined kind; it is not necessary. . . . This is a fundamental point. If Socrates had held the view that the use of the definition of a given kind is necessary to determining whether a given thing is of that kind, he would have committed himself to consequences that are indeed very bad for anyone who makes the discovery and use of definitions an essential part of the search for knowledge.[15]

This latter view is precisely the view of the "Socrates" of *H.Ma.*, *Ly.*, and *Rep.* 354A12ff. And unlike his counterpart of the early, elenctic dialogues, who remains cheerful in the face of his failure to discover the correct answer to the What-is-*F?* question, this "Socrates" is acutely aware of the "very bad" consequences of which Santas speaks: anyone in such a state "might as well be dead" (*H.Ma.* 304E2–3). It is not, however, the view of the Socrates of the early dialogues.

But neither does he hold the view imputed to him by Santas—that definitional knowledge of *F* is a necessary and sufficient condition for *knowing* that anything is an *F* but not a necessary condition for having a *true belief* that something is an *F*. I am advancing a much stronger claim, namely, that although Socrates asserts that definitional knowledge of *F* is a sufficient condition for knowing what actions are *F* in general, he does not assert that it is a necessary condition for *knowing* that any action whatever is an *F*. Hence a person could, in principle, know that something is an *F* without knowing the definition of *F*.

Nor can (A1) be coaxed from the other passages often cited. At *Charm.* 176A6–B1, for example, Charmides does not say that without a definition of Temperance he cannot know that any actions are temperate but only that he cannot know whether *he* is temperate—a remark which is nothing but a more emphatic reaffirmation of the philosophically and psychologically intimidated state of mind to which he had already given vent at 159D1–6. We would be on textually thin ice indeed were we to elevate this embarrassed, boyish utterance to the status of a methodological axiom involving the full generality of (A1)—especially in view of the disconcerting fact that from 159C3–160B5 Socrates and Charmides had both proved remarkably adept at predicating "is temperate" of a host of actions.[16] Provided that Charmides is willing to assent to the general principle—itself a glaring violation of (A2)[17]—that Temperance is noble (*kalon*), which he is, Socrates can effortlessly demonstrate that "in all bodily activities" such as writing, reading, and playing the lyre (159C3–D6) as well as in the "searchings and deliberations of the soul" such as learning, remembering, and understanding (159E1–160B1) quickness and agility are "clearly better than," *and hence more temperate than,* slowness and quietness. Similarly, at *La.* 190B7–C2 Socrates does not put forth the completely general assertion that if you do not know the definition of *F,* you cannot know anything whatever about *F* or that anything whatever is an *F.* His claim is very specific and heavily qualified: if you do not know the nature of virtue, you cannot usefully advise anyone about how best to achieve it. Again, at *Eu.* 15C11–E2 when he mockingly declares that it is Euthyphro's uncommonly firm grasp of what the Holy is (*ti esti to hosion*) which enables him to know "precisely what is holy and unholy," he is again asserting only that definitional knowledge of *F* is a sufficient condition for knowing what things are *F,* not that it is a necessary condition. I conclude that there are no compelling textual reasons for ascribing (A1) to Socrates.

III. TWO POST-GEACH PROPOSALS AND BEYOND

But it is not enough to ransack the early dialogues for passages in which Socrates encourages his interlocutors to search for definitions by means of examples or employs them himself. Granted, Socrates makes copious and diverse use of examples; but what is their epistemic status?

Two mutually exclusive accounts have recently appeared, both based on the view that Socrates disavows all moral knowledge. According to one—the True Belief Theory (hereafter TB)—Socrates' appeals to examples and counterexamples should not be taken as knowledge-claims but as embodying true moral beliefs. According to the other—the Correct Use Theory (hereafter CU)—these same Socratic appeals should be taken neither as knowledge-claims nor as belief-claims.

First, CU. Recently championed by R. M. Hare, this strategy invests Socrates' philosophical method with a Wittgensteinian twist designed to place him on "safer ground."[18] In employing his examples and counterexamples, Socrates is not advancing truth-claims but appealing to the "linguistic fact" that such utterances, *whether true or false,* constitute "what we would say." In support of this interpretation Hare offers the following gloss on *Rep.* 331C5–9:

All of us would call the act of giving back weapons to a madman "not right"; this universal opinion, whether or not it is correct, is certainly not self-contradictory; so the definition which makes it self-contradictory, must be wrong. [H]ence a linguistic hypothesis about the meaning of a word . . . is refuted by showing that the linguistic facts do not square with it.[19]

But this account is at variance with the texts on every point. First, in casting Socrates in the role of an examiner of linguistic *hypotheses,* it misreports what he explicitly claims to be doing whenever he engages in elenctic argument and overlooks one of its announced conditions. "Contentiously eager to know what is true and false" (*Gorg.* 505E3–7), Socrates will enter into disputation only if his interlocutor is willing to lay himself on the line by saying what he really believes:

> Callicles, do not fancy that you should play games with me, and give me no haphazard answer contrary to your real opinion. (*Gorg.* 500B5–C1)[20]

His interlocutor may neither advance theses which he does not hold nor concur with those propounded by Socrates unless he sincerely assents to them. Having secured such a thesis, Socrates relentlessly applies the elenchus in an effort to determine whether it can withstand scrutiny and is therefore certifiable as an elenctically justified truth-claim. He does not appear noticeably interested in ascertaining what his interlocutor finds it necessary to say in light of certain alleged "linguistic facts."

Second, although Socrates periodically assures his interlocutor that he is simply "following the argument wherever it leads," this universally acclaimed profession of philosophical malleability should not be taken in any naively literal sense. Socrates does not passively follow the argument wherever *it* leads. The direction the argument takes is not vouchsafed to the elenctic practitioner by a presiding Cosmic Logos in relation to which he is merely the linguistically attuned and morally neutral medium. It is wholly dependent on the systematically operative, sometimes unargued, and often even unstated methodological assumptions and substantive assertions of the practitioner himself, e.g. his views about the nature and role of definition in philosophical analysis, his implicit ontology and epistemology, his theory of human nature, his first-order moral judgments, and his analogies between morality and the crafts. These factors determine the "direction" in which the argument leads. They are not only constitutive of the conceptual framework within which the discussion takes place, they also specify the preliminary substantive propositions about which the practitioner will attempt to elicit agreement from his interlocutor as well as the subsequent propositions required as premises entailing the negation of the theses targeted for refutation.

Ostensibly concerned with Socrates, CU in fact presents us with a philosophical method which is radically different from that of the early dialogues and which presupposes an equally radically different conception of philosophy itself and the reasons for engaging in it. In transforming the truth-seeking and unabashedly revisionist elenctic method into a use-clarifying and purely descriptive form of conceptual analysis, it leaves us with a Socrates who is all but unrecognizable—who, in effect, argues as follows: "Look here, Cephalus, you don't really want to say that it is just to return weapons to a madman, do you? Such a claim flouts ordinary language."

It is, of course, true that the unleashing of the madman counterexample by which Socrates executes the speediest refutation in the entire Platonic corpus is prefaced by an expression of his complete confidence that it will be endorsed by everyone (*Rep.* 331C5). But this is neither an empirical appeal to *consensus gentium* nor a logical appeal to Correct Use.[21] His confidence derives not from his expectation that the counterexample will accord with everyone's linguistic intuitions but from his philosophical conviction that it can itself withstand elenctic scrutiny and that he therefore has elenctic justification for asserting what everyone else would presumably be prepared to assert without such justification, namely, that the moral judgment "It is just to return weapons to a madman" is false. Far from trying to convict Cephalus of linguistic aberration, he is forcing him to choose between competing truth-claims. Cephalus must either affirm that it *is* just to return the weapons because the true definition of Justice is exactly what he said it is, or he must concede that it would be unjust to do so and withdraw his definition *as false*. He is refuted only if he opts for the latter. Which, of course, he does. But what if Cephalus had refused to budge, clung to his definition, and retorted, "Yes, it *is* just to return the weapons because, mad or not, they are his weapons"? Would this force us to conclude that in the very act of advancing a morally bizarre assertion Cephalus successfully undercuts Socrates' intended refutation? Apparently so. For, according to CU, in dealing Cephalus this *reductio*, Socrates has played his last logical trump and is left with an empty hand.

Something is very wrong here. Although the application of the elenchus begins with an attempt to secure agreement about some premise or premise-set, it is not shortcircuited if agreement is withheld; it is only delayed. If his interlocutor will not accept *q* as a counterexample to *p*, Socrates will either secure agreement about some more fundamental premise, *r*, or premise-set, *r* and *s*, which entails *q*, resume the argument, and demonstrate that *q*, to which his interlocutor has just assented, entails *not-p* (as he does at *La.* 196E1–199E12); or he will ignore *q*, secure agreement about some new premise, *s*, or premise-set, *s* and *t*, resume the argument, and demonstrate that it, too, entails *not-p* (as he does at *Gorg.* 482C4–516D5). Socratic counterexamples have no inherently "normative" status. He employs them not because they enshrine the logical bedrock of Correct Use, nor because they constitute the categorial framework of our language by appeal to which justification comes to an end and our practices take over, nor because it was by attending to such paradigmatic cases that his interlocutors originally learned the meanings of the terms in question. He employs them because these examples and counterexamples, together with the moral predications he makes about them, embody the best by way of truth-claims that he has been able to achieve by the practice of the elenctic method and which therefore serve as the touchstone against which all other alleged truth-claims are tested. By relying on theory-laden terms like "paradigm" and "linguistic facts," CU obscures all this and inadvertently foists upon Socrates a view of philosophy and philosophical discovery that is alien to him.

TB offers the very solution declined by CU. Convinced that Socrates holds (A1) and (A2), and thereby commits the Socratic Fallacy, its proponents try to mitigate the disastrous epistemic consequences by arguing that although he and his interlocutors have no definitions and hence cannot *know* what actions are courageous, temperate, or just, they can still have *true* moral *beliefs*. And that is precisely the epistemic status of the examples which Socrates accepts from his interlocutors and of the counterexamples which he employs against them.[22]

When confronted with the texts, however, TB fares no better than CU. Its apparent cogency derives from the fact that the concepts of knowledge and true belief occur in both the early and middle dialogues. Its central flaw lies in the contention that despite innovative metaphysical and epistemological developments in the middle dialogues concerning the respective objects of knowledge and true belief, the concepts of knowledge and true belief themselves are elucidated in fundamentally the same way and play identical epistemic roles. This is not so.

Proponents of TB speak rather loosely about *the* distinction between knowledge and true belief—as if this were a single distinction in the early and middle dialogues which, given Plato's increasingly frequent excursions into metaphysics and epistemology, is gradually elaborated: implicit but detectable at *Cr.* 44C6–47D5 and *Gorg.* 454B3–E9, somewhat more explicit at *M.* 97A6–98C3, and fully explicit at *Rep.* 476B3–478E7. This overlooks the fact that while the terms *epistēmē* and *orthē doxa* (or *pistis*) occur in the pre-*Meno* dialogues, they are not employed in the technical epistemic senses which they acquire in the *Meno* and post-*Meno* dialogues and which are presupposed by TB, that is, as connoting a greater or lesser cognitive achievement on the part of someone and hence a correspondingly greater or lesser degree of epistemic reliability on the part of the propositions he affirms. In the *Crito* Socrates draws a sharp contrast between those who know and those who believe, but only to remind Crito that of the diverse and fluctuating opinions of "the multitude" (*tēs tōn pollōn doxēs melei*, 44C6–7) he should respect the "useful" views (*tas chrēstas*) of the wise (*tōn phronimōn*), that is, those who know (*tō epistatē*) and understand (*epaionti*), and disregard the "useless" views (*tas ponēras*) of the foolish (*tōn aphronōn*, 47A7–B11). He is not propounding an important epistemic distinction but simply trying to dispel Crito's worries about how his reputation will suffer among Athenian rumormongers chattering about his failure to arrange Socrates' escape from prison. Similarly, at *Gorg.* 454B3–E9 the terms *epistēmē* and *pistis* are employed to draw an equally non-technical distinction between two kinds of persuasion: that which produces knowledge of the kind possessed by experts (masters of a *technē*) and that which produces belief without knowledge of the kind possessed by non-experts (sophists) who rely on rhetoric.

Socrates does not, of course, *deny* that some of his interlocutors have true moral beliefs, beliefs which, *if submitted for elenctic testing,* could survive; but he attaches no epistemic importance to them. It is not enough to believe propositions which happen to be true. Until the person holding such beliefs submits them for elenctic interrogation and discovers that they can survive, he necessarily lacks all epistemic warrant for believing them. Unless they are "buckled fast and clamped together . . . with arguments of steel and adamant" (*sidērois kai adamantinois logois, Gorg.* 508E6–509A2), and thus "become" knowledge, they remain unstable and are not an acceptable stopgap for the knowledge which, by liberating its possessor from the powerful solicitations of desire and appetite, is virtue. Hence while acknowledging the empirical fact of true moral beliefs, Socrates denies their theoretical importance and practical efficacy. Given his exclusively practical philosophical interests, urgent sense of discharging a divinely appointed mission, and views about the decisive role of knowledge in living the moral life, he opted for a different distinction—not between those who have knowledge and those who have true beliefs, but between those who have knowledge and those who do not.

It is not until *M.* 97A6 that we discover signs of a different philosophical mentality at work. Here we encounter the wholly unprecedented and decidedly un-Socratic claim that "for the purpose of acting rightly" true moral beliefs are "as good a guide (*hēgemōn*) as" knowledge (*M.* 97B5–7). This Socratic heresy is a clear forecast of the "Socrates" of the *Republic* who no longer thinks that those who lack knowledge should undergo elenctic cross-examination until, with their ignorance exposed, they take up the philosophic quest. By this time the state of mind called true belief is no longer the morally precarious plight of those whose assertions lack theoretical justification. It has become a *laudable* state of mind to be inculcated in all but the select few capable of attaining knowledge. Such views are utterly foreign to the pre-*Meno* Socrates who would have repudiated the central moral thesis on which the entire *Republic* is based—that virtue is achievable without knowledge by holding true moral beliefs on the authority of the philosopher-king and by performing one's function in the ideal state. For him, there can be no virtue without knowledge.[23] By importing these later views into the pre-*Meno* dialogues, TB misconstrues the purpose of the elenctic method—which is not to turn ignorance into belief or dubious belief into true belief but to turn true belief into knowledge and thereby escape from the unstable realm of true belief altogether.

Nor do the pre-*Meno* dialogues distinguish knowledge from true belief on the ground that each has a distinct object. That is also a later innovation of which the Socrates of the early dialogues knows nothing. In the pre-*Meno* dialogues the distinction between knowledge and true belief is a distinction between states of mind: if you have knowledge, the propositions you affirm will not run away like the statues of Daedalus but "stand fast" (*Eu.* 11B9–E5, 15B7–C3). In the post-*Meno* dialogues, on the other hand, the object of knowledge is the separately existing Form while the object of true belief is the sensible particular inextricably embedded in the world of flux. To know is no longer simply to affirm propositions bound by arguments of steel and adamant; it is to contemplate an eternal and transcendent *eidos*. The epistemic distinction between knowledge and true belief is grounded in the metaphysical distinction between the two worlds, and the "infallibility" of knowledge is parasitic on the immutability of its object—"the real" (*to on*) (*Rep.* 476E4–479E6, *Phdr.* 247C3–E6, *Sym.* 210E2–211D1). It is the character of the intentional object of knowledge, the Form, not the dialectical ability of the possessor of knowledge, which defines knowledge and invests knowledge-claims with their authoritative status. Just as changing sensible particulars "fall short" of unchanging intelligible Forms, so true belief, whose object is those very particulars, "falls short" of knowledge.

Socratic knowledge, that is, knowledge in the pre-*Meno* dialogues, neither has nor requires this transcendent metaphysical grounding. It is irreducibly propositional in character, and the same proposition serves as the object of both knowledge and true belief. That Socratic *epistēmē* and *orthē doxa* not only do, but must, have the same object—for different persons at the same time and, more importantly, for the same person at different times—is strictly entailed by Socrates' conception of knowledge and how it is acquired. Only if the proposition which serves as the object of *epistēmē* (for the person who knows that a is *F*) is identical with that which serves as the object of *orthē doxa* (for the person who truly believes that a is *F*) can the belief-claim "become" a knowledge-claim if and when its possessor justifies it with "arguments of steel and adamant." This claim is echoed—for the last time before giving way to the middle-period view that knowledge and true belief have distinct objects—at *M.* 98A3–4, a passsage which, though surrounded by doctrines absent from the pre-*Meno* dialogues—the theory of Recollection and belief in the immortality and pre-existence of the soul—retains the earlier Socratic view that knowledge and true belief have the same object and that true beliefs remain unstable until they are "tethered by working out the reason"[24] (*heōs an tis autas dēsē aitias logismō*) after which they acquire stability and "become" knowledge (*epeidan de dethōsin, prōton men epistēmai gignontai, epeita monimoi*).

Like knowledge in the middle dialogues, Socratic knowledge is ideally knowledge of the *eidos;* but our only hope of attaining it is by submitting theses for elenctic interrogation. Socratic *eidē,* however, are not separately existing Forms but common characters "present in" those particulars that "have" (*echon*) them (*Eu.* 5D3). Although Socrates has neither an explicit metaphysical theory of Forms nor an explicit epistemological theory as to how they can be known, he conducts the search for definitions in a way which suggests that our only access to the *eidos* is *via* its propositional counterpart—a Socratic definition whose *definiendum* is the relevant moral term and whose *definiens* purports to be an elenctically certifiable explication of the form "The *F* is such and such." Were they ever forthcoming, such definitions would constitute the highest kind of knowledge recognized by Socrates. At the same time, it cannot be emphasized too strongly that this is not the only kind of knowledge that he recognizes. Socratic knowledge is not coextensive with definitional knowledge. Nor do all knowledge-claims presuppose it. Lacking Socratic definitions, one need not therefore despair of all moral knowledge and settle for true moral beliefs. A second (and lower) kind of knowledge is available to anyone whose *non*-definitional assertions can withstand elenctic scrutiny: propositions either of the form "a is *F*" (which predicate some moral term of an action or person) or "The *F* is *Y*" (which predicate some moral quality of a virtue, for example, "Temperance is noble," or—to avoid tangential skirmishes involving Pauline predication—of an action or person exhibiting that virtue, for example, "Whatever or whoever is temperate is noble.")

Furthermore, contrary to TB (as well as to CU and the traditional interpretation), Socrates explicitly avows some moral knowledge of this second kind:

i. *Apol.* 29B6–7: "But I know (*oida*) that to do wrong and to disobey my superior . . . is wicked and dishonorable."

ii. *Gorg.* 486E5–6: "I know well (*eu oid'*) that if you agree with the opinions held by my soul, then at last we have attained the actual truth."

iii. *Gorg.* 512B1–2: "[H]e knows (*oiden*) that it is not better for an evil man to live, for he must needs live ill."

iv. *Prot.* 357D7–E1: "[Y]ou know yourselves (*iste pou*) that a wrong action which is done without knowledge is done in ignorance."

v. *Rep.* 351A3–6: "[I]f justice is wisdom and virtue, it will easily . . . be shown to be also a stronger thing than injustice, since injustice is ignorance—no one could now fail to know that" (*oudeis an eti touto agnoēseien*).

There is no getting around these passages.[25] Far from being "quite exceptional"[26]— mere textual curiosities to be marvelled at and then dismissed—they are the rock on which TB founders, a disproof of the thesis that Socrates claims no moral knowledge whatever.

But the case for ascribing some moral knowledge to Socrates does not depend on this handful of texts containing a tiny range of strong epistemic verbs such as *oida, epaiō, epistamai,* or *gignōskō.* In addition to these passages in which Socrates advances explicit knowledge-claims there are numerous others which contain implicit knowledge-claim indicators, that is, semantically different but epistemically equivalent modes of expression: for example, when Socrates asserts that his thesis has been "proved true" (*apodedeiktai hoti alēthē elegeto, Gorg.* 479E8); that "the just man has revealed himself to us (*hēmin anapephantai*) as good and wise and the unjust man as ignorant and bad"

(*Rep.* 350C10–11); that the previous argument "has rightly compelled them to agree (*orthōs anankasthēnai homologein en tois emprosthen logois*) that no one does evil voluntarily" (*Gorg.* 509E4); that "the sound-minded and temperate man, being, as we have just demonstrated (*hōsper diēlthomen*), just and brave and pious, must be completely good" (*Gorg.* 507C1–5); and that "we can now tell who are our friends, for the argument shows us (*ho gar logos hēmin sēmainei*) that it must be those who are good" (*Ly.* 214D8–E1). Similarly, when in response to Polus' admission that it will be difficult to refute the Socratic thesis that, of all evildoers, those who escape punishment are the unhappiest, Socrates replies, "Not difficult . . . but impossible, for the truth is never refuted" (*Gorg.* 476B10–11), this strong epistemic claim need not be confined to the particular thesis under discussion but is applicable to any thesis which, bound by arguments of steel and adamant, is supported by the full weight of the elenchus. And the Socratic corollary—"unless you or one still more enterprising than yourself can undo [these arguments], it is impossible to speak aright other than I am now speaking" (*ouch hoion te allōs legonta ē hōs egō nun legō kalōs legein, Gorg.* 509A3–4)—can be generalized so as to cover a wide range of elenctically justified propositions. Such passages disclose the Socratic criterion of non-definitional moral knowledge which is operative throughout the early dialogues. That criterion is elenctic justification. Hence we may legitimately ascribe moral knowledge to Socrates in any passage in which that criterion is satisfied. It follows that in the absence of explicit contextual disclaimers we are justified in concluding that Socrates advances all such propositions as *known truths.*

In restricting all knowledge-claims to the null class of Socratic definitions and propositions derivable from them and relegating all other assertions, including elenctically justified assertions, to the epistemic sub-class of true moral beliefs which remain "tentative" and always "up for discussion,"[27] TB overlooks something else. The irreducibly propositional character of Socratic knowledge entails that even definitions of the kind envisaged by Socrates, were they ever forthcoming, would remain equally tentative. Even if Socrates and his interlocutors were well supplied with Socratic definitions which had *so far* survived elenctic scrutiny, they would still not enjoy the infallible, non-tentative knowledge of the middle dialogues. For the object of their knowledge would not be a separately existing *eidos* of which they have a "direct vision" but a propositional explication of that *eidos* which, however it may have fared in the past, is always open to future refutation.

In addition to this textual evidence there is a philosophical reason for ascribing some moral knowledge to Socrates.[28] If, with TB, we deny this, then while he may have some true moral beliefs, we cannot on his own grounds *assert* that he does. That this is so may be seen by asking how, within the context of Socratic thought, we are to determine whose moral beliefs are true. What is Socrates' criterion of a true moral belief? Not elenctic justification, for that is his criterion of non-definitional moral knowledge. But while not itself the criterion, it yields one: to have a true moral belief is to affirm a moral judgment identical with that affirmed by the person who has moral knowledge. In short, the criterion is *agreement with* the "expert in right and wrong" (*epaiōn peri dikaiōn kai adikōn*), the "one authority who represents the actual truth" (*ho heis kai autē hē alētheia, Cr.* 48A6–7). But if TB is correct in claiming that neither Socrates nor his interlocutors has any moral knowledge, then there are no moral experts and hence no non-vacuous criterion by which to determine whose moral beliefs are true—a situation which, far from constituting an improvement upon ignorance, is a form of it. That is why Socrates thinks that we must move beyond belief—even true belief—to knowledge. It remains true that the propositions which Socrates affirms today may prove elenctically unjustifiable tomorrow, but that is not sufficient to call them into question. Having renounced the quest for the absolute certainty that comes with infallibility, he is prepared to live with that risk.

This, then, is Socratic *epistēmē*—the knowledge which, by providing theoretical understanding and the resultant education of desire, brings with it those affectional readjustments which enable its possessor to achieve the only human happiness worth having and of which no one is voluntarily ignorant. In the *Republic* Plato was later to pursue with almost unparalleled moral earnestness the question of how the "philosophi-cal element" in the soul can be preserved against the corrupting influence of evil and mediocrity, and recommended a rigorous program of study culminating in a synoptic vision of reality—the world of "true Being" which every soul pursues "with an intuition of its nature, yet . . . unable to apprehend it adequately" (*Rep.* 505D11–E2). In Socrates' hands the claims are more modest and metaphysically chaste. But while the language is not his, he shares the concern. A corresponding exhortation resounds through the early dialogues enjoining men to rise above the opinions of "the Many." In the end the gentle irony and unsparing criticism converge on the same goal—not simply to call men to virtue but to hover about them like a gadfly, never allowing them to rest content with what they believe and with what they are, even if what they believe is not wholly false and what they are is not wholly ignoble. Yet in the attempt to improve one's soul, one must start where one is—with the fallible and piecemeal insights of examples and particular cases. The road to knowledge begins with what is before one's very eyes, and one embarks upon it not, as the later Plato would have it, by a vertical flight of the soul in which one by degrees takes leave of the sensible world in search of a more exalted metaphysical object but by a horizontal expansion of the understanding—by discoursing with Socrates about matters as commonplace as who is taking whom to court. As the elenchus brings greater understanding, the propositions one affirms will grow less confused, less prone to inconsistency, less vulnerable to counterexamples. In this way true belief is gradually turned into knowledge.

It is, of course, open to anyone to disagree with Socrates about any or all of this. But no critique can carry conviction unless it manages to convey the power of his moral vision and respond to it at the same level of experience, forgoing the easier project of detecting alleged "fallacies" in his alleged "thought." I have no doubt that (A1), (A2), and (B*) are fallacious. For all I know, they may be morally harmful as well. But whatever they are, they are not Socratic.

NOTES

This essay is a revised version of a paper presented to Professor Gregory Vlastos' NEH Seminar "The Philosophy of Socrates" at the University of California at Berkeley, Summer, 1983. I am grateful to him for encouragement and painstaking criticism. For further valuable commentary, I am indebted to Paul Woodruff and an anonymous referee for the *American Philosophical Quarterly*.

1. "Plato's *Euthyphro:* An Analysis and Commentary," *The Monist,* 50 (1966), pp. 369–82.
2. Ibid., p. 372. I.e. in the sense that it is morally injurious to persuade someone that he "must suspend judgment as to whether swindling is unjust until he has water-tight definitions of 'swindling' and 'unjust.'" P. T. Geach, *Reason and Argument* (Berkeley, 1970), p. 40.
3. Ibid.
4. By "Socrates" I mean the Socrates of Plato's early dialogues including *Apol., Charm., Cr., Eu., Gorg., H.Mi., I., La., Prot.,* and *Rep.* I through 354A11 but excluding *Eud., H.Ma., Ly.,* and the remainder of *Rep.* I. Concerning this distinction within the traditionally recognized early dialogues I accept Vlastos' classification of the latter as post-elenctic, "transitional" dialogues between Plato's early and middle periods. (See "The Socratic Elenchus," *Oxford Studies in Ancient Philosophy,* 1 (1983), pp. 25–28, 57–58.) Given this schema, the *Meno,* long regarded as *the* transitional dialogue, must be viewed as containing further explorations of the logical, methodological, and epistemological innovations already present in them. Chief among these innovations is the unambiguous (and decidedly un-Socratic) assertion of (A): at *H.Ma.* 304D8–E3: "How can you know whose speech is beautiful or the reverse—and the same applies to any action whatever (*allēn praxin hēntinoun*)—when you have no knowledge of beauty?" (Cf. 286C5–D2); at *Ly.* 223B4–8: "[W]e have made ourselves rather ridiculous today . . . for our hearers will carry away the report that though we conceive ourselves to be friends . . . we have not yet been able to discover what we mean by a friend" (*oupō de hoti estin ho philos hoioi te egenometha exeurein*); and at *Rep.* 354C1–3: "[I]f I don't know what the just is, I shall hardly know whether it is a virtue . . . and whether its possessor is or is not happy." This so-called "priority of definition" thesis is also explicitly asserted in full generality at *M.* 71B3 where "Socrates" declares: "I have no knowledge about virtue at all" (*ouk eidōs peri aretēs to parapan*), for "how can I know a property of something when I don't even know what it is?" Accordingly, a distinction must be made between the "Socrates" of these dialogues (a thinker whose views are often radically at odds with those of his counterpart in the early dialogues and who does indeed commit the Socratic Fallacy) and the Socrates of the early dialogues (who, as I will argue, does not).
5. The phrase is Wittgenstein's. See *The Blue and Brown Books* (Oxford, 1958), p. 19.
6. Nor is he the last. See R. E. Allen, *Plato's 'Euthyphro' and the Earlier Theory of Forms* (London, 1970), pp. 71–72, 78, 115–17, and *The Dialogues of Plato,* vol. I, tr. with analysis by R. E. Allen (New Haven, Conn., 1984), pp. 33–34, 142; M. F. Burnyeat, "Examples in Epistemology: Socrates, Theaetetus and G. E. Moore," *Philosophy,* 52 (1977), pp. 381–98; H. F. Cherniss, "The Philosophical Economy of the Theory of Ideas," in *Studies in Plato's Metaphysics,* ed. by R. E. Allen (London, 1970), pp. 1–12; N. Gulley, *The Philosophy of Socrates* (London, 1968), p. 9; W. K. C. Guthrie, *A History of Greek Philosophy* (Cambridge, 1969), vol. III, p. 352; T. Irwin, *Plato's Moral Theory* (Oxford, 1977), pp. 40–41, and *Plato Gorgias* (Oxford, 1979), pp. 113, 221, 224; G. Santas, "The Socratic Fallacy," *Journal of the History of Philosophy,* 10 (1972), pp. 127–41, and *Socrates* (Boston, 1979), pp. 116–17, 311–12; C. C. W. Taylor, *Plato Protagoras* (Oxford, 1976), pp. 212–13; and P. Woodruff, *Plato Hippias Major* (Indianapolis, 1982), pp. 139–41.
7. See I. M. Crombie, *An Examination of Plato's Doctrines* (London, 1962), vol. I, p. 57; P. Friedländer, *Plato* (Princeton, N.J., 1964), vol. II, p. 85; R. Robinson, *Plato's Earlier Dialectic* (Oxford, 1951), p. 51; and W. D. Ross, *Plato's Theory of Ideas* (Oxford, 1951), p. 16. Robinson speaks for many in declaring that "the impression vaguely given by the early dialogues as a whole is that there is no truth whatever about [*F*] that can be known before we know what [*F*] is."
8. See J. Burnet, *Plato's Euthyphro, Apology of Socrates and Crito* (Oxford, 1924), p. 37; P. Shorey, *What Plato Said* (Chicago, 1933), p. 157; and A. E. Taylor, *Plato: The Man and His*

Work (London, 1937), p. 47. G. Grote is one of the rare exceptions. He endorses neither (A) nor (B) and goes to great textual lengths to show that Socrates "never altogether lost his hold on particulars." *Plato and the Other Companions of Socrates,* vol. I, 2nd ed., (London, 1867), p. 326. Cf. pp. 307, 327, 477–80, 491, 498.

9. Dissenters include R. E. Allen, *Plato's 'Euthyphro,'* pp. 89, 115–16; R. M. Hare, *Plato* (Oxford, 1982), pp. 38–42; A. Nehamas, "Confusing Universals and Particulars in Plato's Early Dialogues," *Review of Metaphysics,* 29 (1975), pp. 287–306; H. Teloh, *The Development of Plato's Metaphysics* (University Park, Penn., 1981), pp. 20–21; G. Vlastos, "Socrates' Disavowal of Knowledge," *Philosophical Quarterly,* 35 (1985), pp. 23–26; and Woodruff, *Plato Hippias Major,* pp. 139–41. See also Burnyeat, Irwin, and Santas (cited in note 6).

10. That Socrates' appeal to examples leads straight to self-contradiction is limpidly, albeit inadvertently, exhibited by Guthrie who, after claiming that, for Socrates, "until [the meaning of *F*] has been fixed, so that we have a standard . . . to which the individual actions and objects can be referred, we shall not know what we are talking about" (*History,* p. 352), adds that in searching for a definition of *F* "the first [stage] is to collect instances to which both parties agree that the name [*"F"*] may be applied." *Socrates* (Cambridge, 1971), p. 112. That is, in searching for a definition we are to consult the very examples that we cannot identify until we have one.

11. As a corrective to the "priority of definition" thesis, it is worth observing that of the thirteen traditionally recognized early dialogues only six even raise the What-is-*F*? question. The elenchus is conducted more often without it than with it.

12. I am not at this point claiming that these "identifications" of courageous, temperate, and holy actions count as knowledge-claims. I will consider this interpretation of their epistemic status (together with its denial) in Section III.

13. *Eu.* 4E13–17 is an exception.

14. At *Gorg.* 474D3–9 Socrates asks Polus whether he "looks to nothing" (*eis ouden apoblepōn*) in calling fine things "fine," but he is not invoking the *eidos* as standard. Rather, one looks to see whether they are called "fine" because of their usefulness or because of some pleasure they afford (*kata tēn chreian . . . ē kata hēdonēn tina*). Similarly, when Socrates asks what Nicias "has in view" as he defines Courage, he is not alluding to the *eidos* as standard but querying him about whether he thinks that Courage, Justice, and Temperance are all "parts" of virtue. (*La.* 198A4–5) Nor does he allude to it at *Charm.* 175D6–E2 or *Prot.* 360E6–361D6.

15. *Socrates,* p. 116. Cf. p. 69.

16. See n. 13.

17. Three further violations of (A2) occur at *Charm.* 160E9, E11, and E13 as well as at *La.* 192C5–7, 8–9, amd 192D7–8. Other violations of both (A1) and (A2) are found at *Cr.* 54D4–6, *Gorg.* 474B2–4, *Prot.* 329E6–333B4, and *Gorg.* 470D9–11.

18. *Plato,* p. 42. Cf. Woodruff (*Plato Hippias Major*): "The 'Socratic' Fallacy is supposing that a person cannot use a word correctly unless he can define it. That is a fallacy but Socrates does not commit it." (p. 139) However, Woodruff's apparent espousal of CU is rendered problematic by his simultaneous appeal to Socrates' "body of tested opinion." (p. 140)

19. Ibid.

20. Cf. *Cr.* 49D1–3, *Prot.* 331B6–D1, *Gorg.* 491A7–9, and *Rep.* 346A2–5.

21. Although Socrates' counterexamples are carefully calculated so as to elicit the immediate assent of his interlocutors, this is not an appeal to "what we would say." At *Gorg.* 471E2–472A1 he declares: "[Y]ou are trying to refute me . . . like those . . . in the law courts. For there one group imagines it is refuting the other when it produces many reputable witnesses to support its statements. . . . But this method of proof is worthless toward discovering the truth." When the elenchus requires it, Socrates thinks nothing of flouting the

"linguistic facts" by affirming propositions that are universally denied or by denying propositions that are universally affirmed: e.g. that it is worse to do than to suffer wrong, that no one does evil voluntarily, and that one ought never to return evil for evil.

22. See Burnyeat, Irwin, Santas (cited in n. 6), and, more recently, G. Klosko, *The Development of Plato's Political Theory* (New York, 1986), pp. 30–34.

23. Hence I cannot accept Santas' contention that, for Socrates, true moral belief is sufficient for virtue. *Socrates,* pp. 192–93.

24. In "working out the reason" one discovers the cause *(aitia)*, i.e. the F—the *mia idea*—"by which" all Fs are F. *(Eu.* 6D11)

25. Although Socrates frequently disavows all moral knowledge, he also occasionally avows some. If recent contributions to the literature prove anything, it is that on the vexing question of whether Socrates claims any moral knowledge purely textual considerations are inconclusive: not because there is insufficient evidence for either view but because there appears to be sufficient evidence for both. If, as the growing consensus among contemporary commentators suggests, Socrates' disavowals are sincere (as opposed to "feigned," "ironic," "deliberately provocative," etc.), then in avowing what he simultaneously disavows he is either contradicting himself or asserting these apparent contradictories in different senses. See G. Vlastos, "Socrates Disavowal," and R. Kraut, *Socrates and the State* (Princeton, N.J., 1984), pp. 267–79.

26. Irwin's assessment of *Ap.* 29B6–7. *Plato's Moral Theory,* p. 58.

27. See Burnyeat, pp. 386–87.

28. And, strange as it may seem, to some of his interlocutors as well. See *Prot.* 357D7–E1 and *Rep.* 351A3–6.

FURTHER READING

Benson, H. H. 1990. "The Priority of Definition and the Socratic Elenchus." *Oxford Studies in Ancient Philosophy* 8:19–65.

Geach, P. T. 1966. "Plato's *Euthyphro:* An Analysis and Commentary." *Monist* 50:369–82.

Irwin, T. 1977. "Socratic Method and Moral Theory." *Plato's Moral Theory: The Early and Middle Dialogues,* 37–101. Oxford.

Nehamas, A. 1986. "Socratic Intellectualism." *Proceedings of the Boston Area Colloquium in Ancient Philosophy* 2:275–316.

Santas, G. 1972. "The Socratic Fallacy." *Journal of the History of Philosophy* 10:127–41.

Vlastos, G. 1985. "Socrates' Disavowal of Knowledge." *Philosophical Quarterly* 35:1–31.

Woodruff, P. 1987. "Expert Knowledge in the *Apology* and *Laches:* What a General Needs to Know." *Proceedings of the Boston Area Colloquium in Ancient Philosophy* 3:79–115.

8

Misunderstanding the "What-is-F-ness?" Question

HUGH H. BENSON

Over a decade ago Alexander Nehamas successfully called into question a long-standing tradition in Socratic scholarship.[1] According to this tradition, the initial answers to Socrates' "What is F-ness?" question (the WF-question) frequently reflected a confusion between universals and particulars.[2] The interlocutors frequently provided concrete particulars, when what was asked for was a universal.[3] Nehamas persuasively argued that such a view misreads the interlocutors' initial attempts to answer the WF-question. They do not provide concrete particulars. They provide universals, albeit universals that are not sufficiently broad to answer the question correctly. In carefully examining these initial attempts and showing that the answers are universals, not concrete particulars, Nehamas has provided a real service.[4] Unfortunately, he has also raised a real problem—a problem which has not been sufficiently noted or sufficiently resolved. After briefly reviewing Nehamas' argument, I will describe the problem and offer a solution.[5]

A REVIEW OF NEHAMAS' ARGUMENT

Nehamas' argument presupposes a clear distinction between universals and concrete particulars. Unfortunately, drawing such a distinction is not as easy as one might suppose.[6] We can, however, adopt the following intuitive, if not completely accurate, Aristotelian account.

> Something is a universal just in case it is predicable of a plurality of things, and something is a concrete particular just in case it is not.[7]

Thus, for example, Socrates, Laches, and Socrates' standing his ground at Delium are concrete particulars (the first two are concrete particular objects, the third is a concrete particular action), while human, standing one's ground at Delium, and courage are all universals (the first is predicable of at least Socrates and Laches, the second of at least Socrates' standing his ground at Delium and Laches' standing his ground at Delium, and the third is paronymically[8] predicable of at least all four). Notice that on this account of the distinction universals and concrete particulars are mutually exclusive. While a universal may be more or less particular (courage and standing one's ground at Delium are more particular, because predicable of fewer things, than are virtue and standing one's ground, respectively), it can never be a *concrete* particular.

Given this distinction between universals and concrete particulars, we can quickly run through Nehamas' argument. In the dialogue named for him, Euthyphro's initial attempt to answer the "What is holiness?" question is as follows:

(T1) I say that the holy is that which I now do, prosecuting the wrong-doer whether concerning murder or temple-robbery or doing any other wrong of this sort, whether this person happens to be your father or your mother or anyone else such as this, and not to prosecute is unholy. (5d8–e2)

Euthyphro's answer here is straightforward: the holy is prosecuting the religious wrong-doer. But prosecuting the religious wrong-doer is clearly not a concrete particular. It is predicable of a number of actions (e.g., Euthyphro's prosecution of his father, and Meletus' prosecution of Socrates). In fact, the point of most of (T1) is to suggest that it is not even a very particular universal. Euthyphro does not merely say that the holy is prosecuting one's murderous father, itself a universal because predicable of Euthyphro's and others' prosecutions of their murderous fathers; he says that the holy is prosecuting the religious wrong-doer, which is predicable not only of concrete particular prosecutions of murderous fathers, but of concrete particular prosecutions of temple-robbing mothers, of Herm-mutilating strangers, and of many others.

It is true that Euthyphro begins his answer by saying that the holy is that which he now does, but Nehamas correctly explains this as resulting from the context of the "What is holiness?" question (p. 290). Socrates is asking him to say what holiness is in order to justify his present action. Thus, Euthyphro answers: I am justified in acting as I am because I know that my present action is holy. I know that it is holy because I know that it is a concrete particular of the universal prosecuting the religious wrong-doer and I know that prosecuting the religious wrong-doer is what the holy is.[9]

In the dialogue named for him, Laches' initial attempt to answer the "What is courage?" question is as follows:

(T2) This is not difficult to say; for if someone remaining in the ranks is willing to face the enemy and not flee, know well that he is courageous. (190e4–6)

Again, Laches' answer is clear: Courage is remaining in the ranks and facing the enemy without fleeing. Equally clearly, remaining in the ranks and facing the enemy without fleeing is not a concrete particular. On the contrary, it is truly predicable of numerous fifth-century Athenian and Spartan hoplites.

Finally, in the dialogue named for him, Meno's initial attempt to answer the "What is virtue?" question is as follows:

(T3) This is not difficult to say. First, if you want a man's virtue, it is easy to say that it is being able to manage the city's affairs, to treat well one's friends, to harm one's enemies, and to avoid suffering harm oneself. If you want a woman's virtue, it is not difficult to say that she must manage the household well, preserve its possessions, and obey her man. And there is another virtue for a child, both male and female, and for an older man, and, if you wish, for a freeman and for a slave. And there are many other virtues besides, so that one is not at a loss to say what virtue is. (71e1–72a2)

Unlike Euthyphro and Laches, Meno does not give a single answer to the WF-question. But he does not give a plurality of concrete particulars either. Instead, he gives a plurality of universals. He says that "manly" virtue is managing the affairs of the city, treating well one's friends, harming one's enemies, and avoiding harm to oneself. Managing the affairs of the city, treating one's friends well, harming one's enemies, and avoiding harm oneself, however, are presumably truly predicable of a number of successful fifth-century Athenian politicians. Managing the household well, preserving its possessions, and obeying one's man, which he says constitute "womanly" virtue, are universals, unfortunately probably truly predicable of a number of fifth-century Athenian women. He does not tell us what the other virtues are; if he had, there is every reason to think his answers would have been of the same form. They would have been universals, not concrete particulars.

In all three of these cases, then, the interlocutors do not initially respond to the WF-question by providing a concrete particular, thereby revealing their confusion concerning universals and particulars. All three of these answers are universals, albeit not sufficiently general universals to count as correct answers. But these are the primary texts for the tradition.[10] Surely, Nicias' "Courage is wisdom" (194d4–5; cf. 194d8–9), Charmides' "Temperance is a kind of quietness" (159b5–6), Cephalus' "Justice is truth-telling and paying one's debts" (331c1–5), Polemarchus' "Justice is rendering to each his due" (331e3–4), and Thrasymachus' "Justice is the advantage of the stronger" (338c2) are not answers in which what is provided is a concrete particular. Thus, Nehamas is surely correct to conclude that the interlocutors do *not* "tend to provide concrete instances of the universal in question rather than a definition, however inadequate, of the universal itself" (p. 287). Not only do the interlocutors not *tend* to do this, it appears that they never do. In fact, the point seems so obvious that it is difficult to imagine how the tradition arose in the first place.

THE PROBLEM

We can begin to see how the tradition might have arisen, if we turn to the problem which Nehamas' point engenders. As Nehamas is quick to point out, we need not be surprised when, for example, Charmides' initial answer to the WF-question is the right sort of answer, a universal, not a concrete particular. So is every other interlocutor's initial response, including Euthyphro's, Laches', and Meno's.[11] Why, then, does Socrates object in these last three cases, and only in these cases, that his interlocutors have misunderstood the question?

After Laches answers the "What is courage?" question by saying that courage is remaining in the ranks and facing the enemy without fleeing, Socrates blames himself for the fact that Laches has failed to answer the question that he meant to ask.

(T4) You speak well, Laches; but perhaps I am to blame, by not speaking clearly, for your failure to answer the question I meant to ask, but a different one. (190e7–9)

(T5) This is what I meant just now when I said that I was to blame for your failure to answer well, by not asking well. (191c7–8)

This leads him to ask the question more clearly (191e9–11) and when Laches does not yet completely understand (191e11–12), Socrates appeals to the example of the "What is quickness?'' question in order to clarify his meaning. Laches follows this clarification with his second attempt at answering the ''What is courage?'' question.

(T6) It seems to me now that courage is an endurance of the soul, *if it is necessary to mention the thing which is essential in all these cases* (192b9–c1; emphasis added)

suggesting that Laches now has understood the question. This suggestion is not spoiled by Socrates. For he does not blame his speaking unclearly for the inadequacy of Laches' second answer.

In the *Euthyphro,* Socrates follows the initial answer that holiness is prosecuting the religious wrong-doer by saying:

(T7) Try now to say more clearly what it is I just now asked you. For, my friend, you have not taught me sufficiently when I asked what the holy is, but you said to me that this happens to be holy which you are now doing, in prosecuting your father for murder; (6c9–d4)

(T8) Remember that I did not ask you to teach me one or two of the many holy things, but this form itself by which all the holy things are holy. (6d9–11)

Euthyphro follows this by saying that *if this is what Socrates wants* (6e7) (cf. (T6)), then holiness is what is dear to the gods, his second attempt to answer the ''What is holiness?'' question. This leads Socrates to say

(T9) Very nice, Euthyphro, as I wanted you to answer, so you have answered. Whether you have answered truly, I do not yet know. (7a2–4)

This last passage is instructive. Euthyphro's initial answer fails to be an appropriate answer, but (T9) makes clear that its inappropriateness does not lie in its failing to be true. Euthyphro's second answer does not suffer from the same inadequacy as his first: unlike his first attempt, he has now answered as Socrates wants. And yet, whether his second answer is true remains to be examined. (T9) makes clear, then, that, according to Socrates, Euthyphro's initial answer is not merely materially incorrect. It is in some way formally incorrect.

Finally, Socrates responds to Meno's initial answer by saying

(T10) While seeking one virtue, I have found a swarm of virtues posited by you (72a6–7),

which after appealing to the bee-analogy he explains

(T11) Even if the virtues are many and various, nevertheless they all have some one and the same form, through which they are virtues and at which it is appropriate to look for the one answering the request to make clear what virtue happens to be. (72c6–d1)

Meno, however, does not yet completely understand Socrates' question.

(T12) Soc.: Or don't you understand what I say?
        Meno: I think I understand, but perhaps I do not grasp what is being asked as I wish. (72d1–3)

And so, Socrates attempts to explain it further by appealing to the examples of strength, size, and health. Meno, however, appears to be peculiarly thick-headed. His third attempt to answer the WF-question appears to suffer from the same misunderstanding.

(**T13**) Again, Meno, we have suffered the same thing; again, we have found many virtues while seeking one, although in a different way. (74a7–8)

Socrates follows this with the longest explanation of his WF-question to be found anywhere in the corpus: 74b–77a.

In all three of these dialogues the suggestion is the same. According to Socrates there is something peculiarly wrong with Laches', Euthyphro's, and Meno's initial attempts to answer the WF-question, something from which their subsequent answers do not suffer.[12] This is explicit in the *Euthyphro* at (T9), but it is clearly suggested in the *Laches* and *Meno* by Socrates' assumption that the two interlocutors have misunderstood the question. His assumption is confirmed by Laches' own admission a bit later (191e11–12) and Meno's uncertainty in (T12). It is because Laches and Meno do misunderstand his question that Socrates attempts to explain it by appealing to the examples of quickness, bee-ness, strength, size, health, shape, and color. The only other dialogue in which Socrates attempts to explain his WF-question is the *Hippias Major*.

Comparing this dialogue with the *Laches, Euthyphro,* and *Meno* will prove instructive. At 287c–d Socrates explains to Hippias that in asking him "What is fineness?" he means to be asking him "What is that thing by which all fine things are fine?" Hippias claims to understand the question (287e2–3), and offers his first answer.

(**T14**) A fine maiden is fine. (287e4)

(T14) is the fourth passage frequently cited on behalf of the traditional view that the initial answers to the WF-questions are concrete particulars, not universals. But notice that Socrates does not object to (T14) in the same way he has objected to the initial answers of Euthyphro, Laches, and Meno. He has already explained his WF-question and Hippias has claimed to understand it. Socrates takes him at his word. He does not, therefore, object to the formal character of the answer. Rather, he objects to Hippias' initial answer in a similar way to the way in which he objects to Euthyphro's *second* answer.

(**T15**) Then, upon being asked what the fine is, do you reply with something which is no more fine than mean, as you yourself admit. (*Epeita . . . erōtētheis to kalon apokrinēi ho tunchanei on . . . ouden mallon kalon ē aischron;* 289c3–5; cf. *Eu.* 8a10–12: *Ouk ara ho ēromēn apekrinō . . . ou gar touto ge ērōtōn, ho tunchanei tauton on hosion te kai anosion*).

It is because Socrates does not object to (T14) in the same way that he objects to Euthyphro's, Laches', and Meno's initial answers that Nehamas must be right that both Hippias and Socrates understand (T14) in something like the following way:

Being a fine maiden is the fine.

So understood, however, even Hippias' initial attempt to answer the WF-question is not a concrete particular. Being a fine maiden is truly predicable, fortunately, of many women.

This brief digression concerning the *Hippias Major* exhibits how the traditional interpretation provides an answer to the problem with which this section of the essay began. It is a virtue of the tradition that we can explain why Socrates' response to the initial answers of Euthyphro, Laches, and Meno is so different from his response to the initial answer of Charmides, for example. Socrates thinks that Laches and Meno have misunderstood his question because, like Euthyphro, they have given formally incorrect answers. They have all provided concrete particulars, when in order to provide an even potentially correct answer to his WF-question one must provide a universal. Nehamas has helpfully shown us that this explanation will not suffice. Euthyphro, Laches, and Meno do not provide concrete particulars. Unfortunately, Nehamas has not supplied an alternative explanation. It will be the purpose of the remainder of this essay to do just that.

THE PROBLEM RESOLVED

In order to explain why Socrates objects to Euthyphro's, Laches', and Meno's initial answers in the way that he does, given Nehamas' correct account of those answers, we need to draw more carefully than we have so far the distinction between formally and materially correct answers. We can do this by borrowing from the work of Belnap and Steel on the logic of questions.[13]

According to Belnap and Steel a which-question,[14] which for present purposes can be identified with Socrates' WF-question,[15] can be usefully divided into two parts: its subject and its request. The *subject* of a which-question presents the alternatives from which a respondent is to choose in giving his response by means of a matrix and one or more category conditions. Thus, to use one of their examples, the alternatives presented by the subject of the question "Which primes lie between 10 and 20?" are determined by the matrix

x is a prime between 10 and 20

and the category condition

x is an integer.

That is, the respondent must choose his answer from propositions of the form "x is a prime between 10 and 20," where what is substituted for x is an integer.

The *request* of a which-question specifies the number of the alternatives to be selected and whether or not that selection is to be complete.[16] Thus, for example, the question "What are two examples of primes between 10 and 20?" requests that exactly two alternatives be selected without the commitment that these are the only primes between 10 and 20.

According to Belnap and Steel, an answer that fails to satisfy the category condition makes a category mistake (p. 33). Thus, for example, to answer the question "What are two examples of primes between 10 and 20?" with the proposition "A triangle and a square are primes between 10 and 20 and there are others" would be to make a category mistake. It would not simply be to give an incorrect answer. It would be to give an incorrect *kind* of answer. Analogously, to give as an answer the proposition "13 is a prime between 10 and 20 and there are others" or "13 and 17 are primes between 10 and 20 and there are no others" would be to violate the request of the question. The first violates the number-of-alternatives constraint and the second violates the completeness constraint. Thus, these two answers too would not be merely incorrect answers: they would be incorrect kinds of answers. Both of these sorts of mistakes might reasonably be called formal mistakes, while an answer which satisfied the category condition and the request of the question but failed to satisfy the matrix would be materially incorrect.

Armed with this distinction between formally and materially incorrect answers, we can now see how the traditional view explains why Socrates takes Euthyphro's, Laches', and Meno's initial answers to his WF-question to suggest their misunderstanding of the question. The subject of the WF-question presents its alternatives by means of the matrix

(m) is F-ness[17]

and the category condition

(c1) x is a universal.

According to the tradition, Laches and Euthyphro give answers of the form "x is F-ness" whose substitution instances are concrete particulars, not universals, and thereby violate the category condition. They make a category mistake. Thus, Socrates concludes that they have misunderstood his question. They have given an answer which is not even among the alternatives presented by the question. How, though, are we to explain Socrates' response, given that, as we have seen, these answers do not violate the category condition "x is a universal?"

Perhaps we have simply failed to specify sufficiently the category conditions presented by the subject of the WF-question. As I have said the alternatives are presented by means of a matrix and one *or more* category conditions. Perhaps, we simply need to specify other category conditions presented by the WF-question which Euthyphro's, Laches', and Meno's first answers violate. This is not, however, an altogether promising approach.

It is true that Belnap and Steel permit a considerable degree of flexibility in specifying the category conditions,[18] but if the distinction between formal and material correctness is not to become uninteresting, there must be some fairly non-arbitrary constraint on what can count as a category condition. One fairly natural constraint, suggested by the name "category condition" itself, is that the predicate position of a category condition can be filled only by the name of some fairly pre-theoretical kind. A kind is pre-theoretical, in the sense I have in mind here, just in case whether a thing is a member of that kind can be determined without already knowing a great deal about the material correctness of the answer to the question.[19] Thus, for example, while supplementing (c1) with

(c2) x is true of all and only F-things

would serve to explain Socrates' response, (c2) hardly serves to restrict the substitution instances of x to any pre-theoretical kind. A similar difficulty besets

(c3) x is not a kind of F-ness.[20]

In both cases it is not so much that the conditions fail to pick out a set of entities composing some natural kind. One can certainly imagine developing a theory committed to such kinds of things. The difficulty is that such a categorization can hardly be thought to be pre-theoretical. It is difficult to imagine that one could be in any position to determine that an answer failed to satisfy (c2) or (c3), without knowing a great deal about the material correctness of the answer to the relevant WF-question. But if the distinction between formal and material correctness is to be the least bit interesting, we need to be able to recognize the formal adequacy or inadequacy of an answer long before determining its material adequacy or inadequacy. Thus, supplementing the category condition in these ways would serve to spoil the formal/material distinction.

There is a second difficulty for this approach: we run the risk of supplementing the category condition with conditions whose violations would *not* be viewed by Socrates as a formal error. Thus, for example, as I will suggest, although Socrates objects to Meno's second answer on the grounds that it fails to satisfy (c2), he does not regard the answer as formally incorrect (cf., also *La.* 197c, 193c, *Charm.* 161d–e, *Ly.* 212b, *H. Ma.* 288b–e). It would appear, then, that failure to satisfy (c2) does not amount to formal incorrectness according to Socrates. And so, supplementing the category condition with (c2) would be inappropriate.

In the end, however, I must concede that should there be no other way to resolve the difficulty engendered by recognizing that the initial answers of Euthyphro, Laches, and Meno do satisfy the category condition ''x is a universal,'' we would be compelled to resolve it by supplementing the category condition. Doing so, however, would, I suspect, have the unfortunate consequence of making the intuitive and straightforward distinction which Socrates appears to be making in response to those answers considerably less intuitive and straightforward. Fortunately, there is another approach for resolving this difficulty.

Consider Meno's initial answer at (T3) and Socrates' response at (T10) and (T11). Meno has answered by providing a number of universals. Socrates objects that only one universal was sought. That is, Socrates understands his WF-question to require an answer which species only one thing, while Meno has offered an answer specifying a number of things. Adopting Belnap and Steel's terminology, Socrates understands his WF-question to consist of a request which specifies that only one of the alternatives be selected. Meno, however, has misunderstood the question and takes its request to permit that a number of alternatives be selected. It is as if Socrates had asked Meno ''What is one example of a prime between 10 and 20?'' and Meno had answered ''13 *and* 17.'' Meno has not merely failed to give a correct answer: he has failed to give the correct kind of answer. Meno's answer is formally, not merely materially, incorrect.

But this is not the only point Socrates makes in explaining his question to Meno here. It is not simply that his question calls for an answer which specifies only one thing; it also requires that the thing be the same in every case. That is, the answer must refer to the unique thing that is virtue. Once again, we can use Belnap and Steel's terminology to clarify the point. The point Socrates is making is that the request of his WF-question specifies that only one alternative be selected and that the selection be complete. In such a case the request specifies the uniquely true alternative. It is this condition which Euthyphro's and Laches' initial answers and Meno's third answer violates. Before seeing this, let us quickly glance at Meno's second answer.

At *Meno* 73c, Socrates once again asks his ''What is virtue?'' question, hoping that by now Meno has understood the question. Meno responds as follows:

(T16) What else is it than the ability to rule over men, if you seek the one thing which holds in every case? (73c9–d1)

The answer is formally correct. ''The ability to rule over men'' is an appropriate substitution instance of the matrix ''x is virtue.'' It satisfies the category condition ''x is a universal." It provides the correct number of selected alternatives specified by the request, that is, it selects only one alternative, and finally the *eiper* clause displays Meno's commitment to the completeness of this selection. According to Meno the one and only universal which can be substituted for the x in "x is virtue" resulting in a true answer to the question, "What is virtue?" is "the ability to rule over men." Thus, as I understand the logic of the WF-question, Meno's second attempt is formally correct. Socrates seems to understand the logic of his question similarly. He does not object to this answer on the grounds that it is the wrong kind of answer. Instead he suggests that it is the right kind of answer, but the wrong one of that kind.

> (T17) That is indeed what I seek. But is the virtue of a boy and a slave the same as the ability to rule over a master? (73d2–4)[21]

Notice that whether an answer is formally correct is not always self-evident. This is not because formal correctness relies on an extensive background theory, but because in ordinary conversation our answers are frequently ambiguous. This is especially the case when it comes to the answer's completeness commitment. Thus, for example, when in response to the question "What are the primes between 10 and 20?" I say "13 and 17," whether this answer is formally correct will depend upon whether I have intended the answer "13 and 17 are primes between 10 and 20 and there are no others" or "13 and 17 are primes between 10 and 20 and there are others." In the former case, my answer will be formally correct but materially incorrect; in the latter case, it will be formally incorrect.[22] Normally the context of the conversation would make clear that I intended the former answer. But, one can imagine contexts in which I should be understood to have intended the latter answer, and so to have misunderstood the question.[23] What is noteworthy about (T16) is that the *eiper* clause makes Meno's completeness commitment explicit. He cannot reasonably be thought to have intended that there were other equally true alternatives that might have been selected. He cannot, then, be reasonably thought to have misunderstood the question.

Secondly, notice that the number of alternatives to be selected together with the completeness request of the WF-question, leads to the most controversial presupposition of that question. If we assume that every well-formed question has a true answer, then the well-formedness of the WF-question presupposes that *there is* one and only one true alternative to be selected which can be substituted in the matrix "x is F-ness" and satisfies the category condition "x is a universal." Such a presupposition many Sophists, especially of the Gorgianic stripe, would want to deny.[24] It is not insignificant, then, that when Socrates attempts to explain the request of his WF-question to Meno, whose association with Gorgias has already been mentioned, we find him providing an argument, however inadequate, that there is one and only one true alternative to be selected in answering the "What is virtue?" question.[25]

We can now quickly see how Euthyphro's and Laches' first answers and Meno's third answer fail to be formally correct. All three answers are appropriate substitution instances of the matrix "x is F-ness," satisfy the category condition "x is a universal," and provide the correct number of selected alternatives, one. None of them, however, satisfies the completeness requirement.

In the *Euthyphro,* immediately after Socrates complains that Euthyphro has failed to teach sufficiently what the holy is, that is, in effect, that he has failed to answer the question Socrates meant to ask, (T4), we get the following exchange.

(T18) EUTH.: But, I have spoken truly, Socrates.
SOC.: But, Euthyphro, you would say that there are many other things that are
        holy.
EUTH.: There are indeed. (6d6–8)

We discover here that Euthyphro did not intend that "prosecuting the religious
wrong-doer" is the only alternative that might have been selected in order to answer
the "What is holiness?" question. Other alternatives might have been selected, although
they presumably would not have been as relevant to the particular case at hand. (T18),
of course, is immediately followed by (T8), Socrates' reminder that he did not
ask for one or two holy things, but the form itself by which all holy things are
holy.

Similarly in the *Laches,* after Socrates apparently agrees that the one who remains in
the ranks and fights the enemy is courageous (cf. the *isōs* at *Eu.* 6d6), he asks Laches
what he thinks of those who fight the enemy not remaining, but fleeing like the
Scythians. Laches replies

(T19) The cavalry fight [courageously] as you say, the infantry fight [courageously] as I
        say. (191b5–7)

Again we discover that, according to Laches, in the case of cavalry-fighting another
answer to the "What is courage?" question would have been appropriate. His answer,
remaining in the ranks and fighting the enemy, was only one of a number of appropriate
alternatives which might have been selected had he been thinking of other types of
fighting. He did not intend his answer to be complete, but only to be one example of what
courage is. Socrates goes on to point out that he does not even intend it to be a complete
answer to the question "What is courage in the case of the infantry?" to which Laches
readily agrees. Socrates, thereupon, blames himself for not asking the question clearly,
(T5), and, after expanding considerably the kinds of actions in which courage can be
exemplified (191c8–e7), attempts to explain what his "What is courage?" question is
requesting (191e9–192b8).

Finally, we come to Meno's third attempt to answer the "What is virtue?" question.
Meno says

(T20) Justice is virtue. (73d9–10)

Socrates' next two questions immediately reveal that Meno did not intend his answer to
be complete. Meno quickly admits that what he meant was that justice is *a* virtue (*aretē
tis* 73e1). That is, he intended "justice" to be only one of a number of true substitution
instances of the matrix "x is virtue."[26] Others which might have been selected are
"temperance and wisdom and magnificence and very many others" (74a5–6). It is
appropriate, then, that once again Socrates objects to Meno's answer on the grounds that
it is the wrong kind of answer, (T13), and attempts to explain it to him.

This last passage, however, highlights an unfortunate inadequacy of the account I
have put forward. I have been attempting to provide a relatively straightforward and non-
arbitrary distinction between formal and material correctness which can explain why
Socrates responds to the various answers to his WF-question as he does. With this
passage from the *Meno* a certain sort of arbitrariness has sneaked back in. Given a
particular understanding of the answer, whether it is formally and/or materially correct is

non-arbitrary. But whether an answer is understood as complete does appear to allow for a certain degree of arbitrariness.

Compare Socrates' response to Meno's third answer with his response to Hippias' first. Both answers are preceded by an explanation of the WF-question. Both answers are preceded by the suggestion that the interlocutor understands the question. Hippias explicitly claims to understand it, while Meno provides a formally correct answer at (T16). Nevertheless, Socrates understands Hippias' answer to be committed to completeness and Meno's not.

Frequently there are features of the context of the question and answer which will suggest, and even sometimes require, one understanding rather than another. Thus, for example, Euthyphro's, Laches', and Meno's readiness to assent to there being F-things not covered by their initial answers might reasonably be thought to suggest that they did not intend their answers to be complete. That the things Socrates cites subsequent to their answers are F-things meets with no resistance and requires no argument. Nevertheless, I see no reason to deny that there will be contexts in which how the answer is to be understood is radically under-determined. Which understanding Socrates chooses in these cases will be fairly arbitrary. It may simply depend on how charitable Socrates feels toward the interlocutor. This is not a defect of my account. If anything, it is a defect of ordinary conversation. It is both a virtue and a vice of Plato's method of philosophical exposition.

CONCLUSION

I have attempted to draw our attention to a problem which arises when we correctly recognize that, contra the tradition, no interlocutor attempts to answer the WF-question by providing a concrete particular. The problem is why does Socrates respond so differently to the initial answers of Euthyphro and Laches and to Meno's first and third answers than he does to any other answer, whether from these interlocutors or others. The solution I have proposed borrows heavily from Belnap and Steel's work on the logic of questions, but it should not be thought to rely essentially upon this work. The solution can be put less formally: Socrates has asked Euthyphro, Laches, and Meno a question of the form "What is the one and only universal that is F-ness?" but he understands their initial answers to be of the form "x is a universal that is F-ness but there are others." They have not given concrete particular instances of F-ness, but they have nevertheless misunderstood his question. They have failed to grasp its presupposition. Socrates, thereupon, sets out to make the question clear. This is what is new, or, at least, controversial, about Socrates' question: it has only one answer.[27] Euthyphro, Laches, and Meno understood perfectly well that Socrates' question required a universal for an answer. What they failed to understand was that only one universal would do.

NOTES

I wish to thank Michael Hand, Alexander Nehamas, Gregory Vlastos, and Roslyn Weiss for their useful comments and criticisms of earlier versions of this essay. Of course, any errors or obscurities that remain are mine alone. Finally I would like to thank the National Endowment for the Humanities and Gregory Vlastos for the Summer Seminar, "The Philosophy of Socrates," held at the University of California, Berkeley, 1988, during which this essay was put in its present form.

1. A. Nehamas, "Confusing Universals and Particulars in Plato's Early Dialogues," *Review of Metaphysics* 29 (1975), 287–306. (Henceforth, all references to Nehamas are to this essay.) By "Socrates" in this essay, I refer to the Socrates of Plato's early dialogues (see n. 5). While I am inclined to believe that the "Socrates" of these dialogues is the historic one, none of the subsequent argument depends on this belief.

2. In an influential paper Vlastos calls the Socratic question the "What is F?" question (G. Vlastos, "What Did Socrates Understand by his 'What is F?' Question," in *Platonic Studies* [Princeton, 1976], 410–17; see also R. Robinson's "What is x?" question in *Plato's Earlier Dialectic* [Oxford, 1953], followed by G. Santas, *Socrates* [London, 1979]). I believe, however, that such a name for his question is misleading. It invites the following substitution instances: "What is courageous? holy? just?" These, however, are potentially misleading. As a result I prefer to call the Socratic question "the 'What is F-ness?' question." ("The 'What is the F?' question" would do just as well.)

   My point here is not that Socrates could not have asked his question in the predicative form. As Professor Nehamas has suggested to me in correspondence, Euthyphro's answer in (T1) and Laches' answer in (T2) suggest that he could. (Professor Vlastos had also made a similar suggestion.) Rather, my point is simply that referring to the Socratic question as "the 'What is F?' question" invites a misunderstanding that referring to it as "the 'What is F-ness?' question" does not. That Socrates might have agreed is suggested by *H. Ma.* 287d3–6 and the fact that in those dialogues in which the WF-question is explicitly raised (see n. 5) Socrates always introduces it by substituting into the open question either a noun (*La.* 190e3, *andreia; Charm.* 159a10, *sōphrosunēn;* and *M.* 71d5, *aretēn*) or a substantive (*Eu.* 5d7, *to hosion; H. Ma.* 286d2, *to kalon;* and *Rep.* 354b4–5, *to dikaion*).

3. On behalf of the tradition Nehamas cites J. Burnet, *Plato's Euthyphro, Apology of Socrates, and Crito* (Oxford, 1924), 32; R. E. Allen, *Plato's Euthyphro and the Earlier Theory of Forms* (New York, 1970), 70; and I. M. Crombie, *An Examination of Plato's Doctrines* (London, 1962), 44.

4. See, e.g., M. C. Stokes, *Plato's Socratic Conversations* (Baltimore, 1986), 62, and P. Woodruff, "Expert Knowledge in the *Apology* and *Laches:* What a General Needs to Know," *Proceedings of the Boston Area Colloquium in Ancient Philosophy* (1987), 25, n. 25 who recognize Nehamas' service.

5. The WF-question, it should be noted, is not omnipresent. Of the fourteen traditionally accepted early dialogues (in alphabetical order: *Apol., Charm., Cr., Eud., Eu., Gorg., H. Ma., H. Mi., I., La., Ly., Mx., Prot.,* and *Rep.* I) only five unqualifiedly raise it: *Charm., Eu., H. Ma., La.,* and *Rep.* I. (In the case of *Rep.* I the WF-question is not explicitly raised until the end (354b4–5), although, it is clearly an attempt to answer this question.) The *Lysis* might be included in this list because it does attempt to answer a related question: What is a friend?, although this question is never explicitly raised. The *Protagoras* and *Gorgias* also raise the WF-question to a certain extent, but it is clearly not their primary concern (see, e.g., *Gorg.* 462c10–d2 and *Prot.* 312c1–4). Finally, the first third of the *Meno,* a dialogue which is usually considered transitional, raises the WF-question.

6. See esp. P. F. Strawson, "Particular and General," and N. Wolterstorff, "On the Nature of Universals," both in M. J. Loux (ed.), *Universals and Particulars: Readings in Ontology* (New York, 1970).

7. See, e.g. *De Int.* 7, 17a38–b1, *Met.* B4, 999b34–1000a1, and Z13, 1038b16. I should not be thought here to endorse the view that this is Aristotle's account of this distinction. See H. H. Benson, "Universals as Sortals in the *Categories,*" *Pacific Philosophical Quarterly* (1988), 282–306.

8. See *Cat.* 1, 1a12–15.
9. My view of the context of the "What is holiness?" question differs in important ways from Nehamas' view. But for the purposes of the present argument these differences can be set aside. We agree that Socrates is prodding Euthyphro to answer his "What is holiness?" question in order to make good on this claim to know that his prosecution of his father is holy. I discuss this issue further in "The Priority of Definition and the Socratic *Elenchus*," *Oxford Studies in Ancient Philosophy* (1990), 19–65.
10. I here postpone discussion of *H. Ma.* 287e4; see pp. 127–28.
11. Nehamas (249) notes Santas' surprise: "All the definitions [of temperance in the *Charmides*] have the generality required of a Socratic definition. Unlike most typical Socratic dialogues where a definition is sought, Charmides and Critias do not begin by giving the wrong *kind* of definition . . . somehow they seem to know the sort of thing that Socrates is after, which is rather surprising in the case of Charmides at least since he just met Socrates for the first time." (G. Santas, "Socrates at Work on Virtue and Knowledge in Plato's *Charmides*," in *Exegesis and Argument* (Van Gorcon, 1973), 110.)
12. I recognize that Socrates does sometimes object to subsequent answers on the grounds that they are answers to the wrong questions (see, e.g., *Eu.* 8a–b and *H. Ma.* 289c–d). But to raise this objection is not necessarily to object that the answers are of the wrong sort. Every incorrect answer, whether it is the right kind or not, can be understood as a correct answer to some question.
13. N. Belnap and T. Steel, *The Logic of Questions and Answers* (New Haven, 1976).
14. Which-questions are distinguished from whether-questions in virtue of their presentation of alternatives. Whether-questions present a finite set of alternatives, which set is explicitly (or nearly explicitly) contained in the question. For example, the whether-question "Is it raining or snowing?" presents the alternatives "It is raining" or "It is snowing" as the only alternatives from which the respondent can choose. Which-questions "present their alternatives by reference to a matrix and one or more category conditions" (Belnap and Steel, 22).
15. Accuracy demands that I point out that Socrates' WF-question should really be identified with Belnap and Steel's equivalence version of what-questions (82–84). Discussing the WF-questions in these terms, however, would only serve to complicate the otherwise simple points to be made here. As a result throughout this essay I will be understanding the WF-question as a which-question. The resulting inaccuracy is more than made up for, I believe, by the relative ease and clarity of the explanation.
16. I here leave out the distinctness condition for the sake of brevity.
17. Santas' (*Socrates,* 59–96) valuable contribution to understanding the WF-question concentrates primarily upon filling out the details of the matrix and drawing out its presuppositions (see esp. 72–83). This is important for determining which answers will count as materially correct, not which answers will count as formally correct. As a result for the purposes of this essay I can be content with the very general matrix "x is F-ness." For related discussions, although put in different terms, see P. Woodruff, *Plato: Hippias Major* (Indianapolis, 1982), and R. Kraut, *Socrates and the State* (Princeton, N.J., 1984). There is obviously a great deal of similarity between the account I provide in this essay and Santas' important study. The present account differs from his in at least three ways (ordered from least to most important): 1. I borrow from a more recent and, I believe, more perspicuous account of the logic of questions. 2. Santas is apparently unpersuaded by Nehamas' argument. 3. As a result, he is not concerned about the different ways in which Socrates responds to his interlocutors' answers.
18. Belnap and Steel are adamant about pointing out that they are not in the business of specifying for a given English which-question the correct logical structure. Rather they are only committed to the view that such a question has a logical structure consisting of a matrix and one or more category conditions, whatever they may be, determining its alternatives, and a

selection size specification and completeness claim, whatever they may be, determining its request. Thus, they permit us a considerable amount of flexibility.

19. The distinction that I am drawing here is a matter of degree (n.b. the *"fairly* pre-theoretical" and "knowing *a great deal* about the material correctness''): the less pre-theoretical a kind is, the less appropriate is the category condition that employs it.

20. This is, I believe, the most popular way of resolving our difficulty, insofar as one is aware of the difficulty: Socrates' interlocutors reveal their misunderstanding of the WF-question by giving kinds of F-ness rather than F-ness itself. See, e.g., Santas, *Socrates,* who seems to think that Euthyphro's first answer violates both (c1) and (c3): "It is clear from this answer that Euthyphro is selecting from a set of alternatives that consist of individual actions and types of actions and that he is taking himself to be giving a few examples of actions or types of actions that are holy or possibly a complete list of actions or types of actions that are holy" (78).

21. Note the slight parallel with *Eu.* 6e7–7a3 and *La.* 192b9–c3.

22. Note that the ambiguity does not lie in the question. "What are *the* primes between 10 and 20?" is equivalent to, although perhaps slightly less perspicuous than, "What are *all* of the primes between 10 and 20?"

23. I have been told that it is difficult to imagine such a context. Consider, then, the following example. I am conversing with France's foremost mathematician. She speaks English, but not very well. I ask her "What are the primes between 10 and 20?" and she responds "13 and 17." In this case, it seems to me much more plausible to suppose that she has misunderstood my question and intended the answer "13 and 17 are primes between 10 and 20 but there are others" than that she thinks that 13 and 17 are the only primes between 10 and 20.

24. R. S. Bluck (*Plato's Meno* [Cambridge, 1961] 201) seems to think that in the special case of *aretē* at any rate, it is not a presupposition that even the common man would be prone to accept. He writes "it was not supposed that *aretē* would be the same for a woman as for a man, or indeed that *aretē* would be the same whatever one's age," and cites Pindar, *Nem.* 3, 72ff. and A. W. H. Adkins, *Merit and Responsibility: A Study in Greek Values* (Oxford, 1960), 190.

25. N.B. Neither Laches nor Euthyphro, neither of whom have any sophistic leanings, require an argument.

26. Another way of understanding Socrates' objection here is that Meno has misunderstood the matrix of the WF-question. As I have explicated the question its matrix is "x is F-ness," but Meno might seem to understand it to be "x is an F-ness." I have no strong quarrel with this objection, but it does I believe have some difficulty in accounting for why Socrates says in (T13) that the third answer suffers from a similar difficulty as the first.

27. See Nehamas, 303 and Santas, *Socrates,* 83.

FURTHER READING

Nehamas, A. 1975. "Confusing Universals and Particulars in Plato's Early Dialogues." *Review of Metaphysics* 29:287–306.

Robinson, R. 1953. "Socratic Definitions." *Plato's Earlier Dialectic,* 49–60. Oxford.

Santas, G. 1979. *Socrates,* esp. 59–135. London.

Vlastos, G. 1976. "What Did Socrates Understand by His 'What is F?' Question?" In *Platonic Studies,* 2d ed., ed. G. Vlastos, 410–17. Princeton, N.J.

Woodruff, P. 1982. *Plato: Hippias Major,* esp. 136–60. Indianapolis, Ind.

9

Elenchus and Mathematics:
A Turning-Point in Plato's
Philosophical Development

GREGORY VLASTOS

At some time in the course of his life Plato acquired such thorough knowledge of mathematics that he was able to associate in the Academy on easy terms with the finest mathematicians of his time, sharing and abetting their enthusiasm for their work.[1] The *Academicorum Philosophorum Index Herculanensis* (ed. Mekkler, p. 17) goes so far as to picture Plato as "masterminding" (*architektonountos*) the researches of his mathematical colleagues. This we may discount as eulogistic blow-up. Not so its further statement that Plato "set problems" to the mathematicians. Elsewhere[2] I have argued for the credibility of the well-known report in Simplicius:[3]

> **T1 Simpl.,** *in de Caelo* **488.21–24:** "Plato had set this problem to those engaged in these studies: What uniform and ordered motions must be hypothesized to save the phenomenal motions of the wandering stars?"

There is no good reason to doubt that Plato had been the first to project the idea that the apparently inconstant motions of the planets could be accounted for by compositions of invariantly constant circular motions proceeding in different planes, directions, and angular velocities. If Plato could hit on this powerful and fertile notion which "under the name of the Platonic axiom was to dominate theoretical astronomy for twenty centuries"[4] and could propound it in a form which would strike Eudoxus and other practicing astronomers not as a pretty fancy but as a workable hypothesis, he must have been accepted by them as no dabbler in their business but as a student of their subject who understood it so well that his vision of progress in it might even be at certain points ahead of theirs.

But even if all those reports had perished, we would still be in a position to know that by the time Plato came to write the middle books of the *Republic* he had studied mathematics in depth. We could infer this directly from the place he gives it in the studies he prescribes for the rulers-to-be of his ideal polis. A whole decade of their higher education, from their twentieth to their thirtieth year, he reserves for the mathematical sciences of the day—number theory, geometry, celestial kinematics,[5] and theoretical harmonics—for just these subjects to the exclusion of every other, even philosophy.[6]

From this prescription, coupled with Plato's stated rationale for it, we could infer two things:

> *First,* that by this time Plato's own mathematical studies had been sufficiently far-ranging and thorough to convince him that this was no subject for amateurs: if philosophers are to benefit from it, they must invest in it effort as intense and prolonged as that expected nowadays from those preparing for a vocation as research mathematicians.
>
> *Second,* that it was in the course of pursuing such studies himself and to some extent *because* of them that Plato had reached the metaphysical outlook that characterized his middle period.

The first inference is self-explanatory. The second I base on Plato's testimony to the power of mathematics to yield more than intellectual training—to induce a qualitative change in our perception of reality which may be likened to religious conversion:

> **T2 *Repulic* 521C1–523A:** "Shall we next consider how men of this quality are to be produced and how they may be led upward to the light, as some are fabled to have ascended from Hades to the gods? . . . This will be no matter of flipping over a shell, but the turning about (*periagōgē*) of the soul from a day that is as dark as night to the true day."

Immediately after saying this Plato proceeds to locate this turn-about of soul in the study of mathematics:

> **T3 *Republic* 521C10–523A3:** "Should we not ask which study has this power? . . . What is that study, Glaucon, that pulls the soul away from becoming to being (*mathēma psuchēs holkon apo tou gignomenou epi to on*)? . . . It seems to belong to those studies we are now investigating which naturally lead to insight, for in every way it draws us towards reality (*helktikōi onti pantapasin pros ousian*), though no one uses it aright."

This passage comes immediately after the political corollary of the allegory of the Cave has been drawn, namely, that only those redeemed from the ontological bemusement (476Bff.) which is the common lot of unregenerate humanity, only those privileged few, may be trusted with the absolute power over their fellows to be enjoyed by Plato's philosopher kings. What the passage purports to disclose is how this soul-transforming change can come about—how creatures of time and sensuality may be liberated from the empire of the senses, translated into another form of life in which love for timeless truth will dwarf other desires and ambitions. Improbable as such a mutation may seem, impossible as it would certainly be in Plato's view for the mass of mankind, it can nonetheless be achieved, he believes, by those who study mathematics with the seriousness, the concentration, the prolonged application which is implied by that ten-year immersion in the science.

That only those twice-born souls would Plato credit with competence to make authoritative judgments on matters of right and wrong could be inferred from his conviction that in the moral domain, no less than others, bona fide knowledge requires apprehension of eternal forms. But Plato does not leave this as a matter of inference. He insists that critical discussion of the basic concepts of morality is prohibitively risky for the populace at large, and not only for them—even for the philosophers-to-be prior to the completion of mathematical propaedeutics. Only after their decade of mathematical studies should they be permitted to enter discussions of right and wrong:

T4 *Republic* **539A8–B2:** "If you don't want to be sorry for those thirty-year-olds[7] of yours, you must be extremely careful how you introduce them into such discussions. One lasting precaution is not to let them have a taste of it while they are still young."

for if they come to it unprepared they would be sure to be corrupted. Premature exposure to such inquiry will undermine the beliefs about right and wrong inculcated in them from childhood and they will lose their moral bearings: they will be "filled with lawlessness" (583E4).[8]

Where in the annals of Western philosophy could we find a sharper antithesis to this restriction of ethical inquiry to a carefully selected, rigorously trained elite than in the Socrates of Plato's earlier dialogues? Not only does he allow question-breeding argument about good and evil to all and sundry, he positively thrusts it on them. He draws into his search for the right way to live the people he runs into on the street, in the marketplace, in gymnasia, convinced that this outreach to them is his god-given mission:

T5 *Apology* **28E:** "The god has commanded me that I should live philosophizing, examining myself and others."

The central theme of this "philosophizing" is that for each and every one of us, citizen or alien,[9] man or woman,[10] the perfection of our own soul must take precedence over every other concern: money, power, prestige, and all other non-moral goods are trivial by comparison with the awful importance of reaching that knowledge of good and evil which is the condition of moral excellence and therewith the condition of happiness. Such knowledge one cannot expect to get from Socrates or from anyone else, living or dead. One must seek it for oneself by "examining" one's own moral beliefs and those of others:

T6 *Apology* **38A:** "The unexamined life is not worth living by man."

He invites everyone to join in this cooperative inquiry—most particularly the young,[11] from whom he gets a warm response.[12]

The method by which Socrates "examines himself and others," which I shall be calling "the elenchus" throughout this paper, involves a form of argument which Aristotle calls "peirastic":[13] a thesis is refuted when, and only when, its negation is derived "from the answerer's own beliefs" (*ek tōn dokountōn tōi apokrinomenōi, Soph. El.* 165b3–5). And the only constraint Socrates imposes on his respondents, apart from giving answers that are short and to the point, is that they should say only what they believe:

T7 *Gorgias* **495A:** "Callicles, you'll ruin our previous arguments and will no longer be examining the truth with me if you speak contrary to what you believe."[14]

Aristotle (loc. cit.) contrasts the "peirastic" form of argument with another which he calls "dialectical," whose premises are "reputable opinions" (*endoxa*).[15] Peirastic argument could easily be mistaken for this alternative, since Socrates says nothing about the epistemic status of the premises from which he deduces the negation of the refutand: so long as he is himself satisfied, for whatever reason, that those premises are true, he accepts the interlocutor's agreement to them without proceeding to ask or give any reasons for them in that argument. *A fortiori* he does not appeal to their being "reputable opinions," though this is in fact what most of them are, and a superficial observer could easily get the impression that he always argued from such premises. That impression would be groundless. Socrates does not say or imply any such thing. That multitudes, with "wise" men of high repute at their head, subscribe to an opinion would leave Socrates cold. Opinions matter for him only if they are the interlocutor's own:

> **T8** *Gorgias* **427B–C:** "If I cannot produce one man—yourself—to witness to my assertion, I believe that I shall have accomplished nothing on the matter we are debating. Neither will you, I believe, if you do not bring this one man—myself—to witness for your assertions, letting all those others go."

The only other form of argument which Aristotle distinguishes from the "peirastic" as firmly as from the "dialectical" is the one he calls "demonstration" (*apodeixis*). This he defines as follows:

> **T9 Aristotle,** *Topics* **100a27–b21:** "There is demonstration when the premises are true and primary (*ex alēthōn kai prōtōn*). True and primary are those which yield conviction not through some other thing but through themselves (*ta mē di' heterōn alla di' hautōn echonta tēn pistin*). For in regard to the first principles of knowledge one should not proceed to ask the reason why (*ou dei epizēteisthai to dia ti*): each of the first principles should yield conviction by itself (*autēn kath' heautēn einai pistēn*)."

What Aristotle is saying is best grasped with reference to the axiomatized science geometry was coming to be by his time:[16] as Greek mathematicians understood their science, the axioms[17] constitute the reason which can be given for every proposition in it while, short of an infinite regress, no further proposition could be given in that science as the reason for any of them. For such indubitably certain termini to inquiry there is no place at all in Socratic elenchus. Here no opinion is ruled out for being out of line with principles "known through themselves." Every thesis, no matter how offbeat, is a fit subject for "examination" if put forward seriously as the speaker's personal belief. What could be more perversely eccentric than Thrasymachus' thesis that justice is the interest of the stronger, or Callicles' view that to do injustice is more honourable (*kallion*) than to suffer it? But Socrates debates both without the least reluctance—in fact, with enthusiasm: he is overjoyed to have the chance to investigate propositions which he thinks many believe or half-believe in their heart while they lack the outspokenness[18] to own up to them in public.

From this description of the elenctic method as practice of peirastic argument four things follow:

1. In form the method is adversative. Declining at the start of an elenchus to give his own answer to the question under debate, Socrates' formal role in any given argument is not to defend a thesis of his own but only to "examine" the interlocutor's.[19]

2. But since Socrates' real purpose is not merely to search out and destroy his interlocutors' conceit of knowledge but to advance the search for truth, if he is to find it by this method, while professing to know nothing, he must worm it out of *them*. He must derive it from true premises, accepted as such by his interlocutors. Hence the strategic import of the "say what you believe" rule. If his interlocutors were to decline compliance with this rule, Socrates would have no purchase on them; his argumentative procedure would be stymied.[20]

3. Since Socrates does expect to discover truth by this method, he must be making an exceedingly bold assumption which he never states[21] and, if he had stated it, would have been in no position to defend,[22] namely, that side by side with all their false beliefs,

his interlocutors always carry truth: somewhere or other in their belief system Socrates can expect to find true beliefs entailing the negation of each of their false ones.[23]

4. It follows, finally, that the elenchus is a *truth-seeking device which can not yield certainty,* if only because at the start of any given elenctic argument Socrates cannot be certain that the interlocutors do in fact have the true beliefs from which the contradictory of each of their false ones may be deduced.[24] He assumes they do, and the assumption proves true time and again. But its track-record of unbroken success in the past does not guarantee it will succeed again in the future. It may have triumphed a thousand times and go down to defeat in the first elenchus after that.

This shortfall in certainty, inherent in the elenctic method, which only a self-deluded thinker could have failed to sense and only a dishonest one could have wished to conceal, is our best clue to what Socrates meant by declaring that he had no knowledge. As I have intimated elsewhere[25] the declaration is cast in the form of a "complex irony"—that peculiarly Socratic figure of speech in which the speaker both does and does not mean what he says. If certainty were the hallmark of knowledge (as it had been, still was, and would continue to be for centuries to come in the main line of Greco-Roman philosophy[26]), the Socrates of Plato's earlier dialogues[27] and of Aristotle's testimony[28] would wish to renounce knowledge absolutely, though only to reclaim it in another sense of the word, never invoked by any philosopher[29] before him, in which "knowledge" does not entail certainty, and may, therefore, be used to mean simply justified true belief— justified by the highly fallible method of elenctic argument. In the *Gorgias* and the dialogues which precede it,[30] the renunciation of certainty does not deter Socrates from using that method day in, day out, relying on it to vindicate the moral theses on whose truth he stakes his life. The chanciness of his method does not cause the least wavering in his conviction that those theses are true. At the conclusion of his argument against Polus he declares:

T10 *Gorgias* **475E:** "So I spoke *the truth* when I said that neither I nor you nor any other man would rather do than suffer injustice."

About the parallel thesis that to do injustice is *ipso facto* to forfeit happiness, he tells Polus:

T11 *Gorgias* **479E8:** "Has it not been proved that what I said was *true?*"

What then are we to make of the fact that this method, to which Socrates is committed down to and including the *Gorgias,* should be dropped in the *Lysis* and the *Hippias Major?*[31] This shedding of the elenchus Plato makes no effort to explain or justify. He does not even mention it. He indicates it by dramatic means, pairing Socrates with interlocutors who no longer give him any fight. In the *Lysis* they are teen-agers, with no mind of their own on the theses he puts up to them[32] and, in any case, too well-bred and deferential to their older friend to cross anything he says. In the *Hippias Major* the interlocutor is mature enough, and more—a man of parts, *inter alia* accomplished mathematician and astronomer—but hopelessly inept in dialectical argument. His answers to the "What is F?" question are so wild as to be wholly devoid of philosophical interest;[33] Socrates makes short shrift of them, invests little effort in their refutation. When interesting answers are introduced at long last, they come not from Hippias but from Socrates. Hippias welcomes each of them as they are put up, and is resentfully surprised when Socrates then turns against them. Here, as also in the *Lysis,* the promising theses are proposed by Socrates, and refuted by Socrates. So in these dialogues Socrates is only half Socratic: the searcher remains, the elenctic critic has been cashiered. What we see of Socrates here is what Leavis tells us Wittgenstein's lecture audiences witnessed in Cambridge: "the sustained spontaneous effort of intellectual genius wrestling with its self-proposed problems." This was all very well for Wittgenstein. But *he* had not said he had received a divine mandate "to live philosophizing, examining [himself] *and others*" (T5), declaring he would be faithful to that mandate, even at a cost to his life (*Apol.* 29C–30C). All through the Elenctic dialogues Socrates has done just that, examining himself via examining others, testing his own beliefs against the ones he refutes to vindicate his own. But now we see him dropping the two-in-one operation, turning his critical acumen only against his own proposals, examining only himself.[34]

The change is no less marked in *Euthydemus*. The visiting sophists are depicted as so outrageously and irresponsibly eristic that, try as he may, Socrates finds it impossible to lock horns with them in any kind of serious argument. So he gives up. In each of two long segments of the dialogue he turns his back on them, giving all his attention to Cleinias, a beautiful boy, who hangs on his lips. Here for the first time in Plato's corpus we see Socrates unloading his philosophizing on the interlocutor in the form of protreptic discourse[35] expounded in flagrantly non-elenctic fashion as a virtual monologue.[36] Socrates starts it off by laying down an indubitable truth, a proposition which, he says, it would be "ridiculous" (*katagelaston*) and "senseless" (*anoēton*) to question—strange departure from his practice in Elenctic dialogues, where every thesis in moral philosophy is open to challenge. He proceeds to develop his thought entirely by himself, modifying it solely in response to caveats of his own. When the interlocutor is allowed at last an independent voice[37] it is only so he can interject something Socrates wants said but could not have put into his own discourse without digressing abruptly from its line of thought. So here, as in the *Lysis* and the *Hippias Major* the elenchus has been jettisoned. Moral doctrine of the highest import—the core of Socrates' moral philosophy[38]—is propounded in the *Lysis* and the *Euthydemus* unchallenged by an opponent.

I submit that to make sense of so drastic a departure from what Plato had put into his portrayals of Socrates from the *Apology* to the *Gorgias,* we must hypothesize a profound change in Plato himself. If we believe that in any given dialogue Plato puts into the persona of Socrates only what at the time he himself considers true,[39] we must suppose that when that persona discards the elenchus as the right method to search for the truth this occurs because Plato has now lost faith in that method himself. This could have happened to him only after the *Gorgias,* where Socrates is still supremely confident that the elenchus is the final[40] arbiter of moral truth. Why then the disenchantment with the elenchus at just this time in Plato's life? What could have happened in his intellectual development to account for this momentous change? Since Plato doesn't tell us, we have to guess, that is, resort to a hypothesis. Mine is that now, in mid-career, Plato himself has taken that deep, long plunge into mathematical studies he will be requiring of all philosophers when he comes to write Book 7 of the *Republic* and that the effect is proving as transformative of his own outlook as he believed it would be of theirs. Direct evidence for this hypothesis we do not have. But of indirect evidence there is no lack. To find it in abundance we need only turn to the first dialogue in which the impact of these new studies on the content and method of his philosophizing is allowed to surface freely: the *Meno.* Here Plato's new enthusiasm bubbles out all over the text.

When Socrates announces[41] that all learning is "recollecting" and is asked if he has any way of showing (*endeixasthai*) that this startling proposition is true (82A5–6), he replies:

T12 *Meno* 82A–B: "Call one of your attendants, any of them will do, and I shall show this to you in his case (*en toutōi soi epideixōmai*)."

What follows is the most sustained stretch of geometrical reasoning in the whole of Plato's corpus. Meno is to observe that the boy will "discover" (*aneurēsei*)[42] the answer to a geometrical problem: find the side of a square which will duplicate the area of a given square whose side is two feet long. The interrogation which follows has been thought a paradigm of Socratic elenchus.[43] Is it? Yes and No. Yes, where the boy's mistakes are being corrected. When he guesses that the side of the desired square is 4 feet long, or 3 feet long, he is shown that either of these answers must be wrong *because* each contradicts the boy's claim that the area in each case duplicates that of the given square with agreed upon area of 4 square feet: the boy is brought to understand that if the side were 4 (or 3) feet long its area would be 16 (or 9) square feet, and 16 (or 9) is not twice 4. In correcting those two answers in just that way Socrates produces true-blue elenctic argument: false answer P is eliminated because P contradicts Q, and Q is what the answerer himself accepts as true. But how far does this take the boy? Only as far as convicting him of error. Elenchus is good for this, and only this. It does not begin to bring him to the truth he seeks. He could have gone on till doomsday trying out different integers or ratios of integers to be shown their falsehood by the same process, and none of this would have brought him an inch closer to the true answer. In Greek mathematics, which recognizes only integral numbers,[44] no integer or ratio of integers could yield the answer to Socrates' question. The problem admits of no arithmetical solution.[45] But it does admit of a geometrical one. This answer no elenctic badgering could have elicited from the boy.[46] To bring him to it Socrates *must shed the adversative role* to which persistence in elenctic argument would have kept him. Shed it he does. Extending the diagram, he plants into it the line that opens sesame, and *then* the boy "recollects" that the side of a square whose area is twice that of a given square is the diagonal of the given square.

What is so obviously new here is the resort to geometry. But let us note that this episode in the dialogue is not presented as deserting moral inquiry for mathematics. Its whole purpose is to illuminate the process by which according to this new, all-too-Platonic Socrates, *all* inquiry—and therefore all moral inquiry—must proceed:

T13 *Meno* 81D: "For *all* inquiring and learning is recollecting."

As novel as is the theory of recollection itself and as significant an indication of the lines along which Plato's philosophical development is now moving is the fact that geometrical discovery is being taken as paradigmatic "recollection"[47] and therewith that knowledge of geometry is taken as the paradigm of all knowledge, including moral knowledge.

The same is true of a piece of geometry Plato had brought into the *Meno*, earlier on. To show by example how a "What is F?" question should be answered Socrates had put up a geometrical paradigm. Picking "figure" as the definiendum, he proceeds:

T14 *Meno* 76A4–7: "Is there something you would call a 'plane' (*epipedon*), and something else which you would call a 'solid' (*stereon*) as they do in geometry (*hōsper en tais geōmetriais*)? . . . From this you can understand what I mean by 'figure' (*schēma*). For of every figure I would say: that which is the limit of a solid (*stereou peras*) that is figure."

Contrast the line he had taken in the *Laches,* when giving the interlocutor a model to show him what sort of answer is required for a "What is F?" question. The example he had used there is *tachutēs,* "quickness" or "swiftness," a word in everyday speech, without scientific pretension;[48] and the model definition offered for it had been built up with bricks from the same kiln: the cases he wants it to cover are quick actions of "hands or legs or mouth or voice or thought." And the definiens he offers is a rough-and-ready, home-made job, owing nothing to scientific theorizing:

T15 *Laches* 192B: "The quality[49] of doing much in little time (*tēn en oligōi chronōi diaprattomenēn dunamin*), both in speaking and in running and in all other things, is what I call 'quickness.'"

Not so in the *Meno.* The term to be defined here, *schēma,* occurs both in common speech and in scientific discourse—one could use it to refer to, say, the shape of a shield *or* to that of an intricate geometrical construction; Socrates cold-shoulders the former usage, ignores it completely, reminding his interlocutor that the critical words he will be using to produce the definition will be lifted from geometry: *hōsper en tais geōmetriais.* That reference is not gratuitous. The vague way in which those words were used in common speech—*epipedon* for flat, level ground, *stereon* for something firm, rigid, solid— would have disqualified them for the purposes of his definition. So he insists on that highly specialized use of *epipedon* and *stereon* to denote abstract magnitudes, stripped of all physical properties except those implied by their extension in two or three dimensions—a sense which would never enter the head of people using those words in everyday life.

And what is the provenance of the definition in T14? Almost certainly some contemporary geometrical axiom-set. From the scraps of the Eudemian history of geometry that survive in Proclus[50] we know that steps towards the axiomatization of geometry, first taken late in the fifth century by Hippocrates of Chios,[51] were continuing with growing success in the fourth.[52] By the end of the century they would reach the definitive axiom-set which has survived in Euclid's *Elements.* Compare then what Euclid does by way of defining *schēma.* He takes it in two jumps, using "limit" (*peras*) to define "boundary" (*horos*), and "boundary" to define "figure":

T16 Euclid, *Elements I,* Definition 13: "Boundary is that which is the limit of something (*horos estin ho tinos esti peras*)."

T17 Ibid., Definition 14: "Figure is that which is contained by a boundary (*schēma esti to hupo tinos ē tinōn horōn periechomenon*)."

Why this more protracted procedure? It is dictated by the architectonics of Euclid's treatise which defers solid geometry to its latest books. So it is understandable that Euclid should want to make no reference to "solid" until then: he will start off Book 11 by defining the term. But the source on which Plato is drawing when composing the *Meno* would be much earlier—two generations or more before Euclid, in the period when the axiomatization of geometry is making steady progress, but is still nowhere near the level it will reach in Euclid. At this earlier point in the development of geometrical axiomatics no need has been felt to avoid mention of the term "solid" from the very start. So we get the one in T14, more expeditious than Euclid's in T16 and T17. Its use by Plato shows that by the time he came to write the *Meno* he was so familiar with this branch of geometry that he found it natural to turn to it for a model of successful definition.

In the same context we get another novelty in Plato's writing: bringing in Empedocles' theory of effluences as the physical cause of sensation, he takes cognizance of physical speculation no less than of geometry. Socrates offers Meno a definition of "color" which incorporates the Empedoclean theory.[53]

> **T18** *Meno* **76D:** "Color is an effluence from figures commensurate with vision and apprehensible to sense."

Expecting Meno to like this definition, Socrates teases him for fancying it—he calls it "theatrical" (*tragikē*), a sneer. With the geometrical definition in T14 he has no fault to find. The physical one in T18 he treats with condescension. Here again Plato is holding up geometry as paradigmatic science.

He does this on a grander scale in the part of the dialogue which follows the interrogation of the slave-boy. Reinstating the old Socratic question, "Can virtue be taught?" he announces that he is going to "investigate it from a hypothesis," identifying as follows the provenance of this phrase and explaining what he takes it to mean:

> **T19** *Meno* **86E4–87B2:** "By 'investigating from a hypothesis' (*ex hupotheseōs skopeisthai*) I refer to the way the geometricians frequently investigate. When they are asked, for example, as regards a given area, whether it is possible for this area to be inscribed in the form of a triangle in a given circle, they may reply: 'I don't yet know whether this area is such as can be so inscribed. But I think that a certain hypothesis would be helpful for that purpose. I mean the following: If the given area is such that when it has been applied [as a rectangle] to the given straight line in the circle, it is deficient by a figure similar to the one which is applied, then I think that one alternative results, while, on the other hand, another results if it is impossible for what I said to be done. So, setting up a hypothesis (*hupothemenos*), I shall tell you what will follow from it for the inscription of the given area in the circle—whether or not the inscription is possible.' "[54]

An adequate commentary on this passage would require an essay longer than the present paper all to itself. I restrict myself to the bare minimum of comment required for any argument.[55]

1. The geometrical example is ostentatiously technical. To understand its mathematics the reader would have needed considerable proficiency in a branch of Greek geometry, the "application of areas," to which modern histories of mathematics refer as "geometrical algebra."[56] Plato could certainly have chosen a simpler example. He is preening himself on his own expertise in geometry, warning his readers that if they have not already done a lot of work in that science they will be unable to follow him, and this will be their loss, not his: to keep up with the best he has to offer they must learn geometry. Though the detail of the mathematics is left obscure, the logical structure of the recommended method is entirely clear: When you are faced with a problematic proposition p, to "investigate it from a hypothesis," you hit on another proposition h (the "hypothesis"), such that p is true if and only if h is true, and then shift your search

from p to h, and investigate the truth of h, undertaking to determine what would follow (quite apart from p) if h were true and, alternatively, if it were false. To adopt this procedure as a methodological model for research in moral philosophy is *to scuttle the elenchus:*[57] adherence to the model would entail systematic violation of the "say only what you believe" rule, which forbids debating an unasserted premise, while "investigating from a hypothesis" requires it. More generally: if one were to model method in moral philosophy on method in geometry one would be shifting definitively out of peirastic into demonstrative argument, and hence aiming to achieve in moral inquiry the certainty achievable in mathematical proof. For if you are practicing the geometrical method of "investigating from hypothesis" by tying the truth of p to that of h, you will be aiming to demonstrate that p is true (or false) because it is a necessary consequence of h which may be finally known to be true (or false) *because it (or its contradictory) is a necessary consequence of the axioms of the system.*[58]

2. The use to which Plato's new Socrates wants to put this method is made clear at once. To continue the citation in T20:

> **T20 *Meno* 87B2–4:** "Just so, let us say about virtue: Since we know neither what it is (*hoti estin*) nor of what sort it is (*hopoion ti*), let us investigate from a hypothesis (*hupothemenoi auto skopōmen*) whether or not it is teachable."

The problematic proposition is p: Virtue is teachable.

The hypothesis to investigate p is h: Virtue is knowledge.

And h we know to be a cardinal Socratic doctrine.[59] Here Socrates argues first for h (87D–89C), then[60] against it (96D–98C).[61] Neither argument is complete. In neither case is it pushed back to end-of-the-line *archai:* Plato's epistemology is still in the making, still heavily programmatic; we can't expect too much all at once.[62] But what we do get in the text is quite enough to show that as between the two arguments, one for h, the Socratic doctrine, the other against it, the latter carries the day: Socrates satisfies himself that for governing action aright true belief is as good as knowledge:

> **T21 *Meno* 98B–C:** "And isn't this right too: when true opinion governs (*hēgoumenē*) a course of action what it produces is in no way inferior (*ouden cheiron apergazetai*) to what is produced by knowledge? Hence in regard to action true belief is no worse or less beneficial than is knowledge."

When this conclusion is reached a whole row of Socratic dominos will have to fall,[63] including the fundamental conviction that

> **T8:** "The unexamined life is not worth living by man."

For if true opinion without knowledge does suffice to guide action aright, then the great mass of men and women may be spared the pain and hazards of the "examined" life: they may be brought under the protective custody of a ruling elite who will feed them true beliefs to guide their conduct aright, without allowing them to inquire why those beliefs are true. Access to the critical examination of questions of good and evil, right and wrong, may then be reasonably withheld from all but the elite, and even from them until they have finished the mathematical studies which will prepare them for enlightenment (T4). So in the *Meno* we see Plato well started on a course that will take him to the other extreme from the convictions he had shared with Socrates in the Elenctic dialogues: the doctrine of the philosopher-king looms ahead.

But if Plato's mathematical studies are to be invoked to explain the fact that the elenctic method, so vibrantly alive in the *Gorgias* and before it, goes dead in the *Lysis, Hippias Major,* and *Euthydemus,* would we not expect that some positive sign of this new preoccupation of Plato's will show up somehow or other *in* those three dialogues— not only after them, in the *Meno?* So we would, and in two of them the expectation is not disappointed.

A clear sign of what we are looking for occurs in the *Hippias Major.* It enters so inconspicuously that its import could easily pass unnoticed (as it in fact has in the scholarly literature).[64] It slips in as one of several examples of a point of logic. Socrates tries to get Hippias to see that there is a sort of attribute such that if each of two things has it in isolation from the other then each may, or may not, also have it when conjoined with the other; and, conversely, such that if things do have it in conjunction, each may or may not have it in disjunction:

> **T22** *Hippias Major* **303B–C:** "[A] If I am strong and so are you, then both of us are strong. If I am just, and so are you, then both of us are just. And if both of us are just, then so is each of us. Is it similarly true that if I am beautiful and so are you, then both of us are beautiful; and if both of us are, then so is each? Or is it [B] like the case of even numbers: of two numbers which are even when taken together [i.e., when added] each could be an even number or again each could be odd; and again, as in the case of (magnitudes) which are severally irrational, but when taken together[65] may be either rational or irrational (*kai au arrētōn hekaterōn ontōn tacha men rhēta ta sunamphotera einai, tacha d' arrēta*)."

Still on the track of the "What is F?" question for F = "beautiful," Socrates is undertaking to determine in which of two classes of attributes this particular F falls, identifying the two classes by example. Citing "strong" and "just" as examples of class [A], he proceeds to cast about for examples of class [B]. Whole numbers serve this purpose to perfection: from the fact that, $x + y = 10$, which is an even number, we cannot tell whether or not x and y are even or odd: two even numbers would yield that sum, and so would a pair of odd ones. This example from elementary arithmetic, familiar even to children, would have sufficed to make the point. Not satisfied with that, Socrates goes on to pick a second example. And where does he find it? In an area which at this time (the 'eighties of the fourth century) was at the frontier of mathematical research, where only a mathematician, like Hippias, would have any idea of what the talk of "rational" and "irrational" magnitudes is all about. Plato writes with a lordly insouciance for the fact that those technical terms would mystify the layman, and does not deign to explain the theorem to which he is referring (simple enough for one who understands irrationals), namely, that a suitably selected pair of irrational magnitudes (say, the segments of the "golden section," produced by cutting a line in "extreme and mean ratio")[66] would have a rational (geometric) sum, while a differently selected pair of irrationals (say, $\sqrt{3}$ and $\sqrt{5}$) would have an irrational one. Here again, as in the more complicated geometrical example in the *Meno* (T19), Plato gives clear evidence that his mathematical studies have taken him far from the interests and competences of his old teacher.

In the *Euthydemus* he does more of the same, though in a very different way, speaking through young Cleinias:[67]

T23 *Euthydemus* **290B–C:** "No craft whose work is hunting goes further than pursuing and bagging its quarry. When [its] craftsmen have caught what they are after, they are not competent to use it themselves. And while hunters and anglers hand over their catch to cooks, geometricians and astronomers and number-theorists (*logistikoi*)—for they too are hunters: for they are not engaged in creating figures, but in discovering reality[68]—hand over their discoveries to the dialecticians, if they are not altogether stupid, since they themselves know only how to hunt, not how to use, them."

Here. Plato names three of the four sciences which will constitute the curriculum of higher studies in Book 7 of the *Republic* and assures the people who are doing the work in each of them that while they do "discover reality," they are in no position to know what use is best made of their findings: this should be left to the *dialektikoi*, the masters of philosophical argument.[69] If Plato is what we know him to be—a sober, responsible thinker, not given to empty boasting—he would not be making this extraordinary claim unless he already felt when he wrote the *Euthydemus* that his own understanding of mathematical science had already advanced so far as to entitle him to appraise the results reached by its experts and to rule on how they should be used.

Thus in the *Hippias Major* and the *Euthydemus* there is solid, if tantalizingly brief, evidence for the hypothesis that Plato was already well advanced in mathematical studies by the time he came to write those dialogues in which the elenchus goes dead. But in the *Lysis,* where it is equally defunct, there is no allusion to mathematics at all.[70] Does this present a difficulty for my hypothesis? Not if we fix in the *Gorgias,* as we should, the *terminus post quem* of this new development in Plato's intellectual life.[71] This dialogue is the natural turning-point. For while knowledge of advanced mathematics is displayed here no more than in any earlier work of Plato's,[72] contact with geometry shows up,[73] well-motivated by the fact that the *Gorgias* can be dated on good internal evidence[74] soon after Plato's first journey to Syracuse.[75] There, Cicero tells us, "he devoted himself to Pythagorean men and studies," spending much time with Archytas of Tarentum and Timaeus of Locri."[76] The latter is a shadowy figure.[77] Not so the former. From the first-hand evidence preserved in every history of Greek geometry[78] we know that Archytas was a perfectly brilliant mathematician. We know too that he was a leading statesman of his city, a democracy like Athens,[79] elected and re-elected "general" year after year.[80] Here is a new model philosopher for Plato, giving him everything he might have missed in his old one: Socrates had recoiled helplessly from Athenian politics, convinced it was irremediably corrupt. Archytas enters with stunning success the political fray in his own city. And Socrates had recoiled from metaphysics, while Archytas was a master metaphysician in the Pythagorean tradition.[81] Socrates, Xenophon assures us,[82] advised against the study of advanced mathematics, while Archytas was at the forefront of mathematical discovery.[83] If it was this personal association with Archytas that gave the impetus[84] to Plato's mathematical studies, we could hardly expect instant results. To his philosophers in their twenties Plato was to allow all of ten years to become accomplished mathematicians. If Plato himself were coming to this science in his forties, he might well be allowed an interval of more than that many months to go as far. The natural place for the *Lysis* is early in that interval, when his mathematical studies are advancing but have not yet reached so far as to make him want to go public with this new accomplishment. Give him another year or so and he will be giving signs of it in those all-too-brief sallies in the *Hippias Major* and the *Euthydemus* and then copiously and at deliberate length in the *Meno*.

That Plato's encounter with geometry was to prove no passing infatuation, but a love-match, a life-long attachment as deep as it was intense, is not hard to understand. We know how susceptible he was to beauty. Is any product of the human imagination more beautiful than are some of the proofs in Euclid? The elenchus is a messy business by comparison. Still more appealing to him, if that were possible, would be the epistemic achievement of Greek geometry and number-theory. These disciplines with their application to astronomy and harmonics, are the domain in which the Greek aspiration to scientific knowledge had achieved its most assured success. Whereas in other areas—natural philosophy, medicine—there was no stable consensus, all was in controversy,[85] brilliant inventions galore, but nothing so settled that it could not be unsettled by the next strong voice to come along, in mathematics stable bases (the "elements" of the science) had been ascertained from which ever new discoveries could be proved, eliciting agreement among all qualified investigators to be incorporated in a common body of knowledge. Here Plato would see inquirers within reach of a deductive system in which every statement justifiable by rational argument is derivable from premises which are "evident to all" (*Rep.* 510C)[86]—all except talented cranks[87]—and confer similar indubitability on every conclusion drawn therefrom by necessary inference, all of those results constituting statements which, in Aristotle's phrase (*Po. An.* 75b15) "could not be otherwise."

Would it be any wonder if when the groundswell of this triumphant enterprise reached Plato it should sweep him away from his Socratic moorings and start him on the journey from the "Socrates" of the Elenctic dialogues, in whom disciple and teacher had thought as one, to the "Socrates" of his middle period, pursuing un-Socratic projects to anti-Socratic conclusions, the great love of his youth still alive in his heart,[88] but his mind no longer in thrall?[89]

ENDNOTE A: MATHEMATICAL TEXTS IN ELENCTIC DIALOGUES

In the *Gorgias* Socrates distinguishes number-theory[90] from calculation[91] as follows:

> **T A1** *Gorgias* **451A–C:** "If someone were to ask me about any of the arts I mentioned a moment ago, 'Socrates, what is the art of number-theory?' I would tell him . . . that it is an art which achieves its effect through speech. And if he continued, 'And what is that art about?' I would say that it is about the even and the odd, regardless of how numerous each may be. And if he then asked, 'What is the art you call "calculation"?' I would say that it too achieves its effect through speech. And if he then asked me all over again, 'And what is *it* about?' I would say . . . 'In other respects it is the same as number-theory—both are about the same thing, the even and the odd—but they differ in this: calculation determines the quantity of odd and even, both relatively to themselves and in relation to each other.'"

In the *Hippias Minor* (366C) Socrates calls Hippias a master of *logistikē* because he can tell more quickly than anyone what is three times seven hundred. That this should be considered a fine accomplishment is understandable, for unlike grammar and "music," *logistikē* was not a school subject. Even so, in this highly developed commercial society some skill in computation would be within everyone's reach. *Arithmētikē*, on the other hand, unlike what is called "arithmetic" nowadays, is a theoretical pursuit. It engages in general investigations of number, proving theorems applying to any numbers, odd or even, such as those in Euclid 9.21ff., which, it has been plausibly held[92] preserve fragments of archaic Pythagorean number-theory. Here are the first three:

> **T A2 Euclid,** *Elements* **9: Proposition 21:** "If even numbers, as many as we please, be added together, the sum is even." **Proposition 22:** "If odd numbers, as many as we please, be added together, and their multitude is even, the sum will be even." **Proposition 23:** "If odd numbers, as many as we please, be added together, and their multitude is odd, the sum will also be odd."

We may reasonably assume that in Socrates' life-time such elementary theorems would be widely known to educated Greeks. One would not need much mathematical background to understand that an even-numbered set of odd numbers, say {3, 5}, has an even sum, while an odd-numbered set of odd numbers, say {3, 5, 7}, has an odd sum, and to follow the number-theoretical proofs of these propositions: a look at Euclid 9.21ff. will show that they are simplicity itself. That Socrates would know that much mathematics and hence would be in a position to explain the difference between *logistikē* and *arithmētikē* in the terms he uses in A1, as also previously in *Charm.* 166A, can be taken for granted. No one would wish to suggest that he had been a mathematical illiterate.[93] We can safely assume that he had learned some mathematics before his concentration on ethical inquiry had become obsessive.[94] But it is one thing to have learned quite a lot of elementary geometry and number-theory, quite another to have the knowledge of advanced developments in those subjects which is displayed casually in that remark about irrationals in the *Hippias Major* (T22), elaborately and ostentatiously in the *Meno* in the reference to the method of "investigating from a hypothesis" in geometry and in the accompanying geometrical construction (T19). Even if Socrates had learned all of the geometry there was to learn in his twenties and thirties, that knowledge would not begin to account for the mathematician he is made out to be in these passages unless he had come abreast of the new developments which occurred when he was in his middle years or later: the axiomatization of geometry began with Hippocrates of Chios in the last third of the fifth century,[95] when Socrates was in his fifties and sixties; the theory of incommensurability was developed early in the fourth century when he was already dead.[96]

In the *Euthyphro* we have positive evidence that in Elenctic dialogues Socrates does not have the same ready access to geometrical axiomatics which enables him to produce ad hoc the model definition of "figure"[97] in the *Meno*. To explain the part/whole relation of "piety" to "justice" Socrates invokes that of "even" to "number" and then proceeds to define "even" as follows:

> **T A3** *Euthyphro* **12D:** "If you were to ask me, 'Which part of number is the even, and what is that number?' I would say: 'It is that *number which is not scalene but isosceles.*'"

If the way "even" was being defined in contemporary geometry had been at Socrates' finger-tips, he would have surely offered Euthyphro a much simpler and better definition. This is the one in Euclid:

T A4 Euclid, Book 7, Definition 6: "An even number is that which is divisible in two [equal] parts."[98]

In Greek mathematics which recognizes only integers as numbers, this definition is flawless. And this is the very one to which Plato himself will resort after acquiring the mathematical knowledge he desiderates for all philosophers. The one he tosses out in the *Laws* anticipates Euclid's verbatim:

T A5 Plato, *Laws* 895E: "We may designate one and the same thing either by its name 'even,' or by its definition, *'number divisible in two [equal] parts.'*"

The advantage of this definition over the one in T A3 leaps to the eye: it is so much neater and more direct, rendering unnecessary resort to the undefined terms "scalene number," "isosceles number" for the purpose of defining "even number."[99] As portrayed in the *Euthyphro* Socrates is sadly deficient in the mathematical know-how his namesake proudly displays in the *Meno*.

ENDNOTE B: PLATO AND THEODORUS

T B1 Diogenes Laertius 3.6: "[A] As Hermodorus states, at the age of 28 Plato, with certain other Socratics, withdrew to Megara to Euclides.[100] [B] Next he departed for Cyrene to Theodorus the mathematician, and thence to Italy to the Pythagoreans Philolaus and Eurytus; and thence he went to Egypt to the prophets, where Euripides is said to have accompanied him."

Entirely credible is the story of Plato's journey to Megara after Socrates' death, in part [A] of this text, and also elsewhere in Diogenes Laertius (2.106), there too on the excellent authority of Hermodorus. But what confidence can we repose in the tale in part [B], which affords no clue as to its source? The gossipy tale of a grand tour of the southern Mediterranean, which takes Plato to Cyrene,[101] Italy and then Egypt discredits itself by picking as Plato's companion on this journey none other than Euripides, who had died some eight years before the tour could have begun. There is no mention of travel to Cyrene prior to the one to Sicily and Italy in the earlier report in Cicero (*de Rep.* 1.10.16; *de Fin.* 5.29.87), nor yet in the *Index Herculanensis* (ed. Mekkler) 6–7.[102] But while Plato's travel to Cyrene to make contact there with Theodorus seems to rest on nothing better than doxographic gossip, there is no reason to doubt the report elsewhere in Diogenes which represents Plato as having received instruction from Theodorus:

T B2 Diogenes Laertius 2.102: "There have been 20 persons named 'Theodorus.' . . . The second was the Cyrenaic, the geometrician whose auditor Plato became."

This could have occurred after Plato's first journey to Syracuse, on his return to Athens, where Theodorus' presence is well attested (*Tht.* 143Dff.; *Soph.* 216Aff.; *Pltc.* 257A–B).

How close was this relation to Theodorus? The nearest Plato comes to giving some indication of it comes in the following snatch of dialogue in the *Theaetetus:*

T B3 *Theaetetus* 145C–D: Socrates to Theaetetus: "You are getting some instruction in geometry from Theodorus?" Theaetetus: "Yes." Socrates: "And also in astronomy and harmonics and number-theory?" Theaetetus: "I am eager to learn from him.'' Socrates: "I too, my boy—from him and from anyone else whom I believe to have some knowledge of such things (*kai par' allōn hous an oiomai ti toutōn epaiein*). I do moderately well, in general. But I am puzzled about one small thing which I would like to investigate with you and these people.''

Theodorus is represented as only one of those to whom "Socrates" (*alias* Plato) would be eager to turn for instruction in mathematics.[103] And as the dialogue proceeds we sense the absence of any close or intimate bond with Theodorus, who is portrayed as aloof from Plato's philosophical interests. When Socrates tries to draw him into the argument, he is rebuffed:

T B4 *Theaetetus* 165A1–2: "At a rather early age I turned away from bare arguments to geometry (*ek tōn psilōn logōn pros tēn geōmetrian apeneusamen*).''

Robin's gloss on *ek tōn psilōn logōn* here [104] "raisonnements tout formels, vides de substance,'' brings out the lack of interest in philosophical argument suggested by the reference to him in Plato's text. The attraction Plato could have felt for Archytas, who fused enthusiasm for mathematics with dedication to philosophy, he could hardly have felt for Theodorus.[105]

NOTES

1. His association with the leading mathematicians and his zest for their science is amply attested in Eudemus, *Geōmetrikē Historia*, fr. 133 (Wehrli), *ap.* Proclus, *Commentary on the First Book of Euclid's Elements* (Friedlein) 64ff. at 66.8–67.20. On Plato as a mathematician, see in general B. L. van der Waerden, *Science Awakening*, tr. A. Dresden (1961), 138–42 and passim; Thomas L. Heath, *A History of Greek Mathematics* (1921), vol. 1, chapter 9 on Plato. For detailed discussion of controversial points see especially H. Cherniss, "Plato as a Mathematician,'' *Review of Metaphysics* (1951), 393ff., (reprinted in H. Cherniss, *Collected Papers* (Leiden, 1977), ed. L. Taran).
2. G. Vlastos, *Plato's Universe* (1975), 60 and 110–11.
3. On the authority of Sosigenes whose information arguably derives from Eudemus.
4. E. J. Dijksterhuis, *The Mechanization of the World Picture* (1961), 15.
5. For Plato's conception of astronomy as celestial kinematics see especially A. D. P. Mourelatos, "Astronomy and Kinematics in Plato's Project of Rational Explanation,'' *Studies in the History and Philosophy of Science* (1981), 1–32.
6. *Rep.* 7, 518B–531B; 537B–D. For brief comment see the explanatory remarks interspersed in Cornford's translation of the passage (*The Republic of Plato* [Oxford, 1945]); and J. Annas, *An Introduction to Plato's Republic* (1981), 171–76.
7. Who are now about to start the course in dialectics, the final lap of their higher education.
8. The importance of this passage for the contrast between the Socratic and Platonic view of moral education, all too often missed by earlier commentators, is brilliantly highlighted in M. Nussbaum, "Aristophanes and Socrates on Learning Practical Wisdom,'' *Yale Classical Studies* (1980), 43ff.; "Plato charges his teacher (ironically, in his teacher's own *persona*) with contributing to moral decline by not restricting the questioning-process to a chosen, well-trained few. . . . Plato, with Aristophanes, believes that for the ordinary man questioning [of moral values] is destructive without being therapeutic'' (88).
9. "Anyone of you I happen to meet . . . everyone I meet, young and old, alien and citizen . . .'' (*Apol.* 29D, 30A).
10. Women are not in the public places where Socrates could reach them. Not so in Hades, where

those barriers are obliterated: "It would make me inconceivably happy to have discussion with the men *and women* there . . ." (*Apol.* 41C).

11. The elderly Lysimachus, casting about for advice on the education of his son, is told by Laches: "I am surprised you are turning to us for advice on the education of young men and not to Socrates . . . who is always spending his day in places where young men engage in any noble study or pursuit" (*La.* 180C).

12. Lysimachus tells the company: "When these boys are talking among themselves at home they often speak of Socrates, praising him warmly" (*La.* 180E). Young Charmides tells Socrates: "There is much talk about you amongst us boys" (*Charm.* 156A).

13. Cf. G. Vlastos, "The Socratic Elenchus," *Oxford Studies in Ancient Philosophy* (1983) [hereafter "SE"], 42, n. 39.

14. See also *Cr.* 49C–D; *Prot.* 331C; *Gorg.* 500B; *Rep.* 346A. This is a standing rule of elenctic debate, mentioned only when there is special need to bring it to the interlocutor's notice. Thus in the *Gorgias* there is no allusion to it in the whole of Socrates' argument with Gorgias and with Polus. In the *Prot.* nothing is said about it until the sophist reveals that he is unaware of the constraint (331C). In the *Crito,* Socrates brings it up (49C–D) only when it is critically important that Crito should realize that in giving his agreement he stands with Socrates *contra mundum*.

15. In the Revised Oxford Translation of Aristotle (1984), edited by Jonathan Barnes, this translation of *endoxa* supersedes "generally believed opinions" in the previous one, which I had followed uncritically in *SE* (cf. n. 13). M. F. Burnyeat, "Good Repute," *London Review of Books* (November 6, 1986) argues convincingly that the new rendering comes closer to capturing the intent of Aristotle's definition of *endoxa* ("what is believed by all or by most or by the wise and, of these, by all or by most or the most distinguished and most reputable," *Top.* 100a29–b23).

16. Cf. the quotations from Proclus in nn. 51 and 52.

17. I use the "axioms" here and hereafter for the indemonstrables of a deductive system, be they definitions, postulates, or "common notions" (as the last are called in Euclid; *axiōmata* in Aristotle).

18. *Parrēsia*. Callicles is fulsomely praised for it, Polus reproached for lacking it (*Gorg.* 487A3, B1, D5).

19. In the Elenctic dialogues (listed in n. 30) when Plato wants to show Socrates attacking a Socratic thesis he hands over the thesis to an interlocutor, making him its proponent for the duration of that dialogue. So in the *Laches* (194Eff.): Nicias is made the spokesman for the definition of courage which we know to be Socratic (Socrates argues for it in the *Prot.* [360C–D] and uses it there with deadly effect against Protagoras). Alluding to its Socratic provenance (194D), Nicias is left holding the bag: he is made its sole sponsor in this dialogue, required to defend it *against* Socrates. Though Socrates is intensely self-critical, confiding that he is always more eager to examine himself than others (*Charm.* 166C–D), the formalities of elenctic argument prevent him from making any of his own doctrines the target of elenctic refutation by himself.

20. On two occasions Socrates tolerates a breach of the rule, though only as a *pis aller* (to circumvent the evasive tactics of an uncooperative interlocutor) and only *pro tem.*, as at *Prot.* 333Cff. (on which cf. *SE,* 37–38), *Rep.* I, 349Aff., resuming the application of the rule when it comes to the kill.

21. Though he may make statements which *imply* it: see T21, T22, T23, T24(b) in *SE* (cf. n. 13).

22. He couldn't without turning epistemologist and metaphysician, ceasing to be the moralist, pure and simple, which he remains throughout Plato's earlier dialogues where only moral truths are treated as elenctic theses (*SE,* 33). Exceptionally, Socrates debates an epistemological notion, as in the case of *epistēmē epistēnēs kai anepistēmosunēs* in the *Charmides* (167A–169B), but only because it had been proposed (166E) as a definiens of *sōphrosunē;* doing his

best to discredit the proposal he leaves the question unresolved ("I have no confidence in my ability to clear up such matters," 169A).

23. Proposition A. in *SE*, 52ff.

24. For a fuller statement of the reasons for the deficit in certainty in elenctically grounded knowledge, see G. Vlastos, "Socrates' Disavowal of Knowledge," *Philosophical Quarterly*, 35 (1985) ([hereafter *"SDK"*], 1ff. at 18–19).

25. G. Vlastos, "Socratic Irony," reprinted in this volume 66ff. at 72; *SDK*, 30–31.

26. Thus from *de omnibus quaeritur, nihil certi dicitur*, Cicero (*Acad.* 1.46) infers that Plato's position was sceptical—not materially different from that of the out-and-out sceptics of the New Academy, Arcesilaus and Carneades: Cicero is taking it for granted that if Plato renounces *certainty*, he is renouncing *knowledge*. Cf. T25 in *SDK*, Democritus fr. B117 (Diels-Kranz [hereafter "DK"]): we know nothing with certainty ("truth is in the depths"), *ergo* we know nothing.

27. *Apol.* 21B–D and passim.

28. *Soph. El* 183b8, *hōmologei gar ouk eidenai*.

29. I say "by any *philosopher*," not "by *anyone*"; non-philosophers (and even philosophers when off their high horse, speaking and thinking with the vulgar) would have had no hesitation in saying e.g., "I know my friend won't lie to me," while realizing perfectly well that in such matters as these epistemic certainty is unavailable.

30. As I have previously noted (*SE*, 57–58) commitment to the elenctic method as the final arbiter of truth in the moral domain is common and peculiar to ten dialogues which, for miscellaneous reasons, have been often thought by a wide variety of scholars to constitute the earliest segment of the Platonic corpus: *Apol., Charm., Cr., Eu., Gorg., H.Mi., Ion, La., Prot., Rep. 1* (listed in alphabetical order). I call these "Elenctic" in contradistinction to the "Transitional" ones (*Ly., H.Ma., Eud.*) in which the elenctic method is discarded while consistency of moral doctrine is maintained (cf. n. 38). In the *Gorgias* I see a major chronological landmark, for I consider it the last of the Elenctic dialogues, concurring with the widely held opinion (accepted also by C. Kahn, "Did Plato Write Socratic Dialogues?," reprinted in this volume 35ff., despite his radical deviation from common views on other points) that on good internal evidence, it may be dated at, or close to, Plato's return from the first journey to Sicily: see E. R. Dodds, *Plato's Gorgias* (1958), 19ff.; T. H. Irwin, *Plato's Gorgias* (1979), 5–8.

31. I have so argued in *SE*, 57–58 (Appendix on "The Demise of the Elenchus in the *Eud., Ly., and H.Ma.*"). I renew the argument more briefly here.

32. They follow sheep-like wherever he leads. When he takes a position they agree; when he objects to the position they agree with the objection.

33. One could scarcely imagine less promising answers to the question "What is that by which *all* beautiful things are made beautiful?" (288A8–11 and passim) than "a beautiful girl" (287E), "gold" (289E), and the still more naively parochial one (too long to quote) at 291D–E.

34. Elsewhere (*SDK*, 23, n. 54) I have argued that a further problematic feature of the *Lysis*, and of the *Hippias Major* becomes explicable when they are viewed as transitional between the *Gorgias* and the introduction of transmigration and anamnesis at *M*. 81A–E: the emergence here of the so-called "Socratic Fallacy" (the doctrine that knowledge of the definition of "F" is a *necessary* condition of knowing whether "F" can be predicated of anything whatever [*Ly.* 223B; *H.Ma*. 304D–E] or whether anything whatever can be predicated of it [*M*. 71A–B and 80D–E]; and also *Rep*. 354C, in the terminal paragraph of Book 1, best understood as a later addition to Book 1, since it contradicts 350B10–11: *SDK*, 23–26). See now the new study of the topic by J. Beversluis, "Does Socrates Commit the Socratic Fallacy?," reprinted in this volume, 107ff.

35. Protreptic speeches in an elenctic dialogue we get also in the *Gorgias* (511C–513C; 517B–519D; 523A to the end) in great abundance, but there only after hard-won elenctic argument

had established the great truths by which the interlocutor is then exhorted to live, while here the exhortation has swallowed up the argument.

36. So it remains during the whole of its first part (278E–280D) and at the start of the second (288D–290A). Here again, as in the *Lysis,* the interlocutor's attitude to Socrates is docility itself: the yes-man of the middle dialogues has made his entry into Plato's corpus.

37. 290B–D: to be cited (in part) and discussed under T23.

38. In the *Ly.* Socrates lays out the doctrine of the *prōton philon:* there is a supreme object of desire, such that all other things we may desire would be vain except in so far as that "first" object is reached (219B–220B). In the *Eud.* he teaches (1) that the only thing desired by all persons only for its own sake is happiness, and (2) that for the attainment of happiness all goods *become evil* unless controlled by moral wisdom. One can hardly imagine stronger moral claims. In (2) the Socratic doctrine of the Sovereignty of Virtue (see G. Vlastos, "Happiness and Virtue in Socrates' Moral Theory," *Proceedings of the Cambridge Philological Society* 30 (1984), 181ff. at 186–189) is pushed further in the words I have italicized than in any expression of that doctrine in Elenctic dialogues. But while heretofore Socratic doctrine had been maintained against fierce opposition (as in *Gorg.* 467Cff., *Rep.* 352Bff.), it is now uncontested by an interlocutor.

39. This is the grand methodological hypothesis on which my whole interpretation of Plato is predicated (with the qualification that in the *Symposium* and the *Parmenides* he creates a new voice—Diotima in the former, Parmenides in the latter—to supersede his Socrates *pro tem.*)

40. It should go without saying that Socrates may have any number of reasons for believing that, say, to suffer injustice is always better than to do it. But when it comes to the crunch he never brings up any of these. When the issue is joined with those who think his claim absurd and warn him that he is basing his life on a lie, he looks to the elenchus, and to nothing but that, to vindicate the truth of his position.

41. 81A–C. The search for a definition, pursued in the familiar Socratic way (a replay of the elenchus to show it dead-ending), lands in impasse (80D–E). A radically new start is called for. Thereupon a *deus ex machina* is unveiled: the glorious doctrines of transmigration and its pendant, *anamnesis,* are revealed.

42. A great point is made of this: "Watch whether you find me teaching and laying it out for him (*didaskonta kai diexionta autōi*) instead of querrying his own opinions (*tas toutou doxas anerōtōnta*)" (84D). How so, when Socrates' questioning takes the boy *to* the solution step by step? I have suggested a reply—too long to reproduce here in full—in "Anamnesis in the *Meno,*" *Dialogue* 4 (1965), 143ff. The main point is that the boy, required to give *his own* opinion in answer to Socrates' questions, is in no position to base it on what he sees, or guesses, Socrates thinks is the right answer. When he does try doing so he gets his fingers burned: both of his mistakes are due to his having placed unthinking trust in suggestions he reads into what Socrates has said (83B6–7; 83D3–5): the boy must say only what he judges to be true *for his own reasons,* prepared to defend it against Socrates. So when the interrogation reaches the point where Socrates fills out the diagram, giving a graphic presentation of the correct solution, the boy is in no position to say that this *is* the right answer unless he accepts it for reasons other than the suggestions made to him by Socrates both verbally and through the diagram: he must accept it only because *he has some understanding,* however rudimentary, *of the reasoning which warrants that conclusion.* (For fuller discussion see especially A. Nehamas, "Meno's Paradox and Socrates as a Teacher," reprinted in this volume, pp. 310–14; M. F. Burnyeat, "Wittgenstein and Augustine *De Magistro,*" *Proceedings of the Aristotelian Society,* suppl. 61 (1987), 1ff. at 8–24.)

43. T. H. Irwin, *Plato's Moral Theory* (1977), 139: "the examination of the slave-boy is a scale-model of a Socratic *elenchos.*" Same view in A. Nehamas, "Socratic Intellectualism," *Proceedings of the Boston Area Colloquium in Ancient Philosophy* 2 (1986), 16. It is expressed, or implied, in virtually all scholarly comment on the passage.

44. In Euclid "number" is *defined* as "a multitude composed of units (*to ek monadōn sunkeimenon plēthos, Elements* 7, Df. 2). A glance at the definitions cited ad loc in Heath, *The Thirteen Books of Euclid's Elements,* 2d ed. (New York, 1926), vol. 2, 280, will show that from the Pythagoreans in the fifth century B.C. to Theon of Smyrna in the second A.D. this remains constant throughout their variations.

45. Nor does Socrates imply that it does. But the language he has to use in explaining the problem to the boy could hardly fail to suggest it to him: "Now if this side were 2 feet long and that side the same, how many [square] feet would the whole area be?" (82C). He continues using numbers when correcting the boy's mistakes. Only when he reaches the point at which the boy is put on the track of the right solution (84D) does he stop assigning numerical values to the sides of the proposed square to identify possible answers to the problem.

46. Only by imagining a preternaturally precocious slave-boy coming to the interrogation with the positive thesis that all lengths are commensurable (instead of the mere ignorance of the fact that they are not) could we set Socrates a task which he could solve by elenctic means, sc. helping the boy rediscover the proof of the irrationality of the square root of 2 in Euclid, *Elements* 10, Appendix 27 (Heiberg).

47. When Plato's epistemology has matured, as it will by the time he comes to write the middle books of the *Republic,* he will be qualifying this first starry-eyed view of geometry, insisting that the axioms of geometry are not the first principles (*archai*) which unphilosophical mathematicians take them to be: they should be regarded as "hypotheses" which are themselves in need of justification; mathematicians who treat them as final truths are only "dreaming about reality" (*oneirōttousi peri to on,* 533 B–C). In the *Meno,* no such caveats are even hinted at.

48. In scientific discourse one would be more likely to speak of *tachos* instead; thus Eudoxus' astronomical treatise was entitled *peri tachōn* (Simplicius, *Comm. on Aristotle's De Caelo* 492.31ff.). See L. Brandwood, *A Word-Index to Plato* (Leeds, Eng., 1976) *s.v. tachos* for many examples in contexts of cosmological or astronomical or molecular theory in Plato; *tachutēs* occurs only once in such contexts in Plato (*Pltc.* 284E5).

49. For this rendering of *dunamis* see G. Vlastos, *Platonic Studies,* 2d ed. (Princeton, N.J., 1981), 413.

50. Cf. n. 1 (hereafter to be cited as "Proclus").

51. He "compiled elements (*stoicheia sunegrapse*) the first of those recorded to have done so," Proclus 66.1–8—a pioneering venture of whose contents we know nothing.

52. Proclus 66.18–67.14: "At this time also lived Leodamas of Thasos [whose close association with Plato is reflected in the story that Plato taught him the method of analysis: Proclus 211.19–23], Archytas of Tarentum, and Theaetetus of Athens, by whom the theorems were increased and brought into a more scientific system (*eis epistēmonikōteran sustasin*). Younger than Leodamas were Neoclides and his pupil Leon, who added many discoveries to those of their predecessors, so that Leon was able to produce a system of elements (*ta stoicheia suntheinai*) more adequate in respect of both their number and their utility for demonstrations (*tōi te plēthei kai tēi chreiai tōn deiknumenōn*) . . . Amyclas of Heraclea, one of Plato's companions, Menaechmus, a pupil of Eudoxus, who also associated with Plato, and his brother Dinostratus made the whole of geometry still more perfect. . . . Theudius of Magnesia [member of the Academy] . . . produced an admirable system of the elements (*ta stoicheia kalōs sunetaxen*) and made many partial theorems more general."

53. Plato has no quarrel with it *qua* physical theory. He builds it into his own in the *Timaeus* (67C).

54. The translation, containing items whose meaning is controversial, follows in all essentials the one in Heath, *Greek Mathematics,* 299.

55. For further comment see e.g., Heath, *Greek Mathematics,* 298ff.; V. Karasmanis, "The Hypothetical Method in Plato's Middle Period" (Ph.D. diss., Oxford, 1987), 73ff.
56. See Proclus 420.23ff.; Heath, *Euclid's Elements,* 1.343–44; van der Waerden, *Science Awakening,* 118ff.
57. To my knowledge, this claim has not been made in previous discussions of Plato's hypothetical method. It does not seem to have been realized that this method junks the "say only what you believe" rule (cf. T7 and n. 14) which precludes argument from unasserted premises, characteristic of both Zenonian and eristic practice (*SE,* 29, 35–36) and always normal in philosophical discussion, where the use of counterfactual premises is common and entirely unobjectionable.
58. This point is not spelled out in the text, understandably so: Plato is not undertaking a complete description of *ex hupotheseōs skopeisthai.* His mathematician readers would not need to be told that in their science when the logical convertibility of *p* with *h* had been established, the question of the truth of *p* would be left hanging in the air until it could be determined whether or not *h* is a "hypothesis worthy of acceptance" (*hupotheseōs axias apodexasthai, Phdo.* 92D), which could only be finally done by referring to the axioms.
59. *Prot.* 361B: Socrates holds that all the virtues are knowledge, "insisting" on it (or "urging it," *hōs su speudeis). La.* 194D: (Nicias speaking) "I have often heard you say that each of us is good in those things in which he is wise, bad in those in which he is ignorant." For Aristotle this is the crux of Socrates' moral psychology: *EN* 1145b23–27; *EE* 1215b2–9; *MM* 1182a15–26.
60. There is no foundation for Robinson's view (*Plato's Earlier Dialectic,* 2d ed. (Oxford, 1953), 116–17), followed by Karasmanis (*Hypothetical Method,* 85 and 99, n. 24), that the hypothetical procedure ends at 89C. The only reason given for this surprising claim is that "after 89 neither the word 'hypothesis' nor any methodological remark occurs in the dialogue" (Robinson, loc. cit.). This is true, but irrelevant. Plato is under no obligation to keep naming the method he is using or making methodological remarks about it.
61. It should be noticed that *only* this segment of the sequal to the argument *pro h* is directed against *h:* the long section, 89D–96C, argues not against *h,* but against *p* (its conclusion at 96D10, "Hence virtue is not teachable," is obviously the negation of *p*). So the inconclusiveness of the reasoning in 89D–96C (there are no teachers of virtue, *ergo* virtue is not teachable—lame argument, from *non esse* to *non posse*) does nothing to discredit the attack on *h* at 96D–98C: a perfectly solid argument, concluding that knowledge is not a necessary condition of right action (T21), from which it follows that knowledge is not necessary for virtue, as Socrates had thought (his theory makes no provision for controlled right action if the appropriate cognitive component is lacking).
62. It would be reasonable to allow for substantial development between the *Meno* (where the new theory of forms has not yet been formulated) and the *Phaedo* (where it is presented explicitly as the foundation of Plato's metaphysics: 65Dff., 100Bff.); so too *a fortiori* between the *Meno* and the middle books of the *Republic* (cf. n. 47).
63. The break-away from the earlier Socratic view is carried further in the immediate sequel (99B–100A): in the *Gorgias* Socrates had damned Athens' best leaders along with its worst (518C–519A: cf. G. Vlastos, "The Historical Socrates and Athenian Democracy," *Political Theory* 11 (1983), 495ff. at 501). Plato now recognizes Pericles as the "magnificently astute" (*megaloprepōs sophon,* 94B) statesman he surely was (*oudenos hēsson gnōnai te ta deonta kai hermēneusai tauta,* Th. 2.60.5), allowing now for inspired statesmen (as Socrates had allowed for inspired poets: *Apol.* 22C, *Ion* 534B) who achieve much that is excellent (*kala*) by divine grace (*theiai moirai*) without benefit of craft or science. (For a different reading of the passage, using vituperation in the *Gorgias* to undercut eulogy in the *Meno,* unwarrantably homogenizing their respective viewpoints, see R. S. Bluck, *Plato's Meno*

(Cambridge, Eng., 1961), 368ff.; also T. H. Irwin, *Plato's Moral Theory* (Oxford, 1977), 317, n. 22, rebutted by R. Kraut, *Socrates and the State* (Princeton, N.J., 1984), 301–4.)

64. I know of no previous notice of the fact pointed out in *SDK* (26, n. 65) that T22 is "the first clear indication in his corpus that Plato is now abreast of advanced mathematics."

65. I.e., added geometrically, since, as I explained (n. 44), in Greek mathematics numbers are defined as discrete aggregates ("multitudes of units"), hence irrationals, not qualifying as numbers, are not susceptible of arithmetical addition. But they *are* susceptible of geometrical addition: thus two irrational line-segments may be joined to form a continuous one, segmented only by a dimensionless point. This has not been understood in the scholarly literature: D. Tarrant (*The Hippias Major Attributed to Plato; With Introductory Essays and Commentary* (Cambridge, Eng., 1928), 83) remarks that "the use of the terms here is clearly inaccurate, for two *arrēta* cannot become *rhēta* by addition;" P. Woodruff (*Plato: Hippias Major* (Indianapolis, Ind., 1982), 87) that "Socrates may be enticing Hippias with a falsehood." (There is no textual foundation for the view [E. de Strycker, "Une énigme mathématique dans l'*Hippias Majeur*," *Mélange Émile Boisacq* (Paris, 1937) 317ff.; 1941, 25ff.] that Plato is referring to the *product*, rather than the *sum*, of the two quantities: as W. R. Knorr (*The Evolution of the Euclidean Elements* (Boston, 1975), 296, n. 77) points out, "the term *sunamphoteros* is regular for 'sum'; and *amphotera* had just been used in the parallel case of odd numbers having an even sum.)

66. As pointed out in Heath, *Greek Mathematics*, 304, with references to Euclid *Elements* 2.11 and 13.6 (cf. also Heath, *Euclid's Elements*, 1.137 and 3.19). For an additional illustration of suitably selected irrationals having rational or irrational sums, see Knorr, *Evolution of the Euclidean Elements*, 276.

67. Cf. n. 69.

68. *Ou gar poiousi ta diagrammata hekastoi toutōn, alla ta onta aneuriskousin.* My translation is mainly after Cherniss, "Plato as a Mathematician," 422.

69. At this point Plato must have felt that to credit Socrates with such a task, so alien to the purely moral inquiries in which he had been wholly absorbed heretofore in Plato's portrayal of him, would place too heavy a strain on the dramatic consistency of the persona of the protagonist. So he presents the thought as an inspired fluke, a prompting from "higher powers" to a young innocent (291A).

70. Though there is to natural philosophy, paralleling the citation of Heraclitus (DK B82, B83) in the *H.Ma.* (289A–B): Socrates now finds wisdom in the writings of "those who discourse on nature and on the universe" (*hoi peri phuseōs te kai tou holou dialegomenoi, Ly.* 214B). Nothing of the kind happens in the Elenctic dialogues. The nearest thing there to an allusion to natural philosophy is in saying he knows nothing "great or small" about such things when protesting the "nonsense" he is made to talk as a natural philosopher in the *Clouds* (*Apol.* 19C–D).

71. Cf. n. 30.

72. The description of number-theory as "investigating how numerous are the odd and the even both relative to themselves and relative to each other (*kai pros hauta kai pros allēla pōs echei tou plēthous,* 451C), regurgitating verbatim the one at *Charm.* 166A, does not presuppose advanced knowledge of mathematics: see Endnote A. Nor does the concurrent description of the subject-matter of astronomy as "the movements of the stars and the sun and the moon and of their relative speeds" presuppose more than a rudimentary understanding of what is going on in that science.

73. The continued proportion, "as cosmetics is to gymnastics, so is the sophistical to the legislative art, and as cookery to medicine, so is rhetoric to justice" is said to be in the style of the geometricians (*eipein hōsper hoi geōmetrai*) (465C: cf. *Pltc.* 257B); in no previous Elenctic dialogue does Plato say that he is speaking like the geometricians. At the peak of the

argument which confutes Callicles Socrates tells him: "It has escaped you that geometrical equality has great power among both gods and men; you go in for *pleonexia* because you neglect geometry" (508A).

74. See the references to Dodds and Irwin in n. 30.

75. We have no reliable report of any earlier journey outside the Greek mainland: see Endnote B.

76. *Acad.* 1.10.16. The connection established with Archytas was to enable Plato to "bring about relations of friendship and hospitality" between Archytas and Dionysius II ([Plato], *Ep.* 7, 350A–B: this letter is a good source of information about the events it describes; if Timaeus of Tauromenium [c. 356–260 B.C.] "used it in the writing of his history," G. R. Morrow, *Plato's Epistles* (Indianapolis, Ind., 1961), 37–39, it was read and thought trustworthy less than a century after Plato's death).

77. We have no information about him independent of Plato's description of the eponymous dialogue's protagonist: "second to none in wealth and birth, had held the highest and most reputable offices in his city and reached the peak of all philosophy" (*Tim.* 20A).

78. His solution of the problem of the duplication of the cube by an elegant construction in three dimensions, as described by Eudemus (DK A.14 *ap.* Eutocius, preserved in Archimedes, vol. 3.84 of his works [ed. by Heiberg]). For appreciative elucidation of its mathematics see e.g., van der Waerden, *Science Awakening*, 150–51, writing about it with uninhibited enthusiasm ("Is this not admirable? Archytas must have had a truly divine inspiration when he found this construction").

79. Though a decidedly more conservative one: Aristotle, *Pol.* 1320b9–16.

80. "He held the office of general seven times, though no one else had held it in his city more than once, because the law forbade it" (D. L.8.79). For his political views see DK 47. B3, comparing *to ison exein* here with *hē isotēs hē geōmetrikē* at *Gorg.* 508A.

81. Fragments 1, 2, 3 in DK. (For recent defense of the authenticity of fr. 1 see A. C. Bowen, "The Foundations of Early Pythagorean Harmonic Science: Archytas, Fragment 1," *Ancient Philosophy* 2 (1982), 79ff.; C. Huffman, "The Authenticity of Archytas Fr. 1," *Classical Quartlery* 35 (1985), 344ff.)

82. *Mem.* 4.7.2–3: "In the case of geometry he said one should pursue it until one was competent to measure a parcel of land. . . . He opposed carrying the study as far as the hard-to-understand proofs (*mechri tōn dussunetōn diagrammatōn*), though he was not himself unfamiliar with these." For comment see n. 94 in Endnote A.

83. He is named as the teacher of Eudoxus in Diogenes Laertius (8.86).

84. This, and exposure to Archytas' philosophical writings, is all we are in a position to say on the basis of the available evidence. How much of Archytas' philosophical or mathematical thought Plato absorbed at this time we have no way of knowing: see Endnote B, n. 105, and cf. Knorr, *Evolution of Euclidean Elements,* 89.

85. To Xenophon it seems a babble of doctrinaire in-fighting, speculative dogmas clashing in stark contradictions: "Some hold that being is one, others that it is infinitely many; some that everything is in flux, others that nothing changes; some that all things are generated, others that nothing is generated and nothing perishes" (*Mem.* 1.1.14). Cf. Isocrates 15 (*Antidosis*) 268.

86. "Assumptions, treated as the self-evident starting-points of mathematical deductions," G. E. R. Lloyd, *Magic, Reason and Experience* (Cambridge, Eng., 1979), 114. (I cannot follow the different interpretation of this text he adopts in "Plato on Mathematics and Nature, Myth and Science," *Humanities* 3 (1983): 12ff.)

87. Protagoras denying that the tangent meets the circle at (just) one point is not a mathematician opting for a finitist geometry, but a contrarian dogmatizing from the sidelines. Claims to have squared the circle come not from working geometricians (Hippocrates of Chios does not square the circle but lunes inscribed in it [Simplicius, *in Phys.*, 60.22ff; see Lloyd, "The

Alleged Fallacy of Hippocrates of Chios,'' *Apeiron* 22 (1987) 103–28.]) but eristics or sophists, Bryson (*A. Po. An.* 75b40), Antiphon (*A. Phys.* 185a14–17), provoking Aristotle's retort that it is not the geometrician's business to rebut such claims, ''for they are addressed to the many, who do not know what [proof] is, or is not possible, in a particular [subject]'' (*Soph. El.* 172a5–7).

88. No dialogue composed before the *Phaedo* records greater depth and intensity of affection.

89. This essay recycles a paper read to a colloquium on Greek mathematics at King's College, Cambridge, in 1984 under the title, ''When did Plato become a mathematician?'' It was given in 1986 under the present title at Cornell as a Townsend Lecture and in 1987 as a Whitehead Lecture at Harvard and as a paper at a colloquium on classical philosophy at the University of Pennsylvania. For comments which prompted revisions I owe thanks to discussants on those occasions and also to exceedingly helpful criticisms from John Ackrill, Myles Burnyeat, G. E. R. Lloyd, and Friedrich Solmsen. But for views expressed here I alone may be held responsible.

90. *Arithmētikē,* the science of number.

91. *Logistikē,* the art of computation, application of mathematical knowledge or skill to reach a determinate quantitative result. Cf. Socrates' request to the slave-boy: ''How much is twice two? Calculate and tell me (*logisamenos eipe*).'' *M.* 82B.

92. Van der Waerden, *Science Awakening,* 108ff., adopting a surmise by O. Becker.

93. Compare the condition of college-educated adults nowadays who have learned high-school geometry and algebra and may have even had Freshman analytic geometry and calculus but had lost interest after that.

94. If Xenophon's remark (*Mem.* 4.7.3: cf. n. 82) that Socrates was not himself unfamiliar with ''the hard to understand proofs'' in geometry has some basis in fact, as is entirely possible, it would fit perfectly the hypothesis that Socrates had studied mathematics in his youth, absorbing much of the mathematical knowledge available at the time, but had dropped those studies thereafter.

95. Those first moves of his (cf. n. 51) cannot have come long before the cascading developments in this area in the fourth century (n. 52).

96. The pioneering work in the exploration of irrationals by Theodorus, proving the irrationality of the roots of 3, 5, etc., up to 17 on a case by case basis (*Tht.* 147D–148B; cf. M. F. Burnyeat, ''The Philosophical Sense of Theaetetus' Mathematics,'' *Isis* 69 (1978), 489ff. at 494–95), is naturally dated not long before the generalization of those proofs in a systematic theory of incommensurables by Theaetetus in the first third of the fourth century (he died young in 369 B.C.).

97. T14.

98. I follow Heath (*Euclid's Elements,* 281 and passim) in assuming that the parenthetical augment is required to render the sense of *dicha diairoumenos* in mathematical contexts.

99. Heath (*Greek Mathematics,* 292) charges the definition in A3 with a graver fault: ''a defective statement unless the term 'scalene' is restricted to the case in which one part of the number is odd and the other even,'' thus implicitly using the definiendum in the definiens. We cannot positively convict the definition in A3 of such gross circularity, since we do not know how Socrates would have defined ''scalene'' if called upon to do so.

100. Founder of the Megarian school; in the Platonic corpus: narrator in the *Theaetetus;* present at the death-scene in the *Phaedo* (59C).

101. Mentioned also by two other late sources, Apuleius (1.3) and Olympiodorus (*in Plat. Gorg.* 41.7), also without any clue as to *their* source.

102. Cf. W. K. C. Guthrie, *A History of Greek Philosophy* (Cambridge, Eng., 1975), 4, 14–15; Riginos: *The Anecdotes concerning the Life and Writings of Plato, Platonica* 11 (Leiden, 1976) 63–64.

103. Knorr, *The Evolution of Euclidean Elements,* 88–89), following earlier suggestions by

H. Vogt and P. Tannery, hypothesizes a uniquely close relation to Theodorus, maintaining that the latter had been ''Plato's master in mathematics''; he holds that it was from Theodorus that Plato had derived ''his basic conception of the field of mathematics . . . and a deep respect for matters of mathematical rigor.'' But B3 makes a pointed reference to the fact that there were other mathematicians to whom ''Socrates'' could also have turned for instruction in their area of expertise. There is no good reason to suppose that Plato had failed to take advantage of those other opportunities and learn as much, or more, from those others. Theodorus does not appear in the Eudemian history in Proclus (cf. T1) among the mathematicians who were close to Plato.

104. In the note ad loc. in his translation, *Oeuvres Complètes* (Paris, 1950).
105. But neither am I proposing Archytas as Plato's preceptor in mathematics nor yet as his model in metaphysics. Cf. n. 64.

FURTHER READING

Benson, H. H. 1987. ''The Problem of the Elenchus Reconsidered,'' *Ancient Philosophy* 7:67–85.

Brickhouse, T. C. and Smith, N. D. 1984. ''Vlastos on the Elenchus.'' *Oxford Studies in Ancient Philosophy* 2:185–96.

———. 1991 ''Socrates' Elenctic Mission.'' *Oxford Studies in Ancient Philosophy* 9.

Kraut, R. 1983. ''Comments on Vlastos.'' *Oxford Studies in Ancient Philosophy* 1:59–70.

Polansky, R. 1985. ''Professor Vlastos' Analysis of Socratic Elenchus.'' *Oxford Studies in Ancient Philosophy* 3:247–60.

Vlastos, G. 1983. ''The Socratic Elenchus.'' *Oxford Studies in Ancient Philosophy* 1:27–58.

———. 1983. ''Afterthoughts.'' *Oxford Studies in Ancient Philosophy* 1:71–74.

10

The Unity of Virtue

TERRY PENNER

The thesis of this paper is highly unusual, yet it is perfectly straightforward. It is that when Socrates said "Virtue is one," he meant it quite literally! True, the conventional philosophical wisdom—which has infected classicist interpreters of Socrates as well as philosophical interpreters—renders a literal reading of the doctrine quite impossible. But the conventional philosophical wisdom is both mistaken as philosophy and anachronistic as exegesis of Socrates.[1] So there is every reason to look around for an alternative interpretation of Socrates—and what more natural than that he meant what he said? My task, then, is both philosophical and exegetical. I concentrate on the philosophical half of the task in Sections I and II of the chapter, setting forth the philosophical assumptions which have traditionally been made and showing that it is unnecessary to make them, and sketching in by contrast the alternative interpretation I am proposing. In Section III, I show how, on the literal interpretation, Socrates' arguments in the *Protagoras* purporting to show that "Virtue is one" are much improved over what they have usually been supposed to be. In Section IV, the literal interpretation is extended to the *Laches* and the *Charmides*, and the single entity in question, virtue, identified with the knowledge (science) of good and evil. The further characterization of this single entity, and of its place in a Socratic theory of action and motivation, is promised for a later paper.

I

The so-called doctrine of the "unity of the virtues," which turns up in some, though not all, of Plato's earlier, "Socratic" dialogues, is almost always taken to be a disguised equivalence and not an identity. That is, it is taken simply as

(1) Men are brave if and only if they are wise
    if and only if they are temperate
    if and only if they are just
    if and only if they are pious,

and not as the stronger

(2) Bravery = wisdom = temperance = justice = piety.

162

(2) is stronger than (1) because it entails but is not entailed by (1). It is not entailed by (1) since it carries ontological implications not carried by (1)—for example,

> (3) "Bravery," "wisdom," "temperance," "justice," and "piety" are five different names of the same thing   *Socrates*

and

> *courage*
>
> (4) In addition to brave men there is such a thing as (bravery.)

Is a bully Brave? — No! Why? Because Brave is = to wisdom

(3) is the natural metalinguistic version of (2), given the usual assumptions about identity and reference. And (4) is entailed by (2)—though not (1)—when taken together with

> (4a) There are brave men
>
> (4b) If there are brave men and if there is such a thing as bravery, then bravery is not identical with any brave men.

Now there are very strong textual reasons for preferring (2) to (1) as an interpretation of Socrates. To give just one example, there can be little doubt that, using *ousia* or *prāgma* for "thing," Socrates accepts (3) in the *Protagoras*.[2] Why, then, is it practically impossible to find an interpreter who attributes the doctrine of "the unity of the virtues" to Socrates in this stronger form?[3]

At first blush, it might seem that interpreters fear the ontological implications of (2) which we have just noticed. We might picture them asking: how could Socrates seriously have subscribed to (3) and (4)? After all, was it not *Plato* who waxed metaphysical, "separating" the Socratic universal? Unfortunately, there is some serious confusion in these questions. For no interpreter can avoid the ontological implications of the so-called "What is *X?*" questions:[4] questions of the form

> (5) What is that one thing, the same in all cases, by virtue of which brave men are brave?[5]

But consideration of the "What is *X?*" question is no blind alley. Here we will find the underlying reason for the rejection of (2). For the "What is *X?*" question is generally taken (especially by those who accept [1]) to be a request for meanings. "What is bravery?" on this view seeks the meaning of "bravery." In the light of (5), it is easy to see that such interpreters are committed to something like

> (6) In addition to brave men, there must be such a thing as bravery—that is the meaning of "bravery"—by virtue of which brave men are brave.

From this we see immediately why these interpreters prefer (1) to (2). For since nothing could be more obvious than that

> (7) The meaning of "bravery" $\neq$ the meaning of "wisdom,"

it follows—if "bravery" has the same reference in (7), (6), and (2)—that (2) is false. Accordingly, it has been concluded that what Socrates means by the doctrine of "the unity of the virtues" must be not the identity (2), but the equivalence (1).

An exactly parallel argument results if for "the meaning of 'bravery'" in (6)–(7) we substitute "the essence of bravery" or "the universal bravery"—at least on the most usual accounts of essences and universals. For on these accounts,

(8) The essence of bravery = the essence of wisdom if and only if "bravery" and "wisdom" are synonymous—that is, if the meaning of "bravery" = the meaning of "wisdom."

And similarly for universals.[6] Hence even those who prefer talk of essences or universals to talk of meanings characteristically endorse the equivalence (1) rather than the identity (2) as an account of "the unity of the virtues." For brevity's sake, I will follow the hint of (8) and speak of the proponents of meanings *or* essences *or* universals (on the usual interpretations) as all holding "the meaning view."

In this paper, my aim will be to show that in the doctrine of "the unity of virtues," Socrates intended the stronger (2). That is, as long as he held (1), he also held (2), and (2) was his preferred formulation of the doctrine. For similar reasons, I will also maintain that as long as he held the "Virtue is knowledge" doctrine, he held not just the equivalence

(9) Men are virtuous if and only if they have knowledge,

but also the stronger identity

(10) Virtue = knowledge,

the latter being his preferred formulation of the doctrine. On this view, the bravery which, by (4), exists in addition to brave men is identical with the temperance which exists in addition to temperate men, and so forth. But how can this be?

The answer to this question requires a completely new approach to the "What is *X?*" questions of the early dialogues. My singling out of assumption (6) of the meaning view will already have suggested this. To defend this approach in detail would take me too far afield for present purposes. So I will simply claim as evidence of its correctness (for the dialogues I consider) the way it works in passages relevant to this paper. What I maintain is this. When Socrates asked "What is bravery?" and so forth, he did not want to know what the meaning of the word "bravery" was, nor what the essence of bravery was, nor what the universal *bravery* was. His question was not (what has become) the philosopher's question, the question patiently explained to students reading Plato in introductory philosophy courses; it was not a request for a conceptual analysis (as usually conceived: the generating of a certain set of analytic truths about bravery).[7] His question was rather the *general's* question, "What is bravery?"—that is, "What is it that makes brave men brave?" The general asks this question not out of interest in mapping our concepts, but out of a desire to learn something substantial about the human psyche. He wants to know what psychological state it is, the imparting of which to his men will make them brave.[8] But then the general does not know in advance whether or not the psychological state in question will also make his men act wisely. If it does, then Socrates (on the view I am presenting) will have been right. Bravery, the psychological state which makes men brave, will be identical with wisdom, the psychological state which makes men wise. Such, I will maintain, was the question "What is bravery?" for Socrates.

The following comparison may help the reader to see how I understand Socrates' treatment of such questions as "What is bravery?" "What is virtue?" Do not imagine the Ryle of the late 1940s asking "Well, what is a feeling, really?" Instead, imagine the Freud of the early 1890s asking "Well, what is hysteria, really?" Here we have, I take it, something like a contrast between conceptual questions about psychology and substantial questions about psychology, to be answered not by logical analysis, but by finding a true psychological theory. Interpreters have treated Socrates' questions as conceptual questions, whereas I am suggesting that they are substantial questions. (The question "What is water?" would be a conceptual question if what it asks is what people mean by "water"; it is a substantial question if what it asks is what a true scientific theory says water is. Thus the correct answer to the conceptual question could not have been "H_2O" prior to Dalton; but if a true chemical theory says that water is H_2O, then "H_2O" *was* the correct answer to the substantial question before Dalton—even though no one knew it was.)

The issue, then, is this. The meaning view takes the reference of "bravery" in "What is bravery?" to be the meaning of "bravery" or the universal *bravery,* and so forth—what we might call an *abstract entity.* And since, as was explained already, the identity conditions of meanings or universals and so forth are very narrow, "Virtue is one" must be turned into an equivalence. By contrast, I take the reference of "bravery" in "What is bravery?" to be simply *that psychological state which explains the fact that certain men do brave acts*—what we might call a *theoretical entity.*[9] And since the identity conditions for psychological states are presumably wider than synonymy, we can suppose that two non-synonymous virtue-words refer to the same psychological state. Thus on my view "Virtue is one" can be taken as an identity.

I must now explain my choice of the *Protagoras, Laches,* and *Charmides* for detailed discussion. First, we must be clear about the scope of my thesis. Where Socrates denies any of the following,

> In order to be virtuous a man must have knowledge (that is, be knowledgeable)
>
> All just men are pious
>
> All brave men are wise,

there is clearly no argument against my identity version of "Virtue is knowledge" or of "Virtue is one"; for these denials are equally denials of the equivalence versions. In fact, on any view, it must be admitted that Socrates sometimes denies "Virtue is knowledge" and "Virtue is one." For the equivalence (9) is denied at *Meno* 96Eff., and the equivalence (1) is denied at *Eu.* 11E4–12E7,[10] and again (I would say) at *Eud.* 281B4ff.[11] So there can be no requirement that I answer for an absence of the identities (2) and (10) in these three dialogues. Our question can only be: where, as in the *Protagoras,* Socrates plainly does intend to be asserting "Virtue is knowledge" or "Virtue is one," is he merely asserting the weaker equivalences (1) and (9), or is he asserting the stronger identities (2) and (10)? It is clear that the *Laches* and *Charmides* are relevant here, whereas nothing very decisive either way turns up in such other indisputably early dialogues as the *Lysis, Ion, Apology, Crito,* and *Hippias Minor.* The *Gorgias,* which is a transitional dialogue to the middle period dialogues,[12] would evidently respond to investigation of our question. But for reasons of space, I will say no more about it than I do in the next paragraph.

I must now say a word about those dialogues where the denials of "Virtue is knowledge" or "Virtue is one" occur (on *either* the identity view *or* the equivalence view). Here is a possible explanation. In the *Euthyphro, Euthydemus,* and *Meno,* Socrates—or perhaps we should say "Socrates-Plato," since the *Meno* is a dialogue clearly transitional from Socrates to Plato—begins to attend to the popular or "demotic" virtues, those virtues which do not require knowledge or wisdom (cf. *Phdo*. 68C–69D, 82AB; *Rep*. 430C, 500D; and also the startling *Statesman* 305E–310A, where temperance and bravery are treated as *inimical* and *opposite* to each other!). If my conjecture is correct, that the *Euthyphro, Euthydemus,* and *Meno do* represent this transition to the consideration of the demotic virtues, then it is posible that "Socrates-Plato" still thought that *real* virtue (Plato's "philosophic virtue": cf. *Rep*. 505A) was one. Such an interpretation certainly sits well with the way in which Socrates treats *wisdom* at *Eud*. 279Dff., *justice* at *H. Mi*. 375D–376C, *Rep*. I, 353E, and *temperance* in the *Charmides* (at least as treated in Sec. IV) and in the *Gorgias* (506D5–507C3). In the *Gorgias* temperance is clearly a psychological state—a *taxis* or *kosmos* of the soul which is evidently the causal explanation of men's acting piously, justly, bravely, wisely, and so forth. Each of the passages cited treats the virtue in question as though it were the paramount virtue or even the only virtue. It is natural to suggest that here Socrates speaks of "real temperance," "real wisdom," or "real justice"—and that in so doing he speaks of just one thing—the science of good and evil, the ruling art.

Evidently, the unity of "real virtue" could be pursued into the middle and later dialogues of Plato. I shall here, however—for the sake of space and relative completeness of argumentation—confine myself to arguing my thesis for the earlier, "Socratic," period, before demotic virtue arises, and apropos solely of the *Protagoras, Laches,* and *Charmides*. It will, I hope, be clear enough along what general lines I would adapt and argue my thesis for other dialogues.

II

I must now attempt to disarm a fundamental philosophical objection to my interpretation. This is that if we just think in a common-sense way about the reference of "bravery," "wisdom," and so forth, we will see that the references must be dispositions—on the one hand the disposition to brave behavior, on the other the disposition to wise behavior. So bravery and wisdom, being dispositions to different kinds of behavior, must be different dispositions. Thus even leaving aside considerations of whether or not the "What is *X?*" question is a request for meanings, it can be seen that Socrates could not have thought that "bravery" and "wisdom" refer to the same thing. Surely, then, "Virtue is one" must be interpreted as the equivalence (1) rather than the identity (2)?

The objection presupposes (*a*) that dispositions are numerically distinct if and only if they lead to different kinds of behavior, and (*b*) that brave behavior and wise behavior are different kinds of behavior. Now without questioning assumption (*b*), it seems to me that the objection can be met *either* by accepting (*a*) and denying that bravery and wisdom are dispositions, *or* by denying (*a*). To make this clear I shall present two possible conceptions of bravery and wisdom, on one of which they will be dispositions of the type envisaged by the objection, and on the other of which they will not be such dispositions. I shall not inquire which conception properly deserves the name "disposition." (I am not, of course, saying that these are the only possible conceptions of bravery and wisdom.)

On the first conception, bravery and wisdom may be called "tendencies." And we will lay it down that tendencies are numerically distinct if and only if they lead to different kinds of behavior. On the second view, bravery and wisdom may be called "motive-forces" or "states of soul." And we will lay it down that the *same* motive-force or state of soul can result in different kinds of behavior. Given these two views about bravery and wisdom—call them the tendency view and the motive-force or state of soul view—we can perhaps agree on the following as a possible account of Socrates' doctrine of "the unity of the virtues."

> Socrates thought that all and only those men with tendencies to brave actions had tendencies to wise actions (these actions being in general different from the former actions). But he may have believed that all of these tendencies sprang from the same motive-force or state of soul (e.g., a certain kind of knowledge).[13]

The difference, then, between the two views is simply over whether to use the words "bravery" and "wisdom" for the tendencies on the one hand or for the motive-force or state of soul on the other.

Thus the fundamental philosophical objection to my interpretation of Socrates' doctrine comes to this—that "bravery" and "wisdom" *must* be words for tendencies and *cannot* be words for motive-forces or states of soul. Looked at in this way, the objection seems little better than a piece of linguistic dogmatism. What precludes the possibility of the general we met with in Section I asking "What is bravery?" and meaning thereby "What is it that these men have, that makes them so *brave* in combat? And how can I impart it or inculcate it in other men?" Would Freud have been precluded from asking "What is hysteria?" when he sought thereby an *explanation* of hysterical behavior? What the general and Freud seek is neither label nor meaning but *explanation*. They are asking, surely, about inner motive-forces or states of soul. So what we have here is surely the possibility of "bravery" and "hysteria" sometimes referring to motive-forces or states of souls. Moreover, it is conceivable that the motive-force or state of soul about which the general asked also led to other tendencies (e.g., tenderness to friends). Then we would have an analogue to the identity of bravery and wisdom in the identity of the motive-force or state-of-soul bravery with the motive-force or state-of-soul tenderness to friends.

Nor can it be maintained that Socrates would have found odd the idea of bravery as more than a tendency. After all, his pupil Plato identified bravery as a certain psychic structure. Why couldn't Socrates have found possible the identifying of bravery with a psychic state?

Some further philosophical remarks may be in order about tendencies as characterized here. First, the tendency view will often simply collapse into the meaning view. This happens if kinds of behavior are regarded as distinct if and only if the words for the kinds of behavior are non-synonymous. This account of dispositions and kinds of behavior has been common in analytical philosophy, if rarely explicit. On this account, tendencies could be incorporated into (8) along with universals and essences. But then the tendency view would not have to be independently refuted. Second, it may be remarked that it has been common for contemporary philosophers of science, at least since 1932,[14] to identify such physical dispositions as solubility with certain physical structures. If solubility is a tendency, then, of course, it cannot be a physical structure. But if solubility is that which substances have that leads to their actually dissolving in certain circumstances, then it can be such a structure.[15] By contrast, it has been common in that tradition of analytical philosophy which has contributed most to the study of Plato and Aristotle—ordinary language philosophy—to identify dispositons with what I have called tendenices. According to Ryle, and on the tendency view, it can be no part of the truth conditions of a statement about solubility that there be some physical explanation of the tendency to dissolve—for example, in terms of physical structures of some kind. That would be an empirical matter, not a matter of "what we mean by" our disposition talk. For many philosophers of science, however, *whatever* "we mean by" our disposition talk, the truth conditions of disposition statements will at least often implicitly include a clause to the effect that "there exists a physical (or scientific) explanation of the behavior in question"—whether or not that explanation can, at this stage of science, be given a more explicit characterization. Such philosophers evidently regard the assumption that lawlike behavior has an explanation as essential to any semantics they adopt for a language; for the sake of this consideration, they are prepared to drop considerations of "what we mean by" our disposition statements. This position seems to me an eminently reasonable one, though I will not directly argue its merits here.[16] All I need for my present purposes is (a) that this *is* a reasonable position; and so (b) it is appropriate to consider whether Socrates held such a position. In accordance with this position, I will sometimes refer to motive-forces or states of soul as "explanatory entities." Third, it seems to me uneconomical to suppose, as the objection must, that, in addition to brave behavior and the motive-force or state of soul which explains that behavior, there is such a thing as the tendency to brave behavior. For the proponent of the tendency view cannot do without reference to behavior or to the relevant explanatory states—unless he wishes to deprive himself of the possibility of finding explanations for the lawlike behavior that is involved. But once one *does* have reference to the behavior and to the explanatory states, what sentences referring to tendencies cannot be adequately paraphrased into sentences referring to the behavior and to the explanatory states? But as we can see from (4), the tendency view will be committed to this unjustified ontological extravagance.

Of course, we will expect there to be predicate words dividing behavior into kinds. Normally we will want to distinguish admirable actions both by the kinds of human qualities which the agents exhibit (motive-forces or states of soul) and by the kinds of situations in which they occur. Simply by way of example, let us speak of that one thing which, on Socrates' view, is named by all of "bravery," "wisdom," and so forth as "practical wisdom." Then a brave action might be an action such as a man of practical wisdom would do in a situation of danger, a temperate action an action such as a man of practical wisdom would do in a situation of temptation, and so forth. Perhaps the following fable about the development of our ideas of actions, men, and virtues will make things clearer. Imagine that we begin (i) by classifying acts simply as "good acts in situations of danger," (ii) abbreviate this to "brave acts," then (iii) classify certain men as "brave men" according to their tendencies, and (iv) call that thing in them which makes them brave "bravery," and (v) try to find out more about it. We may even then (vi) come to redraw the boundaries of brave acts in the light of theories we have about bravery. Notice that although we referred to *tendencies* in (iii), the reference could be eliminated by substituting for "according to their tendencies" something like "if they have the requisite quality for doing brave acts in the approprite circumstances"; and the requisite quality could be identified with the motive-force or state-of-soul bravery.[17]

In the light of these remarks, I will ignore the tendency view in the sequel, and concentrate simply upon the meaning view as the (philosophical) rationale for reading Socrates' words as though he intended the equivalences (1) and (9), and pit against it the motive-force or state-of-soul view as the philosophical rationale for reading Socrates' works as though he intended the identities (2) and (10).

III

In this section I begin by analyzing the different ways in which Socrates and Protagoras claim in the *Protagoras* that "Virtue is one." This analysis will show us that Socrates meant by this dictum my identity (2), that wisdom = temperance = bravery = and so forth. I then go through all the revelant skirmishes between Socrates and Protagoras over the ways in which virtue is one. The first argument on this topic, the argument from resemblance, will prove to be relevant only to the least plausible part of Protagoras' interpretation of "Virtue is one," and will do nothing toward establishing Socrates' interpretation of the dictum. The first two arguments relevant to how Socrates takes the dictum, the argument from opposites and the argument from confidence, will be shown to be much more plausible on the motive-force or state-of-soul view than on the meaning view. The conclusion of the *akrasia* argument, which I call the argument from "that by virtue of which," is the third relevant argument, and it confirms my view on both the "unity of the virtues" and the "What is *X?*" question. The same applies to the final argument of the dialogue, the argument from "Virtue is knowledge."

With the exception of the discussion of the teachability of virtue (at 318A1–328C2), the main philosophical parts of the *Protagoras* (329B5–334C5, 349A6–361D6) are given over to a dispute between Socrates and Protagoras as to the way in which virtue is one (329C6–D1). Protagoras' position, as it is progressively articulated by Socrates, is as follows:

> **(P1)** Wisdom, temperance, justice, piety, bravery are parts of virtue—parts in the way mouth, nose, eyes, ears are parts of the face, and not parts in the way the parts of gold are parts (being no different from each other or from the whole, except in largeness or smallness).
>
> **(P2)** Wisdom ≠ temperance ≠ justice ≠ piety ≠ bravery.
>
> **(P3)** The parts of virtue, like the parts of the face, each have their own peculiar power (*idian dunamin*); both the parts themselves and their powers are unlike each other.
>
> **(P4)** As one might expect from (*P1*) and (*P3*), men can partake in some of these parts of virtue without partaking in all of them—indeed, some men are brave but unjust, some just but not wise, and so forth.[18]

Socrates' position is generally agreed[19] to be expressed by the words (329C8–D1) translated as

> **(S1)** "Justice," "temperance," "piety" [and so forth] are names of one and the same thing,

which is evidently simply a metalinguistic version of

> **(S2)** Justice, temperance, piety [and so forth] are the same thing, are one.[20]

As I remarked at the beginning of the paper, (S1) and (S2) would naturally be supposed to be simply formulations of the identity statement (2). I hold that, in the *Protagoras, wherever Socrates is arguing for his (S1)–(S2),* he intends it in this natural and obvious way, as an identity statement. The emphasized qualification means that the first skirmish between Socrates and Protagoras (at 330B6–332A1) is irrelevant, since it is concerned only with the refutation of Protagoras' (P3), and this is insufficient to establish Socrates' (S1)–(S2)—*as Socrates well knew.*[21] By contrast, all of the other arguments in the *Protagoras* about the way in which virtue is one will turn out to be arguments against (P2)—that is, for (S1)–(S2); that is, (2). (And incidentally, it is an immediate point against the equivalence interpretation of [S1]–[S2] that it must read "different" in [P2] as "non-identical"—see note 18—but cannot read "one and the same" in [S1]–[S2] as "identical.")

(*i*) *The argument from opposites* (Prot. *332A3–3B6*). Here the meaning view and the tendency view make the argument distinctly odd, and perhaps even unintelligible, whereas on the motive-force or state-of-soul view it makes reasonable sense. Socrates starts from

(11) Wisdom and folly are opposites,

and wants also to get

(12) Temperance and folly are opposites.

For he thinks he can use

(13) To each single thing there is but one opposite

in order to get—since folly is a single thing—

(14) Wisdom = temperance.

Now on the meaning view,[22] this argument is scarcely intelligible. For on that view, what is an opposite of what is settled by the meanings of words,[23] so that (14) would be grossly absurd—inferred only by means of a blatant equivocation on "folly" in (11) and (12). Moreover, Socrates' argument for (12)—from

(15) For certain values of *"F"*—for example, folly, strength, weakness, speed, slowness—one acts *F*-ly [if and] only if one acts with or by *F,* and one acts oppositely [if and] only if one acts with or by the opposite,

and

(16) Men who act foolishly act oppositely to men who act temperately

—could only be a begging of the question. How could one establish (16) independently of just those intuitions which are present in (12)?

On the motive-force or state-of-soul view, however, the argument is perfectly intelligible. What Socrates wants to get to is the idea that in ethics there are *two opposites only.* One is the single thing referred to by both "wisdom" and "temperance" (that is, virtue), and the other the single thing referred to by "intemperance" and "folly" (that is, vice). Under the influence of virtue one will act temperately (and bravely), under the influence of vice one will act foolishly (and impiously). On this view, the argument from (16) to (12) will be an argument from the way men act[24] to the motive-forces or states of soul which bring about these actions. And without these restrictions due to considerations of meaning, it *will* make sense to suppose that folly may turn out to be the opposite of temperance, that wisdom may turn out to be identical with temperance. So on this view we *do* have an intelligible and non–question-begging argument from (16) to (12).[25]

(ii) The argument from confidence (Prot. *349D2–351B2*). At first sight, this argument may seem simply an argument about what equivalences (and other universal statements) are true of brave men, wise men, and so forth.[26] This view may be especially tempting since Protagoras introduces the argument in terms of his (*P3*) and (*P4*). Bravery, he says, is very dissimilar to other virtues, since you will find many unjust, impious (and so forth) men who are nevertheless brave. And the part of Socrates' argument at which he appears to object (350C6–D2) appears to be a universal statement about brave men. But this first sight is misleading. Socrates' method of defense here is attack. He will show this part of the equivalence denied in (*P4*)—that men are brave only if they are wise—to be true by arguing for the stronger identity "Bravery = wisdom." To be more precise, he will show that the explanation of a man's brave actions is wisdom: that what it is that makes a man brave is identical with what it is that makes him wise. The relevant part of the argument goes like this:

(17) Certain men, divers, are confident in diving into wells because they know [what they are doing]; and similarly it is the skilled horsemen who fight confidently on horseback, the skilled peltasts who fight confidently with the light shield.

And in general,

(18) Those who know what they are doing are more confident than those who do not;

and

(19) Those who know are more confident once they have learned [what they are doing] than they were before learning.

The thrust of (17), (18), and (19) is this:

(20) The most reasonable explanation of the confidence exhibited by men who know what they are doing is just that knowledge: it is knowledge that makes men who know what they are doing confident.

Of course (17), (18), and (19) do not together entail (20). It is rather that Socrates believes that (20) gives the best answer available to the question why (17), (18), and (19) should be true.[27] (*dioti* and *dia* at 350A2, the force of which is captured in [17] by the "because," give the tip-off here, a tip-off that recent scholars have tended simply to ignore. Our next argument will see this *dia* figuring again, in an undeniably explanatory way, and right where the meaning view would least like to see it.)

On this understanding, the rest of the argument is easily intelligible. What Socrates does is to argue that the ignorant confident are not brave, but rather mad (350B1–C2). So, since it is granted (349E2) that

(21) All the brave are confident,

we have isolated the class of brave men as the class of knowing confident men. Hence our explanation in (20) can now be seen to cover the whole range of brave men. And this is to say that we can identify their bravery, that which makes them brave, as knowledge. Hence since Socrates uses "knowledge" here interchangeably with "wisdom," we get:

(22) Wisdom = bravery.

(350C4–5: *kata touton ton logon hē sophia an andreia eiē:* "according to this argument, wisdom is bravery.")

As confirmation of this interpretation, we may notice that Protagoras takes the argument to be in effect as we have said. For he remarks that from (21), (18), and (19)— which are just the premises singled out as crucial on our interpretation—Socrates wants to infer (*en toutōi oiei:* 350D4–5) the identity (22): "bravery and wisdom are the same thing" (*tauton:* 350D5, cf. 351A1, 4, and also 350D6, E6). And this natural reading is strengthened when we see knowledge spoken of (351A2, 7) as an explanatory entity (a motive-force or state of soul) in Protagoras' remarks that

Power comes from either knowledge or from madness and passion,

and

Confidence comes from science (*technē*) or from passion and madness,

whereas

Bravery comes from the natural constitution and good conditioning [the state, not the process] of souls.

These are clearly explanatory remarks, on a par with my (20). (In fact, Protagoras' reply to Socrates is just this: that although Socrates has explained certain kinds of confidence in men's actions, as he could explain a certain power trained wrestlers have, the best explanation must be a fuller one. Socrates can no more divorce the explanation of the actions of brave men from the natural constitution and good conditioning of their souls than he could divorce the explanation of the strength exhibited by strong men from the natural constitution and good conditioning of their bodies.) "Knowledge," "science," and "wisdom" are clearly being taken by Protagoras at least as singular terms, and in this he is certainly taking himself to be following Socrates. When Socrates tries again a little later to argue the identity of wisdom and bravery, the agreement he slyly gains from Protagoras that knowledge is something "strong," "lordly," "ruling" enough to "master" pleasures, fear, anger, pain, love, and so forth (352B3–D3) is but another instance of this use of singular terms for explanatory entities. (On the equivalence view, what is it that is strong and lordly?) The cumulative evidence for this argument is surely overwhelming: Socrates is operating with, and is understood by Protagoras to be operating with, the motive-force or state-of-soul view, and attempting to establish identities.

(iii) *An argument concerning "that by virtue of which"* (Prot. *360C1–7*). The preceding two arguments, in showing the superiority of the motive-force or state-of-soul view to the meaning view, have read the "with or by"[28] locution of "Men act bravely with or by bravery" as causal or explanatory rather than as epistemological or semantic. In the principle (15), "acting *F*-ly or by *F*" means *not* that it is by seeing that the meaning of

"F" is instantiated in an act that one sees that the act is done *F*-ly, but rather that it is the quality *F* which makes men act *F*-ly. The present argument will confirm that reading. Simultaneously, it will confirm my view of the "What is *X?*" question—that that question is not a request for the meaning of a word or a request for an essence or a universal (on what I have called the usual view of essences and universals) as in (6), but rather a request for a psychological account (explanation) of what it is in men's psyches that makes them brave. For the "What is *X?*" question is often put as "What is that single thing by virtue of which (with or by which) the many *F* things are *F?*"; and I will be arguing that that too is a causal or explanatory question rather than an epistemological or semantical one.

That Socrates at least sometimes so intends such locutions as "with or by" or "that by virtue of which" is absolutely clear, I think, from the tail end of the *akrasia* argument in the *Protagoras* (360C1–7). The argument begins with just such a premise as the one with which we have been concerned:

(23) The cowardly are cowardly because of cowardice.

We do not have to wait long to see that the "because of" here is non-trivial. For Socrates appeals to the empirical-psychological argument[29] earlier (that no one acts contrary to what he knows to be the best alternative open to him) to say that men are cowardly because of their ignorance of what is fearful and what is not fearful, so that

(24) The cowardly are cowardly because of ignorance.

But therefore,

(25) Cowardice = ignorance.

Obviously the argument is that "cowardice" and "ignorance" must name the same motive-force or state of soul since either name goes into

(26) The cowardly are cowardly because of . . .[30]

So the "because of" here is clearly non-trivial; it is part of some substantial psychological theorizing.

From (25), Socrates goes on to identify the opposite of ignorance, namely wisdom, with the opposite of cowardice, namely bravery. And evidently to say this is to say that there is just one set of opposites involved, each opposite admitting a number of names. Socrates continues, "Now, Protagoras, do you still believe that there are men who are most ignorant, yet most brave?" What this remark shows is that, as before (see the beginning of argument [*ii*]), Socrates' strategy is to refute Protagoras' (*P3*) and (*P4*) by establishing the identity (*S1*)–(*S2*). A few lines later (361B1–2), confirmation of this appears when Socrates speaks of his thesis as that "all these things are knowledge— justice, temperance and bravery." That this does indeed express an identity will be even clearer from the next argument.

(*iv*) *The argument from "Virtue is knowledge"* (Prot. *360E6–361D6*). This argument continues from the preceding one, and focuses on the way in which the conclusion of the *Protagoras* treats *aretē* ("virtue") as a singular term. For consider the treatment of "Virtue is (is not) knowledge" as it occurs between Socrates and Protagoras at 361B1–

6. Protagoras' position has a form most naturally characterized as the denial of an identity,

Virtue is something other than (*allo ti ē*) knowledge,

so Socrates' position,

All [these] things [justice, temperance, bravery] are knowledge, and Virtue is entirely [or: as a single whole] knowledge,

would naturally be characterized as an identity. It is perfectly possible from a linguistic point of view to treat Protagoras' position as the denial not of an identity but of a universal predication:

The virtues are not cases [or types] of knowledge

(cf. the not quite parallel 330B4). But this does not fit so very well with the consistently singular use of the terms for virtue and knowledge in the context. For apart from their appearances in the singular here, it is also the case that the pair

Virtue is knowledge

Virtue is teachable

in 361A6–B6 are treated as instances of answers to the characteristic pair of questions

What is X (virtue itself)?

Is X Y (is virtue teachable)?

But in the first question (*ti pot' estin auto*[31] *hē aretē:* 360E8) as in the second (*pōs pot' echei ta peri tēs aretēs*), the words for virtue or "virtue itself" are singular terms. So too 361C5–6: *epi tēn aretēn hoti estin, kai palin . . . peri autou eite didakton eite mē didakton*. It is one and the same entity which is *both* referred to as "virtue itself" and about which one asks "Whatever is it (*ti pot' estin*)?" *and* about which Socrates asks whether or not it is teachable. But it is common ground to the meaning view and to the motive-force or state-of-soul view that the *"X"* in "What is X?" does duty for a singular term (see the discussion of [5]–[7] at the beginning of Section I). Therefore, in all of the following sentences, "Virtue" and (therefore) "knowledge" should be read as singular terms (and also, in consequence, as having the same reference):

Virtue is knowledge,

Virtue is teachable,[32]

Justice, temperance, bravery are all knowledge.

But this means that we can affirm (from the first and third of these) that, for Socrates,

(10) Virtue = knowledge,

(2) Bravery = wisdom = temperance = justice = piety, and also[33]

(2*) Bravery = wisdom = temperance = justice = piety = virtue = knowledge.

Thus once more we get identities for "Virtue is knowledge" and "Virtue is one."

We can also now see that "Virtue is knowledge" is the Socratic answer to the question "What is virtue?" (though "knowledge" must doubtless still be expanded somewhat). Yet we have just seen in the preceding argument that Socrates holds "Virtue is knowledge'' on the basis of substantial psychological beliefs. So in the *Protagoras* at least, the question ''What is virtue?'' is a request for a psychological account of virtue (and not a purely semantical or purely epistemological one). On the meaning view, ''Virtue is knowledge''—that is, (10)—would have to be analytic, a matter of the meaning of ''virtue''—implausible in itself—whereas the unity of virtue doctrine—that is, (2*)—is always taken to be synthetic. But is it really plausible that (10) should be analytic, (2*) synthetic?

I conclude that the motive-force or state-of-soul view makes better sense of all four of these arguments in the *Protagoras* than the meaning view. In the next section, we will come to the same conclusion about the lead argument in each of the *Laches* and the *Charmides*.

IV

I now respond to the challenge to say more about this single entity which makes men brave, wise, temperate, just, pious, virtuous, knowledgeable. It is the knowledge of good and evil. This becomes obvious, I think, from the chief argument of the *Laches* (197E10–199E12). Nicias' proposed account of bravery (194E11–195A1) is:

(27) Bravery is the science (*epistēmē:* knowledge) of things terrible and confidence-inspiring.

From this account and Socrates' own (198B4–C5) explanation of the terrible as what causes fear, fear being the expectation of future evils (and *mutatis mutandis* for the confidence-inspiring), Socrates deduces that

(28) Bravery is the science of future goods and evils.

But he says—and those who have followed me thus far will note this statement about an identity and the use to which it is put in deducing the conclusion—that

(29) The same science is of the same things whether past, present, or future.

Therefore,

(30) Bravery is the science of all goods and evils.

This gives Nicias only two choices, Socrates says (199C3–D2). *Either* (27) expresses only one-third of the account of bravery, and so is not the correct account of bravery, or

(30*) Bravery is the whole of virtue.

Would Nicias like to switch his view and assert (30*)? But no, Nicias would not. For Nicias believes that

(31) Bravery is a (proper) part of virtue.

This latter belief is the first premise Socrates elicits from Nicias in this argument (198A1–9), and the premise in which he rubs Nicias' nose at the end of the argument (199E3–12). It seems clear that Socrates is telling us we must either give up (27) or give up (31). But there is the strongest possible evidence in the text of the *Laches* (what need to mention *Prot.* 360C2–D5?) that Socrates endorsed (27) as a true account of bravery.[34] Surely, then, Socrates is telling us to reject (31). Bravery is the whole of virtue—that is,

(32) Bravery = virtue = the science of goods and evils,

which readily goes together with our identity (2) to yield the desired result.

(Just to reinforce the present conclusion, and to further confirm the interpretation of the unity of virtue doctrine offered in this essay, let us notice that on the meaning view, Socrates has reduced Nicias' "definition" to absurdity. But since, as we have seen [n. 34], [27] and [28] are unobjectionably Socratic, the meaning view must say that—in adducing [29] as relevant to the meaning of "bravery" [the essence of bravery, and so forth] which is being given in [28]—Socrates is tripping Nicias up with a crude [and absurdly irrelevant] fallacy, and that he was quite wrong to think the choice in the argument was between [27] and [31]. On this view, Nicias should have replied with:

[29*] Bravery is the science of all goods *qua* science of future goods,

and Socrates' silly little argument would have fallen apart.[35] But why suppose that Socrates is committing a crude fallacy when he can simply be uttering what stands a fair chance of being true—namely, that

[33] That which makes us good at dealing with future goods = that which makes us good at dealing with all goods [as good civil engineers know both about past bridges and future bridges],

and making a quite unobjectionable substitution of expressions for identicals in the context "Bravery is . . ."?)

The *Charmides* will yield a similar conclusion. The chief argument here (169D2–175B2) shows difficulties in Critias' account of temperance as the knowledge (science) of what one knows and does not know (169D6–7, 170A3–4).[36] The first difficulty (169D9–171C9) is that it is not clear how the temperate man could know that another person has the science of medicine without himself having that science. And if temperance is not the knowledge *of* what one knows and does not know, but simply the knowledge *that* one knows or does not know (any particular thing) (170D1–3), by what conceivable means could the man who possesses this knowledge *test* anyone's knowledge or ignorance?[37] But this difficulty is simply waived for the crucial second difficulty: even granting that there is such a thing as this knowledge (science) *of* what one knows and does not know (along with the knowledge *that* one knows or does not know whatever it is), would it in fact be of benefit to us (172C6–D10)? Would it in fact turn out to be a flawless guide to life, both for us and those we rule over (171D6–8, 172A5 with 161E10–162A5); would the Utopia of my dream (says Socrates: 173A7–D5) come about with the human race all living knowledgeably and happily under the rule of this science? Well, if all this *were* to come about, which of the many sciences would be the one that would make us happy (173D8–174A11)? Arithmetic? Medicine? No, the science of good and evil (174B11–D7)—*that* is what we must have if the other sciences are to benefit us. So, Socrates says to Critias (174A10–11, D3–4),

(34) Your temperance, the science of all sciences and ignorances is *not* the science which makes us happy, whose work is to benefit us.

So, since medicine and all the other (departmental) sciences do everything else for us, your temperance is useless. So our inquiry into temperance, the finest of all things, has not gotten us anywhere (175A9ff.).

It should now be clear what Socrates is doing in considering this second difficulty.

He is not simply giving a further refutation of an account of temperance already shot down by the first difficulty. And he is not just aimlessly dragging in references to a science which makes us happy, a science without which medicine and the other sciences will not benefit us. All of this comes out not just in the enthusiasm with which Socrates dwells upon the benefits which temperance should bring us, but also in the reason why (34) is false. The reason why (34) is false is that it is *another* science which makes us happy, whose work it is to benefit us—the science of good and evil. This, surely, is that "finest thing of all" (175A11), that temperance which leads a city to be well run (161E10–162A8, referred back to at 175A3–5). Socrates is telling us that

(35) Temperance = the science of good and evil

= the science which makes all other sciences beneficial

= the science of making oneself and others happy

= the science of ruling a city or household.[38]

Putting together our results from the *Laches* and the *Charmides*, we have again the unity of virtue, as well as a further characterization of the single entity referred to in that doctrine. Moreover, the *Laches* makes it a little clearer why the science of good and evil (goods and evils) = the science which makes all others beneficial (195C7–D9). It is because the doctor's knowledge about a sick man is confined to what makes him sick or healthy, what will cure him, and so forth. He has no special knowledge, however, on the question whether in the sick man's circumstances it would be better or worse for him to be cured.[39] This knowledge belongs to the science of good and evil. (It is evident from the *Charmides* passages we have been considering that this knowledge is, in germ, the political art of the *Euthydemus* and *Republic*.[40] This science has a long and interesting development in Plato's thought; but I do not attempt to trace that development in this essay.)

A further argument that the single entity in question is the science of good and evil can be gained from the *akrasia* argument of the *Protagoras* (351B3–357E8). The whole of that famous argument is there simply to provide a premise needed for argument (*iii*) (360C1–7, cf. C7–D5) discussed in Section III—namely,

(24) The cowardly are cowardly because of ignorance.

(Recall that the whole section from 349D2–360E5 is concerned with Socrates trying to prove that bravery = wisdom, against Protagoras' claim that some men may be brave without being wise: see esp. 349D2–8, 359A7–B6). But now what is this ignorance? A glance at 360B6–7 with 359D4–6 and at 358E2 with 358C1–5, 357D3–E2 will show that this ignorance is the lack of the measuring art, the science which measures the relative magnitudes of present and future goods and evils, not being deceived by the effects of time perspective (356C5ff.), the science which the rational part of the soul will have in *Republic* X (602CD). It is, in short, the science of good and evil.[41] And so, the wisdom about what is terrible and what is not, which bravery is identified with at 360D4–5 as a result of the premise just cited, is (what we should in any case have expected from the *Laches*) the science of good and evil. (And notice that the wisdom about what is terrible and what is not must be identical with wisdom *simpliciter* if Socrates is not to be giving a quite irrelevant argument against Protagoras' claim that there are men who are brave *but not wise*.) Once again bravery = wisdom = the science of good and evil.

CONCLUSION

The position I am arguing for, and the position I am arguing against, may be conveniently summarized as follows. On the usual views, there are two kinds of unity which virtue has. One is the identity of an *eidos* or Form (in some suitably nonmetaphysical sense of ''Form,'' to keep Socrates' views distinct from those of Plato's) in the many instances and even in the different species of virtue, and one is the identity of the *extensions* of the different species of virtue, together with the nonidentity of the species themselves. On my view there is just one kind of unity involved: it is one and the same (explanatory) entity being talked about in each of

Virtue = bravery = wisdom = knowledge = temperance = and so forth.

and

Bravery is found in all brave men acting bravely.

On the usual views, the latter proposition must be analytic, the former synthetic. On my view, neither proposition is analytic; each is a substantial truth of psychology. Indeed, for my part, I doubt that there is a philosophically useful analytic-synthetic distinction to be made.[42] So I am happy not to find myelf asking at what point Socrates seeks the analytic truths that answer his ''What is *X?''* questions. I also doubt that there are any good grounds for finding the distinction in the Socratic dialogues,[43] though this is not the place to argue the point in detail. The present essay offers some support for this view, however, by showing that one can do without the distinction in at least some areas of Socratic thought.[44]

In specifying the single entity to which the virtue-words refer, I have said of it little more than that it is an explanatory entity and that it is identifiable as the knowledge (science) of good and evil. In particular, I have left open the question whether this knowledge (science) is more appropriately described as a ''motive-force'' or a ''state of soul.'' Indeed, it may seem strange to think that knowledge, by itself, could be a motive-force in any way. To show that this is a possibility would send us on a long detour through the treatment of reason and knowledge in Socrates and Plato. I believe, in fact, that the Socratic concepts do not stand in any simple relation to ours. But showing this will require further studies.[45] Fortunately, the results of the present chapter are relatively independent of those studies.

NOTES

My research was supported by grants from Princeton University and the University of Wisconsin, for which I am most grateful. Versions of the essay were read at the University of Wisconsin, the University of Toronto and the University of British Columbia, and comments from my audiences there have been very helpful in reformulating various parts of the essay. I was also forced to a number of useful reformulations by comments from an anonymous referee and from the editors of the *Philosophical Review*. I am also indebted to Dennis Stampe and Richard Kraut, who gave me the benefit of their comments on earlier drafts. And my debt to Gregory Vlastos in Socratic studies generally, especially from numerous conversations, has been enormous, and I gratefully acknowledge it here.

1. See nn. 42 and 43.
2. *Prāgma* 330C1, 4, D4, 331A8, 332A5, 349B3, 4–5, C1 and also 330D5 with D8–E1 and

360E8. *Ousia:* 349B4. At least 330C4, D4, 5, 331A8 are explicitly in Socrates' terms (and not in terms we could expect only Protagoras to accept), and this justifies us in finding the 349 uses also as Socratic. That is to say, the indications are that to consider whether virtue is *hen ti*, some single thing, is to consider whether it is *hen prāgma, mia ousia*—one thing, one being (also translated as "essence," "substance"). By the end of the essay it will be clear that I understand the Socratic uses of such words as *ousia, eidos, metechein, etc.* as more akin to Hippocratic uses of *eidos, phusis* and *metechein* than to, say, middle Platonic uses.

3. The equivalence view can be found at its finest in G. Vlastos (ed.), *Plato's Protagoras* (Indianapolis, 1956), p. liv, n. 10; p. xxxv. Other examples are E. R. Dodds (ed.), *Plato's Gorgias* (Oxford, 1959), *apud* 507A4–C7; R. E. Allen, *Plato's Euthyphro and the Earlier Theory of Forms* (New York, 1970), pp. 84 with 94; G. Santas in *Philosophical Review* 73 (1964), p. 157; Michael J. O'Brien, *The Socratic Paradoxes and the Greek Mind* (Chapel Hill, 1967), p. 129, n. 16; and (perhaps?) N. Gulley, *The Philosophy of Socrates* (London, 1968), pp. 153–163. The stronger identity view seems, however, to have been held (at least some of the time) by a number of earlier scholars—e.g., J. Burnet, *Greek Philosophy, Part I, Thales to Plato* (London, 1914), sec. 134; A. E. Taylor, *Socrates* (Anchor Books Ed.; New York, 1954), pp. 144–145; *Plato, the Man and His Work* (Meridian [6th] ed.; New York, 1956), p. 247; and (closest to a literal view, though he thinks most of Socrates' arguments fallacious) J. Adam (ed.), *Platonis Protagoras* (Cambridge, 1893). The identity view was held in antiquity by Antisthenes, the Megarics, and Menedemus the Eretrian—all Socratics. (See E. Zeller, *Socrates and the Socratic Schools*, trans. by Oswald J. Reichel [London, 1877] for references to the minor Socratics.) It is probably Socrates (as Burnet, but not Zeller, thinks) to whom Isocrates attributes the identity view in *Helen*, I.i. Aristotle, however, thought that for Socrates the virtues were sciences (*EN* 1144b17ff., *EE* 1216b2ff.).

  Many scholars—e.g., Shorey in *The Unity of Plato's Thought* (Chicago, 1903), ch. 1, and the great Zeller—have simply fudged the issue. Such phrases as "reduced all the virtues to knowledge," "all the virtues *consist in* knowledge of some kind" (Zeller, p. 143), "Virtue *has a unity in* knowledge" (Adam, p. 128), *"From that point of view* they *become merged into* one" (Burnet, sec. 134), "Each [virtue] *involves* the other" (Shorey, ch. 1), *"To this extent* the definition of a particular virtue is at the same time the definition of any particular virtue" (Gulley, p. 153), are favorites of the fudgers. Others seem simply confused (e.g., Taylor, *ibid.*, who takes the quite preposterous view that what the doctrine meant was that the virtue words were all synonymous). Once the equivalence view is clearly stated, however, as in Vlastos, there can be little excuse for failing to face the issue squarely.

4. See Richard Robinson, *Plato's Earlier Dialectic*, 2nd ed. (Oxford, 1953), ch. 5.

5. "The same in all cases": *Eu.* 5D1, *M.* 72C2, *La.* 191E10–11, etc. "By virtue of which": the dative of the relative pronoun, *Eu.* 6D11, *M.* 72E4–6, *Prot.* 332B4–7 (discussed later). "That because of which" (*dia*) is used with the preceding locution at *M.* 72C8 (two uses of this locution in the *Protagoras* are also discussed subsequently). Interpreters have assumed that these locutions were to be used to much the same purpose—namely, that indicated in (5) throughout the early dialogues.

6. This account of the identity conditions of universals is clearly formalized in Rudolph Carnap's great work, *Meaning and Necessity* (2nd ed.; Chicago, 1955). R. E. Allen's Socratic "essences" (pp. 109, 110, 112, 113–114) are entities with the same identity conditions as those of meanings.

  A clear alternative to this account of properties, similar to the conception of properties employed in this essay, is to be found in Hilary Putnam, "On Properties," in N. Rescher et al. (eds.), *Essays in Honour of Carl G. Hempel* (Dordrecht, 1969), pp. 235–254. It will be evident that I have been greatly influenced by the writings of both Putnam and Hempel.

7. Again the clearest proponent of this meaning view is Vlastos. Because his introduction to the *Protagoras* does not discuss the "What is *X?*" question, his commitment to the meaning view

is evidenced there only in the sharp deductive-empirical distinction maintained there (see n. 27). But his commitment to the meaning view of the "What is *X?*" question emerges clearly enough in "Anamnesis in the *Meno,*" *Dialogue* 4 (1965), pp. 155–159: the question is about concepts or meanings, and can get in reply only analytic truths. See also "Justice and Psychic Harmony in the *Republic,*" *Journal of Philosophy* 66 (1969), p. 507; and in its earlier version, *Journal of Philosophy* 65 (1968), pp. 669, 670, notice the equivalence signs. (It is true that the latter two articles do not in themselves commit Vlastos to the meaning view for the earlier dialogues.) See also W. K. C. Guthrie, in *The Greek Philosophers* (New York, 1950), pp. 76–78.

Further documentation of the meaning view is scarcely necessary. It is pretty well universal. Greekless readers of the Jowett translation should be warned, however, wherever they see the word "meaning," to check a more modern translation.

8. It is clear that the general tone of the *Protagoras* and *Laches* directs us to the general's question. In the *Laches,* the whole problem is: how to train the sons of Melesias and Lysimachus. It is on this question—which is surely a general's question—which first Laches and Nicias, and then Socrates, are invited to pronounce. It is a defect of the meaning view that it has to make Socrates shift the question to the philosopher's question. Notice also the intermediate question by which, at 189D–E, we get from "How should we educate our sons?" (cf. 179B–D, 185E) to "What is bravery?" (cf. 190BC).

> What is that which, when added (*paragignesthai*) to a man makes (*poiein*) him more brave or virtuous (as the power of sight, added to eyes, makes them see).

Paragignesthai here plainly has little to do with *parousia* and *methexis* as usually understood in the middle dialogues (a relation between certain metaphysical entities, or even abstract entities like meanings, and sensible particulars). It has to do in general with enabling (cf. the power of sight), and in particular with teaching, inculcation, what one does to improve someone. Moreover, the example Socrates gives to illustrate how bravery is "the same in all these brave men"—namely, quickness—is explicitly said to be a *dunamis*, a power (192 AB). This is surely no accident (cf. n. 38 on the *Charmides*). Similarly, in the *Protagoras,* the teachability of virtue is a practical concern (309A–319A, 361D4).

9. Notice that this theoretical entity is no more (and no less) metaphysical or "separated" than, say, the hot, the cold, the wet, and the dry in which humans "partake" in Hippocratic accounts of health and illness (see, e.g., *On Anc. Med.,* c. 14). This is, I think, a further advantage of my view over the meaning view.

10. This is clear from the examples there: fear is "broader" than awe, wherever we have the odd we have number but not vice versa. Allen (p. 84) recognizes this conflict with the *Protagoras* doctrine even read as an equivalence. Those who agree with my arguments later in the paper may suggest that Socrates here intends to be denying that piety is a proper part of justice. But the text gives absolutely no indication that Socrates thought anything wrong with this premise.

11. Here there is just one thing good in itself, wisdom (= knowledge), and one bad thing, ignorance. All other things normally called "goods"—wealth, strength, honor, bravery, temperance—cause more harm than good without wisdom (cf. *M.* 87E5–88D1, esp. 88B6). The clear implication is that bravery and temperance are as detachable from wisdom as wealth is. It is hard to see how Allen can cite this as an instance of "mutual implication" of the virtues (p. 99, n. 2).

12. E.g., Dodds, pp. 18–30; W. D. Ross, *Plato's Theory of Ideas* (Oxford, 1951), ch. 1.

13. See, e.g., G. C. Field, *The Philosophy of Plato* (London, 1949), pp. 17–19; W. T. Stace, *A Critical History of Greek Philosophy* (London, 1920), p.149.

14. See, e.g., Rudolph Carnap, "Psychology in Physical Language," in A. J. Ayer (ed.),

Logical Positivism (Glencoe, 1959), pp. 172ff. Similar views appear in later Carnap and Hempel without the verificationism of this article.

15. Bruce Aune, *Knowledge, Mind and Nature* (New York, 1967), pp. 109ff., and note his application of this point to the relation between pain and pain-behavior.

16. They are easily discernible in Nelson Goodman, *Fact, Fiction and Forecast* (Cambridge, Mass., 1955), chs. 1 and 2.

17. I would expect this account—in so far as it proves applicable to *Rep.* 441–444—to yield a rather different reading from that in David Sachs's classic article, "A Fallacy in Plato's *Republic*," *Philosophical Review*, 72 (1963), 141–158 (reprinted in G. Vlastos [ed.], *Plato* [New York, 1970], vol. II), and in Vlastos' reply, "Justice and Psychic Harmony in the *Republic*," *Journal of Philosophy* 66 (1969), pp. 505–521. But I cannot here raise the question of its applicability to the *Republic*.

It will not have escaped notice that I am assuming, for the dialogues I consider, that the names "bravery," "temperance," "virtue," etc. are used *by Socrates* for properties of *men* rather than for properties of *actions*. We should expect this from the Greek use of *aretē* ("virtue") for men only and not actions, from virtue being knowledge, a property of men. We should also expect this where the intent of the dialogue is protreptic (how are men to be made brave, wise, etc.?) or for testing someone's mettle (e.g., Charmides). This assumption is false of the *Euthyphro*, however (see esp. 5C9–D2, 6D3 with 6D10–E6). Socrates probably had no clear *theoretical* position on the relations between these two kinds of properties (cf. *Eu.* 7A6–8). Yet even with the *Euthyphro*, where Socrates does allow Euthyphro to come closest to what he, Socrates, thinks about piety (14B8–C3 with 13B4–11), it is again a kind of knowledge, and so a quality of men (*hupēretikē tis* [sc. *technē*]). The *Charmides* is instructive in just this way. Charmides' first account of temperance and also his third account (= Critias' first account) are of temperance as a quality of actions. But Socrates brings each of them quickly around to qualities of men (159B7–8, leading to 160D5–E5, and 164A2, leading to 165B4). Similarly, in *Rep.* I, where Polemarchus and Thrasymachus both begin speaking of the justice which actions have, Socrates quickly gets them on to justice as a *technē* (332C5ff., 340C6ff.).

On this point, as on the preference of what I call "motive-forces or states of soul," to what I call "tendencies," I find an ally in Myles F. Burnyeat, "Virtues in Action," in G. Vlastos (ed.), *Socrates* (New York, 1971), which unfortunately came into my hands only after I had completed this essay.

18. For (*P1*), see 329C7–8, D4–E1. For (*P2*) and (*P3*), see 330A3–B6; and for the distinctness of (*P2*) and (*P3*) see 332A2–5, 349B3–6 and the bridge (332A2–4) between the attack on (*P3*) at 330B6–332A1 and the attack on (*P2*) at 332A4–333B5. Notice also the contrast between 330A3 (*allo . . . allo*) and 330A6–B6 (*hoion*). For (*P4*), see 329E2–6. I associate (*P4*) with (*P1*) and (*P3*) since (*P2*) would be compatible with the "parts of gold" model while (*P1*) is not and (*P4*) probably is not.

19. See the contrast at 329C5–D1, 349B1–6, and cf. Adam, p. xx with 192, 190, 172, 171, 135, 128; Vlastos, *Plato's Protagoras*, p. liv, n. 10; Allen, pp. 84, 94.

20. At 350D5, Protagoras takes Socrates to be arguing that "bravery and wisdom are the same thing (*tauton*)."

21. At 331A1–B4, (*P2*) is at issue; and he seems to admit here that the earlier argument "refuted" only (*P3*): *schedon ti tauton on*, cf. 331B4–6: *ētoi tauton . . . ē hoti homoiotaton . . . hoion . . .*

22. Again in any of the versions I have described above in Secs. I and II.

23. See, e.g., Dodds, *apud Gorg.* 507A7; Rosamund Kent Sprague, *Plato's Use of Fallacy* (London, 1962), p. 28 n.; Adam, p. 135, seems simply confused.

24. Similarly, the much-maligned argument for (16) is about actions primarily. This runs as follows:

(16a) Men who act not rightly act not temperately (332B1–3).

(16b) Men who act foolishly act not rightly, and therefore act not temperately (B1–2).

(16c) Whenever men act, if they do not act temperately, they act intemperately (implied by Burnet's reading *ē tounantion* at 332A8).

The argument from these premises to (16) is a valid argument. There seems no reason not to suppose all three are intended as generalizations from experience. In particular we need not suppose that (16c) involves a confusion of contraries with contradictories. (Before true belief began to figure in Plato's ethics, knowledge and ignorance, and so virtue and vice, would be without intermediates.) Then all three premises, (16a)–(16c), would be substantial claims about actions leading to the substantial claim (16) about actions.

25. Unfortunately, in the actual argument from (16) to (12), Socrates jumps the gun. For the principle (15) on which he depends does not justify the inference to (12), but only to

(12*) He who acts with or by folly acts with or by the opposite of temperance.

Nevertheless, the error involved is almost certainly not noticed by Socrates, since it is a rather sophisticated one, and one which the wording of (15) and (16) makes it hard to see through. (The gap between [12*] and [12] is clear if we see that moving from [12*] to [12] removes the possibility of inserting an "also" between "folly" and "acts" in [12*]. I am indebted here to my colleague, Louis F. Goble.)

26. So it is taken by Vlastos, pp. xxxi–xxxvi; Adam, pp. 172–176; Kent Sprague, p. 96.

27. In C. S. Peirce's theory of "abductive inference" or in recent accounts of "theoretical inference," scientific reasoning is represented neither as deduction nor as induction by simple enumeration. See, e.g., Gilbert H. Harman, "The Inference to the Best Explanation," *Philosophical Review*, 74 (1965), 88–95; Peter Achinstein, "Inference to Scientific Laws," in *Minnesota Studies in the Philosophy of Science* (Minneapolis, 1971), 5, 87–104.

Vlastos' introduction to *Plato's Protagoras* simply assumes that every argument must proceed either by deduction or by induction by simple enumeration. Wherever possible, Socrates' arguments are fitted into a deductive mold—though always with scrupulous scholarly caveat (e.g., p. xxxii, n. 27 with n. 30). Wherever Socrates uses any empirical argumentation, Vlastos simply rejects it (e.g., p. xxxvii: "Has Socrates then done some empirical research into the psychology of divers, cavalrymen, peltasts . . . ?''). But Vlastos himself (rightly) does not hesitate to judge Socrates empirically wrong (p. xliv). It is noticeable that while all substantial psychological claims receive this treatment, Vlastos has no such objections to Socrates weaving substantial *moral* claims (pp. xlvii–li) into his definitions. (There must be a sharp evaluative-descriptive distinction at work here.) What I would urge is that psychological insights (if such they be) are inherently no more liable to be false than moral insights.

In respect of these assumptions, Vlastos differs from most other recent interpreters of Socrates only in his greater clarity and explicitness.

28. See n. 5. The dative case is what is in question at 332B1–7, at B8, *hupo* at C1–E2.

29. See Vlastos, pp. xxxvii–xliii, esp. p. xxxix.

30. For (25), cf. Adam, p. 190. That (26) captures Socrates' intentions is clear from a more literal rendering of the Greek formulated by (23): "This [thing] because of which . . . is . . .'' (360C1, cf. C5).

31. For the unusual neuter, Adam refers us to *Crat.* 411D, *Tht.* 146E. Thus Burnet's comma after *auto* is unnecessary.

32. Socrates of course claims here that Virtue is *not* teachable, which he notes as paradoxical given his belief that virtue is knowledge. The key to this apparent paradox is, I think, that (*i*) There are no teachers of virtue (*Prot.* 319–20; cf. *M.* 89–96) and (*ii*) Socrates, being ignorant, is yet the wisest man in Greece (*Apol.* 21Aff.). In short, it is a paradox only on the assumption that someone has knowledge (of the relevant kind) and someone has virtue. In the *Meno*,

where the identity of virtue with knowledge is given up, the latter half of this judgment is softened, and some are allowed to have virtue by a divine dispensation as mysterious as the rhapsode's ability to speak about Homer (*M.* 96Eff., cf. *Ion* 533Cff.). R. S. Bluck, *Plato's Meno* (Cambridge, 1961), pp. 23–25 with 3, seems to stop just short of this suggested resolution of the paradox.

33. As is obvious from the fact once "bravery," "wisdom," etc. all name one and the same entity, so will "virtue" simply be a name of that entity.

34. The argument for (27) is that given

    (27A) Each person is good with respect to those things with respect to which he is wise

and

    (27B) The brave man is good

we can infer

    (27C) Bravery is a certain kind of wisdom (knowledge, science).

But (27A) and (27B) are Socratic (194D1–3; and 192C5–D8, 193D4, cf., e.g., *Charm.* 159D8; *Gorg.* 466B6, 470C2–3, 476B1–2) and so is the inference from these to (27C) (194D6–9, E8). So unless we suppose that Socrates rejected the specification, at 194E11, from (27C) to (27), we must surely suppose that (27) is also Socratic.

35. I have already given an argument against the meaning view in the *Laches* at n. 8. (The meaning view is employed with considerable skill in Gerasimos Santas, "Socrates at Work on Virtue and Knowledge in Plato's *Laches*," in Gregory Vlastos [ed.] *Socrates* [New York, 1971]—reprinted from the *Review of Metaphysics* 22, 1969. See esp. p. 184, n. 5 ["What is bravery?" not the general's question], 187 [bravery as a "concept"], 199–200, 208 [factual vs. conceptual]. On p. 204, Santas makes as his main objection to Socrates' argument something analogous to our [29*]. On p. 202, we see that Santas' views lead him to some unusual chronological machinery: the *Euthyphro* earlier than both *Laches* and *Protagoras,* the *Laches* leading to the *Protagoras,* and then in the *Republic* a reversion to the *Euthyphro*'s denial of the unity of virtue! Nevertheless, I did find some judgments confirming my views— on pp. 187, 206 [Socrates seeks the quality brave *men* have rather than the quality brave *acts* have: see n. 17], 195, n. 10 [Nicias' account of bravery is Socratic], and 202–203 [Socrates gives up (31) rather than (27)]. It is hardly surprising that Santas finds Socrates rather confused in his alleged attempts to give the meaning of "bravery.")

36. This account is introduced as "temperance is knowing *one*self" (164D4, 165B4, 169D7). It then becomes the science of *it*self and all other sciences (166C2–3, E5–8, 167A6–7, C1–2, 169B1 and D4 with B6–7), which is explicated as in the body of the paper. At 169D7, the knowledge of what one knows and does not know is given as the account of temperance *or* (= i.e.) knowing oneself. At 169D9–E8, Socrates gives an argument for saying that one who has the knowledge which is knowledge of *it*self will know *him*self, an argument which has often been viewed with suspicion (see, e.g., T. G. Tuckey, *Plato's Charmides* [Cambridge, 1951], pp. 33ff.).

37. This passage shows clearly the high standards for knowledge which lay behind Socratic ignorance—a subject very much in Socrates' mind in the examination of temperance as self-knowledge (see 165B5–C2 and esp. 166C7–D2). Cf. n. 32.

38. It is clear that all that stops Tuckey (pp. 80ff.) from asserting this conclusion (he accepts that [30] above is Socrates' "definition" of bravery in the *Laches*) is Tuckey's *own* belief that "the knowledge of good and evil" is *also* the "definition" of virtue, whereas temperance is merely "a particular manifestation" of virtue (p. 88). Tuckey is evidently lapsing here into what I call the tendency view. It cannot be said that the resulting account is consistent.

    Further confirmation of the motive-force or state-of-soul view in the *Charmides* comes from the causal account which must be given of the question "What is temperance?" there. Thus at 158E7–159A3, temperance is a state of soul entering into the causal explanation of how some people know what temperance is. Where Critias and Charmides try to say what temperance is in terms of actions, Socrates redirects them to causal states (e.g., 160D5–8, E3–5) or states of soul (164A1–3, 165B4).

39. Notice how, in this evidently Socratic answer which Nicias gives, he uses "terrible or not" (195C9, D8, E5 and esp. 195D4) interchangeably with "better or not" (195C9–D1, D4, 196A2), in line with Socrates' account at 198B4–C5.

40. Cf. also *Ly.* 207D–210D, *Prot.* 318A–319B, *Gorg.* 464B, 501A–C with 503A, 510Aff. I do not want to suggest that Socrates had more positive beliefs about this science than he actually did. E.g., he may have felt genuine logical difficulties over it in a few places—e.g., *Eud.* 291B4–293A6 with *Ly.* 219C7–221A5. But he certainly seems to have thought there was such a science (even if no one at present possessed it: n. 32), and that he could say *some* things about it and the benefits it would yield.

41. I am ignoring here the complications arising from the fact that Socrates uses "good" interchangeably with "pleasant in the long run."

42. The most that I think can be done for the supposed distinction is done in Hilary Putnam, "The Analytic and the Synthetic," *Minnesota Studies in the Philosophy of Science* (Minneapolis, 1962), III, 358–397. What is done there is not enough to make the distinction of any interest to interpreters of Socrates.

Vlastos and Santas provide classic examples of exploitation of the analytic-synthetic distinction (see nn. 7, 27, 35).

43. Socrates does indeed distinguish universal truths from particular truths. But where does he distinguish *among* universal truths those which are synthetic or empirical, and those which are analytic or conceptual, even in practice, let alone in theory? (Empirical knowledge is not explicitly short-changed by Plato earlier than the *Phaedo;* and those who say that empirical knowledge is *implicitly* short-changed in the recollection theory of the *Meno* will usually be just those who take the recollection theory there to be already Platonic, and no longer Socratic.)

44. I do without the distinction in another area in my paper, "Socrates on Virtue and Motivation" [in E. N. Lee, A. P. D. Mourelatos, and R. M. Rorty (eds.) *Exegesis and Argument* (Assen, 1973), pp. 133–151.]

45. See the paper mentioned in n. 44. I have also investigated the question in a hitherto unpublished paper on the transition from the Socratic to the Platonic treatment of *akrasia.*

FURTHER READING

Ferejohn, M. T. 1982. "The Unity of Virtue and the Objects of Socratic Inquiry." *Journal of the History of Philosophy* 20:1–21.

Vlastos, G. 1981. "The Unity of Virtue in the *Protagoras.*" In *Platonic Studies,* 2d ed., ed. G. Vlastos, 221–65. Princeton, N.J.

———. 1981. "Socrates on 'The Parts of Virtue.'" In *Platonic Studies,* 2d ed., ed. G. Vlastos, 418–23. Princeton, N.J.

Woodruff, P. 1976. "Socrates on the Parts of Virtue." *Canadian Journal of Philosophy* suppl. 2:101–16.

11

Socrates' Use of
the Techne-Analogy

DAVID L. ROOCHNIK

It has long been recognized that Socrates' use of both the term and concept of *technē* in arguments that are analogical in structure is crucial in Plato's early dialogues.[1] Indeed, entire commentaries have made an interpretation of the "techne-analogy" (TA) a central motif. Recently this was the case in Irwin's *Plato's Moral Theory*. The TA also figured prominently in Sprague's *Plato's Philosopher King* and Kube's *Techne und Arete*.[2]

Where there is interpretation there is disagreement, and this issue is no exception. Here the question under debate is, in what sense did Plato intend the TA to be understood? Most important, did he intend it to be read as a conceptual outline of a theoretical project? To clarify this question, consider *Apology* 20a–c, Socrates' account of his conversation with Callias. If Callias' two sons were colts or calves, he would hire a horsetrainer or farmer as their "overseer" (*epistatēs:* 20a8) to make them excellent in their specific virture. His sons, however, are men. Who, then, is knowledgeable (*epistēmōn*) about the human, the political, virtue (20b4–5)? Callias responds that Evenus of Paros, a sophist, has this techne (20c1). Socrates' irony makes it certain that he thinks Evenus has no such knowledge. In addition, he claims he himself does not possess it. Thus, the analogy is left as follows: as the horsetrainer is to the virtue of colts, so X is to the virtue of human beings. If *hippikē*, the techne of horsetraining, is substituted for the horsetrainer, X refers to a kind of knowledge.

Did Plato believe that the X, moral knowledge, could be unambiguously supplied? If so, how strictly is X to be conceived as analogous to horsetraining? Does it have, for example, a determinate and "separable" *ergon*—a result that is conceptually and physically distinct from both the "technician" and his techne? Is it teachable and precise? Does its possessor become an authority to whose judgments laypersons should submit? In sum, does the analogy provide a model by which a conception of moral knowledge is to be framed?[3] Scholars disagree. Irwin's account is at once the most extreme and most lucid. He believes the analogy is meant so strictly that on the basis of it he attributes to Socrates a moral theory, one of whose axioms is, "virtue is simply craft-knowledge" (*PMT,* 7).[4] Vlastos disagrees with his former student and thinks the analogy is only partial. "For though Socrates certainly wants moral knowledge to be in some respects like that of carpenters . . . he knows that it is radically different in others.''[5] Gould would agree.[6] Klosko argues against Irwin to the effect that there is no substantial evidence for attributing ''a technical conception of virtue'' to Socrates.[7]

The importance of this debate should be emphasized, for the position taken on it will determine a commentator's conception of what Plato meant by moral knowledge (or virtue), and so will heavily influence an entire interpretation. I suggest, however, that a preliminary step in dealing with this question has generally been overlooked. In order to understand how (or if) the TA frames a conception of X, moral knowledge, we must clearly understand the analogy's first term: what is the nature of Platonic techne? First of all, how should this word be translated? Is Irwin's ''craft'' accurate? In English ''craft'' connotes knowledge that is productive in nature, so the question can be reformulated: does Platonic techne refer to productive knowledge? Again, Irwin answers yes and this thesis proves to be utterly pivotal in his argument.[8] Since he takes techne to be productive and moral knowledge to be strictly analogous to techne, he takes moral knowledge to be productive. As a result, moral knowledge requires a product, namely happiness (*eudaimonia*), as an end to which virtue prescribes instrumental means. As the Vlastos/Irwin debate clearly shows, this is an interpretation with which many readers are quite uncomfortable, for it confounds the more orthodox belief that Plato valued virtue as an end in itself.[9] Being uncomfortable, however, is not sufficient. Irwin's argument, as more than one critic has noted, is marvellously coherent.[10] If it is to be attacked, the criticism should be levelled at the initial thesis, namely that techne is exclusively and unambiguously productive.

In this paper I challenge Irwin's interpretation and translation of ''techne'' as ''craft.'' I argue that for Plato ''techne'' does not exclusively refer to productive knowledge. Instead, it is a much more flexible term covering a wide range of different kinds of arts, sciences, and crafts. At one extreme of this spectrum there is the type of knowledge upon which Irwin's interpretation so heavily relies, that which leads to the production of artefacts. At the other, there is that which I shall term theoretical knowledge and which is best exemplified by mathematics. There are, of course, numerous modalities of knowledge somewhere in between these two extremes. These, however, will not be discussed. If it can simply be shown that techne has (at least) two distinct branches, then it follows that the first term of the TA is equivocal and the analogy cannot be used to frame an unambiguous moral theory. In Part 1, I make this basic argument. In Part 2, I explore its ramifications and describe for what purpose the TA is used.

1

What does it mean to call a techne productive? Techne, however it is translated, is essentially a kind of knowledge. When it is productive it issues in a product (*ergon*), a distinct item whose being is contingent upon the activity of the producer. The *ergon* is separate from the possessor of the techne (the ''technician'') and the techne itself. The house built by the carpenter is conceptually and physically distinct from both the carpenter and carpentry. Furthermore, there is no measure of the carpenter's skill other than the house. The house, we may say, ''speaks for itself'' as the final repository of all that the carpenter knows. As such, the value of carpentry is strictly instrumental, for without houses the carpenter (qua carpenter) is both meaningless and without worth.[11]

Theoretical knowledge, on the other hand, has no product. Socrates uses the metaphor of hunting to describe it: "No part of actual hunting covers more than the province of chasing and overcoming; and when they have overcome the creature they are chasing, they are unable to use it. The huntsmen or the fishermen hand it over to the caterers and so it is too with the geometers, astronomers, and calculators—for these also are hunters, since in each case they do not produce (*poiousi*) their diagrams, but discover the realities of things (*ta onta*)" (*Eud.* 290b–c).

A similar characterization of theoretical knowledge as hunting, or more generally as a kind of acquisition, can be found in the *Sophist* (219c4). The object of theoretical knowledge does not depend for its existence on the knower. It is not made. Furthermore, as indicated by the example of the mathematical technai, its object is invariable: it can only be apprehended and not effected. As a result, the value of theoretical knowledge is not instrumental: its worth derives solely from itself.[12]

My argument against Irwin will be made succinctly by noting that Plato repeatedly uses the word "techne" to label such theoretical knowledge. (See *Eud.* 290b4, *Soph.* 219c9.) Thus, the phrase "theoretical techne" should be introduced into the Platonic lexicon. As we shall see, Plato consistently illustrates such techne with examples taken from mathematics. For an elaboration of this point, consider a passage from the *Charmides.*

The issue is, what is moderation (*sōphrosunē*)? Critias offers as a definition, "self-knowledge" (*to gignōskein heauton:* 164d4). Socrates attacks this very general statement in typical fashion, namely by reformulating it: "If moderation is a knowing something (*gignōskein ti*) it obviously would be a certain *epistēmē* and about something; right?" (165c4–6)

I leave *epistēmē* untranslated. This word, normally translated as "science," is used throughout this passage interchangeably with "techne."[13] What Socrates demands here is that if moderation is to be interpreted as a mode of knowledge, then it must be an *epistēmē* and so be about something particular (*tinos*), that is, it must have a determinate object. For example, he says, medicine is an *epistēmē* about health (168c8), the *ergon* it produces. Similarly, houses are identified as the object or product of housebuilding (165d5) and cloaks of weaving (165e7). Such identification is said to be similarly possible "in the other technai" (165d6).

If this were the entire passage, Irwin would be correct. But there is more, for Critias objects. He claims that Socrates has falsely homogenized the technai and asks: "Tell me, what is the product of the calculative (*logistikē*) and the geometrical techne which is such as a house is to housebuilding or a cloak is to weaving?" (165e5–7).

The calculative techne refers to that branch of mathematics which calculates or performs operations such as addition or multiplication. Socrates admits that Critias has spoken the truth (166a3), but adds: "Each of these *epistēmai* is an *epistēmē* about something which happens to be other than the *epistēmē* itself. For example, the calculative techne is, in some way, about the even and the odd, it is about the multitude which they make with themselves and with each other" (166a4–7).

The point Critias makes is that not all *epistēmai* (or technai) are productive. Mathematics provides the examples to substantiate this. Socrates agrees, but insists that even the mathematical technai have objects conceptually distinct from themselves. Later he will argue that it is just this absence of a specifically distinct object which makes self-knowledge, interpreted on the model of a techne, untenable.

Irwin makes the following comment about this passage:

> We might think that 166a5–b3 recognizes that *logistike* can be *tou artiou kai tou perittou* (about the even and the odd) with no product. But the phrase *plethous hopos echei pros hauta kai pros allela* (the multitude which they make with themselves and with each other) suggests the product—the right answer is a result of the calculations distinct from the steps of calculations themselves. Socrates does not then recognize Aristotle's distinction between *poiesis* (production) and *praxis* . . . though this is no doubt Aristotle's source. (*PMT*, 227)

This comment is misleading in two related respects. First, the passage does allow for non-productive techne. Second, Plato does recognize an Aristotelian distinction. It is not, however, between *poiesis* and *praxis,* but between theory and production. More precisely, it is between what Aristotle terms theoretical and productive *epistēmai*.[14]

Irwin's argument is that since calculation has a right answer distinct from the steps leading to it, it is productive. This is doubtful. The *ergon* of a productive techne is a contingent item both conceptually and physically separate from the producer's activity and knowledge. (Even the flute player's music, while not possible if the flute is absent, is still in some sense physically distinct from the flute.) In the typical calculative problem, $4 + 12 + 19 = 35$, the result is, first of all, not contingent, but a matter of necessity. Second, unlike the carpenter's house or the flute player's music, 35 does not "speak for itself" as the measure of the calculator's techne. A house is the unique product of the unique process that produced it. 35 is not only the answer to $4 + 12 + 19$, but equally the answer to $10 + 25$. Also, it is the incorrect answer to $12 + 25$. In other words, qua result 35 is meaningless in and of itself and so it cannot be used to measure the calculative techne. It is an invariable object which is understood as the proper answer to a specific problem. The calculative techne allows us to understand the entire sequence of steps, as well as the result, of the addition. It does not have instrumental value, at least not in relation to its specific object.

It is of course true that, like a house, 35 is conceptually distinct from the steps that compute the sum of 4, 12, and 19. But this is only a minimal point of analogy with a productive process. If Irwin were correct, it would follow that *all* sequential reasoning that issues in answers would be productive. Since most reasoning fits that description, a consequence of Irwin's argument is that most reasoning is productive in nature. Since we have already seen that Plato does conceive of purely theoretical reasoning, Irwin's position must be rejected.

There is much textual evidence to suggest that at every stage of Plato's career "techne" has a multi-faceted meaning and that in most discussions its two extreme cases, the productive and theoretical-mathematical technai, are highlighted. For example, in the *Gorgias* Socrates states: "Of all the technai some consist mostly of production (*ergasia*) and require little speech, some require none at all but accomplish their work in silence, such as painting and sculpture" (450c7–10).

Other examples mentioned in this passage include medicine (450a2) and gymnastic (450a5). Painting and sculpture are obvious examples of productive technai, that is, their *erga* are artefacts. It is not easy to classify medicine and gymnastic. In some sense, they too are productive. For example, medicine's product is health. But is health truly analogous to the carpenter's house? Both are contingent upon the activity of the technician, but the fact that the patient is not passive as building materials are, but active in the process of regaining his health, surely suggests a difference. Fortunately, it is not necessary here to pursue this question, for the following passage is sufficient to establish the central thesis of my argument: "Others of the technai which accomplish their purpose entirely through speech and, one might say, are in need of little or no product (*ergon*) in addition, such as arithmetic, logistic, geometry, and draughts" (450d3–7).

Although there are again ambiguities here, one point is clear: the mathematical technai require no product.[15] Consequently, both here and in the *Charmides* the two extreme versions of techne, the productive and the theoretical, have been identified.

In the *Hippias Minor* a similar identification is possible. Hippias is described as the wisest of all men with respect to the technai (368b). In his listing of the great sophist's accomplishments, Socrates mentions such typical crafts as jewelrymaking, shoemaking, and weaving (368c–d), and such mathematical technai as calculation (366c), geometry (367d), and astronomy (368a). These passages make clear the flexibility of "techne" and, most importantly, its capacity to embrace both productive and theoretical knowledge.

In both the *Sophist* and the *Statesman* we find the Eleatic Stranger, the master of division, dividing the technai. In the former he says, "of all the technai there are two forms" (219a8). Some are productive (*poiētikē:* 219b9), such as agriculture and imitation. Their objects are characterized by the fact that they did not exist before the producer brought them into existence. Other technai are acquisitive (*ktētikē:* 219c7). This branch is exemplified by the "whole class of learning (*mathēmatikon*) and of acquiring knowledge as well as money-making, fighting and hunting" (219c2–4). None of the objects here are produced: they exist independently of the technai apprehending them. Acquisition, as mentioned previously (and as argued by Rosen)[16] is a metaphor for theory. This is made clear by the first two of the Stranger's examples. *"To mathē-matikon,"* which here probably refers to learning in general, nevertheless has the obvious connotation of mathematics.

In the *Statesman* the division is said to include all the *epistēmai* (258e5) and is between the "practical" (*praktikē*) and the "intellectual" (*gnōstikē*). Despite the use of the word "practical," the following passage clearly shows what actually is at issue here. "The (technai) concerning carpentry and handicraft in general possess *epistēmē* which, as it were, is inherently related to its applications and together they make bodies come to be which did not exist before" (258d8–e2).

The mention of carpentry and the last clause of the passage make the meaning here unmistakable. The Stranger refers to productive techne. He explains the intellectual side of the division by saying: "Are not arithmetic and certain other kindred technai free from applications and do they not supply knowledge alone?" (258d4–6).

A final example comes from the *Philebus*. This passage (55dff.) is too complex to be analyzed at length here. Two features of it should, however, be noted. There is a division between productive (*demiourgikon*) knowledge (*epistēmē*) and that which "concerns education and support" (55d2). This phrase is ambiguous, but it becomes clear that with it Socrates refers to mathematics (see 56c5ff.). Again, a whole spectrum of knowledge is described here. We find, for example, applied mathematics in varying degrees of purity. But the essential thesis of my argument is once again confirmed: with "techne" Plato, in both his early and later works, does not refer exclusively to productive knowledge. He also conceives of mathematical knowledge, that knowledge without a produced *ergon,* as a counterpoint to the typically productive crafts.

To summarize: there are several modalities of techne. Two in particular, the productive and the theoretical, are consistently highlighted in the dialogues. This is a point that has been noted by commentators before. Brumbaugh, for example, in his extensive listing of the kinds of technai Plato employs as illustrations, makes it clear that they include both productive and mathematical kinds.[17] Thayer notes that the most frequent types of techne mentioned are "mathematics and medicine."[18] These commentators, however, have glossed over the possible philosophical significance of this insight. Thayer, like Irwin, wants to argue that techne is the model for moral knowledge held by Plato. But what precisely does this assertion entail? We have already seen how the assumption that techne is essentially productive has great bearing on the interpreter's conception of Platonic moral knowledge. Thayer and Brumbaugh do not discuss this point, nor do they consider the ramifications that the first term of the TA has on the significance of the analogy. While I believe Irwin is wrong concerning the productive nature of Platonic techne, he must be credited with having seen the importance of taking a stand on this issue, and then having consistently argued from his initial thesis.

One could argue, as does Lesses, that virtue is analogous to techne on the basis of similarities such as being purposive, organized, and involving knowledge of both ends and means.[19] This may well be correct. If so, however, "techne" should not be translated as "craft," but simply as "knowledge," for these characteristics are sufficiently broad to describe virtually all types of reliable and non-controversial knowledge. If this is the case, then from a theoretical perspective the TA becomes utterly uninformative: it simply states that virtue is moral knowledge, and that moral knowledge is knowledge. I conclude from this that the TA should not be read as Irwin does: the purpose of the analogy is not to establish a theoretical model of moral knowledge.

2

If the TA is not meant by Plato to be a conceptual outline of moral knowledge, what is its function? It has, I suggest, two, both of which are dialectical in nature: exhortation and refutation. By describing the function of the analogy as dialectical, I mean that it can only be understood within the context of the dialogical argument in which it is used. As a result, to isolate it from its context and treat it simply as a conceptual schema is to distort it. The *Crito* provides a paradigmatic instance of the first usage and will serve to clarify further what I mean by a dialectical reading of the TA.

In the *Crito* Socrates attempts to dissuade his old friend from committing a terrible mistake, namely breaking the law. Crito offers the following arguments, roughly paraphrased, to justify Socrates' escape. Crito will lose an irreplaceable friend (44b); he will gain the reputation of being a selfish man unconcerned with the plight of his friends (44b–c, 45e); by choosing not to escape Socrates is fulfilling the desires of his enemies (45d) and abandoning his children (45c). These arguments are largely based on Crito's emotional response to what he perceives as a dire situation. Even worse, they contain explicit appeals to *doxa,* a word he uses several times (see 44b9, 44c2, 44d2, 45e2, 46a1). Even though he has long been an associate of Socrates, Crito has learned very little, for he has forgotten the essential distinction between knowledge and *doxa.*

Socrates is most concerned to point out to Crito that not all *doxai* are the same. Some, those belonging to the wise, are worthwhile; the rest, those belonging to the foolish, are not. If, for example, an athlete is in need of an exercise regimen he does not randomly consult the man on the street for advice. He enlists the services of the doctor or trainer. Analogously, when in need of guidance on right or wrong actions, one should not rely on unexamined *doxa,* but find the man knowledgeable on these matters. The analogy here runs, as the trainer is to the body, so X is to moral actions. The X is not supplied. (See 47c–d.)

Irwin says the following about this passage: "The expert in a particular craft offers authoritative guidance supported by a rational account; and Socrates argues that we should seek someone equally authoritative in morals" (*PMT,* 71). The text, however, does not quite support such a reading. The only safe inference that can be made about the passage is that the analogy is used here to impress upon Crito the fact that *doxai* are not all the same, and that as a result knowledge and not *doxa* ought to be cultivated and pursued. The TA is valuable in communicating this, but there is no real evidence that Socrates' use of the analogy is intended to accomplish anything more. In particular, there is no reason to believe that the TA is meant to be taken strictly as an outline of a theoretical project. Its first term, as argued already, is equivocal and so the analogy is, at best, partial. Moral knowledge is analogous to techne only insofar as both are knowledge of some sort. The door is thus left open for any number of interpretations of the nature of moral knowledge. It may be productive or theoretical. It may also be "non-technical" or dialectical. The manner in which the analogy is here posed even permits moral knowledge to be thought of as a desirable, but unattainable, *telos.* It is not the goal of this essay to determine which of these options is genuinely Platonic. Instead, my discussion is prefatory to a complete analysis of the TA and, more important, Plato's conception of moral knowledge. One point, however, is now clear: Irwin is too eager to read this passage as if its sole import were as an axiom of a systematic moral theory. A procedure that is more reliable is to restrict our interpretation to what the TA actually *does* in the dialogue, and that is to encourage Crito not to submit to the lures of *doxa.*

Socrates' use of the analogy in the *Crito* is protreptic and therapeutic. As indicated, Plato has supplied enough information about Crito to permit the reader to understand that he is non-philosophical. The technai Socrates mentions to him are easily conceived examples of pre-philosophical knowledge at work, for their results are both visible and impressive: the trainer knows what to do when an athlete sprains his ankle. Mentioning them to Crito serves to remind him that, in his everyday life, he does not act as if *doxai* are homogeneous. His behavior contains what might be called an "implicit belief," namely that knowledge does exist and is superior to opinion. As Brumbaugh puts it, the technai "become an onstage testimony for the possibility of some 'knowing' which is not purely subjective or relative."[20] The TA exhorts Crito to learn from such testimony and to extend his implicit belief to the sphere of moral knowledge.

Structurally similar to this passage is *Laches* 184e–185e. Irwin cites these lines to justify the following assertion: "He (Socrates) demands an expert craftsman in moral training" (*PMT,* 71). The main interlocutor in this section of the *Laches* is Lysimachus. He is a somewhat pathetic and apparently weak old man. He admits having recorded no deeds worth boasting of. For this, however, he does not blame himself, but his father for not having trained him properly (179c). Despite the fact that he has lived in the same deme as Socrates he does not know who he is. For this he blames his age and Socrates

(181c). Lysimachus has a terrible memory and admits he cannot follow complex discussions (189d). Most telling of all is that after Nicias and Laches present their verdicts on the value of hoplite training for young men, he wishes to decide the issue by having Socrates cast a final vote. He is willing to go along with the majority (184c–d). In short, he is a pliable old man, susceptible (like Crito) to the whims of *doxa*. Once again, for our purposes his most prominent feature is that he is not the least bit philosophical.

Socrates says (to Melesias) that, as opposed to taking a vote on matters of education, the question "must be decided by *epistēmē* and not by the majority" (184e7). If we were delibertaing what medicine to use as an eye-salve we would enlist the services of the expert on eyes, the ophthalmologist. If the debate were over bridling a horse, we would consult the horsetrainer. Since education concerns the souls of young men, the question becomes "if someone among us is *technikos* concerning the treatment of the soul and is able to treat it beautifully (*kalōs*) and has had good teachers" (185e4–6). Irwin says of these three lines that "the *Laches* explicitly sought the craft which someone could learn to become virtuous" (*PMT*, 102). This is hardly explicit. Socrates is asking a question. Again, the most we can safely infer is that Socrates is concerned to point out to Lysimachus that *doxai*, even those on which a majority agree, are not of equal worth. Once again, the techne Socrates mentions to his non-philosophical interlocutor is an easily grasped example of knowledge at work. Socrates' use of the TA commits him only to the proposition that moral knowledge is desirable and should be sought; it does not commit him to a theoretical conception of that knowledge. (For further examples see the Appendix.)

The second principal use to which Socrates puts the TA is refutation. A good example is *Charmides* 165c4–e2, which was discussed earlier. Irwin believes that this passage is evidence for the following assertion: "In the *Charmides* he (Socrates) argues that temperance is not modesty; he does not ask if it is wise modesty, but considers what kind of craft it must be . . . he must assume it is no more than a craft" (*PMT*, 70). This is a peculiar rendition of the passage, for the definition here under consideration is no longer modesty, but Critias's "knowing oneself" (165b2). To this Socrates asks, "if moderation is a knowing something it obviously would be a certain *epistēmē* and about something; right?" (165c4–6). Socrates has reformulated Critias's definition by insisting that "self-knowledge" be interpreted on the model of an *epistēmē*. Hyland believes that the final clause in the sentence above, *"ē ou,"* (translated as "right?") is important for it leaves open the possibility that Socrates himself does not believe that the knowledge that is moderation is explicable via the model of the *epistēmai*.[21] Critias rejects this potentially fruitful option, and proceeds on the basis of the TA. This is what causes his downfall, since an object analogous to health or houses cannot be located for "self-knowledge." Indeed, much of the remainder of the dialogue explores the *aporiai* that ensue if one explicates temperance through the TA. As Klosko puts it, "Exactly what the *Charmides* establishes is not clear, but it seems to damage the CA [craft analogy] more than support it."[22]

If the *Charmides* does damage the TA, more precisely, if it shows that the analogy cannot be read as providing a theoretical conception of moral knowledge, why and how is it being used? Critias is a man who needs to be refuted. As historical figures both he and Charmides were infamous as intemperate villains. From the outset, then, this dialogue is permeated by a profound irony. Much like Meno, Critias' epistemic arrogance parallels his political viciousness.[23] Thus, there is a need to defeat him in a public argument in order to inform the audience (and the readers) where, in Plato's estimation, this man went wrong. The TA provides a useful tool for doing this. It forces Critias to formulate his knowledge claim in the most unambiguous terms available, that is, those belonging to the typical technai. Once so formulated, Socrates can demand that Critias' definition be explicated as clearly as medicine. By here employing techne as a model of knowledge Socrates brings about the downfall of Critias' definition, as well as his public humiliation.

It is clear that in some sense Socrates does adopt techne as the operative model for knowledge in this refutation. But in what sense does it operate? As mentioned, the *Charmides* is a profoundly ironic work and I suggest that the TA as it occurs here is part of that irony. Critias is neither a reflective nor a moral man. Consequently, it is reasonable to assume he has spent little time wondering about the nature of moral knowledge. The conception of knowledge he thus adopts is that belonging to the ordinary, pre-philosophical world, namely the typical techne (of both the productive and theoretical variety). The refutation proceeds on the basis of Critias' conception of knowledge. In other words, Socrates adopts the standpoint of his interlocutor in order to demonstrate its weaknesses. He does so, not to articulate a moral theory, but to refute Critias and instruct his listeners. Again, the refutation leaves open the question of the nature of moral knowledge, for it is not apparent that moral knowledge is anything like a typical techne. The more philosophically inclined among the audience are thus invited to pursue just this question: what is moral knowledge?

Socrates frequently uses the TA to refute his interlocutors in the manner suggested. Indeed, I would argue that this is the function for which the analogy is most commonly used. In lieu of the extensive argumentation required to substantiate such a claim, the Appendix supplied below will list what I take to be the relevant supporting passages.

To conclude: it has been demonstrated that there is little evidence for Irwin's reading of the TA. In other words, the analogy is not used in order to present a conceptual model of moral knowledge. Instead, its function is dialectical. Armed with his analogy, Socrates exhorts those interlocutors who are not committed to the active search for knowledge, and refutes those who believe they have already found their answers. The first term of the analogy, "techne," does not refer to a specific kind of knowledge: most important, it does not refer exclusively to productive knowledge. Thus, it should not be translated as "craft," but simply as "knowledge." The TA, then, does not describe the nature of moral knowledge; it makes it clear that such knowledge is desirable and should be sought, but it does not, of itself, obviate the difficulty of determining what Plato thought moral knowledge really was.

APPENDIX

The following material does not provide conclusive evidence for the thesis maintained in this essay. For this a thorough discussion of each of the dialogues would be required. Instead, its goal is heuristic. The TA repeatedly occurs throughout the Platonic dialogues and the textual material listed suggests its principal functions. (It should be noted that several of the dialogues listed are considered spurious. For the sake of completeness I nonetheless include them.)

I. The TA used for exhortation.
   1. *Crito* 46c–47d. Socrates exhorts Crito.
   2. *Laches* 184e–185e. Socrates exhorts Lysimachus.
   3. *Protagoras* 311b–313a. Socrates exhorts Hippocrates to consider what Protagoras teaches.
   4. *Theages* 123b–124c. Socrates exhorts Theages to clarify his conception of wisdom.
   5. *Alcibiades* I, 106c–109a. Socrates exhorts Alcibiades to clarify in what sense he wishes to advise the Athenians.
II. The TA used for refutation.
   A. Definitions of individual virtues.
     1. *Laches* 192d–193d. Laches' definition of courage.
     2. *Laches* 195a–195c. Nicias' definition of courage (by Laches).[24]
     3. *Euthyphro* 13a–14b. Euthyphro's definition of piety.
     4. *Charmides* 165c–176d. Critias' definition of moderation.
     5. *Republic* 332d–334c. Polemarchus' definition of justice.
     6. *Republic* 341c–343a. Thrasymachus' definition of justice.
   B. General knowledge claims.
     1. *Ion* 531b–533d. Ion's claim to the rhapsodic techne.
     2. *Gorgias* 447–461. Gorgias' claim to the rhetorical techne.
     3. *Euthydemus* 291b–293a. Ctesippus' claim for the kingly techne.[25]
     4. *Amatores* 134d–135a. The unnamed lover's definition of philosophy.
     5. *Cleitophon* 409a–410e. Socrates' claim to teach justice.[26]
III. The frequency of "techne."
"Techne" is used, in all its inflections, 675 times in the dialogues.[27] In addition, there are 187 occurrences of words derived from it. I would argue that "techne" is used most frequently when the TA is operative, specifically when it is being used in refutations. There are seven dialogues in which "techne" occurs at a rate of 1.0 times per Stephanus page or higher:
   1. *Cleitophon:* 4.0 uses of "techne" per page.
   2. *Ion:* 3.0.
   3. *Amatores:* 2.4.
   4. *Statesman:* 1.5.
   5. *Phaedrus:* 1.2.
   6. *Gorgias:* 1.0.
   7. *Sophist:* 1.0.
In addition, *Republic* Book 1, contains 28 uses of "techne" in its 28 Stephanus pages, for a rate of 1.0.

What is interesting about this list is that it shows how frequently "techne" is used during refutations. For example, the *Cleitophon, Ion,* and *Amatores* are each devoted, almost entirely, to refutation. The *Gorgias* can be divided into three distinct sections in which Socrates talks first with Gorgias, then Polus, and, finally, Callicles. The first section, 447–61, is devoted to refuting the large claims Gorgias makes for himself and his professed techne. "Techne" occurs 45 times in this section, for a rate of 3.2 per page. When the interlocutor shifts to Polus, a student of Gorgias who thus has a lesser claim to make for himself, the rate drops to .6 per page. When Callicles, a man who is *not* a rhetorician and so does not profess to have a techne, takes the stage, the rate drops to .4.

In the *Phaedrus,* "techne" is used 48 times between 260 and 274 (3.4 times per page). This section is devoted to refuting Lysias' claim to having a genuine *technē tōn logōn.*

It has long been observed that *Republic* Book 1 seems to be independent of, and probably earlier than, Books 2–10. It is not necessary to invoke a chronological thesis to explain the disparity between the use of "techne" in Book 1 (1.0 per page) and the later books (.2 per page). Book 1 finds Socrates refuting Polemarchus and Thrasymachus, men who believe they know what justice is. In the remaining Books the interlocutors shift to Glaucon and Adeimantus, young men who make no knowledge claim but who rather seek to be enlightened by Socrates.

It is also interesting to note that the only dialogues in which "techne" is not used are the *Crito, Lysis,* and *Parmenides.* The exhortation of Crito (see I, 1) takes place by means of examples and does not actually use the word "techne." In both the *Crito* and the *Lysis* Socrates converses with men (or boys) who have no knowledge claim to make.

Finally, consider the *Meno.* "Techne" is used only when Socrates converses with Anytus, a man convinced he knows what is just. Meno, at least insofar as we take his paradox seriously, has no knowledge claim to make.

To conclude once more, this outline is heuristic. The goal of this essay has, however, been met. It has been demonstrated that the evidence for Irwin's reading of the TA is not compelling. What may broadly be called a dialectical reading has been suggested as an alternative. With this use of the analogy, Socrates is not committed to a theoretical or technical conception of moral knowledge, but only to the proposition that moral knowledge is something good which should be sought. Such a search should no doubt be methodical, and Plato does give the reader many indications of how it is undertaken. What is perhaps most necessary to remember here is that particular arguments should not be isolated from their dialectical contexts. This is especially true of the TA. It is extremely important for Socrates in several of the dialogues. However, without fully analyzing the context in which it makes its many appearances and considering to what end Socrates employs it, its real significance and role in the dialogues will be missed.

NOTES

I am grateful to the Earhart Foundation for a research grant that made this paper possible and to two anonymous readers whose criticisms were valuable.

1. Hereafter I will not italicize *technē,* nor its plural, *technai.* "Techne" refers to the word itself: without the quotation marks I refer broadly to the concept of techne. All my citations of Plato are from Burnet's edition, and translations are either my own or from the Loeb Classical Library.

   With the name "Socrates" I refer *only* to the character appearing in Plato's early dialogues. The later dialogues, in which Socrates is not the principal speaker, involve a unique set of hermeneutical problems and I mention them only in passing.

2. Terence Irwin, *Plato's Moral Theory* (Oxford: Clarendon Press, 1977). Rosamond Kent Sprague, *Plato's Philosopher King* (Columbia, S.C.: University of South Carolina Press, 1976), Jorge Kube, *Techne und Arete* (Berlin: de Gruyter, 1969).

A large number of works discuss the TA. Irwin's bibliography is a good guide to this literature. My abbreviation "TA" is a variation of Irwin's "CA."

3. See H. S. Thayer, "Models of Moral Concepts of Plato's Republic." *Journal of the History of Philosophy* 7 (1969): 247–62.

4. *PMT* refers to Irwin's *Plato's Moral Theory*.

5. Gregory Vlastos, "The Virtuous and the Happy," *TLS,* 24 February 1978, 232–33.

6. John Gould, *The Development of Plato's Ethics* (Cambridge: Cambridge University Press, 1955). See especially 39–41.

7. George Klosko, "The Technical Conception of Virtue," *Journal of the History of Philosophy* 18 (1981): 98–106.

8. Many commentators use "craft" to translate "techne." One of the great virtues of Irwin's work is that he makes explicit what is often implicit in other commentaries.

9. I refer to an exchange of letters between Vlastos and Irwin that took place in *TLS* on 17 March 1978, 21 April 1978, 16 June 1978, 14 July 1978, 14 August 1978.

10. Miles Burnyeat, in his review of *PMT* in the *New York Review of Books,* 27 September 1979, 56–60, rightly calls it a "developmental story of extraordinary coherence" (59). This is not, however, to call it true.

11. See Aristotle, *EN* 1105a25–31 for this point. I would argue that Plato's division of the technai is a precursor of Aristotle's more familiar tripartition of the *epistemai*.

12. See Aristotle, *EN* 1177b1–5 and *Pol.* 1325b14–22.

13. This claim will be demonstrated in the course of the analysis of this and other passages.

14. See Aristotle, *Met.* 1025b20–30.

15. E. R. Dodds, in *Plato's Gorgias* (Oxford: Clarendon Press, 1959), explains the inclusion of draughts here by describing it as a "game of pure skill" (197).

The phrase "little or no product" obviously requires interpretation. Which of the technai have need of a little product, and which are entirely free from such need? Again, the purpose of this essay is not to delineate the entire range of Platonic techne (although this would be a very useful project); instead, its goal is simply to establish that non-productive techne is a real possibility in the dialogues. It is interesting to note that Irwin in his commentary on the same dialogue, *Plato's Gorgias* (Oxford: Clarendon Press, 1979), doesn't even comment on this passage.

16. See Stanley Rosen, "Plato's Myth of the Reversed Cosmos," *Review of Metaphysics* 23 (1979): 59–86. Since this division in the *Sophist* later includes all the activities of the sophists, it is perhaps an overstatement to say that acquisition is simply a metaphor for theory. It is, however, a broad category under which theoretical knowledge can be subsumed. *Eud.* 290b–c makes this clear.

17. Robert Brumbaugh, "Plato's Relation to the Arts and Crafts," in *Facets of Plato's Philosophy,* ed. by W. H. Werkmeister (Amsterdam: van Gorcum, 1976), 40–49.

18. Thayer, "Models of Moral Concepts," 250.

19. Glenn Lesses, "Virtue as Techne in the Early Dialogues," *Southwest Philosophical Studies* 7 (1982): 93–100.

20. Brumbaugh, "Plato's Relation to the Arts and Crafts," 46.

21. Drew Hyland, *The Virtue of Philosophy* (Athens: Ohio University Press, 1981). See pp. 96ff. Although I agree with Hyland, it must be admitted that *ē ou* in the dialogues regularly meets with an affirmative response.

22. Klosko, "The Technical Conception of Virtue," 102.

23. For an excellent discussion of the Meno's character, see Jacob Klein, *A Commentary on Plato's Meno* (Chapel Hill: University of North Carolina Press, 1967), 35–38.

24. Unless indicated otherwise, Socrates is the speaker in these passages.

25. It is unclear who the speaker is here.

26. In "The Riddle of Plato's Cleitophon," *Ancient Philosophy* 4 (1984): 132–46, I have discussed this largely ignored dialogue at length.
27. All statistical information was generated by the Ibycus computer system at Princeton University. The late Arthur Hanson, a special friend, was typically warm and generous when he introduced me to this new techne. If this paper has any real merit, I should like to dedicate it to his memory.

FURTHER READING

Irwin, T. 1977. *Plato's Moral Theory: The Early and Middle Dialogues,* esp. 37–176. Oxford.
———. 1988. "Repy to David L. Roochnik." In *Platonic Writings, Platonic Readings,* ed. C. L. Griswold, 194–99. New York.
Klosko, G. 1981. "The Technical Conception of Virtue." *Journal of the History of Philosophy* 19:98–106.
Roochnik, D. L. 1988. "Terence Irwin's Reading of Plato." In *Platonic Writings, Platonic Readings,* ed. C. L. Griswold, 183–93. New York.

12

Socrates the Epicurean?

T. H. IRWIN

1. A CONFLICT IN THE *REPUBLIC*

At the end of *Republic* I Socrates persuades Thrasymachus that the just and virtuous person will do well, live well, and be happy (353e4–354a4). Socrates at once admits that the conclusion is premature, and that he ought to have examined the nature of justice before deciding whether or not the just person is happy (354b1–c3).

The rest of the *Republic* might seem to promise a fuller defense of Socrates' claim that justice secures happiness. For Glaucon and Adeimantus claim to "renew the argument of Thrasymachus" (358b7–c1), with a better statement of his objections to justice; and we expect them to ask Socrates for a better defense of the thesis maintained against Thrasymachus.

We do not get what we expect. Glaucon and Adeimantus do not ask Socrates to show that justice by itself makes the just person happy. They ask him to show that justice by itself makes the just person happier than the unjust (361c3–d3). And it is this comparative claim that Socrates defends in the main argument of the *Republic,* in Books II–IX.

The thesis of Book I and the thesis of II–IX are vitally different. For the second thesis leaves open a possibility that the first thesis excludes. It is possible for A to be happier than B even though neither A nor B is happy; and so when Plato argues that the just person is in all circumstances happier than the unjust, he does not imply that the just person is happy in all circumstances.[1] He allows that happiness may have components that are not infallibly secured by justice. Though the second thesis is hard to believe, it is easier than the first.

Plato probably sees the difference between the two theses. In Book X he claims that justice leads to happiness because it normally secures honors, rewards, and other external benefits in this life, and invariably secures the favor of the gods (612a8–614a8). Here Plato assumes that justice by itself does not secure happiness, and rejects the strong thesis defended at the end of Book I (the "sufficiency thesis").

Plato has a good reason for making Socrates in Book I defend the sufficiency thesis. On this point as on others, Book I presents a Socratic argument for comparison and contrast with the rest of the *Republic*. For the early dialogues clearly commit Socrates to the sufficiency thesis.[2] In rejecting it Plato rejects a central element of Socratic ethics.

In later antiquity the interpretation of Socrates' and Plato's views about virtue and happiness remained a controversial matter. Chrysippus criticizes Plato for doing away with justice and any other genuine virtue by recognizing such things as health as goods (Plutarch, *De Stoicorum Repugnantiis* 1040d). On the other hand, the later Stoic Antipater wrote a book arguing that Plato maintained the Stoic thesis that only the fine is good (*Stoicorum Veterum Fragmenta* iii, Antip. 56). Among later Platonists Plutarch seems to accept Chrysippus' interpretation of Plato, and so finds that Plato and Aristotle agree on this point against the Stoics. On the other side Atticus ascribes to Plato a view much closer to the Stoic position, and so contrasts him sharply with Aristotle: "He [sc. Aristotle] deviated from Plato first of all on the common and greatest and most decisive point, by failing to observe the measure of happiness and failing to agree that virtue is self-sufficient for this [sc. measure]" (ap. Eusebius, *Praeparatio Evangelica* 794c6–d2).[3] "While Plato shouted and proclaimed on each occasion that the most just person is the happiest, Aristotle refused to allow that happiness follows on virtue unless one is fortunate in family and physical beauty and other things" (794d10–13). Here Atticus assumes unwisely that Plato's acceptance of the comparative claim commits him to acceptance of the sufficiency thesis.

Albinus is equally unwary; he reasonably finds in the *Euthydemus* a commitment to the Stoic thesis that only the fine is good, but claims that Plato has demonstrated this most of all in the whole of the *Republic;* "for he says that the man with the knowledge we have mentioned is the most fortunate and happiest," even in adverse circumstances (*Eisagōgē* 181.7–9).[4] "Most fortunate" is Albinus' addition to the *Republic* (perhaps under the influence of *Euthydemus* 282c9), and he assumes that the *Republic*'s comparative claim is equivalent to the sufficiency thesis.

This conflict in the interpretation of Plato is implicitly associated with different views on the relation of Plato to Socrates. It is highly probable that the Stoics recognized, as Cicero did (*Parad.* 4), the Socratic origin of their views on virtue and happiness. The Stoics are partly inspired by the Cynics, and the Cynics by Socrates. But Chrysippus' debt to Socrates does not lead him to ascribe the Socratic view to Plato; nor does his dispute with Plato lead him to ascribe the Platonic view to Socrates. Chrysippus' care in distinguishing Socrates from Plato contrasts sharply with Cicero's argument for finding the Socratic position in Plato; Cicero appeals to the *Gorgias* and the *Menexenus,* raising no question about whether these present Plato's views (*Tusc. Disp.* V. 35–36).

I want to suggest that Chrysippus is right in his interpretation of Plato and right to distinguish Socrates from Plato. But to see why Plato disagrees with Socrates we must see why Socrates believes the sufficiency thesis. If we can find his reasons we will perhaps also see the claims that Plato could not accept.

2. SOCRATES' CLAIMS

To show that the sufficiency thesis is Socratic we can appeal to earlier dialogues.

1. In the *Apology* Socrates affirms that a better person cannot be harmed by a worse (30c6–d5), and that no evil at all can happen to a good person, either in life or in death (41c8–d2).

2. In the *Crito* Socrates affirms an essential premise of his argument about disobedience and injustice, that living well, living finely and living justly are the same

thing (48b8–9). Since living well is the same thing as living happily, Socrates assumes that anyone who lives virtuously (i.e. finely and justly) ensures his happiness.

3. In the *Gorgias* Socrates argues that the virtuous and just person acts finely and does well, and thereby is happy (507b8–c7).

4. In the *Charmides* Socrates asks what sort of knowledge temperance is. If it is merely the knowledge of knowledge and ignorance, it will not produce happiness, since only the knowledge of good and evil will do that (173d3–5, 174b11–c3). It is assumed that the knowledge of good and evil ensures happiness; and if virtue is identical to that knowledge, virtue must ensure happiness.

5. The same assumption is made in the *Euthydemus*. Though we find it hard to describe the product of the kingly craft, we take it for granted that there is a craft securing happiness.[5]

This evidence commits Socrates fairly clearly to the sufficiency thesis. The first three passages are the clearest. The last two are less clear; for the crucial assumption appears in an argument that runs into difficulties, and we might say that Socrates wants to expose the assumption as a source of the difficulties. But the first three passages show that he cannot easily reject the assumption.

3. QUESTIONS ABOUT HAPPINESS

To see why Socrates accepts the sufficiency thesis we must consider especially his conception of happiness. His views on virtue are comparatively clear, since inquiries into the nature of virtue are his main concern in the early dialogues. It is remarkable, however, that he never thinks it is worth asking what happiness is. A search for a definition would apparently be rather useful; but he never seems to feel the need of it. The *Republic* displays some of the same insouciance. At the end of Book I Socrates admits that his conclusion is premature; he cannot claim to know that justice ensures happiness until he has said what justice is. But he says nothing similar about happiness; and the *Republic* never offers any explicit account of the nature of happiness.

To see where Socrates and Plato fail we must turn to Aristotle's discussion of happiness in *EN* I. Aristotle notices that people all identify happiness with the highest good, but disagree about what happiness is (1095a17–22), and offer different candidates—virtue, honor, pleasure and so on. But he thinks these disputes are tractable because we can agree on something intermediate between the very general claim about the highest good and the disputed claims about candidates for happiness. His solution of the disputes proceeds through three stages:

1. Formal criteria for the highest good—completeness and self-sufficiency (1097b20–21).
2. A conception of happiness meeting these criteria—activity of the soul according to virtue in a complete life (1098a16–18).
3. A candidate for the happy life—the life according to the specific actions and states of character described in the *EN*.

These three stages make disputes more tractable. Even if we do not initially agree on the successful candidates we can agree on formal criteria, and use our agreement to form a conception of happiness that allows us to reduce our initial disagreement about candidates, by asking if they conform to a conception of happiness that meets the formal criteria. Aristotle practices this method on the lives of pleasure, honor, and virtue to show that each of them is an unsuccessful candidate.[6]

Even this rough idea of Aristotle's method of argument suggests what is missing in Socrates and Plato.[7] They offer us many third-stage remarks, about candidates for happiness. Sometimes they offer second-stage remarks; Aristotle's argument about the human function is partly anticipated in *Republic* I. But they offer no explicit first-stage remarks to show us the appropriate formal criteria for happiness.[8] If, however, we are to understand Socrates' reasons for his third-stage claim that virtue is sufficient for happiness, we would like to find the implicit criteria and conception that might support it. We must ask him Aristotle's questions. Since Socrates does not ask them himself, we must rely on some inference and speculation to decide how he probably answers them. I will offer one account of his position, and try to explain why I think it is preferable to the most plausible alternative I can think of. But whether or not my account is right, I think it draws attention to a series of questions about Socratic ethics that need closer study.[9]

4. CRITERIA FOR HAPPINESS

When Socrates argues with interlocutors holding common-sense views, he must begin from these views, and either appeal to them in his own argument or explain why he rejects them. In the earlier dialogues Socrates does not always show that he sees how controversial some of his claims are. The Socratic Paradox, e.g., is taken for granted in the *Laches,* but defended only in the *Protagoras* and *Meno.*[10] Similarly, the sufficiency thesis is assumed in several dialogues; but only the *Gorgias* indicates that Socrates thinks it is paradoxical (470c–e), and only the *Euthydemus* defends it. We should not assume either that Socrates (or Plato) must have had a clear defense in mind when he first put forward the thesis or that the defense must have come later than the first statement of the thesis. If we attend to the *Gorgias* and *Euthydemus,* we can see that at least sometimes Socrates both sees that the thesis needs defense and defends it. He would be unwise to assume his view without argument; common beliefs about happiness and virtue do not make the sufficiency thesis seem obviously true. We should therefore see how Socrates might argue from common beliefs to show that his interlocutor must accept the sufficiency thesis.

The *Euthydemus* is our best source for such an argument, but it fails us at one essential point. Socrates does not begin with a statement of the criteria and conception he accepts in his claims about happiness. To see how the argument works, however, we must try to see his criteria and conception.

He begins with an assumption that he takes to be uncontroversial, that happiness is what we all want (278b3–6).[11] We achieve happiness by gaining many goods (279a1–4), and Socrates' list of goods is also meant to be largely uncontroversial (279a4–7). The reputed goods include bodily and social advantages, possessions and good fortune (279a4–c8); Socrates recognizes some room for dispute about the virtues and wisdom, but includes them too (279b4–c2).

To see the point of this list of goods we can usefully turn to Aristotle. In *Rhetoric* I. 5 he presents ''by way of illustration . . . what happiness is, to speak in general terms, and from what things its parts [sc. come about]'' (1360b7–9). He offers something closer

to common-sense views than he offers in the *Ethics,* where his views on the right formal criteria and conception influence his presentation of common sense; and for our purposes the less sophisticated account in the *Rhetoric* is especially useful. To show what happiness is Aristotle offers four answers. It is "(1) doing well together with virtue, or (2) self-sufficiency of life, or (3) the pleasantest life together with safety, or (4) prosperity of possessions and bodies together with the power to protect them and act with them; for practically everyone agrees that happiness is one or more of these things" (1360b14–18). After presenting these conceptions of happiness Aristotle offers a list of its parts, rather similar to the list of reputed goods in the *Euthydemus.* He explains why they seem to be parts: "For in this way someone would be most self-sufficient, by having both the internal and external goods, since there are no other goods beside these.
. . . Further, we think it proper for him to have power and fortune, since that will make his life most secure" (1360b24–29).

Aristotle suggests that the reputed goods are plausibly taken to be parts of happiness because they make someone self-sufficient; he has all the goods he could want, and needs none to be added. He is secure in so far as his good fortune protects him against sudden reversals and loss of happiness. Self-sufficiency and security are plausible formal criteria for happiness (1360b14–18), and they justify the common conception of happiness as consisting in the possession of all the goods there are.

In the *Euthydemus* Socrates' attitude to the popular candidates for happiness is far more critical than Aristotle's. He agrees with the popular view that it must include all the goods there are; but he claims that wisdom is the only good, and is therefore necessary and sufficient for happiness. To see if Socrates is right we should appeal to the formal criterion assumed by the popular candidates. If Socrates cannot show that his candidate for happiness achieves self-sufficiency and security, then he violates an apparently reasonable formal criterion for happiness. He must either challenge this criterion or show that his own candidate for happiness satisfies it.

5. SOCRATES' ARGUMENT

Socrates argues for the conclusion that wisdom is the only good and makes a person happy. We have every reason to suppose that he takes the conclusion seriously; for he identifies virtue with wisdom, and we have seen that he takes virtue to be sufficient for happiness. To justify his conviction about happiness he needs to show that there is no genuine part of happiness that is not secured by virtue, and that therefore the reputed goods that are independent of virtue are not elements of happiness at all. (Let us call these "external goods," remembering that in Socrates' final view they are really not goods at all.)

But though the conclusion is important the argument raises grave doubts; its faults seem to be recurrent, gross, and obvious.

Socrates rejects the external goods in two stages. First he argues that good fortune is not an element of happiness that is independent of wisdom, because wisdom by itself secures all the good fortune that is needed (279c9–280a8). Next he argues that none of the external goods is a good at all, because it is their right use that secures happiness, and only wisdom ensures their right use (280b1–281e5).[12]

First Socrates considers good fortune. He mentions two types of crafts: (a) flute-playing, writing, and reading; (b) generalship, navigation, and medicine (279d8–280a4). Though he does not mention it, a difference between (a) and (b) is fairly clear; the Stoics, following Aristotle, formulate it as the difference between stochastic and non-stochastic crafts (*Stoicorum Veterum Fragmenta* III. 19). In (a) fortune seems to be needed to prevent antecedent ill fortune. An expert writer cannot produce good writing without the appropriate material; and we may think that the supply of it is sometimes a matter of fortune. But once he has it, the competent exercise of his craft ensures the right result. In the crafts listed in (b) fortune also seems to be needed to prevent subsequent ill fortune. A pilot might exercise his craft quite competently with the right material, but still a sudden and unpredictable storm might sink the ship.

Keeping in mind these two areas of ill fortune we can examine Socrates' argument. He wants to show that good fortune need not be added to our list of goods once we include wisdom, since wisdom ensures the sort of success for which we wrongly think good fortune is needed. He argues:

1. In each case the wise person has better fortune than the unwise (280a4–5).
2. Genuine wisdom can never go wrong, but must always succeed (280a7–8).
3. Therefore wisdom always makes us fortunate (280a6).

In this argument Socrates seems to move without warrant to steadily stronger claims. Since (3) is supposed to eliminate good fortune as a distinct good apart from wisdom, Socrates should show that wisdom provides all the success that is normally taken to require good fortune. But all he shows in (1) is that wisdom ensures more success, other things being equal, than we can expect if we lack it. The claim in (2) seems stronger. Socrates seems to ignore the problem of antecedent ill fortune with both types of crafts; and even if this point is waived, he seems to ignore subsequent ill fortune in crafts of the second type. We might agree with Socrates that bad writing with a good pen on good paper indicates lack of the writer's craft; but we need not see any lack of craft in a pilot's failure to save his ship from an unpredictable storm. It is just this sort of failure that we avoid only if we have good fortune. These objections seem to show that Socrates is not entitled to (2), if it is understood in a strong enough sense to imply (3). Apparently, then, Socrates tries to prove that good fortune, as an external good distinct from wisdom, is unnecessary for happiness, but in trying to prove this ignores those very cases that seem to show why we need good fortune.

Socrates now argues that the other external goods are not really goods; and he needs to show this, since these external goods seem to depend at least partly on good fortune, which Socrates has just argued is unnecessary for happiness. In Socrates' view, the only real good is wisdom, and so this turns out to be the only good that we need for happiness. He argues:

1. It is possible to use the external goods well or badly (280b7–c3, d7–281a1).
2. Correct use of them is necessary and sufficient for happiness (280d7–281e1).
3. Wisdom is necessary and sufficient for correct use (281a1–b2).
4. Therefore wisdom is necessary and sufficient for happiness (281b2–4).

This is the conclusion that Socrates needs. But he strengthens it by a further defense of (1) and (2):

5. Each external good used without wisdom is a greater evil than its opposite, and each used by wisdom is a greater good than its opposite (281d6–8).

6. Therefore each external good and evil is in fact neither good nor evil (281e3–4).
7. Therefore wisdom is the only good and folly the only evil (281e4–5).

At (3) and (4) two possibilities need to be considered:

(a) Given a reasonable supply of external goods, wisdom is necessary and sufficient for happiness.
(b) Whatever external goods we may have or lack, wisdom is necessary and sufficient for happiness.

In his examples Socrates considers only cases that allow (a); he remarks that a supply of money and other external resources is still liable to misuse. He might say that wisdom guarantees the right use, not the initial resources; then he would have to concede the role of antecedent fortune, and would simply be ignoring the role of subsequent fortune in the exercise of some crafts. But if he concedes the role of antecedent fortune, he cannot maintain his claim to have eliminated fortune as a distinct contributor to happiness. The elimination of fortune requires the strong claim in (b). And for this strong claim Socrates seems to have given no sufficient argument.

A further question arises in (5)–(7). When Socrates says in (5) that health, for example, is a greater good than sickness if it is guided by wisdom, we might suppose he means that health, in these circumstances, is a good and otherwise is not. In that case Socrates can deny, as he does in (6), that health taken by itself (*auto de kath' hauto*) is a good, and allow that it is a good when it is guided by wisdom. But if that is what (6) means, the transition to (7) is blatantly unwarranted, since (7) says that health is not a good at all.

We have two ways out of this unwelcome result:

(a) In (7) Socrates only means that health is not a good by itself, and needs wisdom added if it is to be a good.
(b) In (5) he does not mean that health is a good.

While (a) might seem to be a more reasonable conclusion, it would not fulfill Socrates' main aim in the whole argument; for the reasons we have already seen, he must show that wisdom is necessary and sufficient for happiness, and hence the only real good.

If we look again at (5), we can see that Socrates is not committed to regarding health as a good. If we adapt his remarks to show that health is a greater good, we will say: if wisdom leads health, health will be a greater good than sickness to the extent that it is more able to serve its leader when the leader is good (cf. 281d6–7). This account of how health is a greater good does not imply that health is good; "greater good" may simply mean "more of a good," that is, "closer to being a good." The explanation in "to the extent . . ." says that health is more able to serve wisdom. If a wise person wants to act he will often find it easier to act as he wants to if he is healthy than if he is sick.[13] Socrates, then, can consistently claim that health is not a good. But he surely has not justified this claim, or the sufficiency thesis; for he has not shown that virtue can do without a level of health that is not within its control.

After finding such serious flaws in this argument in the *Euthydemus* we might remind ourselves that the dialogue as a whole is concerned with eristic, and suggest that even the protreptic passages are not free of the fallacious argument that is rife in the rest of the dialogue. But if we dismiss the argument we will have dismissed our best evidence of

Socrates' defense of the sufficiency thesis. Before we dismiss it we ought to see if Socrates can reasonably appeal to assumptions about happiness that make some of his moves less clearly illegitimate.

At this point we need to examine Socrates' criteria and conception more closely. For our previous objections will collapse if Socrates can justify two claims:

1. When we plan for happiness, we can always count on having the right material, so that antecedent ill fortune can be ignored.
2. Happiness is the sort of end that is infallibly secured by the correct exercise of wisdom.

To justify these two claims Socrates needs to show that he can defend them from a conception of happiness that satisfies reasonable formal criteria. If we return to Aristotle's general account of happiness Socrates seems to be wrong; for the completeness, self-sufficiency, and security of happiness seem to require just those goods that are exposed to antecedent and subsequent ill fortune. Socrates needs to show that he need not accept these inferences from the formal criteria.

6. HAPPINESS AND DESIRE

Aristotle takes happiness to be the self-sufficient and secure life. He assumes that self-sufficiency and completeness imply each other; for the list of reputed goods achieves self-sufficiency because it includes all the goods there are (1360b26).

But how is completeness to be achieved? Both Socrates and Aristotle assume, first, that happiness is what we all want, and, second, that whatever else we want we want for the sake of happiness (*Eud.* 278e3–279a4).[14] If we are concerned with happiness because it is what we want, it will be complete in so far as it achieves all we want, and self-sufficient if it lacks nothing that we need to achieve all our desires. Aristotle sometimes explains the completeness of happiness in this way, saying that it is what we must attain to fulfill our desire (*EE* 1215b17–18).[15]

If we accept this account of completeness and self-sufficiency, the formal criterion of happiness seems to explain why we need the external goods, and why the loss of them will prevent happiness. If I lack the resources to satisfy my desires, or ill fortune interferes with their execution, I lose happiness because I have my desires frustrated. The elements of my happiness, on this view, must include all that I need for the satisfaction of my desires; and hence they must include the external goods.

This conclusion, however, is open to challenge, for a reason that is briefly stated by Hume. Hume denies that the failure of metaphysical ambitions is a ground for unhappiness or discontent: ''For nothing is more certain than that despair has almost the same effect upon us with enjoyment, and that we are no sooner acquainted with the impossibility of satisfying a desire, than the desire itself vanishes'' (*Treatise,* Introd.). Hume draws our attention to a familiar fact, that we do not necessarily think ourselves unhappy simply because we cannot fulfill clearly unfeasible desires that we might have had or once did have. When we see that a desire is unfeasible we give it up, and once we have given it up, we no longer suffer the unhappiness of frustrated desire.

If we attend to Hume's point we can reply to the claim that external goods must be elements of happiness. The loss of these goods seems to cause unhappiness because it makes some of our desires unfeasible, and it will cause unhappiness if we retain the unfeasible desires. But the rational person will react by giving up the desires that have become unfeasible; once he has given them up, he is no longer unhappy because they are unsatisfied. The loss of external goods seems to cause no loss of happiness, and the external goods are therefore not necessary for happiness.

In reply to Socrates we might urge that Hume is not right about every case; even if we realize a desire is unfeasible and that we would be better off if we gave it up, we may retain it, and so continue to suffer the unhappiness resulting from its frustration. While this might be a fair objection to Hume, Socrates can hardly accept it. Since he accepts the Socratic Paradox, he believes that everyone's desires are all concentrated on his own happiness and the means to it; as soon as we see that an action does not promote our happiness we will lose the desire to do it. Socrates' moral psychology offers him a strong defense of Hume's claim.

Just as the loss of external goods does not by itself cause unhappiness, their presence does not by itself secure happiness. We can still misuse them; and however many we have, we may have such extravagant and unfeasible desires that we are still unsatisfied. In favorable conditions as well as unfavorable we need feasible desires; and once we have them, we can secure happiness through the fulfillment of our desires.

We have seen, then, why external goods are neither necessary nor sufficient for happiness; and at the same time we have seen why the appropriate sort of wisdom will secure happiness. A wise person will see that he is better off with feasible desires; and if changing external conditions make some of his desires unfeasible, he will give them up. By adapting his desires to suit the external conditions, he will secure his happiness whatever the conditions may be.

A wise person is indifferent to external goods in so far as he does not regret their loss, and sees that they are neither necessary nor sufficient for his happiness. But he does not ignore them altogether. For they are means to the satisfaction of some desires he has. If the wise person wants a Rolls-Royce, and has the money to buy it, the money will help him to satisfy his desires, and for that it will be useful to him. But if he loses the money, he will not suffer a loss of happiness, since he will adapt his desires to suit his reduced resources.

We have traced a conception of happiness that accepts the Aristotelian formal criteria, and interprets them in a particular way that leads to a non-Aristotelian conclusion, that external goods are not elements of happiness, and so are not genuine goods. Aristotle leaves himself exposed to this sort of argument as soon as he identifies completeness and self-sufficiency with the complete fulfillment of desires; for then it seems quite reasonable to adapt our desires in ways that secure their satisfaction.

On further consideration we may even think the formal criteria demand the adaptive strategy. For Aristotle recognizes security as a formal criterion of happiness; and security seems to him to require a reasonable supply of external goods, which in turn requires good fortune. We might challenge Aristotle's inference and claim that only an adaptive strategy properly fulfills his formal criterion. For the happiness of a wise and well-adapted person seems far more secure than the condition of someone who depends on the continuation of good fortune; dependence on external conditions makes our well-being insecure; and such an insecure condition can hardly count as happiness. From the formal criteria of happiness we have reached a conception of happiness as the complete fulfillment of desire, and an adaptive strategy for achieving that fulfillment. Let us call this an adaptive account of happiness; we have seen why it presents a plausible challenge to the common-sense view that regards external goods as elements of happiness.

7. SOCRATES' ACCOUNT OF HAPPINESS

I have sketched an adaptive account of happiness to show how it can plausibly be derived from the common-sense criteria presented by Aristotle. I now suggest that this sort of account is presupposed in the *Euthydemus*. If Socrates relies on an adaptive account of happiness, he can answer our previous objections relying on external circumstances. He is free to ignore antecedent fortune; for the wise person needs no particular external goods, but only needs to find the desires that are feasible in the circumstances. If he suffers subsequent ill fortune, that will not threaten his happiness either; he will simply have discovered that some of his desires are unfeasible, and so will eliminate them. Socrates can justifiably claim that wisdom by itself secures all the good fortune that is needed for happiness, and that while favorable conditions (e.g., being healthy rather than sick) make it easier to fulfill the desires I have, they are unnecessary for happiness and do not contribute to it in their own right.

If an adaptive account of happiness allows this defense of Socrates' argument, we have some reason to suppose he accepts or presupposes it. This is not a decisive reason; we may be able to find other accounts of happiness that explain this argument as well or better. To explain the argument we should both be able to refer to formal criteria for happiness that Socrates might be expected to assume, and be able to answer the objections that arise at different stages in Socrates' argument. I cannot think of any other account of happiness that will pass these tests as well as the adaptive account passes them; and therefore I am inclined to attribute the adaptive account to Socrates.

The implicit presence of an adaptive account in the *Euthydemus* is one reason for ascribing it to Socrates. But clearly we will have much better reasons if we can find other evidence to support us, and we will have to think again if we find conflicting evidence in other dialogues.

One argument in the *Lysis* assumes that the good person, as such, is sufficient for himself and to that extent needs nothing else (215a6–8). This assumption is not clearly challenged in the dialogue; and we can see why Socrates accepts it if he believes that happiness is complete satisfaction and accepts the sufficiency thesis.

In the *Apology* Socrates suggests that death is a good thing even if it is like a permanent sleep (40a9–e4). There are few days or nights in our lives in which we have lived better or more pleasantly than in the nights of dreamless sleep (40d2–e2). Though Socrates first assumes that death involves non-existence (40c6), his praise of death does not rest on this assumption; and so he forgoes the Epicurean argument that nothing bad can happen to us when we do not exist and are unaware of anything.[16] His argument is a different one—that death is actually good for us because it is so similar to a condition that is evidently better and pleasanter than most others. This claim is intelligible if an adaptive account of happiness is assumed; for in dreamless sleep we have no unsatisfied desires. The more seriously we take this account of happiness, the more seriously we will take Socrates' praise of death.

In the *Gorgias* Callicles claims that happiness requires large and demanding appetites and their satisfaction (491e5–492c8). Socrates asks him to consider the view that "those who need nothing are happy" (492e3–4).[17] Callicles rejects this view because it would imply that rocks and corpses are happiest of all (492e5–6). Since Socrates has just suggested that a wise person will be temperate and self-controlled, the conception of happiness that Callicles rejects is plainly the Socratic conception.

Socrates says he wants to "persuade you to change your mind and to choose, instead of the unfilled and unrestrained life, the life that is orderly and adequately supplied and satisfied with the things that are present on each occasion. But do I persuade you at all actually to change your mind ⟨and agree⟩ that the orderly people are happier than the unrestrained?" (493c4–d2). In this last sentence we might take Socrates to be definding only a comparative claim (cf. 494a2–5), so that he is not committed to the stronger claim that the self-sufficient people are actually happy. The merely comparative claim, however, is not enough for the *Gorgias*. Socrates had already asserted the sufficiency thesis against Polus (470e9–10), and he reasserts this claim against Callicles (507b8–c4).[18] If he maintains the adaptive account of happiness, his argument is clear. For he takes virtue to result from temperance, and therefore to result from wise planning that removes demanding and extravagant desires (503c4–6). An adaptive account of happiness strongly supports the sufficiency thesis; without such an account the thesis is left with very weak support.

Here as in the *Euthydemus* we ascribe the adaptive account to Socrates because he needs it; and such an argument is less than conclusive. We are better off in the *Gorgias,* however; for here Socrates mentions an adaptive account of happiness, and closely links it to his claims about virtue and happiness. It is striking that in the *Gorgias* he fails to distinguish the sufficiency thesis from the comparative thesis that is defended in the *Republic;* and the dialogue offers only the adaptive account to support the sufficiency thesis.

These remarks in dialogues apart from the *Euthydemus* encourage us to believe that an adaptive account of happiness is not confined to this one dialogue. Indeed they suggest that whenever Socrates appeals to a conception of happiness to support his argument, he appeals to a conception that finds happiness in the complete satisfaction of desire. An adaptive account of happiness is an important, though largely implicit, element of Socratic doctrine.

I have suggested that the claims made in the *Euthydemus* about external goods are properly explained by the adaptive account of happiness accepted in the *Gorgias*. It is worth remarking, then, that this connection between the two dialogues may have occurred to the author of the pseudo-Platonic *Eryxias*. The argument here asks whether such external goods as wealth are really goods or really useful. The argument in the *Euthydemus* is used to show that these goods are not always beneficial (403a2–c5). Later Socrates claims that the happier and better person is the one who requires fewer external goods (405b8–c6). Just as the healthy person is better off and needs less than the sick person, so the person with fewer desires is better off than the person with many desires who needs large resources to satisfy them (405c6–406a3).

This argument fills the gap left in the *Euthydemus,* by explaining why the wise person, who knows how to use external goods and therefore will make the best use of those he has, will also be successful and happy, no matter how few of them he has. Part of his wisdom is his knowledge that he does not need any particular level of them to secure his happiness, and that he secures his happiness by satisfying the desires that fit the external goods available to him.

We do not know who wrote the *Eryxias* or when. But it is worth mentioning for our purposes, since the author echoes both the *Euthydemus* and the *Gorgias,* and sees how they might be combined. I think the connections he finds reflect an important Socratic assumption. It is easy to suppose that the *Eryxias* reflects the influence of Cynic and Stoic arguments. But we need not assume this; it is an intelligible, and to this extent not unintelligent, development of Socratic views.

8. INTERPRETATIONS OF SOCRATIC HAPPINESS

If Socrates accepts an adaptive account of happiness, we can perhaps understand better why he does not inquire curiously into the nature of happiness. He realizes that his views about virtue and knowledge and their relation to happiness are controversial; but he might well believe that a conception of happiness as completely satisfied desire is fairly uncontroversial, and that an adaptive strategy is a reasonable conclusion from it. We can support Socrates by noticing that these claims might not seem bizarre to all his contemporaries.

The *Menexenus* recognizes self-sufficiency as a source of happiness. A person's happiness is most secure if the things that promote it depend on himself rather than on the good or bad fortune of others; and such self-sufficiency is the mark of the temperate, brave, and wise person (247e5–248a7). I mention this passage not because I imagine that this funeral speech is meant to express distinctively Socratic doctrine, but for just the opposite reason. Such a remark in a speech consisting mostly of moral platitudes suggests that an adaptive account of happiness would not be bizarre and unintelligible (even if it was not immediately obvious) to someone with ordinary views about happiness. This is not to say that Socratic ethics is free of paradox; it certainly outrages common sense at some points, but its aims are not alien to common sense.

Some of Democritus' remarks on happiness suggest that one of Socrates' contemporaries could accept an adaptive account. He says: "If you do not desire much, a little will seem much to you; for a small desire makes poverty equipollent with wealth" (B 284). For similar reasons he advises us to "keep our minds fixed on what is possible, and be satisfied with what is present" (B 191, DK p. 184. 9–10; cf. *Gorg.* 493c6–7). The claim about equipollence is just what Socrates needs to explain why recognized goods are not really goods, and why their loss is not really a harm; if I reduce my desires I will no longer miss the wealth I have lost, and my reduced resources will serve me just as well.[19]

Democritus' advice makes it easy to infer that an adaptive account of happiness will also be ascetic, advising us to reduce our desires to the minimum. Xenophon associates self-sufficiency and requiring nothing with Socratic asceticism (*Mem.* I. 2. 14, 6. 10). In fact, however, the connection between an adaptive account and asceticism is not simple. If asceticism requires the actual cultivation of limited and undemanding desires in all conditions, it does not follow from an adaptive account of happiness. If I can easily afford a steak and would prefer it over a bowl of porridge, an adaptive account of happiness does not require me to prefer the porridge; it simply requires me to give up the desire for steak it I cannot satisfy it. Still, we can see why in some conditions Socratic adaptiveness might require the actions that would be required by Cynic asceticism. We might, therefore, both deny that Socrates is a Cynic ascetic and suggest that his adaptive account of happiness made it easy to regard him as an ascetic.

The Cynic and ascetic interpretation of Socrates' views on happiness provoked a reaction. As Augustine remarked, the unclarity of Socrates' views encouraged disagreement among professed Socratics.[20] Augustine was reasonably puzzled that the anti-hedonist Cynics and the hedonist Cyrenaics could both claim to be Socratics.[21] But the dispute is intelligible if Socrates accepts an adaptive account. For while the Cynics interpret this ascetically, Aristippus points out that self-sufficiency and independence does not require abstention from pleasures when they are available. Like Socrates' temperate person who is satisfied with "the things present on each occasion" (*Gorg.* 493c6–7; cf. Democ. B 191), he "enjoyed the pleasure of things present, but did not labor in pursuing enjoyment of things not present" (D.L. II. 66).[22] While Aristippus' version of hedonism would have surprised Socrates, he legitimately rejects the ascetic inferences drawn from Socrates' claims about happiness and self-sufficiency.

The philosopher who agrees most closely with Socrates on this issue is probably neither Antisthenes nor Aristippus, but Epicurus. I am not concerned here with Epicurus' hedonism, but with the account of happiness that forms his particular version of hedonism. Epicurus clearly accepts an adaptive account of happiness, and therefore cultivates independence of external conditions: "We count self-sufficiency as a great good, not so that in all circumstances we will use only a few things, but so that a few things will suffice us if we do not have many, genuinely convinced that those who enjoy luxury most pleasantly are those who need it least" (D.L. X. 130).[23] Epicurus' advice sounds quite similar to Democritus'; but, unlike Democritus, he sharply rejects the ascetic inference supporting Cynicism. At the same time he clarifies Socrates' claim about self-sufficiency. Socrates left himself open to Cynic and Cyrenaic constructions, but committed himself to neither.[24] Epicurus best appreciates the role of an adaptive account in Socrates, and its consequences for the wise person's attitude to external circumstances. As we will see, the Epicurean position also captures some of Socrates' claims about the virtues, and reflects some of the difficulties in them.

9. THE SUFFICIENCY OF VIRTUE

We turned to the *Euthydemus* to understand the account of happiness that is assumed in the sufficiency thesis. Having seen how Socrates conceives happiness we can now return to this thesis.

Socrates needs to connect wisdom with virtue. We have seen why knowledge of good and evil will be sufficient for happiness, if an adaptive account of happiness is accepted. For the wise person will be the one who knows that an adaptive strategy secures happiness; and this wisdom will secure his happiness. If we agree with Socrates in identifying virtue with the knowledge of good and evil, it follows that virtue is sufficient for happiness.

But we may still wonder how this conception of virtue is connected with the particular sorts of actions and states of character that both common sense and Socrates count as virtuous. Can Socrates explain why the wise person will characteristically be unafraid in battle, moderate in his appetites and demands, and unwilling to cheat or steal?

We can see the main line of argument if we consider why someone might be attracted to intemperate, cowardly, or unjust action. If I am thinking about my happiness I might suppose that a particular vicious action will secure me some external good that I need to be happy, and that I will reduce my happiness if I deny myself that good. If I cheat, I can get the money I think I need to satisfy my desires; and if I do not cheat, and forgo the money, then apparently I lose something I need for happiness. An adaptive account implies that this argument is mistaken. If I forgo an external good, I simply need to adapt my desires to new circumstances, and I will not necessarily forgo any happiness.

Socrates insists strongly that a virtuous person will allow nothing to count against doing the virtuous action, no matter what the cost may be; the only question he need ask himself is what the virtuous action is, and his answer to that question should guide his action (*Apol.* 28b5–9).[25] His account of happiness makes this pattern of choice quite reasonable; since the virtuous person will not see any threat to his happiness if he pays the price of virtuous action in loss of external goods, he need not concern himself with this price in deciding what to do. If Socrates were to choose an external good over the virtuous course of action, he would be choosing an action that is bad for him, and he refuses to do this; that is why he refuses to propose an alternative to the death penalty (*Apol.* 37b5–e2).[26] For the same reason a good person cannot be harmed; no loss of external goods will threaten his happiness.

When Socrates makes these strong claims about virtue, he is not allowing himself a rhetorical exaggeration or an expression of unwarranted faith. He is drawing attention to a consequence of an adaptive account of happiness. A virtuous person can certainly suffer the loss of external goods; such losses require him to change his desires; but they do not threaten his happiness, since he adapts his desires to fit the circumstances.

If this is a defensible account of Socrates' claim about virtue, one consequence is worth noticing. It is easy to suppose that if Socrates thinks virtue all by itself is sufficient for happiness, then he must attribute some intrinsic value to virtue; it might be identical to happiness, or a part of happiness whose presence is causally sufficient for the presence of the other parts. If, however, Socrates holds an adaptive account of happiness, he can maintain the sufficiency of virtue without attributing any intrinsic value to it.

10. THE VALUE OF EXTERNAL GOODS

We may hesitate to accept the sufficiency thesis because it seems to imply that no external good is worth pursuit at all; since these alleged goods do not promote happiness, they will not be genuine goods, and so apparently not worth pursuit. This objection was raised against the Cynics and Stoics who supported the sufficiency thesis. If we ascribe the thesis to Socrates we may well suppose he is open to the same objection; and if the objection seems cogent, we may hesitate to ascribe the thesis to him.

We may hesitate still more when Socrates sometimes seems to admit that external goods are goods. Sometimes he lists them as goods without hesitation (*Gorg.* 467e4–6, *M.* 78c5–d1, *Ly.* 218e5–219a1). He says he would wish neither to do nor to suffer injustice (*Gorg.* 469c1). He allows the reflective pilot to wonder if he has benefited or harmed people by saving them from drowning (*Gorg.* 511e6–512b2). He even claims that virtue is the source of wealth and any other goods there are (*Apol.* 30b2–4).[27]

To admit that Socrates regards external goods as genuine goods introduces conflict with some of his other views:

(a) He explicitly contradicts this view in the *Euthydemus* (281e3–5).

(b) If the sufficiency thesis is true, and if nothing is good without contributing to happiness, then external goods cannot contribute to a virtuous person's happiness.

(c) We avoid this conflict if we say that external goods make the virtuous person happier than he would be without them, and that this is what makes them goods, though even without them he would be happy. But if they are goods, then the loss of them should harm the virtuous person, and we are in conflict with the claim that the good person cannot be harmed.

We can remove any appearance of conflict if we deny either that (i) Socrates makes virtue the only good, or that (ii) he accepts the sufficiency thesis, or that (iii) he thinks the good person cannot be harmed. Alternatively, we can understand the claims about external goods so that they are consistent with (i)–(iii).

In the first three passages listed (*Gorg.* 467e etc.) Socrates simply asks his interlocutor about commonly recognized goods, and nothing in the argument depends on his agreeing with the interlocutor that these are genuine goods. The passages therefore provide very weak evidence for reinterpreting his explicit statement in (i). When he says he would not wish to suffer injustice Socrates refrains from saying he would wish not to suffer it.[28] He has no reason to wish for it, since suffering injustice is in itself no benefit to him, and he can say this even if not suffering injustice is no benefit to him either.[29] These passages do not require us to reinterpret (i).

But there is a broader reason for wanting Socrates to modify (i); we do not want Socrates to be a Cynic, believing that he has no reason to choose external goods over their opposites. It is worth noticing, then, that Socrates can consistently maintain that health is preferable to sickness without rejecting (i)–(iii). As we have seen, he is entitled to say that if I have a feasible desire, I have reason to choose a means to its fulfillment, and such a means is useful to me. To this extent Socrates could say that the means are instrumental goods. However, it is easy to suppose that if they are instrumental goods, I will be worse off without them; and in Socrates' view this is false. If I lack instrumental means to satisfy a desire I will just give up the desire, and I will be in an equally good position to achieve my happiness.

If, then, Socrates holds an adaptive account of happiness, he has some reason for allowing that external goods are goods (they are sometimes instrumental means to the fulfillment of my desires) and some reason for denying this (their presence or absence makes no difference to my happiness). Sometimes he compromises between these two claims by speaking in comparative terms. Just as in the *Euthydemus* he says health is a greater good than sickness for a virtuous person, he says the person who is killed unjustly is less wretched and pitiable than the one who kills unjustly (*Gorg.* 469b3–6), and that doing injustice is a greater evil than suffering it (509c6–7). We might insist that these comparative terms do not imply that external goods and evils are genuine goods and evils, even if the presence of one and absence of the other counts as a benefit (509d1).[30] But it may be better to allow that Socrates does count external goods as genuine goods, and then to insist that they do not make a virtuous person any happier than he would be without them. We need not, then, be surprised to find apparent evidence of Socrates' speaking both ways; and we need not infer that he must reject (ii) or (iii).

11. CONFLICTING VIEWS ON HAPPINESS

I have tried to show that Socrates holds an adaptive account of happiness, and that it is consistent with his recognition of reasons for choosing external goods. But even so I doubt if he sticks consistently to an adaptive account. Some of his remarks seem to require a different view that seems irreconcilable with the sufficiency thesis.

In the *Crito* Socrates compares justice in the soul with health in the body; he wants to show that it is not worth living with an unjust soul, and to show that he appeals to Crito's agreement that it is not worth living (*bioton*) with a diseased body (47d7–e5). The same claim about health is affirmed still more strongly in the *Gorgias*. There Socrates argues that it does not benefit a person to live with his body in bad condition, since he is bound to live badly (505a2–4).[31]

These claims raise difficulties for the view that virtue is sufficient for happiness. For apparently the virtuous person could be in bad health; if bad health deprives him of happiness, it cannot be true that no evil can happen to him, and his wisdom cannot make good fortune unnecessary for his happiness.

At the same time, these claims raise wider questions about the nature of happiness. Socrates might maintain a conception of happiness as the complete fulfillment of desire, and argue that bodily sickness inevitably frustrates desires that we cannot help having; in that case he must admit the failure of an adaptive strategy for securing happiness. Alternatively, he might allow that we could cease to desire the health we cannot have, and still insist that we are unhappy because of how we are, not because of how we feel about it. In this case Socrates must reject the conception of happiness as complete fulfillment of desire. He will have to interpret the formal criterion of completeness and self-sufficiency as requiring fulfillment of our nature and capacities, not just of our desires.

It is worth asking whether this ''Aristotelian'' conception of happiness, referring to fulfillment of our nature and capacities, explains more of Socrates' claims than we have explained with the adaptive account. The main difficulty is its failure to explain the sufficiency thesis. Socrates appeals to the Aristotelian conception to suggest that virtue is necessary for happiness (*Cr., Gorg.* locc, citt.), but it is not easy to see how it could also support the sufficiency thesis.

In *Republic* I Plato highlights this difficulty by relying on the Aristotelian conception. Socrates asks, ''Will the soul achieve its function well if it is deprived of its proper virtue, or is this impossible?'' (353e1–2). Thrasymachus agrees, as Crito did, that it is impossible, so conceding the necessity of virtue for doing well. But Socrates infers, ''It is necessary, then, for a bad soul to rule and attend badly, and for a good one to do all these things well'' (353e4–5).[32] This abrupt and illegitimate inference from necessity to sufficiency has no parallel in earlier dialogues; and though the *Republic* refers again to the Aristotelian conception (445a5–b4), Plato does not repeat the fallacious inference. Its presence in Book I may be a further sign of his self-consciousness in that book. Believing (as the rest of the *Republic* shows) that Socrates is right in appealing to the Aristotelian conception, Plato sees that this will not justify the sufficiency thesis; and so he abandons the sufficiency thesis in the rest of the *Republic*.

The Aristotelian conception, then, will not by itself explain Socrates' major claims about virtue and happiness. To explain these claims it is reasonable to ascribe the adaptive account to him as well. We have no reason to believe that Socrates sees the conflict between these two views.

12. OBJECTIONS TO SOCRATES

I have argued that an adaptive account of happiness explains the sufficiency thesis. But this result does not imply a satisfactory defense of virtue. Some unwelcome results of Socrates' views show what might be wrong both with his account of happiness and with his claims about virtue.

The problem about virtue is a special case of a general problem in the adaptive account of happiness. This account tells us what to do with desires that we have; satisfy the feasible ones and get rid of the unfeasible. It does not tell us how to choose between two equally feasible sets of desires. Indeed it must tell us that from the point of view of happiness there is nothing to choose between them. If I have the resources and capacities to be a musician, a politician, or an athlete, and I want to be one, the adaptive account of happiness does not forbid me to try. But it does not explain why I should not want to do nothing but lie in the sun or torture insects. The choice between these two lives will have to depend on other grounds than happiness.

This conclusion might not surprise us. For it is not obviously false that an admirable and a deplorable life can make different people equally happy. But Socrates seems to think that happiness should be our sole and sufficient guide in deciding between different ways of life; and if happiness leaves so many questions open, it seems to be an inadequate guide for him.

If we apply this point to Socrates' claims about virtue, we can see where he faces questions. An adaptive account of happiness explains the sufficiency thesis. In Socrates' view, a virtuous person has seen that his happiness requires him to have flexible or feasible desires; he therefore cultivates these desires and eliminates others, and so ensures the satisfaction of his desires. He therefore ensures his happiness, and loss of external goods is no threat to it. To this extent Socrates can defend his claim that the virtuous person cannot be harmed and will be happy. He will not lose any happiness by being brave, temperate, and just.

The same sort of argument shows why an opponent such as Crito or Callicles or Thrasymachus is wrong to suppose that happiness requires vicious action or vicious character. I will believe that happiness requires me to be unjust or intemperate or cowardly if I want the external goods secured by these vices, and I believe that these goods are necessary for my happiness. But if I believe this, I must accept a mistaken, non-adaptive account of happiness.

Socrates can argue, then, that virtue is sufficient for happiness and vice is unnecessary for happiness. But this argument seems to give him no reason to be virtuous rather than non-virtuous. He may convince me that my happiness does not require me to profit at my neighbor's expense. But I can still be happy if I am indifferent to my neighbor's interests or unconcerned about the other people fighting in the battle beside me. If my desires are flexible and feasible, I can secure happiness for myself even if I refuse to do any of the actions of the just and brave person. And if I feel greedy or malevolent or cruel or extravagant, an adaptive account of happiness does not prohibit the satisfaction of these inclinations.

This philosophical weakness in Socrates' position helps to explain the historical puzzle we mentioned earlier—the sharp conflict between the views of professed Socratics about the right account of happiness. Socrates' adaptive account endorses neither the Cynic nor the Cyrenaic view; but it is hard to see how Socrates can deny that both views satisfy his account, or how he could justify preference for one view over the other. The sharp conflict between the Socratic schools reflects their common acceptance of a Socratic assumption, and, as Plato (in the *Philebus*) and Aristotle see, we can resolve this conflict only by rejecting the shared Socratic assumption.

Socrates, then, offers a weak defense of virtue. Though the sufficiency thesis may seem to recommend virtue rather strongly, it does not; for being virtuous is at best one of many possible results of an adaptive strategy.

Even if we agree with Socrates that the happy person has no need to violate the accepted rules of virtuous action, we need not agree that such a person is really virtuous. Mere absence of temptation to vicious action is not the same as a positive desire to do virtuous action; and we might argue that the positive desire is necessary for virtue. Further, we might argue that only the right sort of positive desire is sufficient for virtue; perhaps the virtuous person must value virtue and virtuous action for themselves, not simply as instrumental means.

We might even doubt that virtuous lives will normally be a subset of happy lives. Will a just person not desire to promote other people's good, and will his desire, in unfavorable conditions, not be frustrated? It looks as though a virtuous person will be less happy, according to Socrates' conception of happiness, than someone who is wrongly indifferent to the results of virtuous action.

For these reasons we might doubt if Socrates has an adequate defense of virtue. If he has no answer to our objections, it does not follow that he is wrong. It may be our estimate of virtue that is wrong. But the objections should at least encourage us to reconsider Socrates' case. Especially they should encourage us to reconsider the adaptive account of happiness.

At this point we might argue that if the adaptive account of happiness leaves Socrates open to such objections, we have good reason for doubting that he accepts it. And indeed this would be a good reason, if we also had good reason to believe that Socrates both sees these objections and sees their bearing on his account of happiness. But we have no good reason to believe either of these things.

13. PLATO'S REPLY TO SOCRATES

We may now return to the beginning of the argument, and the conflict between *Republic* I and the rest of the *Republic*. I have argued for these conclusions:

1. Socrates believes the sufficiency thesis maintained in *Republic* I.
2. He believes it because he accepts an adaptive account of happiness.
3. Such a conception makes just lives at best a proper subset of happy lives.

I now suggest a further conclusion:

4. Plato rejects the sufficiency thesis because he rejects the adaptive account of happiness.

Plato sees that it is reasonable to maintain an apparently weaker claim about virtue to avoid the price that must be paid for Socrates' stronger claim. The most plausible defense of the sufficiency thesis rests on an adaptive account of happiness. Once an adaptive account is rejected, the sufficiency thesis must be rejected; and Plato defends instead the comparative claim about virtue and vice.[33]

To show that Plato rejects an adaptive account of happiness, we need to understand the implicit criteria and conception assumed in the *Republic*. In particular we need to understand Plato's reasons for claiming that the people with unjust and disordered souls must all be unhappy. If we examine these reasons, we will see that Plato's claims about unjust people rest on an account of happiness that is not purely adaptive.

I will not defend this suggestion here. I have simply suggested why Plato might have good reasons for rejecting Socrates' sufficiency thesis. The thesis should be rejected not simply because it is counter-intuitive, but also because it rests on an account of happiness that is more deeply in error. When we see that Socrates' account of happiness leads him into error, we learn an important Socratic lesson that Socrates apparently has not learned himself; we need a clearer account of what happiness is supposed to be, and what would be a plausible candidate for happiness. This is the lesson that Plato and Aristotle learn, to different degrees. Once they examine happiness more carefully, they abandon Socrates' sufficiency thesis.

NOTES

An earlier version of this essay was read to the Society for Ancient Greek Philosophy in December 1984, and benefited from questions raised on that occasion. Questions from audiences at Colgate University and at William and Mary College, especially from Daniel Little, helped me to improve a still earlier version. I have also benefited from criticisms by Gail Fine, and from a very helpful correspondence with Gregory Vlastos. I am especially indebted to the papers by Vlastos and Zeyl cited in the notes.

1. I translate *eudaimonia* by "happiness." This use of the comparative marks one difference between *eudaimōn* and the English "happy"; the comparative suggests that *eudaimōn* has the logic of "straight" and (significantly) of "complete."
2. One way to explain the parallels between *Rep.* I and the Socratic dialogues is to regard it as a Socratic dialogue. I think this solution is unnecessary, and that some evidence of self-consciousness in *Rep.* I suggests that Plato wrote it deliberately as an introduction to the *Republic*. See part 11.
3. Edited by E. H. Gifford (Oxford 1903, 5 vols.). Atticus' views are discussed by J. Dillon, *The Middle Platonists* (London 1977), p. 25.
4. Edited by K. F. Hermann in *Platonis Dialogi*, vol. 6 (Leipzig 1884). See Dillon, p. 299.
5. Socrates assumes that *hētis hēmas onēsei*, 288e1–2, is equivalent to *hēn edei kektēmenous hēmas eudaimonas einai*, 289c7–8; cf. d9–10, 290b1–2, 291b6, 292b8–c1, e5.
6. On the role of the formal criteria in this chapter see *EN*, trans. T. H. Irwin (Indianapolis 1985), note on 1095b14ff.
7. Some hints exploited by Aristotle appear in *Phil.* 20b8–22c4, in terms partly derived from *Rep.* 505b5–d1. Helpful remarks on formal criteria: N. P. White, "Goodness and Human Aims in Aristotle's Ethics," in *Studies in Aristotle*, ed. D. J. O'Meara (Washington, D.C. 1981), pp. 225–46, at pp. 231, 234f.
8. I believe that in the *Protagoras* Socrates is seriously committed to hedonism (some grounds for this belief are ably urged by J. C. B. Gosling and C. C. W. Taylor, *The Greeks on Pleasure*

[Oxford 1982], pp. 58–68). It is important to explore the connections of the view of happiness that I attribute to Socrates with the discussions of hedonism in the *Protagoras* and *Gorg*. But I ignore the *Protagoras* here, because I would like my arguments to be independent of the dispute about hedonism, and because hedonism offers us only a conception of happiness that still leaves us to look for the criteria that justify it.

9. My treatment of Socrates' views on happiness in *Plato's Moral Theory* (Oxford 1977) is open to criticism for not having faced these questions. It is justly criticized by Gregory Vlastos, "Happiness and Virtue in Socrates' Moral Theory," *Proceedings of the Cambridge Philological Society* NS 30 (1984), 181–213, at p. 207 note 54, and by D. J. Zeyl, "Socratic Virtue and Happiness," *Archiv für Gesch. der Phil.* 14 (1982), pp. 225–38. In this essay I don't defend the claim that Socrates *does* take virtue to be merely instrumental to happiness and not an intrinsic good, but the weaker claim that the sufficiency thesis is compatible with the purely instrumentalist conception of virtue. (See Part 9, last paragraph.)

10. See Irwin, *Plato's Moral Theory*, p. 72.

11. Socrates identifies *eu prattein* with *eudaimonein*, 280b6.

12. In examining reputed goods Socrates does not distinguish instrumental from intrinsic goods. Indeed he does not describe *eudaimonia* or *eu prattein* as an *agathon* at all in the *Euthydemus;* and it might be argued that here he confine *agatha* to instrumental goods. The same is true of *Gorg.* 467c–468e. Sometimes *agatha* may seem to include intrinsic goods, *Gorg.* 494e9–495b4, 499e5, *Prot.* 355c3–8 (contrast *Gorg.* 496b5–6). But this is not certain; I can see no clear reason for denying that, e.g., the pleasures mentioned in these passages are considered as goods because they are instrumental to happiness. If this is so, then the claim in *Rep.* 357b5 that some goods are goods because they are chosen for their own sakes reflects a departure from the Socratic conception of goods. The claim that happiness is not a good is not unparalleled; Aristippus (D.L. II. 87) may be exploiting a Socratic distinction to draw an un-Socratic conclusion.

13. In *M.* 88c6–d1 Socrates concedes that external goods are in some circumstances actually beneficial. His claim here is different from the one in the *Euthydemus,* though either claim is consistent with his main claims about virtue and happiness. See Part 10.

14. The second assumption is not explicit in the *Euthydemus;* but no other object of wish (*boulometha,* 278e3) and no other basis for choice than happiness is mentioned. Here, in apparent contrast to *Gorg.* 467c ff., *agatha* are not said to be objects of *boulēsis.*

15. This is not a complete or fair account of Aristotle's conditions for happiness. (This passage, e.g., raises a question about the relation between being *haireton* and filling desire.) But the fact that he speaks in these terms about happiness shows how someone might interpret the demand for completeness.

16. This passage is, quite reasonably, adapted to Epicurean use and strangely conflated with some of the dualism of the *Alc.* in *Ax.* 365d–366a. See D. J. Furley, "Nothing to Us?" in *The Norms of Nature,* ed. M. Schofield and G. Striker (Cambridge, Eng., 1986).

17. Here *deisthai* includes both wanting and needing. We might think it is important to distinguish the two, to insist that someone who does not want anything may still need some things, and to urge that only not needing anything is a reasonable condition for the self-sufficiency that is relevant to happiness. But for Socrates the distinction will be unimportant, since what we need for happiness is just what we need for the complete satisfaction of our desires; when we have no unsatisfied desires, then, in his view, we will need nothing.

18. I doubt if Socrates or Plato is (as often alleged) either confused by or deliberately exploiting any ambiguity in *eu prattein*. See *Plato: Gorgias,* tr. Irwin (Oxford 1979), p. 223.

19. This apparent evidence of a contemporary view may be challenged; see Z. Stewart, "Democritus and the Cynics," *Harvard Studies in Classical Philology* 63 (1958), 179–91. It is one of the fragments derived from Stobaeus, and sometimes taken to be contaminated by Cynicism. At the same time this claim fits well with Democritus' belief in the unimportance of

fortune and the importance of wisdom and one's own efforts; cf. B 119 and the well-attested B 3. The occurrence of the term "equipollent," *isosthenea,* otherwise attested only in later Greek, may provoke doubts, but perhaps should not. It is a technical term of Skeptical argument (though this is not its only use); but this may be an example of a Skeptical term introduced by Democritus. For another example of such a term see P. De Lacey, *"Ou Mállon* and the Antecedents of Ancient Scepticism," *Phronesis* 3 (1958), 59–71. The appeal to equipollence may indeed be connected with the use of *ou mállon,* since both can be connected with a doctrine of indifferents; see, e.g., Sextus, *Pyrr. Hypotyp.* III. 177 (cited by De Lacey, n. 19).

20. "Quod [sc. summum bonum] in Socraticis disputationibus, dum omnia movet, adserit, destruit, quoniam non evidenter apparuit, quod cuique placuit inde sumserunt et ubi cuique visum esse constituerunt finem boni" *(Civ. Dei* VIII. 3).

21. "Sic autem diversas inter se Socratici de isto fine sententias habuerunt ut (quod vix credibile est unius magistri potuisse facere sectatores) quidam summum bonum esse dicerent voluptatem, sicut Aristippus; quidam virtutem, sicut Antisthenes" (loc. cit.; cf. XVIII. 41).

22. Probably the force of *parontón* is partly temporal, reflecting Aristippus' views about prudence and the future. But it should also refer to Socrates' and Democritus' use of the term, for what is available and feasible.

23. I translate Cobet's attractive though unnecessary emendation *arkómetha (chrómetha,* codd.), which makes the connection with the *Gorgias* and Democritus especially clear.

24. The difference between the Socratic and the ascetic position is overlooked by E. R. Dodds, *Plato: Gorgias* (Oxford 1959), on 492e3.

25. This passage is appropriately stressed by Vlastos, "Happiness," p. 188, as evidence of Socrates' belief in the "sovereignty" of virtue over other goods.

26. In saying that it would be bad for him to *choose* imprisonment as a penalty Socrates does not imply that there would be anything bad about imprisonment in itself. For a different view of this passage see Richard Kraut, *Socrates and the State* (Princeton 1984), p. 38 n.

27. Vlastos, "Happiness," p. 208 n. 66, follows J. Burnet, *Euthyphro, Apology, Crito* (Oxford 1924), ad loc., in translating "from virtue wealth and the other things become goods" (taking *agatha* as predicate). This provides a less exact balance with the previous clause ("virtue does not come to be from wealth"); and the other translation, if I have explained it correctly, does not commit Socrates to praise of money-making. If Burnet's translation is accepted, then this will be a passage where Socrates allows goods whose loss does not leave a person any less happy.

28. Vlastos, p. 198, and Kraut, p. 38 n., explain the passage differently.

29. Vlastos, p. 192f., understands Socrates in *Apol.* 30c6–d5 to mean that death or imprisonment or dishonor would be some harm to him, but a much smaller harm than doing injustice, and when Socrates says that a better man cannot suffer harm from a worse (30c9–d1) Vlastos takes him to mean that he can suffer no major harm. We might be forced to suppose that Socrates does not mean exactly what he says if we had compelling reason to adopt Vlastos's view in other passages, but this passage taken by itself must be *prima facie* evidence against Vlastos' view, and I doubt if other passages require us to take Socrates to be speaking inexactly here. As I will explain, even if Socrates were to admit that these external goods are goods, he would not have to admit that their loss makes him any less happy, and therefore would not have to admit that their loss harms him (even if he also concedes, at first sight paradoxically, that their presence benefits him).

30. Kraut, p. 38 n., may be over-confident in claiming that "469b3–6 suggests that someone who is unjustly killed is to be pitied" and that "at 509c6–7 he [sc. Socrates] calls suffering injustice an evil."

31. Zeyl, "Virtue," rightly cites these passages as evidence for Socrates' views on happiness; but he does not discuss their bearing on the sufficiency thesis.

32. On *eu prattein* in this argument see n. 18. The inference (indicated by *ara,* 353e4) from necessity to sufficiency is still invalid whatever we decide about the use of *eu prattein.*
33. Plato's rejection of the Socratic Paradox gives him a further reason for rejecting Socrates' account of happiness (see n. 10), though it would not by itself justify him in rejecting the conception of happiness as fulfillment of desires.

FURTHER READING

Brickhouse, T. C., and Smith, N. D. 1987. "Socrates on Goods, Virtue, and Happiness." *Oxford Studies in Ancient Philosophy* 5:1–27.

Irwin, T. 1977. *Plato's Moral Theory: The Early and Middle Dialogues,* esp. 37–176. Oxford.

Vlastos, G. 1984. "Happiness and Virtue in Socrates' Moral Theory." *Proceedings of the Cambridge Philological Society* NS 30:181–213.

Zeyl, D. J. 1982. "Socratic Virtue and Happiness." *Archiv für Geschichte der Philosophie* 14:225–38.

13

Socratic Piety
in the *Euthyphro*

MARK L. McPHERRAN

A persistent and much debated issue in the interpretation of the *Euthyphro* is whether the dialogue is merely a peirastic inquiry or a source of positive Socratic doctrine on the nature of piety.[1] The majority of commentors favor the latter view and have produced various reconstructions of the positive Socratic doctrine of piety they find implicit in the text following the "aporetic interlude" (*Eu.* 11b–e).[2] A few prominent scholars have raised objections to this constructivist approach.[3] R. E. Allen, for instance, taking the Socratic profession of ignorance to heart, holds that the *Euthyphro* "bears its meaning on its face," and that (hence) it neither states nor implies a definition of piety.[4] Lazlo Versenyi, another anticonstructivist, argues more cogently that no definition of piety involving reference to the gods may be culled from the dialogue's explicit statements (*contra* all the constructivists), and that in fact, the notion of piety towards which Socrates is directing Euthyphro is a thoroughly secular one, identical to the whole of virtue.[5]

It seems to me that the anticonstructivists are wrong, and that most of the interpretations the constructivists have offered involve the mistaken use of textual references which do not plausibly bear on the views of the historical Socrates,[6] and/or do not do justice to a reasonable understanding of Socrates' profession of ignorance, his claims to be pursuing a god-ordered work, and the evidence of his somewhat traditional religious practices and beliefs. In the following, I argue for a cautiously constructive view of Socratic piety derived from the *Euthyphro*, which is consonant with a reasonable conception of the historic Socrates.

1

Following the aporetic interlude of the *Euthyphro*, Socrates offers to aid (*sumprothumēsomai*) Euthyphro in the search for a definition of piety (*hosios; Eu.* 11e3–5).[7] Socrates initiates this assistance by raising the question of whether justice and piety are coextensive concepts (such that all and only just acts are pious acts) or whether justice is a broader concept than piety such that piety is a "part" of justice (so that pious acts are a subset of just acts; *Eu.* 11e4–12d5). Subsequent to his careful explanation to Euthyphro of these alternatives, Socrates secures Euthyphro's free assent to the second proposition that piety is a part of justice. Socrates' explanation, and his illustrative use of the relation of odd-numberedness to number (*Eu.* 12c6–8), make it clear that both he and Euthyphro accept that as a consequence there may exist just acts which are neither pious nor impious.[8] With this established, the search then begins for the characteristic which differentiates pious justice from the remainder. Although Euthyphro's claim that piety is the part of justice having to do with our service to the gods (*therapeia theōn; Eu.* 12e5–8) is shortly defeated (*Eu.* 12e1–13d4), it seems evident that the proposition only fails on Socrates' view because of the problems ("one little point"; *Eu.* 13a1) he raises for Euthyphro's use and interpretation of the term *therapeia.* Socrates says, for instance (*Eu.* 12e3–4), that if Euthyphro identifies for him the part of justice that piety is, he will then be able to understand adequately (*hikanōs*) what piety is,[9] and after having made this attempt, he *congratulates* Euthyphro for having "spoken well" (*kalōs . . . phainēi legein; Eu.* 12e9).[10] This much, then, seems a Socratically acceptable *claim* about piety:

P₁ Piety is that part of justice having to do with the relation of men to the gods.

There are many additional reasons for attributing a belief in P_1 to Socrates. It is Socrates himself who introduces the view that piety is a part of justice, and claims to do so as an *aid* to the definitional search (*Eu.* 11e3). It is also significant that Socrates keeps the form of P_1's answer constantly before Euthyphro for the remainder of the dialogue,[11] and it remains unrefuted throughout the dialogue (I do not, however, think that *every* unrefuted claim in a Platonic dialogue represents positive doctrine).[12] Socrates might wish to mislead Sophists at such length, but not, one would think, such a confused soul as Euthyphro. This would seem to be especially true where there exists a possibility of some harm coming to someone (viz., Euthyphro's father) if Euthyphro comes to perceive himself to be a victim of mere eristics. In any case, it would be odd to view this section of the dialogue as an attempt to reduce Euthyphro to a state of *aporia,* since Euthyphro has already confessed his confusion in the aporetic interlude.[13] Socrates does not generally pursue trickery for simple enjoyment, and it is hard to see how an insincere Socratic commitment to P_1 throughout the dialogue would be of any pedagogic value. It is of further significance that P_1 *follows* the aporetic interlude: a familiar feature of Plato's dramatic style is for positive doctrine to be suggested following such interludes in the discussion (e.g., *Protagoras, Phaedo, Phaedrus, Theatetus*).[14] With all this, then, we have compelling internal evidence that Socrates finds P_1 to be true, though not definitional, of piety.[15]

The attribution of P_1 to Socrates has further support external to the *Euthyphro.* Both P_1 and *Euthyphro* 12e5–8 make clear that while piety is a form of justice concerned with the relation of men to the gods, there is another distinct part of justice concerned with the relation of men to other men. This division of justice into two kinds of just relations according to two different sets of relata is suggested by *Crito* 54b–c, *Laches* 199d–e, and especially *Gorgias* 507a–b, where Socrates asserts that a man doing his duty to *men* act justly and doing his duty to the *gods* acts piously.[16] Furthermore, Socrates' division of the virtue wisdom into two sorts, human and divine, suggests that he would also divide another virtue such as justice into two "parts" on the basis of their respective domains of concern: man-to-man versus man-to-god.[17] Finally, Xenophon (*Mem.* 4.6.2–5) represents Socrates as analyzing legal conduct into two subclasses, where pious persons are therein defined as those who know what is lawful in respect of the gods (in contrast to what is lawful in respect of men).[18] This again supports the view that Socrates would have found it natural to divide justice into two subclasses, human secular justice and divine justice (piety). To what extent Xenophon can be trusted on this is a live issue. Still, given the other evidence, it would be odd if it did not have some credibility, especially given the widespread, if unclear, traditional connection between being *dikaios;* and being *hosios/eusebēs.*[19]

2

Statement P_1, as we saw, was derived from Euthyphro's first attempt (12e5–8) to specify the nature of the relationship between men and gods which would constitute just relations. That attempt may be represented as:

P_2 Piety is that part of justice which is our tendance (*therapeia*) to the gods.

Socrates attempts to clarify the term *"therapeia"*[20] by means of a craft analogy (13a1–d4). *"Therapeia,"* it is shown, can imply a kind of knowledge whose practice aims at the substantive improvement of that which is tended. This in turn implies that the subject to which tendance is given lacks both self-sufficiency and excellence, and that the agent is superior to that subject in some aspect of power or knowledge. These implications are incompatible with Euthyphro's conception of the gods' and man's relative powers, which, in accord with popular belief, represented the gods as vastly superior to men in respect of knowledge, power, self-sufficiency, and enjoyment.[21] It is on these grounds that P_2 is rejected by Euthyphro. In addition, Socrates gives some indication (13c–d) that he would find P_2 objectionable on the same grounds.[22]

By the replacement of the objectionable term *"therapeia"* (a "little" matter, says Socrates at *Eu.* 13a1–2) with *"hupēretikē"*—a term which does not imply the improvement of a subject—Euthyphro produces (13d3–8) a candidate for a definition of piety much more consonant with (I shall argue) both traditional and Socratic belief:

Piety is that part of justice which is a service (*hupēretikē:* along the lines of servants to masters) of men to the gods.

Both Socrates and Euthyphro are portrayed in the craft-analogy sequence which follows (13d–e) as reasoning by analogy (naturally enough) from the fact that many human *hupēresiai* which help with some *ergon* are productive of some end result, to the implicit conclusion that all human services aim at helping those they serve to achieve the result which defines the professional activity of those helped; for example, the service to a shipbuilder is the service which aids him to build a ship. With this general principle before him, Euthyphro is then asked to specify precisely the nature of that "most beautiful work" (*pankalon ergon*) for which the *gods* must then desire our assistance (13e–14a). Euthyphro tenaciously avoids answering this question which, significantly, is asked *three* times.[23] To this Socrates responds clearly and emphatically that Euthyphro had just "turned aside" at the very moment he was *close* to giving a *briefer* answer (than he did), which would have given Socrates all the information he needed about piety. Many scholars have found this powerful evidence for ascribing to Socrates a belief in something like the following:

P₃ Piety is that part of justice which is a service (*hupēretikē*) of men to the gods, assisting the gods in their work (*ergon*), a work which produces some good result.

To this I would add the claim that Socrates also believes that pious acts please the gods. This claim was left in place at *Euthyphro* 9e and was accepted to be a *pathos* of piety at 11a, and is thereafter left unrefuted.[24] Notice too that at 9e Socrates seems to hint that a statement allowed to pass through the discussion unchallenged would be one accepted by both of them. Finally, it is Socrates who implies (*Eu.* 11a6–b1) that Euthyphro *has* (in fact) identified an attribute of piety. The anticonstructivists wishing to deny this and P₃ to Socrates are thus left with the task of reconciling the Socrates who insists that people state what they truly believe with the deceptive Socrates their anticonstructivism forces on them. Moreover, there are several other considerations that support our attributing P₃ to Socrates.

To begin, all the evidence in support of P₁ serves as support for P₃, whose form it preserves and from which it derives. Like P₁, for instance, P₃ is left unrefuted at the end of the dialogue.[25] As distinct from P₁, and constitutive of P₃'s improvement over P₁, P₃ makes use of the concept of a service assisting a work which produces something good. Such a motif is a typical methodological model of Socrates, characteristic of his teleological outlook and use of craft-analogies.[26] Socrates later emphasizes that this question of service to the gods is of the greatest importance to him (*Eu.* 14d4–7)[27] and, significantly, urges Euthyphro to specify the nature of our service to the gods no fewer than six times between 13e6 and the end of the dialogue.[28] Plato also credits Socrates with conceiving of our relation to the gods as being a kind of master-slave relation (*Phdo.* 62d–63d; *I.* 53e; *Parm.* 134d–e; *Alc. I* 122a) as does Xenophon (*Mem.* 1.4.9–12). This represents, as well, what the Greeks usually had in mind when discussing a *therapeia theōn*.[29] Nonetheless, this evidence remains at best suggestive until we see its confirmation by the historical touchstone of the *Apology*.

The argument which connects the *Euthyphro* to the *Apology* has convincingly been made elsewhere,[30] and it should be enough to point out that the dramatic setting and internal remarks of both combine to present a historically continuous characterization of Socrates. The *Apology* emphatically portrays in careful detail a Socrates who both conforms to traditional religious practice and belief, and who has a divine mission which is the result of a pious (*euseboien*) duty to follow a god's commands (*Apol.* 30a). This mission is thus a service to the god(s) (*tēn emēn tōi theōi hupēresian; Apol.* 30a6–7, cf. *Apol.* 23b–c)[31] producing good results (*Apol.* 30a5–7), such as the improvement of those who are persuaded by Socrates to care for their souls and do what is right (*Apol.* 30a–b, 36c–d; *Cr.* 47d–48d: cf. *Eu.* 14e11–15a2). It would be hard to produce stronger evidence that Socrates in fact believes P₃ to be true. Nonetheless, as Socrates himself sees, P₃ is not definitional of piety, and is thus left incomplete by the conclusion of the discussion.

There have been numerous interpretations attempting to make good P₃'s deficiencies by characterizing the work and produce of the gods, thereby inferring the nature of our service to them (see n. 2). Unfortunately, these attempts either impute Platonic doctrine to Socrates, or ignore Socrates' ambivalence concerning the precise work and nature of the gods, or discount the claim that piety is but a *part* of the justice mentioned in P_1 and P_3 (or some combination of these). In section 3 I will suggest and defend a hypothetical completion of P_3 that I think Socrates would have endorsed.

Returning to the text, it remains to discuss Euthyphro's "wrong-turning," which introduces the conception of piety as a kind of knowledge or craft of proper giving to (which is again a service; *hupēresia*) and requesting from the gods (a kind of *emporia*) (*Eu.* 14b2–7, 14c4–15b5). This section we should see as primarily a transition to a somewhat different matter which Socrates is forced to follow—as he suggests (14c3–4)—by the rules of elenctic discourse,[32] but whose course he shapes in pursuit of the unresolved issue of P_3; that is, the nature of our service to the gods. Here the service is identified as a "giving" to the gods of prayerful praise and sacrifice, for which we may hope to receive the good things we request. Though Euthyphro concedes that there is nothing *artful* in giving someone what they do not need, he nonetheless maintains (rather inconsistently) his earlier position (13b13–c2) that while our gifts cannot *benefit* the gods, they can still *please* them (which wouldn't seem to be a *need* on their part). With this answer, Socrates concludes that they have returned to the definition of piety which was rejected in the first portion of the dialogue (at *Eu.* 10e9–11b5).

The logical details of this section deserve careful treatment, but here I will only contend that it represents a digression in the discussion. In evidence of this is the reluctance of Socrates to pursue Euthyphro's new definition and Euthyphro's own apparent inconsistency mentioned above. In addition, Socrates only helps to advance Euthyphro's definition in order to clarify Euthyphro's own initial reply to his quest for the completion of P_3. Since Euthyphro is not portrayed as having any philosophical acumen, the dialogue does not then seem to argue for this approach.[33] Furthermore, this section has moved—by Euthyphro's casting his "wrong-turned" answer in terms of the "know-how" pious people would have—from a consideration of the nature of pious *acts,* the dialogue's primary concern,[34] to that of the *knowledge* pious *persons* would have. This is not to imply that genuine piety cannot be characterized in terms of knowledge or that some of that knowledge will not include knowledge of orthodox religious practices. Socrates would affirm both these claims, and the dialogue makes clear that Euthyphro's attempted definition has only been rejected on the grounds that it is incompatible—taken as a *definition*—with the earlier rejection of the same claim.[35] Socrates never doubts in this section *that* pious actions is a virtuous relationship of men and gods, with benefits accruing to the worshipper (cf. *Eu.* 14e11–15a2) and pleasure accruing to the gods. Furthermore, it is left open for Socrates to affirm at this point that though *full* and *certain* knowledge of piety would necessitate a knowledge of *how* our acts of sacrifice, prayer, and obedience to their commands *are* a service to those gods (*what* about them is pleasing), no human may possess knowledge so extensive or certain. Nevertheless, he may claim, there *are* practical standards to guide us in the performance and identification of pious acts. P_3, he could claim, gives us a general foundation which will allow us to rationally derive what pragmatic knowledge we *need* (what we could be content with; 14c2–3) for the pious conduct of our everyday lives. It is this view, I shall argue (in section 3), which the discussion surrounding P_3 intimates and which Euthyphro—shrouded in his eccentric religious dogmatism—has failed to appreciate. I will also show how this view bears on Euthyphro's justification of his prosecution of his father on the grounds of its piety (*Eu.* 3e–6a). Before doing so, however, I must first defend P_3 against four anticonstructivist challenges.

1. Burnet, Allen, and Versenyi have argued that nothing like P$_3$ can be attributed to Socrates, since it is not possible in the context of the dialogue to specify an *ergon* (and product) which piety serves.[36] Versenyi takes this line of argument further by claiming that the reason for this is that the gods, being perfect, cannot be conceived to have any *ergon:* "If the gods are already as good as possible and possessed of all that is good for them, then . . . [t]hey can have no ends still outstanding . . . and thus no rational motivation for action."[37]

This misses the mark. While the perfect gods of Versenyi *are* no doubt incompatible with P$_3$, there is no evidence that such perfect beings were the gods of either Socrates or the majority of his fellow Greeks. One can import *Platonic* text (e.g., *Rep.* 381b–c, *Sym.* 202c–d) to the contrary (as Versenyi, surprisingly, does),[38] but such a tactic is not even helpful for conclusively establishing *Plato's* views. In the *Phaedrus* (247a), for instance, each god *is* said to have his own *ergon.* In any case, there is good evidence that Socrates believed in divine activity (e.g., that they give us commands and gifts; *Apol.* 33c, 41d).[39]

Aside from all this, Versenyi's argument contains a confusion. Though perfect gods themselves may be incapable of improvement in their own natures, from this it follows that such gods do not now act only if we suppose them to act solely out of rational *self-interest* so as to have already achieved all their desires. But it is possible that it could be in the rational interest (self-regarding or otherwise) of the gods to have left *some* of their ends outstanding. The accomplishment (improvement) of *these,* unlike the improvement of their natures, we *could* be in a position to help achieve (e.g., they could have left the world or our souls unfinished).[40]

2. Versenyi has argued against the coherence of our performing a service (*hupēretikē*) to the gods (as in P$_3$) along similar lines as those above.[41] Such a service implies that those assisted by us are benefited, yet Euthyphro rejected the previous definition of piety as a *therapeia theōn* (P$_2$) precisely on the grounds that the gods could *not* be benefited and thereby improved. The notion of a *hupēretikē* is thus just as incompatible with the gods' self-sufficiency as was that of a *therapeia theōn.*

If this argument is correct, it is then very curious that Socrates should *not* have leapt upon this repetition of a previous "wrong-turning" rather than pursuing (as he does) for a full Stephanus page a much more obscure point (viz., the god's *ergon*), and does not return to drive home what—on Versenyi's interpretation—would be a very simple elenchus.[42] Such neglect (on this account) is made all the more malicious by Socrates' remark that Euthyphro was close to a satisfactory answer by his pursuit of the question concerning the god's *ergon.* Versenyi's argument, then, has the effect of portraying Socrates as an ineffective and deceitful teacher. Worse than that, it renders him guilty of impiety, since in the *Apology,* he claims (under the threat of impious perjury) to be pursuing a service to the god (e.g., 22a, 23b, 30a).[43] Irrespective of this, Versenyi's objection fails on grounds similar to those in point 1.

Socrates' rejection of *therapeia* seemed to rest on two implications of that term: that the gods lack in their nature self-sufficiency and excellence, and that men are superior to them in some respect (the respect in which it is that *man* may improve the gods). The concept of *hupēretikē* clearly lacks the second implication, and so Versenyi is apparently claiming that the only service we could perform for the gods would be a service which would (*per impossibile*) improve the nature of the gods. But it does not follow from the concept of *hupēretikē* that by assisting the gods in their work ("their functioning") we thereby improve their capacity to function (their nature, as *therapeia* was taken to imply), "and thus their very being."[44] It is quite within the realm of Greek religious conceptions that the gods should delegate to us the performance of some beneficial and god-pleasing service which they are quite sufficient in themselves to perform, but from which they abstain (e.g., as a parent might—for various reasons—allow his child to bring him a cup which he is quite able to get on his own).

3. Taking *hupēretikē* to imply a "slavish, ignorant, and utterly submissive" kind of service, Versenyi argues that accepting something like P$_3$ would undercut Euthyphro's and the city's claim to know—and thus prescribe—pious behavior; it would also, he implies, undercut our having *any* knowledge of piety at all.[45] On the other hand, if we *can* have knowledge of the gods' *ergon,* and that *ergon* is the fostering of goodness in human life (say through philosophical activity), then any references to the gods in the definition of piety (as in P$_3$) are gratuitous. This is so, Versenyi claims, because of the lesson of the first half of the dialogue we are supposed to have learned: that to know what is pious is to know what is just in human life, and *that* knowledge one can have independently of and without reference to the gods or their love. Piety, on *this* view, is then not a part (as in P$_3$), but the whole of moral virtue, for whose performance we all have the necessary intrinsic motivation, and which is what it is whether or not the gods even exist.[46] This secular account of piety is furthermore inconsistent (according to Versenyi) with the notion of serving the gods in the subordinate fashion of *hupēretikē*. By serving human justice we serve ourselves, and this is a relation between equals (in fact, he says, if the gods' work is realizing the good in human life, that seems to make them *our* servants).[47]

To this tortured line of reasoning Socrates can (and would, I shall later argue) respond that it is precisely Euthyphro's and the city's claim to know with certainty what pious actions *are* that he wishes to undercut, and that if *hupēretikē* has this effect, so much the better. Indeed, such an undercutting is the thrust of the entire dialogue. It also perfectly accords with Socrates' constant confession that he lacks all divine (certain) knowledge and can only reasonably hope for *human* (fallible) wisdom. In comparison with the knowledge of divine things we are indeed ignorant (cf. *Apol.* 23a–c), but this need not imply complete ignorance about piety, as Versenyi suggests. If we understand P$_3$ as it stands, and it is true, then we understand something about piety.[48]

The remainder of Versenyi's argument is based on the supposition that the gods' *ergon*—if they had one—would be the accomplishment of the good in *human life*. Versenyi provides no argument for this crucial supposition, which arbitrarily delimits the class of the gods' good acts to those in human life. Further, by making this supposition, and thus identifying piety with the whole of human justice. Versenyi also contradicts all the evidence for P$_1$ and P$_3$, since both P$_1$ and P$_3$ imply that some just acts need not be pious. Of course, if the gods' *ergon* is simply the establishment of good in the *universe,* the possibility remains open that some of the tasks involved in helping them to attain that end might simply be a matter of following the gods' orders without knowing their reasons. In such a case, any remotely clear notion of piety must involve reference to the gods.

Even if we suppose the *ergon* of the gods to be simply the establishment of the good in *human* life (and are thus able to serve the gods' ends by a knowledge that involves no reference to them), it does not follow that an attempted *definition* of "piety" may ignore these gods. For example, though my father may not wish for anything but *my* good, and though the acts of filial piety he sanctions are only those acts productive of such good, that does not entail that the meaning of "filial piety" is the same as "the son pursuing his own good." Rather, an act of filial piety would seem to crucially involve an *intention* to satisfy parental desires. Analogously, the difference between a piously just act and one which is merely secularly just could simply be that in the former case one acts with the *intention* to please and honor the gods.[49] Finally, I take Versenyi's last point to be a *reductio* of his own position. Since making piety the whole of virtue on Versenyi's account *would* suggest a relation to the gods of equality or superiority, we ought not to make such an identification.

4. Versenyi recognizes that the conclusion of the first part of the dialogue—that "the god-pleasing" is not definitive of piety—still leaves open the possibility that all and only god-pleasing acts are those which are pious. I have earlier argued in section 2 that this claim would probably be acceptable to Socrates. In order to preclude the attribution to Socrates of even so minimally a positive claim as this about piety, Versenyi presents an argument which, when generalized, would falsify all the statements of the *Euthyphro* concerning the relation of men and gods. On his account, both the early and middle dialogues,[50] and especially the *Lysis,* make it clear that love (as a desire for what is lacking) is irreconcilable with perfection, and that therefore the (perfect) gods cannot love anything. Furthermore, if they cannot love anything, and since all rational activity is rooted in rational love, they cannot act at all, be pleased by (for this implies lack) or care about anything, or thus be the givers of what is good to men.[51]

Socrates, however, clearly believes that the gods act and have given men good things. Versenyi has also not established that Socrates' gods *are* perfect, or that he had any beliefs entailing this, or that (having such beliefs) he was aware of that entailment, or (being so aware) that he would have seen Versenyi's inference.[52] It is also doubtful that Versenyi may establish such claims on the basis of middle dialogue text, which on the whole is not directly relevant to issues concerning *Socratic* belief. As for the *Lysis,* it is regarded as a *late* early dialogue, and so what positive doctrine it contains is much more likely than the material of the *Apology* (in which the gods *have* desires) to import Platonic doctrine into the Socratic portrayal. The *Lysis* is also aporetic and makes it clear that Socrates no more *believes* that perfection and action are irreconcilable than that he doesn't. In fact, by the end of the dialogue, Socrates has consciously led Lysis and Menexenus by the nose to conclude not only that "those who are already good are no longer friends to the good" (214e–215b: one of Versenyi's pieces of "evidence"), but also its contradictory that "none are friendly with the good by the good" (222d). It would be hard to find as clear a case of eclectic data-gathering.

With the preceding, then, the claim that P_3 represents a Socratic belief emerges unscathed. It remains to be seen whether and how Socrates himself would characterize the nature of the gods' *ergon* and our service in its behalf. In the following section I provide this answer and use it as the canvas for a sketch of Socratic piety.

3

Let us return to the dialogue and ask what answer would have satisfied Socrates when he asked Euthyphro to specify the *pankalon ergon* of the gods. Close inspection of the text at this point (13e–14c) might suggest that Socrates uses a false analogy to mislead

Euthyphro. While it is true that different human professions have a *chief* (*kephalaion*) result, it is not a necessary consequence that the gods *qua* gods then have a single characteristic product. Indeed, as a traditionalist, Euthyphro should persist in his initial answer (13e12) that they produce *many* fine things (being many different gods, after all). However, when pressed by Socrates, he does not insist on this, but goes on to a new conception of our relations with the gods (one of *emporia:* 14a–b). Why, then, does Socrates press this, and why does Euthyphro not repeat his earlier answer? Because, as the earlier discussion has indicated (6d–10a), Socrates believes, and has convinced Euthyphro as well, that piety is one thing the gods must *all* agree about if piety is to be an objective feature of acts. If then, piety is a service which helps (as in P_3), there must be at least some project commonly agreed upon by the gods which pious actions serve to promote.

What then is this "chief" *pankalon ergon?* The answer to this—the "chief part" of P_3 outstanding, on Socrates' view (as he puns)—should be, I submit, that we *cannot know* (other than that it is good). This—and not some constructivistic speculation—is just the answer we should expect from a man who claims not to have any wisdom of things "more than human" (*Eu.* 6a–b, *Apol.* 20e) had only by god (*Apol.* 23a), and who is quite conscious of this shortcoming (e.g., *Apol.* 20d).[53] By such "divine wisdom" I interpret Socrates to mean a kind of *infallible* and *complete* knowledge: such a certain and complete understanding of piety would be certain knowledge of the definition of piety, wherein the terms of its definiens are mutually entailing with the definiendum "piety," and where the definition constitutes a *complete* explanation of why instances of piety are pious (see n. 15). Such a definition of piety *would* require a specification of the gods' *ergon,* and yet the complete specification of that *ergon* would seem a prerogative of the gods: only *they* can know with completeness and certainty what their *ergon* is. This profession of ignorance is also what we should expect Socrates to be attempting to elicit from such a person as Euthyphro, whose claim to know things more than human and to be guided thereby in the performance of serious actions leaves Socrates in awe (*Eu.* 4a–5d). Euthyphro is even so presumptuous as to think that actions permissible for Zeus himself are likewise permissible for him.[54] Since Euthyphro *is* ignorant of piety, it is then part of Socrates' mission to force him to concede that—like Socrates himself—he lacks infallible and even fallible knowledge of the gods' *ergon.* This response would be in accord with Socrates' claim that a satisfactory answer would have been much briefer than the one Euthyphro offered (*Eu.* 14b8–c1). Furthermore, Socrates presents a subtle *modus tollens* for the view that piety is not completely known by using the evidence of Euthyphro's own ignorance: he states that if *anyone knows* what piety is, it is Euthyphro (*Eu.* 15d2–3). Thus, by having repeatedly demonstrated Euthyphro's ignorance, Socrates is here perhaps informing us that *no person knows* (completely and infallibly) what piety is.[55]

Besides having discredited Euthyphro's claim to a complete understanding of piety, Socrates has also thereby undermined Euthyphro's justification of his attempt to prosecute his father for the murder of a laborer. That is, since Euthyphro does not understand what piety is, its relation to the gods, or the precise nature of the gods, he cannot justify his action by simply appealing to its evident piety or to the behavior of the gods (*Eu.* 5d–6a). Furthermore, by having acknowledged that (as in P_1) piety is but a part of justice concerned with our relation to the *gods,* Euthyphro can no longer straightforwardly claim that the prosecution of his father for an act concerning another *man* is just by *reason* of its piety and the danger of religious pollution (*Eu.* 4b–5a). Rather, the case now appears to be a matter whose merits can only be determined on the grounds of *secular* justice.[56]

It is thus probably more than just an attempt at an ironic parallel that Plato presents both Euthyphro and Socrates to be involved in court cases whose crucial concern is pious action.[57] The implicit message intended by tying these two cases together (see especially *Eu.* 15c–16a) would seem to be this: in virtue of P_3 (and P_1), charges concerning the piety or impiety of a person's actions are not matters of secular justice. Further, since we as mere humans cannot complete P_3 and so cannot know precisely what acts serve the gods, we should acknowledge that we cannot confidently know whether someone's acts are pious or impious. Hence, just as Euthyphro's father ought not to be prosecuted for a crime against another man on the basis of the alleged impiety of his actions (or the impiety of failing to prosecute him), neither should Socrates be charged with impiety.[58] Such a charge is both inappropriate—since the real issue would seem to concern whether Socrates corrupts other *men*—and unwarranted, given our very fallible and incomplete understanding of the gods, as well as Socrates' claim that (in accord with P_3) he obeys divine commands.

However, whether or not this moral is implied by the *Euthyphro,* my primary thesis remains unaffected: given that the implicit answer of the *Euthyphro* is that P_3 is true and yet cannot be fully completed by mortals, then neither the constructivists nor anti-constructivists have been correct. I will now adduce further evidence in support of my view, and offer a sketch of the pragmatic guidelines to pious action Socrates understood P_3 to warrant.

According to P_3, we may credit Socrates with the beliefs that (1) pious acts are a species of just acts, (2) whose performance is a service to the gods (which pleases them), (3) which assists them with their work productive of a good result, and now, (4) that all these elements exist in the context of a limited agnosticism that precludes their specification in full detail. An elaboration of (1) through (3) and a mapping of the *extent* of that agnosticism are hampered by a lack of unequivocal evidence on the subject of Socratic piety, but this is the portrait I find most plausible: in Socrates we find what might be called a species of theist who believes that there *are* gods, but that our understanding of their nature and relation to us is extremely limited. Full knowledge of the gods is simply not within the power of finite human understanding to achieve. Nonetheless, we can and should acknowledge the great morality, knowledge, and power of the gods, and doing so is a sign of the proper intellectual humility which is partially constitutive of pious wisdom; that is, a recognition that our relation is in fact one of servant to great unseen master. Because of their excellence, the gods—who for Socrates may be addressed by their traditional names—do not bear all their traditional descriptions. They are, for instance, wholly moral and so—unlike the gods of Greek traditon—do not quarrel (*Eu.* 6b–d. *Phdo.* 62c–d). Socrates would hold the acts of traditional sacrifice to be pious, but not to constitute the whole of orthodox religious practice as he conceives it, which additionally includes the practice of philosophy. Thus, for Socrates there is no radical split between the life of philosophy and that of true religion. Both call for virtuous acts and a clear understanding through philosophy of their differing spheres of influence. I will discuss the connection between Socratic piety and the practice of philosophy at length later.

Socrates is also somewhat traditional in belief. He holds that we do receive goods from the gods, that they deserve our gratitude and honor, that we owe obedience to their commands, and that pious acts are productive of good things. Furthermore, there are occasions on which our human knowledge may be supplemented by divine and nondiscursive sources of information such as dreams, divinations, and divine voices. These sources are not, however, to be regarded as providing standard methods of inquiry. Finally, I would hypothesize that all the elements listed are fully integrated in the thought and practice of Socrates, and thus in his belief in the unity of the virtues; for example, to the extent that we understand the nature of pious relations between men and gods, we likewise understand the nature of right relations between men, and conversely.[59]

Socratic agnosticism is founded upon the distinction between human and divine wisdom or knowledge, where it is only the former fallible sort of knowledge that we may properly lay claim to (*Apol.* 23a). The field of human wisdom comprises the knowledge of human affairs, including the knowledge (fallible) of virtue; it does not extend to the full and infallible apprehension of divine objects such as gods, or facts such as whether or not dying is *certainly* good (*Apol.* 42a), whether the life of philosophy *certainly* achieves something (*Phdo.* 69d), or what it is the *gods* call themselves (*Crat.* 400d). Thus, neither does it extend to the complete and infallible understanding of the definition of piety, since that would require a complete and infallible knowledge of the gods' *ergon*. To strive after such knowledge in the hope of actually obtaining it is futile. Socrates, for instance, castigates the Sophists and nature philosophers for attempting to be ''wise in a wisdom more than human'' (*Apol.* 20e), an attempt he has given up (cf. *Apol.* 20e, *Phdo.* 97b–101a, *Phdr.* 229e, *Mem.* 1.1.11–16).[60] Lacking such knowledge (e.g., of future events) we should pray for no specific thing, since we cannot know (with certainty) if the fulfillment of our prayer would be a good for us or not (*Mem.* 1.3.2). This is so, since divine wisdom is a property of the gods (*Apol.* 23a–b; *Mem.* 1.1.6–8, 1.1.9, 1.1.13) and we must thus be content with the investigation of human matters (*Mem.* 1.1.9, 1.1.16), for to do otherwise is ridiculous and irrational (*Phdr.* 229e–230a, *Mem.* 1.1.8–10).[61] Socrates has such human wisdom, as the priestess of Delphi testifies (*Apol.* 21a), and he demonstrates it by recognizing the worthlessness (the fallibility) of human wisdom in respect of divine wisdom (*Apol.* 23a–c). The pursuit of this wisdom— that sort which is practically obtainable—is not to be denigrated, however, for it is the wisdom proper to fallible men. In some cases, of course, the pursuit of human wisdom will amount to an effort to obtain the most complete knowledge about divine matters which is humanly possible (human wisdom), but this effort should be conducted with the recognition that we cannot obtain certain (divine) knowledge of these matters.[62] Such incomplete and fallible knowledge is constitutive of the human wisdom Socrates seeks to gain by means of the elenchus.

To this point the characterization of Socrates' theism has been negative. What kind of gods are those we serve in accordance with P$_3$? An initial appraisal of the evidence indicates that Socrates' claims concerning the gods were at least compatible with the Greek religious traditions of his time. Socrates apparently believes that real gods exist (*Apol.* 35d, 42a; *Cri.* 54e; *Phdo.* 62b) and that they may be called by the same names as the gods of the state (*Apol.* 26b–c, *Eud.* 302c,[63] *Mem.* 1.1.10–11). These gods are completely moral (*Apol.* 21b; *Phdo.* 62d–63c)[64] and knowledgeable (*Cr.* 54c; *Apol.* 42a; *Mem.* 1.1.19, 1.4.18), and so should not be described as identical in nature to the gods of popular belief. Also, since Socrates subscribes to a dualist epistemology, that suggests that he does not view the gods as intervening extensively in the everyday life of men. Because of our weak epistemological powers, on the other hand, they ought not to be confidently described in detail, and so should not be identified with the metaphysical beings of the nature philosophers (*Mem.* 1.1.11–13).[65] Thus Socrates may be said to plot a course between the confused traditionalism of his day and the overconfident intellectualism of the Sophists and nature philosophers. Rather than denying belief in the gods, Socrates renders them *more* believable by eliminating their non-sensical squabbles while simultaneously emphasizing the role reason plays in the moral life: it is, again, part of Socrates' goal to show that people like Euthyphro may not invoke traditional divine behavior to justify their course of action. This is so, since aside from the belief that the gods are good, the specifics of divine behavior (including their chief *ergon*) and their nature are not accessible to us. Rather, we must admit our inability to obtain divine knowledge and search for the human knowledge of what constitutes just behavior between men.

Socrates is not simply a purified traditionalist, however. The charge of impiety we find in the *Apology* (24b) and which is confirmed in the *Euthyphro* (3b–d) indicates that the Socratic pantheon also includes a notorious demonic force, the *daimōn*. This divine voice (*Apol.* 31c–d) is negative in its advice (dissuading rather than prescribing),[66] and gives advice which is primarily personal, practical, and particular (*Apol.* 41c–d, 40a; *Eud.* 272e; *Phdr.* 242b–d; *Tht.* 151a; *Mem.* 1.1.4–5). Thus, Socrates may add to P_3 agreement with Euthyphro that he at least receives fine things from the gods; namely, advice on certain occasions. It is clear that Socrates does regard this advice as useful (*Apol.* 31d) and good (*Apol.* 40c–d), which may or may not be subject to rational confirmation in this life. For instance, it can be so confirmed when it advises against a life of politics (*Apol.* 31c–33b) and claims Socrates to be the wisest of men (*Apol.* 21a), but is not when it concerns the fate of the soul after death (*Apol.* 40b–c). On the whole it serves Socrates as a source of personal conviction in pursuing a correct course of action, and may be supplemented by philosophical reflection.

Such information, which may include that gained by divination and poetic inspiration (cf. *Apol.* 22b–c; *I.* 534e; *M.* 99c; *Mem.* 1.1.2, 1.1.6–10, 1.4.16) should be considered a form of human knowledge, for though it comes from a non-human source, it is often empirically confirmable.[67] Furthermore, Socrates would hardly find such information useful or consoling, as he does, if he considered it mere conjecture and not a source of knowledge, but only a kind of hunch. Also, since Socrates conceives of the gods as our masters, it is (then) reasonable for him to expect those gods to give their servants—both himself and *others* (*Mem.* 1.4.15–19)—good advice. This good advice in turn may be expected to contribute to the attainment of our principal good, the improvement of our souls, by providing us with information and encouragement relevant to the making of good moral judgments (*Mem.* 1.4.18–19).[68]

Socrates believes that we receive more than gifts of knowledge from the gods; he also believes (traditionally) that the gods care for us, and demonstrate that care by providing us with all manner of good things (*Eu.* 15a; *Apol.* 41c–d; *Mem.* 1.4.5–19),[69] including well-designed bodies and the very precondition of our moral excellence and happiness: the best type of soul (*Mem.* 1.4.13–14). Such care should not be identified with the chief *ergon* of the gods, however. Though they have an *ergon* according to P_3 (cf. *Mem.* 1.4.5, 1.4.10–12), as we have seen, its specification is a task for which human epistemic powers are not adequate.

Having observed that for Socrates there *are* gods, whose *ergon* is good, and who give us many good things, we come to the task of specifying the nature and requirements of our service (*hupēretikē*) to the gods. In accord with this sense of service—that we are servants to masters of quite another station and unable to specify their *ergon*—we may not state with any confidence what final end our service helps the gods to achieve. Nonetheless, Socrates clearly specifies what the practical guidelines of that service are, and what goods redound to us from conforming to them. The texts indicate that he understands this service to include acts of traditional sacrifice and worship and especially obedience to the gods' commands, all of which, as we saw, please them in their performance (cf. *Mem.* 4.3.17). Socrates, for instance, obeys a divine command to philosophize (*Apol.* 28d–e, 23b, 29b) taking precedence over all others, which helps the cause of god (*Apol.* 23b–c; with no implication that what it achieves is somehow beyond the power of the gods to effect).[70]

As for the evidence that Socrates thought traditional sacrifice to be a pious service, we have only one clear instance in the Platonic corpus (viz., the request at *Phdo.* 118a that a cock be offered to Asclepius). Nonetheless, we cannot conclude from this that Socrates did not sacrifice on a regular basis. Indeed, we may infer from Socrates' modest mode of life and Xenophon's explicit claims, that Socrates' sacrifices were humble (*Mem.* 1.3.3). If so, we need not expect Plato to have dwelt on the matter.[71] In any case, *Euthydemus* 302c, *Phaedrus* 229e, and numerous references in Xenophon's *Memorabilia* (1.1.2, 1.1.19, 1.3.64, 4.3.16–17, 4.6.4–6) all testify to some extent to Socrates' orthodox religious behavior. Although Xenophon's claims may well exaggerate the extent of Socratic orthodoxy out of apologetic fervor, he nonetheless seems to confirm a degree of traditional practice independently testified to in Plato.

Finally, the philosophical justification for the performance of sacrifice *and* the following of divine commands is implicit in P$_3$: Socrates would have endorsed the moral imperative of filial piety (including gifts and praise), and thought it a species of human justice. By analogy, then, we are obligated to perform acts of respect, gratitude, and obedience to our heavenly ancestors and masters (though we cannot know what benefits they derive from it [aside from pleasure]). Beyond this, what makes our obedience a matter of *justice per* P$_3$? The early dialogues do not address this issue, but in Xenophon Socrates argues that we are obligated to be pious on the principle that since we receive many gifts from the gods we owe them in return what it is ours to give (e.g., sacrifices and obedience) (*Mem.* 4.3.15–17). Though this is again Xenophon, it seems just the sort of argument Socrates might offer, for it parallels the argument in the *Crito* (48d–54d) for our obligation to our civil "master," the laws of the state. Socrates may argue on such lines that since we have received many blessings from the gods since birth, we have thereby entered into an implicit contract with them to obey their commands. Furthermore, as servants, we are the *property* of the gods (*Phdo.* 62a–63a): therefore, the gods have a claim on our service as the right of property owners (cf. *Apol.* 29b). Finally, we have prudential grounds for satisfying our obligations, given that the gods are both moral and omniscient.[72]

This analysis also shows how piety is a virtue, and provides the basis for showing why Socrates conceives of philosophy as a pious duty. Given that we have entered into an implicit contract with the gods, since it is virtuous to keep our contracts it is virtuous to be pious. As a virtue, pious activity naturally gives good results: just those which the gods give us and whatever end is served by our service. Beyond that, there is the good for ourselves and others we accomplish by the practice of right philosophy. Socrates is convinced, after all, that his service to the gods is one of the greatest gifts Athens could have.

One might get the impression from reading the *Apology* that Socrates sees the practice of philosophy as a special—not general—obligation imposed in his particular case by an order of the god. However, while he does see himself under orders, other passages indicate that he also views philosophy as a task everyone ought to undertake, for it improves us and makes life worth living (*Apol.* 29e–30b, 36c, 38a). Does Socrates then think that philosophy is a pious activity only for himself, whereas for others it is a matter of non-pious prudence? I think not, and for somewhat different reasons than are usually derived from the *Euthyphro* to show that philosophy is a pious obligation. Such arguments usually simply identify *the ergon* of the gods as the attempt to instantiate goodness in the world, then suppose that philosophy is the service which does this, and so conclude in uniformity to P_3 that piety is nothing other than philosophy.[73] Now I think that Socrates would have found it a likely and worthy belief—one which has or would withstand the test of the elenchus—that *an ergon* of the gods is to promote the establishment of goodness in the world, and that as an activity which helps in this, philosophy is thus probably a pious activity. Nonetheless, he would object to those arguments (such as the one just stated) which presuppose as (i) an item of infallible knowledge that (ii) the establishment of goodness in the world is *the* (only or primary) *ergon* of the gods. As I have already argued, Socrates would find it presumptuous to identify with certainty the nature of the gods' *ergon*. Furthermore, doing so in the manner of the argument above undercuts P_3, for if our *pious* service is *simply* to help instantiate the good in the world, then there would not seem to be any non-pious just acts (*contra* P_3), and as Versenyi argues, any reference to the gods in P_3 then begins to appear superfluous.

Thus, it seems to me that Socrates may well have held philosophical activity to be the primary (though not sole) form of pious activity for reasons additional to those which involve an identification of the gods' *ergon*. One such reason might be that since the gods are probably wholly good, it is a compelling hypothesis that they desire our virtuous happiness. Since philosophical activity in both its constructive and destructive modes aims at the production of this, and since our service to the gods would seem to call for us to satisfy their desires, philosophical activity is pious. Moreover, it is only possible to be a pious person by having a fallible human knowledge of piety; that is, a non-dogmatically held claim to a knowledge recognized to be fallible which one would therefore always be willing to submit to the elenchus. This knowledge of piety involves the belief *that* P_3 is true *and* not completable in this mortal life, a tentative claim as to why that is so, and elenctically tested beliefs as to what rules of pious action ought to be endorsed. I have briefly explained what those pragmatic rules are and what it is in P_3 that might justify them. But given the requirement that we understand that P_3 cannot be completed in this mortal life, it follows that the practice necessary to know this is then pious itself on derivative grounds. This practice is simply the elimination *via philosophy* (in its destructive mode) of the epistemological conceit most men have. That is, again, the conceit that we mortals might possess the certain knowledge of divine things (the god's *ergon*) which *would* complete P_3, whereas all that is vouchsafed to us is fallible knowledge.

Philosophical practice in its constructive mode is in turn the justification by means of the elenchus of those beliefs—such as the belief that P_3 is true and not completable—constitutive of human wisdom.[74] This activity is pious, as I suggested, because it is productive of the virtuous happiness which good gods desire for us. Insofar as this is likely to be a matter of concern to the gods, this constructive aspect of pious philosophical activity demands that we serve the gods by putting our faith only in those beliefs which we have rigorously tested *via* the elenchus. Additionally, we should always regard such bits of human wisdom with a humility and caution which will always consent to their re-testing by elenctic procedures.[75] This active humility and caution are called for, since as Socrates' practice of the destructive mode of the elenchus has repeatedly demonstrated (*Apol.* 21b–23b), men are constantly in danger of supposing they have certain knowledge of both divine and human matters, and that they are thus in no need of improvement. Euthyphro serves as a paradigm case of this danger. Such an attitude is impious and is therefore to be guarded against because (again) it represents a lack of knowledge of what is true about piety (that P_3 is not completable by mortals) and because it impedes men from serving the (likely) desire of the gods that we improve souls and produce virtuous happiness.

It is thus part of the preceding account that it is impious to suppose—contrary to the correct understanding of piety—that we mortals may possess divine wisdom. Hence, in the *Euthyphro* it is precisely Socrates' pious activity to attack the impiety underlying Euthyphro's presumptuous claims which take divine things to be possible objects of certain knowledge for mortals and a reliable source of moral justification. Philosophy on the Socratic model is then a prime case of pious activity designed to reveal the real epistemic state of affairs between men and gods. This activity returns us to a state of human wisdom and the correct appraisal of what that activity is epistemically worth. Piety is also linked to the rest of the virtues by philosophy. That is, the human knowledge of the virtues sought by philosophy is only possible by performing a pious activity which, if performed correctly, results in the proper knowledge of piety.

Socrates' methodological skepticism emerges from the preceding as the expression of a piety (as Socrates himself claims) more sincere than traditional Greek piety, which presupposes an extensive knowledge of the gods (*Apol.* 35d). It is also an activity grounded in faith in the power of the elenchus to win for us some measure of human wisdom, as well as a faith in that divine certainty by which the fallible worth of human knowledge is recognized. Socrates, therefore, emerges from the *Euthyphro* as not only a hero of critical rationality, but of a kind of religious faith as well: it might be said that by rejecting more than we, he out-believed us all.

NOTES

I wish to thank the National Endowment for the Humanities and all my fellow seminar members in the 1983 NEH Summer Seminar on the philosophy of Socrates for providing me with the stimulating environment in which this essay was written. I am particularly indebted to the director of the seminar, Gregory Vlastos, for his comments on an earlier draft of this essay. I also wish to extend my gratitude to my colleague, Charles Chiasson, and an anonymous referee for the *Journal of the History of Philosophy* for their constructive criticisms of earlier versions of my essay.

1. See W. G. Rabinowitz, "Platonic Piety: An Essay Toward the Solution of an Enigma," *Phronesis* 2 (1958): 112–14 (hereafter cited as "Platonic Piety"), for a partial history of this

issue, the discussion of which extends from Thrasyllus of Alexandria to a recent article by C. C. W. Taylor, "The End of the *Euthyphro*," *Phronesis* 27 (1982): 109–18 (hereafter cited as "The End").

2. Among the constructivists are J. Adam, *Platonis Euthyphro* (Cambridge, 1902); H. Bonitz, *Platonische Studien* (Berlin, 1866), 233–34; T. Brickhouse and N. Smith, "The Origin of Socrates' Mission," *Journal of the History of Ideas* 4 (1983): 657–66 (hereafter cited as "Socrates' Mission"); J. Burnet, *Plato's Euthyphro, Apology of Socrates and Crito* (Oxford, 1924), 82–142 (hereafter cited as "Plato's *Euthyphro*"); P. Friedländer, *Plato*, 3 vols. (New York, 1964), 2:82–91; W. A. Heidel, "On Plato's *Euthyphro*," *TAPA* 31 (1900): 173ff.; T. Irwin, *Plato's Moral Theory* (Oxford, 1977), 1–131; B. Jowett, *The Dialogues of Plato*, 4 vols. (Oxford, 1953), 1:303–08; Rabinowitz, "Platonic Piety"; P. Shorey, *What Plato Said* (Chicago, 1933), 74–80; A. E. Taylor, *Plato, the Man and His Work* (New York, 1927), 146–56; C. C. W. Taylor, "The End"; and G. Vlastos, "The Unity of the Virtues in the *Protagoras*," in *Platonic Studies* (Princeton, 1981): 221–69 and 427–45 (hereafter cited as "Unity"). For further references, see Rabinowitz, "Platonic Piety," 113, n. 4, and L. Versenyi, *Holiness and Justice: An Interpretation of Plato's Euthyphro* (Washington, D.C., 1982): 111, n. 4 (hereafter cited as "Holiness").

3. See, e.g., R. E. Allen, *Plato's Euthyphro and the Early Theory of Forms* (New York, 1970) (hereafter cited as "The Early Theory"); J. Beckman, *The Religious Dimension of Socrates' Thought* (Waterloo, 1979) (hereafter cited as "The Religious Dimension"); G. Grote, *Plato and Other Companions of Socrates*, 4 vols. (London, 1888), 1:437–57; and Versenyi, "Holiness."

4. "The Early Theory," 67; see also 6–9. Curiously, Allen nonetheless finds little difficulty in discovering most of Plato's theory of Forms in a text which is perfectly coherent without such an attribution (employing, instead of Forms, universals [abstract qualities]). Those very principles of interpretation which Allen endorses (9) sanction the constructive claim concerning piety I will derive from the text. Cf. Versenyi, "Holiness," 16.

5. "Holiness," 104–34; cf. Versenyi's other work relevant to this topic, *Socratic Humanism* (New Haven, 1963); C. C. W. Taylor, "The End," 117–18, also holds a view which makes piety identical to the whole of virtue. Beckman, "The Religious Dimension," 51–54, argues in a manner similar to Versenyi and Taylor that no definition of piety may be derived from the explicit statements of the text. Rather, he claims, Socrates argues implicitly that "real" piety is nothing but the *whole* of justice, for whose understanding and definition no gods are required. Irwin, *Plato's Moral Theory*, 22, seems to hold this view as well.

6. A star instance of this is Heidel, "On Plato's *Euthyphro*," 174, who defines piety as the "intelligent and conscious endeavor to further the realization of the [Platonic!] Good in human society, as under God" (my brackets).

7. I will assume, as most commentators do, that *hosios* and *eusebēs* are used synonymously in the dialogue.

8. Cf. Vlastos, "Unity," 231, 435–36, who accepts this interpretation.

9. Vlastos, ibid., 228, n. 17; Rabinowitz, "Platonic Piety," 114.

10. See the Vlastos–Irwin dispute over whether or not this is to be read as an endorsement of Euthyphro's attempt; Vlastos, "Unity," 434; Irwin, *Plato's Moral Theory*, 301, n. 57.

11. Noted by Rabinowitz, "Platonic Piety," 115.

12. By making this point I am not, then, endorsing the mistaken (I believe) "Bonitz principle" that whatever remains unrefuted in Platonic text represents positive doctrine; Bonitz, *Platonische Studien*, 233–34; cf. Adam, *Platonis Euthyphro*, xii; Heidel, "On Plato's *Euthyphro*," 171. For criticisms of this principle, see R. E. Allen, "The Early Theory," 6; Versenyi, "Holiness," 111, n. 3.

13. I take this point from Brickhouse and Smith, "Socrates' Mission," 661.

14. As noted by Rabinowitz, "Platonic Piety," 114. This, and the points noted by nn. 12 and 13,

are at least obstacles to Allen's claim, "The Early Theory," 5, that no substantive issue in the interpretation of the *Euthyphro* turns on its dramatic structure. Taylor, "The End," 112, notes that other dialogues contain clear hints of a conclusion not explicitly drawn (e.g., *Charm*. 174d–75a). For the possible connection of the *Euthyphro* to the *Theatetus* see Allen, 7.

15. What would count as a definition of some concept for Socrates is a thorny issue. But what he seems to be after (ideally) is a relation of mutual entailment between definiendum and definiens, where the definiens of "F" gives a complete explanation of why any x *is* F, such that any instance of an F-thing can be thereby recognized as being F. See also the beginning of section III; cf. G. Santas, *Socrates* (London, 1979): 97–135.

16. As Taylor, "The End," 110, notes: "Ordinary Greek idiom would naturally appropriate the term *Dikaiosunē* as the name for the virtue of social relations with human agents, and it is in accordance with that usage that the good man is described at *Gorg.* 507b as one who would do right by men. . . . It is unnecessary to suppose any difference of doctrine between that passage and the *Euthyphro*."

17. *Apol*. 20e, 23a–b.

18. Pious acts, on this view, would be those we ought to perform, doing so in accordance with the laws governing the relations of men and gods.

19. Cf. K. J. Dover, *Greek Popular Morality* (Berkeley, 1974), 247–48, and A. W. H. Adkins, *Merit and Responsibility* (Oxford, 1960), 133. As Dover notes (247–48): "The formal conjunction of *hosios* with *dikaios* was sometimes augmented by reference to *"both* gods *and* men,"* as if recognizing a distinction between divine law and man-made law." Irwin, *Plato's Moral Theory*, 22, points out that piety had a well-established association with justice for Hesiod, Solon, and Aeschylus, among others; cf. Taylor, "The End," 110. It is useful to note Aristotle's connection of impiety with injustice at *EN* 1122a5–7.

I should note that despite the strength of the case for P_1, there is one serious objection to it. P_1 differentiates pious justice from non-pious justice, and yet at *Protagoras* 331a6–b8 we find Socrates claiming that "justice is pious" (i.e., that there is no non-pious justice). Much is made of this difficulty by those who subscribe to T. Penner's view in "The Unity of Virtue," *Philosophical Review* 82 (1973): 35–68 [reprinted in this volume], that the unity of the virtues is a thesis asserting their *identity:* e.g., Irwin, *Plato's Moral Theory*, 22; Taylor, "The End," 116–18. In defense of that view, they reject any constructivistic interpretations of the text which employ the substance of P_1 (in their arguments, both Versenyi and Taylor unjustifiably *assume* that piety *is* the whole of virtue. Taylor, however, tries to retain a sense of P_1 by maintaining that piety is virtue "under a certain aspect" (viz., the relation of man to the gods)). Vlastos, "Unity," 224–28, on the other hand, utilizes the evidence of the Socratic commitment to P_1 as partial grounds for the rejection of Penner's interpretation. An adequate discussion of this dispute goes far beyond the practical limits of this paper. Nonetheless, the weight of the evidence for P_1 we have seen, together with the observation that the dialogue seems primarily interested in the piety of *acts* (noted by I. M. Crombie in *An Examination of Plato's Doctrines*, 2 vols. (New York, 1962), 1:211; see also n. 34) leads me to endorse the Vlastos solution to this apparent incompatibility.

In brief, this solution allows us to analyze the claim of the *Protagoras* to be the claim that someone is a just *person* if and only if he is a pious *person* (and likewise for the other virtues [Vlastos, "Socrates On 'the Parts of Virtue,'" in *Platonic Studies* (Princeton, 1981): 418–23]). On the other hand, P_1 should only be taken to claim that while all pious *acts* are just, a just *act* (of any sort of person) need not also be a pious one (e.g., repaying a small loan; cf. Vlastos, ibid., 421, n. 5, on the concept of virtue's "parts"; cf. P. Woodruff, "Socrates on the Parts of Virtue," *Canadian Journal of Philosophy*, supplementary volume 2 (1976): 101–16).

20. Which can simply mean the correct treatment of any class of beings; see Burnet, "Plato's *Euthyphro,*" 135; Versenyi, "Holiness," 100.
21. This analysis is derived from the excellent discussion by Versenyi, ibid., 100–102.
22. Socrates does not press P_2 upon Euthyphro and would have found it "surprising" for Euthyphro to maintain it. As shown later, the evidence indicates that Socrates also believed in gods vastly superior to men in power and knowledge.
23. As Rabinowitz, "Platonic Piety," 115, has noted, the fact that Socrates is *pressing* Euthyphro to produce the gods' *ergon* constitutes evidence of Socrates' commitment to something like P_3.
24. Again, no endorsement of the Bonitz principle is intended. See n. 12.
25. See nn. 24 and 12.
26. Noted by Brickhouse and Smith, "Socrates' Mission," 660–61; see also W. K. C. Guthrie, *Socrates* (Cambridge, 1971), 136–39.
27. Noted by Rabinowitz, "Platonic Piety," 115. Although this remark as a whole has some flavor of irony to it, that is explicable on the grounds that by this point in the dialogue it is quite reasonable to portray Socrates as becoming bored with Euthyphro's avoidance of the question. Socrates, giving up the hope of eliciting a useful answer, is perhaps playfully needling Euthyphro on his pretensions to divine knowledge.
28. *Eu.* 13e6, 13e10–11, 14a9–10, 14d6, 14e9–15a4, 15a7–8.
29. *Od.* 11.225; *Erga.* 136 (as noted by Versenyi, "Holiness," 102).
30. E.g., Heidel, "On Plato's *Euthyphro,*" 169; "Socrates' Mission," 657–66; Beckman, "The Religious Dimension," 42.
31. In the *Apology* Socrates often refers to his service to the god as a *latreia,* but like *hupēretikē,* this connotes the work of, among other things, a servant for a master. Note also that though the term *keleuō* at *Apol.* 30a5, commonly translated as "command," does have several other possible translations, it is this sense of the term which should be preferred, given Socrates' likening of his situation to a man's being on station at a military post (*Apol.* 28e–29a).
32. Not to mention Plato's artistic considerations: this is the move which finally leads the discussion full circle, back to Euthyphro's earlier rebuffed claim that piety is what pleases the gods.
33. Crombie, *An Examination of Plato's Doctrines,* 1:211.
34. Crombie's observation, ibid., 209: "There are two ways of expressing an abstract noun in Greek: firstly one can use the definite article with the neuter of the appropriate adjective ('the holy'), and secondly one can use a noun formed from the adjective ('holiness'). It is natural to use the first form for the thing-abstract and the second for the person-abstract, and this the *Euthyphro* does. Socrates begins by asking for a definition of the thing-abstract; the primary subject of the dialogue is the quality attaching to objects and actions which makes them holy." The evidence for this claim includes the fact that the dialogue begins with a concern over whether or not Euthyphro's *act* of prosecuting his father is pious (*Eu.* 4e–5a, 5d–6a, 8a–e) and the charge that Socrates has *acted* impiously by "making new gods and not believing in the old ones" (2a–3e, 12e). In addition, Socrates requests that Euthyphro state what piety and impiety are with reference to the act of murder and all other cases (*acts*), specifying whether "the holy [is] always one and the same thing in every *action (praxei)*" (5c9–d2) and what the form of holiness is that is found in every holy *action* (6d9–e1). This latter concern continues right up to the aporetic interlude (11b–e), which is followed by a concern over what sort of *acts* of service to the gods would constitute pious *action* (12e–14a). Socrates then turns the discussion of piety as a kind of knowledge *back* to a discussion of what sort of *actions* this knowledge calls for (14d–15b). The dialogue then concludes by returning to the topic of whether or not Euthyphro's *act* of prosecuting his father and Socrates' *actions* are pious or not (15c–16a).

35. See P. T. Geach, "Plato's *Euthyphro*," *The Monist* 3 (1966): 369–82, who argues (rightly, I think) that this incompatibility is not something Euthyphro is logically committed to (381).
36. Burnet, "Plato's *Euthyphro*," 137; Allen, "The Early Theory," 6–7, 5–8; Versenyi, "Holiness," 107–10. Allen maintains that the dialogue takes no stand on the issue of piety's *ergon*, since none of the virtues have products. Burnet similarly argues that the *Euthyphro* contains the suggestion that there is no *ergon* achieved by piety since piety is not a specialized art but a condition of the soul. But as Brickhouse and Smith note, "Socrates' Mission," 7, "Socrates' frequently drawn analogies between virtues and crafts make little sense if crafts produce *erga*, but virtues do not."

As will be seen, my own position relies on the notion that though we cannot (with certainty) specify the *ergon* of the gods, that does not prevent us from attributing P_3 (as a *pathos* of piety) to Socrates.
37. Versenyi, "Holiness," 110. He derives this line of reasoning (122) from *M.* 77c–78b.
38. Ibid., 109. This is surprising because of Versenyi's condemnation of those constructivists who import Platonic, rather than Socratic, doctrine into their theses (107).
39. See also *Phdr.* 229e, *Mem.* 1.3.2. Even the gods of Aristotle, after all, have an *ergon* (viz., *noēsis*), sublime though it may be *EN* 1178b9–30).
40. This latter task is Taylor's specification of the gods' *ergon*, "The End," 113: "There is one good product they can't produce without human assistance, namely, good human souls." Unfortunately, he provides no evidence for attributing this claim to Socrates. In fact, it seems to me that Socrates would not have held the gods so powerless in any sphere of activity. Rather (he would think), the gods have left our souls unfinished in respect of goodness for whatever reasons they have, though it is still in their power to produce such good human souls. However (for Socrates), it is not within the grasp of fallible *human* wisdom to understand why they refrain from doing so.
41. Versenyi, "Holiness," 104–11.
42. In fact, Socrates cannot, since as the discussion of piety conceived of as *emporikē* reveals (*Eu.* 14b–15b), Euthyphro has become educated on this matter, and thus does not allow himself to be interpreted as suggesting that we further the excellence of the gods (by giving gifts).
43. Socrates insists at *Apol.* 35d that perjury is impious. Socrates also testifies that he has a service to the gods, but by crediting Socrates with the additional belief that such service is incompatible with the nature of the gods (since Versenyi would hardly think that Socrates is missing his own point), Versenyi—very implausibly—must then discount all of Socrates' talk concerning his divine mission as ironic. "Holiness," 111–12n.7. Thus we see his motivation for doing so, i.e., to avoid just the sort of objection to his rejection of *"hupēretikē"* I have given in the text.
44. Versenyi, ibid., 109.
45. Ibid., 104, 107–8. I say "implies" because Versenyi does not clearly assert this, but requires it for his dilemma (107–8), to be formally valid.
46. Ibid., 86, 104–10; see also "The Religious Dimension," 51–54; "The End," 113–18.
47. Ibid., 104–9.
48. If we assume that the gods are much more knowledgeable beings not "of this world" (as both Socrates and Versenyi would), then that does suggest that we can't fully know the reasons (ends) of the gods, which on the model of P_3 suggests that we can't *fully* understand the piety of actions. By analogy, servants might not be in a position to fully know the reasons of their masters, and so not fully understand the nature of their service. But that need not keep them from knowing enough to recognize and perform particular acts which are "master-pious." Cf. *Mem.* 1.4.4; Geach, "Plato's *Euthyphro*," 381.
49. I derive this point from Geach, ibid., 381.
50. Viz., *Ly.* 221–222a, 217a–218c, 214e–215b, 210c–d; *Sym.* 200b–e, 202b–d, 203e–204a; *Rep.* 334c.

51. Versenyi, "Holiness," 120–23.
52. Or, seeing it, that he would not have rejected one of his other entailing beliefs so as to save the gods from being thought indifferent and inactive. In any case, I do not see how Versenyi makes his attribution of a belief in perfect gods compatible with the statement of Socrates' alleged agnosticism (*Crat.* 400d) which Versenyi calls "the most likely candidate" for an accurate account of Socrates' religious beliefs, "Holiness," 123.
53. My attention was first drawn to this point by Brickhouse and Smith, "Socrates' Mission," 661–62, and in conversation with them.
54. See R. F. Holland, "Euthyphro," *Aristotelean Society Proceedings* 82 (1981–82): 3.
55. For the reasons given, I interpret Socrates' remark to be more than just an *ad hominem* attack on Euthyphro.
56. This, however, is not provided for by Athenian legal practice, which, as noted by Burnet, "Plato's *Euthyphro,*" 83, "only took cognizance of homicide in so far as it created a religious pollution." This explains Socrates' remark at the end of the dialogue that it would be unthinkable for Euthyphro to initiate a prosecution of his father for murder without knowing what piety is (*Eu.* 15d). That is, it would be unthinkable for *someone like Euthyphro* who seems to agree with Athenian legal practice and whose only apparent justification for his prosecution is the danger of religious pollution posed by a failure to prosecute (4b–c). The question of whether or not Euthyphro's father still ought to be prosecuted on non-religious grounds is thus left open (note that there is some question whether or not Euthyphro's father even committed the act in question, *Eu.* 4d).
57. Note, additionally, how the two cases are made to seem more analogous than they might by Plato's treating the *two* charges of impiety and corruption of the *Apology* (24b–c) as *one* charge of impiety: Socrates is said to corrupt the young *by* making new gods and not believing in the old ones (*Eu.* 2c–3b).

     My discussion of Euthyphro's legal case and n. 58 owe much to a very interesting paper by R. Weiss, "Euthyphro's Failure," *Journal of the History of Philosophy* 24 (1986): 437–53.
58. Hence, one moral Plato may be suggesting in this dialogue is that the Athenian practice of prosecuting people for impiety ought to be abandoned. Socrates, he seems to be telling us, is especially unjustly charged with impiety if the basis of those charges lies in Socrates' doubts (*Eu.* 6a–d) concerning the sorts of quarreling gods Euthyphro ignorantly appeals to in justification of his legal case. These same gods may well have not been taken very seriously by much of the Athenian populace, and if so, the charges against Socrates are unfairly brought (see Adam, *Platonis Euthyphro,* xviii–xix). All this accords with and helps to explain the common intuition that the *Euthyphro* was written with more than Plato's usual degree of apologetic intent (cf., e.g., Versenyi, "Holiness," 153).
59. This, of course, is in essence the Vlastos interpretation of the doctrine of the unity of the virtues (in "Unity"), which I have not attempted to argue for in this paper. See n. 19.
60. Socrates would seem at *Apol.* 20e to be referring back to not only Sophists such as Gorgias (mentioned at 19e) but also those who inquire "into things below the earth and in the sky" who, due to the portrait of him in *The Clouds* of Aristophanes (19b–c), he has been confused with; e.g., the nature philosopher Anaxagoras, who does have a theory about a thing "in the sky," viz., the sun (*Apol.* 26c–e). Socrates has "no disrespect for such knowledge, *if anyone really is versed in it*" (*Apol.* 19c5–8, my italics). See also *Phdo.* 97b–101a for Plato's portrait of Socrates' disappointments with Anaxagoras' theories. Two of his more important and relevant points there would seem to be that as far as Socrates was concerned Anaxagoras was not well-versed in the knowledge of divine things he laid claim to, and that his theories didn't provide a knowledge of the proper ends of human—not divine—action (i.e., he didn't possess human wisdom). Although the *Phaedo* is a middle dialogue, this section clearly purports to give us a relatively accurate picture of a period in Socrates' youth (cf. e.g., *Eu.* 5a, which

supports the attribution to Socrates of a youthful—and now past—interest in the "divine things" of the nature philosophers).

61. While I appeal to middle dialogue text in my characterization of Socratic piety, I have been careful to use it only to supplement citations from early dialogues (esp. the *Apology* and *Euthyphro*) and/or Xenophon's *Memorabilia*. My use of citations from the *Memorabilia,* in turn, has been generally limited to supporting points which are independently testified to by material from the Platonic *corpus*. In those few cases where this is not true, the citations generally corroborate a previously supported point, or the point is not crucial to my thesis.

62. Since, on Socrates' view, the gods presumably know everything (human and divine) with certainty and we in turn may know some facts (fallibly) concerning the gods (e.g., that P_3 is true), the difference between human wisdom and divine wisdom would not seem to lie primarily in there being different objects of knowledge (human and divine) appropriate to each sort of wisdom. Rather, it is the degree of epistemic reliablility which distinguishes the two: a man may only hope for a knowledge about any state of affairs which will at best remain fallible relative to the infallible knowledge had by the gods. In certain cases, however—like that of the *ergon* of the gods—the *explanation* for the impossibility of our having certain knowledge is to be specifically found in the fact that the gods are divine metaphysical entities not as knowable for men as are, say, facts having to do with material objects and the practices of human society (e.g., the knowledge of horse training). Also, the differentiation of human wisdom from divine wisdom for Socrates seems to be connected with his emphasis upon the importance of the pursuit of human ethical wisdom, whose human subject matter takes precedence for him over questions concerning the nature of the divine objects (e.g., the sun) studied by the nature philosophers (complete and certain knowledge of which would be a kind of divine wisdom) (see n. 58; *Mem.* 1.1.11–16).

63. This passage provides evidence that Socrates had his own altars and family prayers, from which it seems reasonable to infer that he prayed to the gods of the state at least in name.

64. They must be completely moral, since we saw it admitted that the gods can't themselves be improved (*Eu.* 13c–d). This view is also suggested by Socrates' remarks concerning the behavior of the traditional gods at *Eu.* 6a–d.

65. See n. 60. Of course, given Socrates' youthful attraction to Anaxagoras' *Noûs* (*Phdo.* 97b–98a), it is possible that Socrates might have been willing to entertain as a hypothesis that it is *Noûs* which is named by all the traditional names of the gods. This would depend, however, on how confident Socrates was in his use of the plural "gods" (cf., e.g., *Phdo.* 62b–c).

66. Although if one follows Xenophon religiously—as I am not inclined to do—the *daimonion* also prescribes (see, e.g., *Mem.* 1.1.4).

67. Socrates, for instance, sets out to test the claim of the Oracle. This also follows from Socrates' general claim that human (fallible) knowledge is the best we can hope for. That it should be regarded as human, and so, *fallible* knowledge, may be argued for in particular by a consideration of *Apol.* 40b–c. There the divine sign does not oppose a course of action that threatens Socrates with death, and Socrates regards that as excellent grounds for supposing his death not to be an evil. Nonetheless, at *Apol.* 42a Socrates then claims that it is in fact *unknown* whether death will be a happier prospect for himself than continued life will be for the court.

It should be noted that just before *Ion* 534e Socrates says that the "inspired" poet is "out of his mind" and that "intelligence is no longer in him." In the *Meno* Socrates also says that those who are "inspired" "don't understand anything they say" (99c). Nonetheless, keeping in mind how the pronouncement of the Oracle served as a source of knowledge for Socrates—once properly interpreted by philosophical investigations—the ravings of the poets might also serve as sources of information for others.

68. I am unable, however, to find textual evidence in the early dialogues of anyone other than Socrates profiting from such advice.

69. The claim that this citation from Xenophon accurately represents Socratic doctrine has been disputed; see, e.g., W. Jaeger, *The Theology of the Greek Thinkers* (Oxford, 1947), 167.

70. Socrates also obeys the exhortation of a recurring dream (*Phdo.* 60d–61c), and such dreams he regards as containing the commands of a god (*Apol.* 33c).

71. There is no *need* for testimony to this effect in the *Apology* either, for the charges against Socrates concern an alleged lack of orthodoxy (and of teaching to that effect), not a failure to sacrifice. *Plato* would also not be likely to think that such testimony would be a philosophically relevant matter to bring up in the *Apology,* just because of its irrelevance to this issue of one's possessing the correct *intellectual* attitude to the gods. Plato surely recognizes that truly impious people may still sacrifice. Xenophon, on the other hand, should not be expected to distinguish clearly between practice and belief, and in his zeal to defend Socrates before everyone, to emphasize his sacrificial practice. This is just what we find in the *Memorabilia* (e.g., *Mem.* 1.3.1–4).

72. None of these consideration imply that our service to the gods is a kind of *emporia,* which Socrates *seems* to discount ironically (*Eu.* 14e–15a).

73. E.g., Heidel, "On Plato's *Euthyphro,*" 174; Taylor, "The End," 113–18.

74. Recent important papers on the constructive role of the elenchus are G. Vlastos' "The Socratic Elenchus" and "Afterthoughts on the Socratic Elenchus," R. Kraut's "Comments on Professor Vlastos' 'The Socratic Elenchus,'" all in *Oxford Studies in Ancient Philosophy* 1 (1983), and Brickhouse's and Smith's "Vlastos on the Elenchus," *Oxford Studies in Ancient Philosophy* 3 (1984): 185–95.

75. As an anonymous referee has pointed out to me, Socrates even subjects the pronouncement of the Oracle that no one is wiser than he to an exhaustive examination. Brickhouse and Smith, "Socrates' Mission," 659–65, have proposed an interesting explanation for Socrates' puzzling interpretation of the Oracle's claim as a *command* of the god (Apollo) to carry out this examination (*Apol.* 21b–22a). They argue, in essence, that Socrates' interpretation of the Oracle's claim is predicated upon a notion of piety similar to the one I am proposing, insofar as Socrates conceived of piety (prior to the Oracle's pronouncement) as a duty to serve the gods in the manner of slave to master, promoting what is good. On their view, the god has said something Socrates finds mysterious and paradoxical (*Apol.* 21b), and since anything a master might say to his servant *could* conceal a demand for some sort of service on the slave's part, Socrates conceives it to be part of his pious obligation—a religious duty—to discover the meaning of the god's claim.

FURTHER READING

Brickhouse, T. C. and Smith, N. D. 1989. *Socrates on Trial,* esp. 87–99. Princeton, N.J.

Cohen, S. M. 1971. "Socrates on the Definition of Piety: *Euthyphro* 10a–11b." *Journal of the History of Philosophy* 9. Reprinted in *The Philosophy of Socrates,* ed. Gregory Vlastos, 158–76. Garden City, N.Y.

Geach, P. T. 1966. "Plato's *Euthyphro:* An Analysis and Commentary." *Monist* 50:369–82.

Taylor, C. C. W. 1982. "The End of the *Euthyphro.*" *Phronesis* 27:109–18.

Versenyi, L. 1982. *Holiness and Justice: An Interpretation of the Euthyphro.* Washington, D.C.

Weiss, R. 1986. "Euthyphro's Failure." *Journal of the History of Philosophy* 24:437–53.

14

Ho Agathos as *Ho Dunatos* in the *Hippias Minor*

ROSLYN WEISS

This essay is an attempt so to construe the arguments of the *Hippias Minor* as to remove the justification for regarding it as unworthy of Plato either because of its alleged fallaciousness and Sophistic mode of argument or because of its alleged immorality.[1] It focuses, therefore, only on the arguments and their conclusions, steering clear of the dialogue's dramatic and literary aspects. Whereas I do not wish to deny the importance of these aspects to a proper understanding of the dialogue—on the contrary, in a dialogue so heavily laden with irony and caricature,[2] these aspects are necessarily more significant than they are in other dialogues—I do think there is something to be gained from concentrating on the arguments themselves. Although there can be little doubt that Socrates is up to something in the *Hippias Minor,* the task of determining just what he *is* up to can only be simplified by clarifying the arguments *first*.

The *Hippias Minor* has traditionally been thought to contain two independent arguments,[3] each having its own paradoxical conclusion. The first argument begins, it is said, when Hippias characterizes the two Homeric heroes Achilles and Odysseus as the true man (*ho alēthēs*) and the false man (*ho pseudēs*) respectively. Through its discovery that both the false man and the true man have *dunamis,* it results in the paradox that the false man and the true are identical. The second argument, on this view, leaves the subject of *ho alēthēs* and *ho pseudēs* and compares instead all sorts of agents in intentional and unintentional action. Finding that the intentional agent is in every case better than the unintentional, the argument concludes that the intentional evil-doer is also better than the unintentional. Viewing the dialogue as thus containing two distinct topics treated in two self-sufficient arguments is perhaps not the best way to understand it.

First of all, Socrates does not himself take this approach. He sees the two arguments as being intimately related, through a proposition which, in some sense, spans them both. The proposition that voluntary *liars* are better than involuntary[4] belongs, for him, to the first argument as a direct consequence of it; but it belongs no less to the second, for the second argument is itself occasioned by Hippias' resistance to this proposition.

And secondly, we have reason to question the conclusiveness of the first paradox. For if we regard the first argument as establishing absolutely the identity of the true man and the false, it is difficult to understand why the discussion proceeds, as it does, to consider whether it is Achilles or Odysseus who *actually* tells lies. If the true man and false were identical, what difference would it make? The following interpretation, therefore, constitutes an attempt to maintain the integrity of the dialogue by viewing all its parts as related to a single topic: who is the truly superior man?[5]

Let us begin by looking at the first stage (363a1–369b7). On the usual interpretation, this stage includes one self-contained argument (beginning after a brief and inconsequential reference to Achilles and Odysseus) leading to a paradoxical conclusion, as follows. (1) The false man (*ho pseudēs*) is the man with the power, ability, and wisdom to be false in the matters in which he is false. (2) Only the man who has the power, ability, and wisdom in the matters in which he is false can be false. (3) The true man (*ho alēthēs*) is the man with the power, ability, and wisdom to speak truthfully in the matters in which he is true. (4) Only the man with the power, ability, and wisdom to speak truthfully can be true in the matters in which he is true. (5) The same man who, because of his power, ability, and wisdom can speak truthfully in a given matter (e.g., calculation, geometry, astronomy, and indeed all the arts and sciences) can, for the same reason, speak falsely in that matter, therefore (6) *ho alēthēs* and *ho pseudēs* are the same.

Each of these steps appears in the text. But the argument presented in this way is surely fallacious. For if *ho alēthēs* and *ho pseudēs* in (6) are understood (as they normally would be) to mean the man who typically tells the truth and the man who typically lies, respectively, then even if they are each capable of speaking both truthfully and falsely in a given matter (4), it does not follow that each typically *actually* speaks both truthfully and falsely in that matter. *Ho alēthēs* and *ho pseudēs* may share a common ability without being identical. In Mulhern's terms, the argument fails because of a confusion of *dunamis*-terms, terms which denote ability, and *tropos*-terms, terms which denote typical behaviour.[6]

Mulhern, who is representative of the many scholars who charge the *Hippias Minor* with patent equivocation and abuses of language, finds support for his unique characterization of this abuse in a pun on the word *polutropos*. *Polutropos,* which Hippias regards as the special trait of Odysseus, itself contains the word *tropos*, which for Mulhern signifies the typical behaviour of a person, the way he is, his character. But though it contains the word *tropos*, *polutropos* is itself not a *tropos*-term but rather a *dunamis*-term; it does not signify a person's typical behaviour but rather an ability or capacity to behave a certain way.[7] Thus he rejects Jowett's and Fowler's translation of *polutropos* as "wily," which he considers to be a *tropos*-term, a term suggesting typical behaviour, and replaces it with "resourceful," which he feels preserves the *dunamis*-nature of *polutropos* by limiting it to one's capacity and ability. According to Mulhern, then, the paradoxical conclusion of the argument—that *ho alēthēs* and *ho pseudēs* are the same—is ultimately attributable to a confusing of *tropos*-words with *dunamis*-words as well as assigning a *tropos*-sense to *dunamis*-terms and vice versa.

On Mulhern's view, Hippias initiates the confusion. He takes the *dunamis*-term *polutropos* and stipulates *pseudēs* as its meaning. But *pseudēs* is a *tropos*-term, one which distinguishes between Achilles and Odysseus in terms of how they regularly behave, their respective *tropoi*, rather than in terms of their *dunameis*, their abilities. But Socrates compounds the problem by using *polutropos* to stipulate a meaning for *pseudēs* at 365e1–2,[8] thereby setting the stage for the reduction of *pseudēs* from a *tropos*- to a *dunamis*-adjective. When at 366b4–5 *hoi pseudeis* become *hoi sophoi te kai dunatoi pseudesthai, pseudēs* ceases to denote one who habitually lies and denotes instead one who has the power to lie. These shifts of meaning inevitably lead the argument into paradox when it concludes that the same man is both *alēthēs* and *pseudēs, alēthēs* and *pseudēs* being taken once again in their initial *tropos*-sense.

Indeed, in order for the conclusion to strike us as paradoxical, *alēthēs* and *pseudēs* must be understood in the *tropos*-sense; only thus will the conclusion read: The truthful man and the liar are the same man. But before we can be certain that this is indeed how the conclusion *ought* to read, we should see if there is ample justification for assuming that Socrates really brings back the *tropos*-sense of *alēthēs* and *pseudēs* on which this reading depends.

As Mulhern has shown, *pseudēs* is reduced to a *dunamis*-adjective at 366b4–5. But from that point on, the dialogue gives not the slightest indication that Socrates in any way regrets this. On the contrary, the text confirms his satisfaction. Once the stipulation that *hoi pseudeis* are *hoi sophoi te kai dunatoi pseudesthai* is made and agreed upon, Socrates ceases to ask questions of definition and proceeds immediately to employ the *dunamis*-sense of *pseudēs* in his illustrations. The assumption that *alēthēs* and *pseudēs* revert to their *tropos*-sense in the conclusion is thus not supported by the text, but seems to be based on nothing more than that this is their ordinary sense. Since, however, new *dunamis*-meanings for these terms were specifically stipulated, this assumption loses what plausibility it might otherwise have had.[9]

If this reasoning is correct, the conclusion retains the *dunamis*-sense of *alēthēs* and *pseudēs*. With this sense, though it reads: The truthful man and the false are the same, it means: The man skilled at speaking truthfully and the man skilled at speaking falsely are the same man;[10] the paradox vanishes.

An analysis similar to this is presented by T. Gomperz who believes the argument to be valid as long as it is understood hypothetically, as follows: If knowledge and ability are the only factors involved in determining whether one is a liar or a truthful man, then the liar and the truthful man are indeed identical.[11] According to Hoerber, too, the conclusion rests on the basis of the admission that *dunamis* is the essential attribute of the truthful man and the deceptive one.[12]

This view leaves Socrates vulnerable on two counts. First, if we say that the argument rests on a hypothesis or an admission which may or may not be true or justified (the implication being that surely it is *not* true or justified, for *is* the essential attribute or factor in the true man and the false really their ability, their *dunamis?*), then even though the validity of the argument remains intact (as Gomperz points out), the conclusion is not certain.

Secondly, as Mulhern could contend, this analysis does not really preserve even the argument's validity, for it ignores Hippias' first stipulation, that is, that *polutropos*, a term designating ability, is to be identified with *pseudēs*, a term which ordinarily describes a man's character. Thus, even if the conclusion does not understand *alēthēs* and *pseudēs* in their usual *tropos*-sense, the argument is none the less invalid because it still contains at least two shifts of meaning (1) from the *dunamis*-term *polutropos* to the *tropos*-term *pseudēs* (365b7–c2), and (2) from *pseudēs* in the *tropos*-sense to *pseudēs* in the *dunamis*-sense (366b4–5), though not the third in which *pseudēs* reverts once more to its initial *tropos*-status.

There may be, however, one way of preserving both the validity of the argument and the truth of the conclusion, by claiming that the argument contains *only dunamis*-terms. Rather than a confusion between *dunamis*-terms and *tropos*-terms, rather than a reduction of the former to the latter and of the latter to the former, what we encounter here is the conspicuous absence of *tropos*-adjectives and the consistent employment of the *dunamis*-sense of *dunamis*-terms as well as a *dunamis*-sense of terms generally considered to be *tropos*-adjectives in everyday discourse. Neither Socrates nor Hippias is to be accused of equivocation; they both use *polutropos* and *pseudēs* throughout as *dunamis*-concepts. From 365b4–5, where Hippias first links *haplous* with *alēthēs* and *polutropos* with *pseudēs*,[13] to 366b4–5, where *hoi pseudeis* become *hoi sophoi te kai dunatoi pseudesthai*, Socrates takes great pains to ascertain that Hippias does indeed literally identify *polutropos* and *pseudēs*, taking both to denote an ability to lie, viewing both as *dunamis*-concepts.[14]

This analysis, even if correct, encounters two major difficulties. Mulhern's account had the merit of making sense of Hippias' identification of *polutropos* and *pseudēs:* since Hippias wished to maintain that *polutropia* is the mark of an inferior man, he needed to supply this otherwise neutral *dunamis*-term with a negative sense. He accomplished this by equating it with the *tropos*-term, *pseudēs*. On the above analysis, however, which insists that *pseudēs* is not a *tropos*-adjective at all in this first argument of the *Hippias Minor,* how can we explain what Hippias hoped to achieve by equating *polutropos* with it?

Furthermore, if both Socrates and Hippias are aware that they are using only *dunamis*-adjectives throughout the argument, the conclusion should strike neither as being paradoxical or problematic. Why, then, does Hippias balk at the suggestion that *ho alēthēs* and *ho pseudēs* in the *dunamis*-sense are the same man?

In order to answer these questions, we must examine the argument in context. At the beginning of the dialogue, we find Socrates trying to determine whether Homer meant Achilles or Odysseus to be the better man. He turns to Hippias because of Hippias' alleged expertise as an interpreter of Homer. Based on his knowledge of the Homeric text, Hippias asserts that Nestor was the wisest, Achilles the bravest, and Odysseus the *polutropōtatos* of the men who went to Troy. Since the term *polutropos* is not clear to Socrates, Hippias acquires the twofold task of (*a*) interpreting it, and (*b*) assigning it a value, ideally the value Homer intended it to have.

For Hippias, *polutropos* is from the first a pejorative word. Hence, Jowett's and Fowler's "wily"[15] is a suitable translation of *polutropos* when Hippias says it. Were this not so, it would be difficult to see why Hippias regards it as obvious that Homer's characterization of Odysseus as *polutropos* makes Odysseus the lesser of the two heroes. For Socrates, on the other hand, it seems that *polutropos,* at least initially, designates a neutral ability, probably meaning something like Mulhern's "resourceful." Thus he cannot understand why Hippias believes that Homer made Odysseus, but not Achilles (364e5–6), *polutropos,* until Hippias explains that since Achilles is *haplous* and *alēthēs,* he could not possibly be *polutropos,* for *polutropos* and *pseudēs* distinguish Odysseus.[16] At this point Socrates realizes that he and Hippias do not share the same conception of *polutropos,* and so, if the discussion is to proceed, he must adjust his conception of *polutropos* to match that of Hippias.

Socrates asks first if Hippias means to identify *polutropos* with *pseudēs* (365b8). When Hippias answers that he does, Socrates (unlike Mulhern!) does not immediately assume that he knows what Hippias has in mind. And so, he continues to inquire: is *ho pseudēs* different from *ho alēthēs* (366c3–4)? Is he *dunatos* in what he does (365d6–7)? Is he *polutropos* and *dunatos* (365e1–2)? Does he deceive by *panourgia* and *phronēsis*

(365e3–4)?[17] Is he ignorant or wise (365e10)? And Hippias answers: *ho pseudēs* differs from *ho alēthēs* (365c1–2); he is *polutropos* and *dunatos* (365e2);[18] he deceives by *panourgia* and *phronēsis* (365e4–5); he knows what he is doing (365e8); he is wise—not ignorant (365e10). But Hippias also adds a few unsolicited qualifications of his own. He says of the *pseudeis: Dunatous egōge kai mala sphodra alla te polla kai exapatān anthrōpous* (365d7–8); *dia tauta kai kakourgousin* (365e8–9); *Sophoi men oun auta ge tauta, exapatān* (365e10–366a1).

Hippias' expansion of his answers beyond the simple "yes" or "no" required by the questions makes this a very significant and revealing exchange. Socrates, on the one hand, keeps asking if the *pseudēs* are *dunatoi, phronimoi, sophoi,* etc., repeatedly emphasizing the neutral *dunamis*-sense of *pseudēs;* he even goes so far as to ask if the *pseudeis* are *polutropoi* (365e2). Hippias, on the other hand, although readily agreeing that his *pseudeis* are *dunatoi, phronimoi, sophoi,* and *polutropoi,* and thus equally affirming the *dunamis*-status of *pseudēs,* insists, however, that the *dunamis* of a *pseudēs* is of a special kind. It is, in particular, an ability, a skill, a know-how, a wisdom, to deceive and do mischief.

Herein lies the key to our first difficulty. The difference between the positions of Socrates and Hippias is not the difference between *tropos*-concepts and *dunamis*-concepts, between terms indicating typical behaviour and terms indicating skill, but rather the difference between two kinds of *dunamis*-concepts, one of which is neutral and the other of which is negative. It is a question of where to place the emphasis in the phrase *dunatous exapatān anthrōpous*; for Socrates, the emphasis belongs on the *dunatous,* for Hippias, on the *exapatān.* Thus, by introducing *pseudēs* as a synonym for *polutropos,* Hippias, though indeed aiming at giving *polutropos* a negative sense, was not substituting a *tropos*-adjective for a *dunamis*-adjective; he was not saying that *ho pseudēs* is a "liar," that is, one who typically lies. Instead, he was supplying the *dunamis* of *ho pseudēs* with a particular content, a content which he thought negatively coloured the *dunamis* itself; though he was indeed saying that *ho pseudēs* is essentially a skilful man, he was furthermore contending that the skill of a *pseudēs* is limited to lying and deceit. Hence, for Hippias, *polutropos,* like "wily" in English indicates a special kind of skill, skill at trickery and deceit. But like *polutropos* in Greek, "wily" is a *dunamis*-term, a term primarily indicating skill, and though it has negative connotations, it is not, as Mulhern believes, a *tropos*-concept concerned with typical behaviour.

It is instructive to note that Hippias does not present Achilles as able or powerful. As the complete opposite of Odysseus, he is said to be *haplous,* an interesting word with a range of meaning comparable to that of *polutropos;* it may mean either "simple" (the opposite of *polutropos* when it means "resourceful"), or "straightforward" (the opposite of *polutropos* when it means "wily"). Presumably, then, when Socrates is puzzled about the meaning of *polutropos* and asks Hippias (364e5–6): *ho Achilleus ou polutropos tōi Homerōi pepoiētai?,* it is because he as yet views *polutropia* as a neutral ability. But when Hippias answers: *Hēkista ge, ō Sōkrates, all' haploustatos kai alēthestatos,* he is simultaneously affirming both the pejorative nature of *polutropos* and the superiority of being *haplous.* The gap between Odysseus and Achilles consists, for Hippias, of the difference between *polutropos* and *haplous.*

This point puts us in a better position to confront our second difficulty. If, as the present interpretation suggests, the argument contains only *dunamis*-terms and hence does not equivocate, the conclusion too contains only *dunamis*-terms and so loses its air of paradox; it now states simply that the man skilled at truth-telling and the man skilled at lying are the same man. But why would Socrates wish to prove so innocuous a proposition? And why would Hippias object to it? Perhaps because it is precisely this that Hippias denied in reserving *polutropos* exclusively for Odysseus and describing Achilles as *haplous*. By linking *alēthēs* with *haplous,* Hippias in effect denies to Achilles (and to *ho alēthēs* in general) the ability and skill to lie.

It is now possible to explain why Socrates twice asks Hippias if (Homer thinks that) *ho alēthēs* and *ho pseudēs* differ (365c3–4; 366a5–6). On the standard interpretation in which *ho alēthēs* and *ho pseudēs* are rendered "the truthful man" and "the liar" respectively, the conclusion that they are the same is so startling that it gains nothing (and perhaps even loses something) by Hippias' having, in the course of the argument, twice affirmed that they differ. Indeed, when earlier we set forth the standard interpretation, it contained no mention of *ho alēthēs* differing from *ho pseudēs* because there was no place to put it; it had no apparent connection to what preceded it or to what followed it. But on the present interpretation, the distinctness of *ho alēthēs* and *ho pseudēs* is crucial. For if, as Hippias asserts, *polutropos* and *pseudēs* are interchangeable (both meaning having the ability to lie), and if, as he furthermore grants, *ho alēthēs and ho pseudēs are different,* then it follows that one who is *alēthēs* does not have the ability to lie and is not *polutropos*. What the rest of the argument is devoted to is the refutation of the notion that *ho alēthēs* does not have the ability to lie.

The argument is as follows:

1. *polutropos* = *pseudēs*.
2. *ho pseudēs* and *ho alēthēs* are different.
3. *ho pseudēs* is the man best able to speak falsely.
4. *ho alēthēs* is the man best able to speak truthfully.[19]
5. In any art or science, the man best able to speak truthfully is the wisest and ablest in that field.
6. In any art or science, the man best able to speak falsely is the wisest and ablest in that field.
7. In any art or science, the man best able to speak truthfully is the man best able to speak falsely, that is, the wisest and ablest man.
8. The man best able to speak truthfully and the man best able to speak falsely are the same man, that is, the wisest and ablest man.
∴ 9. The same man is both *pseudēs* and *alēthēs*.
∴ 10. If Odysseus is *pseudēs* he is also *alēthēs*.
∴ 11. If Achilles is *alēthēs* he is also *pseudēs*.
∴ 12. Achilles and Odysseus are not opposed to one another but are alike.

Perhaps the most striking thing about this argument as it now appears is that three of the four concluding propositions, (9), (10), and (11) flatly contradict proposition (2). Without proposition (2), these would have been either paradoxical results (on the standard interpretation of *alēthēs* and *pseudēs*) or trivial ones (on the present interpretation). But with proposition (2), a proposition which Socrates twice makes a point of establishing, they become instead important steps in the *reductio ad absurdum* of Hippias' notion that by using *polutropos* pejoratively [as synonymous with *pseudēs* (1)], by regarding it specifically as the power to deceive and lie, he can prove the inferiority of Odysseus to Achilles. The final proposition, (12), is thus the decisive rejection of even *this polutropos* as a means of distinguishing between Achilles and Odysseus. By proclaiming the similarity between the two men even on this account of *polutropos,* it declares (*a*) that having the wisdom and power to speak falsely does not brand a man as inferior, and (*b*) that, on the contrary, wisdom and power to speak falsely make the man who has them good in whatever area he has them.[20]

Thus, what Socrates arrives at in this first stage of the *Hippias Minor* is not the paradoxical and scandalous view that the man who typically lies is the same as the man who typically tells the truth (as would be the case were *alēthēs* and *pseudēs* interpreted in their *tropos*-sense), but rather the reasonable view that since the man who is able to lie in a given art or science (*ho pseudēs* as a *dunamis*-term) is the same as the man who is able to speak truthfully in the same art or science (*ho alēthēs* as a *dunamis*-term), both men are *polutropoi,* and neither, with respect to his ability alone, is better or worse than the other.[21] Indeed, in all the arts and sciences, the man with the ability to speak falsely is the good man.

The next stage, Stage II (369b8–373c6), is a transitional one in which Socrates inquires whether it is Odysseus the *polutropos,* or Achilles, who is seen in Homer actually telling lies. As was remarked earlier, it is difficult to see why the question would come up at all if the conclusion of the first argument is that liars and truth-tellers are the same. If they are the same, then whoever is found to be the actual liar is also found to be the actual truth-teller and is thus no worse than the one who does not actually lie.

On the proposed view, however, the final result of the first stage was not the equation of the habitual liar and the habitual truth-teller, but the decisive elimination of *polutropos,* when identified with *pseudēs* in the *dunamis*-sense, as the criterion for distinguishing Achilles from Odysseus. The next logical step would be either (*a*) to look for a new differentiating criterion, or (*b*) to see if *polutropos* was perhaps misinterpreted. Though Socrates never gets to suggest an alternative interpretation for *polutropos,* he does choose (*b*); he questions the propriety of identifying *polutropos* with *pseudēs.*

He reasons as follows: given Homer's characterization of Odysseus as *polutropos,*[22] one would expect, on the view that *polutropia* indicates skill at lying, that Odysseus— not Achilles—is the one who actually lies, especially if only one of them does. But Hippias provided no proof that Odysseus lies other than a passage (*Iliad* 9.308f.) in which Achilles accuses him of such—not one in which he is seen actually to lie.[23] On the other hand, within just fifty lines of that passage, another is found (*Iliad* 9.357f.) in which it is Achilles who lies. If *polutropia* really indicates skill at lying, and if Achilles alone actually lies, why would Homer call Odysseus *polutropos?*[24] Indeed, Socrates argues further that not only is Achilles the one who actually lies, but that it is he who does so *ex epiboulēs* (371a2).[25] In fact, he is so clever (*phronein*) that he outdoes Odysseus in pretending (371a4–6).[26] Hippias disagrees, asserting that Achilles, when he speaks falsely, does so *ouk ex epiboulēs . . . all' akōn* (370e6–7), but Odysseus, when he speaks falsely, does so *hekōn te kai ex epiboulēs.* Furthermore, Achilles speaks falsely only because he is *anapeistheis* (371e1),[27] whereas Odysseus, whether he speaks truthfully or falsely, speaks *epibouleusas* (371e3).[28]

This contrast between Odysseus, the intentional liar, and Achilles, the unintentional, sets the stage for the introduction of the topic to be discussed in the third and final stage of the *Hippias Minor,* that is, if it is the intentional or the unintentional *wrongdoer* who is superior. As was suggested previously, the contrast between the intentional and unintentional *liar* constitutes the link between the first part of the dialogue and the last.

For Socrates assumes that the superiority of the intentional liar to the unintentional was established by the argument of Stage I (*ouk arti ephanēsan hoi ekontes pseudomenoi*[29] *beltious ē hoi akontes?* —371e7–8), and it is Hippias' denial of this that leads to the resumption of the discussion.

It is not at all surprising that Socrates feels that the superiority of the intentional liar has been more than amply demonstrated in Stage I. Given Hippias' concessions that (*a*) the ablest man in calculation, geometry, and astronomy and in all the *technai* and *epistēmai* is he who is able to speak falsely in these matters (366e1–367a5), (*b*) only the man who does what he wishes when he wishes (*hos an poiēi tote ho an boulētai, hotan boulētai*—366b8–c1)[30] is *dunatos* (366b7), and (*c*) the *agathos* is the *dunatos* (367c5–6),[31] the inference that the intentional liar[32] (i.e. the liar who lies when he wishes and only then) is better than the unintentional (who, as *adunatos,* cannot, of course, be *agathos*), surely stands on firm ground.

What is perhaps more surprising is that Hippias denies the inference. One possibility that suggests itself is that Hippias does not make the connection between the kind of falsehood discussed in Stage I, that is, falsehood in the arts and sciences, with the falsehood of Odysseus and Achilles in Stage II which he regards as a clear case of wrongdoing.[33] (Were it not wrongdoing, why would Achilles' only defence be the unintentionality of the act?) Indeed, it is Hippias who restates the contrast between Odysseus and Achilles, previously stated by Socrates in terms of voluntary and involuntary *pseudesthai,* in terms of voluntary and involuntary *adikein* (371e9).

It is interesting to note that Socrates expresses no doubts about the proposition that the voluntary *liar* is better than the involuntary; he therefore regards the case for Odysseus' superiority as closed: *Ameinōn ar' estin, hōs eoiken, ho Odusseus Achilleōs* (371e4–5). But when Hippias replaces this proposition with: *hoi hekontes* adikountes *kai hekontes epibouleusantes kai kaka ergasamenoi beltious an eien tōn akontōn* (371e9–372a2), Socrates claims to be greatly confused and confesses a tendency to change his mind. At the same time, however, despite Hippias' horror and his own professed uncertainty, Socrates states that at least for now it does seem to him that voluntary evildoers are superior. Furthermore, he attributes his present condition to the previous argument, as he says: *aitiōmai de tou nun parontos pathēmatos tous emprosthen logous aitious einai, hōste phainesthai nun en tōi paronti tous akontas toutōn hekasta poiountas ponēroteros ē tous hekontas.*

In so saying, Socrates both establishes a connection between the first and third stages of the dialogue and explains this connection: it is because the argument of Stage I suggests that one who acts involuntarily in anything is worse than one who acts voluntarily (*tous akontas . . . tous hekontas*), that he is now inclined to believe that even involuntary *wrongdoers* are worse than voluntary (372e2–3).

But even though there is this definite link between Stage I and Socrates' present predicament, it is surely not as rigorous a connection as that between the first argument and the superiority of voluntary *liars*. For, as noted earlier, Socrates regards the superiority of *hoi hekontes pseudomenoi* as an obvious consequence of the previous argument and hesitates not at all in affirming it as such. This would seem to indicate that for Socrates, if not for Hippias, what is true about *hoi hekontes pseudomenoi* is not necessarily true about *hoi hekontes adikountes.*[34] It is in order to explore the new possibility that intentional *adikountes* are like all other intentional ''doers'' discussed up to this point (including intentional liars) that Socrates resumes the discussion.

Let us proceed then to Stage III. The argument of this third and final stage of the *Hippias Minor* invites Hippias to compare (*a*) one who intentionally does poorly with one who does poorly unintentionally in all forms of bodily exercise requiring strength and/or grace, for example, running and wrestling; (*b*) organs which are intentionally defective with organs which are unintentionally defective[35]—voices, feet, eyes, ears; (*c*) instruments with which one does poorly intentionally with those with which one does poorly unintentionally, for example, rudders, musical instruments, horses, and dogs (here regarded as instruments for man's use); and (*d*) *psuchai* which intentionally exercise their skills badly with those which exercise their skills badly unintentionally, such as the *psuchai* of archers, users of the bow, physicians, flute-players, lute-players, and slaves.[36] In each instance, Hippias agrees that the first in the pair is preferable to the second. With this granted, Socrates proceeds to ask Hippias about ''our'' *psuchai;* are they analogous to the other *psuchai* discussed; are those that do wrong voluntarily superior? Anticipating the conclusion that *hoi hekontes adikountes* will turn out to be better than *hoi akontes,* Hippias jumps the gun and denies it. But Socrates goes on with the argument:

1. Justice is either a power (*dunamis tis*), knowledge (*epistēmē*), or both.
2. If justice is a power (of the soul), the more powerful the soul, the more just.
3. If justice is both power and knowledge, then the wiser and more powerful soul will be the more just.
4. The soul which is more powerful and wiser is the better.
5. The better soul is better able to do both good and evil (since it is more powerful and wiser).
6. The soul which does bad intentionally does shameful things (*aischra*) by power and art (*technē*).
7. Acting unjustly (*adikein*) is doing bad things (*kaka*).
8. The abler and better soul acts unjustly intentionally.
9. The bad soul acts unjustly unintentionally.
10. The good man has the good soul.
11. The bad man has the bad soul.
12. The good man acts unjustly intentionally.
13. The bad man acts unjustly unintentionally.
∴ 14. He who sins (*hamartanōn*) and does shameful and unjust things (*aischra kai adika poiōn*) is the good man (*ho agathos*).

There are two important ways in which this argument goes further than the argument in Stage I. First, it leaves no doubt that in each of the four categories considered the action being done is bad. In case, as we suggested, Hippias did not connect the falsehood discussed in Stage I with doing bad (and for this reason, once he did perceive the lying of Odysseus and Achilles as bad, he resisted Socrates' assertion in Stage II that intentional liars are superior), Socrates in Stage III positively eliminates the possibility of viewing the actions he discusses as anything but bad. Thus, the runner who runs slowly intentionally is not doing something good, but rather something *kakon kai aischron* (373e1) in the race. Similarly, he who is better does with his body *ponēra* (374b2) intentionally. In terms of grace, the better man assumes *ta aischra kai ponēra schēmata* (374b6). Blinking is a *ponēria* (374d3) of the eyes, senses act *kaka* (374e1), a man steers *kakōs* (374e4), one rides horses *kakōs* (374a2), one produces *ta ponēra* with horses, and so, in all the arts and sciences, the *psuchē: ta kaka ergazetai kai ta aischra kai examartanei* (375c1–2).

Secondly, Socrates states that whatever is better is better because it is good, and whatever is worse is worse because it is bad.[38] In Stage I, the comparison between two able men, *ho alēthēs* and *ho pseudēs*, showed that they were the same and that *ouden ameinōn ho alēthēs tou pseudous* (367c8–d1). But here, in Stage III, where the comparison is between the intentional evildoer and the unintentional, not only is the former better than the latter, but the former is also good and the latter bad.[39] Hence, when discussing the runner, Socrates says not only that the better (*ameinōn*—373d6) runner runs slowly voluntarily, but that the good (*agathos*—373e4) runner does.[40] Similarly, when Hippias says he would prefer the intentionally unmusical voice since it is better, Socrates asks (374c5–6): "And would you choose to possess goods (*tagatha*) or evils (*ta kaka*)?" Also, with regard to the senses, those which involuntarily perform poorly are undesirable *hōs ponēras* (374e1), and those which voluntarily perform poorly are to be desired *hōs agathas* (374e2). Although the argument generally emphasizes better/worse rather than good/evil, this is probably because of the form of the hypothesis it tests, that is the intentional wrongdoer is *better than* the unintentional, phrased also in comparative rather than absolute terms. As the argument makes clear, however, the one which is better is better because it is good; the one which is worse is worse because it is bad.

Having said this, let us inquire if the argument is valid. As was the case in Stage I's argument, here too the fallacy of which the argument is accused is equivocation. The commonly alleged equivocations are on the words (*a*) *agathos*, which may mean either good at something or morally good, (*b*) *ameinōn*, which may mean either better at something or morally better, and (*c*) *hekōn*, which may refer either to one's ability or to what one desires.[41] If there is equivocation, one must consider (as the critics indeed have) whether or not the equivocation is intentional on Plato's part and, if so, what purpose it serves and if it is justified. Not all those who accept the equivocation agree on its purpose and justification. Some accuse Plato of sophistry because of it,[42] others excuse it on the grounds that Hippias deserves no better,[43] some think it a device to trap opponents,[44] others a challenge to the reader.[45]

However, as in Stage I, it seems more likely that the words are used in *one* (probably non-standard) sense consistently. It is perhaps unfair to impose on *agathos*, for example, our expression "morally good," when such an imposition is not supported by anything in the argument. If the argument generally uses *agathos* to mean "good at something" or "good for something," then perhaps this is the meaning it intends throughout. But the question then arises with regard to *ho agathos* himself: is he not "morally" good? The answer can only be that in terms of Stage III he is none the less also "good at" something, that is, justice.[46] Similarly, the "better" man, soul, instrument, sense, or athlete is *ameinōn*, understood as the comparative of the *agathos* which means "good at" or "good for" something. *Hekōn*, too, when attached to the commission of acts, is probably unambiguous, always indicating that the acts are done *only* when the agent wishes; it denotes neither sheer ability nor pure desire. It does, however, imply that one has the ability to carry out one's desire.

It must be conceded that it is somewhat more difficult to be certain that there is no equivocation in Stage III than it was in Stage I, for there, unlike here, a great deal of space was devoted to questions of definition. But even in Stage III, this view has some measure of confirmation. We have, for one thing, Socrates' own satisfaction with the argument to reassure us. For although he voices strong doubts about the conclusion (*oude gar egō emoi* [*sunchōrēsō*]—376b8), he has little doubt that it is compelled by the argument (*anankaion . . . ek tou logou*—376b8–c1). It seems fair to say that Hippias, too, shows no resistance during the argument, at least not until he grasps its implications (375d3–6). We shall assume, then, that since the argument is not nonsensical when the words *agathos, ameinōn,* and *hekōn* are understood throughout in the senses stipulated here, and since it receives the approval of both Socrates and Hippias, though neither is pleased with its conclusion, that there is no equivocation. This assumption, of course, completely relieves us of the task of either defending or prosecuting Plato for his alleged intentional (or even unintentional) equivocation.

We are free then to proceed to consider the point of the argument. Here the job is simpler because the argument accomplishes precisely what it sets out to, to prove that the intentional wrongdoer is better than the unintentional. Though the final conclusion is put in absolute rather than relative terms, that is the man who does wrong intentionally is *ho agathos* rather than *ameinōn* than the man who does so unintentionally, this is easily accounted for by the earlier stipulation that whatever is better/preferable is so because it is good.

One fascinating thing about the argument is that the word *adikein* is conspicuously absent from the exchange until Hippias introduces it (as he did in Stage II as well) at 375d4. Socrates uses the term *hamartanein* or *examartanein* for ''doing the wrong thing,'' or else either *poiein* or *ergazesthai* + *ta kaka, ponēra,* or *aischra,*[47] through 375b8–c2, where he says: *kai talla panta ta kata tas technas te kai tas epistēmas, ouchi hē ameinōn hekousa ta kaka ergazetai kai ta aischra kai examartanei, hē de ponērotera akousa.*[48] At 375c3, when Socrates considers the *psuchai* of slaves, he introduces for the first time in Stage III the term *kakourgousas* (375c5),[49] which he continues to use in the case of ''our'' *psuchē,* saying: *Oukoun beltiōn estai, ean hekousa kakourgēi te kai examartanēi, ē ean akousa?* (375d1–2). But it is Hippias who recasts this comparison in terms of *hoi adikountes,* declaring: *Deinon mentan eiē, ō Sōkrates, ei hoi hekontes adikountes beltious esontai ē hoi akontes* (375d3–4).

What is striking about all this is how closely it resembles what took place in Stage II. There, as we pointed out, Socrates inferred from the argument of Stage I that voluntary *pseudomenoi* are better than involuntary, but Hippias was shocked by an inference of his own invention, that voluntary *adikountes* are better than involuntary. In Stage III, as well, Socrates infers from his *epagoge* that the soul which *hekousa kakourgēi* is better than *akousa,* but Hippias protests against an inference he himself originates, that is, once again, that *hoi hekontes adikountes* are better than *hoi akontes.*

It is interesting to note, further, how similarly Socrates reacts to Hippias' introduction of *hoi adikountes* here and earlier. In Stage II, Socrates found that the argument of Stage I inclined him to believe that *hoi hekontes adikountes* are superior, but he still felt that this startling superiority required further investigation; hence Stage III. And here, within Stage III itself, Socrates again says that he thinks the superiority of *hoi hekontes adikountes* follows from what was said (375d5) (and is even surprised that Hippias does not think so—375d7), yet he continues his *elenchus,* beckoning Hippias *palin d' apokrinai* (375d7–8). But if Hippias has already grasped the conclusion, why does Socrates go on?

It seems that what we have here is a sample of Socratic intellectual honesty. Though the Socrates of the *Hippias Minor* has been accused of deceit and sophistry, he has surely been unjustly maligned. Twice in the argument Hippias prematurely concludes that voluntary *adikountes* are superior, but neither time does Socrates let the discussion go at that. And it is not as if he keeps the argument going until he gains Hippias' approval, for though the argument ends, *that* never happens. What we witness here is Socrates continuing the *elenchus* until he is satisfied that the conclusion has adequate support from the argument, not being content merely to "trap" Hippias.

What, then, does Socrates think is lacking in the argument? Why is the *epagoge* thus far unable to support the conclusion? The easiest way to see what is missing is to see what Socrates supplies. What he supplies is the proposition that *dikaiosunē* is a *dunamis, epistēmē,* or both. Indeed, without this proposition, (1) we could not appreciate the similarity between *adikein* and, say, *kakourgein, hamartanein,* or *pseudesthai;* (2) none of the cases drawn upon in the *epagoge* would parallel *hoi adikountes* and thus what is true of them would not necessarily be true of *hoi adikountes;* (3) *hoi hekontes adikountes* could not be conclusively shown to be better; and (4) we could not know who is the good man.

(1) Unless *dikaiosunē* were a *dunamis, epistēmē,* or both, we could not appreciate the similarity between *adikein* and all other forms of wrongdoing. In Stage I, where the form of wrongdoing dealt with was speaking falsely, it was shown that the good man is the man with the ability to speak falsely as well as truthfully. But it was always understood that the ability to speak falsely as well as truthfully occurs in specific areas of expertise. Hence, Socrates asks Hippias to review all his arts and sciences and those of others and see if he can discover in any of them a difference between *ho alēthēs* and *ho pseudēs* (368e1–369a2), confidently predicting that he cannot. And furthermore, "the good man" (*ho agathos*) is everywhere equivalent to the good artist or scientist, that is, the man skilled in a particular field. Hence, the good and wise arithmetician is also called the good man (376c6), as is the good and wise geometer (367e4). Thus, in Stage I, *ho agathos,* like *ho alēthēs* and *ho pseudēs,* is an incomplete expression, requiring specification of the art or science in which the man is skilled. In the conclusion of Stage I, where *ho alēthēs* (Achilles) and *ho pseudēs* (Odysseus) are compared, the implication is that since truth-telling and lying take place within the various *technai* and *epistēmai,* whenever either possesses skill in lying, he simultaneously possesses skill in truth-telling because he is an expert in the matter in which he is able to speak falsely or truthfully at will. For the same reason, in Stage II, the man who lies intentionally is the better man, for he is the expert in the field in which he lies.

Similarly, in Stage III, where intentional as opposed to unintentional wrongdoing is discussed, the wrongdoing (*hamartanein, poiein kaka, ergazesthai ponēra, kakourgein,* etc.) always takes place within an area of *epistēmē* or an area which requires *dunamis.* Thus, one may do ill in running (i.e., run slowly) and in other bodily exercises, or something may fulfil its function poorly (e.g., an eye its seeing, etc.), or something may be used for performing a particular skill poorly (e.g., a rudder for steering, a horse for riding, an archer's soul for hitting the target, a physician's soul for healing, a slave's soul, presumably, for fulfilling his master's will, etc.). And, as Hippias agrees, when someone performs some art badly or some instrument is used badly intentionally, he/it is the better.

But, when the discussion turns to *hoi adikountes,* the problem arises that these wrongdoers apparently do not perform badly within a *technē* or *epistēmē* which requires *dunamis,* but rather simply do wrong. However, unless they do wrong within *technai* and *epistēmai,* they are unlike all the wrongdoers thus far considered. In order to dispel this glaring difference, a *technē* or *epistēmē* must be found for *hoi adikountes,* and the one Socrates comes up with is *dikaiosunē.*

(2) Unless *dikaiosunē* were a *dunamis, epistēmē,* or both, none of the conclusions reached about the cases used in the *epagoge* would necessarily apply to *hoi adikountes.* Since the entire *epagoge* is based on doing wrong within an art or science or being used in performing some function badly, unless *adikein* were also doing wrong in the sense of misusing a skill or performing badly within an art or science, anything proved by the *epagoge* would not apply to it. Therefore, Socrates must stipulate a skill or science in which *ho hekōn hamartanōn* would be *ho hekōn adikōn;* he stipulates *dikaiosunē.*

(3) Unless *dikaiosunē* were a *dunamis, epistēmē,* or both, *hoi hekontes adikountes* could not be conclusively shown to be better. Only in skills, arts, and sciences were the intentional wrongdoers found to be better. Hence, intentional *adikountes* could not be proved better unless their wrongdoing occurred within a specific field. The specific field in which *hoi adikountes* do badly is *dikaiosunē.* With a field thus specified, Socrates is able to resume his former terminology, making *adikein* equivalent to *kaka poiein* (376a5), and calling the good man *ho . . . hekōn hamartanōn kai aischra kai adika poiōn* (376b5).

(4) Unless *dikaiosunē* were a *dunamis, epistēmē,* or both, we could not know who is the good man. In all the arts and sciences, the good man is the good artist or scientist, the man with skill or ability in his area of expertise. But to find simply *ho agathos* (as opposed to the good geometer, astronomer, flute-player, slave, etc.), we need to find the skill of man *qua* man. This is *dikaiosunē.* [50]

Of course, one might wish to suggest that the good man is the man who does *kala* and *dikaia.* But this will not help us to choose between the intentional and unintentional *adikōn.* Interestingly, the *epagoge,* in a sense, provides for *two* definitions of the good man, one in terms of doing just deeds, and one in terms of doing unjust deeds intentionally, when it defines the good runner in *two* ways: the good runner is both the one who *eu theōn* (373d1) and the one who *hekōn to kakon touto ergazetai kai to aischron* (373e4–5). Thus, by analogy, if justice is an art or science or skill, the good man would be the one who does just things and/or the one who does bad things intentionally.

It is very important that we distinguish these two senses of *ho agathos.* For although an examination of the activities of a man will suffice to determine whether or not he is *ho agathos* in the first sense—if he regularly performs *ta kala* and *ta dikaia* he *is ho agathos* in this sense and if not, not, such an examination will help not at all in discovering whether or not a man is *ho agathos* in the second sense. A man may do good things *or* bad things and still be *ho agathos* in this second sense, for what is at stake is skill, and skill is determined not by result but by the control the agent has over the result. Thus what we need to examine is the intentionality or unintentionality of the deed—whether good or bad—in order to decide if the agent is *ho agathos* in the sense at issue here. A man who performs *kala* and *dikaia* may or may not be *ho agathos* in this second sense; only if he performs these good acts *intentionally* is he *ho agathos. Anyone* may perform good acts unintentionally, but one who does so is certainly not *agathos.* [51]

Assuming, then, that the argument is valid and the conclusion which indeed follows from the argument is that *ho agathos* is he who sins intentionally, it becomes necessary to ask if this outcome is really scandalous.

If we attend closely to the dialogue, we discover that, throughout, it is the superiority or inferiority of the agent (or of his instrument or soul) which is the issue—not that of the act performed. There is no suggestion anywhere that, for example, the intentional *lie* is better than the unintentional,[52] but rather that the intentional *liar* is better because more skilled. Similarly, running slowly intentionally is not said to be better than running slowly unintentionally, but rather it is said that he who runs slowly intentionally is the better runner. Thus, whereas it would be disgraceful indeed if intentional injustice were better than unintentional, and *a fortiori*, if it were good, it is surely not so *deinon* for the better man, the more able man, to be the one who commits injustice voluntarily.[53]

It is this point which enables the *Hippias Minor* to plead innocent to the charge of immorality. For in locating the goodness or badness of the agent in the intentionality or unintentionality with which he performs his acts[54] rather than in the value of the acts themselves, the *Hippias Minor* is never compelled to attempt to purge an evil act of its evilness: on the contrary, the dialogue insists upon the badness of all the acts it considers.[55] Indeed, the arguments of both Stage I and Stage III go no further than to assert that the better (or good) man in all *technai* and *epistēmai* is the one who is *dunatos* and *sophos*.

Ho agathos of the *Hippias Minor* is thus not the standard *agathos* who is judged on the basis of his actions. Since the agent in this dialogue is judged solely on the basis of his skill, things may be said with impunity about this man that could not be said so freely about the ordinary *ho agathos*. We need only bear in mind that *ho agathos* here is "the man *skilled at* justice"—not "the just man."

Having come this far, we face the problem of determining what Plato's purpose could possibly have been in having Socrates reach a paradoxical-sounding conclusion about a non-standard *agathos*. And, of course, if this conclusion is valid based on premises elicited by Socrates himself, we must wonder why he is dissatisfied with it.[56] If Plato claims no more than that the good man is wise and able and hence does wrong only intentionally, why does he have Socrates wonder if there are any such men (*eiper tis estin houtos*—376b5–6)? These difficulties, as stated at the outset, are beyond the scope of this essay, which has attempted only to lay the groundwork for the inquiry into them.

NOTES

1. It is difficult to maintain, as only very few nineteenth-century scholars nevertheless have, that the *Hippias Minor* is actually spurious, particularly since Aristotle mentions and discusses it (*Met.* 4. 29. 1025a6–13), but it is likely, as Paul Friedländer remarks, that "without the explicit testimony of Aristotle, probably few critics would consider the *Hippias Minor* a genuine Platonic work." See Friedländer's *Plato*, trans. H. Meyerhoff (Princeton: Princeton University Press, 1964), ii, 146.

2. Besides these there are also (*a*) the shocking conclusions reached in the dialogue, (*b*) the *aporia* with which the dialogue ends, and (*c*) Socrates' alleged "hint" at 376b5–6 (*eiper tis estin houtos*) that the dialogue's conclusion is not to be taken seriously (since no one actually does do wrong intentionally), all of which cry out for interpretation. But none of these,

nor the irony and caricature, affects the validity of the arguments or the morality of their conclusions.

3. See, e.g., R. G. Hoerber, "Plato's Lesser Hippias," *Phronesis* 7 (1962), 121–31, who thinks that this view is supported by Eudicus' appearing twice in the dialogue, once in the beginning and once in the middle, thereby dividing the dialogue into two parts. In general, Hoerber is fascinated by the dialogue's twos: two propositions, two Homeric heroes, two famous Socratic doctrines (i.e. "No one does wrong willingly" and "Virtue is knowledge"), two characters carrying on the discussion, and two appearances by Eudicus. In my opinion, however, Eudicus' appearance confirms the dialogue's continuity, its integrity, rather than its duality.

4. The term "involuntary liars" may seem peculiar, if not outright self-contradictory, for a "liar" is normally one who intentionally speaks falsely in order to deceive. However, it does seem a suitable translation of *hoi akontes pseudomenoi,* which may be just as peculiar an expression in Greek as "involuntary liars" is in English. The intended sense is, of course, "involuntary speakers of falsehoods."

5. Interestingly, R. K. Sprague who, in her *Plato's Use of Fallacy* (London: Routledge, 1962), also emphasizes the unity of the dialogue when she claims that the *Hippias Minor* "consists of a single argument (with variations)," p. 65, offers an analysis of the earlier part of the dialogue which is very similar to the one proposed here (see Sprague, pp. 66–70). Hence her interpretation is not embraced by our reference to the "usual" or "standard" interpretation. The major (and irreconcilable) difference between her interpretation and mine, however, is that she believes that the dialogue contains equivocation and I do not.

6. J. J. Mulhern, "*Tropos* and *polytropia* in Plato's *Hippias Minor,*" *Phoenix* 22 (1968), 283–8. There are, of course, other ways of characterizing the equivocation in the first argument. Hoerber emphasizes the dialogue's pervasive confusion, which he regards as Plato's way of challenging his readers. The pairs of terms he thinks are intentionally confused in the first argument are *dunatoi/sophoi* and *panourgia/phronēsis.* Sprague says that Socrates uses two ambiguous terms in the first argument: (*a*) "power," which can be either for good or for evil, and (*b*) "wiliness," which can be either the shiftiness of the false man or the intellectual ability which enables such a man to carry out his designs. Like Hoerber, she also sees the equivocations as intentional (pp. 67–8).

7. The term *tropos* is found at 365b3–4, where Hippias says that the *tropos* of Achilles and Odysseus as set forth by Homer is such that Achilles is *alēthēs* and *haplous,* and Odysseus *polutropos* and *pseudēs.* This passage, however, does not seem to support Mulhern's view that Plato makes an intentional pun on *polutropos,* for the way in which he uses *tropos* does not suggest that he restricts it to words describing man's typical behaviour; on the contrary, it seems that, for Plato, a man's *tropos* is any way in which he can be characterized.

8. Mulhern excuses Socrates' equivocation as an expression of his justified objection to Hippias' mixing of *dunamis*- and *tropos*-concepts in distinguishing Achilles and Odysseus (p. 287).

9. With respect to arithmetic and calculation, Hippias, who is able to tell falsehoods *dunatōtata* (366d6), is thus the *pseudēs peri logismon* (367c5); in geometry, the man who *mē dunamenos pseudesthai* is not *pseudēs* (367e5–6); in astronomy, *ho agathos astronomos pseudēs estai, ho dunatos pseudesthai* (368a4–5).

10. This precisely parallels what is said in the astronomy example: *kai en astronomiai ara eiper tis kai allos pseudēs, ho agathos astronomos pseudēs estai, ho dunatos pseudesthai . . . Ho autos ara kai en astronomiai alēthēs te kai pseudēs estai* (368a3–7).

11. T. Gomperz, in *Greek Thinkers,* trans. L. Magnus (London, 1920), ɪɪ, 296, takes this argument to be a *reductio ad absurdum* of the idea that all that is involved in action is knowledge; choice of ends is important, too.

12. Hoerber, p. 126.

13. On the proposed interpretation, as we shall see, the comparison Hippias draws between

Achilles and Odysseus has far more bearing on the argument than it had on the standard interpretation in which the comparison was merely a literary device to introduce the argument but did not actually affect it. On the present interpretation, however, Hippias' description (in Homer's name) of Achilles as *haplous*—usually rendered "simple"—and *alēthēs,* and of Odysseus as *polutropos* and *pseudēs* will play a crucial role.

14. There is a difference between the claim of Gomperz and Hoerber that the argument rests on the hypothesis that the essential factor or attribute of a truthful or false man in his *dunamis* and the claim made here that the substantives "truthful" (*alēthēs*) and "false" (*pseudēs*) are throughout the argument shorthand for "the man skilled at speaking truthfully" and "the man skilled at lying," respectively. Whereas, in the former case, one may sensibly ask "Is it true that the essential attribute of a truthful man is his *dunamis* to speak truthfully?," in the latter, it is nonsense to ask "Is it true that the essential attribute of a man skilled at truth-telling is his skill at truth-telling?" In the former case, Socrates can perhaps be blamed for missing the essential nature of *ho alēthēs* and *ho pseudēs;* in the latter, since he is only ascertaining what Hippias means by *pseudēs,* blame would be entirely out of place.

15. "Wily" is a suitable translation of *polutropos* because (*a*) it suggests the cleverness which is essential, and (*b*) it is a word which, while having an appropriately pejorative taint, does not go so far as to become a *tropos*-adjective like, say, "wicked" or "treacherous."

16. Hoerber points out that when this word characterized Odysseus in the first line of the *Odyssey,* it probably meant "much travelled," "much wandering," though Hippias takes it in its other sense meaning "crafty," "shifty," "clever," or "versatile" when equating it with *pseudēs* (pp. 124–5). But Mulhern makes a distinction even within this second sense between *dunamis*- and *tropos*-terms; he would probably consider "crafty" and "shifty" *tropos*-terms, and "clever" and "versatile" *dunamis*-terms, like his own "resourceful."

17. At this point, Socrates has not yet finished probing Hippias' intention in identifying *polutropos* and *pseudēs.* While it is true that the question: "Does *ho pseudēs* deceive *hupo panourgias kai phronēseōs tinos?*" may suggest that the skill of the *pseudēs* is not part of the very meaning of *pseudēs* but is merely *that with which* the *pseudēs* does his deceiving, since the cross-examination is not yet complete, it is too soon to decide. By 366b4–5, however, Socrates is asking not merely if *hoi pseudeis* are *sophoi* but if they are *hoi sophoi te kai dunatoi pseudesthai* and receiving an unequivocal *nai* for an answer.

18. It is incorrect to say here, as Gomperz does, that Socrates "wrings" this admission from Hippias (p. 291). Considering that Hippias equates *polutropos* with *psuedēs,* it is very reasonable for Socrates to ask if *pseudēs* are *dunatoi* and Hippias answers readily—with no hesitation—that they are.

19. This is the crucial move (367c6). It flatly contradicts Hippias' association of *alēthēs* with *haplous,* for here the good man and *ho dunatos* are one and the same. (See n. 31). Cf. Sprague, who presents a similar analysis of the argument in general (pp. 66–70), and also perceives this is the crucial move (p. 68).

20. Thus Socrates in effect denies what Hippias (and Homer on Hippias' interpretation) had affirmed, i.e. that *ho alēthēs* is *haplous.* On the contrary, *ho alēthēs* is *polutropos.*

21. This is in fact a return to Socrates' initial position that both are *polutropoi,* only now *polutropos* means "having ability *in lying.*" But, for Socrates, things have not really changed at all.

22. This he does in line 1 of the *Odyssey.*

23. Although Hippias could no doubt have found passages in which Odysseus does lie (particularly in the *Odyssey*), had Plato allowed him to cite those, Socrates' question here would not make sense.

24. There is thus no reason to believe that in seeking the man who actually lies, Socrates returns to a *tropos*-sense of *polutropos.* He merely regards actual lying as an indication of possible skill at lying.

25. Indeed, Socrates is aware that it is not enough to show that Achilles actually lies in order to show that he is *polutropos*, presumably because even people who are not *polutropoi* do lie—out of ignorance; he must show that Achilles' lying is voluntary. This accounts for the *ge* when Socrates says: *ho de Achilleus polutropos tis phainetai kata ton son logon; pseudetai goun* (370a1–2); the fact of lying is not more than an indication that *polutropia* may be present in the liar.

It is important to point out here that the first argument, as it was presented on the "usual" interpretation, contained as its second premiss the statement: "Only the man who has the power, ability, and wisdom in the matters in which he is false can be false." This seems to contradict what is being said here, i.e. that many people lie without being powerful or wise. On the revised analysis of the first argument, however, the word *pseudēs* no longer means "one who lies," but rather "one who is skilled at lying." Thus, at 366b6–7, when Socrates says: *Adunatos ara pseudesthai anēr kai amathēs ouk an eiē pseudēs,* he is to be understood as saying not that one who has no skill and is ignorant cannot lie, but rather that one who has no skill and is ignorant cannot be a *pseudēs,* a man skilled at lying.

26. The emphasis on Achilles' superiority to Odysseus in cunning shows that it is Achilles who is *dunatos* even in lying, and hence Hippias must surely be mistaken in his claim that *polutropos* means skilled in lying: if it does, why does Homer call Odysseus—rather than Achilles—*polutropos?*

27. Hippias means by this that Achilles had no intention of deceiving, "but the force of external circumstances had brought his actions into disaccord with his words; it was the desperate position of the army that had prevented him from withdrawing, as he had threatened," Gomperz, p. 292. As Socrates will show, if this is the case, then Achilles is indeed the *inferior.* Although Gomperz thinks this is a just defence of Achilles on Hippias' part, that is beside the point, for Achilles manifests the inability to tell the truth whenever he wishes. (This case, in which Achilles is prevented from telling the truth by "external circumstances," is not the same as the case of extenuating circumstances described by Socrates earlier (366b), i.e. being prevented by disease or some such thing; in which case, it could, presumably, still be true that one is skilled. In Achilles' case, however, there is a definite lack of ability.)

28. This certainly shows that Hippias is concerned not with Odysseus' *tropos* but with his *dunamis* with *how* Odysseus speaks—both when he is and when he is *not* lying.

29. *Pseudomenoi* is the word used for liars; *tropos* is reserved for those skilled at lying, *hoi pseudeis = hoi hekontes pseudomenoi.*

30. Cf. 366b2–3: *poteron legeis dunatous einai pseudesthai ean boulōntai.*

31. Cf. 366d3–5: Socrates asks Hippias if he is only wisest and ablest in arithmetic and calculation, or if he is also the best, and Hippias says he is also the best. Socrates makes sure there that Hippias sees a connection between wisest and ablest, on the one hand, and best, on the other, so that the connection between *agathos* and *dunatos* is not new.

32. Even though *hekōn* is not used but rather *boulomenos pseudesthai, akōn* is used (367a3) as the opposite of *boulomenos* to mean, with respect to lying, "not (only) when one wishes to," *akōn* implies *to mē eidenai*—not knowing (367a3).

33. There is, of course, no excuse for this because if he does not see all cases of lying as bad, there was no point in his substituting *pseudēs* for *polutropos.*

34. Socrates seems aware of the change because, when he states his present belief, he talks of *kai adikountes kai pseudomenoi kai exapatōntes kai hamartanontes hekontes* (372d5–6). As we shall see, *hoi adikountes* require a stipulation beyond what *hoi hamartanontes* do, although both of these are new to the discussion. Interestingly, this is the last time we see Achilles and Odysseus in the dialogue; by dropping their names, Socrates also signals that a new topic is beginning.

35. Socrates speaks of these as doing the actions themselves, except in the case of eyes, *with* which the blinking is done voluntarily.

36. Though not specified, the skill of slaves is presumably to carry out their master's wishes well.
37. *Technē* substitutes for *epistēmē* here, with *dunamis,* in both cases, being the alternative. There is no change in meaning implied. Hoerber attempts to show that Socrates distinguishes between Hippias' *technai* and the previously discussed *epistēmai* such as arithmetic, geometry, and astronomy (368b1–2), but drops the distinction when it flies past Hippias (375b8–e1), p. 126. The fact is, however, that Socrates never distinguishes between the two terms in this dialogue. He does not distinguish Hippias' crafts from *epistēmai,* but rather calls those crafts *epistēmai,* asking Hippias to consider with respect to *pasōn tōn epistēmōn* if the same principle holds. The *epistēmai* he goes on to enumerate are all Hippias' *technai.*
38. Perhaps this is what W. K. C. Guthrie (*A History of Greek Philosophy* IV, Cambridge, 1975, p. 195) means when he accuses Socrates of "treating as absolute contraries what are matters of degree only."
39. This is foreshadowed in Stage I where the good man is the able man just as the ablest and wisest man is the best. See n. 31.
40. There are two definitions of the good runner, (1) he who runs well (373d2), and (2) he who runs slowly—*bradeōs* (= poorly *kakōs* 373d3), intentionally (373e4).
41. Guthrie sees equivocation on *agathos* which can mean either good, as a technical accomplishment, or morally good; the equivocation on *hekōn* confuses "able and willing" with "able" alone (p. 195). Hoerber sees confusion between *ameinōn* and *beltiōn,* only the latter of which has moral connotations, p. 127. (If this is true, it is very difficult to see why Socrates uses *beltiōn* about instruments!) Mulhern characterizes the equivocation on (*a*) *agathos,* such that it can be either neutral (good at something—*a dunamis*-concept), or evaluative (a *tropos*-concept), (*b*) *hekōn,* such that it can either refer to what is in our power (a *dunamis*-concept) or to what we normally wish (a *tropos*-concept), and (*c*) *ameinōn,* such that it can be either the comparative of the *dunamis*-sense of *agathos* or that of its *tropos*-sense. Applied to the voluntary wrongdoer, the one who has it in his power to do wrong is indeed the better in the *dunamis*-sense, but one who normally wishes to do bad is probably not better in the *tropos*-sense, p. 288. For Sprague, the major fallacy is the move from powerful (to do evil), to powerful, to better (morally); so it turns out that he who does evil voluntarily (i.e. because he has the power) is better (morally) than he who makes mistakes involuntarily, p. 77.
42. G. Grote, in *Plato and the Other Companions of Sokrates* (London, 1865) 1:394, following Steinhart, thinks that the historical Socrates did use the Sophistic style of speaking. Cf. p. 258.
43. Mulhern, for example, excuses the equivocation because he thinks Hippias confuses *tropos*- and *dunamis*-terms (p. 286).
44. Apelt. *Platonische Aufsätze* (Leipzig, 1912), p. 205.
45. Hoerber, p. 128.
46. Sprague believes that there is equivocation in the argument because "no other activity than the activity of being a man has been specified for him [i.e. the good man] to be skillful at," p. 75. Once we see, however, that Socrates has indeed specified *justice* as that at which the good man is skilled, we are no longer forced to say that *agathos* is used in the conclusion to mean "morally good."
47. Even in the case of running where *to thein* is used, Socrates makes a point of ascertaining that this too is a kind of *poiein* or *ergazesthai* (373d7–9).
48. According to R. Robinson, in *Plato's Earlier Dialectic* (2nd ed. Oxford, 1953), p. 39, the only two cases in Plato where an *epagoge* is the main step (i.e. the step before the conclusion) in an argument are the two long arguments in the *Hippias Minor.* This, however, is not strictly true because, certainly in Stage III, there is a universal statement made before the case of *hoi hekontes adikountes* comes up, though the argument does go back to a particular case, i.e. that of slaves' souls, before deducing the conclusion. Nevertheless, the conclusion that the better

soul is the one that does wrong intentionally does not derive strictly from particular co-ordinate cases, but rather relies upon what is the case in *talla panta ta kata tas technas te kai tas epistēmas* (375b8–c1). Similarly, in Stage I, before concluding that *ho pseudēs* and *ho alēthēs* are the same in terms of Achilles and Odysseus, Socrates asks about *ho alēthēs* and *ho pseudēs* in *all* the arts and sciences (368a8–369a2).

49. The verb *kakourgeō* appears in only three places in the dialogue, (1) at 365e8–9, where Hippias says that *hoi pseudeis* have knowledge and therefore *kakourgousin*, (2) at 373b4–5, where Hippias, accusing Socrates of being troublesome in argument, says that Socrates *eoiken hōsper kakourgounti,* and (3) here, at 375c5–d1, where the soul that intentionally *kakourgēi* is seen to compare favourably with the soul that does so unintentionally. In an interesting way this word unites the dialogue, appearing once in the discussion of *ho pseudēs,* once in the discussion of the voluntary versus involuntary *deceiver,* and once in the discussion of voluntarily versus involuntarily wrongdoing souls (here). As we can see, each of these corresponds to the particular topic of one of the three distinct stages in the *Hippias Minor.*

50. Another attempt at viewing *dikaiosunē* as a craft is found in *Republic* 1.334a, and there the concern is to specify its use, since it is assumed that all crafts are useful for some purpose. The end result is a paradox similar to the one in the *Hippias Minor,* namely, that the just man turns out to be some kind of thief, i.e. a man who is good at stealing as well as guarding money.

51. To amplify this point, let us turn to a remark by Guthrie: "One might ask anyway why Hippias should agree at once that justice must be "either a power or knowledge or both." Can it really be supposed to follow from his previous admission that no action can be performed unless one has the power and skill to perform it, justice being seen as a form of action?," p. 195, n. 3. The "previous admission" of which Guthrie speaks is not at all what he says it is, i.e. that no action can be performed unless one has the power and skill to perform it. On the contrary, actions can be performed without one's having the skill and ability to perform them, i.e. one can perform them when one does not wish to, or involuntarily. Thus, unless one is capable— skilled at lying—one may tell the truth inadvertently when one wishes to lie. Only in order to be a *pseudēs* in the *dunamis*-sense, does one need to be *dunatos;* one does not need to be *dunatos* just to lie. It is not that anyone who lies must be able to lie, it is that anyone who lies whenever he wishes to lie must be able to lie. Thus Socrates says (367b2–3), *eiper mellei pseudēs esesthai, hōs su arti hōmologeis, dunaton einai pseudesthai,* but does not say, *eiper mellei pseudesthai . . . dunaton einai pseudesthai.* Also, of course, justice is not seen as a "form of action"; it is a power or knowledge in the soul. Doing noble or ignoble deeds is the action to which this power corresponds.

52. In *Rep.* 8. 535e, Socrates maintains that the unintentional lie is to be despised by the rulers who love truth just as much as the intentional. We may assume, then, that if the lie spoken from ignorance is no better than the lie spoken willingly, the lie spoken willingly is certainly to be condemned.

   Confusing the voluntary *lie* with the voluntary *liar* is perhaps what caused E. Hamilton and H. Cairns, eds., *The Collected Dialogues of Plato* (Princeton, 1963) to say, in their introduction to the *Hippias Minor,* that this dialogue "is inferior to all the others. . . . It turns upon voluntary and involuntary wrongdoing, Hippias maintaining that it is better to do wrong unintentionally than intentionally and Socrates taking the opposite side," p. 200. Shorey, too, in *What Plato Said* (Chicago, 1933), says: "The *Hippias Minor* issues in the paradox that if virtue is knowledge, and the virtues may be compared in Socratic fashion with the arts and sciences, then it is better to do wrong knowingly than without knowing it, for induction shows that in every science and craft the good artist is the one who can most skillfully and most certainly do wrong if he chooses," pp. 86–7. It does not really follow, however, that if the good artist is the most skilful at doing wrong it is better to do wrong willingly, and in the *Hippias Minor* there is no suggestion that it does.

53. This is reminiscent of Donald Ogden Stewart's burlesque of Emily Post, *Perfect Behavior*

(1922; rpt. Philadelphia, 1977) which begins with the definition: "The perfect gentleman is he who never unintentionally causes pain," p. 1.

If one accepts the idea that the scandalousness of the conclusion is seriously reduced with the appreciation of the difference between the goodness of a voluntary wrongdoer and the goodness of voluntary wrongdoing, Aristotle's criticism of this passage loses some of its force. Aristotle attempts to drive a wedge between *ton dunamenon pseusasthai* (*Met*. 4. 29. 1025a8) and *ton hekonta phaulon* (a9), but when one realizes that the two are equivalent, especially since there is no mention of the deed but only of the doer, the importance of the distinction disappears. Of course, when the comparison is put in terms of the voluntary and involuntary wrongdoer rather than the man able or unable to do wrong, the conclusion has the more paradoxical sound which Plato no doubt intended. But one must always bear in mind that these terms are introduced in the dialogue by Hippias—not by Socrates; Socrates never himself goes beyond *hoi hekontes pseudomenoi*. Cf. Grote, p. 398, who agrees with Aristotle. (It must be said that Aristotle hopelessly jumbles the arguments of the *Hippias Minor,* claiming that the identity of the false man and the true is based on the two assumptions that (*a*) the man more skilled at lying is the false, and (*b*) the good man does wrong willingly. Of course, the second assumption appears in the dialogue only *after* the identity of the true man and the false has been established.)

54. In Stage III it is not even usually the agent himself who is discussed. Indeed, only in the case of the runner and wrestler (and other masters of bodily exercise) is the man himself considered. After these there are voices, feet, rudders, musical instruments, horses, dogs, and all sorts of souls, and it is not until Socrates says that *ho agathos agathēn psuchēn echei* (376b3–4) that a man re-enters the picture. This may be significant, for had Socrates asked Hippias if he prefers a physician who prescribes the wrong drug intentionally to one who does so unintentionally, Hippias may well not have known which to choose. But with the alternatives put in terms of souls, the choice is easy: the better soul is the soul that can do whatever it wishes, be it good or bad; that physician's soul is better which prescribes the wrong drug intentionally. This applies even to the just man as the craftsman of justice. Indeed, first his soul is discussed and only later, after the admission that the good man has the good soul, is the good man (*ho agathos*) said to be he who sins voluntarily. This connection between the soul and its possessor is made only for justice.

55. Cf. Xenophon, *Mem.* 4.2. 19–20, where Socrates asks the identical question and again speaks not of intentional and unintentional deception, but rather of intentional and unintentional deceivers, and here too the act is specified as bad: *exapatōntōn epi blabēi,* ruling out the possibility that the goodness of the intentional doer depends on the goodness of the deed done intentionally.

56. As Gomperz notes, "Socrates does not disguise his dissatisfaction with the conclusion, in spite of the necessity with which it appears to flow from the discussion leading up to it," p. 294. Not everyone, however, believes that the conclusion is disapproved of by Socrates despite his having said that it is. Aristotle quotes the *Hippias Minor*'s paradoxes without giving any indication that Plato or Socrates did not believe them (*Met*. 4. 29. 1025a6–13). Xenophon, too, has Socrates bring up the identical point in *Mem*. 4.2.19–20 in terms of liars and deceivers. Many modern scholars as well have taken as Socratic the view that intentional wrongdoers are better than unintentional. Grote, for instance, considers this view to be one of Plato's and Socrates' "startling novelties in ethical doctrine," p. 393.

FURTHER READING

Burnyeat, M. F. 1971. "Virtues in Action." In *The Philosophy of Socrates,* ed. Gregory Vlastos, 209–234. Garden City.

Hoerber, R. G. 1962. "Plato's Lesser Hippias." *Phronesis* 7:121–31.
Mulhern, J. J. 1968. *"Tropos* and *Polytropia* in Plato's *Hippias Minor." Pheonix* 22:283–88.
Sprague, R. S. 1962. *Plato's Use of Fallacy.* London.
Zembaty, J. S. 1989. "Socrates' Perplexity in Plato's *Hippias Minor."* In *Essays in Ancient Greek Philosophy III: Plato,* ed. J. P Anton and A. Preus, 51–70. Albany, N.Y.

15

Socrates on Desire for the Good and the Involuntariness of Wrongdoing: *Gorgias* 466a–468e

KEVIN McTIGHE

In the *Gorgias* Socrates forces his interlocutor Polus to agree that neither orators nor even the tyrants whom they emulate have any great power at all. I would like to examine the logic and dramatic context of the argument for this rather strange claim. Doing so will help clarify (1) Plato's thesis that all men desire the good and (2) the role this thesis plays in the Socratic Paradox "No One is Voluntarily Unjust."

The argument runs as follows (466a9–468e5). Tyrants (or orators) are typically able to do whatever they please: for example, they can expropriate, banish, or even murder their opponents. Thus they do what seems good to them (*ha dokei autois*). Doing *what seems good,* however, must be distinguished from doing *what one desires* (*ha boulontai*). For all men desire *the good.* And so if a particular action, either in itself or in its consequences, happens actually to be bad (i.e., harmful to the agent), how can it be what one desires to do? In accordance with the familiar argument of the *Republic,* Socrates claims that the kind of action characteristic of the tyrant—unjust action—is in fact always harmful to the agent (cf. 460e6, 481b5). Granted this claim it seems to follow that the tyrant doesn't desire to do the thing he typically does do; or, put another way, doesn't do what he desires to do. Hence he is powerless. For how can anyone who (typically) fails to do what he desires be considered powerful?[1]

Now it seems to follow from the above considerations that unjust action is never what *any* agent desires to do, tyrant or no. Isn't that to say, then, that the unjust agent always acts against his desire, or against his will—which is to say *involuntarily?* The view that no one is voluntarily unjust is, of course, a "Socratic Paradox."[2] Does the foregoing argument constitute its basis? Later on in the *Gorgias,* when Socrates has occasion to refer to this Paradox, he does in fact connect it to the claim about desire raised originally in the context of the question whether or not tyrants are powerful. He asks his interlocutor Callicles to affirm the earlier findings that "no one desires to act unjustly, rather all those who act unjustly do so involuntarily" (*mēdena boulomenon adikein, all' akontas tous adikountas pantas adikein:* 509e5–7). It would appear then that he takes the

Paradox to rest squarely on the claim that no one desires to do anything that happens to be bad for him, together with the claim that injustice is bad for all agents.

I shall focus here on the claim (DG henceforth) that 'doing what one desires' must be distinguished from 'doing what seems good to one,' from which it is supposed to follow that if what one does happens to be bad, then he does it without desiring to do it. From antiquity onwards commentators have generated four more or less distinct interpretations of what exactly is meant by DG, all of which assume that Plato holds it as a serious doctrine. Most are of the belief that, whatever its precise meaning, DG must somehow be essential to the Paradox—as seemingly indicated by Socrates' remark to Callicles.[3] Others believe that in any case it is an outcome, or perhaps supportive, of Socrates' fundamental intellectualism.[4] Another common view is that DG is, after all, intended to (and does) support Socrates' contention that tyrants are powerless.[5] Some scholars rest content in assuming that it must have *some* theoretical significance, for otherwise Plato would not have Socrates present it.[6]

All these views are mistaken. In what follows I first examine the received interpretations of DG. We shall then see that the arguments Socrates gives for DG and the claim that tyrants are powerless have been misunderstood; that they are quite bad arguments, logically, although quite good from the perspective of what he is trying to accomplish with Polus. It will emerge that DG itself is actually inconsistent with Plato's considered view of what "desire for the good" means and that, despite what Socrates says to Callicles, Plato cannot intend us to lift it from its context in the Polus episode. By thus disposing of the view that DG is a serious doctrine, we shall clear the way for a better understanding of the argument underlying the Paradox.

I

Perhaps the most widespread interpretation of DG is that Plato intends it to display the following conception of *boulēsis* or "desire."[7] *Boulēsis* has as its object *the* good: only that which is actually (by nature) good, both as means and end, never that which merely seems but isn't good. This is due to the intimate association of "desire" with the "true self" which directly perceives the good. The agent's conscious self, however, may be oblivious of its reality; hence he acts wrongly. Thus, with the *Gorgias* in mind, F. M. Cornford speaks of Plato's belief in a

> true self [whose] peculiar form of desire, always directed at the good it can perceive, he
> called by a special name, "wish" (*boulēsis*). When we act wrongly, we do what we like,
> but not what we wish; the insight of the true self is for a moment obscured.[8]

Cornford fails to justify his linking of "wish" with the "true self," a concept which appears nowhere in the *Gorgias*. Later scholars have done so, however, by citing evidence from other dialogues. Thus the true-self-cum-*boulēsis* has been identified by some with the "true man" of *Alc*. I 130c5–6, by others with the immortal rational being which, according to *Rep*. 611b9–612a3, is the soul in its true nature.[9] In the latter passage the soul is said to possess "philosophy" (*philosophian:* 611e1), understood in the sense of an instinctive longing or impulse (*hormēs:* e4, cf. e2) to mingle with the divine and eternal being to which it is akin, presumably by way of contemplation of the forms.[10]

M. J. O'Brien draws on another text from the *Republic:*

Plato wants to emphasize [in the *Gorg.*], as elsewhere, that a "desire for the truly good" is something all men have all the time. . . . [T]he [unjust] man does not understand the nature of the good. But his soul grasps it after a fashion. . . . [O]nly the presence in Polus and Callicles of a real desire for the good, whose nature they "divine," makes worthwhile Socrates' attempts to win them over.[11]

O'Brien here alludes to *Rep.* 505d5–506a2, where Plato argues that although men may choose to have merely the external appearance of justice, no one is ever satisfied with merely the appearance of good things. Men rather seek or pursue what *are* good things (*ta onta zētousin*). And the good is "that which every soul pursues and for the sake of which does everything" (d11–e1). The agent himself—unless of course he is wise— neither has knowledge of the good, nor consciously desires it. Nevertheless his soul "divines" or intuits (*apomanteuomenē:* e1) the good, and it is this intuition which directs the soul's search. O'Brien takes it that this search is just the *Gorgias'* notion of *boulēsis* expressed in different terminology.[12]

The same holds true for the *erōs* of the *Symposium*. Says O'Brien: "The theory of Eros . . . cannot be divorced from the ethical principle that no man wishes evil and all wish the good. Eros *is* this same universal wish."[13] This would explain why Diotima momentarily lapses into what O'Brien calls "the language of the *Gorg.*" In the course of explaining to Socrates what it is that lovers will have when they attain their object, she describes love as a *boulēsis* for good things, which is common to all men (cf. 205a5– 206a5). This proves that all men are lovers, despite the popular belief that only some are. Thus love itself just is "every sort of desire (*epithumia*) for good things and happiness" (205d2). Although *epithumia* is used here instead of *boulēsis*, this is not surprising, since "Plato . . . varies his choice of [terms for desire] according to the associations he wants to create . . . and the intensity of the emotion he wants to suggest."[14]

If the good, then, is that which the agent desires and loves, how shall we describe his choice of something which happens not to be good? He may tell us that it is what he desired to do. But his action cannot be what he *desired* to do. And just this, moreover, is the basis of the Paradox according to which wrongdoing is involuntary. The Paradox thus turns out to involve the special or "restricted" sense of "desire" which emerges from DG.[15] Denying the propriety of standard usage, Socrates stipulates that *boulesthai* (or *boulēsis*) has as its object only what is actually and really good. He does so in accordance with certain facts about the soul, namely that it has a "true self" which somehow intuits and longs for the good. Hence, as one scholar puts it: "Plato does not agree that [the wrongdoer] is fulfilling some mistaken wish; rather, he is not fulfilling his wish at all, since he is deceived about the object of his desire."[16] Some commentators present evidence that Plato adheres to the "restricted" sense of *boulesthai* in dialogues other than the *Gorgias*.[17]

I shall call this sort of view the neoplatonic interpretation of DG. For the ideas which Cornford and the others cited attribute to Plato at *Gorg.* 466eff. are among those which Plotinus[18] and various of his followers[19] not only held for themselves but, so it seems, ascribed to Plato *qua* author of the *Gorgias*.

A view of more recent origin is that of K. Steinhart, according to whom DG expresses a distinction between "die Willkür" (arbitrariness) and "der vernünftige Wille" (the rational or ethical will).[20] The unjust man does what seems good and yet always fails to achieve the good that is the object of his rational will. The latter is not thought to be any sort of profound longing residing unconsciously in the soul, as it was on the neoplatonic view. All men "really" (im Grunde doch) will the good in that as rational beings they are capable of discriminating actual, unconditional goods/ends from indifferent or evil ends: the rational will is present in men *implicite*.[21] Steinhart is consciously adapting what are Hegelian categories; let us call his the "Hegelian" interpretation of DG.[22]

In somewhat the same vein, although quite differently motivated, is the view of N. Gulley.[23] Gulley wants to explain why it is that, at *Gorg*. 509c8–510a5, Socrates denies that the desire (*boulēsis*) to avoid injustice is sufficient for successfully avoiding it, claiming instead that a certain power and skill are needed as well. In particular what does this imply for our understanding of the way in which *boulesthai* functions in the Paradox as stated at 509e5–7, wherein *akōn* is apparently equivalent to *mē boulomenos?* Since Socrates has stipulated that the object of "desire" is the agent's true good, Gulley says, it seems surprising that possession of this "desire" would *not* be sufficient, barring external constraint, for avoiding injustice. For the agent who "desires" the good surely must already have knowledge of what is good (how else would he desire it, given Plato's insistence that such knowledge is necessary and sufficient for virtuous or good action?). But if so, how can he fail to live virtuously? Gulley takes the problem here to be an erroneous assumption: that *boulēsis* is a desire which the agent *has* for the good and which implies his own knowledge of the good. It must rather be the desire he *would* have *if* he were knowledgeable of the good and thus able to judge the actual worth of a proposed action. Thus: "No one acts against what he would wish to do if he knew what was 'really' good."[24] At least this is the thought Socrates is aiming to express. If so, then it is no longer a puzzle why he should deny that *boulēsis* is a sufficient defence against wrongdoing.

A problem remains, however. In the text Socrates ascribes an actual *desiring,* in the present tense, to all agents. In the statement of the Paradox at 509e5–7 the same sort of ascription recurs: no one commits injustice "desiringly" (*boulomenos*). Gulley sees the problem and calls this ascription, dictated by DG, an "awkward interpretation" by Plato of the Paradox. It is due to an analogy between moral and professional behavior:

> Just as the bad runner "really" wants to win the race and loses it "against his will," so Plato assumes, the morally bad man "really" wants to do what is good and does wrong "against his will" . . .

The analysis, however, is pressed too far:

> . . . in speaking of what the morally bad man "really" wants, the natural way to specify it is as what he believes to be right.[25]

Despite the awkwardness, however, Gulley believes that DG is presupposed in all other dialogues that refer to the Paradox with the single exception of the *Protagoras*.[26] Thus the Paradox requires DG and the desire ascribed to the agent by DG is to be construed in hypothetical terms, notwithstanding the absence of the hypothetical formulation in the text. Let us call this the "hypothetical" interpretation of DG.[27]

The most recent interpretation of DG amounts to a radical departure from traditional views. An attempt has been made to construe the argument without recourse to the notion of a "true self" or even of an actual good defined independently of the agent's preferences and alleged to be the object of ''desire'' in a restricted or hypothetical sense. According to G. Santas, the agent does things he does not want to do

> if in fact these things were to lead to the agent's possessing bad things: for according to the theory [which Socrates is expounding] a man would do these things for the sake of possessing good things (*in a relativized version, for the sake of what he thought best for himself*); and yet these things turn out to lead to the possession of bad things and so are things which according to the theory no one wants to do.[28]

Santas seems to mean something like this: if the tyrant's activities were to lead to some result *which he regarded as harmful,* such as his own assassination, Socrates would say that although his action seems good to him, it is not what he really desires to do—even if he goes ahead and does it.[29] Just what importance this point is supposed to have for Plato is left obscure.[30] At any rate let us call this the ''subjectivist'' interpretation of DG, since the ''good'' that is supposed to be really desired by the agent is simply that which *he holds to be* good: as Santas puts it, it is a ''relativized version.''[31]

So far the received views. Which, if any, deserves to be favored? Unfortunately none of them has paid much attention to the actual structure of the argument for DG. Let us examine this structure before going any further.

II

The argument at *Gorg.* 467c–468e may be reconstructed as follows.

1. All action is such that if a person does something, he desires only that for the sake of which he acts, not the action itself. (proven by induction: 467c5–e1)
2. Everything is either good, bad, or neither good nor bad (intermediate): things in the latter category lead sometimes to good, sometimes to bad consequences, and thus may be derivatively good or bad. (assumption: 467e1–468a4)
3. All men do intermediate things (e.g., walking, running, expropriating, slaughtering) in pursuit of the good, i.e., for the sake of what they hold to be good for themselves (e.g., skill, health, wealth), but not for the sake of [what they hold to be] intermediate or bad things. (assumption: 468a5–b8)
4. Hence we desire good things, not intermediate or bad things. (by 1, 2, 3: 468c5–7)
5. Hence if a certain action is beneficial or good for the agent [either in itself or in its consequences], he desires to do it, but if it is intermediate or bad, he doesn't desire to do it.[32] (by 4?: 468c2–8)
6. If someone does certain things, thinking they are better for him, he does what seems good. (assumption: 468d1–5)
7. However, if those things happen in fact to be bad, he does not do what he desires. (by 5?: 468d5–7)
8. Power is always something good. (assumption: 468e1–2)
9. Hence his ability to do these things is not power. (by 7, 8: 468d7–e3)
10. Hence it is possible for a person to do what seems good and yet not have power or do what he desires. (by 6, 7, 9: 468e3–5)[33]

It is putting it mildly to say that this argument is problematic.

Step (1), first of all, seems not only to be supported by what is itself a bad argument, but also in any case to be false and—moreover—to contradict step (5). The supporting argument is that no one desires, for example, to drink bitter medicine, or take dangerous sea voyages. When we do these things it is health or wealth that we desire, that is, the ends in view. It is concluded that it holds true of *all* purposeful action that if the action is a means, we do not desire it, rather only its end. But the examples are clearly loaded. If the medicine were sugar-coated, or the sea voyage on a luxury liner, we might desire to take them for themselves, not merely for their ends. Moreover, doesn't step (5) assert that if a particular action is good—perhaps just as a means—then even if it is painful in itself the agent still desires to do *it*?[34] Such cases remind us of Aristotle's discussion in *EN* III.1 of the criteria for involuntariness: the example he uses is jettisoning cargo to save a ship. In some sense we are constrained to do this, but at the same time we desire and choose it and it is in our power to do otherwise. It is "more like the voluntary than the involuntary" (1110b6).[35] At any rate it seems absurd to deny that useful actions *not* painful in themselves are ever the objects of desire. What is even stranger is the discrepancy, with respect to this, between steps (1) and (5).

A more interesting problem arises with steps (4) through (7). It involves an equivocation.

Step (4) says, roughly, that all men desire the good. From this Socrates infers, roughly, that if one's action is bad, then it is false that one desires to do it. It is clear from step (7) that the antecedent clause here means "if one's action *happens to be really* bad, regardless of how the agent conceives it at the time." Is this inference valid? In what sense might the agent not have desired X, if he in fact did X? Is it that one performs badly only under some sort of compulsion?

The inference is invalid. The problem has nothing to do with compulsion, however. It is due to the fact that "desire" is a verb of so-called propositional attitude, which occasions a certain ambiguity over which Socrates' argument rides roughshod. Verbs of this stripe introduce a context, commonly called "opaque," in which (among other things) the substitutivity of co-referring terms may not be assumed to be valid. For when we ascribe desires to a person, we sometimes fix the content of the desire as *he* does or would fix it, sometimes not. In the former case, substitutivity frequently fails; and one cannot have it both ways at once.

For example, given the statements:

1. Oedipus wants to marry Jocasta.
2. Jocasta is Oedipus' own mother.

we would still hesitate to infer that:

3. Oedipus wants to marry his own mother.

We know that was the furthest thing from his mind. Thus it is the attitudes and beliefs of the agent about the object of his desire which we assume to govern his desire. He wants Jocasta only under certain descriptions which he himself thinks true of her. But he does not necessarily want her under *any* description which just happens to be true of her. We thus give a *de dicto* interpretation of the verb "wants."

Although in general we hesitate to allow such inferences, there are nevertheless exceptions. With opaque contexts it is quite legitimate for the speaker in effect to stipulate, implicitly or otherwise, that co-referring terms may be substituted *salva veritate:* in this case the context becomes "transparent." For example we can imagine

Zeus saying to himself, while Oedipus is busy proposing to Jocasta, "It looks like Oedipus wants to marry his own mother!" We should accept Zeus' statement as true, and when we do so we assume the *de re* interpretation of the verb. Of course, on the *de dicto* interpretation, Zeus' statement is false. Note then that such statements are ambiguous.

Let us return to Socrates' arguments: in his claim that all men desire the good are we to give a *de dicto* or a *de re* reading of "desire?" Given the manner in which he has won Polus' support for this claim, it can only be given the *de dicto* reading, which is after all the natural reading. What exactly is this "good" which all agents supposedly desire? Socrates names what he has in mind: popular goods like skill, health, wealth and the like [cf. step (3)] together with the derivatively good intermediate means for their sake [cf. step (5)]. This "good" then is defined according to the agent's conceptions of just what are the things in life worth aiming at and just what are the best means of attaining them in particular choice situations. In accordance with a long-standing tradition, let us call this "good" the "apparent good."[36] Socrates' claim, then, that all men desire the good means that they desire the apparent good. A more precise, if still inadequate formulation would be:

> The agent at time *t* desires and chooses *x* in preference to *y*, *iff* he believes at time *t* that *x* is better for him than *y*.[37]

Now the inference from this, in step (5), to the statement that if a particular action is bad, the agent doesn't desire to do it, is in itself innocuous. If we assume that the antecedent falls under the scope of the main verb, this is just to say that no one desires what he conceives to be bad. Yet it is clear from step (7) that this assumption about the antecedent must be incorrect. For the mere fact that an action happens to be bad—regardless of how the agent himself conceives it at the time—is now sufficient for his not desiring it.[38] Clearly the verb in the original claim is no longer being given the *de dicto* but rather the *de re* reading. For now it is imagined that one's "desires" are tied not to actions under the descriptions "good for me"—apparently good actions—but to those actions that are in fact actually good—whether or not the agent knows or believes it. On this reading Socrates' claim now amounts to: all men desire the *actual* good. Only on this reading is the inference from (5) to (7) a valid one.

What Socrates does, then, is in effect equivocate over the two readings; and on this fallacy rests the proof that doing what seems good is non-equivalent to doing what one desires. For on the *de dicto* reading "doing what one desires" *is* (at least extensionally) equivalent to "doing what seems good to one" or "doing the apparent good." Polus is tricked when, after agreeing that all men desire the apparent good, he is oblivious when Socrates tacitly shifts to the *de re* reading and pretends that the *de dicto* is no longer valid—even though it was the very reading presupposed at the beginning of the argument. On the *de re* reading the apparent good is not necessarily desired—true—but only on that reading.

An alternative way of formulating the problem is to say that the conclusion of the argument entails the denial of one of its own premises. All desire is for the apparent good, it is initially argued: which is just to say that men, both the wise, and the ignorant, desire *what seems good* to them. But then the remarkable outcome (DG) is that doing what seems good is not equivalent to doing what one desires, after all.[39]

There is still more. Note that Socrates, in addition to putting forward DG as a general doctrine, states that as a matter of fact tyrants (or orators) do not do what they desire

(466d6–e2). The manner in which he puts this involves yet a further equivocation. On the *de re* reading of the desire claim it is the "actual" good which is the object of desire. Now just what is this actual good? It is not yet *the* good, that is, the good-by-nature subscribed to by Socrates and Plato, for the utility of the distinction between apparent and actual good is not restricted to the ethical objectivist. No matter what account one cares to give of the cognitive status of value statements, it is still possible to say that a given agent mistakes his apparent good—what he judges he should do in a particular situation—for his actual good. This will likely be true of him in those situations in which he has a defective grasp of the actual consequences of his act. For example, if we expect that the tyrant's ongoing expropriation of his enemies will result in his own assassination, we might say that his "actual good" requires some action other than the one he is performing. But we do not thereby commit ourselves to objectivism. We might very well ascribe to this actual good the status of a subjective preference.[40]

We know, of course, that Socrates' version of "good" is objective in status. Thus we know that when he blanketly asserts that tyrants do not do what they desire, that is, their actual good, the latter is defined not according to the agent's own conceptions (or ultimate preferences) but rather according to what is good in the nature of things. So too the "bad." The tyrant's actions are unjust and Socrates holds that unjust action is bad for any agent, regardless of what he may think, and regardless of whether it does or does not have only its intended consequences.

Thus a further equivocation has become visible. Socrates shifts, in steps (4), (5), and (7), from:

all men desire the apparent good

to:

all men desire the actual good

to:

all men desire *the* good.

Only on this last does it follow that tyrants, in acting unjustly, never do what they desire to do.

The argument at *Gorg.* 466a–468e is thus fallacious in several ways.

III

We are now in a position to criticize the received interpretations of DG. They ignore, first, the presence of fallacy. Although this is a weakness, it is not necessarily fatal: perhaps the fallacies escaped Plato himself. Nevertheless the received accounts each suffer from crucial shortcomings.

The subjectivist interpretation correctly recognizes that the *de re* construal of "all men desire the good," on which Socrates' argument in part turns, is consistent with supposing that what men "really" desire are simply the ends which they *conceive* to be good. As we just saw, the mere distinction Socrates makes between "what one desires" and "what seems good" does not require in itself that it is *the* good which is desired. What undermines this interpretation is, as we saw in addition, that the blanket claim that tyrants do not do what they desire, made by Socrates in the course of arguing for DG, does imply that it is *the* good that is supposedly desired by all agents. This must be explained.[41]

Both the hypothetical and Hegelian interpretations do try to account for this; yet in so doing they succumb to a different pitfall. According to the latter, not doing "what one desires" means not exercising one's implicit (rational) will; according to the former, not doing what one would do if he had knowledge of what is actually (by nature) good. The problem with both is that the desire referred to in Socrates' argument is neither implicit nor hypothetical, but fully actual. Its subject is not man *qua* rational being but all men *qua* engaging in any action whatsoever. What Socrates *says* is not that on certain conditions we *would* desire the good, but that in all action we *desire* it. The unjust or irrational agent is no exception. Nor does Gulley's attempt to explain away the non-hypothetical language succeed. The suggestion that Plato presses too far the analogy between moral and professional behaviour is ad hoc—without any foundation in the *Gorgias* or elsewhere[42]—and in any case intrinsically unconvincing. What possible reason could there be for Socrates to resort to non-hypothetical language if what he *means* is the hypothetical claim and if it is clear, as of course it is, that Polus does not understand the claim in this sense? Note further that, if the hypothetical claim were indeed what Socrates means, the argument for DG would still fail in its stated purpose. For the fact that doing what seems good is not necessarily the same as doing what one would desire to do given full knowledge is not at all inconsistent with Polus' claim that it is the same as doing what one desires to do; but it was this that Socrates challenged.

Is the neoplatonic interpretation of DG correct? In its favor is the fact that DG clearly does attribute to all men a real desire for *the* good—a fact which helped undermine the rival interpretations. And even if it is true that DG turns on an equivocation over different readings of a verb of propositional attitude, followed by an equivocation over different senses of "actual good," this does not necessarily stand in the way. It is at least possible, one could say, that at the time of writing the *Gorgias* Plato (wrongly) believed that his theory justified his ascribing these equivocations to Socrates; and perhaps he was not conscious of them as such.

Nevertheless it can be shown that the neoplatonic view does not underlie DG. First, and most importantly, the evidence is tenuous—or so I shall argue—that Plato ever really held such a view at all. Second, there is at least one respect in which it is clearly incompatible with the text of DG. Third, its construal of *boulesthai* as having a "restricted" sense trivializes the thesis about desire. Let us take these in reverse order.

If we commit Plato to the view that *boulesthai* necessarily has *the* good for its object we thereby commit him, in effect, to stipulating a non-standard meaning for the word. This in turn reduces the thesis that desire is for the good to logical vacuity. Thus if it should happen that X is bad and yet someone seems to desire X, this cannot count as evidence against the thesis. For by definition he does *not* desire it (it's bad): counter-examples are logically ruled out. What ought to be a controversial thesis, that all desire is somehow for *the* good, becomes true by definition and reduces to: all desire for *the* good is for *the* good.[43]

The neoplatonic view has it that *boulēsis* is in some way united with, or governed by, an intuition of the good. But then the proponents of this view have no way to account for the fact, which ought to them to be curious, that according to the argument in the text (cf. above, steps [5] and [7]) it follows that the agent who does X *bouletai* X *iff X is in fact good*. That the agent be in any noetic state whatever, conscious or unconscious, is evidently unnecessary: it is sufficient that his action be good. Thus if an ignorant agent happens to perform a genuinely good action (by chance, say), the argument requires us to say that he *bouletai* it.

The most serious threat to this interpretation of DG, however, is the lack of compelling evidence that Plato held anywhere the sort of view it ascribes to him. The *boulēsis* of the *Gorgias*, it was alleged (see pp. 264ff.), is what Plato calls *erōs* in the *Symposium;* it is supposed to be comprehended in the psychology of the *Republic;* and alluded to in passages from these and other dialogues which seem to use *boulesthai* in the "restricted" sense. All these claims, some of which are plausible, are false. Examination of the evidence will help us to uncover the view Plato actually does hold. We shall meet with a remarkable fact: that for Plato *exactly the opposite of DG* is the case. For doing what seems good *is* the same as doing what one desires.

In *Sym.* 205a5–206a5 Diotima says that all men are lovers, because all men desire (*boulesthai*) good things, and love (*erōs*) just is "every sort of desire (*epithumia*) for good things (*agathōn*) and happiness" (205d2). Now what are these *agatha* which Diotima is referring to? She gives three examples of the desires she means to classify under the rubric of *erōs:* the desire to make money, the desire to excel in athletics, and the desire to gain wisdom or knowledge (205d4–5). Clearly only the last of these could qualify (for Plato) as an actual good by itself, such as to ensure genuine happiness. On the other hand all three are apparent goods.[44] What Diotima does, then, is identify all desires for apparent goods as *erōs*, or forms of *erōs;* and it is not surprising that she speaks of *epithumia* as well as *boulēsis*. The latter is *not* tied to *the* good, as it is in the *Gorgias;* it has a standard sense. All that Socrates in the *Gorgias* calls "doing what seems good," rather than being denied the name of *erōs*—which it would have to be were it true that *erōs* = *boulēsis* in the restricted sense—is instead emphatically awarded it. There is, finally, no trace of any "true self."

What then of *Rep.* 505d5–506a2, wherein Plato states that all men "seek what really are good things" and describes the good—*the* good—as "that, then, which every soul pursues (*diōkei*) and for its sake does all that it does, with an intuition of its reality (*apomanteuomenē ti einai*) . . . ." (Shorey, trans.)? From this text, if from any, the neoplatonic account of DG would seem to draw strength; yet it is not so.

First of all the context suggests that Plato does not mean the good things which men seek happen to be the things which are actually—objectively—good. To be sure, he says that when it comes to *agatha,* men seek *ta onta.* But this gets its meaning from the contrasting case—men's behavior in regard to justice and nobility. The point is that all men take questions about the good seriously, but not so in the other case. Whereas men are frequently content merely to appear to be just—according to what they *conceive* justice to be—no one is content merely to appear to possess good things. All men seek *actual instances* of good things—what they *conceive to be* actual instances of good things.[45] Thus once again it is the apparent good that comes into focus, just as it did in the initial steps of the *Gorgias* argument.[46] But there is no trace of the notion that *the* good is somehow the object of desire.[47]

What then of the rest of this passage? Does it not plainly indicate that what the soul (the "true self?") pursues is nothing other than *the* good itself? Yes; but this notion of "pursuit" is perhaps more subtle than has been supposed. It is an interesting fact about *Rep.* 505d5ff.—one that should trouble the neoplatonic interpreter of DG—that not only is there no reference to *boulēsis,* there is not a single term which straightforwardly carries the meaning "desire" of some sort anywhere in this text. Now if Plato in fact believes that the soul *desires the* good, why doesn't he say it? Why does he instead say "pursues?" One possibility of course is that by "pursues" he implies "desires," since normally one pursues X only if one desires X. (This, it could be said, is evident from the *Gorgias* argument itself, in which "pursue" and "desire" are used more or less interchangeably, as at 468b1.) Another possibility is that "pursues" does not imply "desires" but rather something else, in which case the absence of any claim that the soul desires *the* good forces one to consider that perhaps Plato does not hold such a view after all. The latter alternative is correct.

Plato's meaning is as follows. The soul "pursues" the good in that, as 505d11–e1 goes on to say, it does all that it does "for the sake of this [sc. *the* good] (*toutou heneka*)."[48] This latter is the key notion; and it implies a metaphorical, not a literal "pursuit." The "action-for-the-sake-of" relation which the soul has to *the* good points simply to an *explanation by final clause* of the soul's activity, rather than to any faculty of wish or desire or love somehow drawing the soul towards the good. The good, for Plato, has final causality with respect to the natural order (cf. *Phdo.* 97b8–99c6; *Rep.* 509b6–10; *Tim.* 29a, 30a, 46de, 68e–69a). The fact that all men desire and seek the *apparent* good, referred to in the lines preceding, is then explained by the relationship which *the* good has to the soul. We might say that the good brings it about that men, *qua* having a soul, necessarily seek what they judge to be good. The man who attains knowledge of what *is* good is thus enabled to desire and choose *it.*[49]

If this is correct, the prepositional phrase . . . *heneka* . . . expresses final causality, as in Aristotle. The soul acts "for the sake of" the good, but this does not mean that the good is its "end in view" or that it somehow "sees" or "knows" the good in any sense. This is confirmed by the lines that follow. The soul does indeed act *apomanteuomenē ti einai.* But what this means has been misunderstood. On the neoplatonic view this phrase captures the soul's *noēsis* of the good, the "intuition" which underlies its true desires. Can the phrase bear such a weight? Now the motivation for so construing it is understandable. The operative assumption is drawn, one can say, from common sense: for X to be an object of desire, the agent must somehow know or at least be able to identify X for what it is: how else can he desire it? There must then be a way in which the "true self" knows the good.[50] The problem, however, is that our phrase likely means no more than "surmising what it is," that is, conceiving that the good is constituted by such and-such.[51] It is clear from what follows that this surmise is far from being a kind of knowledge. For the soul is "yet baffled (*aporousa*) and unable to apprehend its nature adequately, or to attain any stable belief about it as about other things . . ." (505e1–3, Shorey, trans.). The soul which is baffled is hardly any true self.

Thus there is no basis for imposing on Plato's scheme any sort of impulse or desire in the soul for *the* good, or any notion of "pursuit" in the strict sense. We might, if we wish, speak here of a "teleological lure" on the part of the good and imagine that Plato *could* have characterized his final good as "like a beloved object."[52] But he does not do so, even though in the *Symposium* he does characterize the desire and pursuit of (apparent) good as "love." The "lure" exercised by the final good is only metaphorical, and the metaphor is not even Plato's. The soul, although it acts for the sake of the good, does not (necessarily) either know or desire it.

Nor is *Rep.* 611b9–612a3 of any help. It is true that Plato here describes the soul as having a true nature, in effect attributing to it a kind of true self. Moreover he refers to the "impulse" (*hormē*) of the soul, its "philosophy," to mingle with true being. But none of this yields the requisite desire for the good.

The idea that the rational part of the soul has desires of its own appears already in *Rep.* 581b5–8, where it is applied in one of several arguments intended to show that the just man is happiest. This part of the soul is to be called "lover of learning and lover of wisdom" (*philomathes dē kai philosophon*), insofar as it has a natural desire or *appetite* (cf. *epithumia:* 580d8) for knowledge. It may very well be that the impulse mentioned in the later passage is somehow linked to this. But in any case neither the one nor the other desire is linked to desire for *the good,* or a desire whose object is alone that which is "really" wanted in a practical context. For in the one case the object is said to be knowledge, in the other that which knowledge is of—true being, or the Forms. Desires so conceived do not match the scope of *boulesthai* as conceived according to DG. The latter has, primarily at least, *actions* for its object. But actions do not range among the objects of the "philosophical" *epithumia* or *hormē*. Furthermore it is acknowledged in the *Republic* that there are other *epithumia* in the soul besides those of the reasoning part, and yet nothing to indicate that their objects are not "really" wanted. It is most difficult to believe that Plato could have identified the *boulesthai* of DG with the *Republic*'s philosophical appetite.

Let us turn, finally, to the claims (see p. 265 and n. 17) that Plato in certain places uses *boulesthai/boulēsis* in the same "restricted" sense found in DG, according to which it has all and only *the* good for its object. The assertion that these terms are used *consistently* in this fashion is pure silliness. Here are three counterexamples (from among dozens): *Gorg.* 511b3–5, Socrates insisting that a tyrant may slaughter a man, *an boulētai,* but he will be an evil man slaying a good one; *Rep.* 445a5–b4, where even the possibility that he can do whatever he wishes (*ho an boulēthēi:* b2) is held to be insufficient (NB!) for rendering happy the life of one with a disordered soul; *Tht.* 201a8. As for the particular passages alleged to show at least an occasional use of the restricted sense, none convinces. It would be tedious to discuss them individually; suffice it to say that examination will reveal that if there is any explicit tie to "the good," nothing suggests that anything other than the *apparent* good is meant.[53]

Thus the neoplatonic interpretation of DG cannot, any more that its rivals, explain why Socrates says that all men desire *the* good and only that. The problem is not simply, however, that the *Symposium* and *Republic* texts we have examined show no trace of such a view. The fact is that the view which they do express is this: human action is motivated by the desire all men have for what they conceive to be good. Now as we saw earlier, this view—although premissed within the very argument for DG—is just what the conclusion of that argument *denies*. What are we to make of this?

Let me now suggest that the idea that all desire is for the *apparent* good is in fact Plato's considered view in dialogues perhaps earlier than the *Gorgias,* as well as in the *Symposium* and *Republic,* which are perhaps later.[54] It will be found at, for example, *Ly.* 216c–220b, *Eud.* 278e–282a, *Prot.* 358cd, and *Meno* 77b–78b—if, at least, one attends carefully to what these passages do and do not say.[55] We are then faced with the peculiar circumstance that not only is DG based on fallacy—but the argument poses at the outset Plato's considered view of the object of desire, only to contradict it in the end!

One way out might be to imagine that when Plato wrote the *Gorgias* he departed from his earlier view about desire and then later returned to it. One might then add that in the process of changing his mind he succumbed to a sadly fallacious argument. I shall suggest what I believe is a more plausible hypothesis.[56]

Let us now turn to a feature of DG which has generally escaped attention: the fact that it arises within a dramatic context. We shall find that DG, as peculiar as it is, is yet only one of a series of like oddities occurring in Socrates' conversation with Polus in 466aff. These oddities demand a common explanation, which I shall try to give. Let us then review the conversation a little more closely.

Can Socrates really believe that rhetoric is so worthless?, wonders Polus. Isn't public opinion right, that orators—like tyrants—are among the most powerful people there are? Socrates, however, denies this. They may be able to do whatever they please, as Polus insists, but this does not prove that they are powerful. Moreover, Socrates thinks Polus himself doesn't say any differently (*ouch hōs ge phēsin Pōlos:* 466e4). Polus protests that he *does* hold that to do whatever one pleases is tantamount to having great power. Wait, asks Socrates, doesn't Polus conceive power to be something good for its possessor? Having secured assent to this, he presents Polus with a simple argument designed to show him that he does *not* accept the account of power he thinks he does. That argument is roughly as follows:

1. Power is (always) something good for the agent. (Polus' belief: 466b6–8, e6–10)
2. Power is the ability to do whatever one pleases. (Polus' belief: 466e1–5)
3. Hence the ability to do whatever one pleases is (always) something good for the agent. (by 1 and 2)
4. But unintelligent agents sometimes harm themselves by doing whatever they please. (Polus' belief: 466e9–12)
5. Hence 3 is false. (by 4)
6. Hence either 1 or 2 or both are false. (by 5)
7. Polus still agrees that 1 is true. (assumed by Socrates)
8. Hence Polus must deny 2: that is, that power is the ability to do whatever one pleases. (by 6 and 7: 466e4)[57]

The argument is valid, and so Polus "says" otherwise than he did at first. Due to his holding inconsistent beliefs about power and the consequences of unintelligence, Socrates has succeeded in getting him to contradict himself. As for the issue at hand, his claim that orators are powerful is now jeopardized. He will have to offer something more than simply the fact that they can do whatever they please. Clearly, given his commitment to 1, he will have to show that orators have a way of guaranteeing that what they please—what *seems* best to them—really is best. Only then can they be said to have power.

At this point Socrates acknowledges that if Polus can prove that orators have intelligence (*nous*) (or that rhetoric is a *technē*, craft), that will suffice to refute Socrates' claim that they are powerless (466e1–467a9).[58] Thus he appears to accept the claim:

PI A person has power *iff* he has the ability to do whatever he pleases and is intelligent.

Now Polus has no reason to reject PI or to evade Socrates' challenge, even though it is a different account from what he thought he believed. For of course he thinks orators *are* intelligent. Now that Socrates and Polus stand on the common ground afforded by PI, one might expect the discussion to turn—rather, turn back—to issues pertaining to the relation between rhetoric, craft, and intelligence.[59] In this way the initial problem about orators and power could perhaps be resolved. But no such thing occurs.

Instead what happens (467a8–c4) is that Socrates loses interest in the question whether orators are intelligent, and presses a rather different question. That is: can orators do *whatever they desire?*[60] Polus thinks that orators are powerful and Socrates will be satisfied that this is the case, if it can be proved that they do whatever they desire. Polus' response is one of sputtering frustration; it is easy to see why. Hasn't Socrates already insisted, and gotten Polus to agree, that for orators to be called powerful it is not enough that they have the ability to do whatever they please? And isn't doing whatever one pleases the same as doing whatever one desires? Why then does he presume now that the latter *would* be a sufficient basis for calling orators powerful? It must seem to Polus that Socrates has roundly asserted the very point he took such pains to deny a moment before.

In what follows, as we know, Socrates once again succeeds in getting Polus to contradict what at first seemed self-evident to him. Agreeing to each step of DG, Polus admits that doing whatever one pleases is not equivalent to doing what one desires and that only if the agent satisfies the latter description is he powerful. What should we now expect to happen? We might expect the discussion to revert to the issue which ostensibly motivated the presentation of DG in the first place: whether or not tyrants/orators are powerful.

But this in fact does not happen. That issue is quietly dropped. At 468e6ff. the discussion turns to another topic: whether unjust action ever benefits the agent.[61]

Let us pause to take stock of certain peculiarities. First, the apparently erratic manner in which Socrates steers the argument: instead of allowing Polus to try to prove (on the basis of the account of power which Socrates himself had suggested) that orators are intelligent and hence powerful, he forces on him the strange claim that they never do what they desire. Is this intended to clarify the problem, or promote its solution? At any rate it doesn't: for Socrates has to stop to show that doing what seems good is non-equivalent to doing what one desires. And then the whole issue is simply forgotten, the "problem" left unsolved.

Second, consider the claim that power is always something good for the agent. Polus accepts this strong claim, at least at Socrates' bidding; and Socrates himself makes use of it in refuting him. Does Socrates himself actually hold this view? Does he really believe, further, that powerful people are all intelligent, as implied by PI? Here is how he defines power in the *Hippias Minor:* "every man has power who does that which he wishes at the time he wishes" (366b7–c1). No mention at all of its goodness, or of its restriction to the intelligent.[62] Is there any evidence that Plato (or Socrates) holds power to be an intrinsic good, or something always worth having? The evidence points to the contrary. In the *Euthydemus* Socrates argues that popularly conceived goods such as power, health, wealth, fame are not *reliably* good: when used by the ignorant agent, as of course they often are, they lead to self-harm, so that in themselves they are neither good nor evil. The only thing *always* good is wisdom.[63] This account of popular goods is common in Plato and there can be little doubt that it is his considered view.[64] If so, it seems puzzling that at this point in the *Gorgias* Socrates should agree with Polus' view that power, whatever its precise definition, is always good—rather than argue against it.[65] It is also puzzling that he should endorse PI, which rules out ignorant agents from ever *being* powerful.

Third, let us pause to consider what Socrates is doing in the first place. Whereas in the context of an investigation of rhetoric it would certainly make sense for him to question the goodness of power, why should he be at all concerned to deny that orators and tyrants are powerful? To doubt that tyrants, of all people, have great power seems silly.

Thus *Gorg.* 466aff. presents a series of puzzles. If DG is not only fallacious but inconsistent with Plato's considered view of the object of desire, so too is the claim that power is always a good thing inconsistent with his considered view of the status of popular goods, and PI inconsistent with a rather straightforward presupposition of the latter view, that is, that some unintelligent people are powerful. The issue ostensibly under investigation seems trivial in the first place; and the manner in which it is handled seems strangely erratic. How are we to account for all this?

V

A crucial and so far tacit assumption has been that, in questioning Polus and being in turn questioned by him, Socrates intends a sincere investigation of rhetoric or, more precisely, of the power which orators are thought to enjoy. A corollary of this assumption would be that Plato licenses his audience to regard the arguments Socrates gives as philosophically motivated and thus capable of being related more or less straightforwardly to other of his doctrines. These assumptions are false. Once we see why this is so, the puzzles dissolve: the fallacies and even the un-Platonic elements may be accounted for. The problem lies in our understanding of Socrates' aims in conversing with Polus. Could it be that these aims are satisfied by a method that permits such things?

Although the issue of the nature of Socratic dialectic is vast and controversial, nevertheless our progress to this point requires that we say something about it. I propose in the following to compare briefly the Polus episode with the Gorgias episode that precedes it in regard to the character and aim of the method Socrates follows in each. My treatment will be sketchy and incomplete, although I hope that it will support the claims made in the previous paragraph.

The conversation with Gorgias is as follows. Having gotten him to agree to give brief answers, Socrates begins to question him concerning the nature and scope of the rhetoric which he claims to teach (449c9ff.). Various definitions are advanced by Gorgias and then rejected as being either too wide or too narrow. Throughout the discussion, however, Socrates repeatedly emphasizes that he is not directing himself against Gorgias personally. His questions are rather for the sake of the argument (*ou sou heneka alla tou logou*), because he thinks it a great evil for anyone, but himself above all, to have false beliefs concerning the matter at hand (453a8–b4, 453c1–4, 454b8–c5, 457c4–458b3). Gorgias accepts this and commends Socrates' procedure (454c6, 458b4–5). Eventually the following definition is reached: "Then it seems rhetoric is the producer of persuasion which yields conviction but not instruction in the matter of just and unjust" (454e9–455a2). But it seems this is still too narrow: Socrates elicits the admission that it is not only justice and injustice concerning which rhetoric produces conviction but in fact all things, in particular the subject matters of all other crafts (455a8–459c5). This broadening prepares for the sequel, wherein Socrates shows that certain beliefs held by Gorgias are mutually inconsistent. Does the orator possess knowledge of the crafts concerning whose subject matters he produces conviction in his audience? Gorgias must of course deny this. The upshot is embarrassing: that the orator is convincing only to the ignorant, not to those who *do* possess such knowledge. Gorgias tries to save face by saying that concerning justice and injustice, at any rate, the orator—at least if he is taught by Gorgias—*does* have knowledge (460a3–4). This claim, however, turns out to be inconsistent with other statements that he has already made or else now admits to: (1) he who knows what is just is just; (2) he who is just never desires to act unjustly; (3) some orators use rhetoric for unjust ends. For together the four claims yield the contradiction: it is and is not possible for an orator to act unjustly (460a5–461a7).[66] Socrates admits, finally, that he had for some time expected an inconsistency to emerge and yet that to discover on which side of the question the truth lies (*tauta oun hopēi pote echei*) will require a very long discussion (461a7–b2). Before he can go on, however, he is interrupted by Polus; the conversation with Gorgias is never resumed.

What exactly has Socrates been doing with Gorgias? Is it the same sort of thing he is about to do with Polus? We note that Gorgias has been refuted, in the sense that he has been shown to contradict himself. Polus will likewise be refuted. Is such a refutation precisely the goal of Socratic dialectic? As is well known, R. Robinson has argued that the method portrayed in the Socratic dialogues (*Gorgias* included) is—notwithstanding Socrates' protestations to be simply "following the *logos*"—a purely destructive method of questioning (the "elenchus") designed to elicit contradictory assertions from the interlocutor. Its purpose is educational: to instill awareness of ignorance, at least a necessary condition for moral and philosophical improvement.[67] Robinson supports this view by referring us to certain passages in the Platonic corpus identified by him as "discussions of the elenchus."[68] Others, in particular G. Vlastos and T. Irwin, have argued that the Socratic dialectic is on the contrary a positive or constructive method of *investigation,* not simply an educational elenchus, and that neither Socrates' disclaimers of knowledge nor his claims to be pursuing the *logos* are insincere. By its means the philosopher rationally supports or emends his own convictions, even if he is unable thereby to gain knowledge in the strict sense.[69] These (respectively) "destructive" and "constructive" interpretations, as opposed as they are, nevertheless share an important assumption. This is that the dialectic is monolithic, so to speak: Socrates does basically the same sort of thing with whomever he converses. This I think is false, as our material from the *Gorgias* will show. And yet despite their sharing this particular assumption, neither the destructive nor the constructive interpretation ought to be completely rejected. I suggest that with Gorgias the dialectic is of a sort that is constructive in aim, whereas with Polus it is indeed of the opposite sort. The reason for the difference has to do with the fact that the two interlocutors are rather different sorts of people.

Whatever else Gorgias is, he is—or so he is regarded by Socrates—capable of a sincere regard for the truth. He may suffer from "complacency (448a, 449cd), pomposity (451d, 455d), and naive vanity (449a, 463cd)" (Dodds), but it is difficult to dismiss as no more than ironic the respectful tone Socrates adopts with him.[70] Gorgias is not only willing to answer Socrates' questions, but to answer them briefly, thus freely renouncing his preferred rhetorical modes. His intelligence seems unquestionable and he is, after all, in *some* sense an "expert" in what he professes to do. When Socrates so emphatically claims to want to discover the truth about rhetoric, and not to refute Gorgias—and when Gorgias accepts these claims—it seems perverse to construe the one as "ironic" (read *hypocritical*) and the other as a mere dupe. It does not seem possible that when Socrates says such things, Plato doesn't mean us to regard him as sincere.[71] To be sure, insofar as Gorgias does suffer from complacency or vanity Socrates must believe both that he will be refuted and will benefit from the refutation. He has reason both to expect and value the negative outcome. As he himself explicitly points out to Gorgias (461a1–2), however, the refutation is a *foreseen consequence,* not the intended aim of the dialectic. Note further Socrates' emphasis on the fact that the negative outcome is merely provisional. Determining *tauta oun hopēi pote echei* (461a7)—that is, which claim(s) of those admitted by Gorgias should be rejected in order to resolve the discovered inconsistency—would be a lengthy matter, as Socrates (rightly) notes, without at all implying that he wishes to drop the matter. All indications are thus that with Gorgias Socrates engages in a sincere investigation of the nature of rhetoric.

Yet it appears otherwise in the case of Polus. That Socrates thinks so, and why, is at any rate evident. Note first his reaction to Polus' rude attempt at the start of the dialogue to usurp the place of Gorgias—his teacher—as Chaerephon's and Socrates' interlocutor (448aff.). Rather arrogantly insinuating himself on the excuse that Gorgias must be fatigued from his earlier rhetorical display, he is quickly dismissed by Socrates on account of his evident inability to answer the question asked (what is it that Gorgias does?) without begining a long speech. With this Polus' character is already defined in sharp contrast with that of Gorgias. He is one who is so thoroughly convinced of the unimpeachable value of his profession and of his own competence that he is simply unable to participate in a *questioning* of that profession. All that he is able to do, vainly and ludicrously, is to attempt to display his alleged skills (thus he waxes encomiastic). Later on when he interrupts a second time (461bff.), and thereafter throughout the whole episode, we see repeatedly the signs of his conceit. Although he certainly has the desire to be heard, he has no need to investigate, so he thinks. Beliefs opposed to his own appear to him not just incorrect but obviously so, and his own views self-evidently true (cf. 461b3–c4, 462a5–7, 468e6–9, 470c4–5, 473e4–5). At 462a7 he seems to harbor no doubt whatsoever that he will succeed where he thinks Gorgias has failed, nor at 466a4ff. does he think it will be very difficult at all to rescue rhetoric from Socrates' condemnation of it as flattery. If eventually he submits to being questioned, it is only because he cannot conceive that Socrates seriously believes what he is saying and wants to know really what he means (cf. 467c3–4, 471e1, 474c2–3). Thus in his attitude towards and motives in joining the conversation, Polus differs significantly from Gorgias. Corresponding to this difference is a profound difference in Socrates' own motives for conversing with him.

It appears no longer to be the case, as it was with Gorgias, that Socrates is pursuing the truth of the matters discussed or that his motive is to rid himself of the evil of false belief. It seems now that he *is* directing himself against the person of the interlocutor. Surely it is no accident that the disclaimers stated so emphatically to Gorgias are nowhere to be found in the Polus episode: not once does Socrates reassure Polus that he is arguing, as it were, *ou sou heneka alla tou logou,* or that he had expected a contradiction to emerge, or that further investigation will be needed. His silence in regard to these matters is only honest. For his motivation in conversing with such a one as Polus is not to discover truth or falsehood or to support in any way his own convictions by subjecting either them or their denials to cross-examination. Instead the dialectic is in a certain way destructive in intent: destructive not (necessarily) of any false beliefs the interlocutor may have concerning the matters under discussion but rather of the false belief he has *about himself*—that he is wise and hence in no need to engage in further investigation.

The character and aim of this sort of dialectic are made clear in a passage from the *Sophist*. Although it does not mention Socrates by name, Robinson is surely right to think that it must reflect in *some* way on the Socrates of the early dialogues. Certain educators, says the Stranger,

> have convinced themselves that all ignorance is involuntary and that he who thinks himself wise would never be willing to learn any of those things in which he thinks he is clever. . . . They question a man about the things about which he thinks he is talking sense when he is talking nonsense, then they easily discover that his opinions . . . contradict one another about the same things in relation to the same things and in respect to the same things. But those who see this grow angry with themselves and gentle towards others and this is the way they are freed from their high and obstinate opinions about themselves. . . . [T]hose who [so] purge the soul believe that the soul can receive no benefit from any teachings offered to it until someone by cross-questioning reduces him who is cross-questioned to an attitude of modesty, by removing the opinions that obstruct the teachings, and this purges him and makes him think that he knows only what he knows, and no more (230a5–d4, Fowler, trans.)

This "purgative" dialectic, dubbed "noble sophistic" (*gennaia sophistikē* 231b8), has the single purpose of "removing the opinions that obstruct the teachings," that is, the opinions which constitute the self-conceit of the interlocutor.[72] It is a protreptic, not an epistemological method. He who is firmly convinced of his wisdom is induced to contradict himself solely in order for him to confront and acknowledge his actual ignorance. Repeatedly Socrates emphasizes the necessity of this humbling recognition in order for genuine philosophical pursuit to be possible.[73] The claim in the *Sophist* is that one best gains such a recognition by being made to contradict himself in public.

Now a person such as Gorgias, able to participate sincerely in the question-and-answer examination of his own profession, has to that extent implicitly acknowledged at least the possibility that his views may be overturned. But such a one as Polus, conceited to an extreme, is unable and unfit to take part in such an investigation. Therefore he is subjected to what is by design a "purgation" of his conceit. The character of the dialectic changes accordingly.[74] Since Socrates is arguing now not for the sake of the *logos* but for the sake of Polus, he has no reason necessarily to adhere to the standards of logic or fair play—and possibly reason not to. To achieve his ends the practitioner of the purgative method may find it simply more efficient to argue fallaciously, to admit into discussion theses he regards as false, and in general to steer the discussion from moment to moment in whatever direction is conducive to eliciting self-contradiction—rather than "follow the *logos* wherever it may lead," or agree only to what he regards as true, or strive for logical cogency. Admittedly these options are not explicitly recognized in our passage from the *Sophist*. Yet they are consistent with the goals it describes and their availability is surely alluded to in the title conferred on the purgative method: it is after all *sophistic*, however noble.

Thus when Polus insists that orators, like tyrants, have great power, Socrates quickly denies that it is so. He has thereby begun to maneuver Polus into contradicting himself on the question of power; for this it does not matter that the issues first turned to are in fact silly.[75] Although Polus never quite reaches the point of formally contradicting his claim that orators have great power (as we saw, this "issue" is left unresolved at 468e), Socrates succeeds in getting him to deny certain assumptions which underlie his claim and which at first seem self-evident: (1) that one has great power just in case he is able to do whatever seems good; (2) that doing whatever seems good is the same as doing whatever one wants. It doesn't matter that these assumptions are perfectly legitimate. Nor that the denial of (1) rests on grounds which Socrates himself does not accept (i.e., that power is always actually good for its possessor, hence that the ability to do whatever seems good must be conjoined with intelligence in order to *be* power). Nor that the denial of (2) is both fallacious and contradictory of Socrates' own characterization of the object of desire. Nor is the course of the discussion in 466aff. really erratic at all: in its seemingly random transitions it proceeds expeditiously towards its goal. It may be that the fallacies and distortions are bad in themselves; but if so, Socrates must think, the good here outweighs the bad.[76]

I do not mean to imply that Socrates is right about this. Is it so clear that the experience of self-contradiction has protreptic force in itself? Can we say that Plato's portrayal of Socrates arguing in the ''sophistic'' mode was not liable to create misunderstanding on the part of the reader? Surely the kind of humiliation which Polus suffers may lead rather to greater resentment of Socrates than to any desire to pursue philosophy Socratically: cf. *Apol.* 22e–23a, *Tht.* 167e–168b. As for its results on Polus, nothing is indicated in the *Gorgias,* although it is difficult not to come down on the side of scepticism. Moreover, if the above interpretation of the Polus episode is correct, then Socrates' arguments have unfortunately been misconstrued for quite some time. Yet it is perhaps unclear whether it is Plato or rather his readers who bear the greater responsibility for this.

VI

If my argument so far is correct, then DG is irrelevant to Platonic moral theory. Hence it is irrelevant to the Paradox, ''No One Is Unjust Voluntarily.'' This is a result, however, which requires further clarification and support.

On first blush it seems that the very text of the *Gorgias* stands in the way of this result. As noted at the outset of this essay, Socrates asks Callicles at 509e5–7 to reaffirm the conclusion reached earlier with Polus: ''No one desires to act unjustly, but all those who act unjustly do so involuntarily.'' Does this not imply that wrongdoers, according to Socrates, act involuntarily simply in virtue of their *not desiring* the unjust action? This in turn would imply, as many interpreters of Plato have thought (cf. Sec. I), that DG is required for the Paradox: if something is in fact harmful, then no one desires it, injustice is harmful and thus no one desires it.

It would be absurd at this point, however, to place any weight on Socrates' just cited remark. The preponderating evidence is that DG is not, nor is intended by Plato to be, a cogent argument or one that is even consistent with his own view of desire. Note in any case that Socrates does *not,* strictly speaking, infer the *alla* clause which contains the Paradox from the initial clause which requires DG. Rather he has found, I suggest, a device which enables him to introduce the Paradox into the discussion with Callicles (for purposes we need not consider here). The link between ''not desired'' and ''involuntary,'' although specious in itself (so I will argue), is nevertheless superficially plausible and hence rhetorically effective. I shall now try to clarify just how ''involuntary'' should instead be taken.

Let us assume in accordance with our previous findings that, unless he is externally coerced or perhaps akratic,[77] the unjust agent in Plato's analysis straightforwardly does what he desires to do: that which appears good overall to him. What is it that makes his action *involuntary?*

Santas in a well-known paper derives the Paradox from three doctrines which he finds in the text of the *Gorgias*. His approach is, I think, basically correct; yet some difficulties which remain in his discussion should be cleared away. The three doctrines are:

[1] [M]en desire only good things.

[2] [M]en do what they do not for its own sake but because they think it is better for them.

[3] [D]oing what is just is . . . good for the agent (whereas injustice is harmful).[78]

Santas, it is clear, rightly construes the "good things" that are the object of desire according to (1) as the *apparent* good.[79] It is not so clear, however, either that (2) is held by Plato or that it is really necessary for the derivation: why couldn't certain actions be desired for their own sakes consistently with their being involuntary?[80] In any case the evident crux, as Santas himself recognizes, is that from these doctrines it does not at all follow that:

(4) Men who act unjustly do not desire or "will" to do so.

All action, even unjust action, is motivated by the agent's desire for what he conceives to be good: it is desired, even if in fact it is harmful. Now this is indeed a problem if "involuntary" must be taken to be equivalent to "unwilled" or "undesired." But this is a mistake. To see this let us first consider what *does* follow from the above three (or two) doctrines:

(4') Men who act unjustly do not do so knowing or believing that their action is harmful to them.

Wrongdoers may very well do what they desire to do—but they are always ignorant of the harm their action causes them. Could it perhaps be that it is the agent's ignorance, not an absence of desire or will, that constitutes the basis of the Paradox? But what is the precise connection, if any, between ignorance of self-harm (or any other sort of ignorance) and involuntariness?

Santas remarks that

"willingly" and "involuntarily" may be bad translations [sc. for *boulomenon* and *akontas,* respectively, in 509e6].[81] . . . [I]t is clear that Plato does not mean that these people act reluctantly or that they are forced to do injustice; he means that they act in ignorance that what they do is unjust or harmful to them or both.[82]

This seems to suggest that if Plato uses the term "involuntary" without implying that the action was in some sense against the actual will or desire of the agent, then he is not using the term in its normal sense: for all that he means is that the agent is ignorant in the stated respects. But this is not quite right. Plato does not *mean* that unjust agents are ignorant in certain ways: what he says is that their action is involuntary. It is very unclear that he holds "involuntary" to be synonymous with "performed in ignorance that it is unjust or harmful or both"; or that, in his view, involuntariness necessarily implies the presence of such ignorance; or that he is confused. Nor is there the slightest problem with the cited translations. The problem, if there is one, lies in the argument itself—or rather our understanding of it.

I suggest that we construe "involuntary" in the Paradox in the following way. Plato's claim is that the unjust agent is *exempt from blame*. This is what makes it a Paradox![83] Moreover, it is false—and not just for Plato—that involuntary action is necessarily or even normally action that is in some way against or in conflict with the desires of the agent.

In the case of unjust action it is simply the presence of a certain kind of ignorance in the agent that, for Plato, forms the *basis* of its involuntariness. It may help to note that in regard to the general criterion of ignorance, Socrates and Plato (and Aristotle after them) were hardly innovators. Aristotle's discussions of exculpatory ignorance (cf. *EN* III.1, V.8, *EE* II.9) are an attempt to clarify and elaborate a standard which had long held appeal to Greek common sense and had become embedded in the legal tradition.[84] It was the very criterion upon which Socrates' and Plato's Paradox had already, in some form, implicitly relied. We might call it the agent's *relevant ignorance,* that is, ignorance of relevant features of his action. The difficultly, of course, lies in the account to be given of "relevant." Which kinds of ignorance are exculpatory and which not? On what is the distinction to be based? It is in relation to these questions that the Paradox must be interpreted and judged; the peculiar notion of desire that emerges from DG has nothing to do with it.

In regard to this Santas states that what gives "plausibility" to the Paradox is the fact that "the people in question [sc. unjust agents] would not have acted unjustly and would not have wanted to, if they had . . . knowledge [sc. that their action is unjust or harmful to them or both]."[85] According to this suggestion Plato holds that ignorance *either* that one's action is harmful to oneself *or* that one's action is unjust is exculpatory. The reason is that in the case of all unjust agents the presence of either sort of ignorance would render true the hypothetical proposition:

> If the agent had not been ignorant (in such a way), he would not have desired or chosen to act as he did.

This suggestion seems to be on the right track. Nevertheless it is problematic as it stands. First of all, it presupposes that in Plato's view one may know that an action is unjust and yet not know that it is harmful.[86] This is perhaps not true. Even if that possibility were a real one, however, it would obviously be false—on Platonic grounds or any other—that *every* unjust agent who happens to be ignorant that his action was unjust would not have desired to act as he did if only he had known *this* (i.e., and not also that it was harmful as well). Let us then revise the hypothetical proposition as follows:

> H If the unjust agent had known or believed that his action was harmful to him, he would not have desired or chosen to act as he did.

This proposition is clearly true of all unjust agents. For all men, whether unjust or not, do only what they conceive to be good for themselves.

The suggestion that H (or something close to it) gives plausibility to the Paradox is not unique to Santas. Gulley argues that the basis for the claim that injustice is involuntary is Plato's view (based on DG) that the agent does not do what he desires to do; and that this means that he acts "against what he would wish to do if he knew what was "really" good."[87] As we saw, this attempt to interpret DG by construing the agent's desire for *the* good in hypothetical terms fails. Nevertheless that failure does not affect the present suggestion, which entirely dispenses with DG. Put in a form which conspicuously omits any use or even mention of DG, the suggestion was put forward as early as the second century A.D.: it is present in extant texts of the Middle Platonists Albinus and Apuleius. Thus Albinus, while insisting that virtue is always voluntary, defends Plato's view that vice is always involuntary (*to tēn kakian akousion huparchein*) thus:

> For who would freely choose to possess the greatest of evils in the most noble and honorable part of himself? If a person is attracted to evil, first of all it will not be attractive to him as an evil but rather as something good. Even if a person has recourse to evil, such a one is entirely deceived insofar as he hopes to extract a greater good by means of a lesser evil, and in this way he will proceed involuntarily. For it is impossible for anyone to be attracted to evils, and to desire them, unless it is out of hope for good or else fear of a greater evil.[88]

Vice is involuntary not because it is not desired, but because the vicious agent is necessarily deceived, that is, ignorant, concerning the harm he possesses in his soul. Otherwise he would never choose to be in such a condition. Even if he recognizes that his condition (or action) is to some extent evil, he must still be ignorant that it is the *greatest* of evils and necessarily evil overall. For no one desires anything that is not conceived to be good overall. I believe that this is a correct account of Plato's view. It happens to have a firm textual basis: *Lg.* 731c1–d5, which (unlike *Gorg.* 466a9–468e5) deserves to be ranked as definitive for the understanding of the Paradox.

It should be clear, then, that the claim as to what the agent, given certain circumstances, would not desire to do does not serve to explicate any sense in which he does not in fact desire or will his act. The suggestion should rather be—and for Albinus it is—that the truth of such a claim is required for and supportive of the doctrine that injustice is involuntary, where "involuntary" means "exempt from blame" and the criterion for involuntariness is a certain kind of ignorance (ignorance of self-harm). The point to emphasize is that an action can be involuntary and yet still *desired in an unqualified sense*.

It is not clear, however, that in Plato's view proposition H shows by itself that ignorance of self-harm makes unjust action involuntary. A case might be made that the success of *any* ascription of involuntariness—on whatever grounds—necessarily requires that the agent, given the alleged exculpating factor, would not have desired or chosen to act as he did.[89] But is that all that is required? In what Aristotle calls a "mixed" case of compulsion, for example being compelled on pain of suffering some great loss to perform a wicked deed, it may be true that the agent would not have desired to act as he did had he not been compelled. Yet as Aristotle's discussion of such cases makes clear, this may not be enough to excuse him: if his action was sufficiently heinous, we may blame him just as we may have praised him for refusing to submit and so incurring the great loss. This suggests the possibility that, also in cases where ignorance is the criterion, something more might be needed. At any rate isn't a state of ignorance, or perhaps persistence in such a state, possibly something that the agent freely chooses or is somehow responsible for? (For an example take someone's choosing, in a game of Russian roulette, not to know that the next chamber is loaded.) If that were ever true in the case of self-harm, then the truth of H would be insufficient to justify the ascription of involuntariness. For the latter might be defeated by the fact that the agent is still to be blamed for his own ignorance. There are texts, however, in which Plato explicitly denies that *any* state of ignorance can be considered voluntary.[90] This claim surely deserves to be included in any reconstruction of the theory underlying the Paradox.

In sum I have tried to show, *contra* the majority opinion, that the Paradox does not depend on the peculiar notion of desire that emerges from the argument at *Gorg.* 466a–468e. That is, it does not rely on any notion that the agent could not have desired or willed to perform X if X was unjust and hence objectively harmful. The Paradox depends rather on the much less peculiar notion that

(1) All men desire the apparent good, that is, what they conceive to be good for themselves,

which together with the basic Socratic claim that

(2) Unjust action is always harmful to the agent,

yields the result that

(3) Every unjust agent is ignorant that his action is harmful to himself.

Then in part on the basis of H, that is

(4) For every unjust agent, if he had not been ignorant that his action was harmful to himself, he would not have desired or chosen to act as he did,

and in part on the basis of

(5) Ignorance is always involuntary,

Plato concludes that

(6) Ignorance of self-harm is always exculpatory of the unjust agent.

It then follows from (3) and (6) that

(7) No one commits injustice voluntarily.

Is the reasoning underlying the paradox cogent? This argument can and of course has been challenged in various ways. Thus the doctrines expressed in (1) and (2) have struck many as dubious; the former suffering (it is alleged) from inability to account adequately for weakness of will and implying (it is alleged) an objectionable psychological egoism, the latter resting upon a kind of moral objectivism that many today find repugnant. I cannot contribute to these debates here.[91] Instead I will end by mentioning one problem which I do not think has received the attention it deserves.

Let us suppose for a moment, with Aristotle, that Plato's doctrines (1) and (2) are correct. It follows that the unjust agent is ignorant that he is harming himself. But is this ignorance necessarily *relevant* ignorance? That is, does (6) necessarily follow from (4) and (5)?

As is well known, Aristotle argues that only "particular" ignorance is relevant to ascriptions of involuntariness. By this he means ignorance of the peculiar circumstances, nature, and objects of one's action: "(1) the agent, (2) the act, (3) the object or medium of the act, and sometimes also (4) the instrument (e.g., a tool), (5) the aim (e.g., saving life), and (6) the manner (e.g., roughly or gently)" (*EN* 1111a3–6, Thomson, tr., cf. *EE*

1225b1–8). Aristotle denies that what he calls "ignorance of the universal" (*hē* [*agnoia*] *katholou*) is exculpatory. He seems to identify this sort of ignorance with ignorance of "one's advantages" (*ta sumpheronta*) and argues that when displayed in moral choice such ignorance causes vice in the first place and is precisely what is *subject* to blame. After all, he says in effect, every wicked agent is "ignorant of what he ought to do and refrain from doing" (*ha dei prattein kai hōn aphekton*), so that such ignorance cannot be a criterion for distinguishing those whose action is involuntary from those whose action is not so (cf. 1110b28–33). What Aristotle here denies to be exculpatory seems to resemble closely what Plato in the reasoning underlying the Paradox holds to be such: ignorance of self-harm. At any rate there is little doubt, although he mentions no names, that his discussion of ignorance is intended in large part to refute the Paradox put forward by Socrates and Plato.[92] Does it?

Some writers on the Paradox, for example, Gulley and Santas, presume without argument that Aristotle's criticism is correct.[93] This is too interesting an issue to be decided without argument. Perhaps the interpretation given here of the notion of involuntariness in the Paradox has helped to clarify the real issues involved.

NOTES

1. A rough formalization is given below, p. 267.
2. Cf., in addition to *Gorg.* 509e5–7, *Prot.* 345d6–e6; *Tim.* 86d5–e3; *Lg.* 731c1–d5, 860d5. I will refer to it as "the" Paradox. Of course it is only one of several interrelated claims generally labelled "Socratic Paradoxes." These include: virtue is knowledge; to have one virtue is to have them all; weakness of the will is impossible.
3. This view is found above all among proponents of what I label the "neoplatonic" and "hypothetical" interpretations: Santas, Gulley, Cornford, O'Brien, many others (see Sec. I). Cf. also the late Stoic revival of the Paradox, e.g. in Epictetus, *Disc.* I. xvii. 13–14 with II. xxvi. 1–2 (clearly reminiscent of the *Gorg.*), IV.i. 1–5.
4. So M. Mackenzie: "The distinction between 'what I think I want' and 'what I truly want' ensures that choice will be intellectual, such that bad choice is a matter solely of mistake, good choice of correct judgment," *Plato's Theory of Punishment* (New York 1981) [= Mackenzie] 161. She is echoing a long-standing view: cf. M. O'Brien, *The Socratic Paradoxes and the Greek Mind* (Chapel Hill 1967) [= O'Brien] 91. It may be rejected immediately. DG is neither necessary nor sufficient for the thesis that "choice is intellectual." Not necessary, as is clear from the *Protagoras,* in which the argument that moral failure is due to error neither needs nor resorts to any such distinction. Nor is it sufficient. For "doing what seems good" must still involve motivation by way of desire of some sort: if not "desire," then (say) "apparent desire." But then for all that DG says, choice might depend merely on which of the two happens to have greater motivational pull, "desire" or "apparent desire." At any rate it is unclear to begin with that either Socrates or Plato is "intellectualist" in the sense of holding that choice is *solely* intellectual.
5. Cf. the Arethan scholium on 466e (Greene 473); Boethius, *De Consol. Phil.* Bk.IV, Pr.2. More recently: J. Gould, *The Development of Plato's Ethics* (Cambridge 1955) [= Gould] 51; I. M. Crombie, *An Examination of Plato's Doctrines:* Vol. I (London 1962) [= Crombie] 246; N. Gulley, "The Interpretation of 'No One Does Wrong Willingly' in Plato's Dialogues," *Phronesis* 10 (1965) [= Gulley] 83; O'Brien 87–8; A. Spitzer, "The Self-Reference of the *Gorgias,*" *Philosophy and Rhetoric* (1975) 16–17; T. Irwin, *Plato: Gorgias* (Oxford 1979) [= Irwin] 139, 145–46 (who, however, denies that the argument about power is valid); Mackenzie 138–39.

6. Cf. W. H. Thompson: "The distinction . . . is sufficiently obvious . . ." *The Gorgias of Plato* (London 1871) viii; G. Nakhnikian, "The First Socratic Paradox," *Journal of the History of Philosophy* 11 (1973) 15; G. Santas, *The Philosophy of Socrates* (London 1979) [= Santas] 224–5.

7. It is a curious fact that with few exceptions (Dodds, for one) commentators seem to think that Plato uses the noun *boulēsis* in *Gorg.* 466a–468e. This is false—the text has only the verb *boulesthai*. The error seems trivial; yet the reification may contribute to the non-trivial error (so I shall argue) of extracting from the argument the notion of a special kind of faculty in the soul, *"boulēsis."*

8. *Cambridge Ancient History,* Vol. VI, ed. J. B. Bury, J. A. Cook, and F. E. Adcock (Cambridge 1927) 306; cf. *Before and After Socrates* (Cambridge 1932) 51.

9. Cf. Gould 47–55; R. Cushman, *Therapeia* (Chapel Hill 1958) [= Cushman] 185, 194–95; E. R. Dodds, *Plato: Gorgias: A Revised Text with Introduction and Commentary* (Oxford 1959) [= Dodds] 235–36, who notes that DG "is perhaps only fully intelligible in the light of Plato's later distinction between the 'inner man' . . . and the empirical self which is distorted by earthly experience (cf. *Rep.* 611bff.) . . ."; A. W. H. Adkins, *Merit and Responsibility* (Oxford 1969) 305, 309. J. Moline, *Plato's Theory of Understanding* (Madison, Wis. 1981) [= Moline] 71–73 assumes that Plato held to the tripartite division of the soul when he wrote the *Gorgias* and cites *Rep.* 585ce and 611bc as showing that the *logistikon* of Book IV is in fact one's "real self," and its desires one's "real desires." All this is at least debatable. It is simply incorrect, however, to say that in the *Gorgias* Plato "alleges that what one really wants is wanted by one's most real part" (71); and wildly false that an apparent-wants/real-wants distinction is "frequently invoked" by Plato (ibid.). As for the "true self," it seems clear that Plato holds that there is such a thing (see D. Gallop, *Plato: Phaedo* [Oxford 1975] 88). What is at issue is its relation to a special kind of *desire for the good.*

10. This kinship and longing are referred to in *Phdo.* 79a6–80b6, cf. 84a7–b4; *Tim.* 90a2–d7; perhaps *Phil.* 58d.

11. O'Brien 217–18 n. 15; cf. 158, where the "true self" is at least implicit in his analysis. His claim that only the concept of a real desire for *the* good could render intelligible Socrates' dialectic is shared by R. E. Allen, "The Socratic Paradox," *Journal of the History of Ideas* 21 (1960) 263–64, who also reminisces *Rep.* 505de. It may be dismissed immediately. Socrates needs no more than that (1) all men desire the apparent good; (2) there is a determinate, genuine good capable of being known by all men; (3) dialectic enables one to attain knowledge of this good. On (1) see pp. 269ff.

12. So too Nettleship implicitly in *Lectures on the Republic of Plato* (London 1901, repr. 1962) 234, and N. R. Murphy, *The Interpretation of Plato's Republic* (Oxford 1951) [= Murphy] 47, who invents Greek that is not in the text of *Rep.* 505; Cushman loc cit.

13. O'Brien 224 (my emphasis); cf. 91.

14. O'Brien 225–26.

15. That DG shows a "restricted" sense of "desire" is claimed by O'Brien 89, 91 and before him by O. Apelt, *Platon: Gorgias* (Hamburg 1922, repr. 1955) 171–72; Gould 50; Dodds 236; Santas 315–16 n. 16; Gulley 83; after him by Irwin 141 ad 467b (but cf. ad 467cd); Mackenzie 165 cf. 138 n 14. Cf. Moline 73 who sees not "desire" but rather "involuntary" as the bearer of a "technical, part [sc. of the soul]-related sense." Santas, Gulley, and Irwin, however, express views on DG overall that are quite different from O'Brien's, on which see subsequent discussion.

16. Gould 50, cf. A. E. Taylor, *Socrates* (London 1932) 142; Cushman 185.

17. Plato uses the restricted sense in *Charm.* 167e4–5 (Apelt, Gould 47 n. 1, Cushman, Santas); *Crat.* 420d5, 8 (Gould 55); *Meno* 78a4ff. (Santas *contra* R. S. Bluck, *Plato's Meno* [Cambridge 1961] 259); *Rep.* 577e1 (P. Shorey, *What Plato Said* [Chicago 1933] [= Shorey

I] 504, but cf. the contrary remark in Shorey's Loeb *Rep.* Vol. II [= Shorey II] 358–59, Murphy 47, Dodds); *Laws* 687c9 (Mackenzie 143–44), 687e7 (Apelt, Mackenzie), 688b7 (Shorey II 359), 863e2 (Mackenzie 247). It also appears in the *Def.* 413c8–9 (Gould 47 n. 1, Dodds, Santas). Santas goes so far as to say: "Plato never speaks, to my knowledge, of bad or harmful *boulēsis* . . . neither the intended nor the actual object of [*boulēsis*] can ever be a bad thing," whereas "the object of every desire (*epithumia*) is a pleasure . . . . : and so presumably may be a bad thing." Apelt, Dodds, and O'Brien, however, deny that Plato consistently adheres to the restricted sense. On all this see below, p. 274 and n. 53.

18. Plotinus takes "all men desire the good" to mean that all human action is somehow motivated by an instinctive longing for the good—a longing which proceeds from the very nature of the soul and of which only the agent's "true self," not necessarily his conscious self, is cognizant. In fact, all *things* desire the good. "We must realize that men have lost their awareness of that which from the beginning and still now they long for and desire. For all things desire it [sc. the good = the one] and aspire to it by natural necessity, as though having divined (*apomemanteumena*) that without it they cannot exist (V.5.12.5–9 [the use of "divine" may reminisce *Rep.* 505e1], cf. VI.8.13.11–22, I.6.7.3–44, I.7.1.23, I.8.2.2–4, VI.7.26.6–9). In the case of men this desire is a function of the soul's activity, which is instinctively directed at that which is better and greater: *tēs psuchēs epheseōs pros to kreitton kai agathon* (III.5.9.41, cf. I.4.6.17ff.). Cf. R. Arnou, *Le désir de Dieu dans la philosophie de Plotin* (Paris 1921) 74–92 and passim. Why then do most men choose objects or ends which happen to be bad? As with Cornford et al., the wrong which men do is *undesired.* It is only *the* good which is really desired (*ontōs orekton* [VI.7.20.36], *ontōs erōmenon* [VI.9.9.44], cf. *ho boulētos ontōs bios* [I.4.6.19–20]). When the soul has finally attained the contemplative state, it will "know that this [the good] is what it always desires" (*ginōskein hoti touto estin hou ephieto* [VI.7.34.26, but cf. VI.8.13.20–22]). Not surprisingly, then, Plotinus links *boulēsis* with *nous,* the "true self," for which see I.1, esp. I.1.7.20 and I.1.10.14, together with the interesting argument in VI.8.6.26–45 that, although "what is in our power" (*to eph' hēmin*) is none other than the activity—internal to the soul—of the contemplative mind (*tēn tou nou energeian:* VI.8.3.22, cf. VI.8.5.34–37), such activity is at any rate still a matter of desire—or at least *boulēsis* in the "proper" (*kuria*) sense. Thus he evinces what amounts to the restricted sense. See also the argument in I.4.6.14–24 to the effect that no one desires external (popular) goods, *ei kuriōs tēn boulēsin hupolambanoi* (intended to support their exclusion from his account of happiness). Is it certain that Plotinus was inspired by DG? There is no direct evidence pointing in this case to the *Gorgias.* I know of no commentator on the present passage who has mentioned such a link. Yet certain considerations support it: (1) it is at least a plausible interpretation of DG to say that Socrates means *boulesthai kuriōs;* (2) it would explain why Plotinus speaks of a restricted sense of *boulesthai* only—never of *erān* or *oregesthai* or other desire-terms; (3) the restricted sense appears nowhere, so far as I know, in any other (extant) text which might have influenced Plotinus [On its absence in Aristotle see n. 40. The old Stoic concept of *boulēsis,* as report by Cicero *Tusc. Disp.* 4.6.12 = *Stoicorum Veterum Fragmenta* [hereafter "SVF"] III.438, involves to be sure a certain restricted sense (roughly, "sustained prudent desire" [such as only the sage possesses]); here again, however, its object is quite clearly the *apparent* good (quod bonum videatur); cf. *SVF* III.386 and A.-J. Voelke, *L'Idée de volonté dans le Stoicisme* (Paris 1973) 56–61. On the middle Platonic use of *boulesthai,* see n. 88.]; (4) such a concept *is* explicitly linked with the *Gorgias* by later neoplatonists (see next note), which points perhaps to a continuous tradition to this effect within the school. Is Plotinus' overall interpretation of DG an original one? That is more difficult to say.

19. The Plotinian interpretation is reflected in scholia found on certain manuscripts of the *Gorgias,* perhaps deriving from the lost commentary by Proclus. Cf. esp. the Arethan

scholium on 466e (Greene 473); for the ascription to Proclus, see Dodds 61. Cf. scholia on 466b (Greene 473) and 460c (Greene 141). The restricted sense (without, however, the "true self" linkage of *boulēsis* with *nous*) appears clearly in Olympiodorus' *In Plat. Gorg.; his* comments on DG are of interest. Although adopting a very roundabout way of reconstructing Socrates' argument, as he puts it, *hoti ha bouletai tis prattein, tauta agatha estin* (16.1 = 91.24–5 Westerink). Olympiodorus finally hits on the heart of the matter; *to de telos agathon, kai touto boulometha prattein . . . ei de tis eipoi hoti 'ti oun? ou boulometha kai kakon?'* *eipe hoti 'ou kuriōs, all' epeidē to agathon ē phainomenon estin ē ontōs, estin hote tou phainomenou epithumountes nomizomen to ontōs agathon diōkein; hōste to hou heneka kuriōs to agathon estin'* (16.1 = 93.1–7 Westerink). Someone might try to say that sometimes bad things come to be desired and the reply to him is that there are times when, even if we do desire things that happen to be bad, still we hold that we are pursuing what is actually good; hence the end is strictly speaking *the* good and thus we don't really desire, in the strict sense, things that happen to be bad. The idea here seems to be that it is possible for the agent himself to license a *de re* interpretation of his own "I desire the good," on which "the good" = "the actual good, whatever it is." (Even if this argument were valid, and perhaps it is, the conclusion isn't strong enough: the point that needs to be shown is not that *sometimes* we don't *boulometha* actually bad things, but that we *never* do.) Cf. also *In Plat. Alc.* 39.15–20 = 27 Westerink, 46.15–17 = 31 Westerink.

20. Cf. *Platons sämtliche Werke*, H. Müller, trans., introd. by K. Steinhart, Vol. III (Leipzig 1851) 367–68. He is followed by F. Susemihl, *Die genetische Entwicklung der Platonische Philosophie* (Leipzig 1855) 93, n. 56; and echoed by many others. These include P. Friedländer in *Plato: The Dialogues (First Period)*, trans. H. Meyerhoff (Princeton, N.J. 1964) 255; J. Moreau, with his talk of "bon plaisir" or the "volonté réfléchie" opposed to "toutes nos volitions empiriques" and having "un Bien idéal" as its object, in *La construction de l'idéalisme platonicien* (Paris 1939) 151–53, cf. 157; Murphy 48; I. Dilman, *Morality and the Inner Life: A Study in Plato's "Gorgias"* (London 1979) 31–41.

21. The term *implicite* is used by Susemihl in noting his own agreement with Steinhart; its aptness is evident, cf. next note.

22. *Hegel's Philosophy of Right*, trans. by T. M. Knox (Oxford 1952) para. 258: "[T]he objective will is rationality implicit or in conception, whether it be recognized or not by individuals, whether their whims be for it or not." On the distinction between "Willkür" and "vernünftige Wille" see also paras. 12 (with Addition), 129, 141. One notorious conclusion Hegel draws by way of this distinction is that the criminal necessarily wills to be (justly) punished: "It is his implicit will, an embodiment of his freedom" (para. 100). Presumably then he didn't really—implicitly—will to commit the crime in the first place. Cf. Steinhart 371 n. 54. Was Hegel's distinction inspired to any extent by DG? He does not refer to *Gorg.* 466–68 in *Lectures on the History of Philosophy*. Kant also distinguished between "Wille" and "Willkür."

23. In Gulley. See also his *The Philosophy of Socrates* (London 1968) 120–23. Subsequent references are to the article.

24. Gulley 90.

25. Gulley 90–91.

26. Gulley 92–96. The demarcation of the *Protagoras* is vitiated by the neglect of 345d6–e4, which displays exactly the same "interpretation" of the Paradox that is found in the *Gorgias* and elsewhere. Cf. C. C. W. Taylor, *Plato: Protagoras* (Oxford 1976) 146, 203.

27. Gulley enlists A. E. Taylor, *A Commentary on Plato's Timaeus* (Oxford 1928) 619; and *Laws* 731c (on which see p. 284 and n. 88). Cf. also Santas 317 n. 26 and below, Sec. VI. His explanation of the non-hypothetical language is unique. For an attack on Gulley's views from the perspective of the neoplatonic view, see O'Brien 217–18 n. 5.

28. Santas 224–25, my emphasis, in the chapter "Power, Virtue, Pleasure and Happiness in the

Gorgias,'' apparently written after "The Socratic Paradoxes." The latter presents a rather different interpretation of DG (see previous note) and links it explicitly to the Paradox.

29. I take it that the "bad things" referred to in the quoted passage are to be understood, as in the case of the "good things," in the "relativized" sense: they are bad relative to the agent's own conceptions.

30. He does not relate it to the Paradox, nor to the claim about power.

31. Cf. also J. C. B. Gosling, *The Philosophy of Plato* (London 1973) 27, who seems to express the same view when he says (without argument): "The distinction between 'wanting the good' and 'deeming something good' does not rely on contrasting something which really is good with something apparently so, but on distinguishing wanting some goal and considering something to be a means to it." This is unclear; at any rate Gosling implies that the object of *boulēsis* is the subjectively conceived good, not (necessarily) *the* good. The rest of his discussion, however, seems inconsistent on this point. For he evinces much hesitation over whether in claiming (in the *Gorg.* or elsewhere) that all desire is for the good Plato is making a merely "formal" point (men desire what they conceive to be good) or rather a "substantial" point (there is a single good, which all men desire): cf. 26–28, 38. And he says that the following consideration might motivate Socrates to assume the "substantial" reading: it allows him to reply to the immoralist challenge, Why should anyone care about your kind of goodness, Socrates?, by pointing out that it is no less than what everyone desires: cf. 27. Just which interpretation of DG Gosling is most happy with remains uncertain.

T. Irwin is also subject to vacillations; in his case they are unacknowledged. They concern whether or not Socrates gives a restricted sense to *boulesthai* and what sort of "good" it has for its object. He says that "Socrates is proposing a restriction on the ordinary range of 'want'" (141 ad 467b) and yet also that "Socrates' claim [that we want only the end, not the means] would be trivial if he were proposing to redefine 'want' . . . to mean 'want for itself' rather than 'want' in general, but nothing suggests that this is what he wants to do" (ibid. ad 467cd). These two statements seem mutually contradictory. Irwin continues: "Nor does Socrates suggest any distinction between what a person thinks he wants and his "true will," which is taken to express what he "really wants," whether or not he thinks he wants it (cf. Dodds, Gould, ch. 3). Here the "ends" mentioned are those someone thinks he wants as a result of his actions" (141–42 ad 467cd [the reference to Dodds and Gould is misleading: they *hold* the "true will" view which Irwin without argument is attacking: cf. n. 9]). Yet a few pages later Irwin implies a rather different view of the matter: "Socrates has shown that if I do not have correct beliefs about what is good for me, I lack the power to achieve *my own good, which I want above all . . .''* (146 ad 468cd, my emph.). Is the good that I want above all the good about which I lack correct beliefs? Presumably then it is *the* good. So it is not the case after all that the ends mentioned in Socrates' argument are simply those which a person *thinks* he wants. In *Plato's Moral Theory: The Early and Middle Dialogues* (Oxford 1977) = Irwin II, the same problem arises. Commenting on DG he says: "What everyone really wants . . . is the good to be achieved (*he believes*) by his action. . . . This is simply a statement of the Socratic assumption denying the existence of good-independent desires" (117, my emph., cf. 78). So far this is the subjectivist interpretation. But according to Irwin the denial of "good-independent" desires amounts to this: everyone's desires are all "focused on the final good" (79, cf. 95), which is happiness, but which in content is *not* what they *think* they are pursuing. For Socrates' theory is "an account of what everyone really pursues, not an account of what everyone claims to pursue. . . . People wrongly claim, Socrates thinks, that they pursue recognized goods, health, wealth, and so on as the final good (*Eud.* 280b5–281c5). Their claims are refuted when their choices show that these *do not constitute the final good they seek''* (86, my emph.). It is unclear what he presumes to be the textual basis for this: the *Eud.* passage, the reference to which presumably contains a misprint, is irrelevant. Is it *Gorg.* 466a–468e? At any rate is it *the* good which everyone desires, or what they think to be good?

32. Socrates says that "we don't desire to slaughter, or banish . . . just like that (*haplōs* [= without qualification] *houtōs*), but if these things are beneficial (*ōphelima*) we desire to do them, if harmful we don't desire" (468c2–5). For this construal of *haplōs houtōs,* cf. Dodds ad loc. This phrase is frequently (e.g. Stallbaum ad loc., Santas 224) taken to mean "for their own sake," evidently with a view to Socrates' preceding statement (step 1) that actions are never desired, only ends, and taking "desired" there to mean "desired for their own sakes." But this is probably wrong. I take *ōphelima* to mean "good either as means or end," hence the bracketed addition.

33. Note that the conclusion that the agent in question lacks power is not based directly on the claim that he doesn't do what he desires but rather on the claim that what he does is self-harming. The central idea is thus that power is always good, not that it consists in always doing what one desires (in the sense of "desires" that emerges from the argument). Still, Socrates' remarks at 466d6–e2 and 467a7–10 imply a definitional tie between "doing what one desires" and "having power," so that it is legitimate to put the argument as I did, pp. 263–64.

34. This has been noticed by Nakhnikian 14 and also Irwin 141 ad 467cd, 144–45 ad 468bc, who also says that Socrates seems to deny the possibility of desiring something both as means and end. There is no evidence for this, nor does he offer any. Instead he cites *Ly.* 220ab as showing more clearly that Socrates denies this; but evidence is lacking there as well. Cf. also n. 32.

35. Aristotle, it is true, does not say that the agent *bouletai* such an action—but nor does he deny it. At 1111b26–27 he does remark: *eti d' hē men boulēs tou telous esti māllon, hē de proairesis tōn pros to telos* ("desire is more for the end, whereas choice is of means to the end"); cf. the cross ref. in 1113a15: *hē de boulēsis hoti men tou telous estin eirētai* . . . Can he mean that one doesn't desire the chosen means, not even if the latter is an action *not* painful in itself? He is sometimes taken to mean this and to be repeating the thought of *Gorg.* 467c5–e1 (cf. Stewart ad 1113a15, Gauthier-Jolif 206–7 ad 1113a15–16). But this is probably wrong. Aristotle is here in the midst of arguing the non-identity of desire and choice; his point seems to be not that *boulēsis* is *only* for the end, but that *proairesis*—unlike *boulēsis*—is only for the means. He says that desire is for the end, meaning primarily for the end. Nor does 1113a15 imply otherwise, on which see n. 40.

36. The "apparent" terminology goes back to Aristotle, who bequeathes it to later philosophers such as Aquinas and Leibniz.

37. To ensure that this formulation picks out opaque desires, the context introduced by "believes" must be stipulated to be itself opaque.

38. Expressing the connection between desire and the good by means of (in effect) the biconditional *"iff* it is good, we desire it," thus facilitates the trick. What was at first "if they are bad, we don't desire them, right Polus?" then becomes "if they are *in fact* bad . . . ?" *eiper tunchanei tauta kaka onta:* 468d5–6). Note also that, since the question posed here expects and gets a negative answer, apparently desire is not a necessary condition for action!

39. It is in these terms that Aristotle sees the problem with DG, although that he sees a problem at all has gone unnoticed. At *Topics* 146b36ff. Aristotle warns the dialectical reasoner that

> in dealing with desires . . . you must see whether there is a failure to add the qualification "apparent," for example in the definitions "wish is a desire for the good" [*hē boulēsis orexis agathou*] or "appetite is a desire for the pleasant" instead of the "apparently good or pleasant." For often those who feel desire fail to perceive what is good or pleasant, so that the object of their desire is not necessarily good or pleasant, but only apparently so. One ought, therefore, to have assigned the definition with this qualification (E. S. Forster, tr.).

It is the apparent good—not the actual good—which (by definition) is the object of desire; and inattention to this fact is dangerous. The precise danger is not specified, although it is clear what it is and at *EN* 1113a15ff. Aristotle is explicit, succinctly refuting the very claim about *boulesthai* to which Socrates forces Polus' assent:

> Those . . . who say that what is wished for (*boulēton*) is the really good are faced by the conclusion that what a man who chooses his end wrongly wishes for is not really wished for at all; since if it is to be wished for, it must on their showing be good, whereas in the case assumed it may so happen that the man wishes for something bad (Rackham, tr.).

In other words, the claim is defeated by a *reductio,* since it implies a contradiction: in the case of moral error what is desired is not desired. Although putting the point in this way misses the fact that different readings of "desire" are being employed, the "contradiction" (it is not really that) cited by Aristotle is of course a symptom of that underlying problem. At any rate he comes quite close to seeing that the problem is actually one of different senses of "desire," for he goes on to say that there is still a sense in which it *is* the "really good" which is the object of desire. For it is *haplōs men kai kat' alētheian bouleton.* Yet it must be admitted that his own justification for this *haplōs kai kat' alētheian* is obscure; and perhaps he is simply trading on an ambiguity in the verbal adjective—which may mean either "desired" or "(ought) to be desired." This ambiguity is logically independent of the *de re/de dicto* ambiguity. In any case no real use is made of this *haplōs* sense of *bouletōn* by Aristotle. At 1113a22–b2 he insists that what each person desires is what appears to him to be good (*to phainomenon* [*agathon*]). He points out that this does not at all exclude the possibility of a good by nature—the latter is both actual and apparent (i.e., appearing good to the good man). (This has been misunderstood by many commentators.) It should be emphasized that this is Aristotle's regular view: in addition to the *Topics* passage, see, e.g., *EN* 1136b6–9, 1155b25–26, *EE* 1235b26–30, *De Anima* 432b5–7, 433a23–31, *Rhet.* 1369a2 (contra Dodds 236). Although at times he uses *boulēsis* to mean "rational desire" whose object is good (contrasted with "irrational" *epithumia* or *orexis*) the good is still only the apparent good.

40. Cf. G. H. von Wright, *The Varieties of Goodness* (London 1963) 109.
41. Among modern commentators G. Grote, *Plato and the Other Companions of Sokrates* (New York 1974, orig. ed. 1863) vol. 2, 352 and Irwin 145 ad 468cd deserve credit for noticing a problem in the logic underlying DG.
42. In the *H. Mi.* Socrates argues that the best runner, when he fails in a race, does so deliberately, whereas the worse runner does so involuntarily; and that the same sort of thing holds not only for all craftsmen but for all moral agents as well, so that the morally bad man does wrong involuntarily, but not so the morally good man (cf.373ce, 375d, 376c). Is this what Gulley is thinking of? If so, it is hard to see how it bears on the analogy he ascribes to Plato in the *Gorg.* At any rate the latter involves even more awkwardness than Gulley realizes. Winning the race is *not* what the bad runner "really" wants, rather simply what he wants—in his case there is no bifurcation, analogous to that alleged in the case of the wrongdoer, between a goal which is "really" wanted and some other goal that is not. The suggested analogy thus appears irrelevant.
43. Gould 51 sees this when he admits that the thesis he ascribes to Plato is "in large measure merely analytical." It is unclear why he yet sees in it "a considerable measure of illumination."
44. Diotima places no restriction on just how the money or the athletic excellence are to be obtained or used in order for the desires for them to be labelled *erōs.* Even the most morally vicious businessman, say, is a "lover" in Diotima's sense, although what he desires is actually bad.
45. Cf. also 458a1–6, where the claim that *pantes tōn agathōn epithumousin* is upheld, not rejected (contra Murphy 46 et al.).

46. That the apparent good is meant is seen by B. Jowett and L. Campbell, *Plato's Republic* (Oxford 1894), 301. Against this it might be argued that since the sentence beginning in 505d11 says in part that *the* good is what is pursued, and since this same sentence seems to be an *inference* from the claim that men seek *ta onta agatha*, then the latter phrase must stand for *the* good after all, even if it is ambiguous in itself. However, if I am right (see next note) 501d11ff. involves no inference from d5–10 but is instead a compressed explanation of the point made in those lines about how men behave. Note also that whereas d5–10 concerns "goods" in the plural and the behavior of *men* (cf. *polloi*), d11ff. concerns *the* good in the singular (*ho . . . toutou . . .*) and the activity of the *soul*—indications that something more complicated is involved than a simple inference from "men seek the actual good" to "the actual good is what men pursue."

47. That *ta onta* implies *actual* goodness is wrongly assumed by many commentators: e.g., N. White, *A Companion to Plato's Republic* (Indianapolis 1979) 175–76, 193–94. Shorey in his Loeb edit. ad loc says: "Men may deny the reality of the conventional virtues, but not of the ultimate sanction, whatever it is"; he then refers to *Tht.* 167c, 172ab. If by "ultimate sanction, whatever it is" he means the actual good in the nature of things, then I believe he is wrong about what Plato says here and in the *Tht.* Plato did not hold that all men assume or are logically committed to ethical objectivism.

48. I take the clause *kai toutou heneka panta prattei* in 505d11 to be parenthetical to, and explanatory of, the clause *ho dē diōkei men hapasa psuchē*. For *toutou* instead of *hou* would seem to indicate that *kai* has emphatic, not strictly conjunctive force. Translate: ". . . — indeed for the sake of this it does everything— . . ."

49. What *Rep.* 505de says about *psuchē* is compatible with *Laws* X—where, as A. E. Taylor says, " 'souls' are the real agents which initiate *all* processes, and Plato . . . holds that every soul aims at 'what *it* judges to be *good*' " (his emph.): *A Commentary on Plato's Timaeus* (Oxford 1928) 72. It is not only human action that is due to the soul's choosing and desiring in accordance with its judgment concerning the good, but all natural processes: cf. esp. 896e–897b (where it is certain—from the fact that some souls are said to lack virtue and intelligence—that the *boulesthai* ascribed to souls is simply "desire," not any desire for *the* good.) It is true that neither *Laws* X nor the passages in the *Tim.* concerning the origins of souls (cf. 34c–37c, 69e–70a) yield confirming evidence for my interpretation of *Rep.* 505de. But it is not incompatible with these other texts. It is incidentally very close to the Stoic view: cf. *SVF* III.348 = Cicero, *Tusc. Disp.* IV.6.12.

50. Cf. Augustine, *Conf.* X.20, M. Ficino, *Commentarium in Conv. Plat.* xii.

51. Translations such as "with an intuition of its reality" (Shorey) are perhaps misleading. Inspection of the other three instances of *apomanteuesthai* in Plato (*Ly.* 216d3, *Rep.* 516d2, *Soph.* 250c1) leads one to suspect that, as in the case of the more common *manteuesthai* (cf. *Rep.* 506a6, a8), the term denotes a reasonable, though *fallible* surmise. The term "intuition" wrongly suggests that the object is grasped infallibly.

52. Cf. Aristotle, *Met.* 1072a28, b3: the prime mover is *hōs erōmenon* in that it causes movement without being moved. The phrase "teleological lure" is taken from Cushman 194.

53. Perhaps *Rep.* 577e1 should be discussed, since it is so prominently cited in this connection (cf. n. 17). There the tyrannical soul is said to be like the tyrannized city in that "it will also be the least likely to do what it may want (*ha an boulēthēi*)—that is, the soul as a whole." The qualification must be intended to clarify that even though the appetitive part of the tyrant's soul *does* do what it wants, the other two parts of the soul—which are larger, it being *mikron* (577d4) in comparison—do *not* do what they want. All that is meant, then, is that taken as a whole such a soul has a greater sum of unsatisfied desires (cf. White 224). By implication, moreover, *boulesthai* may be used for the desires of the appetitive part: obviously this is not the *boulesthai* of DG. Santas' remark (cf. n. 17) on the consistency in Plato of the "restricted" sense is incredible. Plato is in general not fond of rigorous verbal distinctions. At

Prot. 340a he even has Socrates mock Prodicus, albeit gently, for his penchant for such distinctions—such as that between *boulesthai* and *epithumein!*

54. This suggestion is nothing new. Santas has seen that Plato's thesis is to be taken this way: see his discussion in "The Socratic Paradoxes" in Santas 187–89. So have others. Yet the problem DG poses for this suggestion has not been recognized.

55. I should note that it is often supposed that Plato in his maturity abandoned the view that all men desire the good, committing himself instead to what some have recently been calling "good-independent" desires, i.e., desires the existence of which is not to be explained by any reference to the agent's beliefs about the good. Thus the tripartite psychology of the *Rep.* is supposed to reject and improve upon Socratic intellectualism, which is allegedly unable to handle weakness of will and psychic conflict. This seems to be based on misunderstandings. But I must beg off from trying to discuss this issue here.

56. Cf. Irwin 139–40 ad 466e, who rightly (I think) denies that Socrates puts forward a weaker claim such as that power is good in some respect that might on occasion be overridden by a greater evil associated with its use.

57. The argument is recapitulated at 467a1–9.

58. Step 4 of the argument has it that intelligence is necessary for successful action; now it is assumed to be sufficient. Further, roughly: "rhetoric is a craft" *iff* "orators have intelligence."

59. Socrates had already argued against the idea that rhetoric is a craft (462–465e). Why does he not ask Polus to reconsider that issue?

60. Socrates had already raised and denied this at 466d5–e2; now he presses it.

61. At 469c3–470a12 the power issue is raised anew; but there is no pretence of a return to the question whether tyrants are powerful. On this passage see n. 75.

62. Here "wishes" is *boulētai*. There is not the slightest indication that Socrates intends the term to be understood in the restricted sense; or, in other words, that power is always good. Irwin 145 ad 468cd says that Socrates, in reaching the conclusion that tyrants lack power, relies upon the *H. Mi.* definition of power. But this entails that power as defined in the *H. Mi.* is always good; and that is false.

63. Cf. *Eud.* 278e–281e.

64. For this well-known argument cf. also *M.* 87c–89a and *Lg.* 631bd, 661a–662b. At *H. Ma.* 295e–296d Socrates argues against the view that power in itself is *kalon.*

65. It might be said that the idea (cf. 466e9–12) that intelligence must be conjoined with doing whatever seems good is in effect at least a near equivalent of the protreptic argument (if we may take intelligence = wisdom). And so it is. But this does not remove the puzzle. For Socrates agrees here to the claim that power is *always good* and uses it to defeat Polus' account of what power consists in—rather than allowing *it* to be defeated by the consideration that power (which *is,* after all, the ability to do "what one wishes at the time that he wishes") is sometimes a bad thing. Nevertheless it is but a short step from the one to the other; and a little later Socrates does tacitly allow the claim that power is always good to be defeated in just this way: 469c3ff. on which see n. 75. Note, however, that *this* requires his *acceptance* of Polus' view of what power is. Later on with Callicles Socrates continues to accept this view, as though he had not earlier denied it: cf. 509c6–511a3.

66. That is, an orator taught by Gorgias. The contradiction arises only if, in regard to (3), Gorgias is understood to admit that even *his own* pupils might use rhetoric for unjust ends. This admission is only implicit, not explicit in 456c8–457c3.

67. Cf. *Plato's Earlier Dialectic* (Oxford 1953, 2nd ed.) 7–15.

68. Cf. Robinson 10. The passages are *M.* 84b, *Apol.* passim, and *Soph.* 229e–230e. I discuss the latter subsequently.

69. Cf. Vlastos, "The Paradox of Socrates," in *The Philosophy of Socrates* (New York 1970) ed.

G. Vlastos 12–15 and for his latest views, "The Socratic Elenchus" *Journal of Philosophy*, 79 (1982) 715–21; Irwin II 38–41, 62–3, 69–71.
70. Cf. Dodds 9.
71. Cf. Vlastos 10 with *Charm.* 166c7–d6, wherein Socrates responds to Robinson's objection (which Plato puts in the mouth of Critias). This is of course not to deny that Socrates is ironic in other ways.
72. The *doxai* referred to at 230d2 (*tas tois mathēmas empodious doxas*) are those referred to at c1–2 (*tōn peri hautou megalōn kai sklērōn doxōn*). What obstructs philosophical growth is self-conceit. Nothing is said here about removing—or supporting—any opinions *other* than those which constitute the self-deceit.
73. Cf. *Apol.* 21d2–7; *Charm.* 167a5–8; *Ly.* 218a2–b1; *M.* 84c4–6; *Sym.* 204a3–7; *Tht.* 210b11–c6.
74. That is, for the duration of the Polus episode. Concerning Callicles I am not so sure. An example from another dialogue is *Ly.* 211e–213c. Notice that I do not in the least wish to deny that doctrines of unimpeachable Socratic credentials are among those which Socrates gets Polus to accept. Important Socratic claims are, of course, found throughout 466–68; it would be most odd if this were not the case. I believe rather the arguments themselves are *ad hominem* to an extreme; they are not intended to offer any support for the ideas which they frequently express. Socrates is quite sincere in saying that the issues surrounding doing vs. suffering injustice are "matters on which it is most honorable to have knowledge and most disgraceful to lack it" (472c7–8, Lamb, tr.). What he does not say is that the present discussion is in any sense a search for such knowledge. Instead he asserts that if he cannot succeed in making Polus "a witness who agrees with the things I say" (472b7–8), he will not have accomplished much. Now this must be ironic. It may *seem* as though Socrates thinks that the mere inability of Polus to evade self-contradiction and having to accept—"vote for"—Socrates' assertions *justifies* him (Socrates) in claiming that they are true: cf. 475e3–476a2. If Socrates really thinks this it would mean that the method he is using with Polus *is* constructive. Does he? It seems unlikely, given Polus' straightforward inanity, that Socrates could really believe that conversing with him is epistemologically advantageous. Appearances to the contrary are due to ironic pretence, as at 476a1–2, where he says that he is happy to ignore the votes of everyone else—all he needs is the single vote of Polus! True, Socrates contrasts Polus' "forensic" methods (according to which, after long speeches, the majority decides) with his own method of securing agreements through question and answer (cf. 471e2–472d1). It's just that he is not at the moment following *that* method, but one which—superficially—resembles it. If he "accomplishes much" with Polus, it will be along the lines of protreptic success, nothing more. For a contrary view see Vlastos, "Was Polus Refuted?" *American Journal of Philology* 88 (1967) 459.
75. The serious question about power is of course whether and in what respect it *is* good and *ought* to be pursued. At 469cff., beginning with what Dodds calls "the Parable of the Lunatic with the Knife," the notion that power is only conditionally good emerges clearly: "So . . . you have come around again [cf. 466e9–12] to the view that if doing what one thinks fit is attended by advantage (*ōphelimōs*) in doing so, this is not merely a good thing but at the same time, it seems, the possession of great power; otherwise it is a bad thing and means little power" (470a9–12, Lamb, tr.). Here "great" and "little" now amount to value terms: and the discussion turns finally to the real question of the criterion for *ōphelimōs:* cf. 470c1–3, with 509c6–511a5.
76. It is inconceivable that Plato is unconscious of the fallacies in DG. How then would he describe or explain them? It seems reasonable to suppose that he would do no worse than Aristotle (cf. n. 40). As for Socrates, note how he carefully alters the claim about desire when repeating it to Callicles at 499e6–500a1: "Polus and I, if you recollect, decided that

everything we do should be for the sake of what is good . . . —that the good is the end of all our actions, and it is for its sake that all other things should be done (*dein . . . prattesthai*) and not it for theirs'' (Lamb, tr.). It was decided rather that the good *is* desired, not that it ought to be. Socrates is not being forgetful; it is simply that the claim he elicited from Polus is not the claim he actually holds.

77. Weakness of will introduces obvious complications. Perhaps, contrary to the Socratic analysis, the weak-willed agent does *not* do what he most desires to do. I leave this issue aside.

78. Santas 191.

79. Cf. 187–89. Yet he strangely fails to see that 509e5–7, taken seriously, implies that the Paradox requires DG, forcing ''good things'' to be read as the good.

80. Santas, cf. Gosling 27, draws (2) erroneously from 467c5–e1 and 468c2–8. See p. 267—with n. 32.

81. So too J. J. Mulhern, ''A Note on Stating the Socratic Paradox,'' *Journal of the History of Ideas* 29 (1968) 601–4.

82. Santas 317 n. 26. His words might be taken to imply that Plato allows the possibility that an agent who does X might be ignorant that X is unjust and yet *not* ignorant that it is harmful. This is of course false; the implication is presumably unintended. He might also be understood to imply that the agent's ignorance *that his action was unjust* would in itself suffice to render his action involuntary. I will argue that this is false.

83. The point of the Paradox is that the following common-sense conviction happens to be false: wrongdoers are normally (if not always) blameable for their wrongdoing; the appropriate response to them is one of anger, resentment, and retributive punishment. Wrongdoers are *never* blameable, according to Socrates and Plato. More or less gentle instruction is what is called for; if punishment is required, it is to be justified teleologically. Cf. *Apol.* 25d1–26a7, where Socrates argues that if he has involuntarily harmed himself (as he must have if he has corrupted the young), then one should not punish (at least not retributively) but rather admonish and instruct him; *Gorg.* 488a2–b1, where he asks Callicles not to cease admonishing him, since if he has not lived his life rightly it was done involuntarily; *Rep.* 336e2–337a2, where he asks Thrasymachus to show pity in place of harshness, since if he has erred it was involuntarily; *Rep.* 589c6. Complicating factors are introduced in *Soph.* 227c7–230d5; *Tim.* 86b1–87b9; *Lg.* 731c1–d5, 860c4ff.; nevertheless they do not, I think, affect the heart of the matter. That Aristotle understood the Paradox in this sense is clear: see pp. 285–86. So too Epictetus, *Disc.* I.xviii.1–10, I.xxvi.6–7, I.xxviii.1–10, II.xxii.36–37; M. Aurelius, *Medit.* IV.3, XI.18, XII.12. Among more recent commentators see Gulley 95–6 (who, however, unjustly excludes this interpretation of ''involuntary'' from the *Gorgias* and earlier dialogues). Irwin 229 ad 509e (implicitly) and O'Brien 218 n. 15 (explicitly) *deny* that ''involuntary'' carries the meaning ''exempt from blame,'' the former saying that Socrates holds not that unjust action is involuntary so much as that it is ''involuntary under the description 'harmful to the agent' '' (cf. equivalent formulations in O'Brien 3, 17 etc.). It is true enough that the lexicographic meaning of *hekōn akōn* is, roughly, ''intentional[ly]''/''unintentional[ly].'' Furthermore, the Paradox does, one may say, *rely* upon the point that the agent does not desire or intend unjust action under the description ''harmful to me.'' But that is simply another way of stating the first step of the argument underlying the Paradox, not the Paradox itself, a thesis which does not primarily concern intentionality, but rather the ascription of blame. That this has not always been clearly grasped is perhaps due in part to the tendency to equate the Paradox with the well-known phrase *oudeis hekōn hamartanei* (cf., e.g., *Rep.* 589c6), or ''No One Intentionally Errs.'' Now this phrase does not capture the Paradox itself (as I have been using ''Paradox''). For *hamartanein* does not mean ''act unjustly'' but rather something like ''make a harmful mistake.'' Thus the phrase amounts to no more than step (1) of the argument for the Paradox (as given previously): no one desires or intends anything conceived to be harmful to himself. Of course we may substitute

adikein for *hamartanein,* given the doctrine that injustice is a form of harmful mistake. But then the rendering of *hekōn* as ''intentionally'' creates a dilemma: for it would suggest that no one intends to commit injustice—which is obviously false. The way out, however, is not to take injustice merely to be ''unintentional under the description . . . ,'' and leave the point at that, but to see that injustice is, according to the Paradox, *exempt from blame.*

84. Cf. Dodds, *The Greeks and the Irrational* (Berkeley 1963) 17; G. Calogero, ''The *Gorgias* and the Socratic Principle *Nemo Sua Sponte Peccat,''* *Journal of Hellenic Studies* 77 (1957) 12–17; and R. Sorabji, *Necessity, Cause and Blame: Perspectives on Aristotle's Theory* (Ithaca 1980) 272–81, 291–92, with the literature there cited.

85. Santas loc cit.

86. Santas argues for this at 192.

87. Gulley 89; cf. pp. 265ff.

88. *Epit.* 31.1 = 151–153 P. Louis: *Tis gar an hekōn en tōi kallistōi heautou merei kai timiōtatōi heloito echein to megiston tōn kakōn? ei de tis epi kakian hormāi, prōton men ouch hōs epi kakian autēn hormēsei, all' hōs ep' agathon; ei de kai paraginetai tis epi kakian, pantōs ho toioutos exapatētai, hōs di' ellatonos tinos kakou apoikonomēsomenos meizon agathon, kai tautēi akousiōs eleusetai; adunaton gar hormān tina epi kaka boulomenon echein auta, oute elpidi agathou oute phobōi meizonos kakou.* Here *kakia* means ''evil'' both in the sense of vice or injustice and in the sense of harm (and ''injustice'' characterizes both the state of the soul as well as his action). That ''involuntary'' has the force of ''exempt from blame'' is shown in 31.2, where it is argued that injustice is still to be punished despite its involuntariness, for punishment is remedial: cf. *Gorg.* 477a2–b1. Note the standard sense of *boulesthai.* The wording of this passage is heavily influenced by *Lg.* 731c1–d5. Cf. also the parallel passages in Apuleius, *De Platone* II.11,17 = 88–89, 94 Beaujeu. The origins of and relation between the *Epit.* and *De Plat.* are still under debate; in fact, so is the attribution of the *Epit.* to Albinus. Cf. C. Mazzarelli, ''Bibliografia Medioplatonica,'' *Rivista di filosofia neoscolastica* 72 (1980) 108–44; 63 (1981) 557–95.

89. Aristotle may be making this point in a less general form when he says that, for ignorance to excuse, the action must cause the agent subsequent pain and regret (*EN* 1110b18–24). This ensures that he would not have acted as he did, had he not been ignorant. Otherwise the action is only ''not voluntary,'' not ''involuntary.''

90. Cf. *Rep.* 382a4–b6, 412e10–413c4; *Soph.* 228c7–8, 230a5.

91. However G. Zeigler, ''Plato's *Gorgias* and Psychological Egoism,'' *The Personalist* 60 (1979) 123–33 seems mistaken in arguing that since *Gorg.* 466–68 has it that all men desire *the* (Platonic) good, not any merely self-regarding advantage, Plato must not be a psychological egoist.

92. Cf. R. A. Gauthier and J. Y. Jolif, *L'Éthique à Nicomaque* (Paris 1959), Vol. II.2, 182ff.

93. Cf. Gulley 91; Santas loc. cit., saying that in view of Aristotle's discussion the Paradox remains ''doubtful at best.''

FURTHER READING

Irwin, T. 1977. ''The *Gorgias:* Problems in Socratic Ethics.'' *Plato's Moral Theory: The Early and Middle Dialogues,* 115–31. Oxford.

Santas, G. 1964. ''The Socratic Paradoxes.'' *Philosophical Review* 73:147–64.

———. 1979. *Socrates,* esp. chs. 6–8. London.

Vlastos, G. 1967. ''Was Polus Refuted?'' *American Journal of Philology* 88:454–60.

———. 1991. ''Does Socrates Cheat?'' *Socrates, Ironist and Moral Philosopher.* Ithaca, N.Y.

Weiss, R. 1985. ''Ignorance, Involuntariness, and Innocence: A Reply to McTighe.'' *Phronesis* 30:314–22.

16

Meno's Paradox and
Socrates as a Teacher

ALEXANDER NEHAMAS

Meno has always been considered as one of the least gifted and co-operative characters in Plato's dialogues. Commentators have disdained him generally, but their greatest disdain is reserved for the agrument he introduces to the effect that all learning is impossible at *Meno* 80d5–9. Shorey, who had no patience for the view expressed in the paradox itself, referred to it disparagingly as "this eristic and lazy argument."[1] Taylor liked neither the argument nor Meno's reasons for bringing it up: "Meno," he wrote, "again tries to run off on an irrelevant issue. He brings up the sophistic puzzle. . . ."[2] Klein thought of the negative influence of the paradox on all desire to learn anything new and wrote that Meno himself "was conspicuously reluctant to make the effort Socrates requested of him. It seems that his behaviour throughout the conversation was in agreement with the consequence that flows from the argument he has just presented."[3] Bernard Phillips, who with many other writers takes the argument itself quite seriously, nevertheless insists that for Meno personally "it is merely a dodge."[4] Even Bluck, who is slightly more sympathetic to Meno than other writers are, cannot approve of him in this instance: "So far as Meno is concerned, this question may be regarded as a convenient dodge, an eristic trick; but for Plato, it had important philosophical implications."[5]

Plato himself certainly took Meno's paradox seriously, as we can see from the care with which he develops his own controversial and complicated solution to the problem (*M*. 81a5–86c2) and from the intimate connection of that solution, the theory of recollection, to the theory of Forms when the latter eventually appears, as it does not in the *Meno,* in Plato's texts.[6] But does Plato take only the agrument, and not Meno himself, seriously? Is Meno merely dodging the issue and trying to win a debating point from Socrates? Is his paradox simply a pretext for Plato to present his own, recently acquired, epistemological ideas?

This view is invested with considerable authority, but does not seem to me to be true. To see that it is not, we must first examine the general situation that prompts Meno to present his paradox as well as the precise wording of his statement. If we can show that Plato thinks that Meno himself has good reason to raise this difficulty then we shall be able to connect this passage with certain other issues, some of which were of considerable importance in Plato's philosophical thinking.

I

The question whether *aretē* is teachable, inborn, or acquired in some other way, with which Meno so abruptly opens the dialogue (71a1–4), was a commonplace of early Greek speculation. That it concerned not only Socrates but also, more generally, the sophistic movement is already indicated by the Gorgianic style of Meno's question.[7] More traditionally, the issue applied not only to *aretē* but also to *sophia* (wisdom); this may appear surprising in view of the fact that Socrates finds it uncontroversial to claim that if *aretē is epistēmē* (knowledge or understanding, often used interchangably with *sophia*) then it is surely teachable (*M*. 87c5–6).[8] Already by the end of the fifth century, the author of *Dissoi Logoi* (403–395 BC) can refer to the "neither true nor new argument that *sophia and aretē* can neither be taught nor learned" (6.1).[9] In a famous passage of *Olympian* II.86–8, Pindar had already claimed that the wise (which in this case refers to the poet) is so by nature, the rest being to him like cacophonous crows in comparison.[10] Isocrates was to argue that *aretē* and *dikaiosunē* (justice) are not purely teachable, without, that is, the proper nature (*Contra Sophistas* 14–18, 21)[11]—a position with some affinities to Plato's view in the *Republic*. Finally, a similar position in regard to *andreia* (courage) is attributed to Socrates by Xenophon at *Memorabilia* III.9.

But though this question was commonplace, there was little, if any agreement as to the nature of what it concerned, the nature of *aretē*. What concerns me is not the specific debate over the distinction between "quiet" or "co-operative" and competitive virtues. Mine is the much simpler point that *aretē* has an immensely broader range of application than its conventional English translation "virtue," while the more recent "excellence" strikes me as too weak and vague. *Aretē* not only applies to more human qualities than "virtue" does, but it also covers features that are in no way specifically human. This is, of course, perfectly clear from *Republic* 352d–354a, where Plato discusses explicitly the *aretē* of instruments and, by implication, that of animals. But this usage is not found only in Plato. Already in Homer, horses are said to possess *aretē* (*Iliad* XXIII.276, 374). Even inanimate objects can have their characteristic excellence: fertile soil (Thucydides I.2.4) and fine cotton (Herodotus III.106.2) are cases in point. If it were not for this, we might do well to construe *aretē* as "success" or as the quality that constitutes or that accounts for it. If nothing else, this would show that the ancient debate is relevant to the many contemporary promises to ensure success, for an appropriate fee, in all sorts of fields and endeavours and which prompt Socratic and Platonic responses from all those who look down upon the notion of success implicit in these promises and upon the endeavours themselves. We may thus be able to answer Jowett, who, construing *aretē* as virtue, claimed that "no one would either ask or answer such a question (as Meno's) in modern times."[12]

In order to account for the application of *aretē* to animals as well as to inanimate objects, it might be better to construe it as that quality or set of qualities, whatever that may be, that makes something *outstanding* in its group. We might even consider it as what accounts for an object's *justified notability*. Both suggestions concern not only intrinsic features of such objects but also, in one way or another, their reputation. And this is as it should be. For from the earliest times on, the notion of *aretē* was intrinsically social, sometimes almost equivalent to fame (*kleos*). That this was so even in late periods is shown by Hypereides, who in his *Epitaph* wrote that those who die for their city "leave *aretē* behind them" (41). Also, an epigraph commemorating the Athenians who fell at Potidaea states that "having placed their lives onto the scale, they received *aretē* in return." [13]

The question, therefore, whether *aretē* can be taught is the question whether one can be taught what it takes to have a justifiably high reputation among one's peers. [14] But this, of course, leaves the prior question unanswered; the term is not non-controversially connected with any particular set of human qualities. We still do not know the proper domain within which one is supposed to be outstanding or, even more importantly, in what being outstanding itself consists.

This last reasonable doubt, expressed in appropriate Socratic vocabulary, suggests that Socrates' own response to Meno's opening question makes rather good sense. In the persona of an imaginary Athenian, Socrates tells Meno not only that he does not know whether it can be taught but also that he doesn't know "in any way at all (*to parapan*) what *aretē* itself is" (71a5–7). [15] Now as long as we think of *aretē* as virtue we have enough intuitions about what that is to think that Socrates' reply must be prompted by metaphysical or epistemological considerations. He, too, we suppose, has a pretty good idea of what virtue is, but insists that he does not in order to make a purely philosophical point about the priority of definition. Yet, though not without important metaphysical implications, Socrates' response to Meno's precipitate question is quite independently reasonable. Meno asks without preamble a commonplace question which nonetheless depends on many disputable presuppositions. Socrates' reaction is, simply, to try to slow Meno and the discussion down. [16]

In light of this, I follow Bluck (209) in taking *to parapan* at 71a6 closely with *oude.* Socrates is disclaiming all knowledge of the nature of *aretē,* and he does exactly the same at 71b4: *ouk eidōs peri aretēs to parapan.* I also take it that his very next point, that one cannot know whether Meno is beautiful, rich, or noble, if one does not in any way (*to parapan*) know who Meno is, is strictly parallel. Socrates is not appealing to a distinction between knowledge by acquaintance and knowledge by description as Bluck (32–3, 213–14) among others, has claimed, nor is he introducing, at least implicitly, a technical distinction between knowledge and belief and claiming that though one can have all sorts of beliefs about the object of one's enquiry, these beliefs cannot become knowledge unless they are supplemented by knowledge of the definition of the nature of the object in question. [17] His point is simple and intuitive: if he has *no* idea who Meno is, how can he answer any questions about him? That this is so is shown by the fact that Meno immediately accepts Socrates' general view, as he should not on either of the two previous interpretations. What he cannot believe is that Socrates is quite as ignorant as he claims to be about the nature of *aretē.*

Nevertheless, and in characteristic fashion, Socrates insists on his ignorance and asks Meno, who claims to know, to tell him what *aretē* is. Meno makes three efforts (71eff., 73cff., 76bff.). But in each case he can only produce many *aretai* instead of the one that Socrates wants in answer to his question. Meno is originally unwilling to agree that *aretē* is one (73a1–5). He then agrees to go along with Socrates without necessarily accepting his view (*eiper hen ge ti zēteis kata pantōn,* 73d1). He finally appears to accept Socrates' arguments to that effect (79a7–e4). Willing as he is to co-operate with

Socrates, Meno is led from thinking that he knew what *aretē* is to being unable to say anything satisfactory about his topic, each time unexpectedly, and in a different way, being shown to make the very same error.

It is only after the failure of his third effort that Meno begins to lose his patience. Even so, he very politely concedes that Socrates seems correct in what he says (cf. 79d5, e4) and rather ingenuously confesses that he cannot answer the question. Through his famous comparison of Socrates to the torpedo-fish, he claims that though he had earlier spoken at length and well about *aretē* his contact with Socrates seems to have robbed him of all ability to do so now (79c7–80b3).

It is very important to notice the exact expression Meno uses at this point:

> *nun de oud' hoti estin to parapan echō eipein.* (80b4)

He admits that he is unable to say even in the most general terms what *aretē* is, that he is totally lost and confused. And by the repetition of the crucial term *to parapan*, through which Socrates had earlier disavowed all ability to lead the discussion, Plato now places Meno, even if against his will, in the very same position which Socrates had eagerly taken up at the opening of the dialogue.

Socrates refuses to return Meno's compliment and offers a simile in his turn (80c3–6). If he has reduced Meno to perplexity, he says, it is only because he is himself perplexed.

> *kai nun peri aretēs ho estin egō men ouk oida, su mentoi isōs proteron men ēidēstha prin emou apsasthai, nun mentoi homoiōs ei ouk eidoti.* (80d1–3)

This passage is important. We should notice, for one thing, the irony of the final phrase, in which Socrates, despite his earlier disclaimer, does after all offer a simile for Meno; though, of course, to say as he does that Meno is "similar to someone who does not know" is literally true.[18] We should also notice that in saying that Meno may have known earlier what *aretē* is, Socrates suggests, equally ironically, that something that is known can actually be forgotten. In one sense this is quite true and it forms the central point of the theory of recollection. But once something comes to be known, once (in Plato's terms) it is recollected, then it becomes more difficult to forget it or to be persuaded to change one's mind about it. This, after all, is how Socrates distinguishes *doxa* from *epistēmē* at 97d6–98b5. True beliefs, he claims, like Daedalus' statues, are always escaping from the soul. But when they are bound down by an "account of the explanation," which, "as we earlier agreed, is recollection" (98a3–5), they are transformed into *epistēmē* and become permanent. There is a serious question here about the sorts of things that, once learned, become permanent. Does Plato believe, for example, that if you know the road to Larissa (97a9–11) you cannot ever forget it? Or would he more plausibly be willing to allow gradations of perrmanence which would prevent geometrical or ethical truths from being forgotten but which would allow lower-level truths to escape the soul either through forgetfulness or through contrary argument? We shall return to this question toward the end of this essay.

Our present passage, 80d1–3, is finally important because it completes the stage-setting for the raising of Meno's paradox. Since Meno has now admitted that he is totally lost with respect to *aretē* and since Socrates has repeated his earlier complete inability to say anything about it, neither of them can even know where to begin the investigation. It is only at this point and faced with yet a further exhortation by Socrates to say what *aretē* is (80d3–4) that the much-maligned Meno raises the not unreasonable question how, if this is indeed their situation, they can possibly go on with the enquiry. In stating the paradox Meno once again repeats Socrates' word *to parapan:* "In what way," he asks, "can you search for something when you are altogether ignorant of what it is?" (80d5–6). Plato has gone to great lengths in order to emphasize Socrates' ignorance and to strip Meno of all claims to knowledge. Given this situation, and far from being a contentious move, Meno's raising of the paradox of enquiry is natural and well motivated.

II

Plato takes Meno's paradox, that you can't look for what you don't know and don't need to look for what you know, very seriously in its own right.[19] In addition, he provides Meno with good reason to raise it. He uses the paradox not only in order to discuss serious epistemological issues, but also to resolve a number of dialectical difficulties to which Socrates' practice had given rise.

Of course, Meno's paradox could easily be put to contentious use, as it was, in two related versions, in the *Euthydemus.* At 275d3–4, Euthydemus asks Cleinias whether those who learn are the wise or the ignorant; at 276d7–8, he asks him whether one learns things one already knows or things one does not. In each case Cleinias is made to contradict himself. Having claimed that it is the wise who learn, he is forced to admit that is has to be the ignorant instead (276b4–5) and immediately following, he is made to concede that in fact those who learn are, after all, the wise (276c6–7). Having claimed that one learns what one does not know, he is forced to agree that what one learns one actually knows (277a8–b4) and, at that point, Dionysiodorus enters the argument and argues that one learns only what one does not know (277e6–7).

Socrates replies on Cleinias' behalf that such paradoxes depend merely on verbal trickery. They equivocate between two senses of *manthanein* (to learn), one involving the acquisition at some time of knowledge that was not at all possessed previously and the other involving the exercising of knowledge that has already been acquired in the past (277e3–278b2). In this he is followed to the letter by Aristotle, who, in *Sophistici Elenchi* 4 (165b30–4), classifies this as a paradox due to verbal homonymy.

When such paradoxes, therefore, are offered contentiously, Plato is perfectly capable of giving them a short and easy reply. His reply in the *Euthydemus* depends crucially and unselfconsciously on the notion of the absolute acquisition of knowledge. But, in the *Meno,* Plato finds this reply deeply problematic. At the very least, he does not think that the paradox to which he can also supply a merely verbal solution has merely verbal force. What, then, accounts for this difference in attitude?

We have already said that Meno uses the term *to parapan* in stating his paradox. Some commentators have taken it that Meno simply overstates his case, and that Plato solves the problem by pointing this out. Their case depends primarily on the fact that Socrates omits this qualification in his restatement of Meno's problem (80e1–5). Thomas, for example, writes:

> This immediately destroys the thrust of the original puzzle for, lacking "parapan," the crucial premise reads "if a man does not have some knowledge" rather than "if a man has no knowledge whatsoever." The reformulated dilemma is consistent with the possession of some knowledge. . . . Plato is not making much of an effort to meet the eristics in

their . . . own terms. How could he, since to do so would be to concede them victory? Why should he, when the dilemma proscribes the possible? One is not obliged to take seriously intellectual chicanery that prohibits us from doing what we already do.[20]

But to assume that this is chicanery and that we can perfectly well do what the paradox denies, being a begging of the question, is itself a prime case of chicanery. Despite the similar views of Moravcsik[21] and Scolnicov,[22] it does not seem to me that Socrates refutes Meno by changing the terms of the argument. He may try to show that we do all possess some knowledge already but he cannot begin from that fact. In this respect, at least, White is correct in writing that there is no substantive difference between Meno's and Socrates' statement of the paradox: "What Socrates does is simply to make clear that Meno's puzzle can be cast in the form of a dilemma" (290 n. 4). The function of *to parapan* is important and ineliminable.

Discussions of this passage often claim that Plato is only concerned with one among the many species of learning. Gregory Vlastos, for example, writes that:

Manthanein . . . is being used in this context in the restricted sense of *learning to have propositional knowledge.* The acquisition of inarticulate skills, though well within the scope of the word in ordinary usage, is tacitly excluded.[23]

Moravcsik also believes that the paradox concerns only "learning taking the form of inquiry" (53). Plato, he continues, is not concerned with the learning of non-intellectual skills, with learning by being told, or with learning by imitation (54).

This is in a way correct, since the *Meno* does discuss only learning by enquiry.[24] But we must avoid the implication, which perhaps these writers themselves do not want, that Plato acknowledges many ways of learning but discusses only one in this context. Instead, Plato seems to hold the view that any learning and *epistēmē* worth the name must be achieved through enquiry and that therefore all learning, not just one particular form of it, must, in Moravcsik's words, "be given direction by the learner himself" (54). Plato is not simply excluding the learning of inarticulate skills from his discussion. Rather, he seems at least implicitly to be denying that inarticulate skills are acquired through learning and that they are therefore, strictly speaking, objects of *epistēmē*. Similarly, he appears to deny that being told or imitation can, in themselves, constitute learning and produce understanding.

But if learning can proceed only through enquiry and if neither Socrates not Meno know how to go on, then their impasse is very serious indeed. Where can the elenchus even begin? In addition, Gorgias, who had been earlier mentioned as a possible teacher of *aretē* and who might have helped the discussion, has already been disqualified. Since Meno accepts his views, it was agreed that to include him in the discussion would have been superfluous (71c5–d5). And in any case, his account of what *aretē* is (71e1–72a5; cf. Aristotle, *Politics* 1. 13. 1260a20–8) did not survive Socrates' arguments.

III

It would seem, then, that for the discussion to proceed, Socrates and Meno are in need of another teacher who might guide them out of their impasse. Such teachers are mentioned later on in the *Meno*. Why does Plato not bring them into the discussion now? Is it simply because he is not interested in the case of learning by being told by another or is the matter, as I shall now try to suggest, considerably more complicated?

Three classes of possible teachers of *aretē* are brought up in the *Meno*: sophists, notably successful citizens, and, in a rather cursory way, poets (89e–96b). The sophists are disqualified because they cannot agree among themselves whether *aretē* can or cannot be taught (95b–c); also because, unlike the case of any other subject, those who claim to teach what *aretē* is are not acknowledged as proper teachers of their subject by others and are even claimed to lack that which they profess to teach (96a6–b1; cf. 91c1–92c5). Good and noble citizens, men like Pericles, Themistocles, Aristeides, and Thucydides, are disqualified because not one of them has been capable of teaching his own sons what *aretē* is (93b–94e); also because they, no less than the sophists, cannot agree on whether this is a teachable topic (95a–b, 96b1–3).[25] Finally, the poets, through a quick examination of Theognis, are summarily dismissed because they cannot even produce internally coherent views on the subject (95c–96a).

These arguments against particular sorts of teachers of *aretē* are common, indeed, commonplace.[26] In addition to them, however, Plato offers a subtler and much more far-ranging argument against any self-professed teachers of success. The argument is implicit in a not very widely discussed passage of the *Protagoras* (313a1–314c2). In this passage, Socrates is warning Hippocrates against going to the sophist for instruction without first thinking the matter through very carefully. In addition, however, this warning involves an important paradox with some serious implications for our own discussion.

Socrates, we said, warns Hippocrates not to rush into Protagoras' company. He describes the sophist as ''a merchant or peddler of the goods by which the soul is nourished'' (313c4–5). The soul, he continues, is nourished by what it learns (*mathē-mata*, 313c7). He then offers an analogy between sophists, so construed, and those who sell any sort of food for the body (*ponēron ē chrēston*) but praise everything they sell indiscriminately (313d1–3). The buyers of such food also lack the necessary knowledge, unless they happen to be experts on such issues, gymnasts or physicians (313d3–5). The same is at least possible in the case of the peddlers of mental nourishment: some of them, too, may well be ''ignorant of whether what they sell is harmful or beneficial to the soul'' (*chrēston ē ponēron pros tēn psuchēn*, 313d8–e1). And the analogy holds further true of their clients, unless one among them happens to be ''a physician with regard to the soul'' (*peri tēn psuchēn iatrikos*, 313e1–2). Now if, Socrates continues, ''you happen to be an expert regarding which of those things are beneficial or harmful, then it is safe for you to buy learning from Protagoras or from anyone else'' (313e2–5). But if not, the danger is great, much greater indeed in this case than in the case of physical nourishment. Physical food can be taken away from the peddlers in a separate vessel and examined by an expert before it is consumed (314a3–b1). But this is not possible with food for thought:

> You cannot carry learning away in a jar. Once you have paid for it you must receive it directly into the soul and having learned it you must leave already harmed or benefited. (314b1–4)

The discussion is at least cautionary, but it makes an additional point. Buying, or more generally receiving, learning presents some specific difficulties of its own. When buying food one can always ask a third party, an acknowledged expert, for advice before the fact and act accordingly. But when buying learning the expert cannot be consulted, so to speak, after the initial transaction. One must determine in advance of all contact whether listening to the sophist or to any other professor of *aretē* is likely to help or harm one's soul. But at least part of the additional problem in regard to learning is that in this case there are no acknowledged experts. And therefore the same difficulty that applied to the sophists will also apply to such putative experts: how is one to tell whether their advice is itself harmful or beneficial?

The predicament gets worse. The dangers involved in approaching the sophist, concerning as they do, what is most dear and precious to us, the soul, are immense. The implication, though it is not explicitly drawn in the text, is that one should not approach such a professor unless one is certain that one knows that what is offered will be beneficial. Now to benefit or harm the soul, is, obviously, to make it better or worse (cf. 318a6–9, d7–e5). And a discussion in the *Laches* adds a special urgency to this connection.

In the *Laches,* Lysimachus and Milesias ask Socrates, Laches, and Nicias whether they should train their sons in armed combat. The two generals having disagreed on this issue, Socrates questions whether any one of them there is an expert (*technikos,* 185a1) on the issue at hand. In typical fashion, he immediately generalizes that issue to apply not only to fighting but to the large question whether the boys will or will not become good (*agathoi,* 185a6). This in turn he construes as the problem of how to make the boys' souls as good as possible (186a5–6). But to know how to accomplish this, he continues, they must know what it is that makes the soul better when it is present in it. And to know this, of course, is to know what *aretē* is (189d–190a).

In order to know whether a course of learning, therefore, will harm or benefit the soul, the expert (*iatrikos, epaiōn*) of the *Protagoras* must, like the expert (*technikos*) of the *Laches,* know what *aretē* is. But if the expert knows this, why bother to go to the sophist at all, why not learn instead from one who has already been determined to know? But the point is that there are no such acknowledged experts. Therefore, learners can only be certain that their soul will not be harmed by the sophist (or by the expert) if they themselves can tell whether such advice or instruction will be beneficial or harmful. But to know this, we have just shown, is to know oneself what *aretē* is. Therefore, unless one already knows what *aretē* is, and thus precisely what sophists claim to teach, one should never approach any professors of *aretē*. The sophists, and all who claim to teach what *aretē* is, are quite useless!

IV

None of the problems discussed here, of course, could ever be problems for Socrates, since he never claimed to teach what *aretē* is. It is true that in *Alcibiades* I Socrates makes some startlingly extravagant claims about his importance to Alcibiades and his political ambitions (105dff.). But his point there, I should think, is to satirize the wooing practices of Athenian men.[27] In general, Socrates steadfastly refuses the teacher's role or function in Plato's early dialogues.[28]

These problems, therefore, could not have seriously disturbed Socrates. But they did become very serious indeed for Plato, who gradually, in the very process of portraying him as refusing that role, came to see Socrates not only as "the best, the wisest, and the most just" man of his generation (*Phdo.* 118a16–17) but also as the ablest, thus far, teacher of *aretē*. For Socrates' sons, like the sons of Pericles, Aristeides, and Themistocles, did little to distinguish themselves in their city. His friends and companions, like the friends and companions of Protagoras and Gorgias, remained mediocre, like Crito, or became vicious, like Charmides, Critias, or especially Alcibiades. Though perhaps ironically motivated, his views on whether *aretē* can be taught did not remain stable. And he certainly was not universally acknowledged as an expert on *aretē*. On the contary, his life no less than his reputation suffered worse in the hands of the Athenians than the lives and reputations of many who, in Plato's eyes, had no claim to *aretē* whatsoever compared to him.

How, we should finally ask, could Socrates be exempt from the paradox that the teacher of *aretē* is useless? How could Plato, the disciple who may have thought he learned something from him, believe that Socrates could be approached even if one did not already know what was good and what was bad?

The answer to this question goes to the heart of Socrates' personality as well as of his method. It is that Socrates, unlike all other teachers of *aretē* does not constitute a danger to his students precisely because he refuses to tell anyone what *aretē* is, especially since he denies having that knowledge in the first place. Whatever claim Socrates has to the teaching of *aretē* lies exactly in his disclaiming any such ability. The contrast around which the *Protagoras* and many other early Platonic dialogues revolve is a contrast between a method that depends on telling one's students what *aretē* is, on transmitting information to them, and one that does not.

But if Socrates' refusal or inability to offer positive views makes it safe to approach him, it generates another problem: how does the elenctic method result in any learning? How do two people who are ignorant of the answer to a given question discover that answer and how do they realize that they have discovered it? If the elenchus presents a serious methodological question, this is it. And this is the very question that Meno raises in the paradox with which we have been concerned.

Plato tries to answer this question in the *Meno* through the examination of the slave and the theory of recollection, though his views on these issues never remain unchanged. In claiming that Meno's paradox is well motivated and that it goes to the heart of Socratic dialectic, I find myself in agreement with Irwin, who writes that "the examination of the slave is a scale-model of a Socratic elenchos, with a commentary to explain and justify the procedure" (139). However, I cannot agree with Irwin on the question of the resolution of the paradox. He thinks that the paradox depends on the view that if I know nothing about an object, I cannot identify it as the subject of my enquiry and I cannot therefore enquire into it at all (138–9).[29] According to Irwin (139), Socrates rejects this view and claims that

> though the slave does not know, he has true beliefs about the questions discussed.
> . . . To inquire into *x* we need only enough true beliefs about *x* to fix the reference of the
> term *"x"* so that when the inquiry is over, we can still see we refer to the same thing.

To support his view, Irwin relies crucially on 85c6–7, where Socrates asks whether one who does not know does not still possess true beliefs about the things he does not know (316 n. 14). But, for one thing, the position of the passage announces it more as an intermediate step of the argument rather than as a conclusion to it.[30] More importantly, the question of identification does not seem to me so crucial to Plato's resolution of the paradox. It is quite true that Plato writes that before the enquiry begins the slave has true beliefs concerning the geometrical problem discussed. But these beliefs were in no way available to him as such at the time. They were mixed together with all sorts of false beliefs, some of which were both elicited and eliminated by Socrates during his questioning. These true beliefs are recovered by the slave at the end of his examination by Socrates; they could not therefore play the identifactory role Irwin asks of them, and which requires them to be there consciously at its very beginning. Further, the knowledge that the slave is said to be eventually able to recover is also said to be in him, just as those true beliefs are (85d3–7). But if this is so, it is not clear that true beliefs are possessed in a particular manner, different from that in which knowledge is possessed and which therefore would enable them to have the different function Irwin's account assigns to them.

For true belief to secure the stable identification of the object of enquiry, it is necessary for it and for knowledge to be independent of each other. But this does not seem to be the case. Plato writes that the slave who now has only belief will acquire knowledge through repeated questioning (85c9–d1). This statement is not by itself very explicit, but it becomes a bit more clear when we connect it to the later discussion of "the reasoning out of the explanation" at 97e–98a. Once this is achieved, Plato writes, true beliefs "become *epistēmai.*" That is, these beliefs do not simply fix the object of which knowledge is to be acquired or, in Plato's terms, recovered; rather once acquired (recovered) themselves they become that knowledge when they have been properly organized and systematized.[31]

But before we offer some tentative remarks about Plato's resolution of the paradox we must raise one further, rather complicated problem. What exactly does recollection cover for Plato? Does it apply to the whole process of learning or only to part of it? Or, not to beg any questions about learning, which part of the slave's examination actually involves him in recollection?

The manner in which Socrates introduces the theory of recollection and his rather general statements at 81d2–3, d4–5, and 82a1–2, suggest that recollection applies to all the different stages that may be, however loosely, associated with the process of learning. Accordingly, we expect that everything that takes place during the slave's examination constitutes an instance of recollection. Socrates strengthens this expectation when he prefaces his examination by urging Meno to see whether the slave will be recollecting or learning from him (82b6–7), and by saying at the end of its first stage that he is only asking questions of the slave and not telling him anything (82e4–6).

But doesn't Socrates teach or tell the slave all sorts of things during their discussion? How else can we construe the questions of 82c7–8 and d1–2 or the leading (that is, misleading) question of 82d8–e2 that prompts the slave to offer one of his many wrong solutions to the geometrical problem? In addition, we must not forget the passages 83c8–d1 and d4–5, where Socrates does not even bother to ask a question but himself draws the inference, marked in each case by *ara,* for the slave.

Bluck, who was exercised by this problem answered, that Socrates does not teach the slave "in the sophistic way, by merely presenting him with propositions that he must accept." He gradually "leads" the slave to the correct solution and at that point the slave is "able to 'see' that what was said was true. The argument is simply that such 'seeing' or comprehension would not be possible if the slave had not had previous acquaintance with the truth . . ." (12).

But is it so clear that there was such a thing as "the" sophistic way of teaching?

And if there were, is Bluck's description of it accurate? Some sophists, Hippias and sometimes Protagoras (*Prot.* 320c2–4), may have taught in this manner. But Euthydemus and Dionysiodorus used a questioning method which, at least superficially, did not differ so drastically from the elenchus.[32] Bluck's appeal to "seeing," in addition, seems to me rather empty. The point is not simply that, especially in the *Meno,* the text gives little warrant to the identification of the slave's understanding with "his feeling of inner conviction" (12). More importantly, it is not clear that, even if such a feeling exists, the slave has it only when he "sees" the right answer and not also when he gives the wrong one. On the contrary, Socrates' comment at 82e5–6 to the effect that the slave now thinks he knows the solution suggests that subjectively there is no difference between merely thinking one has knowledge and actually having it. If there were, and assuming that everyone knows at least one thing, learning should proceed on its own until this feeling of inner conviction is acquired.

In the course of questioning the slave, Socrates produces in him, or elicits from him, a number of false geometric beliefs. In the present case, he continues to clear them out and to replace them by true ones instead. But what if he had not? What if, in particular, their conversation concerned *aretē,* of which Socrates is himself ignorant, and thus the very soul of the slave? Would Socrates not be capable of causing at least as much harm to the slave as the sophists have earlier been said to cause their students unless these already know the answers to their questions?

It is at this point that we should take Socrates very seriously, if rather liberally, when he insists that he does not teach anyone anything. He does not mean that he will ask no obvious or leading questions, or that he will not make statements or even sometimes long speeches.[33] He does mean that he requires his interlocutor to assent only to what he thinks is true, nothing more and nothing less. This is what Vlastos has recently called the "say what you believe" requirement of the elenchus.[34] Socrates' practice is in stark contrast with the method of Euthydemus, despite their apparent similarity. For Euthydemus insists that Socrates answer his quesions in ways with which he is deeply dissatisfied, dropping a number of essential qualifications, in order to prove to him that (again in a way superficially and perhaps deliberately reminiscent of the *Meno*) he has always known everything, even before he or the whole universe came into being, provided Euthydemus "wants it that way" (*Eud.* 295e–296d).

If knowledge consisted in a feeling of inner conviction, Socrates would have been quite dangerous to his interlocutors. For since knowledge and belief, true or false, do not differ subjectively, there might in fact be no way of telling, from the inside, whether a particular answer reached to a problem is true or false. But, of course, Socrates never ends his questioning when he has simply elicited a statement. The major burden of the elenchus is to *test* such statements and Socrates assumes that no false statement can survive these tests. Whether he is engaged in the more negative elenchus of the earlier dialogues or in the more positive investigation of the *Gorgias,*[35] Socrates consistently makes his interlocutors answer for their beliefs. What determines whether a belief is true or false has nothing to do with how the respondent feels and everything to do with that belief's dialectical impregnability.

The elenchus, therefore, depends solely on a dialectical test for truth: a belief is true if it cannot be overthrown by sound, non-contentious argument. To which, of course, one might be tempted to reply: but how can we know that a belief will not be overthrown? Socrates, I think, had no clear answer to this question. Plato may have tried to devise one: we can know this to be the case when we master the whole interconnected set of truths to which our particular belief refers. We have *epistēmē* when we have learned the axiomatic structure of the system in question and can prove any one of its elements.[36]

But even though Socrates' leading questions may be harmless to the slave, his claim that the whole examination involves recollection is misleading for the readers of the *Meno*. The slave only produces a false belief in the first stretch of the argument (82b9–83e3). Are we to infer that coming to have (or recovering) false beliefs is a case of recollection?[37]

By opening the second stretch of the examination by asking Meno to watch how the slave will now properly engage in orderly recollection (82e11–12), Socrates again suggests that the slave will be actually recollecting in what follows. What occurs here, of course, is that the slave is made to realize that he does not know the answer to Socrates' question (82e14–84a2). Are we to infer that recollection applies to the realization that one's beliefs about a topic are false?

Part of the answer to this question depends on the interpretation of Socrates' next question, which occurs in his summary of this second stretch of argument:

Ennoeis au, ō Menōn, hou estin ēdē badizōn hode tou anamimnēiskesthai? (84a3–4)

Thompson construes this as asking "what point on the track of reminiscence he has now reached," and believes that recollection has already begun.[38] On the other hand, we could take the question to concern "what point on the track *to* reminisce he has now reached," in which case Socrates would be saying that the path to recollection is now open, not that recollection has already begun. In that case, we may take his earlier remarks about the slave's recollecting to apply not specifically to the first part of the discussion but, more generally and programmatically, to the whole examination. Recollection may be more restricted than is sometimes supposed.

This impression is reinforced by Socrates' summary of the last section of his questioning. He and Meno agree that the slave has only replied with beliefs that were his own (85b8–9) and that he has true beliefs about what he does not yet know (85c2–7). Socrates now claims that if "someone asks him the same question many times and in many ways" he will finally have as much knowledge about these topics as anyone else (85c9–d1).[39] From this it is clear that the slave still does not have *epistēmē* of the subject and Socrates drives the point home by locating the slave's knowledge in the future in his very next question (*epistēsetai*, 85d3–4). He then goes on to say that it is just this recovery of knowledge which is still all in the *future* for the slave, that is recollection (85d6–7). Recollection thus seems limited to a very small part of the process of learning.

Despite the tension it creates with the general statement at 81d4–5, such a restricted interpretation of recollection fits well with Socrates' later distinction between *doxa* and *epistēmē*: the former, he says, "is worth little until it is tied down by reasoning about the explanation" (98a3–4). And it is *this* (*touto*, 98a4), he continues, that, "as we agreed earlier, is recollection" (98a4–5). But the *aitias logismos,* as far as I can see, corresponds to nothing in the first stages of the slave's interrogation. The only process to which it can be connected is the repeated questioning that will eventually lead to the recovery of *epistēmē* (85c–d) and which we were just now, on independent grounds, considering as a candidate for recollection.

Suppose now that we restrict recollection in this way. Since we are explicitly told that the slave does not yet have any *epistēmē* does it not follow that he has not engaged in recollection in the dialogue? And if this is so, what is the point of his long examination? What has Plato succeeded in demonstrating by its means?

It is quite possible that recollection, strictly speaking, is not shown to occur anywhere in the *Meno*. Nevertheless, I think that the last stage of the slave's questioning, in which Socrates elicits the correct solution to the problem from him, is deeply representative of the process. It represents it, that is, because it is a part of it. The slave, Socrates says, will come to have knowledge "if one asks him the very same questions [or: questions about the very same things] many times and in many ways" (85c10–11). What brings about the *aitias logismos* and transforms *doxai* into *epistēmē* is not a new operation, additional to the eliciting of true *doxa* but rather the eliciting of enough true *doxa* about the subject to make having them *constitute* the *aitias logismos*. The very same true beliefs the slave now has, Socrates claims at 86a7–8, "having been aroused by the questioning, become knowledge" (*epistēmai*).

Plato does not explain how this transformation is to occur, and it is very difficult to know what is involved in the transition. Certainly, simply having many *doxai* about geometry cannot be itself sufficient for *epistēmē*. One must also acquire the ability to organize them systematically, to become able to move from one of them to another properly and on one's own, to know how they are supported by one another. This is one of the reasons Plato emphasizes the role of questioning in the recovery of knowledge. Having the answers to as many questions as one pleases does not constitute *epistēmē* unless one is also capable of answering ever new questions as well as of formulating questions of one's own. The *aitias logismos* and recollection, strictly speaking, consist in this ability, which transcends merely having answers to different questions but which is acquired (or revealed) only in the course of learning them.[40]

Implicitly, true beliefs are in one in just the way that knowledge is supposed to be; explicitly, they enter the process of learning and recollection midway. It is therefore unlikely that Meno's paradox is resolved by appealing to them in order to secure, from the very beginning of the enquiry, reference to the object which the enquiry concerns. Plato seems to deny the claim, on which the paradox depends, that "one cannot search for what one does not know for one does not even know what to search for" (80e5), on slightly different grounds. One does know what one does not know because questioning and the inability to answer continued questions determine that knowledge is lacking. Conversely, the continued ability to answer such questions suggests that knowledge has been reached and that "you have happened upon" what you did not know (80d8). On the other hand, he also denies the claim that "one cannot search for what one knows—for one knows, and one who knows does not need to search" (80e3-5). For one need not know what one knows since knowledge may be, and usually is, forgotten and is brought out only by questioning. Knowledge is reached when what one knew that one does not know is matched with what one did not know that one knows. The role of questioning in bringing this matching about is crucial: Plato's resolution of Meno's paradox is dialectical rather than logical.

V

The dialectical resolution of Meno's paradox, even when supported by the non-dialectical explanation offered through the theory of recollection,[41] does not by itself account for Socrates' continued insistence that he is not, in this or in any other case, engaged in teaching. We have seen that part of this account is that had Socrates been willing to offer positive views on the nature of *aretē,* he should not have been approached any more than the sophists should. But in the *Meno* the question does not concern *aretē* and Socrates is quite aware of the correct answer. Why does Plato insist that the slave must come to it on his own? Why is he so eager to point out that even when Socrates is transmitting information to the slave (which he has him do on a number of occasions) the slave is still only recovering knowledge from within himself?

Plato appears to believe that even in matters that do not concern the soul's welfare as directly as *aretē* does, *epistēmē* cannot and must not be reached through the transmission of information. But knowledge depends essentially on the transmission of information and is itself transmissible. What is crucial to knowledge is that the information in which it consists has been acquired in the proper way, no less and no more. As Bernard Williams has written, in regard to knowledge in general

> not only is it not necessary that the knower be able to support or ground his belief by reference to other propositions, but it is not necessary that he be in any special state in regard to this belief at all, at least at the level of what he can consciously rehearse. What is necessary . . . is that one or more of a class of conditions should obtain . . . conditions which can best be summarized by the formula that, given the truth of p, it is no accident that A believes that p rather than not p.[42]

Though this formulation, as Williams himself admits, needs much further refinement, it seems to me quite true. However, William's conditions are remarkably weaker than Plato's and even explicitly exclude what Plato considers most crucial to *epistēmē*: the ability to "support or ground (a) belief," to give an account, a *logos* of the object of *epistēmē.*[43]

We might want to say that Plato insists upon an unduly restrictive notion of knowledge; but we would do better, I think, to say that when he is discussing *epistēmē* he is not producing unreasonable conditions on knowledge, but rather, quite reasonable conditions on what it is to understand something. For unlike knowledge, understanding involves, in rough-and-ready terms, the ability to *explain* what one understands. By contrast, many items of knowledge, for example, particular facts, are not even the sorts of things to which explanation is applicable in this context.[44]

In the case of mathematical knowledge, at least so far as non-elementary propositions are concerned, Williams accepts "the Platonic view" that such knowledge involves *aitias logismos* which he glosses as "a chain of proof." But he goes on to claim (9) that whether or not having such proof makes true beliefs more permanent, as Plato believes, is irrelevant to the main point

> that the access to mathematical truth must necessarily be through proof, and that therefore the notion of non-accidental true belief in mathematics essentially involves the notion of mathematical proof (the points which the Platonic model of *recollection* precisely serves to obscure).

But Plato's emphasis on the permanence of *epistēmē* is anything but irrelevant. For one thing, the permanence of one's understanding of a topic is in itself a measure of the degree to which one understands it. At some earlier time, I was capable of dealing with quadratic equations; my present total inability to do so strongly argues that I never understood that subject very well. For understanding the nature of quadratic equations is not an isolated act concerning an isolated object; it involves, at least in principle, the understanding of a vast number of mathematical propositions and operations, perhaps of all of algebra. And the more of a field one understands, the more systematically one's abilities with respect to it are organized, the less likely it is that the relevant beliefs will be forgotten: the more likely it is that they will be, in Plato's word, permanent (*monimoi*, 96a6). It is very easy, it is in fact inevitable, to forget whether it rained here three years ago today or to be persuaded that my recollection is wrong. It is also easy to forget how to get from one part of one's country to another. It is easy to forget how to determine the circumference of the circle, if you were only taught it once at school. But it seems more difficult to say that one has forgotten geometry, and almost totally absurd to claim to have forgotten what *aretē* is.[45] The broader and more encompassing the field to which a proposition belongs, the more permanent beliefs concerning that field, once mastered, are likely to be. The more worthy, therefore, that field is, in Plato's eyes, as an object of *epistēmē*.

Plato's model of recollection, though it may obscure Williams' points about knowledge, is crucial in emphasizing the necessity of working out a proof or of reaching any sort of understanding through and for oneself. Knowledge of fact, we have said, is transmissible and the

> mechanism by which knowledge is transmitted is *belief*. More precisely . . . it is sufficient and necessary for the transmission of your knowledge that *p* to me that I *believe you* when, speaking (or writing) from knowledge, you tell me that *p*.[46]

But, as Augustine also saw and argued in the *De Magistro* (40), understanding cannot be handed down in this manner. In an important discussion of this dialogue that connects it to Plato's concerns, Burnyeat describes its main thesis, "that no man can teach another knowledge (*scientia*)," as

> the claim that no man can teach another to understand something. The argument will not be that information cannot be transmitted from one person to another, but that the appreciation or understanding of any such information is something that each person must work out for himself. . . . The conveying of information is not enough for teaching in the sense of bringing the learner to know something.[47]

Burnyeat wants to connect Augustine's view that learning comes about through "first-hand learning, by the intellect or by my own sense-perception" with a number of cases discussed by Plato. He mentions in particular Plato's insistence that the slave in the *Meno* can learn mathematics only through reasoning and with his claim that only someone who has actually gone on the road to Larissa knows the way there (97a–b). He also brings in the view of the *Theaetetus* (201b–c) that only an eyewitness to a crime can have knowledge about it (16). My own view is that Plato considers the examples of the traveller and of the eyewitness not as instances of *epistēmē* but as indispensable analogies by which to explain his view of it. Their function is to highlight the crucial condition that *epistēmē* must be acquired first-hand; and in so far as they satisfy this condition, they may be, catachrestically, considered as cases of *epistēmē*. But in a stricter sense,[48] *epistēmē* applies only to cases which in addition to first-hand acquisition also involve systematization, proof, explanation, or account: this is the *aitias logismos* of the *Meno* and the *logos* of the *Theaetetus* (202d5). Neither the case of the traveller nor that of the eyewitness seems to me capable of satisfying this additional constraint.

What, then, is the difference between *epistēmē* and *orthē doxa?* According to Burnyeat, the case of the eyewitness shows that if he tells me I may come to know much of what he knows himself (though not, of course, on his grounds); still, there will "typically" be other things I will not know because eyewitnesses "nearly always" know more than they tell. What marks the difference between us is the eyewitness' synoptic grasp of something of which I at best know some isolated elements. And Burnyeat (17) concludes that

> the important difference between knowledge and understanding is this, that knowledge can be piecemeal, can grasp related truths one by one, but understanding always involves seeing the connections and relations between the items known.

The conclusion itself is quite correct, but I doubt that the case of the eyewitness testifies in its favour. First, I am not sure that it would be correct to say that the eyewitness does have understanding of what occurs. More importantly, the manner in which Burnyeat constructs his case (through the qualifications "typically" and "nearly always") suggests that he may think that eyewitnesses can on occasion tell all they see. But the difference between the eyewitness and me (if we attribute understanding to the eyewitness) cannot be, as this construal implies, merely one of degree. For if it depends simply on the amount of the information transmitted, then teaching may be after all, at least in principle, a matter of degree: what we would need would simply be a *very good* eyewitness. I think that the problem is caused by taking this case to constitute for Plato an actual instance of *epistēmē*. If, as I suggest, we take it only as a partial illustration of what *epistēmē* involves, then we will not feel it necessary to locate the difference between *epistēmē* and *orthē doxa* through it.

Instead, we can turn to the case of the slave and of mathematical knowledge. For here, the difference between belief (or even knowledge) and understanding is more clearly qualitative. Here, the connections and relations between the objects of knowledge, which were not easy to discern in the previous case, are much more central. For it is these relations and connections that produce understanding, and this limits understanding to fields which, unlike empirical low-level matters, involve them crucially. And it is precisely the mastering of these connections and relations that cannot be transmitted (cf. *Rep.* 518b6–7) because these connections are methods and rules for proceeding in a properly justified manner, from one item of knowledge to another. And even if such rules and methods can be formulated, and in that sense, transmitted, what cannot be transmitted in the same manner is the ability to follow the methods and to apply the rules.[49] And if we can formulate methods and rules for following the previous set, we will again face the question how these new rules and methods are to be correctly applied. The notion of recollection provides Plato both with an account of the inward, first-hand nature of all *epistēmē* and with a way of ending this regress: its power lies in its double contribution to Plato's philosophical purposes.[50]

In relation to *aretē* the connections we have been discussing are what allows one to do the right thing on all occasions and not only sometimes or capriciously. Unless it is in order to fool someone, the geometrician will not consciously produce a fallacious proof of a theorem. And unless it is in order to harm someone, the *agathos* will not willingly do the wrong thing. But part of being *agathos,* of course, is never to want to harm anyone, as Socrates consistently argued in Plato's dialogues. The *agathos,* therefore, will never do the wrong thing.

Socrates, in Plato's eyes, never did the wrong thing, and thus seemed to him to be the best man of his generation. But Socrates steadfastly refused the role of teacher: he claimed not to know how to make people good, and not even to understand at all what *aretē* itself consisted in. For practical and ethical reasons, Socrates had never wanted to tell his students (for students he certainly wanted, and had no less than any of the distinguished sophists) anything about the subject which they wanted to learn from him. For epistemological reasons, Plato came not to want Socrates to have believed that he was capable of doing so. Meno's paradox brought together Socrates' immediate concern with not harming his friends (a rather old-fashioned conception of *aretē* in its own right) with Plato's theoretical interest in the nature of understanding. The theory of recollection, whatever its ultimate shortcomings, succeeded in accounting systematically for both, even if in the process some of the mystery of Socrates gave way to the mysticism of Plato.

NOTES

For comments on an earlier version of this essay, I am grateful to M. F. Burnyeat, Rosemary Desjardins, Steven Strange, and Gregory Vlastos. I must also thank Paul Kalligas, who discussed these issues exhaustively with me and who gave me extensive and helpful comments. The generous support of the Guggenheim Foundation is gratefully acknowledged.

1. Paul Shorey, *What Plato Said* (Chicago, 1983), 157.
2. A. E. Taylor, *Plato: The Man and His Work* (London, 1937), 137.
3. Jacob Klein, *A Commentary on Plato's Meno* (Chapel Hill, 1965), 92.
4. Bernard Phillips, "The Significance of Meno's Paradox," in *Plato's Meno: Text and Criticism,* ed. Alexander Sesonske and Noel Fleming (Belmont, Calif., 1965), 78.
5. R. S. Bluck, *Plato's Meno* (Cambridge, Eng., 1964), 8. Bluck's mixed view of Meno can be found on pp. 125–6.
6. The contrary views of Cherniss and Guthrie have been recently discussed by Michael Morgan, "Belief, Knowledge and Learning in Plato's Middle Dialogues" (unpublished manuscript), 8–9, with full references.
7. Cf. also G. B. Kerferd, *The Sophistic Movement* (Cambridge, 1981), 131–8.
8. Cf. *Prot.* 361a5–b3 and contrast *Eud.* 282c1–8.
9. On the date of the *Dissoi Logoi,* cf. T. M. Robinson, *Contrasting Arguments: An Edition of the Dissoi Logoi* (New York, 1979), 34–41.
10. Cf. *Nemean* III.41.
11. Cf. *Antidosis* 186–92, 274–5. For further referenes, cf. Klein, 39 n. 18.
12. B. Jowett, *The Dialogues of Plato,* 4th ed. by D. J. Allan and H. E. Dale (Oxford, 1953), 252.
13. W. Peck, *Griechische Versinschriften,* vol i (Berlin, 1955), 20.11.
14. The question of the public aspects of *aretē,* though very complicated, has not been widely discussed. My suspicion, though highly speculative and in need of extensive support before it can be taken seriously, is that Plato was centrally concerned with it. Part of his purpose in the *Republic,* I would want (and have) to argue, is to ensure that *aretē* will always have a proper audience, and that those who possess it will necessarily be recognized as such by everyone in their social group.
15. There is considerable irony in putting this reply in the mouth of an imaginary Athenian, since

Anytus is later shown not to have any doubts about the fact that any good Athenian citizen can make another better (92eff.).

16. The abrupt opening of the *Meno* concerns both Bluck (199) and Klein (38). The discussion above may offer an adequate dramatic justification for it.

17. This view has become popular recently. It is supported for example, by Terrence Irwin, *Plato's Moral Theory* (Oxford, 1977), 40–1, 63; by Gerasimos Xenophon Santas, *Socrates* (London, 1979), 188–22, 311 n. 26; and by Paul Woodruff, *Plato: Hippias Major* (Indianapolis, 1982), 138, 141. The issue is much too complicated to be discussed here, and it will occupy me on a further occasion. A careful examination of the passages cited in this connection (*La.* 190b8–c2; *Prot.* 361c3–6; *Charm.* 157e7–159a3; *M.* 100b4–6; *Ly.* 223b4–8; *H. Ma.* 286c8–d2, 304d4–e3; *Rep.* 345b3–c3) has convinced me that Socrates does not, and need not, appeal to the distinction between knowledge and belief in order to justify his views on the priority of definition. The present case is, I think, even more straightforward.

18. Cp. 80d3 with *homoiotatos . . . narkēi,* and cf. Bluck, 271.

19. Cf. Nicholas White, "Inquiry," *Review of Metaphysics,* 28 (1974), 289 with n. 1.

20. John E. Thomas, *Musings on the Meno* (The Hague, 1980), 123, 128–9.

21. J. M. E. Moravcsik, "Learning as Recollection" in *Plato: Metaphysics and Epistemology,* ed. Gregory Vlastos (Garden City, 1971), 57.

22. Samuel Scolnicov, "Three Aspects of Plato's Philosophy of Learning and Instruction," *Paideia* 5 (1976), 52.

23. Gregory Vlastos, *"Anamnesis* in the *Meno,"* *Dialogue* 4 (1965), 143 n.1.

24. Cf. White, and Irwin, 315 n.13.

25. Similar arguments can be found at *Prot.* 319e–320b, *Alcibiades* 118c–119a.

26. Cf.*Dissoi Logoi* 6.3,4.

27. On which see Kenneth Dover, *Greek Homosexuality* (Cambridge, Mass., 1978), 81–100. In the course of the dialogue Socrates insists that he is not telling Alcibiades anything as their discussion proceeds (112dff.) and he readily admits that he, no less than Alcibiades, is in need of an education (124b1–c2). In a final ironic reversal, moreover, the dialogue ends with Alcibiades assuming the teacher's role and assigning to Socrates the student's position (135d–e).

28. Socrates often describes himself as a willing disciple of someone who claims to know something about *aretē;* cf., e.g., *Eu.* 5a3–b7.

29. White offers a related account, more concerned with identifying the object enquired into throughout the enquiry, on 294–7.

30. Cf. Michael Morgan, "An Interpretation of *Meno* 85b8–86b4" (unpublished manuscript, 1982), 8.

31. I have discussed some of the issues involved in this transition in *"Epistēmē* and *Logos* in Plato's Later Thought," *Archiv für Geschichte der Philosophie,* 66 (1984), 11–36.

32. For some material on sophistic teaching methods, cf. Kerford, 59–67.

33. For example, despite his insistence on short questions and answers at *Gorg.* 448e–449a, 449b4–c7, Socrates makes many longer speeches than Gorgias in the course of their conversation (451a3–c9, 452a1–a4, 455a8–e5, 457c3–458c8).

34. Gregory Vlastos, "The Socratic Elenchus," *Oxford Studies in Ancient Philosophy,* 1 (1983), 27–58, with full references.

35. Vlastos' evidence, in "The Socratic Elenchus," for his construal of the elenchus as a method for reaching positive ethical conclusions mainly comes, as he himself admits, from the *Gorgias.*

36. This view is supported in my *"Epistēmē* and *Logos* in Plato's Later Thought" (n. 31).

37. Theodor Ebert, *Meinung and Wissen in der Philosophie Platons* (Berlin, 1974), 83–104, and "Plato's Theory of Recollection Reconsidered: An Interpretation of *Meno* 80a–86c," *Man and World,* 6 (1973), 163–81, thinks that it is because he thinks that Plato believes that

learning is only analogous to recollection, and not an instance of it. But, I think, Plato's view is much stronger than that, and it would be very strange of him to consider that both the recovery of knowledge and the recovery of false beliefs are equally cases of recollection.

38. E. S. Thompson, *Plato's Meno* (London, 1901), 137.

39. Plato radically qualifies this extremely optimistic view, of course, in the *Republic*. The myth of *Er* and the theory of recollection as presented in the *Phaedrus* provide a rationale for his more cautious claims about the ability of people to reach *epistēmē*.

40. Restricting recollection in this way may help account for Socrates' agrument of 96dff. that though *aretē* is beneficial it may still not be *epistēmē* but *orthē doxa* instead and thus not teachable. For recollection provides Socrates' alternative account of teaching and learning. If it applied to the recovery of a single true belief (or to a small number of them), then this recovery would definitely be a matter of teaching, and Socrates would have no grounds for arguing that *aretē* cannot be taught. But if recollection only follows the recovery, or mere possession, of true belief, he may have just such a reason: teaching produces orderly recollection.

41. On the question whether the paradox is resolved primarily by the examination or by the theory of recollection, I agree with Irwin (139 and n. 13; *contra* White, 289, and *Plato on Knowledge and Reality* [Indianapolis, 1976], 40–1): the paradox is disarmed in the examination, and recollection explains how that is possible.

42. Bernard Williams, "Knowledge and Reasons" in *Problems in the Theory of Knowledge*, ed. G. H. von Wright (The Hague, 1972), 5.

43. I have presented a full case for that claim in "*Epistēmē* and *Logos* in Plato's Later Thought"; cf. also Jon Moline, *Plato's Theory of Understanding* (Madison, Wis., 1981), 32–51.

44. This is not to say that the fact, which I know, that it is raining cannot be explained. It is only to say that my knowledge of that (meteorological) explanation has no bearing on whether I know the fact in question. Most people know the latter, when it is the case, and ignore the former.

45. Cf. Hesiod, *Works and Days* 293–4: "He is the very best who understands everything having considered it himself and knows what is good later and to the end" (quoted by Moline, 19; the translation is different).

46. Michael Welbourne, "The Transmission of Knowledge," *Philosophical Quarterly*, 29 (1979), 3.

47. M. F. Burnyeat, "Augustine *De Magistro*" (unpublished manuscript, 1982), 9, 11.

48. This stricter sense, as I proceed to suggest, can be found in the *Meno* and in the *Theaetetus*, contrary to Burnyeat's suggestion, 16.

49. The problem is discussed, but not resolved, by Gilbert Ryle, "Teaching and Training" in *Plato's Meno*, ed. Malcolm Brown (Indianapolis, 1971), 243–6.

50. Recollection does not perpetuate the regress, for the requisite abilities have, according to Plato (85e–86b), always been in the soul.

FURTHER READINGS

Bluck, R. S. 1964. *Plato's Meno*. Cambridge.

Brown, M. S. 1967. "Plato Disapproves of the Slaveboy's Answer." *Review of Metaphysics* 20:57–93.

Irwin, T. 1974. "Recollection and Plato's Moral Theory." *Review of Metaphysics* 27:752–72.

Vlastos, G. 1965. "Anamnesis in the *Meno*." *Dialogue* 4:143–67.

White, N. P. 1974. "Inquiry." *Review of Metaphysics* 28:289–310.

Bibliography

Adam, J. 1902. *Plato's Republic*. Cambridge, Eng.

Adkins, A. W. H. 1960. *Merit and Responsibility: A Study in Greeek Values*. Oxford.

———. 1969. *Moral Values and Political Behavior in Ancient Greece*. New York.

———. 1970. "Clouds, Mysteries, Socrates and Plato." *Antichthon* 4:13–24.

———. 1973. *"Arete, Techne,* Democracy and Sophists: *Protagoras* 316b–328d." *Journal of Hellenic Studies* 93:3–12.

———. 1976. *"Polupragmosune* and 'Minding One's own Business': A Study of Greek Social and Politcal Values." *Classical Philology* 71:301–27.

———. 1978. "Problems in Greek Popular Morality." *Classical Philology* 73:143–58.

———. 1980. "The Greek Concept of Justice from Homer to Plato." *Classical Philology* 75:256–68.

Adkins, Arthur. 1989. "Plato." In *Ethics in the History of Western Philosophy*, ed. Robert J. Cavalier, 1–31. New York.

Alford, Fred C. 1988. *Narcissism: Socrates, the Frankfurt School, and Psychoanalytic Theory*. New Haven, Conn.

Allen, R. E. 1959. *"Anamnesis* in Plato's *Meno* and *Phaedo." Review of Metaphysics* 13:165–74.

———. 1960. "The Socratic Paradox." *Journal of the History of Ideas* 21:256–65.

———. 1970. *Plato's Euthyphro and the Earlier Theory of Forms*. New York.

———. 1971. "Plato's Earlier Theory of Forms." In *The Philosophy of Socrates,* ed. Gregory Vlastos, 319–34. Garden City, N.Y.

———. 1975. "The Trial of Socrates: A Study in the Morality of the Criminal Process." In *Courts and Trials: A Multi-Disciplinary Approach*, ed. Martin L. Friedland, 3–21. Toronto and Buffalo.

———. 1976. "Irony and Rhetoric in Plato's *Apology." Paideia* (Buffalo) 5:32–42.

———. 1980. *Socrates and Legal Obligation*. Minneapolis.

———. 1984. *The Dialogues of Plato*. New Haven, Conn.

Ambrose, Z. Philip. 1983. "Socrates and Prodicus in the Clouds." In *Essays in Ancient Greek Philosophy,* ed. John P. Anton and Anthony Preus, 2:129–44. Albany, N.Y.

Ambrosio, F. J. 1987. "Gadamer, Plato the Discipline of Dialogue." *International Philosophical Quarterly* 27:17–32.

Amory, F. 1981–2. *"Eiron* and *Eironeia." Classica et Mediaevalia* 33:49–80.

———. 1984. "Socrates: The Legend" *Classica et Mediaevalia* 35:19–56.

Anastaplo, George. 1975a. "Citizen and Human Being: Thoreau, Socrates, and Civil Disobedience." In *Essays on Virtue, Freedom, and the Common Good,* ed. George Anastaplo, 203–13, 313–16. Chicago.

———. 1975b. "Human Being and Citizen: A Beginning to the Study of Plato's *Apology of Socrates.* " In *Essays on Virtue, Freedom, and the Common Good,* ed. George Anastaplo, 8–29, 233–46. Chicago.

Anderson A. 1969. "Socratic Reasoning in the *Euthyphro." Review of Metaphysics* 22:461–81.

Anderson, Daniel E. 1967. "Socrates' Concept of Piety." *Journal of the History of Philosophy* 5:1–13.

Anderson, J. K. 1974. *Xenophon.* London.

Anderson, J. M. 1970. "On the Platonic Dialogue." In *Essays in Metaphysics,* ed. C. G. Vaught, 5–17. University Park, Penn.

Andic, M. 1971. "Inquiry and Virtue in the *Meno.*" In *Plato's Meno,* ed. M. Brown, 262–314. Indianapolis.

Annas, Julia. 1985. "Self-Knowledge in Early Plato." In *Platonic Investigations,* ed. D. J. O'Meara, 111–38. Studies in Philosophy and the History of Philosophy. Washington, D.C.

Anselmet, Raymond A. 1978. "Socrates and the *Clouds:* Shaftesbury and a Socratic Tradition." *Journal of the History of Ideas* 39:171–82.

Anton, John P. 1980. "Dialectic and Health in Plato's *Gorgias:* Presuppositions and Implications." *Ancient Philosophy* 1:49–60.

———. 1971. *Essays in Ancient Greek Philosophy 1,* ed. G. Kustas, Albany, N.Y.

———. 1983. *Essays in Ancient Greek Philosophy 2,* ed. A. Preus, Albany, N.Y.

———. 1989. *Essays in Ancient Greek Philosophy 3: Plato,* ed. A. Preus, Albany, N.Y.

Armleder, P. J. 1966. "Death in Plato's *Apology.*" *Classical Bulletin* 42:46.

Arrowsmith, W. 1962. *The Clouds of Aristophanes.* Ann Arbor, Mich.

Astrene, Tom. 1978. "An Analysis of Thrasymachus' True Definition of Justice." *Dialogue* 20:57–63.

Austin, Scott. 1987. "The Paradox of Socratic Ignorance (How to Know That You Don't Know)." *Philosophical Topics* 15:23–34.

Baker, W. W. 1916–17. "An Apologetic for Xenophon's *Memorabilia.*" *Classical Journal* 12:293–309.

Balaban, Oded. 1987a. "The Myth of Protagoras and Plato's Theory of Measurement." *History of Philosophy Quarterly* 4:371–84.

———. 1987b "Relation and Object in Plato's Approach to Knowledge." *Theoria* 53:141–58.

Ballard, E. G. 1965. *Socratic Ignorance: An Essay on Platonic Self-Knowledge.* The Hague.

Bambrough, R. 1960. "The Socratic Paradox." *Philosophical Quarterly* 10:289–300.

———, ed. 1965. *New Essays on Plato and Aristotle.* London.

———. 1972. "The Disunity of Plato's Thought." *Philosophy* 47:295–307.

Barker, Andrew. 1977. "Why Did Socrates Refuse to Escape?" *Phronesis* 22:13–28.

Baron, James R. 1975. "On Separating the Socratic from the Platonic in *Phaedo* 118." *Classical Philology* 70:268–69.

Beatty, Joseph. 1976. "Thinking and Moral Considerations: Socrates and Arendt's Eichmann." *Journal of Value Inquiry* 10:266–78.

Beckman, J. 1979. *The Religious Dimension of Socrates' Thought.* Waterloo, Ont.

Bedu-Addo, J. D. 1983. "Sense Experience and Recollection in Plato's *Meno.*" *American Journal of Philology* 104:228–48.

———. 1984. "Recollection and the Argument from a Hypothesis." *Journal of Hellenic Studies* 104:1–14.

Belfiore, Elizabeth. 1980. *"Elenchus, Epode,* and Magic: Socrates as Silenus." *Phoenix* 34:128–37.

Benardete, S. 1986. "On Interpreting Plato's *Charmides.*" *Graduate Faculty of Philosophy Journal* 11:9–36.

Benjamin, Walter. 1984. "Socrates." *Philosophical Forum* 15:52–54.

Benson, Hugh H. 1987. "The Problem of the Elenchus Reconsidered." *Ancient Philosophy* 7:67–85.

———. 1989. "A Note on Eristic and the Socratic Elenchus." *Journal of the History of Philosophy* 27:591–99.

————. 1990a. "Meno, the Slave Boy and the *Elenchos.*" *Phronesis* 35:128–58.

————. 1990b. "Misunderstanding the 'What is F-ness?' Question." *Archiv für Geschichte der Philosophie* 72:125–42.

————. 1990c. "The Priority of Definition and the Socratic *Elenchos.*" *Oxford Studies in Ancient Philosophy* 8:19–65.

Berns, Laurence. 1974. "Socratic and Non-Socratic Philosophy: A Note on Xenophon's *Memorabilia,* 1:1:13 and 14." *The Review of Metaphysics* 28:85–88.

Berti, Enrico. 1978. "Ancient Greek Dialectic as Expression of Freedom of Thought and Speech." *Journal of the History of Ideas* 39:347–70.

Bertmann, Martin A. 1971. "Socrates' Defense of Civil Disobedience." *Studium Generale* 24:576–82.

Best, Judith. 1980. *"Minos* Reconsidered." *Interpretation* 8:102–13.

Betz, Joseph. 1980. "Dewey and Socrates." *Transactions of the Pierce Society* 16:329–56.

Beversluis, J. 1974. "Socratic Deinition." *American Philosophical Quarterly* 11:331–36.

————. 1987. "Does Socrates Commit the Socratic Fallacy?" *American Philosophical Quarterly* 24:211–23.

Bicknell, P. J. 1974. "Socrates' Mistress Xanthippe." *Apeiron* 8:1–6.

Blakeney, E. H. 1929. *The Apology of Socrates.* London.

Blank, David. 1985. "Socrates vs. Sophists on Payment for Teaching." *Classical Antiquity* 4:1–49.

Blits, Jan H. 1980. "The Holy and Human: An Interpretation of Plato's *Euthyphro.*" *Apeiron* 14:19–40.

————. 1985. "Socratic Teaching and Justice: Plato's *Cleitophon.*" *Interpretation* 13:321–34.

Bloom, A. 1968. *The Republic of Plato.* New York.

Bluck, R. S. 1961. "Plato's *Meno.*" *Phronesis* 6:94–101.

————. 1964. *Plato's Meno.* Cambridge.

Blum, A. F. 1978. *Socrates: The Original and Its Images.* London and Boston.

Blumenthal, H. J. 1973. "Meletus the Accuser of Andicides and Meletus the Accuser of Socrates." *Philologus* 117:169–78.

Bolotin, David. 1979. *Plato's Dialogue on Friendship.* Ithaca, N.Y.

Bonafonte, L. and L. Raditsu. 1978. "Socrates' Defense and His Audience." *Bulletin of the American Society of Papyrologists* 15:17–23.

Bonner, Robert J., and Gertrude Smith. 1938. *The Administration of Justice from Homer to Aristotle.* Chicago.

Bostock, David. 1990. "The Interpretation of Plato's *Crito.*" *Phronesis* 35:1–20.

Boter, G. J. 1986. "Thrasymachus and *Pleonexia.*" *Mnemosyne* 39:261–81.

————. 1988. "Plato, *Meno* 82c2–3." *Phronesis* 33:208–15.

Brann, Eva. 1978. "The Offense of Socrates: A Re-reading of Plato's *Apology.*" *Interpretation* 7:1–21.

Brenk, F. E. 1975. "Interesting Bedfellows at the End of Plato's *Apology.*" *Classical Bulletin* 51:44–46.

Brickhouse, Thomas C., and Nicholas D. Smith. 1982. "Socrates' Proposed Penalty in Plato's *Apology.*" *Archiv für Geschichte der Philosophie* 64:1–18.

————. 1983. "The Origin of Socrates' Mission." *Journal of the History of Ideas* 44:657–66.

————. 1984a. "Irony, Arrogance, and Truthfulness in Plato's *Apology.*" In *New Essays on Socrates,* ed. Eugene Kelly, 29–46. Lanham, Md.

————. 1984b. "The Paradox of Socratic Ignorance in Plato's *Apology.*" *History of Philosophy Quarterly* 1:125–32.

————. 1984c. "Socrates and Obedience to the Law." *Apeiron* 18:10–17.

————. 1984d. "Vlastos on the Elenchus." *Oxford Studies in Ancient Philosophy* 2:185–96.

——. 1985. "The Formal Charges Against Socrates." *Journal of the History of Philosophy* 23:457–81.

——. 1986a. "'The Divine Sign Did Not Oppose Me': A Problem in Plato's *Apology*." *Canadian Journal of Philosophy* 16:511–26.

——. 1986b. "Socrates' First Remarks to the Jury in Plato's *Apology of Socrates*." *Classical Journal* 81:289–98.

——. 1987a. "Socrates' Evil Associates and the Motivation for His Trial and Condemnation." *Proceedings of the Boston Area Colloquium in Ancient Philosophy* 3:45–71.

——. 1987b. "Socrates on Goods, Virtue, and Happiness." *Oxford Studies in Ancient Philosophy* 5:1–27.

——. 1989a. "A Matter of Life and Death in Socratic Philosophy." *Ancient Philosophy* 9:155–66.

——. 1989b. *Socrates on Trial*. Princeton, N.J.

——. 1990. "What Makes Socrates a Good Man?" *Journal of the History of Philosophy* 28:169–80.

——. 1991. "Socrates' Elenctic Mission." *Oxford Studies in Ancient Philosophy* 9.

Brown, J. H. 1964. "The Logic of the *Euthyphro* 10a–11b." *Philosophical Quarterly* 14:1–14.

Brown, M. S. 1967. "Plato Disapproves of the Slaveboy's Answer." *Review of Metaphysics* 20:57–93.

——, ed. 1971. *Plato's Meno*. Indianapolis.

Brown, Malcolm. 1975. "Comments on Brumbaugh's *Meno* for Secondary Schools." *Teaching Philosophy* 1:115–18.

Bruell, Christopher. 1977. "Socratic Politics and Self-Knowledge: An Interpretation of Plato's *Charmides*." *Interpretation* 6:141–203.

——. 1988–9. "Xenophon and His Socrates." *Interpretation* 16:295–306.

Brumbaugh, R. S. 1975. "Plato's *Meno* as Form and as Content of Secondary School Philosophy." *Teaching Philosophy* 1:107–15.

——. 1976. "Plato's Relation to the Arts and Crafts." In *Facets of Plato's Philosophy*, ed. W. H. Werkmeister, 40–49. Amsterdam.

——. 1979. "Plato and Socrates." In *Plato for the Modern Age*, ed. R. S. Brumbaugh, 29–50. Westport, Conn.

——. 1981. "Socrates: The Search for the Self." In *The Philosophers of Greece*, ed. R. S. Brumbaugh, 123–32. Albany, N.Y.

——. 1983. "Doctrine and Dramatic Dates of Plato's Dialogues." In *Essays in Ancient Greek Philosophy, Vol. 2*, ed. J. P. Anton and A. Preus, 174–85. Albany, N.Y.

——. 1989. *Platonic Studies of Greek Philosophy: Form, Arts, Gadgets, and Hemlock*. Albany, N.Y.

Buford, T. 1977. "Plato on the Educational Consultant: An Interpretation of the *Laches*." *Idealistic Studies* 7:151–71.

Burge, E. L. 1969. "The Irony of Socrates." *Antichthon* 3:5–17.

Burger, R. 1981. "Belief, Knowledge, and Socratic Knowledge of Ignorance." *Tuland Studies in Philosophy* 30:1–23.

Burnet, John. 1914. *Greek Philosophy Part 1: Thales to Plato*. London.

——, ed. 1924. *Plato's Euthyphro, Apology of Socrates, and Crito*. Oxford.

Burnyeat, M. F. 1971. "Virtues in Action." In *The Philosophy of Socrates: A Collection of Critical Essays*, ed. Gregory Vlastos, 209–34. Garden City, N.Y.

——. 1977a. "Examples in Epistemology: Socrates, Theaetetus, and G. E. Moore." *Philosophy* 52:381–98.

——. 1977b. "Socratic Midwifery, Platonic Inspiration." *Bulletin of the Institute of Classical Studies* 24:7–13.

————. 1987. "Platonism and Mathematics: A Prelude to Discussion." In *Mathematics and Metaphysics in Aristotle,* ed. A. Graeser, 213–40. Berne and Stuttgart.

————. 1988. "Review of *The Trial of Socrates,* by I. F. Stone." *New York Review of Books* 35:12–18.

Burnyeat, M. F., and J. Barnes. 1980. "Socrates and the Jury: Paradoxes in Plato's Distinction Between Knowledge and True Belief." *Aristotelian Society Supplement* 44:177–206.

Buttrey, T. V. 1981. "Plato's *Apology* 23c and the Anger of the Catechized." *Liverpool Classical Monthly* 6:51–53.

Cahn, S. N. 1973. "A Puzzle Concerning the *Meno* and the *Protagoras.*" *Journal of the History of Philosophy* 11:535–57.

Calder, William M., III. 1961. "Socrates at Amphipolis (Apology 28e)." *Phronesis* 6:83–85.

————. 1972. "Plato's *Apology of Socrates:* A Speech for the Defense." *Boston University Journal* 20:42–47.

Calogero, G. 1957. "*Gorgias* and the Socratic Principle *nemo sua sponte peccat.*" *Journal of Hellenic Studies* 77:12–17.

Calvert, B. 1974. "Meno's Paradox Reconsidered." *Journal of the History of Philosophy* 12:143–52.

————. 1984. "The Politicians of Athens in the *Gorgias* and *Meno.*" *History of Political Thought* 5:1–16.

————. 1987. "Plato's *Crito* and Richard Kraut." In *Justice, Law and Method in Plato and Aristotle,* ed. S. Panagiotou, 17–33. Edmonton.

Candlish, S. 1983. "*Euthyphro* 6d–9b and Its Misinterpretations." *Apeiron* 17:28–32.

Chaplin, M. 1987. "Commentary on Brickhouse's and Smith's 'Socrates' Evil Associates and the Motivation for His Trial and Condemnation'" *Proceedings of the Boston Area Colloquium in Ancient Philosophy* 3:72–78.

Charlton, William. 1988. *Weakness of Will: A Philosophical Introduction.* New York.

Cherniss, Harold F. 1971. "The Philosophical Economy of the Theory of Ideas." In *Plato: A Collection of Critical Essays,* ed. G. Vlastos, 1:16–27. New York.

Chroust, A. H. 1945. "Socrates: A Source Problem." *New Scholasticism* 19:48–72.

————. 1947. "An Anonymous Treatise on Law: The Pseudo-Platonic Dialogue *Minos.*" *Notre Dame Lawyer* 23:47–53.

————. 1952. "Socrates in the Light of Aristotle's Testimony." *New Scholasticism* 26:327–66.

————. 1955. "Xenophon, Polycrates, and the Indictment of Socrates." *Classica et Mediaevalia* 16:1–77.

————. 1957. *Socrates: Man and Myth.* Notre Dame, Ind.

Chen, Chung-Hwan. 1978. "On Plato's *Charmides* 165c4–175d5." *Apeiron* 12:13–28.

Ciholas, P. 1981. "Socrates, Maker of New Gods." *Classical Bulletin* 57:17–20.

Claus, David B. 1981. *Toward the Soul: An Inquiry into the Meaning of 'Psyche' Before Plato.* New Haven, Conn.

Clay, D. 1972. "Socrates' Mulishness and Heroism." *Phronesis* 17:53–60.

————. 1987. "Gaps in the 'Universe' of the Platonic Dialogues." *Proceeding of the Boston Area Colloquium in Ancient Philosophy* 3:131–57.

Cobb, W. S. 1973. "*Anamnesis:* Platonic Doctrine or Sophistic Absurdity." *Dialogue* 12:604–28.

————. 1982. "The Argument of the *Protagoras.*" *Dialogue* 21:713–31.

————. 1986. "The Religious and the Just in Plato's *Euthyphro.*" *Ancient Philosophy* 5:41–46.

————. 1989. "Plato on the Possibility of an Irreligious Morality." *International Journal for Philosophy of Religion* 25:3–12.

Coby, Patrick. 1982. "The Education of a Sophist: Aspects of Plato's *Protagoras.*" *Interpretation* 10:139–58.

————. 1987. *Socrates and the Sophistic Enlightenment: A Commentary on Plato's Protagoras.* Lewisburg, Penn.

Cohen, Cynthia B. 1980. "The Trials of Socrates and Joseph K." *Philosophy and Literature* 4:212–28.

Cohen, Maurice. 1976. "Confucius and Socrates." *Journal of Chinese Philosophy* 3:159–68.

Cohen, S. M. 1971. "Socrates on the Definition of Piety: *Euthyphro* 10a–11b." Reprinted from *Journal of the History of Philosophy.* In *The Philosophy of Socrates: A Collection of Critical Essays,* ed. G. Vlastos, 158–76. New York.

Colson, D. 1985. "On Appealing to Athenian Law to Justify Socrates' Disobedience." *Apeiron* 19:133–51.

————. 1989. *"Crito* 51a–c: To What Does Socrates Owe Obedience?" *Phronesis* 34:27–55.

Congleton, Ann. 1974. "Two Kinds of Lawlessness: Plato's *Crito." Political Theory* 2:432–46.

Cooper, J. M. 1982. "The *Gorgias* and Irwin's Socrates." *Review of Metaphysics* 35:577–87.

Cornford, F. M. 1941. *The Republic of Plato.* Oxford.

————. 1950. *Plato's Theory of Knowledge.* London.

————. 1987. "Plato's *Euthyphro* or How to Read a Socratic Dialogue." In *F. M. Cornford: Selected Papers,* ed. A. C. Bowen, 221–38. New York.

Coulter, C. 1933. "The Tragic Structure of Plato's *Apology." Philological Quarterly* 12:137–43.

Coulter, James Albert. 1964. "The Relation of the *Apology of Socrates* to Gorgias' *Defense of Palamedes* and Plato's Defense of Gorgianic Rhetoric." *Harvard Studies in Classical Philology* 68:269–303.

Croiset, A. *Plato.* Guillaume Budé. Vol. 3, sec. 2. *Gorgias and Meno.* Trans. Louis Bodin. Paris.

Crombie, I. M. 1962. *An Examination of Plato's Doctrines.* London.

————. 1989. "A Dream of Socrates." *Philosophy* 64:29–38.

Cropsey, J. 1986. "The Dramatic End of Plato's Socrates." *Interpretation* 14:155–75.

Daniel, James, and Roland Polansky. 1979. "The Tale of the Delphic Oracle in Plato's *Apology."* *Ancient World* 2:83–85.

Dawson, Miles M. 1974. *The Ethics of Socrates.* New York.

Demand, Nancy. 1975. "Plato and the Painters." *Phoenix* 29:1–20.

Desjardins, R. 1985. "Knowledge and Virtue: Paradox in Plato's *Meno." Review of Metaphysics* 39:261–81.

Devereux, D. T. 1975. "Protagoras on Courage and Knowledge: *Protagoras* 351a–b." *Apeiron* 9:37–39.

————. 1977. "Courage and Wisdom in Plato's *Laches." Journal of the History of Philosophy* 15:129–41.

————. 1978. "Nature and Teaching in Plato's *Meno." Phronesis* 23:118–26.

de Vries, G. J. 1985. "Laughter in Plato's Writings." *Mnemosyne* 38:378–81.

Di Lorenzo, Raymond. 1978. "The Critique of Socrates in Cicero's *De Oratore:* Ornatus and the Nature of Wisdom." *Philosophy and Rhetoric* 11:247–61.

Dilman, Ilham, 1976. "Socrates and Dostoyevsky on Punishment." *Philosophy and Literature* 1:66–78.

————. 1979. *Morality and the Inner Life: A Study in Plato's Gorgias.* Totowa, N.J.

Dixit, R. D. 1980. "Socrates on Civil Disobedience." *Indian Philosophical Quarterly* 8:91–98.

Dodds, E. R. 1959. *Plato Gorgias.* Oxford.

Dorter, Kenneth. 1973. "The *Ion:* Plato's Characterization of Art." *Journal of Aesthetics and Art Criticism* 32:65–78.

————. 1974. "Socrates' Refutation of Thrasymachus and Treatment of Virtue." *Philosophy and Rhetoric* 7:25–46.

————. 1976. "Socrates on Life, Death and Suicide." *Laval Theologie et Philosophie* 32:23–41.

Dover, K. J. 1971. "Socrates in the *Clouds."* In *The Philosophy of Socrates:* A Collection of Critical Essays, ed. G. Vlastos, 50–77. Garden City, N.Y.

————. 1974. *Greek Popular Morality in the Time of Plato and Aristotle.* Berkeley and Los Angeles.

————. 1975. "Freedom of the Intellectual in Greek Society." *Talanta* 7:24–54.

————. 1978. *Greek Homosexuality.* Cambridge, Mass.

Dreisbach, Donald F. 1978. "Agreement and Obligation in the *Crito." New Scholasticism* 52:168–86.

Drengson, Alan R. 1981. "The Virtue of Socratic Ignorance." *American Philosophical Quarterly* 18:237–42.

Dubose, Shannon. 1973. "The Argument Laughs at Socrates and Protagoras." *Tulane Studies in Philosophy* 22:14–21.

Dubs, H. H. 1927. "The Socratic Problem." *Philosophical Review* 36:287–306.

Duff, R. A. 1982–83. "Socratic Suicide?" *Proceedings of the Aristotelian Society* 83:35–48.

Duncan, R. 1974. *"Philia* in the *Gorgias." Apeiron* 8:23–26.

————. 1978. "Courage in Plato's *Protagoras." Phronesis* 23:216–28.

Dybikowski, J. 1974a. "Socrates, Obedience, and the Law: Plato's *Crito." Dialogue* 13:519–35.

————. 1974b. "Was Socrates as Reasonable as Professor Vlastos?" *Yale Review* 44:293–96.

Dyson. M. 1974. "Some Problems Concerning Knowledge in Plato's *Charmides." Phronesis* 19:102–11.

————. 1976. "Knowledge and Hedonism in Plato's *Protagoras." Journal of Hellenic Studies* 96:32–45.

————. 1978. "The Structure of the Law's Speech in Plato's *Crito." Classical Quarterly* 28:427–36.

Ebert, Theodor. 1973. "Plato's Theory of Recollection Reconsidered: An Interpretation of *Meno* 80a–86c." *Man and World* 6:163–80.

Eckstein, J. 1968. *The Platonic Method: An Interpretation of the Dramatic-Philosophic Aspects of the Meno.* New York.

Edmunds, Lowell. 1985. "Aristophanes' Socrates." *Proceedings of the Boston Area Colloquium in Ancient Philosophy* 1:209–30.

Ehrenberg, Victor. 1973. *From Solon to Socrates.* 2d ed. London.

Eisner, Robert. 1982. "Socrates as Hero." *Philosophy and Literature* 6:106–18.

Elias, Julias A. 1968. " 'Socratic' vs. 'Platonic' Dialectic." *Journal of the History of Philosophy* 6:205–16.

Euben, J. Peter. 1978. "Philosophy and Politics in Plato's *Crito." Political Theory* 6:149–72.

Evans, J. Claude. 1990. "Socratic Ignorance—Socratic Wisdom." *The Modern Schoolman* 67:91–110.

Farness, J. 1987. "Missing Socrates: Socratic Rhetoric in a Platonic Text." *Philosophy and Rhetoric* 20:41–59.

Farrell, Daniel M. 1978. "Illegal Actions, Universal Maxims, and the Duty to Obey the Law: The Case for Civil Authority in the *Crito." Political Theory* 6:173–89.

Feaver, D., and J. Hare. 1981. "The *Apology* as an Inverted Parody of Rhetoric." *Arethusa* 14:205–16.

Ferejohn, Michael T. 1982. "The Unity of Virtue and the Objects of Socratic Inquiry." *Journal of the History of Philosophy* 20:1–21.

————. 1984. "Socratic Thought-Experiments and the Unity of Virtue Paradox." *Phronesis* 29:105–22.

————. 1988. "Meno's Paradox and De Re Knowledge in Aristotle's Theory of Demonstration." *History of Philosophy Quarterly* 5:99–118.

Ferguson, A. S. 1913. "The Impiety of Socrates." *Classical Quarterly* 7:157–75.

Findlay, J. N. 1974. *Plato: The Written and Unwritten Doctrines.* London.

Finley, Moses I. 1972. "Socrates and Athens." In *Aspects of Antiquity,* 60–73. London and New York.

Forrester, James W. 1975. "Some Perils of Paulinity." *Phronesis* 20:11–21.

Foulk, Gary F. 1974. "Socrates' Argument for Not Escaping in the *Crito.*" *The Personalist* 55:356–59.

Fowler, H. N. 1926. *Plato: Cratylus, Parmenides, Greater Hippias, Lesser Hippias.* New York.

Fox, M. 1956. "The Trials of Socrates." *Archiv für Philosophie* 6:226–61.

Frede, D. 1986. "The Impossibility of Perfection: Socrates' Criticism of Simonides' Poem in the *Protagoras.*" *Review of Metaphysics* 39:729–53.

Freidlander, P. 1964. *Plato.* Vol. 2. *The Dialogues: First Period.* Trans. H. Meyerhoff. New York.

Frey, R. G. 1978. "Did Socrates Commit Suicide?" *Philosophy* 53:106–08.

Friedman, Joel I. 1982. "Plato's *Euthyphro* and Leibniz' Law." *Philosophia: Philosophical Quarterly of Israel* 12:1–20.

Furley, Wiiliam D. 1985. "The Figure of Euthyphro in Plato's Dialogue." *Phronesis* 30:201–8.

Gadamer, Hans-Georg. 1985. "Religion and Religiosity in Socrates." *Proceedings of the Boston Area Coloquium in Ancient Philosophy* 1:53–76.

Gagarin, M. 1969. "The Purpose of Plato's *Protagoras.*" *Transactions of the American Philological Society* 100:133–64.

———. 1977. "Socrates' *Hybris* and Alcibiades' Failure." *Phoenix* 31:22–37.

Gallop, D. 1961. "Justice and Holiness in *Protagoras.*" *Phronesis* 6:86–93.

———. 1964. "The Socratic Paradox in the *Protagoras.*" *Phronesis* 9:117–29.

Garland, William J. 1976. "Notes on Two Socratic Arguments in *Republic* I." *Apeiron* 10:11–13.

Garrett, R. 1974. "The Structure of Plato's *Euthyphro.*" *Southern Journal of Philosophy* 12:165–83.

Gavin, Bill. 1979. "A Note on Socrates and 'the Law' in the *Crito.*" *Aitia* 7:26–28.

Gavin, William. 1977. "Death: Acceptance or Denial: The Case of Socrates Re-examined." *Religious Humanism* 11:134–39.

Geach, P. T. 1966. "Plato's *Euthyphro:* An Analysis and Commentary." *Monist* 50:369–82.

Gerson, Lloyd P. 1989. "Plato on Virtue, Knowledge and the Unity of Goodness." In *Essays in Ancient Greek Philosophy 3: Plato,* ed. J. P. Anton and A. Preus, 85–100. Albany, N.Y.

Gill, C. 1973. "The Death of Socrates." *Classical Quarterly* 23:25–28.

Glidden, D.K. 1981. "The *Lysis* on Loving One's Own." *Classical Quarterly* 31:39–59.

Gontar, David P. 1978. "The Problem of the Formal Charges in Plato's *Apology.*" *Tulane Studies in Philosophy* 27:89–101.

Gooch, P. W. 1985. "Socrates: Devious or Devine?" *Greece and Rome* 32:32–41.

———. 1987a. "Irony and Insight in Plato's *Meno.*" *Laval Theologique et Philosophique* 43:189–204.

———. 1987b. "Socratic Irony and Aristotle's *Eiron:* Some Puzzles." *Phoenix* 41:95–104.

Gordon, R. M. 1964. "Socratic Definitions and Moral Neutrality." *Journal of Philosophy* 61:433–50.

Gosling, J. C. B. 1973. *Plato.* London and Boston.

Gosling, J. C. B., and C. C. W. Taylor. 1982. *The Greeks on Pleasure.* Oxford.

———. 1990. "The Hedonic Calculus in the *Protagoras* and the *Phaedo:* A Reply." *Journal of the History of Philosophy* 28:115–16.

Gould, C. S. 1987. "Socratic Intellectualism and the Problem of Courage: An Interpretation of Plato's *Laches.*" *History of Philosophy Quarterly* 4:265–79.

Gray, V. J. 1989. "Xenophon's *Defence of Socrates:* The Rhetorical Background to the Socratic Problem." *Classical Quarterly* 39:136–40.

Griswold, C. L. 1986. "Philosophy, Education, and Courage in Plato's *Laches.*" *Interpretation* 14:177–93.

———. 1988a. *Platonic Writings, Platonic Readings.* New York.

————. 1988b. "Plato's Metaphilosophy: Why Plato Wrote Dialogues." In *Platonic Writings, Platonic Readings,* ed. C. L. Griswold, 143–70. New York.

————. 1988c. "Unifying Plato." *Journal of Philosophy* 85:550–51.

Groden, S., trans. 1970. *Symposium.* In *The Symposium of Plato,* ed. J. A. Brentlinger. Amherst, Mass.

Grote, George. 1875. *Plato and the Other Companions of Socrates.* London.

Grube, G. M. A. 1931. "The *Cleitophon* of Plato." *Classical Philology* 26:302–8.

————. 1974. *Plato's Republic.* Indianapolis.

Guardini, Romano. 1948. *The Death of Socrates: An Interpretation of the Platonic Dialogues: Euthyphro, Apology, Crito, and Phaedo.* Trans. B. Wrighton. Cleveland, Ohio.

Guilhamet, Leon. 1985. "Socrates and Post-Socratic Satire." *Journal of the History of Ideas* 46:3–12.

Gulley, N. 1952. "Ethical Analysis in Plato's Earlier Dialogues." *Classical Quarterly* n.s. 2:74–82.

————. 1954. "Plato's Theory of Recollection." *Classical Quarterly* n.s. 4:194–213.

————. 1958. "Greek Geometrical Analysis." *Phronesis* 3:1–14.

————. 1962. *Plato's Theory of Knowledge.* London.

————. 1965. "The Interpretation of 'No One Does Wrong Willingly' in Plato's Dialogues." *Phronesis* 10:82–96.

————. 1968. *The Philosophy of Socrates.* London.

————. 1971. "Socrates' Thesis at *Protagoras* 358b–c." *Phoenix* 25:118–23.

Guthrie, W. K. C. 1962–75. *A History of Greek Philosophy.* 5 vols. Cambridge, Eng.

————. 1971. *Socrates.* Cambridge.

Hackforth, R. 1928. "Hedonism in Plato's *Protagoras.*" *Classical Quarterly* 22:39–42.

————. 1931. "A Corner of the Socrates Problem." *Proceedings of the Cambridge Philological Society* 148–150:2–3.

————. 1933. *The Composition of Plato's Apology.* Cambridge, Eng.

Haden, James. 1969. "On Plato's Inconclusiveness." *Classical Journal* 64:219–24.

————. 1979. "On Socrates, with Reference to Gregory Vlastos." *Review of Metaphysics* 33:371–89.

————. 1984. "Socratic Ignorance." In *New Essays on Socrates,* ed. Eugene Kelly, 17–28. Lanham, Md.

Hadgopoulos, Demetrius J. 1973. "Thrasymachus and Legalism." *Phronesis* 18:204–8.

Hall, J. C. 1968. "Plato: *Euthyphro* 10a1–11a10." *Philosophical Quarterly* 18:1–11.

Hall, R. W. 1971. *"Techne* and Morality in the *Gorgias."* In *Essays in Ancient Greek Philosophy,* ed. J. Anton and G. Kustas, 202–18. Albany, N.Y.

Hamilton, W., trans. 1951. *Plato's Symposium.* Baltimore.

————, trans. 1960. *Plato's Gorgias.* Baltimore.

Hansen, D. T. 1988. "Was Socrates a 'Socratic Teacher'?" *Educational Theory* 38:213–24.

Hare, R. M. 1982. *Plato.* Oxford and New York.

Hart, Richard E. 1984. "Socrates on Trial." In *New Essays on Socrates,* ed. Eugene Kelly, 143–50. Lanham, Md.

Hartman, Margaret. 1984. "How the Inadequate Models for Virtue in the *Protagoras* Illuminate Socrates' View of the Unity of the Virtues." *Apeiron* 18:110–17.

Hathaway, Ronald F. 1970. "Law and the Moral Paradox in Plato's *Apology.*" *Journal of the History of Philosophy* 8:127–42.

————. 1984. "Explaining the Unity of the Platonic Dialogue." *Philosophy and Literature* 8:195–208.

Havelock, E. A. 1972. "The Socratic Self as It Is Parodied in Aristophanes' *Clouds.*" *Yale Classical Studies* 22:1–18.

———. 1983. "The Socratic Problem: Some Second Thoughts." In *Essays in Ancient Greek Philosophy 2*, ed. J. P. Anton and A. P. Preuss, 147–73. Albany, N.Y.

———. 1984. "The Orality of Socrates and the Literacy of Plato." In *New Essays on Socrates*, ed. Eugene Kelly, 67–93. Lanham, Md.

Hawtrey, R. S. W. 1972. "Socrates and the Acquisition of Knowledge." *Antichthon* 6:1–9.

———. 1976. "Plato, Socrates and the Mysteries: A Note." *Antichthon* 10:22–24.

———. 1978. "How Do Dialecticians Use Diagrams—Plato, *Euthydemus* 109b–c." *Apeiron*12:14–18.

Helm, James J. 1981. *Plato, Apology: Text and Grammatical Commentary*. Chicago.

Helmbold, W., trans. 1952. *Plato's Gorgias*. New York.

Handerson, T. Y. 1970. "In Defense of Thrasymachus." *American Philosophical Quarterly* 7:218–28.

Hendley, Brian. 1981–82. "The *Meno* and Modern Education—a Response to Harold Stern." *Educational Studies* 12:425–29.

Henry, Maureen. 1984. "Socratic Piety and the Power of Reason." In *New Essays on Socrates*, ed. Eugene Kelly, 95–105. Lanham, Md.

Higgins, W. E. 1977. "Socrates." In *Xenophon the Athenian*, 21–43. Albany, N.Y.

Hoerber, R. G. 1958. "Plato's *Euthyphro*." *Phronesis* 3:95–107.

———. 1959. "Plato's *Lysis*." *Phronesis* 4:15–28.

———. 1960. "Plato's *Meno*." *Phronesis* 5:78–102.

———. 1962. "Plato's *Lesser Hippias*." *Phronesis* 7:121–31.

———. 1964. "Plato's *Greater Hippias*." *Phronesis* 9:143–55.

———. 1966. "Note on Plato's *Apology* XLII." *Classical Bulletin* 42:92.

———. 1968. "Plato's *Laches*." *Classical Philology* 63:95–105.

Hogan, Richard A. 1977. "The Techne Analogy in the *Charmides*." *Philosophy Research Archives* 3:1225.

———. 1978. "Was Socrates a 'Utilitarian'?" *Auslegung* 5:118–31.

Holland, R. F. 1981–82. "*Euthyphro*." *Aristotelian Society Proceedings* 82:1–16.

Hoopes, James P. 1970. "Euthyphro's Case." *Classical Bulletin* 47:1–6.

Houlgate, L. D. 1970. "Virtue is Knowledge." *Monist* 54:142–53.

Hourani, George F. 1962. "Thrasymachus' Definition of Justice in Plato's *Republic*." *Phronesis* 7:110–20.

Hubbard, B. A. F., and E. S. Karnofsky. 1982. *Plato's Protagoras: A Socratic Commentary*. Chicago.

Huby, P. M. 1957. "The *Menexenus* Reconsidered." *Phronesis* 2:104–14.

Hughen, Richard E. 1982. "Some Arguments in Support of the Socratic Thesis That There is No Such Thing as Weakness of the Will." *Journal of Thought* 17:85–93.

Hutchinson, D. S. 1988. "Doctrines of the Mean and the Debate Concerning Skills in Fourth-Century Medicine, Rhetoric, and Ethics." *Apeiron* 21:17–52.

Hyland, Drew A. 1968. "*Eros, Epithumia*, and *Philia* in Plato." *Phronesis* 13:32–46.

———. 1981. *The Virtue of Philosophy: An Interpretation of Plato's Charmides*. Athens, Ohio.

Irwin, T. H. 1973–74. "Recollection and Plato's Moral Theory." *Review of Metaphysics* 27:752–72.

———. 1977. *Plato's Moral Theory: The Early and Middle Dialogues*. Oxford.

———. 1979. *Plato: Gorgias*. Clarendon Plato Series. Oxford.

———. 1983. "Euripides and Socrates." *Classical Philology* 78:183–97.

———. 1986a. "Coercion and Objectivity in Plato's Dialectic." *Revue Internationale de Philosophie* 40:47–74.

———. 1986b. "Socrates the Epicurean." *Illinois Classical Studies* 11:85–112.

———. 1986c. "Socratic Inquiry and Politics." *Ethics* 96:400–15.

————. 1988. "Reply to David L. Roochnik." In *Platonic Writings, Platonic Readings*, ed. C. L. Griswold, 194–99. New York.

————. 1989. "Socrates and Athenian Democracy." *Philosophy and Public Affairs* 18:184–205.

Jackson, B. Darrell. 1971. "The Prayers of Socrates." *Phronesis* 16:14–37.

James, Gene G. 1973. "Socrates on Civil Disobedience and Rebellion." *Southwestern Journal of Philosophy* 11:119–27.

Jeffrey, Andrew. 1979. "Polemarchus and Socrates on Justice and Harm." *Phronesis* 24:54–69.

Johnson, Curtis N. 1989. "Socrates' Encounter with Polus in Plato's *Gorgias.*" *Phoenix* 43:196–216.

Jordan, James N. 1973. "Socrates' Wisdom and Kant's Virtue." *Southwestern Journal of Philosophy* 4:7–23.

Kahn, C. H. 1976. "Plato on the Unity of Virtues." In *Facets of Plato's Philosophy*, ed. W. H. Werkmeister, 21–39. Amsterdam.

————. 1981. "Did Plato Write Socratic Dialogues?" *Classical Quarterly* 31:305–20.

————. 1983. "Drama and Dialectic in Plato's *Gorgias.*" *Oxford Studies in Ancient Philosophy* 1:75–122.

————. 1986. "Plato's Methodology in the *Laches.*" *Revue Internationale de Philosophie* 40:7–21.

————. 1988a. "On the Relative Date of the *Gorgias* and the *Protagoras.*" *Oxford Studies in Ancient Philosophy* 6:69–102.

————. 1988b. "Plato and Socrates in the *Protagoras.*" *Methexis* 1:33–52.

————. 1988c. "Plato's *Charmides* and the Proleptic Reading of Socratic Dialogues." *Journal of Philosophy* 85:541–49.

————. 1989. "Problems in the Argument of Plato's *Crito.*" *Apeiron* 22:29–44.

Karavites, P. 1973–74. "Socrates in the *Clouds.*" *Classical Bulletin* 50:65–69.

Kauffman, Charles. 1979. "Enactment as Argument in the *Gorgias.*" *Philosophy and Rhetoric* 12:114–29.

Keaney, John J. 1980. "Plato, *Apology* 32c8–d3." *Classical Quarterly* 30:296–98.

Kelly, Eugene, ed. 1984. *New Essays on Socrates*. Lanham, Md.

Kerferd, G. B. 1964. "Thrasymachus and Justice: A Reply." *Phronesis* 9:12–16.

————. 1974. "Plato's Treatment of Callicles in the *Gorgias.*" *Proceedings of the Cambridge Philological Society* 20:48–52.

————. 1981. *The Sophistic Movement*. Cambridge, Mass.

Kimball, Bruce. 1988. "The Inclination of Modern Jurists to Associate Lawyers with Doctors: Plato's Response in *Gorgias* 464–465." *Journal of Medical Humanities and Bioethics* 9:17–31.

King, J. 1976. "Nonteaching and Its Significance for Education." *Educational Theory* 26:223–30.

————. 1987. "Elenchus, Self-Blame and the Socratic Paradox." *Review of Metaphysics* 41:105–26.

Klein, Jacob. 1965. *A Commentary on Plato's Meno*. Chapel Hill, N.C.

Klein, S. 1986. "Socratic Dialectic in the *Meno.*" *Southern Journal of Philosophy* 24:351–63.

Kleve, K. 1983. "Anti-Dover or Socrates in *The Clouds.*" *Symbolae Osloenses* 58:23–37.

Klonoski, Richard J. 1984. "Setting and Characterization in Plato's *Euthyphro.*" *Dialogos* 19:123–40.

————. 1986. "The Portico of the Archon Basileus: On the Significance of the Setting of Plato's *Euthyphro.*" *Classical Journal* 81:130–37.

Klosko, G. 1979. "Toward a Consistent Interpretation of the *Protagoras.*" *Archiv für Geschichte der Philosophie* 61:125–42.

————. 1980. "On the Analysis of *Protagoras.*" *Phoenix* 34:307–22.

————. 1981. "The Technical Conception of Virtue." *Journal of the History of Philosophy* 19:98–106.

————. 1983a. "Criteria of Fallacy and Sophistry for Use in the Analysis of Platonic Dialogues." *Classical Quarterly* 33:363–74.

————. 1983b. "Plato's Utopianism: The Political Content of the Early Dialogues." *Review of Politics* 45:483–509.

————. 1986. *The Development of Plato's Political Theory*. New York and London.

————. 1987. "Socrates on Goods and Happiness." *History of Philosophy Quarterly* 4:251–64.

Kosman, L. A. 1983. "*Charmides'* First Definition: Sophrosune as Quietness." In *Essays in Ancient Greek Philosophy 2*, ed. J. P. Anton and A. P. Preuss, 203–16. Albany, N.Y.

————. 1986. "Commentary on Henry Teloh's 'The Importance of Interlocutors' Characters in Plato's Early Dialogues.'" *Proceedings of the Boston Area Colloquium in Ancient Philosophy* 2:39–44.

Kostman, James. 1984. "Socrates' Self-Betrayal and the Contradiction Between *Apology* and *Crito*." In *New Essays on Socrates*, ed. Eugene Kelly, 107–30. Lanham, Md.

Kramer, Scott. 1988. "Socrates' Dream: *Crito* 44a–b." *Classical Journal* 83:193–97.

Kramm, L. 1986–7. "Plato's *Crito* in Present Perspective." *Philosophical Studies* 31:159–74.

Kraut, R. 1980. "Plato's *Apology* and *Crito*: Two Recent Studies." *Ethics* 91:651–64.

————. 1983. "Comments on Vlastos." *Oxford Studies in Ancient Philosophy* 1:59–70.

————. 1984. *Socrates and the State*. Princeton, N.J.

————. 1988. "Reply to Clifford Orwin." In *Platonic Writings, Platonic Readings*, ed. C. L. Griswold, 177–82. New York.

Kubara, Michael. 1975. "Acrasia, Human Agency and Normative Psychology." *Canadian Journal of Philosophy* 5:215–32.

Lacey, A. R. 1971. "Our Knowledge of Socrates." In *The Philosophy of Socrates: A Collection of Critical Essays*, ed. G. Vlastos, 22–49. New York.

Lee, E. N., A. P. D. Mourelatos, and R. M. Rorty. 1973. *Exegesis and Argument: Studies in Greek Philosophy Presented to Gregory Vlastos*. Amsterdam.

Lesher, James H. 1975. "Theistic Ethics and the *Euthyphro*." *Apeiron* 9:24–30.

————. 1987. "Socrates' Disavowal of Knowledge." *Journal of the History of Philosophy* 25:275–88.

Lesser, Harry. 1980. "Suicide and Self-Murder." *Philosophy* 55:255–57.

Lesses, G. 1982. "Virtue as Techne in the Early Dialogues." *Southwest Philosophical Studies* 13:93–100.

————. 1985. "Is Socrates an Instrumentalist?" *Philosophical Topics* 13:165–74.

————. 1986. "Plato's *Lysis* and Irwin's Socrates." *International Studies in Philosophy* 18:33–43.

Levin, D. N. 1971. "Some Observations Concerning Plato's *Lysis*." In *Essays in Ancient Greek Philosophy*, ed. J. P. Anton and G. L. Kustas, 236–58. Albany, N.Y.

Lewis, M. 1984–5. "An Interpretation of Plato's *Euthyphro*." *Interpretation* 12:225–59, 13:33–65.

Lewis, T. J. 1986. "Refutative Rhetoric as True Rhetoric in the *Gorgias*." *Interpretation* 14:195–210.

Lombardo, Joseph. 1980. "Husserl's Method in Phenomenology and the Socratic Method of Teaching." *Aitia* 8:10–16.

Long, A. A. 1988. "Socrates in Hellenistic Philosophy." *Classical Quarterly* 38:150–71.

Lycos, K. 1987. *Plato on Justice and Power: Reading Book I of Plato's Republic*. Albany, N.Y.

McCoy, W. J. 1975. "The Identity of Leon." *American Journal of Philology* 96:187–99.

MacDowell, Douglas M. 1978. *The Law in Classical Athens*. Ithaca, N.Y.

Mackenzie, Mary Margaret. 1981. *Plato on Punishment*. Berkeley, Los Angeles, and London.

————. 1982. "A Pyrrhic Victory: *Gorgias* 474b–474a." *Classical Quarterly* 32:84–88.

———. 1988a. "Impasse and Explanation: From the *Lysis* to the *Phaedo.*" *Archiv für Geschichte der Philosophie* 70:15–45.

———. 1988b. "The Virtues of Socratic Ignorance." *Classical Quarterly* 38:331–50.

McKim, R. 1985. "Socratic Self-Knowldege and 'Knowldege of Knowledge' in Plato's *Charmides.*" *Transactions of the Americal Philological Association* 115:59–77.

———. 1988. "Shame and Truth in Plato's *Gorgias.*" In *Platonic Writings, Platinoc Readings,* ed. C. L. Griswold, 34–48. New York.

McKirahan, R. D. 1984. "Socrates and Protagoras on *Sophrosune* and Justice (*Protagoras* 333–334)." *Apeiron* 18:19–25.

———. 1985. "Socrates and Protagoras on Holiness and Justice (*Protagoras* 330c–332a)." *Phoenix* 39:342–54.

McLaughlin, Robert J. 1976. "Socrates on Political Disobedience." *Phronesis* 21:185–97.

McPherran, M. L. 1985. "Socratic Piety in the *Euthyphro.*" *Journal of the History of Philosophy* 23:283–309.

———. 1986. "Socrates and the Duty to Philosophize." *Southern Journal of Philosophy* 24:541–60.

———. 1987. "Commentary on Paul Woodruff's 'Expert Knowledge in the *Apology* and *Laches:* What a General Needs to Know.' " *Proceedings of the Boston Area Colloquium in Ancient Philosophy* 3:116–30.

———. 1990. "Comments on Charles Kahn, 'The Relative Date of the *Gorgias* and the *Protagoras.*' " *Oxford Studies in Ancient Philosophy* 8:211–36.

McTighe, K. 1984. "Socrates on Desire for the Good and the Involuntariness of Wrongdoing: *Gorgias* 466a–468e." *Phronesis* 29:193–236.

Maguire, J. P. 1971. "Thrasymachus . . . or Plato?" *Phronesis* 16:142–63.

———. 1973. "Protagoras—or Plato?" *Phronesis* 18:115–38.

Malcolm, J. 1968. "On the Place of the *Hippias Major* in the Development of Plato's Thought." *Archiv für Geschichte der Philosophie* 50:189–95.

Manasse, E. M. 1980. "A Thematic Interpretation of Plato's *Apology* and *Crito.*" *Philosophy and Phenomenological Research* 40:393–400.

Mara, Gerald M. 1988. "Socrates and Liberal Toleration." *Political Theory* 16:468–95.

Martin, G. 1972. "Socrates: On the Interpretation of His Ignorance." Trans. R. D. S. Hartman. In *Value and Valuation: Axiological Studies in Honor of Robert S. Hartman,* ed. J. W. Davies, 107–13. Knoxville, Tenn.

Martin, R. 1970. "Socrates on Disobedience to the Law." *Review of Metaphysics* 24:21–38.

Meridor, Ra'anana, and Lisa Ullman. 1978. "Plato's *Apology* 24a6–b1." *American Journal of Philology* 99:36.

Meyer, Michel. 1980. "Dialectic and Questioning: Socrates and Plato." *American Philosophical Quarterly* 17:281–90.

Meyers, J. I. 1988. "Plato's Geometric Hypothesis: *Meno* 86e–87b." *Apeiron* 21:173–80.

Michaelides-Nouaros, George. 1980. "A New Evaluation of the Dialogue Between Thrasymachus and Socrates." *Archiv für Rechts und Sozialphilosophie* 66:329–47.

Mikalson, J. 1983. *Athenian Popular Religion.* Chapel Hill, N.C., and London.

Miller, Clyde Lee. 1977. "Two Midpoints in Plato's *Protagoras.*" *The Modern Schoolman* 55:71–79.

———. 1978. "The Prometheus Story in Plato's *Protagoras.*" *Interpretation* 7:22–32.

Miller, John F., III. 1971. "The Socratic Meaning of Piety." *Southern Journal of Philosophy* 9:141–9.

Miller, M. 1987. "Commentary on Clay's 'Gaps in the "Universe" of the Platonic Dialogues.' " *Proceedings of the Boston Area Colloquium in Ancient Philosophy* 3:158–64.

Mitscherling, J. 1982. "Xenophon and Plato." *Classical Quarterly* 32:468–69.

Mittelstass, J. 1988. "On Socratic Dialogue." In *Platonic Writings, Platonic Readings*, ed. C. L. Griswold, 126–42. New York.

Moline, J. 1969. "Meno's Paradox." *Phronesis* 14:153–61.

———. 1981. *Plato's Theory of Understanding*. Madison, Wis.

———. 1988. "Plato on Persuasion and Credibility." *Philosophy and Rhetoric* 21:260–78.

Momeyer, Richard W. 1982. "Socrates on Obedience and Disobedience to the Law." *Philosophy Research Archives* 8:1458.

Montouri, Mario. 1981. *Socrates: Physiology of a Myth*. Trans. M. Langdale. Amsterdam.

Mooney, Christopher P. 1984. "The Mystical Dimension of Socratic Piety." In *New Essays on Socrates*, ed. Eugene Kelly, 161–71. Lanham, Md.

Moore, S. 1988. "Democracy and Commodity Exchange: Protagoras Versus Plato." *History of Philosophy Quarterly* 5:357–68.

Moravcsik, J. M. E. 1970. "Learning as Recollection." In *Plato: A Collection of Critical Essays*, ed. G. Vlastos, 1:53–69. New York.

———. 1978. "Understanding and Knowledge in Plato's Philosophy." *Neue Hefte für Philosophie* 15–16:53–69.

Morgan, Michael L. 1989. "How Does Plato Solve the Paradox of Inquiry in the *Meno?*" In *Essays in Ancient Greek Philoosophy 3: Plato*, ed. J. P. Anton and A. Preus: 169–82. Albany, N.Y.

Morris. T. F. 1989. "Knowledge of Knowledge and of Lack of Knowledge in the *Charmides*." *International Studies in Philosophy* 21:49–61.

Morrison, D. 1987. "On Professor Vlastos' Xenophon." *Ancient Philosophy* 7:9–22.

Moutafakis, Nicholas J. 1971. "Plato's Emergence in the *Euthyphro*." *Apeiron* 5:23–32.

Mulgan, R. G. 1972. "Socrates and Authority." *Greece and Rome* 19:208–12.

Mulhern, J. J. 1968a. "A Note on Stating the Socratic Paradox." *Journal of the History of Ideas* 29:601–4.

———. 1968b. "*Tropos* and *Polytropia* in Plato's *Hippias Minor*." *Phoenix* 22:283–88.

Muller, Anslem W. 1977. "Radical Subjectivity: Morality Versus Utilitarianism." *Ratio* 19:115–32.

Murphie, Jeffrie. 1974. "The Socratic Theory of Legal Fidelity." In *Violence and Aggression in the History of Ideas*, ed. P. Weiner and J. Fisher, 15–33. New Brunswick, N.J.

Murray, James S. 1988. "Plato on Knowledge, Persuasion, and the Art of Rhetoric." *Ancient Philosophy* 8:1–10.

Nadler, S. 1985. "Probability and Truth in the *Apology*." *Philosophy and Literature* 9:198–201.

Nakhnikian, G. 1971. "Elenctic Definitions." In *The Philosophy of Socrates: A Collection of Critical Essays*, ed. G. Vlastos, 125–57. New York.

———. 1973. "The First Socratic Paradox." *Journal of the History of Philosophy* 10:1–17.

Navia, Luis, E. 1981a. "A Certain Man Named Socrates." In *An Invitation to Philosophy*, ed. N. Capaldi, 35–56. Buffalo.

———. 1981b. "The Philosophical Impulse: The Case of Socrates." In *The Fundamental Questions*, ed. E. Kelly and L. E. Navia, 1–57. Dubuque, Iowa.

———. 1984. "A Reappraisal of Xenophon's *Apology*." In *New Essays on Socrates*, ed. Eugene Kelly, 47–65. Lanham, Md.

———. 1985. *Socrates, the Man and His Philosophy*. Lanham, Md.

———. 1987. *Socratic Testimonies*. Lanham, Md., New York, and London.

Nehamas, A. 1975. "Confusing Universals and Particulars in Plato's Early Dialogues." *Review of Metaphysics* 29:287–306.

———. 1985. "Meno's Paradox and Socrates as a Teacher." *Oxford Studies in Ancient Philosophy* 3:1–30.

———. 1986. "Socratic Intellectualism." *Proceedings of the Boston Area Colloquium in Ancient Philosophy* 2:275–316.

————. 1990. "Eristic, Antilogic, Sophistic, Dialectic: Plato's Denmarcation of Philosophy from Sophistry." *History of Philosophy Quarterly* 7:3–16.

Nemes, Z. 1978. "On Socrates' Public and Political Attitude." *Acta Classica Universitatis Scientiarum* 14:19–22.

Neumann, Harry. 1968. "Socrates and the Tragedy of Athens." *Social Research* 35:426–44.

————. 1969. "Socrates in Plato and Aristophanes." *American Journal of Philology* 90:201–14.

————. 1970. "Plato's *Defense of Socrates:* An Interpretation of Ancient and Modern Sophistry." *Liberal Education* 56:458–75.

Newman, Jay. 1980. "Philosophy as a Profession." *Aitia* 7–8:18–22.

Nichols, M. P. 1987. *Socrates and the Political Community: An Ancient Debate*. Albany, N.Y.

Nicholson, P. P. 1974. "Unraveling Thrasymachus' Arguments in the *Republic*." *Phronesis* 19:210–32.

Norman, D. N. 1971. "Some Observations Concerning Plato's *Lysis*." In *Essays in Ancient Greek Philosophy,* ed. J. Anton and G. Kustas, 236–58. Albany, N.Y.

North, H. 1966. *Sophrosune: Self-Knowledge and Self-Restraint in Greek Literature*. Ithaca, N.Y.

Novak, Joseph A. 1982. "Plato and the Irrationals." *Apeiron* 16:71–85.

————. 1983. "Plato and the Irrationals—part 2." *Apeiron* 17:14–27.

Nussbaum, Martha C. 1980. "Aristotle and Socrates on Learning Practical Wisdom." *Yale Classical Studies* 26:43–97.

————. 1985. "Commentary of Lowell Edmunds' 'Aristophanes' Socrates.'" *Proceedings of the Boston Area Colloquium in Ancient Philosophy* 1:231–40.

————. 1986. *The Fragility of Goodness: Luck and Ethics in Greek Tradegy and Philosophy*. Cambridge, Eng.

Ober, William B. 1982. "Did Socrates Die of Hemlock Poisoning?" *Ancient Philosophy* 2:115–21.

O'Brien, M. J. 1962. "The Fallacy in *Protagoras* 349d–350c." *Transactions of the American Philological Society* 93:408–17.

————. 1963. "The Unity of the *Laches*." *Yale Classical Studies* 9:131–47.

————. 1967. *The Socratic Paradoxes and the Greek Mind*. Chapel Hill, N.C.

Ogilvy, J. A. 1971. "Socratic Method, Platonic Method, and Authority." *Educational Theory* 21:3–16.

O'Neill, B. 1988. "The Struggle for the Soul of Thrasymachus."*Ancient Philosophy* 8:167–86.

Organ, Troy. 1977. "The Excellence of Socrates." *Darshana International* 17:27–34.

O'Sullivan, J. N. 1976. "On Plato *Apology* 23c–d." *American Journal of Philology* 97:114–16.

Orwin, C. 1988. "Liberalizing the *Crito:* Richard Kraut on Socrates and the State." In *Platonic Writings, Platonic Readings,* ed. C. L. Griswold, 171–76. New York.

Panagiotou, S. 1974. "Plato's *Euthyphro* and the Attic Code on Homocide." *Hermes* 102:422–23.

————. 1987a. *Justice, Law and Method in Plato and Aristotle*. Edmonton, Alta.

————. 1987b. "Justified Disobedience in the *Crito*." In *Justice, Law and Method in Plato and Aristotle,* ed. S. Panagiotou, 35–50. Edmonton, Alta.

————. 1987c. "Socrates' Defiance in the *Apology*." *Apeiron* 20:39–61.

Pangle, T. L. 1985. "The Political Defense of Socratic Philosophy—A Study of Xenophon *Apology of Socrates to the Jury*." *Polity* 18(1):98–114.

————. 1987. *The Roots of Political Philosophy*. Ithaca, N.Y.

Pappas, Nickolas. 1989a. "Plato's *Ion:* The Problem of the Author." *Philosophy* 64:381–90.

————. 1989b. "Socrates' Charitable Treatment of Poetry." *Philosophy and Literature* 13:248–61.

Parke, H. W. 1961. "Chaerephon's Inquiry About Socrates." *Classical Philology* 56:249–50.

Parker, Meg. 1973. *Socrates and Athens*. London.

Parry, R. 1983. "The Craft of Justice." *Canadian Journal of Philosophy*, supp.4:19–38.

Paxson, Thomas D. 1972. "Plato's *Euthyphro* 10a to 11b." *Phronesis* 17:171–90.

Payne, Thomas. 1983. "The *Crito* as a Mythological Mime." *Interpretation* 11:1–24.

Pecorino, Philip A. 1975. "The Midwife's Trickery or on Teaching Philosophy: A Provocation." *Aitia* 3:13–17.

Penner, T. 1973a. "Socrates on Virtue and Motivation." In *Exegesis and Argument: Studies in Greek Philosophy Presented to Gregory Vlastos*, ed. E. N. Lee, A. P. D. Mourelatos, and R. M. Rorty, 133–51. Assen, Amsterdam.

———. 1973b. "The Unity of Virtue." *Philosophical Review* 82:35–68.

———. 1987. "Socrates on the Impossibility of Belief-Relative Sciences." *Proceedings of the Boston Area Colloquium in Ancient Philosophy* 3:263–325.

———. 1990. "Plato and Davidson: Parts of the Soul and Weakness of Will." *Canadian Journal of Philosphy*, supp. 16:35–74.

Peterman, John E. 1984. "The Socratic Suicide." In *New Essays on Socrates*, ed. Eugene Kelly, 3–15. Lanham, Md.

Phillips, B. 1965. "The Significance of Meno's Paradox." In *Plato's Meno: Text and Criticism*, ed. Alexander Sesonske and Noel Fleming, 77–83. Belmont, Calif.

Phillipson, C. 1928. *The Trial of Socrates (with Chapters on His Life, Teaching, and Personality)*. London.

Plochmann, George Kimball, and Franklin E. Robinson. 1987. *A Friendly Companion to Plato's Gorgias*. Carbondale, Ill.

Polansky, R. 1985. "Professor Vlastos' Analysis of Socratic Elenchus." *Oxford Studies in Ancient Philosophy* 3:247–60.

———. 1988. "Reading Plato: Paul Woodruff and the *Hippias Major*." In *Platonic Writings, Platonic Readings*, ed. C. L. Griswold, 200–9. New York.

Principe, Michael A. 1982. "Restraint of Desire in the *Gorgias*." *Southern Journal of Philosophy* 20:121–32.

Prior, William J. 1980. "Relations Between Forms and 'Pauline Prediction' in *Euthyphro* 11e4–12d4." *Ancient Philosophy* 1:61–68.

Quandt, Kenneth. 1982. "Socratic Consolation: Rhetoric and Philosophy in Plato's *Crito*." *Philosophy and Rhetoric* 15:238–56.

Raaflaub, Kurt A. 1989. "Contemporary Perceptions of Democracy in Fifth-Century Athens." *Classica et Mediaevalia* 40:33–70.

Rabinowitz, W. G. 1958. "Platonic Piety: An Essay Toward the Solution of an Enigma." *Phronesis* 3:108–20.

Race, William H. 1979. "Shame in Plato's *Gorgias*." *Classical Journal* 74:197–202.

Rankin, H. D. 1983. *Sophists, Socratics, and Cynics*. Totowa, N.J.

Reeve, C. D. C. 1985. "Socrates Meets Thrasymachus." *Archiv für Geschichte der Philosophie* 67:246–65.

———. 1989. *Socrates in the Apology: An Essay on Plato's Apology of Socrates*. Indianapolis.

Reilly, R. 1977. "Socrates' Moral Paradox." *Southwestern Journal of Philosophy* 8:101–7.

Rhodes, P. J. 1980. "Athenian Democracy After 403 B.C." *Classical Journal* 75:305–23.

Richardson, Henry S. 1990. "Measurement, Pleasure and Practical Science in Plato's *Protagoras*." *Journal of the History of Philosophy* 28:7–32.

Richardson, N. J. 1985. "Early Greek Views About Life After Death." In *Greek Religion and Society*, ed. P. E. Easterling and J. V. Muir, 50–66. Cambridge, Mass.

Rist, J. M. 1975. "Plato's Earlier Theory of Forms." *Phoenix* 29:336–57.

Roberts, J. W. 1984. *City of Socrates: An Introduction to Classical Athens*. London.

Robin, L. 1956. *Platon, Oeuvres Completes*. Paris.

Robinson, D. B. 1986. "Plato's *Lysis:* The Structural Problem." *Illinois Classical Studies* 11:63–84.

Robinson, Franklin, E. 1977. "Plato's *Gorgias:* Socrates' Argument in the Socrates-Polus Colloquy." *Midwest Journal of Philosophy* 5:43–49.

Robinson, Richard. 1953. *Plato's Earlier Dialectic.* 2d ed. Oxford.

Rogers, Arthur Kenyon. 1933. *The Socratic Problem.* New York.

Rohatyn, Dennis A. 1973. "The *Euthyphro* as Tragedy: A Brief Sketch." *Dialogos* 9:147–51.

———. 1980. "Reflections on Meno's Paradox." *Apeiron* 14:69–73.

Roochnik, David L. 1984. "The Riddle of the *Cleitophon.*" *Ancient Philosophy* 4:132–45.

———. 1985. *"Apology* 40c4–41e7: Is Death Really a Gain?" *Classical Journal* 80:212–20.

———.1986. "Socrates' Use of the Techne-Analogy." *Journal of the History of Philosophy* 24:295–310.

———. 1987a. "Plato's Critique of Postmodernism." *Philosophy and Literature* 11:282–91.

———. 1987b. "Plato's Use of *Atechnos.*" *Phoenix* 41:255–63.

———. 1988. "Terence Irwin's Reading of Plato." In *Platonic Writings, Platonic Readings,* ed. C. L. Griswold, 183–93. New York.

Rorty, Amelie Osenberg. 1986. "Commentary on Alexander Nehamas' 'Socratic Intellectualism': The Limits of Socratic Intellectualism: Did Socrates Teach Arete?" *Proceedings of the Boston Area Colloquium in Ancient Philosophy* 2:317–30.

Rose, L. E. 1965. "A Note on the *Euthyphro,* 10–11." *Phronesis* 10:149–50.

———. 1970. "Plato's *Meno* 86–89." *Journal of the History of Philosophy* 8:1–8.

Rosen, Frederick. 1968. "Piety and Justice in Plato's *Euthyphro.*" *Philosophy* 43:105–16.

———. 1973. "Obligation and Friendship in Plato's *Crito.*" *Political Theory* 1:307–16.

Rosivach, Vincent J. 1981. *"Hoi Polloi* in the *Crito* 44b5–d10." *Classical Journal* 76:289–97.

Ross, W. D. 1933. "The Socratic Problem." *Proceedings of the Classical Association:*7–24.

———. 1951. *Plato's Theory of Ideas.* Oxford.

Rossetti, Livio. 1989. "The Rhetoric of Socrates." *Philosophy and Rhetoric* 22:225–38.

Rowe, Christopher. 1976. *An Introduction to Greek Ethics.* London.

Rudebusch, George. 1988. "Plato on Knowing a Tradition." *Philosophy East and West* 38:324–33.

———. 1989a. "Plato, Hedonism and Ethical Protagoreanism." In *Essays in Ancient Greek Philosophy III: Plato,* ed. J. P. Anton and A. Preus. Albany, N.Y.

———. 1989b. "Plato's Aporetic Style." *Southern Journal of Philosophy* 27:539–47.

Santas, Gerasimos Xenophon. 1964. "The Socratic Paradoxes." *Philosophical Review* 73:147–64.

———. 1971a. "Plato's *Protagoras* and Explanations of Weakness." In *The Philosophy of Socrates: A Collection of Critical Essays,* ed. G. Vlastos, 264–98. New York.

———. 1971b. "Socrates at Work on Virtue and Knowledge in Plato's *Laches.*" In *The Philosophy of Socrates: A Collection of Critical Essays,* ed. G. Vlastos, 177–208. New York.

———. 1972. "The Socratic Fallacy." *Journal of the History of Philosophy* 10:127–41.

———. 1973. "Socrates at Work on Virtue and Knowledge in Plato's *Charmides.*" In *Exegesis and Argument: Studies in Greek Philosophy Presented to Gregory Vlastos,* ed. E. N. Lee, A. P. D. Mourelatos and R. M. Rorty, 105–32. Assen, Amsterdam.

———. 1979. *Socrates: Philosophy in Plato's Early Dialogues.* London.

Savan, D. 1964. "Self-prediction in *Protagoras* 330–331." *Phronesis* 9:130–35.

Saxonhouse, A. W. 1988. "The Philosophy of the Particular and the Universality of the City: Socrates' Education of Euthyphro." *Political Theory* 16:281–99.

Sayre, K. M. 1969. *Plato's Analytic Method.* Chicago.

Scaltsas, Theodore. 1989. "Socratic Moral Realism: An Altenative Justification." *Oxford Studies in Ancient Philosophy* 7:129–50.

Scharff, R. C. 1986. "Socrates' Successful Inquiries." *Man and World* 19:311–27.
Schmid, W. T. 1981. "Socrates' Practice of Elenchus in the *Charmides*." *Ancient Philosophy* 1:141–47.
———. 1982. "Philosophy and Moral Commitment." *Ancient Philosophy* 2:134–41.
———. 1983. "Socratic Moderation and Self-Knowledge." *Journal of the History of Philosophy* 21:339–48.
———. 1985. "The Socratic Conception of Courage." *History of Philosophy Quarterly* 2:113–30.
Scodel, R. 1986. "Literary Interpretation in Plato's *Protagoras*." *Ancient Philosophy* 6:27–37.
Scolnicov, S. 1976. "Three Aspects of Plato's Philosophy of Learning and Instruction" *Paideia* 5:50–62.
Scott, Dominic. 1987. "Platonic Anamnesis Revisited." *Classical Quarterly* 37:346–66.
Sedley, D. 1989. "Is the *Lysis* a Dialogue of Definition?" *Phronesis* 34:107–8.
Seeskin, Kenneth. 1982. "Is the *Apology of Socrates* a Parody?" *Philosophy and Literature* 6:94–105.
———. 1985. "Reply to Nadler." *Philosophy and Literature* 9:201–2.
———. 1987. *Dialogue and Discovery: A Study in Socratic Method.* Albany, N.Y.
Senter, Nell W. 1976. "Socrates, Rhetoric and Civil Disobedience." *Southwest Philosophical Studies* 1:50–56.
Sesonske, Alexander. 1961. "Plato's Apology: *Republic* I." *Phronesis* 6:29–36.
———. 1968. "To Make the Weaker Argument the Stronger." *Journal of the History of Philosophy* 6:217–31.
Sesonske, Alexander, and Noel Fleming, eds. 1965. *Plato's Meno: Text and Criticism.* Belmont, Calif.
Shargel, E. I. 1987. "Socrates and Thrasymachus." *Philosophy of Education: Proceedings* 43:327–37.
Sharples, R. W. 1984. *Plato, Meno.* Chicago.
———. 1989. "More on Plato, *Meno* 82c2–3." *Phronesis* 34:220–26.
Shartin, D. 1987. "Commentary on Terry Penner's 'Socrates on the Impossibility of Belief-Relative Sciences'" *Proceedings of the Boston Area Colloquium in Ancient Philosophy* 3:326–32.
Sharvy, Richard. 1972. "*Euthyphro* 9d–11b: Analysis and Definition in Plato and Others." *Nous* 6:119–37.
Shey, H. James. 1971. "Petronius and Plato's *Gorgias*." *Classical Bulletin* 47:81–84.
Shorey, P., trans. 1961. *Plato: The Republic.* In *Plato: The Collected Dialogues,* ed. E. Hamilton and H. Cairns. Princeton, N.J.
Sider, David. 1980. "Did Plato Write Dialogues Before the Death of Socrates?" *Apeiron* 14:15–18.
Siemsen, T. 1987. "Thrasymachus' Challenge." *History of Political Thought* 8:1–19.
———. 1988. "Rational Persuasion in Plato's Political Theory." *History of Political Thought* 9:1–17.
Skousgaard, Stephen. 1974. "Genuine Speech vs. Chatter: A Socratic Problematic." *Kinesis* 6:87–94.
Smith, Michael. 1980. "Did Socrates Kill Himself Intentionally?" *Philosophy* 55:253–54.
Sobel, J. H. 1987. "Cephalus: *Republic* 331c–d." *History of Philosophy Quarterly* 4:281–90.
Soupios, Michael A. 1984. "Reason and Feeling in Plato." In *New Essays on Socrates,* ed. Eugene Kelly, 137–41. Lanham, Md.
Sparshott, F. E. 1957. "Plato and Thrasymachus." *University of Toronto Quarterly* 27:54–61.
———. 1966. "Socrates and Thrasymachus." *Monist* 50:421–59.
———. 1988. "An Argument for Thrasymachus." *Apeiron* 21:55–67.
Spitzer, A. 1975. "The Self-Reference of the *Gorgias*." *Philosophy and Rhetoric* 8:16–17.

Sprague, Rosamund Kent. 1962. *Plato's Use of Fallacy*. New York.

———, 1967. "An Unfinished Argument in Plato's *Protagoras*." *Apeiron* 1:1–4.

———, trans. 1973. *Laches and Charmides*. Indianapolis.

Stenzel, J. 1973. *Plato's Method of Dialectic*. Trans. D. J. Allan. New York.

Stephens, J. 1985. "Socrates on the Rule of Law." *History of Philosophy Quarterly* 2:3–10.

Stern, Herold S. 1974. "Plato's Funeral Oration." *The New Scholasticism* 48:503–8.

Sternfeld, Robert, and Harold Zyskind. 1977. "Plato's *Meno* 86e–87a: The Geometrical Illustration of the Argument by Hypothesis." *Phronesis* 22:206–11.

———. 1978. *Plato's Meno: A Philosophy of Man as Acquisitive*. Carbondale, Ill.

Stocker, M. 1984. "Some Structures for *Akrasia*." *History of Philosophy Quarterly* 1:267–80.

Stokes, Michael, C. 1986. *Plato's Socratic Conversations, Drama and Dialectic in Three Dialogues*. Baltimore.

Stone, I. F. 1987. *The Trial of Socrates*. Boston.

Strauss, Leo. 1972. *Xenophon's Socrates*. Ithaca, N.Y.

———. 1976. "On Plato's *Apology of Socrates* and *Crito*." In *Essays in Honor of Jacob Klein*, 155–70. Annapolis, Md.

———. 1980. *Socrates and Aristophanes*. Chicago.

Strycker, E. de. 1975. "The Oracle Given to Chaerephon about Socrates." In *Kephalaion: Studies in Greek Philosophy and Its Continuation Offered to C. J. Vogel*, ed. J. Mansfield and L. M. de Rijk, 39–49. Assen.

Sullivan, J. P. 1961. "The Hedonism in Plato's *Protagoras*." *Phronesis* 6:10–28.

Sutton, D. F. 1981. "Critias and Atheism." *Classical Quarterly* 31:33–38.

Sweeney, Leo. 1977. "A. E. Taylor on Socrates and Plato." *Southwestern Journal of Philosophy* 8:79–99.

Taran, Leonardo. 1985. "Platonism and Socratic Ignorance." In *Platonic Investigations*, ed. D. J. O'Meara, 85–110. Studies in Philosophy and the History of Philosophy. Washington, D.C.

Tarrant, Harold. 1988. "Midwifery and the *Clouds*." *Classical Quarterly* 38:116–22.

Tatham, M. T. 1966. *Plato's Laches*. New York.

Taylor, A. E. 1952. *Socrates*. New York.

Taylor, C. C. W. 1976. *Plato Protagoras*. Oxford.

———. 1982. "The End of the *Euthyphro*." *Phronesis* 27:109–18.

Taylor, J. H. 1973. "Virtue and Wealth According to Socrates (*Apology* 30b)." *Classical Bulletin* 49:49–52.

Tejera, V. 1978. "Methodology of a Misreading: A Critical Note on T. Irwin's *Plato's Moral Theory*." *International Studies in Philosophy* 10:131–36.

———. 1984a. *Plato's Dialogues One by One*. New York.

———. 1984b. "Ideology and Literature: Xenophon's *Defense of Socrates* and Plato's *Apology*." In *New Essays on Socrates*, ed. Eugene Kelly, 151–59. Lanham, Md.

Teloh, Henry. 1981. *The Development of Plato's Metaphysics*. College Park, Penn.

———. 1986. *Socratic Education in Plato's Early Dialogues*. Notre Dame, Ind.

———. 1987. "The Importance of Interlocutors' Characters in Plato's Early Dialogues." *Proceedings of the Boston Area Colloquium in Ancient Philosophy* 2:25–38.

Tessitore, Aristide. 1988. "Aristotle's Political Presentation of Socrates in the *Nicomachean Ethics*." *Interpretation* 16:3–22.

———. 1990. "Plato's *Lysis*: An Introduction to Philosophic Friendship." *Southern Journal of Philosophy* 28:115–32.

Thayer, H. S. 1969. "Models of Moral Concepts of Plato's *Republic*." *Journal of the History of Philosophy* 7:247–62.

Thesleff, H. 1976. "The Date of the Pseudo-Platonic *Hippias Major.*" *Acta Philologica Fennica* 10:105–17.

———. 1982. *Studies in Platonic Chronology.* Helsinki.

———. 1989. "Platonic Chronology." *Phronesis* 34:1–26.

Thom, Paul. 1978. *"Euthyphro 9d–11b." Philosophical Inquiry* 1:5–70.

Thomas, John E. 1974. "On the Duality of Socrates' What-is-X-Question." *Laval Theologique et Philosophique* 30:21–27.

———. 1976. "Models for Muddles at *Meno* 75a–77a." *The New Scholasticism* 50:193–203.

———. 1980. *Musings on the Meno.* The Hague.

Tigerstedt, E. N. 1977. *Interpreting Plato.* Uppsala.

Tigner, S. 1970. "On the 'Kinship' of 'All Nature' in Plato's *Meno.*" *Phronesis* 15:1–5.

Tiles, J. E. 1984. *"Techne* and Moral Expertise." *Philosophy* 59:49–66.

Tindale, Christopher W. 1984. "Plato's *Lysis:* A Reconsideration." *Apeiron* 18:102–9.

Tofallis, Kypros. 1978. *Socrates: Man and Philosopher.* London.

Tomin, Julius. 1987–88. "Aristophanes: A Lasting Source of Reference." *Proceedings of the Aristotelian Society* 88:83–95.

———. 1987. "Socratic Midwifery." *Classical Quarterly* 37:97–102.

Trainor, Paul. 1988. "Autobiography as Philosophical Argument: Socrates, Descartes, and Collingwood." *Thought* 63:378–96.

Tuckey, T. Godfrey. 1968. *Plato's Charmides.* Amsterdam.

Turner, Frank M. 1981. "Socrates and the Sophists." In *The Greek Heritage in Victorian Britain,* ed. Frank M. Turner, 264–321. New Haven, Conn., and London.

Umphrey, Stewart. 1976a. "On the Theme of Plato's *Laches.*" *Interpretaion* 6:1–10.

———. 1976b. "Plato's *Laches* on Courage." *Apeiron* 10:14–22.

———. 1982. *"Eros* and *Thumos." Interpretation* 10:353–422.

van der Ben, N. 1985. *The Charmides of Plato: Problems and Interpretations.* Amsterdam.

Versenyi, L. 1963. *Socratic Humanism.* Hew Haven, Conn.

———. 1971. "Plato and His Liberal Opponents." *Philosophy* 46:222–37.

———. 1972. "Virtue as a Self-Directed Art." *The Personalist* 53:274–89.

———. 1975. "Plato's *Lysis.*" *Phronesis* 20:185–98.

———. 1982. *Holiness and Justice: An Interpretation of Plato's Euthyphro.* Washington, D.C.

Vlastos, G. 1956. "Introduction." In *Plato's Protagoras,* trans. M. Ostwald, vii–1vi. Indianapolis.

———. 1957. "Socratic Knowledge and Platonic Pessimism." Reprinted from *Philosophical Review* 66:226–238. In *Platonic Studies,* ed. G. Vlastos, 204–20. Princeton, N.J.

———. 1965. "Anamnesis in the *Meno.*" *Dialogue* 4:143–67.

———. 1967. "Was Polus Refuted?" *American Journal of Philology* 88:454–60.

———. 1969. "Socrates on Acrasia." *Phoenix* 23:71–88.

———. 1971a. "The Paradox of Socrates." In *The Philosophy of Socrates: A Collection of Critical Essays,* ed. G. Vlastos, 1–21. New York.

———, ed. 1971b. *Plato, a Collection of Critical Essays I: Metaphysics and Epistemology.* Garden City, N.Y.

———, ed. 1971c. *Plato, a Collection of Critical Essays II: Ethics, Politics, and Philosophy of Art and Religion.* Garden City, N.Y.

———. 1971d. *The Philosophy of Socrates: A Collection of Critical Essays.* Garden City, N.Y.

———. 1974. "Socrates on Political Obedience and Disobedience." *Yale Review* 42:517–34.

———. 1978. "Review of H. Cherniss, *Collected Papers* Ed. L. Taran." *American Journal of Philology* 89:537–43.

———.1979. "On 'The Socrates Story.'" *Political Theory* 7:533–36.

———. 1981a. "The Individual as Object of Love in Plato." In *Platonic Studies,* ed. G. Vlastos, 2d ed., 3–42. Princeton, N.J.

——. 1981b. *Platonic Studies*. 2d ed. Princeton, N.J.

——. 1981c. "Socrates on 'The Parts of Virtue.'" In *Platonic Studies*, ed. G. Vlastos, 2d ed., 418–23. Princeton, N.J.

——. 1981d. "The Unity of Virtues in the *Protagoras*." In *Platonic Studies*, ed. G. Vlastos, 2d ed., 221–65. Princeton, N.J.

——. 1981e. "What Did Socrates Understand by His 'What is F?' Question." In *Platonic Studies*, ed. G. Vlastos, 2d ed., 410–17. Princeton, N.J.

——. 1982. "The Socratic Elenchus." *Journal of Philosophy* 79:715–21.

——. 1983a. "Afterthoughts." *Oxford Studies in Ancient Philosophy* 1:71–74.

——. 1983b. "Classical Greek Political Thought I: The Historical Socrates and Athenian Democracy." *Political Theory* 11:495–516.

——. 1983c. "The Socratic Elenchus." *Oxford Studies in Ancient Philosophy* 1:27–58.

——. 1984. "Happiness and Virtue and Socrates' Moral Theory." *Proceedings of Cambridge Philological Society* 30:181–213.

——. 1985. "Socrates' Disavowal of Knowledge." *Philosophical Quarterly* 35:1–31.

——. 1987. "Socratic Irony." *Classical Quarterly* 37:79–96.

——. 1988a. "Elenchus and Mathematics: A Turning Point in Plato's Philosophical Development." *American Journal of Philology* 109:362–96.

——. 1988b. "Socrates." *Proceedings of the British Academy* 74:87–109.

——. 1991. *Socrates, Ironist and Moral Philosopher*. Ithaca, N.Y.

Vogel, Cornelia J. de. 1955. "The Present State of the Socrates Problem." *Phronesis* 1:26–35.

——. 1963. "Who Was Socrates?" *Journal of the History of Philosophy* 1:143–61.

Wade, F. C. 1971. "In Defense of Socrates." *Review of Metaphysics* 25:311–25.

Wakefield, J. 1987. "Why Justice and Holiness Are Similar: *Protagoras* 330–331." *Phronesis* 32:267–76.

Wallach, John R. 1988. "Socratic Citizenship." *History of Politcal Thought* 9:393–413.

Walsh, James J. 1971. "The Socratic Denial of Akrasia." In *The Philosophy of Socrates: A Collection of Critical Essays*, ed. G. Vlastos, 235–63. New York.

Walsh, John. 1984. "The Dramatic Dates of Plato's *Protagoras* and the Lesson of *Arete*." *Classical Quarterly* 34:101–6.

Walton, Craig. 1978. "Xenophon and the Socratic Paradoxes." *Southern Journal of Philosophy* 16:687–700.

Walton, Richard E. 1980. "Socrates' Alleged Suicide." *Journal of Value Inquiry* 14:287–300.

Warren, Edward. 1989. "The Craft Argument: An Analogy." In *Essays in Ancient Greek Philosophy 3: Plato*, ed. J. P. Anton and A. Preus 101–16. Albany, N.Y.

Watson, Walter. 1984. "The Voices of the God." In *New Essays on Socrates*, ed. Eugene Kelly, 173–79. Lanham, Md.

Weingartner, R. W. 1973. *The Unity of the Platonic Dialogue*. Indianapolis.

Weiss, Roslyn. 1981. "*Ho Agathos* as *Ho Dunatos* in the *Hippias Minor*." *Classical Quarterly* 31:287–304.

——. 1985a. "Courage, Confidence, and Wisdom in the *Protagoras*." *Ancient Philosophy* 5:11–24.

——. 1985b. "Ignorance, Involuntariness, and Innocence: A Reply to McTighe." *Phronesis* 30:314–22.

——. 1985c. "Socrates and Protagoras on Justice and Holiness." *Phoenix* 39:334–41.

——. 1986. "Euthyphro's Failure." *Journal of the History of Philosophy* 24:437–53.

——. 1987. "The Right Exchange: *Phaedo* 69a6–c3." *Ancient Philosophy* 7:57–66.

——. 1990a. "The Hedonic Calculus in the *Protagoras* and the *Phaedo*." *Journal of the History of Philosophy* 27:511–30.

——. 1990b. "A Rejoinder to Professors Gosling and Taylor." *Journal of the History of Philosophy* 28:117–18.

Wellman, R. R. 1964. "The Question Posed at *Charmides* 165a–166c." *Phronesis* 9:107–13.
———. 1976. "Socratic Method in Xenophon." *Journal of the History of Ideas* 37:307–18.
Wengert, R. G. 1988. "The Paradox of the Midwife." *History of Philosophy Quarterly* 5:3–10.
Wenz, P. S. 1973. "Socrates on Civil Disobedience: The *Apology* and the *Crito*." *Transactions of the Wisconsin Academy of Sciences, Arts, and Letters* 61:103–16.
Werkmeister, W. H., ed. 1976. *Facets of Plato's Philosophy*. Amsterdam.
West, Elinor J. M. 1984. "Plato and Socrates: The Men and Their Methods." In *New Essays on Socrates*, ed. Eugene Kelly, 131–36. Lanham, Md.
———. 1989. "Socrates in the *Crito*: Patriot or Friend?" In *Essays in Ancient Greek Philosophy 3: Plato*, ed. J. P. Anton and A. Preus, 71–84. Albany, N.Y.
West, T. G. 1979. *Plato's Apology of Socrates: An Interpretation with a New Translation*. Ithaca, N.Y.
———. 1983. "Defending Socrates and Defending Politics: A Response to Stewart Umphrey." *Interpretation* 11:383–97.
West, T. G., and Grace Starry West, trans. 1984. *Plato and Aristophanes: Plato's Euthyphro, Apology, and Crito and Aristophanes' Clouds*. Ithaca, N.Y.
Weston, A. H. 1951. "The Question of Plato's *Euthyphro*." *Classical Bulletin* 27:57–58.
White, N. P. 1974. "Inquiry." *Review of Metaphysics* 28:289–310.
———. 1976. *Plato on Knowledge and Reality*. Indianapolis.
———. 1985. "Rational Prudence in Plato's *Gorgias*." In *Platonic Investigations*, ed. D. J. O'Meara, 139–62. Studies in Philosophy and the History of Philosophy. Washington, D.C.
Wilcox, J. F. 1987. "Cross-Metamorphosis in Plato's *Ion*." In *Literature as Philosophy/Philosophy as Literature*, ed. D. G. Marshall, 155–74. Iowa City, Iowa.
Wilkes, Kathleen V. 1979. "Conclusions in the *Meno*." *Archiv für Geschichte der Philosophie* 61:143–53.
Winspear, A., and T. Silverberg. 1960. *Who Was Socrtes?* 2d ed. New York.
Wolz, Henry G. 1974. "The Paradox of Piety in Plato's *Euthyphro* in the Light of Heidegger's Conception of Authenticity." *The Southern Journal of Philosophy* 12:493–511.
Wood, Ellen Meiksins, and Neal Wood. 1978. *Class Ideology and Ancient Political Theory: Socrates, Plato, and Aristotle in Social Context*. New York.
Woodbury, Leonard. 1971. "Socrates and Archelaus." *Phoenix* 25:299–309.
———. 1973. "Socrates and the Daughter of Aristides." *Phoenix* 27:7–25.
Woodhead, W. D., trans. 1961. In *Plato: Gorgias. In Plato: The Collected Dialogues*, ed. E. Hamilton and H. Cairns. Princeton, N.J.
Woodruff, P. 1976. "Socrates on the Parts of Virtue." *Canadian Journal of Philosophy*, supp. 2:101–16.
———. 1978a. "Socrates and Ontology: The Evidence of the *Hippias Major*." *Phronesis* 23:101–17.
———. 1978b. "The Socratic Approach to Semantic Incompleteness." *Philosophy and Phenomenological Research* 38:453–68.
———. 1982. *Plato: Hippias Major*. Indianapolis.
———. 1983. *Plato: Two Comic Dialogues: Ion and Hippias Major*. Indianapolis.
———. 1986. "The Skeptical Side of Plato's Method." *Revue Internationale de Philosophie* 40:22–37.
———. 1987. "Expert Knowledge in the *Apology* and *Laches*: What a General Needs to Know." *Proceedings of the Boston Area Colloquium in Ancient Philosophy* 3:79–115.
———. 1988. "Reply to Ronald Polansky." In *Platonic Writings, Platonic Readings*, C. L. Griswold, 210–14. New York.

———. 1989. "Plato's Early Theory of Knowledge." In *Ancient Greek Epistemology,* ed. Stephen Everson, 60–84. Cambridge, Eng.

Woozley, A. D. 1971. "Socrates on Disobeying the Law." In *The Philosophy of Socrates: A Collection of Critical Essays,* ed. G. Vlastos, 299–318. New York.

———. 1979. *Law and Obedience: The Arguments of Plato's Crito.* Chapel Hill, N. C.

Xenakis, Jason. 1955. "Plato on Ethical Disagreement." *Phronesis* 1:50–57.

Xiuliang, Lan. 1984–5. "Hegel's Evaluation and Analysis of Socrates' Proposition 'Virtue is Knowledge.'" *Chinese Studies in Philosophy* 16:22–30.

Yaffe, M. D. 1976–7. "Civil Disobedience and the Opinion of the Many: Plato's *Crito.*" *Modern Schoolman* 54:123–36.

Young, Gary. 1974. "Socrates and Obedience." *Phronesis* 19:1–29.

Zaslavsky, Robert. 1982. "The Platonic Godfather: A Note on the *Protagoras* Myth." *The Journal of Value Inquiry* 16:79–82.

Zeigler, G. 1979. "Plato's *Gorgias* and Psychological Egoism." *The Personalist* 60:123–33.

———. 1980. "Plato's *Euthyphro* Revisited." *Pacific Philosophical Quarterly* 61:291–300.

Zeller, E. 1985. *Socrates and the Socratic Schools.* Trans. Oswald Reichel. 3d ed. London.

Zembaty, J. S. 1989. "Socrates' Perplexity in Plato's *Hippias Minor.*" In *Essays in Ancient Greek Philosophy 3: Plato,* ed. J. P. Anton and A. Preus, 51–70. Albany, N.Y.

Zeyl, D. J. 1980. "Socrates and Hedonism: *Protagoras* 351b–358d." *Phronesis* 25:250–69.

———. 1982. "Socratic Virtue and Happiness." *Archiv für Geschichte der Philosophie* 14:225–38.

Zimmerman, Michael E. 1980. "Socratic Ignorance and Authenticity." *Tulane Studies in Philosophy* 29:133–50.

Zyskind, H., and R. Sternfeld. 1976. "Plato's *Meno* 89c: 'Virtue is Knowledge' a Hypothesis?" *Phronesis* 21:130–34.

Index Locorum